Workplace Hazard Prevention Management

Joel M. Haight, Editor

American Society of Safety Engineers
Des Plaines, Illinois, USA

Disclaimer
While the publisher and authors have used their best efforts in preparing this book, they make no representations or warranties with respect to the accuracy or completeness of the contents, and specifically disclaim any implied warranties of fitness for a particular purpose. The information herein is provided with the understanding that the authors are not hereby engaged in rendering professional or legal services. The mention of any specific products herein does not constitute an endorsement or recommendation by the American Society of Safety Engineers, and was done solely at the discretion of the author. Note that any excerpt from a National Fire Protection Association Standard reprinted herein is not the complete and official position of the NFPA on the referenced subject(s), which is represented only by the cited Standard in its entirety.

Library of Congress Cataloging-in-Publication Data

Workplace hazard prevention management / Joel M. Haight, editor.
pages cm.
Includes bibliographical references and index.
ISBN 978-1-885581-72-3 (alk. paper)
1. Industrial safety. I. Haight, Joel M., editor of compilation.
T55.W667 2013
658.4'08--dc23

2012043230

Managing Editor: Michael F. Burditt, ASSE
Editor: Jeri Ann Stucka, ASSE
Text design and composition: Cathy Lombardi
Cover design: Image Graphics

Printed in the United States of America

18 17 16 15 14 13 6 5 4 3

Workplace Hazard Prevention Management

Contents

Foreword

Safety engineering involves the application of engineering principles to the identification and elimination of hazards. Hazard control is the physical control of various materials, processes, and activities to produce a specific benefit. Successful management of hazard prevention and control depends on successful risk assessment. What had been recognized in practice became recognized in fact with the Supreme Court's 1980 ruling which in effect required OSHA to demonstrate a significant risk before issuing a standard. The Court's ruling did not require OSHA to perform a quantitative risk assessment in every case, but in its ruling the Court implied, and OSHA's policy concurs, that to the extent possible, such assessments should be put in quantitative terms to the extent possible.

Another very important consideration in hazard prevention is human behavior. Human behavior is all too often left out of the equation. It is assumed that the human operator always does the right thing. The human operator must be considered part of the system. One effective control is a permit-to-work system. The permit-to-work system discussed in this book applies the safety management aspects of planning, documentation and training that were learned while developing safe products to the performance of a task that may be unfamiliar and hazardous. Most workers will appreciate having a step-by-step plan to follow while performing unfamiliar, potentially hazardous tasks.

Performance measurement is fundamental to any improvement process, since performance is what you ultimately want to improve. The measures most frequently used by safety professionals include: accident rates, audit scores, and behavioral observation. The quality of any measure is assessed by formal tests of reliability and validity, and we describe some methods to actually conduct tests of reliability and validity. The chapter on benchmarking will take you through an examination of each of the measures listed above. This will enable you to evaluate the measures you are using, understand their limitations, and maximize their effectiveness. Both the reliability and validity issues that arise frequently with accident rates and audit scores are discussed. While these can be overcome to an extent, most practitioners do not take the steps to do this.

In addition to the measures listed above, the chapter introduces the employee safety survey as measure of safety system performance that has very high reliability and validity. While many managers are not comfortable with the use of an opinion survey to measure safety, the evidence of the efficacy of safety surveys is clear. After all, the decisions of people are at the heart of safe work. The survey provides a systematic method to explore the attitudes and beliefs of the workers that will influence the decisions they make, for better or for worse.

The chapter also discusses benchmarking in two contexts. First, without a benchmark, a performance measurement means little. If you are told that someone went 100 miles per hour, that would be very fast on a motorcycle, and very slow in an airplane. Second, when used carefully and properly, as described in the chapter, benchmarking can provide you with important information to improve your own program.

The safety professional must also understand the concept of risk, how it is measured, the financial consequences of ignoring it, and the cost benefits of managing it. Once the basic tools are understood, a strong business case can be formulated for management to reduce and, in some cases, completely eliminate risk. When not possible or financially feasible, there are alternatives, such as insurance. Regardless of approach, if it costs time or money, the case must be made to management.

ABOUT THE EDITOR

In 2009, Joel M.Haight, Ph.D.,P.E., was named Branch Chief of the Human Factors Branch at the Centers for Disease Control and Prevention (CDC)—National Institute of Occupational Safety and Health (NIOSH) at their Pittsburgh Office of Mine Safety and Health Research. He continues in this role. In 2000, Dr. Haight received a faculty appointment and served asAssociate Professor of Energy and Mineral Engineering at the Pennsylvania State University. He also worked as a manager and engineer for the Chevron Corporation domestically and internationally for eighteen years prior to joining the faculty at PennState. Hehasa Ph.D. (1999) and Master's degree (1994) in Industrial and System Engineering, both from Auburn University. Dr. Haight does human error, process optimization, and intervention effectiveness research. He is a professional member of the American Society of Safety Engineers (where he serves as Federal Liaison to the Board of Trustees and the ASSE Foundation Research Committee Chair), the American Industrial Hygiene Association (AIHA), reviewed scientific journal articles and book chapters and is a co author and the editor in chie fof ASSE's *The Safety Professionals Handbook* and the John Wiley and Sons, *Hand book of Loss Prevention Engineering.*

ABOUT THE AUTHORS

Brooks Carder, Ph.D., is a Principal in Carder and Associates, LLC, and a Senior Member of the American Society for Quality.

David A Dodge, P.E., CSP, is a Senior Consultant with Safety and Forensic Consulting.

Jerome F. Fields, M.T., CHMM, is Environmental, Healtha nd Safety Manager for Southern California Aviation.

Mark A. Friend, Ed.D., CSP, is a Professor and Chair of the Department of Applied Aviation Sciences at Embry Riddle Aeronautical University, Daytona Beach, Florida.

Mark D. Hansen, M.S., P.E., CPE, CPEA, CSP, is Director, Portfolio Environmental and Risk Management, Natural Gas Partners.

Mohammad A. Malek, Ph.D., P.E., is a Pressure Systems Manager at the Stanford University–SLAC National Accelerator Laboratory, Menlo Park, California.

John Mroszczyk, Ph.D., P.E., CSP, worked for major corporations such as General Electric before founding his own firm, Northeast Consulting Engineers, Inc., Danvers, Massachusetts. His work includes design, safety, and consulting services for major corporations, small companies, architects, insurance companies, building contractors, and the legal profession.

Steven J. Owen, CET, EIT, is a Master Electrician/Contractor in 44 states, a Chief Code Analyst, and OSHA authorized instructor and Principal CMP3 of NFPA70, as well as the President of National Code Seminars, Birmingham, Alabama.

Patrick T. Ragan, M.B.A., CSP, is Vice President of Quality, Health, Safety, and Environment at Bayer Crop Science in Kansas City, Missouri.

Stephen J.Wallace, P.E., CSP, is the President of Wallace Consulting Services, LLC, in Washington, D.C.

1

Regulatory Issues

Jerry Fields

Learning Objectives

- Develop a knowledge of the regulatory requirements to define risk assessment.
- Be able to describe the gap between risk assessment and risk perception and regulatory requirements.
- Gain a basic understanding of the regulatory risk-assessment process.
- Identify three steps in the process of regulatory risk assessment.
- Understand the policies and regulations that embody environmental and occupational health risks.
- Be able to recognize when to use risk assessments for environmental and occupational risks that may have an impact on the environment, workers, and the public.

THIS CHAPTER PROVIDES an introduction to the subject of regulatory issues in risk assessments and hazard controls. The chapter outlines the reasons that risk assessments are completed, and it discusses some regulations that require risk assessments and some reasons why risk assessments are conducted.

Defining Risk

Risk is the probability (or likelihood) that a harmful consequence will occur as a result of an action. Risk is a function of hazard and exposure. People take risks every day, in many forms—crossing the street, smoking, drinking alcohol, driving a car: the list is endless.

Somehow we catalog all of these risks, deciding some are acceptable while others are not—and not even considering others. According to Bascietto (1998), for a risk to occur there must be a source of risk (hazard) and an exposure to the hazard. Every risk involves a combination of these two factors: (1) the probability of an undesirable occurrence and (2) the severity of that occurrence (Ropeik 2000). For example, for a person who has measles, the risk of death is one in one million (CDC 2003). A *risk assessment* is an analysis that uses information to estimate a level of risk.

Why Assess Risk?

Assessing risks is done to mitigate indefensible, undesired, or unavoidable risk to make operating decisions ("go/no go") and to manage resource distribution for improved control of losses. Risk assessment is "The process of determining the degree of threat that is posed by one or more hazards to one or more resources, or the product of that process" (Lack 2001). Performing risk assessments provides a systemic approach for ranking risks and making decisions and is a tool to help the organization or individual spend money more intelligently (Alijoyo 2004). Risk assessment is not a substitute for conforming to applicable codes, standards, and regulations (O'Brian 2000). Risk assessment considers information describing an actual or potential opportunity for human contact with chemicals or physical objects, the potential level of exposure, the health effects, and the expected degree of harm (Occupational Safety and Health Regulations 2007a). Risk assessments can be performed for hazards and exposures to chemicals and physical agents in the workplace and many other situations (Occupational Safety and Health Regulations 2007a). Many federal and state regulatory programs use or require risk assessments.

Conducting a Risk Assessment

The four steps of a risk assessment are hazard identification (Can this substance damage health?), dose-response assessment (What dose causes what effect?), exposure assessment (How and how frequently do people contact it?), and risk characterization (combining the other three steps to characterize risk and to describe the limitations and uncertainties) (EPA 2001).

Some problems with risk assessments are that crucial parts of assessment come before (initial assumptions) and after (interpreting results) the actual analysis, models drastically simplify what happens in nature, and accurate accident and equipment-failure data are necessary (O'Brian 2000).

There are several regulatory risk-assessment techniques. More rigorous methods may be used when the regulatory approaches are inappropriate or inadequate. According to Jasanoff (1993), assessments are based on local concerns, guidelines, policies, and assessment review.

The Environmental Protection Agency (EPA)

History

In July 1970, the White House and Congress worked together to establish the EPA in response to the growing public demand for cleaner water, air, and land (EPA 1994). Prior to the establishment of the EPA, the federal government was not structured to make a coordinated attack on the pollutants that harm human health and degrade the environment. The EPA was assigned the daunting task of repairing the damage already done to the natural environment and to establish new criteria to guide Americans in making a cleaner environment a reality (EPA 1994).

Mission Statement

The EPA was established in 1970 to consolidate in one agency a variety of federal research, monitoring, standard-setting, and enforcement activities to ensure environmental protection.

EPA's mission is to protect human health and to safeguard the natural environment—air, water, and land—upon which life depends. For 30 years, the EPA has been working for a cleaner, healthier environment for the American people (EPA 2001).

The EPA provides leadership in the nation's environmental science, research, education, and assessment efforts. EPA works closely with other federal agencies, state and local governments, and Indian tribes to develop and enforce regulations under existing environmental laws. EPA is responsible for researching and setting national standards for a variety of environmental programs; it delegates to states and tribes the responsibility for issuing permits, and monitoring and enforcing compliance. Where national standards are not met, EPA can issue sanctions and take other steps to assist the states and tribes in reaching the desired levels of environmental quality. EPA also works with industries and all levels of government in a wide variety of voluntary pollution prevention programs and energy conservation efforts (EPA 1994).

Another federal act to review is the National Environmental Policy Act, which requires risk assessments but is not part of this chapter. (Oliver 2005).

EPA Risk Assessment

After the establishment of EPA, new legislation was developed, implemented, and enforced to regulate chemicals in the environment (EPA 2001). The EPA uses risk-assessment techniques to assess a chemical's capacity to cause harm (its toxicity), and the potential for humans to be exposed to that chemical in a particular situation; for example, workplace or home (EPA 2001).

The most common basic definition of *risk assessment* that is used within the Environmental Protection Agency is "a process in which information is analyzed to determine if an environmental hazard might cause harm to exposed persons and ecosystems" (NRC 1983).

During the 1970s, risk-assessment procedures for all chemicals were reevaluated and improved. More importantly, they were formalized (Oliver 2005). Standardized tests were developed so consistent evaluations could be performed and the scientific basis of regulations could be more easily applied (EPA 2001).

According to the EPA, there are two components that make up the definition of risk assessment: *toxicity*, or dose-response assessment, and *exposure assessment* (EPA 2001). Dose-response assessment is a measure of the extent and types of negative effects associated with a level of exposure. Exposure assessment is a measure of the extent and duration of exposure to an individual. One example of a chemical that was developed based on dose-response assessment data is dioxin (EPA 2001).

The EPA is responsible for developing and providing state and local government agencies with toxicological and medical information relevant to decisions involving public health (EPA 2001). State agencies that use such information include all boards and departments within state EPAs, as well as the Department of Health Services, the Department of Food and Agriculture, the Office of Emergency Services, the Department of Fish and Game, and the Department of Justice (EPA 2001). According to the EPA, risk assessment is the "process by which one attempts to evaluate and predict the likelihood and extent of harm (in qualitative and quantitative terms) that may result from a health or environmental hazard" (EPA 2001). Information comes from scientific studies, historical data, and actual experiences. A risk assessment provides an estimate of risk to workers who have the potential to be exposed to chemical and physical agents at a work site (McGarity and Shapiro 1993). According to Benner (1983), regulatory risk-assessment analysis has built-in safety margins.

A risk assessment provides essential information about the severity and extent of specific environmental problems for use in risk-management decisions (EPA 2001). *Risk management* is the process of deciding how and to what extent to reduce or eliminate risk factors by considering the risk assessment, engineering factors (Can procedures or equipment do the job, and for how long and how well?), and social, economic, and political concerns (McGarity and Shapiro 1993).

Why the EPA Conducts Risk Assessments

Determining environmental standards, policies, guidelines, regulations, and actions requires making decisions (Ropeik 2000). Environmental decision making is often a controversial process involving the interplay of many forces: science, social and economic factors, political considerations, technological feasibility, and statutory requirements (Oliver 2005). Environmental decisions are often time-sensitive, for example when public health is known or suspected to be at risk (EPA 1994).

The EPA conducts risk assessment to provide the best possible scientific characterization of risks based on a rigorous analysis of available information and knowledge, a description of the nature and magnitude of the risk, an interpretation of the adversity of the risk, a summary of the confidence or reliability of the information available to describe the risk, identifying areas where information is uncertain or lacking completely, and documentation of all of the evidence supporting the characterization of the risk (EPA 1994). According to Schoeny, Muller, and Mumford (1998), the EPA then incorporates this risk characterization with other relevant information, such as social, economic, political, and regulatory information, in making decisions in the form of policies and regulations about how to manage the risk. Risk assessment informs decision makers about the scientific implications of the risk involved (Schoeny et al. 1998). Risk assessments that meet their objectives can help guide risk managers to decisions that mitigate environmental risks at the lowest possible cost and that will stand up if challenged in the courts (Schoeny et al. 1998).

Two Types of EPA Risk Assessments

Exposure Assessment

Exposure assessment is accomplished in three basic approaches: analysis of the source of exposure in drinking water or workplace air, measurements of the environment, and blood and urine laboratory tests of the people exposed. Sample analyses of air and water often provide the majority of usable data (EPA 2000). These tests reveal the level of contamination in the air or water to which people are exposed. However, they only reflect concentration at the time of testing and generally cannot be used to quantify either the type or amount of past contamination. Some estimates of past exposures may be gained from understanding how a chemical moves in the environment (EPA 2003).

Other types of environmental measurements may be helpful in estimating past exposure levels. Past levels of a persistent chemical can be estimated using the age and size of the fish and information about how rapidly these organisms accumulate the chemical (CDC 2003).

Analyses of body-fluid levels of possibly exposed people provide the most direct exposure measure. They do not provide good estimates of past exposure levels because the body usually reaches a balanced state, so that there is no longer any change in response to continued exposure (EXTOXNET 1998). Many chemicals are excreted from the body after exposure stops, and the basic understanding of what happens to chemicals in the human body is often lacking for those that do persist. Thus, direct examination of a population may provide information as to whether exposure has occurred but not the extent, duration, or source of the exposure (CDC 2003).

Exposure assessments can be performed reliably for recent events and less reliably for past exposures. The difficulties in exposure assessment often make it the weak link in trying to determine the connection between an environmental contaminant and adverse effects on human health. Exposure-assessment methods will continue to improve, but at the present time there still remains significant uncertainty (EPA 2001).

Dose-Response Assessment

A distinction must be made between *acute* and *chronic* effects when discussing dose-response assessment. Acute effects occur within minutes, hours, or days, whereas chronic effects appear only after weeks, months, or years. The quality and quantity of scientific evidence gathered is different for each type of effect, and the confidence placed in the conclusions from the test results also differs (EPA 2001).

Acute toxicity is easier to deal with. Short-term studies with animals provide evidence as to which effects are linked with which chemicals and the levels at which these adverse effects occur. Often, some human experience is available as a result of accidental exposure. When these two types of evidence are available, it is usually possible to make a good estimate of the levels of a particular toxicant that will lead to a particular acute, adverse effect in humans. This approach is the basis for much of the current regulation of toxic substances, especially in occupational situations (OSHA 2006).

Chronic toxicity is much more difficult to assess. According to Centers for Disease Control (CDC), there are a variety of specific tests for adverse effects such as reproductive damage, behavioral effects, and cancer (CDC 2003). The CDC states that cancer assessment will reveal some of the problems inherent in long-term toxicity assessments and also focus on the health effect that seems to be the biggest public concern.

In cancer assessment, it is not only the chronic nature of the disease but also the low incidence that causes difficulty. Society has decided that no more than one additional cancer in 100,000 or one million people is acceptable, so assessment measures must be able to detect this small increase (CDC 2003). Two types of evidence are utilized to determine the dose of chemical that will result in this change. One is based on experiments on animals, and the other is based on experience with humans (CDC 2003).

To detect an increase of one cancer in a million animals, millions of animals would have to be exposed to environmentally relevant amounts of the chemical (CDC 2003). Consequently, investigations are performed on smaller numbers of animals who have been exposed to very large amounts of a chemical. These large amounts are necessary to produce a high enough incidence of cancer to be detectable in this small population (CDC 2003). The results of these CDC-type studies indicate the levels of a chemical that will cause cancer in a high percentage of the population (CDC 2003).

As a result, this information is used to assess and predict the level of a chemical that will cause cancer in a million animals or, more importantly, in a million humans, by utilizing mathematical models (CDC 2003). There are a variety of mathematical models, and the one generally chosen is that which provides the greatest margin of safety (EPA 2001). In using one of these models, the results are overestimates rather than underestimates of the ability of the chemical to cause cancer (Rhomberg 1997).

The type of evidence utilized in chronic toxicity assessment is known as epidemiological evidence. In this type of study, human populations are carefully observed and possible associations between specific chemical exposures and particular health effects are investigated (CDC 2003). This is not an easy task. There were clinical assessments in 2008 for cadmium and chronium, and for arsenic in 2009. CDC hazard/ assessment goals for 2010 were to address specifics for children age 6 and under for mercury. The CDC had a document with a comment period that closed in January 2011 and held a public forum in February 2011 for the "Development of Health Risk Assessment Guidance," which is still in progress as of this writing (CDC 2008, 2009, and 2010). The task is made even more difficult in cancer assessment by the requirement of detecting very small changes in incidence (one extra cancer in a million people) (CDC 2003).

Epidemiological assessments have been most useful in only certain situations. One is the workplace, where exposure levels to known carcinogens may be elevated, and where the duration of exposure can be determined. According to OSHA, a sizable increase in cancer incidents is needed before a connection can be established. The conclusion that asbestos causes lung cancer is based on this type of situation. An exception to the need for a high cancer incidence rate is where the effect is unique, so that even a few cases are significant. An example of this was the observation that a small number of vinyl chloride workers developed a rare form of liver cancer (CDC 2003). Even with known occupational carcinogens, the question of what happens at low exposures for common environmental chemicals has not been answered (Schoeny et al. 1998).

The techniques available for assessment of chronic toxicity, especially carcinogenicity, provide rather clear evidence as to whether a particular chemical causes a particular effect in animals (CDC 2003). The CDC state that there is great uncertainty about the amounts needed to produce small changes in cancer incidence in humans (EPA 2001). This uncertainty and the difficulties in exposure assessment will continue to make it difficult to draw definite conclusions about the relationship between most environmental exposures and chronic health effects (EPA 2001).

Examples of EPA Risk Assessments

Health Assessment Document for Diesel Engine Exhaust (EPA 2002a)

This assessment examined information regarding the possible health hazards associated with exposure to diesel engine exhaust (DE), which is a mixture of gases and particles. The assessment concludes that long-term (i.e., chronic) inhalation exposure is likely to pose a lung-cancer hazard to humans, as well as damage the lung in other ways, depending on exposure. Short-term (i.e., acute) exposures can cause irritation and inflammatory symptoms of a transient nature, these being highly variable across the population. The assessment also indicates that evidence for exacerbation of existing allergies and asthma symptoms is emerging. The assessment recognizes that DE emissions, as a mixture of many constituents, also contribute to ambient concentrations of several criteria air pollutants, including nitrogen oxides and fine particles, as well as other air toxics. The assessment's health-hazard conclusions are based on exposure to exhaust from diesel engines built prior to the mid-1990s. The health-hazard conclusions, in general, are applicable to engines currently in use, a category that includes many older engines. As new diesel engines with cleaner exhaust emissions replace existing engines, the applicability of the conclusions in this health-assessment document will need to be reevaluated. To obtain a hard copy or CD of the health-assessment document, contact EPA's National Service Center for Environmental

Publications: telephone, 1-800-490-9198 or 513-489-8190; fax, 513-489-8695; mail: NSCEP; P.O. Box 42419; Cincinnati, OH 45242-0419.

Health-Effects Assessment for Mercury (EPA 1993)

This document represents a brief, quantitatively oriented scientific summary of data on health effects. It was developed by the Environmental Criteria and Assessment Office to assist the Office of Emergency and Remedial Response in establishing chemical-specific health-related goals of remedial actions. If applicable, interim acceptable intakes of chemical-specific subchronic and chronic toxicity are determined for systemic toxicants, or q_1 values are determined for carcinogens for both oral and inhalation routes. A subchronic and chronic interim acceptable intake was determined for mercury based on both oral and inhalation exposure. Estimates for mixed alkyl and inorganic mercury alone are presented.

Risk Management Plan

The Clean Air Act Amendments of 1990 require the EPA to publish regulations and guidance for chemical accident prevention at facilities using extremely hazardous substances (EPA, 2001). The Risk Management Program Rule (RMP Rule) was written to implement Section 112(r) of these amendments. The rule, which built upon existing industry codes and standards, requires companies of all sizes that use certain flammable and toxic substances to develop a *risk management program*, which must include the following:

- hazard assessment that details the potential effects of an accidental release, an accident history of the last five years, and an evaluation of worst-case and alternative accidental releases
- prevention program that includes safety precautions and maintenance, monitoring, and employee training measures
- emergency response program that spells out emergency health care, employee training measures, and procedures for informing the public and response agencies (e.g., the fire department) should an accident occur
- EPA's risk management plan (RMP) requires an owner or operator of a covered process to prepare and submit a single RMP that includes
  - conducting an analysis of a worst-case release scenario
  - conducting a hazard assessment
  - implementing a streamlined prevention program (hazard control)

For this process analysis EPA has developed three program levels, and each level requires, at a minimum, the three conditions listed above. The three program levels and the requirements of each are as follows:

1. ***Program One***—Processes with no public receptors within the distance to an endpoint from a worst-case release and with no accidents with specific off-site consequences within the past five years. This program imposes limited assessment requirements and minimal prevention and emergency response requirements.
2. ***Program Two***—Processes that are not eligible for program one or subject to program three. This program requires a streamlined prevention (hazard control) program and requires additional hazard assessment, management control systems, and emergency response procedures.
3. ***Program Three***—Processes not eligible for program one and subject to OSHA's *Process Safety Management (PSM) Standard*, 29 CFR 1910.119, Subpart H, under federal or state OSHA programs or classified in one of ten specified North American Industry Classification Systems (NAICS) codes. Program three requires the owner or operator to develop an OSHA PSM program as the prevention program and requires additional hazard assessment, management control systems, and emergency response procedures (OSHA 1992a).

Summary

Risk assessment is a complex process that depends on the quality of scientific information that is available. Risk assessments are used for assessing acute risks where effects appear soon after exposure occurs. The longer the period of time between exposure and appearance of symptoms, the greater is the uncertainty (EPA 2001) because of the greatly increased uncertainties in exposure assessment and also the problems involved in using epidemiological or laboratory animal results in such cases (CDC 2003).

The mission of the EPA is to protect human health and to safeguard the natural environment (air, water, and land) upon which life depends. To fulfill this mission, EPA develops and enforces regulations that implement environmental laws enacted by Congress. Implementation of environmental laws includes grants and other financial assistance to state and tribal governments carrying out environmental programs approved, authorized, or delegated by the EPA (EPA 1994).

The primary purpose of a risk assessment is to provide data for a risk manager's decision-making process (Oliver 2005). The primary purpose of a risk assessment is not to make or recommend any particular decisions; rather, it gives the risk manager information to consider with other pertinent information to make better decisions (Oliver 2005). The EPA uses risk assessment as a key source of scientific information for making good, sound decisions about managing risks to human health and the environment (Schoeny, Muller, and Mumford 1998). Examples of such decisions include deciding permissible release levels of toxic chemicals, granting permits for hazardous waste treatment operations, and selecting methods for remediation at Superfund sites (Schoeny et al. 1998). It is important to consider other factors along with the science when making decisions about risk management. In some regulations, the consideration of other factors is mandated (e.g., costs). Some of these other factors appear in the following list, which is adapted from the EPA (2001):

1. *Economic factors*—the costs and benefits of risks and risk-mitigation alternatives
2. *Laws and legal decisions*—the framework that prohibits or requires some actions
3. *Social factors*—attributes of individuals or populations that may affect their susceptibility to risks from a particular stressor
4. *Technological factors*—the feasibility, impact, and range of risk-management options
5. *Political factors*—interactions among and between different branches and levels of government and the citizens they represent
6. *Public factors*—the attitudes and values of individuals and societies with respect to environmental quality, environmental risk, and risk management

The EPA, in response to a growing demand for consistent information on substances for use in risk assessments, decision making, and regulatory activities, has updated the Integrated Risk Information System (IRIS). IRIS is an electronic database containing information on human health effects that may result from exposure to various substances in the environment. IRIS was prepared by and is maintained by the EPA's National Center for Environmental Assessment (NCEA) within the Office of Research and Development (ORD).

National Center for Environmental Assessment (NCEA)

The National Center for Environmental Assessment conducts risk assessments of national significance for topics such as

- diesel exhaust
- dioxin
- drinking water and disinfection by-products
- ozone
- particulate matter
- PCBs
- perchlorate
- second-hand smoke (ETS)
- watershed assessment
- World Trade Center disaster site

International Organization for Standardization (ISO)

The International Standards Organization (ISO) was established in 1947. The ISO is based in Geneva and is the world's largest developer of standards. It provides a single set of voluntary standards that are recognized and respected worldwide (ISO 2004). The ISO has developed acceptable standards for all aspects of the workplace.

ISO standards are developed according to three sound principles (ISO 2004):

1. *Consensus*—the views of all interests are taken into account.
2. *Conformity*—global solutions to satisfy industries and customers.
3. *Voluntarism*—based on voluntary involvement of all interests in the marketplace (market-driven).

The ISO has helped to provide a greater acceptance of harmonized international standards, and to improve competition and eliminate barriers to trade as globalization of industries and markets continues to increase (ISO 2004).

The ISO publishes a guide that provides a framework of best practices and procedures that are used by assessment stakeholders, including governmental, private, national, and international systems. This guide for conformity assessment helps to harmonize international practices (ISO 2004). *Conformity assessment* involves checking that products, materials, services, systems, or people measure up to specified requirements.

Environmental Assessment–Management Framework (ISO 14000)

Corporate management manages risk, whether consciously or not, and corporations manage risks on an ongoing basis. By using management systems, corporations are defining the organization's environmental policy. Such policies will include a commitment to continued improvement, prevention of pollution, and compliance with regulations (ISO 2004). A successful program will include routine auditing and review as key elements to continuous improvement. Other elements for a successful environmental ISO 14000 program will be document control, operational control, control of records, management policies, training, statistical techniques, and corrective and preventive action. One of the major requirements in developing a successful ISO 14000 program is to determine the company's risks through a systematic risk assessment (ISO 2004).

Risk Assessment–ISO 14000 Components

There are three very important requirements for risk assessment and risk management and the development of an environmental management system (EMS) (EPA 2001):

1. Develop a procedure to identify all environmental aspects of all operations. Included are activities, products, and services of a company's operations and of those companies (e.g., suppliers, subcontractors) on which they have influence. The company must determine the environmental aspects that have or can have significant impacts on the environment. These significant impacts must be considered when a company develops its environmental objectives. The procedures developed must be maintained.
2. Develop and work toward environmental objectives.
3. Perform management reviews of EMS and make changes to policy, objectives, and all elements of the EMS when needed.

This program requires a preliminary analysis, a risk analysis, a risk evaluation, and risk control following the initiation. All of these elements are required in the development of a successful program (EPA 2001).

A preliminary analysis includes the development of a risk information base that will help to identify possible exposures to loss using risk scenarios.

- A risk analysis includes the estimated consequences of the risk scenarios identified.
- A risk evaluation includes assessing the acceptability of the risks identified.

Risk control includes the identification of feasible risk-control options in terms of effectiveness and costs, and it assesses stakeholders' acceptance of proposed actions, including regulatory compliance.

Occupational Safety and Health Administration (OSHA)

Requirements for Risk Assessment and Hazard Control

Risk assessment, in occupational safety and health regulations, began when the United States Supreme Court ruled in a benzene decision (*Industrial Union Department v. American Petroleum Institute,* 448 U.S.

607, 1980) that the Occupational Safety and Health Administration could not issue a standard without demonstrating a significant risk of material health impairment. As a result of the Supreme Court ruling, risk assessment became standard practice in OSHA rule making for health standards.

Hazard control is the physical control of various materials, processes, and activities to produce a specific benefit. Safety engineering is the control of system hazards having the potential to cause system damage or system operator injury, or to decrease system benefits. When controlling hazards, OSHA requires the use of engineering controls as a primary method for controlling hazards and reducing the risk of injury to workers (OSHA 1995b).

According to OSHA, when engineering controls are not feasible, then administrative controls and/or the wearing of personal protective equipment are to be used to reduce the risk of injury (OSHA 1995b). A major goal of OSHA is to prevent workers from being exposed to occupational hazards. Eliminating the hazard by substituting a less hazardous chemical or by engineering the hazards out of the process or out of the equipment is the most effective method of controlling hazards.

OSHA's approach to risk assessment is guided by the Supreme Court (OSHA 2007a). Following the Supreme Court's interpretations of the OSH Act involving benzene and cotton dust, OSHA may not promulgate a standard unless it has determined that there is a significant risk of health impairment at existing permissible exposure levels and that issuance of a new standard is necessary to achieve a significant reduction in that risk (OSHA 2000). For benzene, a risk assessment relating to worker health is not only appropriate but is, in fact, required in order to identify a significant worker health risk and to determine whether a proposed standard will achieve a reduction in that risk (ACGIH 2002). The Court did not require OSHA to perform a quantitative risk assessment in every case; the Court implied, and OSHA as a policy matter agrees, that such assessments should be put in quantitative terms to the extent possible (OSHA 2007a).

It is assumed that mathematical curves are reflective of biological processes that control the biological fate and action of a toxic compound (ACGIH 2002). Many of these factors have not been quantitatively linked to the mathematical models. Biological factors that may play important roles in the risk assessment are (1) dose of the material at the sensitive tissue; (2) the sensitive tissue(s) itself; (3) the nature of the response(s); (4) rates and sites of biotransformation; (5) toxicity of metabolites; (6) chronicity of the compound (cumulative nature of the material or its actions); (7) pharmacokinetic distribution of the material (especially effects of dose on the distribution); (8) the effect of biological variables such as age, sex, species, and strain of test animal; and (9) the manner and method of dosing the test animals (OSHA 2006).

OSHA estimates of risk can result in exposure difficulties in establishing allowable exposure limits related to dermal exposure (OSHA 1995b). There are a number of reasons why this is impractical, among which are the difficulty of quantifying dermal exposures, the inability to select a reliable biological indicator, and the difficulty in correlating the amount absorbed with a precise adverse health effect (OSHA 1995b). OSHA requires adherence to permissible exposure limits that can reduce surface contamination by reducing the opportunity for skin contact through the use of personal protective clothing and equipment that would aid in preventing dermal exposure (OSHA 1995b).

Process Safety Management

Process safety management of highly hazardous chemicals was developed for the prevention of, or for minimizing the consequences of, catastrophic releases of toxic, reactive, flammable, or explosive chemicals into the atmosphere where they may affect the surrounding community. According to OSHA requirements, an initial process hazard analysis is to be completed by the employer on all processes if any of the processes have a highly hazardous chemical that is listed in OSHA's *Process Safety Management (PSM) Standard* (OSHA 1992a).

There are fourteen key elements of the OSHA PSM Standard. Several of the elements require a risk assessment and methods for hazard control. According to OSHA, process hazard analysis requires the employer to conduct an initial process hazard evaluation on any process covered by this PSM standard (OSHA 1992b). The employer must identify, evaluate, and control the hazards involved in the process. When the PSM took effect, employers had two years to comply with this element of the standard. According to OSHA, employers that plan to start up a new process are to determine if the process will require a PSM program and if it will require a hazard analysis (OSHA 1992b).

Several methodologies can be used by the employer to determine and evaluate the hazards of the process being analyzed. According to OSHA, one very important requirement is that the process hazard analysis is to be performed by a team that is made up of employees with knowledge of the process or processes. Here is a list of acceptable methodologies from OSHA 20 CFR 1910.119:

- what-if scenarios
- checklist
- what-if/checklist combination
- hazard and operability study (HAZOP)
- failure mode and effects analysis (FMEA)
- fault tree analysis

OSHA requires that hazards of the process are to be addressed when using one of these methodologies. If an employer has had a previous incident that had a likely potential to cause a catastrophic event and potential consequences in the workplace, the employer is required to evaluate the hazards and provide applicable hazard controls. These controls can be engineering and administrative controls that are appropriate to the hazards and the early warning devices for the detection of releases.

The employer must establish a system to address any recommendations or findings the process hazard-analysis team develops and ensure that recommendations are resolved promptly. All activities are to be documented. At least every five years from the initial process hazard analysis, the employer is required to update and revalidate the process hazard analysis for consistency with the current process (OSHA 2000).

Confined Space

An OSHA regulation was promulgated for the purpose of protecting employees in general industry from the hazards associated with permit-required confined spaces. The general requirement of the standard was for employers to evaluate their workplace to determine if any spaces are permit-required confined spaces. For this purpose, OSHA has developed a permit-required confined-space decision flow chart (OSHA 1998). A confined space and a permit-required confined space had to meet the following criteria:

Confined Space

a. is large enough and so configured that an employee can bodily enter and perform assigned work
b. has limited or restricted means for entry or exit
c. is not designed for continuous employee occupancy

Permit-Required Confined Space

d. contains or has the potential to contain a hazardous atmosphere
e. contains a material that has the potential for engulfing an entrant
f. has an internal configuration such that an entrant could be trapped or asphyxiated by inwardly converging walls or by a floor that slopes downward and tapers to a smaller cross-section
g. contains any other recognized serious safety or health hazards

OSHA requires employers to conduct a risk assessment. OSHA requires an employee to conduct a pre-entry check of the atmosphere with a calibrated direct-read instrument that will measure the oxygen content and check for flammable gases and for toxic air contaminants that may cause a health hazard for the employee [1910.146(c)(5)(ii)(H)]. According to OSHA 29 CFR 1926.21(b)(6)(i), an employee is required to be instructed in the nature of the hazards involved, precautions to be taken, and the use of personal protective and emergency equipment required (OSHA, 2007b).

Risk Assessments, Risk Characterization, and Regulatory Programs

OSHA believes that risk analysis is a tool necessary for linking sound policy decisions with sound science.

The Superfund Amendments and Reauthorization Act, Title III, also referred to as EPCRA, required states and local jurisdictions to develop emergency response plans. Title III created a procedural obstacle course for OSHA's risk-assessment process and prevented a more flexible case-by-case approach. According to OSHA, it often conducts simplified rule-making sessions to streamline or update standards, but that the present OSHA process of risk assessment requires formalized peer review, which is very time-consuming and makes it difficult to lift the burden on industry (OSHA 1992a).

OSHA regulations often address risks that threaten 1 in 100 exposed workers. For example, OSHA completed a risk assessment of workers exposed to ethylene oxide and concluded that the limits prior to regulations estimated that worker lifetime exposure ranged from 63.4 to 109.3 excess cancer deaths per 100 exposed workers (OSHA 2000). According to OSHA, responsible policy makers would not consider these risks marginal. OSHA estimated that if the implementation of the PSM standard would have been delayed one year, the fatalities would have exceeded 130, and the injuries would have exceeded 750 (OSHA 2007a).

OSHA states that risk assessments depend on the nature of the risk; for example, a risk assessment for a safety hazard differs from a risk assessment for toxins (OSHA 2006). Risk assessments for toxic substances, hazardous physical agents, and safety hazards do follow established scientific principles and nationally recognized guidelines established by the National Academy of Sciences. In conducting risk assessments to establish safety standards, all relevant injury and fatality data and any other relevant information will be reviewed. OSHA invites comment on all aspects of the risk-assessment process at the proposal, during public hearings, and at the final rule stage of a standard's development. An obstacle is that OSHA has to follow prescribed procedures, which do not allow for simple risk assessments, but only for complex and costly analyses in every case. OSHA is required to demonstrate that the regulation addresses a significant risk, that the regulation will substantially reduce that risk, and that it will do so in a feasible and cost-effective manner (OSHA 2007a). The analyses include detailed examinations of regulatory costs, economic impacts, and benefits (OSHA 2000).

Summary

OSHA has a mandate to protect workers before they are injured or become ill. The statutory framework for OSHA imposes both substantive and procedural obligations. OSHA currently has extensive procedural obligations to assess the impact of proposed regulations and justify the need for a regulation, including mandates to conduct detailed risk assessments. OSHA currently does not publicly reveal the policy preferences it uses in risk assessment; doing so would reveal the extent of the uncertainty that may affect risk estimates.

OSHA risk assessment is subject to divergent, socially conditioned interpretations, which may make it difficult to reach consensus concerning the extent of risk posed by a safety or health hazard (OSHA 2007a). The standards of assessing quality in regulatory science are fluid, controversial, and sensitive to political factors (see OSHA Web site).

According to OSHA, risk analysis is a necessary and appropriate tool for linking sound policy decisions with sound science. The agency has experience in conducting risk analyses to support occupational safety and health regulations. The result of OSHA's approach to risk assessment has been the development of a body of regulations that address and reduce significant risks and are both technologically feasible and economically justifiable. Assessment for a safety hazard, such as fatal falls from roofs, differs substantially from those for toxins, such as cadmium, which can cause many forms of disease. In developing risk assessments for toxic substances, hazardous physical agents, and safety hazards, OSHA follows established scientific principles and nationally recognized guidelines, such as those of the National Academy of Sciences. For health standards, OSHA also carefully explains and justifies its choice of risk-assessment models and discusses the weight of the evidence in a comprehensive manner. For safety standards, the agency describes all relevant injury and fatality data and any other information relevant to the assessment of risk.

OSHA takes these steps to ensure that its risk assessments and risk characterizations are as clear and understandable as possible. OSHA invites comment on all aspects of its risk assessments at the proposal, public hearing, and final rule stages of a standard's development (see OSHA Web site).

Before issuing any safety or health regulation, OSHA must demonstrate that the regulation addresses a significant risk, that the regulation will substantially reduce that risk, and will do so in an economically feasible, cost-effective manner (OSHA 1995b).

Consumer Product Safety Commission (CPSC)

History

The Consumer Product Safety Commission (CPSC) is an independent federal regulatory agency created to protect the public from unreasonable risks of injuries and deaths associated with some 15,000 types of consumer products. The CPSC's mission is to keep American families safe by preventing or reducing the risk of injury, illness, or death from primarily household consumer products. The CPSC's empowerment is by way of the older Federal Hazardous Substances Act (FHSA 1960). It regulates consumer products that generate pressure or that are combustible, toxic, corrosive, or radioactive. Its means of product regulation is primarily through label warnings.

The CPSC works to reduce the risk of injuries and deaths from consumer products by:

- developing voluntary standards with industry
- issuing and enforcing mandatory standards, or by banning hazardous consumer products if no feasible standard would adequately protect the public
- obtaining the recall of products or arranging for their repair
- conducting research on potential product hazards
- informing consumers by using the media (written, radio, television), state and local government agency bulletins, private organizations' publications, and by responding to consumer inquires

According to the CPSC's 2002 annual report (2002a), the staff provided technical support for the development of 64 voluntary safety standards. These were handled by three standards-developing coordinating organizations: The American Society for Testing and Materials International (ASTM), The American National Standards Institute (ANSI), and Underwriters Laboratory, Inc. (UL). These standards provide performance safety provisions addressing potential hazards associated with consumer products found in homes, schools, and recreational areas. The CPSC staff continued monitoring conformance to selected voluntary consumer product safety standards.

The Office of Compliance and the regional offices are jointly responsible for identifying consumer products that fail to comply with a specific product safety standard or the CPSC product-related requirements mandated by statute or regulation. CPSC worked cooperatively with responsible companies to obtain voluntary, corrective action plans monitored by the commission.

CPSC does not deal with the types of products covered by the Department of Transportation (DOT), such as cars, trucks, and motorcycles, those covered by the Food and Drug Administration (FDA), including drugs and cosmetics, or those covered by the Department of the Treasury (DOT), such as alcohol, tobacco, and firearms (CPSC 2002).

CPSC and Risk Assessments

In mid-2007 the CPSC was actively engaged in more than 60 voluntary standards-development activities on a wide range of consumer products (CPSC 2007). CPSC provides expert advice, technical assistance, injury and death data and analysis, and supporting research. CPSC submits recommendations concerning new safety standards or modifications of existing standards. Its recommendations are often based on CPSC research, which may include recent injury and death data associated with a product category. CPSC solicits public comment on selected voluntary standards activities by posting its proposed recommendations on the CPSC Web site for a minimum of five days (CPSC 2007). At the end of the posting period, CPSC will consider any comments received before developing final voluntary recommendations.

The commission was established in 1973 with the task of preventing unreasonable injury to consumers from a wide range of consumer products that are purchased every day. During the 1990s, CPSC was best known for its recalls of a number of consumer products that it thought to be unsafe.

In 1990, CPSC released a study on the potential risk of skin cancer from arsenic on treated-wood playground equipment. The CPSC Environmental Working Group provided new data suggesting a more serious risk of cancers such as bladder and lung cancer associated with chromated-copper-arsenate (CCA) (CPSC 2002b). CCA is a mix of chromium, copper, and arsenic and is used generally to prevent infestation of wood by insects and fungus (CPSC 2002b). In 2002, both CPSC and EPA considered issues relating to CCA-treated wood. CPSC studied the amount of CCA released from newly purchased, unused CCA-treated wood used for playground equipment as compared to "used" or "older" wood. The question CPSC raised was how much arsenic are children exposed to when playing on the treated-wood playground equipment (CPSC 2002b). EPA's Office of Pesticide Programs studied the CCA issue and announced a voluntary decision by industry to phase out the use of CCA-treated wood for consumer use by December 31, 2003 (EPA 2002b).

Summary

In 1992, the CPSC issued guidelines for assessing health hazards under the Federal Hazardous Substance Act, which included risk assessment (CPSC 2002b). In these guidelines is a series of default assumptions that are used in the absence of evidence, but are intended to be flexible, to incorporate the latest scientific information. There are provisions to use alternative procedures on a case-by-case basis, provided that the procedures used can be supported by scientific evidence and data. CPSC staff and EPA staff have worked together on several issues related to exposure and potential risk to children and will initiate studies to determine effective methods of reducing the amount of arsenic released from CCA-treated wood (CPSC 2002b).

National Fire Protection Association (NFPA)

History

Modern fire safety codes and standards were developed in the late 1800s by the National Fire Protection Association to address standards for automatic sprinklers. A total of nine different standards for piping size and sprinkler spacing could be found within 100 miles of the city of Boston (NFPA 1995). The situation was considered a plumber's nightmare, and if left unresolved, it would result in an unacceptably high rate of sprinkler-system failures. After a series of meetings, a committee was chosen to review all past meetings, and in November 1896 the National Fire Protection Association was created. Through technical committees, fire codes were developed over the next 70 years, beginning with a code for automatic sprinklers, which was released in 1897 (NFPA 1995).

Today the NFPA uses its consensus-building process with over 60,000 NFPA members worldwide. Of that number, approximately 24 percent are affiliated with fire departments, the remaining being representatives of the private and public sectors in a wide variety of fields (Watts 2002). The standard-making process requires consensus building, which in turn requires a broad-based representation of interested parties. The public comment period is a mechanism to reach beyond the committee to be even more inclusive. Finally, the general membership of the NFPA must approve before any document becomes a standard.

NFPA's mission is "to reduce the worldwide burden of fire and other hazards on the quality of life by providing and advocating {scientifically based} consensus codes and standards, research, training, and education" (NFPA 2008).

Risk Assessment

The NFPA's use of performance-based fire protection changed significantly during the 1990s. These changes evolved because of global competition, the availability of computer-run analysis tools, unique designs for large public facilities, a rise in new technology, and the occurrence of a few major disasters. Most codes and standards developed were previously based on prescriptive concepts that present design solutions that imply, "Build it this way and the design is considered safe." These codes were once adopted and enforced by the local, state, or national jurisdictions having authority. As major losses occurred, the codes were changed or modified. Prescriptive-based codes, however, were grounded in the technology existing at the time they were developed and were not flexible enough as new technologies evolved. In the 1990s, NFPA began developing codes based on performance-based fire protection; these codes focused on design outcomes and not simply design solutions (Rose, et al. 2007).

When developing a performance-based code, NFPA looks at the fire risk when conducting a fire risk assessment. With the perception of risk and the acceptance of a risk, this process is always influenced by the values of all stakeholders. For fire safety the hazards are generally fire, explosion, smoke, and toxicity associated with fire. Some of the stakeholders are regulators, employees, community, investors, emergency responders, facility owners and operators, and insurers. All groups have a chance to comment on the proposed code during the development process over a specified period of time during which modifications will be made before a final acceptance of the code is released.

Summary

NFPA codes go through a long process before a new document is published and released for use. First, a committee reviews a document that has been placed into a revision cycle. The committee then provides a standardized basis for management and business continuity in private and public sectors by providing common elements, techniques, and processes. A collection of comments is gathered from the public comments process before a draft document is produced. At this point the committee members have to approve the new draft document with a two-thirds majority vote of the committee members. The next step is to have a vote of the NFPA membership followed by an approval from the Standards Council (NFPA 2000).

In 2007, NFPA issued the NFPA 1600 standard, which was updated in 2010. NFPA 1600 is a comprehensive risk-assessment process recommended, according to the Praxiom Research Group Limited, for use in disaster management programs, emergency management programs, and business continuity management programs (NFPA 2010).

The purpose of NFPA 1600 is to help the disaster management, emergency management, and business continuity communities to manage disasters and emergencies. Its purpose is to help organizations and jurisdictions to (NFPA 2010):

- *prevent* disasters and emergencies
- *mitigate* disasters and emergencies
- *prepare* for disasters and emergencies
- *respond* to disasters and emergencies
- *recover* from disasters and emergencies

The NFPA standard can be used to:

- establish a new program
- evaluate an existing program

The NFPA standard applies to:

- public disaster management, emergency management, and business continuity programs
- private disaster management, emergency management, and business continuity programs
- not-for-profit disaster management, emergency management, and business continuity programs

American National Standards Institute (ANSI)

History

The American National Standards Institute has served as the coordinator of the U.S. voluntary standards system, which includes industry, standards-developing organizations, trade associations, professional and technical societies, government, labor, and consumer groups (ANSI 1999). It has provided a forum where the private and public sectors can work together toward the development of voluntary national consensus standards. ANSI provides the means for the United States to influence global standardization activities and the development of international standards. It is the dues-paying member and sole U.S. representative of the two major nontreaty international standards organizations—the ISO and the International Electrotechnical Commission (IEC)—via the United States National Committee (USNC) (ANSI 1999).

The history of ANSI and the U.S. voluntary standards system is dynamic. Discussions to coordinate national standards development in an effort to avoid duplication, waste, and conflict date back to 1911. In 1916 the American Institute of Electrical Engineers (now IEEE) invited the American Society of Mechanical Engineers (ASME), American Society of Civil Engineers (ASCE), American Institute of Mining and Metallurgical Engineers (AIMME), and the American Society for Testing Materials (ASTM) to join in establishing a national body to coordinate standards development and to serve as a clearinghouse for the work of standards-developing agencies (ANSI 1999).

ANSI, originally founded as the American Engineering Standards Committee (AESC), was formed on October 19, 1918, to serve as the national coordinator in the standards-development process and as an impartial organization for approving national consensus standards and halting user confusion on acceptability.

ANSI adopted its present name in 1969. Throughout these various reorganizations and name changes, the institute continued to coordinate national and international standards activities and to approve voluntary national standards, now known as American National Standards. Domestic programs were constantly expanded and modified to meet the changing needs of industry, government, and other sectors (ANSI 1999).

ANSI is a private, nonprofit organization that administers and coordinates the U.S. voluntary standardization and conformity-assessment system. Its mission is to enhance U.S. global competitiveness and the American quality of life by promoting, facilitating, and safeguarding the integrity of the voluntary standardization system. The institute represents the interests of its company, organizational, governmental, institutional, and international members through its headquarters in Washington, D.C., and its operations center in New York City (ANSI 1999).

Conformity Assessment

Conformity assessment is defined as "any activity concerned with determining directly or indirectly that relevant requirements are fulfilled" (ANSI 1999). Many of these conformity-assessment activities are applied in today's marketplace, including accreditation, certification, inspection, registration, supplier's declaration, and testing, but the one dimension that ANSI is directly engaged with is accreditation.

The institute provides accreditation services, specifically in product and personnel areas that recognize the competence of bodies to carry out product or personnel certification in accordance with requirements defined in international standards. ANSI accreditation programs are themselves created in accordance with similar international guidelines as verified by government and peer-review assessments.

Summary

ANSI provides accreditation services, specifically in product and personnel areas that recognize the competence of bodies to carry out product or personnel certification in accordance with requirements defined in international standards. ANSI accreditation programs are themselves created in accordance with similar international guidelines as verified by government and peer-review assessments. Furthermore, in partnership with the Registrar Accreditation Board (RAB), ANSI serves the marketplace in the provision of a National Accreditation Program (NAP) for quality and environmental management systems registrars (ANSI 1999).

Continuing pressures in the global marketplace to preclude redundant and costly barriers to trade drive the need for acknowledgment of equivalency across boundaries. Accordingly, ANSI is involved in several international and regional arrangements for multilateral recognition. These include the International Accreditation Forum (IAF), the Inter-American Accreditation Cooperation (IAAC), and the Pacific Accreditation Cooperation (PAC). ANSI is also recognized by the U.S. Department of Commerce via the National Institute of Standards and Technology (NIST) and their National Voluntary Conformity Assessment System Evaluation (NVCASE) program (ANSI 1999).

Conclusion

Regulatory issues for risk assessment involve a complex process that depends on the quality of scientific information available. Conducting risk assessments is best for acute risks where effects appear soon after exposure occurs. Uncertainty becomes greater as the period of time between exposure and appearance of symptoms or activities grows longer. In many circumstances uncertainties can make it impossible to come to a firm conclusion about risk (Stulz 2003).

Risk assessment is a tool used to facilitate decisions about how to optimize the use of scarce resources. Risk assessment provides the basis for determining the risk involved in certain processes and activities, and it provides justification for actions that have been undertaken.

Properly used, risk assessments often provide an essential ingredient in reaching decisions on the management of hazards. The results of a risk assessment are often used to inform rather than dictate decisions and are only one of many factors taken into account in reaching a decision (Ropeik 2000).

The use of risk assessment is not without controversy. For example, an approach based on the assessment of risk could be seen to underestimate the true impact of a problem and could undermine the adoption of precautionary approaches based on anticipating and averting harm (O'Brian 2002).

A risk assessment is a several-step process that, once completed, will provide a basis for establishing and judging tolerable risk. Information and perspectives are gathered while progressing from one stage to another, often requiring early stages of the process to be revisited. The process is iterative. Stakeholders should be involved at all stages, although final decisions may not always be taken by consensus because the various stakeholders may present and hold different or even opposing views. Risk assessment is a combination of analysis and evaluation that leads to a risk decision. All the regulations require risk assessment and revisions to the risk assessment as necessary.

Is risk assessment the only alternative? Does risk assessment ask the tough questions, such as:

- Is the proposed activity needed?
- Is the proposed activity ethical?
- Are secondary and ancillary activities considered as part of the cumulative impact to which humans and nonhumans are exposed at a location?
- Are there sustainable, less damaging, ways to accomplish the same purpose?

According to Mary O'Brian (*Making Better Environmental Decisions*), there are alternative assessments that can be used in tandem with current risk-assessment procedures (O'Brian 2000).

O'Brian (2000) states that safety professionals "identify a specific situation in which alternatives ought to be considered." She gives a few examples: draining a wetland, pesticides that are being used along county roads, and atrazine that is found in the drinking water (O'Brian 2000). Who will conduct the risk assessment and what method will be applied? The EPA has set standards to apply a risk-assessment methodology where the question might be, "Is there an alternative assessment available, and is draining a wetland something that should be done, not that it will be done with a low-risk impact to human beings?"

Important Terms (EPA 2003)

Hazard: Anything, physical or chemical, that can cause harm

Risk: A chance, high or low, that someone will be harmed by the hazard

Risk assessment: A process by which results of a risk analysis or risk estimates are used to make decisions through ranking or comparison

Risk management: Planning, organizing, leading, and controlling assets and activities through specific means that minimize adverse operational and financial effects of losses

References

Alijoyo, Antonius. 2004. *Focused Enterprise Risk Management*. 1st ed. Jakarta, Indonesia: PT Ray.

American Conference of Governmental Industrial Hygienists (ACGIH). 2002. "Guidelines for Classification of Occupational Carcinogenicity." In *Documentation of the Threshold Limits Values and Biological Exposure Indices*. 7th ed. Cincinnati:ACGIH.

American National Standards Institute (ANSI). 1999, modified July 2005. *ANSI Annual Report: Overview and History* (retrieved June 10, 2005). www.ansi.org/

Baird, S., J. Cohen, J. Graham, A. Shlyakhter, and J. Evans. 1996. "Cancer Risk Assessment: A Probabilistic Alternative to Current Practice." *Human Ecological Risk Assessment* 2(1):79–102.

Barton, A., and A. Sergeant. 1998. "Policy before the Ecological Risk Assessment: What Are We Trying to Protect?" *Human Ecological Risk Assessments* 4(4):787–795.

Bascietto, J. J. 1998. "A Framework for Ecological Risk Assessment: Beyond the Quotient Method." In M. C. Newman and C. L. Strojan, *Risk Assessment: Logic and Measurement*, p. 352. Ann Arbor, MI: Ann Arbor Press.

Benner, Jr., Ludwig. 1983. "What Is This Thing Called a Safety Regulation?" *Journal of Safety Research* 14(4): 139–143.

Centers for Disease Control (CDC). 2003. *National Report on Human Exposure to Environmental Chemicals*. NCEH Publication No. 02-0716 (retrieved February 10, 2005). www.cdc.gov/exposurereport/

Consumer Product Safety Commission (CPSC). 2002a. *U.S. Consumer Product Safety Commission Annual Report to Congress* (retrieved January 29, 2008). www.cpsc.gov/cpscpub/pubs/reports/2002rpt.pdf

______. 2002b. "CPSC & EPA Both Consider Issues Related to CCA-Treated Wood." *CPSC Monitor* (September) 7(9).

______. 2007. "Voluntary Standards Activities FY 2007." *Mid Year Report* (October 2006–March 2007). U.S. Consumer Product Safety Commission staff report. Bethesda, MD: CPSC.

Dear, Joseph A. 1995. *The Hearing of the United States House Science Committee on Risk Assessment and Title III of H.R. 9* (retrieved February 15, 2005). www.osha.gov/pls/oshaweb/owadisp.show_document?p_table=TESTIMONIES&p_id=72

Dorfman, Mark S. 1997. *Introduction to Risk Management and Insurance*. 6th ed. Upper Saddle River, NJ: Prentice Hall.

Environmental Protection Agency (EPA). 1993. "Health Effects Assessment for Mercury, EPA/540/1-86/042 (NTIS PB86134533)." Washington, D.C.: Environmental Protection Agency. Prepared in cooperation with Syracuse Research Corp., NY. See also NTIS PB85-123925, PB86-134525, and PB86-134541.

______. 1994. "Model Validation for Predictive Exposure Assessments." Risk Assessment Forum, Washington, D.C. (retrieved June 10, 2005). www.cfpub.epa.gov/crem/cremlib.cfm

______. 2000. *Risk Characterization Handbook*, EPA 100-B-00-002. Washington, D.C.: Science Policy Council.

______. 2001. "Developing Management Objectives for Ecological Risk Assessments," Risk Assessment Forum, Washington, D.C.

______. 2002a. "Health Assessment Document for Diesel Engine Exhaust, EPA/600/8-90/057F." Washington, D.C.: U.S. Environmental Protection Agency, Office of Research and Development, National Center for Environmental Assessment, Washington Office.

______. 2002b. "Questions & Answers—What You Should Know About Wood Pressure Treated with Chromated-Copper-Arsenate (CCA)." *Pesticides: Topical & Chemical Fact Sheets*. Washington, D.C.: EPA (retrieved January 29, 2008). www.epa.gov/oppad001/reregistration/cca/cca_qa.htm

______. 2003. *Framework for Cumulative Risk Assessment*, EPA/600/P-02/001F. Washington, D.C.: Environmental Protection Agency, Office of Research and Development, National Center for Environmental Assessment.

Extension Toxicology Network (EXTOXNET). 1998. "Risk Assessment Background." *Toxicology Information Briefs*. www.extoxnet.orst.edu/tibs/riskasse.htm

Federal Hazardous Substances Act of 1960 (retrieved October 12, 2011). www.epsc/gov/businfo/fhsa.pdf

Finney, C., and R. E. Polk. 1992. "Developing Stakeholder Understanding, Technical Capability, and Responsibility." *The New Bedford Harbor Superfund Forum Environmental Impact Assessment Review*. 15:517–541.

International Standards Organization (ISO). 2004. *Code of Ethics: ISO Action Plan for Developing Countries—2005* (retrieved June 10, 2005). www.iso.com/about_iso/

Jasanoff, Shelia. 1993. "Procedural Choices in Regulatory Science." *Risk: Health, Safety & Environment* 4:143–160.

Kaminski, L., A. Griffiths, M. Buswell, J. Dirsherl, J. Bach, H. Bach, T. Van Dyk, and J. Gibson. 2003. "GICHD—Risk Assessment and Mechanical Application." *EUDEM2-SCOT* 1:335–341.

Lack, Richard W., ed. 2001. *The Dictionary of Terms Used in the Safety Profession*. Des Plaines, IL: American Society of Safety Engineers.

McGarity, Thomas O., and Sidney A. Shapiro. 1993. *Workers at Risk: The Failed Promise of the Occupational Safety and Health Administration*. Westport, CT: Praeger.

______. 1996. "OSHA's Critics and Regulatory Reform." *Wake Forest Law Review* 31(3):587.

National Fire Protection Association (NFPA). 1995. *History: The Birth of NFPA* (accessed June 7, 2010). www.nfpa.org/itemDetail.asp?categoryID=500&item+18020&URL=About%20%NFPA/Overview/History.

______. 2000. *Code Development Process* (accessed June 7, 2010). www.nfpa.org/categoryLIST.asp/category ID=1618URL=Codes%10%Standards20/Cod@0%Development/%20process

______. 2008. Mission statement (retrieved June 8, 2010). www.nfpa.org/categoryList.asp?categoryID=495URL=About%20NFPA/Overview.

______. 2010. NFPA 1600, *Standard for Disaster Management, Emergency Management, and Business Continuity Management Programs*. Quincy, MA: NFPA.

National Research Council (NRC). 1983. *Risk Assessment in the Federal Government—Managing the Process*. Washington, D.C.: National Academy Press.

______. 2009. *Science and Decisions: Advancing Risk Assessments*. Committee on Improving Risk Analysis Approaches Used by the EPA, Board on Environmental Studies and Toxicology, Division on Earth and Life Studies. Washington, D.C.: National Academy Press.

O'Brian, Mary. 2000. *Making Better Environmental Decisions: An Alternative to Risk Assessment*. 4th printing. Cambridge, MA: MIT Press.

Occupational Safety and Health Administration (OSHA). 1992a. 29 CFR 1910.119, Subpart H, *Process Safety Management of Highly Hazardous Chemicals* (retrieved April 1, 2005). www.osha.gov

______. 1992b. CPL 02-02-045 - CPL 2-2.45A. *Process Safety Management of Highly Hazardous Chemicals—Compliance Guidelines and Enforcement Procedures*.

______. 1993. 29 CFR 1910.146, *Permit-Required Confined Spaces*.

______. 1995a. *All about OSHA*, OSHA pamphlet number 2056. Washington D.C.: U.S. Department of Labor.

______. 1995b. *Risk Assessment and Title III of H.R. 9*.

______. 1998. 29 CFR 1910.146, Appendix A."Permit-required Confined Space Decision Flow Chart."

______. 2000. *Process Safety Management*. OSHA Document 3132 (retrieved January 29, 2008). www.osha.gov/Publications/osha3132.html

______. 2006. 29 CFR 1910, Subpart Z, *Toxic and Hazardous Substances* (retrieved November 10, 2007). www.osha.gov

______. 2007a. 29 CFR 1910, Section VI, *General Industry Standards* (retrieved November 10, 2007). www.osha.gov

______. 2007b. 29 CFR 1926, *Safety and Health Regulations for Construction*.

Oliver, James. 2005. "The National Environmental Policy Act." Chapter 18 in *Hazardous Materials Management Desk Reference*. 2d ed. Rockville, MD: Academy of Certified Hazardous Materials Managers.

Rhomberg, L. R., 1997, "A Survey of Methods for Chemical Health Risk Assessment among Federal Regulatory Agencies." Risk Assessment and Risk Management Commission. Washington, D.C.: EPA.

Ropeik, David. 2000. "Let's Get Real about Risk." *Washington Post*, August 6, 2000, p. B1.

Rose, Susan, Stephanie Flamberg, and Fred Leverenz. 2007. *How to Perform a Risk Assessment According to NFPA 1600 ANNEX A* (retrieved November 10, 2007). Praxiom Research Group Limited. www.praxiom.org/risk-assessment.htm

Russell, M., and M. Gruber. 1987. "Risk Assessment in Environmental Policy-Making," *Science Journal* 236:286–290.

Schoeny, R., P. Muller, and J. Mumford. 1998. "Risk Assessment for Human Health Protection: Applications to Environmental Mixtures." In *Pollution Risk Assessment and Management*, pp. 205–234. P. Douben, ed. New York: John Wiley and Sons.

Stulz, Rene M. 2003. *Risk Management and Derivatives*. 1st ed. Mason, OH: Thomson South-Western.

Watts, Jr., J. M. 2002. "Risk Indexing." In *SFPE Handbook of Fire Protection Engineering*. 3d ed. Quincy, MA: NFPA.

Appendix: Further Reading

Alexander, Carol, and Elizabeth Sheedy, eds. 2004. *The Professional Risk Managers' Handbook: A Comprehensive Guide to Current Theory and Best Practices*. Wilmington, DE: PRMIA Publications.

Almand, Kathleen H. 2007. "Fire Risk Assessment as a Tool." *NFPA Journal* (March/April) (retrieved November 10, 2007). www.nfpa.org/publicColumn.asp

Environmental Protection Agency (EPA). Information Quality Guidelines Web site. www.epa.gov/oei/qualityguidelines

______. Quality System Web site. www.epa.gov/quality

______. Risk Assessment Guidelines Web site. www.cfpub.epa.gov/ncea/raf/recordisplay.cfm?deid=55907

______. Science Policy Council Web site. www.epa.gov/osp/spc

Health and Safety Executive (HSE). *Five Steps to Risk Assessment*. www.hse.gov.uk/risk/fivesteps.htm

______. 1992. *Management of Health and Safety at Work: Approved Code of Practice, L21*. Sudbury, Suffolk, UK: HSE Books.

______. 2006. *Essentials of Health and Safety at Work*. Sudbury, Suffolk, UK: HSE Books.

2

Systems and Process Safety

Mark D. Hansen

LEARNING OBJECTIVES

- Become familiar with system safety terminology.
- Be able to recognize various hazardous energy sources and controls.
- Understand the concepts of risk and risk assessment.
- Understand risk mitigation and acceptability criteria.
- Learn about basic design solutions for identified hazards.
- Grasp basic analysis techniques, such as fault tree analysis, event tree analysis, failure modes and effects analysis, hazard and operability studies (HAZOPs), functional and control flow analysis, and sneak circuit analysis.
- Learn the purpose and use of hazard-analysis worksheets and hazard reports.

To SOME, system safety is an arcane tool, but to others it is a tool used daily in the course of doing their jobs. It has received a bad rap over time because many have acquired mental blocks to this style of applying safety to hazard prevention. Even with all the negative press, system safety is a discipline that has been effectively used to eliminate and control hazards (Roland and Moriarty 1983). System safety has saved many lives in the military, NASA, the Department of Energy, and in many commercial applications.

System safety provides a systematic approach to safety. It begins in the conceptual stages of a project and continues through operation and disposal. It involves the following:

- managing the safety program—planning and execution
- analyzing the system for safety problems at all design stages
- identifying design requirements to make the system safe
- recording results.

System Safety Concepts

This systematic approach introduced science to the "Fly-Fix-Fly" methods that the Air Force was already using (Malasky 1975). This involved building a system (airplane), operating (fly) it until something went wrong and caused an accident, fixing (fix) the problem, and then operating (fly) it again until something else broke. This was a costly approach in terms of equipment and human loss. By analyzing an aircraft design for hazards and fixing them during design, the Air Force had fewer accidents (Roland and Moriarty 1983). A systematic approach makes safety more of a science than an art. It catches safety problems during the design phase where they can be corrected more economically.

Safety should not be ensured at the work site alone. It must be ensured ahead of time, beginning with the equipment used and the operations performed. This requires advanced planning for safety from the earliest conceptual stages, and continuous safety awareness and analysis throughout design, construction, and operation. The entire system and its interfaces must be considered. The risks must be identified as much as possible, either eliminated or controlled to an acceptable level of risk, and accepted by management.

Hazard Analysis

The basic purpose of system safety is to identify the risk of a system. This involves analyzing the system to identify the following:

- hazards
- outcomes of potential mishaps (hazard effects)
- the potential mishap's occurrence
- the severity and probability of potential mishaps (risk assessment) and how to reduce the likelihood of the potential mishaps occurring (hazard control)

When analyzing a system for hazards, first, make the task manageable. For simple devices such as a toaster or food processor, it may be easy enough to look at the device as a whole and see the hazards involved. With complex systems such as satellites, space vehicles, or chemical plants, the task may initially seem overwhelming. For these systems, the first step is to break the system down into subsystems and the subsystems into components. Next, one looks at the subsystems and components individually for hazards. Then one should analyze the interfaces of these parts for hazards.

During the conceptual design stages, there is little design detail. One may know only what functions the system performs and what types of subsystems may be involved. Still, it is wise to look at the system and ask, what are the basic hazards associated with the system functions and subsystems? A detailed description of the system should be documented to support any analysis (DOD 2000). This at least allows for pinpointing areas of concern for more detailed analysis later on.

Hazard Cause and Effect

As noted earlier, a hazard is the potential for a mishap. Hence, hazards need to be documented in complete statements—generally with a noun and a verb—that accurately describe a condition or event that could result in a mishap. One-word hazards such as *hydrogen* are not adequate. Hydrogen in itself is not a hazard, but merely an element. It is a component of water. It becomes hazardous only when it is released into an area where it could contact an ignition source (creating the potential for fire or explosion) or when it displaces oxygen in an enclosed space (creating the potential for asphyxiation). A better hazard statement would be the following: "Hydrogen inadvertently released into the laboratory."

One must also be careful not to express the hazard as a mishap. Suppose a hazard is labeled "fire." Usually when there is a fire, there is a mishap. The *hazard* is the condition or event that created the potential for fire. Such a hazard might be expressed as the following: "Inadvertent leakage of gasoline onto the garage floor."

The *hazard effect* is the credible worst-case mishap that could result from an uncontrolled hazardous condition. This describes the potential severity of the hazard. One also needs to estimate the probability of the mishap's occurrence. Often, the probability is determined by an educated guess, rather than by exact methods. The combination of severity and probability yields the risk faced from that hazard. Decision makers can then consider all risk factors to determine which hazards get fixed and how, considering available time and money. Knowing the cause of the hazard helps in identifying hazard controls.

For example, suppose a steel tower is being designed. It is next to a wooden building full of people. Assuming the tower is designed with acceptable safety factors (e.g., design codes, consensus standards), one hazard would be weakening of the steel structure by corrosion. The effect would be collapse of the tower onto the building. The severity would be death or severe injury to the building occupants and loss of building and tower. The cause would be exposure of the steel to humid salt air. The mishap is likely to occur in time. Therefore, this poses a high-risk hazard that needs to be controlled. From the cause, it is obvious that the steel needs to be protected—probably with a corrosion-resistant protective coating. The identified hazard information would be as follows:

- Hazard: Weakened structure due to corrosion in the steel
- Cause: Exposure to humid, salt air
- Effect: Collapse of tower onto building, causing death and injury
- Risk: High severity and probability, high risk
- Control: Paint tower with corrosion-resistant protective coating

When describing hazards, keep the following in mind:

- Make a complete hazard statement that describes a hazardous condition or event. Avoid one- or two-word hazard statements.
- Ensure that there is a logical flow from the cause to the hazard to the effect. The cause should cause the hazard, and the hazard should cause the effect.

The following is an example of an incorrect hazard description:

- Hazard: Oxygen pressure
- Cause: Oxygen leakage due to loosening of fittings, chafing, or excess pressure
- Effect: Injury and/or system damage due to fire

Is "oxygen pressure" a hazardous condition or event? Not if it is properly contained. Does "oxygen leakage" cause "oxygen pressure"? Does "oxygen pressure" cause "fire"? Not only does this hazard statement not state a hazardous condition or event, but further, there is no logical flow from cause to hazard to effect.

In this case, a higher oxygen concentration increases the potential for fire. Therefore, a better hazard statement would be "Oxygen-enriched atmosphere due to oxygen leakage and ignition source present." The revised hazard description could read as follows:

- Hazard: Oxygen-enriched atmosphere due to leakage from oxygen lines and ignition source present
- Cause: Loosening of oxygen fittings, chafing, or excess pressure
- Effect: Injury and/or system damage due to fire

There may be other ways to adequately describe this hazard. The important things are the complete hazard statement and logical flow.

Controlling Hazards

There are three factors to consider in controlling hazards: effectiveness, feasibility, and cost. The hazard control should to be effective in reducing the likelihood of the potential mishap and should not introduce any new hazards into the system. Next, the control must be feasible—not degrade system performance to an unacceptable level. Finally, one must consider cost. Can the organization afford the control? Will there be an adequate payback in risk reduction? (e.g., is the organization spending $100,000 to protect a $20,000 piece of equipment?) Are there hazards with a higher risk that need to be fixed first?

Controlling hazards requires use of an appropriate method (engineering design, interlocks, etc.) (Hammer 1989) to reduce the severity and/or probability of occurrence (DOD Directive 3150.2). For example, one could follow what is known as the hazard-reduction precedence sequence (HRPS). The HRPS may also be called by other names, such as risk-reduction sequence, system safety precedence, or safety precedence sequence.

Whatever the name, the sequence is basically the same. In order of most effective to least effective, the HRPS is as follows:

- Design for minimum hazard.
- Install safety devices.
- Install warning devices.
- Use special procedures.

After using this sequence, there may be some residual risk. *Residual risk* is the risk remaining after controls have been put in place to control the hazard. There are few operations that are risk-free. Management must either accept this risk or go through the sequence again.

Designing for minimum hazards is the safest alternative. However, this may render the system useless or be too costly. Eliminating the explosives from a high-tech smart bomb makes it totally safe, but the bomb cannot perform its intended function. On the other side of the coin, using solid fuel instead of liquid fuel may be a safer alternative for a launching system.

If it is not practical or possible to design the hazard out of the system, safety devices must then be installed. These may include pressure-relief valves to prevent overpressure; interlocks that fail to a safe condition to prevent injuries; safe/arm devices that act like safeties on weapons, protective barriers such as laser beams that, once broken, halt machine operation; and so on. Safety devices are part of the hardware, not dependent on human performance, and are effective to the extent that the hardware is used as designed.

If safety devices are not practical or possible, then warning devices may be installed, such as alarms, signs, and so on. These are effective only to the extent that they are used properly.

Special procedures are the least effective control. This includes not only written procedures, but also personal protective equipment such as protective suits, self-contained breathing apparatuses, and so on. Procedures are effective only to the extent that people follow them. Personal protective equipment is only effective to the extent that it is used properly. Procedures are dependent on human factors and human behavior, which is often unpredictable. Training personnel becomes critically important when relying on safety procedures.

Suppose that a robot is taking parts from a bin and putting them on widgets. One hazard to consider would be:

- Hazard: Fast-moving robot arm around people or equipment
- Cause: Excessive speed and lack of barriers to keep out people and equipment
- Effect: Injury or damage due to impact of robot arm on humans or valuable equipment

Now one must develop hazard controls.

First, consider design measures. One could slow down the robot arm so that impact with personnel or equipment will not cause injury or damage. This may not be practical because it would reduce the robot's productivity.

Safety devices may be more practical. There are several options: put a fence around the robot's operating area, install software-hardware interlocks on the gate so that the robot shuts down when the gate is open, put special mats around the robot so that it shuts off when someone steps on them, pad the robot arm.

If management thinks the safety devices are too costly, then one resorts to warning devices and procedures and policies. These may include painting a yellow line around the robot's operating area, installing a red light that flashes when the robot is operating, and instructing employees not to enter the area. One could also put up a warning sign or develop special procedures for people to follow when around the robot.

The important thing to remember is that once a hazard is identified, steps must be taken to control it. Methods such as the HRPS offer a systematic approach or sequence to go through for finding control measures. What control measures are applied will depend on operational effectiveness, cost, and schedule. The high-risk hazards should be controlled first. Management may have to accept some residual risk even after the controls have been applied.

How to Recognize Hazards

There is no one rule for hazard recognition. Hazards come in many different forms. They can result from design deficiencies, human error, environmental factors, and so on. This section gives several general guidelines that help us recognize hazards. Hazard recognition is important early on in the project and in selecting appropriate hazard-recognition techniques to fit the types of hazards or concerns that one desires to control.

Energy Sources

Most hazards are related to an inadvertent or uncontrolled release of energy. An explosion causes shock waves and kinetic energy of shrapnel, which can cause injury or damage. Uncontrolled electrical energy can cause injury or death and property damage. So the first task is to identify all energy sources. Then one needs to determine what targets (people, objects, environment, etc.) could be injured or damaged by any release of that energy. Look for barriers to harmful energy flow between the source and target. Barriers may be physical (design measures) or administrative (policies and procedures). Figure 1 illustrates the relationship of the energy source, barrier, and target and shows how barriers can prevent injuries from energy sources.

Energy may be of one or more of the following types:

- Mechanical—rotating machinery
- Potential—raised crane load, coiled spring; resulting in kinetic energy—falling or flying objects
- Pressure (pneumatic, hydraulic, acoustic)—stored pressure that could be released
- Thermal—high or low temperatures
- Chemical—toxic or corrosive chemicals, reactants
- Electrical—energy that is used to operate equipment
- Radioactive—energy that is used to provide power

Many systems will contain several energy sources. A high-temperature furnace contains both thermal and electrical energy. Also consider interaction among many energy sources. For instance, a tank of gasoline is next to a house in a lightning-prone area. There are two energy sources—electrical energy from the lightning and chemical energy in the gasoline. If the two interact in the right combination, this could cause a fire or explosion.

The targets are the house and its occupants. A hazard statement for this situation should be written in terms of the energy and targets. Barriers that prevent energy transfer to the targets are the hazard controls.

The hazard could be described as follows:

- Hazard: Leaking gasoline tank next to house in lightning-prone area.
- Cause: Careless placement of gasoline tank
- Effect: Death or injury and damage from fire or explosion
- Controls: Move tank a safe distance from the house, install lightning shield around tank, build a blast wall between tank and house, and abandon house before lightning storm

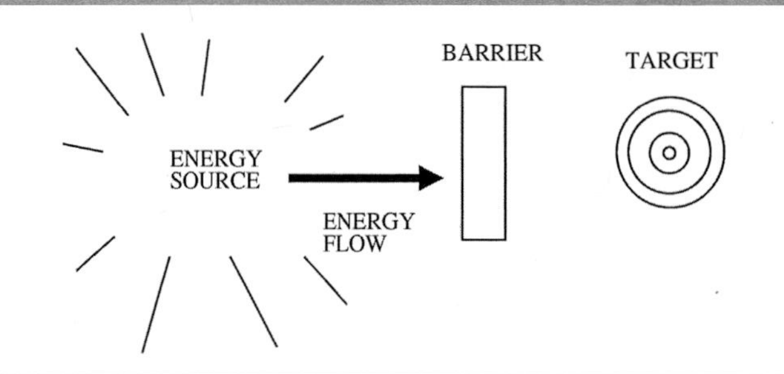

FIGURE 1. Relationships between energy source, barrier, and target (*Source:* Hansen 1993)

Looking for energy sources, targets, and barriers is the best technique to use during the conceptual design stages. One may not see or be able to define all barriers because the design detail is not defined. However, general requirements can be defined. High-energy subsystems are candidates for more detailed analysis later on.

Non-energy-Related Hazards

Examining energy sources enables one to identify most of the serious hazards, but by restricting the process only to energy, one could miss other serious hazards. Such hazards can involve interruptions to normal life functions—for example, asphyxiation, smoke inhalation, or disease—or problems that result from human factors.

- to find such hazards, look for the following:
- presence of inert gas
- potential for loss of breathable atmosphere
- potential for disease
- human interfaces with the system
- software hazards

Software in and of itself is not hazardous. However, it can become hazardous when it interfaces with hardware. Software that controls hardware functions may command an undesired event or condition. Software that monitors hardware may fail to sense or properly process a hazardous condition. There are various methods for analyzing software. It is important that hardware designers identify all software interfaces with the hardware and bring them to the attention of the software designers and analysts. This includes subroutine controls for weapons systems, traffic lights and traffic control, communications systems, cancer irradiation equipment, and so on.

Failures

Many hazards do not result from failures. However, some do. Consider two cases:

1. The failure of safety-critical subsystems—life support, fire alarm or sprinkler, and so on—can cause a hazardous situation. Look at the organization's system to see if it contains any such subsystems. If it does, first, determine the probability that these systems will fail, and then take measures to reduce the probability, if necessary.
2. Component failures can cause hazards or mishaps. For instance, failure of a hydrogen-line coupling can cause hydrogen to leak into a room and create a potential for explosion.

Examine the system to see if any such failures are possible. This can be done in the course of the safety analysis, or one can consult a failure modes and effects analysis, if it is available.

Helpful Hints for Recognizing Hazards

Using the team approach is best. In most cases, no one person can be familiar with all aspects of system design and operation and related hazards. At a minimum, a knowledgeable engineer should analyze the system first and give the results to a safety engineer for review. Consult experts frequently. Experience is invaluable for many reasons, but one should learn from a past history of accidents to avoid repeating them. Inquire about past accidents associated with the organization's system.

Look at all operating modes. Often, a system is scrutinized only while it is in normal operating mode. Problems often do not occur here, but at startup or shutdown. Other examples of operating modes include transport, delivery, installation, checkout, emergency startup and shutdown, and maintenance.

The following is a list of proven methods for finding hazards (Roland and Moriarty 1983):

- Use intuitive engineering sense.
- Examine similar facilities or systems.
- Examine system specifications and expectations.
- Review codes, regulations, and consensus standards.
- Interview current or intended system users or operators.
- Review system safety studies from other similar systems.
- Review historical documents—mishap files, near-miss reports, OSHA-recordable injury rates, National Safety Council data, manufacturers' reliability analyses, and so on.
- Consider external influences, such as local weather, environment, or personnel tendencies.
- Brainstorm—mentally develop credible problems and play "what if?" games: "What could go wrong?" "What is the worst possible thing that could happen?"
- Consider all the energy sources (pressure, motion, chemical, biological, radiation, electrical, gravity, and heat and cold). What's necessary to keep these sources under control? What happens if they get out of control?
- Use checklists such as the hazard category list presented in the following section.

Hazard Categories

The following is a checklist of hazard categories. These are also called *generic hazards*. Note, first, that most are one- or two-word statements and therefore not appropriate for hazard statements. Rather, they are intended as thought joggers. Some of them, such as collision and fire, describe mishaps instead of hazardous conditions or events. In those cases, look for the potential hazard—for example, a drunk driver or bad brakes for a collision. Some are interrelated. For instance, contamination from a corrosive liquid can cause corrosion on a metal structure, which in turn can cause structural failure.

This list is not complete. If one finds hazards that do not fit into any of these categories, add another category to the existing list.

Figure 2 outlines the procedure for using each category as a guide to identifying hazards.

Checklist of Hazard Categories

1. Collision

Collisions are usually thought of as mishaps. Hence, in this category, one looks for the potential for collisions between people and objects or objects and other objects. Collisions often result in injury or death to people and damage to equipment.

Conditions	*Causes*
Structural failure	Inadequate structure
Inadvertent motion (especially in zero-gravity)	Human error
Falling objects	Horseplay
Flying projectiles	Inadequate handling
Lifting equipment	Equipment failure

2. Contamination

Contamination could be a condition, a hazard or hazard cause, or a mishap. When there is a chemical spill, it is usually considered a mishap because at least environmental damage can be involved. Leakage of corrosive material onto a steel structure is a condition that can cause corrosion, which in turn could cause structural failure. Contamination could involve release of hazardous materials (e.g., toxic, flammable, corrosive), dust and dirt particles (causing degraded performance or health problems), growth of fungus, and so on. It could result in death or illness to people, damage to equipment or environment, or loss of resources (e.g., contaminated fuel or water).

Conditions	*Causes*
Presence of hazardous materials	Inadequate containment
Leaks	Human error
Dust or dirt in critical systems or components	Improper handling
Presence of fungi	Environmental factors (rust, wind, sand, etc.)
Materials that off-gas (release vapors)	Worn seals, gaskets, joints
Toxic substances	

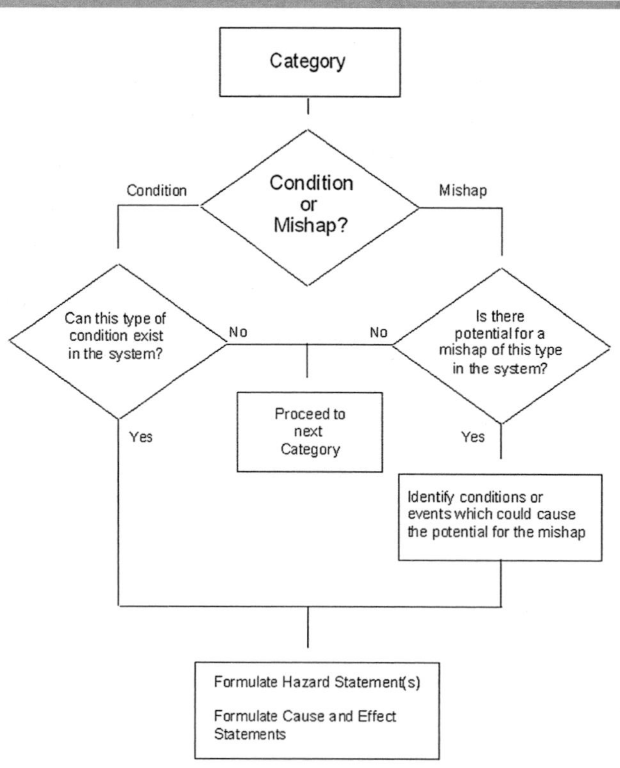

FIGURE 2. Procedure for using each category as a guide to identify hazards (*Source:* Malasky 1974)

3. Corrosion

Corrosion is usually thought of as a condition that could lead to a mishap. It can result from leakage of corrosive or reactive materials (acids, salts, solvents, halogens, etc.) or from other factors, such as galvanic corrosion from joining two dissimilar metals due to a direct current electricity that is chemically generated or exposure to environmental extremes (temperature or humidity). Corrosion can result in death or injury to personnel or in equipment damage (structural or mechanical failure).

Conditions	*Causes*
Presence of corrosive materials	Contamination
	Inadequate corrosion protection
Joining dissimilar metals	Design errors
Stress corrosion	Environmental factors (vibration, temperature)
Polymerization	Hydrogen embitterment

4. Electrical

In this category one looks for conditions that could cause electrical mishaps—shock, arcing, overcurrent, electrical fire, and so on. Such conditions may include potential for people contacting energized parts, sensitive electronics that need overcurrent protection, short circuits, and potential for environmental electricity (e.g., static electricity, lightning, etc.). Mishaps from this category could include death or injury from electrical shock, equipment damage, overcurrent, overheating and burns, or fire.

Conditions	***Causes***
Exposed electrical conductors	Inadequate insulation
Sensitive electronic parts	Worn insulation
Energized casing or parts	Inadequate grounding
Short circuit	Lightning potential
Lightning/static electricity	Contamination
Flammable materials with electrical parts	Damaged electrical connectors

5. Explosion

An explosion is usually considered a mishap. It is a violent energy release that causes a shock wave and flying fragments. It can result from misuse of explosives, increased temperature or pressure, chemical reactions, and so on. Equipment such as pumps, motors, blowers, generators, and lasers can malfunction and explode. Explosions can result in death or injury to people or damage to equipment both from shock waves or shrapnel and from spread of toxic substances.

Conditions	***Causes***
Presence of explosives and ignitors	Improper handling
Reactive chemical processes	Inadequate pressure relief
High temperature/pressure	

6. Fire

Fire is usually thought of as a mishap. The hazards to look for in this category are conditions that could cause a fire. Fuel (some flammable material), an oxidizer (oxygen, nitric acid, nitrogen tetroxide, etc.), and an ignition source (spark, electrical arc, pilot flame, hot surface, etc.) are necessary to cause a fire. Without any one of these, there is no hazard. Generally, the presence of highly flammable materials is a hazardous condition. Oxygen is present in the air. Potential ignition sources are all around—rotating machinery, heaters, faulty electrical wiring, and so on. Only in highly controlled environments can one claim there are no oxidizers or ignition sources. Fire can result in death, injury, or illness to people or damage to property. Most personnel injury results from smoke inhalation (Hammer 1989). Burning some materials, such as plastic, can spread toxic fumes. Review material safety data sheets because there are some situations where no ignition source is needed to result in fire (concentrated hydrogen peroxide and pyrophorics such as aluminum alkyls are examples). Also, some chemicals may include oxygen sources and burn in low- or no-oxygen atmospheres.

Conditions	***Causes***
Presence of flammable materials	Inadequate containment
Organic substances	Careless handling of flammables or oxidizers
Flammable metals	
Chemicals	
Oxidizers	

7. Physiological

This category deals with conditions that could cause health problems in human beings—physical or mental disability, asphyxiation, disease, and so on.

Conditions

Presence of viruses, bacteria, oxygen-deficient atmospheres, carcinogens, mutagens, teratagens, and so on

Rapid pressure or temperature changes

8. Human Factors

Human error can cause hazards or accidents in any of the categories listed. This category is included to emphasize the importance of looking for ways that human error can cause hazards.

Conditions

Too much physical or psychological stress

Hostile environment

Hardware not designed for humans

Inadequate, confusing, or difficult procedures

Untrained or unqualified people

Recent changes

9. Loss of Capability

This could be a condition or a mishap. Loss of some critical function, such as life support, constitutes a mishap resulting in instant death. If there is back-up life support, then loss of the primary system is a condition that could lead to loss of the backup and a resultant mishap. That may require mission abort or system shutdown. If a spacecraft loses reentry capability, its crew is left stranded in space. Loss of capability can result in death or injury to people. Energy systems and their potential problems were mentioned earlier. Consider, along with energy sources, the loss of the energy source. The loss of electrical power in a chemical plant is a very serious concern and hazard.

Conditions	***Causes***
Loss of primary critical function with redundant systems	Failure
Loss of critical monitoring function	Design deficiency
Component failure	Lack of redundancy
Damage	Operator error
Loss of power or energy source	

10. Radiation

The hazard to look for in this category is exposure of people or sensitive equipment to ionizing and non-ionizing radiation. Ionizing radiation includes alpha, beta, gamma, neutron, and x-ray from radioactive substances. Non-ionizing radiation includes laser, infrared, microwave, ultraviolet, and radio waves. Sources include high-energy antennae, radar, video monitors, welding, infrared and ultraviolet lights, and so on. Exposure to radiation can injure or kill people and damage sensitive equipment.

Conditions	***Causes***
Presence of radioactive materials	Inadequate containment
Radiation sources	Inadequate protection
	Careless handling

11. Temperature Extremes

This category represents conditions of high or low temperatures. Such exposure can injure or kill people or damage sensitive equipment. Increased pressure or flammability from increased temperature can result in fire or explosion.

Conditions	***Causes***
Presence of hot or cold surfaces	Inadequate protection
Hot or cold environments	Design deficiencies
Elevated pressure	Careless handling
Flammability, volatility, reactivity	Environmental factors
Reduced reliability	

12. Mechanical

In this category, look for mechanical conditions that could cause injuries such as cuts, broken bones, and crushed body parts.

Conditions	***Causes***
Exposed sharp edges or points	Lack of guards or failure to use
Moving machinery	Inadequate tie-downs
Pinch points/shear points	Design deficiencies
Elevated objects	
Unstable objects	
Crushing surfaces	
Stored energy release	

13. Pressure

This category deals with conditions related to pressure—high pressure or low pressure. The sudden release of pressure causes a shock wave and possible fragments that could injure people and damage equipment. Slow release of pressure can cause contamination. One can find pressure in gases or liquids (hydraulics).

Conditions	***Causes***
Overpressure	Lack of pressure relief
Vacuum	Inadequate pressure relief
Loose pressure line	Inadequate pressure couplings
Hydraulic ram	Metal fatigue
Inadvertent release—toxic or flammable materials	

Risk Assessment

As discussed earlier, risk is a combination of the severity and probability of a potential mishap. It is not enough to look *only* at the severity. A person can think of many worst-case consequences, such as cutting one's throat while shaving, but the chances of those consequences occurring are so remote that he may not want to worry about it. Hence, in setting priorities for safety activities, one must consider the *total* risk involved, not just the severities.

Severity is the worst-case, yet believable, hazard effect. It could range from minor injury and damage to death and system destruction. Severity is usually easy to determine. There is generally little debate about the worst-case outcome of a potential mishap.

Probability is the chance that a specific outcome will occur. The probability can change with the exposure time. Suppose one predicts that there will be an earthquake somewhere in the world tomorrow. He has a chance of being right. However, if one predicts there will be an earthquake somewhere in the world in the next year, he is almost certain to be right. When stating probabilities, one needs to include a specific time period or exposure interval.

It is usually difficult to determine probability. It is often controversial and subjective. Safety people may tend to estimate a high probability of a system mishap, whereas the designers may tend to estimate a low probability (Roland and Moriarty 1983). The actual probability may be between the two. If the mishap would result from a component failure, and one has significant failure-rate data on that component, then one can just use the failure-rate number. If one has significant experience with a similar system, then one can use that experience to estimate a probability.

In many cases, one is dealing with new systems and technology. However, we can still arrive at some kind of probability estimate. The best approach is to develop prototypes and test them. However, this is expensive and not always practical. Another good approach is to run computer simulations. This is cheaper than testing but is only effective to the extent that the computer model is accurate. The least effective, yet least costly, approach is analysis (Roland and Moriarty 1983). For instance, if a structural analysis is performed and it finds that there is a high safety factor, then one can conclude that there is a low probability of structural failure.

Many analysis situations may not be as straightforward as structural analysis. In these cases, one needs to use "engineering judgment." The following are some factors to consider.

How many causes are there to a particular hazard? For example, a safety person is concerned about gasoline puddles in the garage catching fire. The more gasoline cans and tanks there are in the garage, the greater the likelihood that there will be a leak and resultant fire.

What is the maturity of the system and technology? If a firm is designing a new type of spacecraft, using new technology, then there is probably a good chance of a malfunction or mishap because it has not been tested over time (Stephenson 1991).

How long does it take for a hazardous condition to turn into a mishap, and how can it be detected? For example, a company uses a process that can cause an explosion if it reaches a certain temperature. If its temperature rises slowly enough that it will likely be detected, and the process can be shut down before it reaches the critical temperature, then there is a low probability that the explosion will occur.

Probabilities can be expressed quantitatively or qualitatively. If there is numerical data, it can be used (e.g., 0.0002 per exposure hour, once in one million cycles, etc.). If numerical data is hard to get, it can be expressed qualitatively (e.g., likely to occur soon, likely to occur in time, remote, impossible, etc.).

Risk—putting severity and probability together—is often expressed via a matrix. First, severity levels are set up. The following is an example of a severity categorization:

I—Catastrophic; death or total system destruction
II—Critical; serious injury or major property damage
III—Marginal; minor injury or property damage
IV—Negligible; little or no effect

Then we assign probability levels:

A—Likely to occur immediately
B—Probably will occur in time
C—May occur in time
D—Unlikely to occur

Finally, the risk-assessment matrix is set up using the severity levels:

		Probability level			
		A	B	C	D
	I	1	1	2	3
Severity	II	1	2	3	4
level	III	2	3	4	5
	IV	3	4	5	6

One method of expressing risk is to assign a number to each block of the matrix as shown here. The number is called a RAC (risk assessment code).

Risk Assessment and Decision Making

Making decisions about risks is intrinsic to designing in-process safety. Historically, when designing a new process, engineers examined how the system could break down (Roland and Moriarty 1983). They would then determine the impact of system failures, and estimate their likelihood. Evaluating these issues produced a continuous stream of risk-related design decisions. Unfortunately, these decisions were based more on perceptions of risk than on real measurements of risk (Roland and Moriarty 1983).

The result was an unsystematic and incomplete assessment of the design. This led to an inadequate and sometimes cost-prohibitive, or incompatible, risk-reduction solution. When the process for determining the design basis lacked consistency, it was difficult to know whether the same risk-management philosophy supported all of the company's risk decisions.

By designing in-process safety and decision making using a risk-based approach, safety professionals can improve their ability to understand and reduce risk, control costs, and protect their investments and reputations, as well as protect company employees. Risk-based approaches get integrated with the process and can help safety managers translate the technical complexities of risk analysis into clear messages about risks and options for corporate management.

The Concept of Risk

Before continuing, it will be helpful to look at some terms that are often misused when talking about safety and risk. In everyday conversation, people use words such as risk, hazard, and danger interchangeably. For example, crossing the street without looking both ways might be described as "hazardous," "dangerous," or "risky," all meaning pretty much the same thing.

In chemical process-safety design, risk is defined more precisely in terms of the likelihood and consequences of incidents that could expose people, property, or the environment to the harmful effects of hazards (CCPS 2000).

Hazards are potential sources of harm. Examples of hazards include a reactor vessel under high pressure, a very corrosive chemical, and an improperly sized emergency relief valve (CCPS 2000).

Likelihood is determined in terms of two factors: frequency (how often does this happen?) and probability (what are the odds that it will happen?) (CCPS 2000). Likelihood can be determined by using a risk matrix as shown here:

Criticality or Severity Ratings

1 Catastrophic	Loss of containment of substantial amounts of material that may result in an on-site or off-site death, or damage and production loss greater than $1,000,000
2 Severe	Loss of containment of material that may result in multiple injuries or morbidity, or damage and production loss between $100,000 and $1,000,000
3 Moderate	Loss of containment of small amounts of material that may result in minor injury or morbidity, or damage and production loss between $10,000 and $100,000
4 Slight	Loss of containment of small amounts of material that may result in no injuries or morbidity, or damage and production loss less than $10,000

Frequency Ratings

1 Frequent	Likely to occur more than once per year

2 Probable	May occur several times in 1 to 10 years
3 Occasional	May occur sometime in 10 to 100 years
4 Remote	Unlikely to occur, but possible in 100 to 10,000 years
5 Improbable	So unlikely to occur it can be assumed that occurrence is less than once in 10,000 years

Based on the criticality and frequency definitions presented in the preceding ratings, a risk matrix (see Tables 1 and 2) is used to identify a risk rank (DOD 2000). The risk rankings are defined in Tables 1 and 2 (DOD 2000).

Consequences cover specific outcomes or impacts of an incident, such as a toxic vapor cloud that spreads beyond the plant boundary into a neighborhood or an explosion that causes a fatality.

Risks cannot be completely eliminated from industrial processes any more than they can be eliminated from other activities. Instead, the goal of system safety is to consistently reduce risk to a level that can be accepted by all concerned—facility staff, company management, shareholders, surrounding communities, the public, industry groups, and government agencies. For this reason, defining what constitutes *acceptable* and *unacceptable* risk is a critical part of risk-based design.

TABLE 1

Risk-Ranking Matrix

		Frequency Rating				
		1	2	3	4	5
Criticality Ratings	1	1	1	1	2	4
	2	1	2	3	3	4
	3	2	3	4	4	4
	4	4	4	4	4	4

(*Source:* DOD 2000)

TABLE 2

Risk-Ranking Definitions

Ranking Levels	Description	Action Required
1	Very High	Must be mitigated with engineering and administrative controls before continued operation
2	High	Must be mitigated by engineering controls within six months
3	Medium	Must be mitigated by administrative controls within six months
4	Low	Mitigation is optional depending on cost-benefit

(*Source:* DOD 2000)

Steps in Risk Assessment

A risk-based design approach (see Figure 3) integrates safety where it belongs: at each stage in the design cycle, including laboratory, pilot, production design, and operation. This technique can be incorporated into a company's current design approaches because it derives from process-design engineers' characteristic problem-solving methods. Therefore, it can be applied to simple and complex designs.

Systematic risk-based design helps engineers to include system safety in the design at the earliest development stages, where the most cost-effective solutions to safety challenges tend to be found. Risk-based design supports a disciplined thought process and opens the door to creativity and innovation in risk reduction. This increases the range of possible solutions and focuses attention on risk-reducing options that may be overlooked using historical approaches.

This approach traces the most efficient path possible through the risk-assessment process. In the nine steps that follow (Roland and Moriarty 1983), review and reassessment loops come into play only as needed.

1. ***Identify failure scenarios.*** When engineers have established an initial process design, they can address failure scenarios that might require a safety system. Process hazard-analysis techniques and past experience assist in identifying possible failure scenarios.
2. ***Estimate the consequences.*** In this step, designers establish the consequences of the failure scenarios identified in Step 1. These scenarios typically involve quality, safety, health, and environmental impacts. Consequences of interest include fires, vapor cloud explosions, toxic releases, and major equipment damage. Some potential consequences can be determined through direct observation,

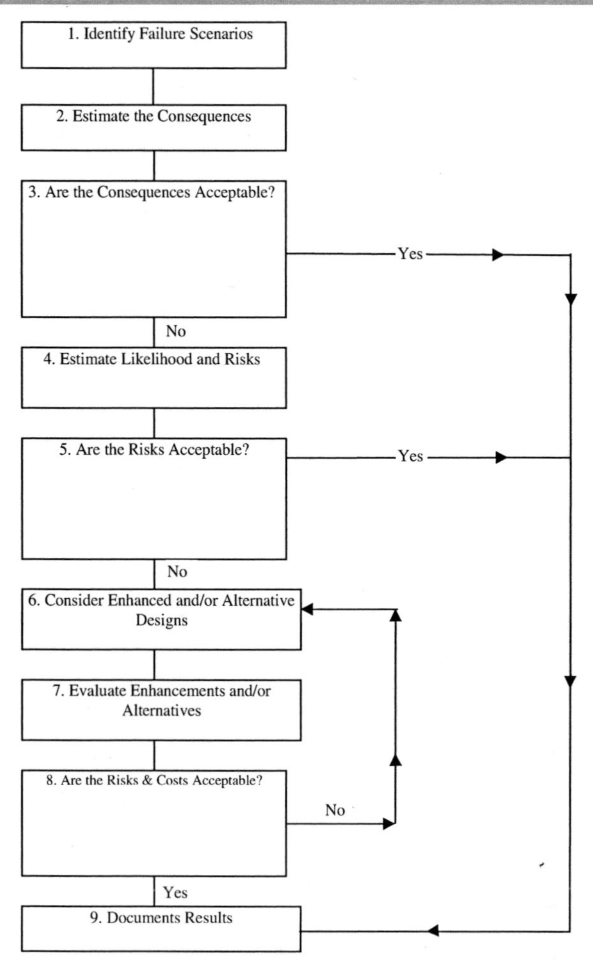

FIGURE 3. Risk-based design approach

engineering judgment, or the use of qualitative consequence criteria. Other cases require experimentation or analytical approaches such as the calculation of maximum hazard distances of vapor cloud dispersion.

3. ***Determine the acceptability of the consequences.*** Accomplishing this requires guidance from established acceptability criteria. These include company-specific criteria, engineering codes and standards, recommended practices, and regulatory requirements.
4. ***Estimate likelihood and risks.*** Estimates of likelihood rest on an understanding of how, and how often, failure scenarios such as those identified in Step 1 might occur. When historical data are available about equipment and processes, these data can be used to estimate failure-scenario frequency. When data are lacking, methods such as fault tree analysis (further described later in this chapter) help in developing quantified estimates. Measures of risk are determined by combining probability and consequence estimates. A detailed review of methods for combining likelihood and consequence estimates to obtain risk measures can be found in system safety literature. Some cases can be resolved through comparisons with similar systems or through the use of qualitative tools such as risk matrices. Others will require quantified approaches such as risk profiles and risk contours.
5. ***Determine risk acceptability.*** Determining risk acceptability means asking, "Can we accept this level of risk?" Guidance on acceptable levels of risk can be gained from established risk criteria. If the criteria indicate an acceptable level of risk, then the design of the process or the emergency-relief system is satisfactory from a risk standpoint. If the criteria indicate unacceptable risk, the next step is to reduce risk through further design refinements.
6. ***Consider enhanced or alternative designs.*** This includes an opportunity to consider the entire process design and define changes that can reduce risk to an acceptable level. The Center for Chemical Process Safety (CCPS) (1992) has classified risk-reduction concepts, in declining order of reliability, as follows: inherently safer (designed in), passive (operates only when a hazard occurs), active (operates whenever the system is operating), and procedural (written procedures).
7. ***Evaluate enhancements or alternatives.*** A design change intended to reduce risk can introduce new failure scenarios and new risks. Therefore, the evaluation of design changes should treat these changes as an integral part of the process. Following Steps 1 through 4, the review should reestimate process risk. The review should also estimate the cost of the proposed changes.

8. ***Determine acceptability of risk and cost.*** As in Steps 3 and 5, established risk criteria can provide guidance on risk acceptability. Cost becomes an issue in this step because, like all designs, system safety designs must meet business criteria. Coupling estimates of cost and risk reduction provides a basis for assessing the cost-benefit trade-off of each alternative design or mitigation solution. The cost-benefit analysis can be qualitative or quantitative. A quantitative approach is especially useful when a large number of competing process-safety systems are being considered. If the analysis yields acceptable risk and cost for a design option, the results should be documented (Step 9). If not, it may be necessary to consider design enhancements and alternatives (Steps 6 through 8).
9. ***Document results.*** The failure scenarios and associated consequence, likelihood, and risk estimates developed during this process document the design basis for process-safety systems and emergency-relief systems. Documentation retains essential information for risk-management situations such as hazard evaluations, management of change, and subsequent design projects. When the findings from Step 3 and Step 5 show that consequences and risk meet acceptability criteria, results still need to be documented. Doing so will cut down on needless repetitions of the analysis and ensure that design or operational changes reflect an understanding of the baseline risk of the design.

Guidelines for Risk Acceptability

Underlying this entire approach is the understanding that risk levels range along a continuum. In most cases, risks cannot be eliminated, only reduced to a level that everyone who has a stake in the activity or process finds acceptable. Because attitudes about the acceptability of risks are not consistent, there are no universal norms for risk acceptability. What your stakeholders view as an acceptable risk will depend on a number of factors, including the following (Post, Hendershot, and Kers 2001):

- ***The nature of the risk.*** Is it a voluntary risk, one that those who are at risk accept, as part of a choice? Or is it involuntary?
- ***Who or what is at risk?*** Does it affect a single person or many people? What about the surrounding environment? Is it an industrial landscape already altered by past uses or a pristine or prized natural setting? Are areas such as schools or residential neighborhoods or resources such as water at risk?
- ***To what degree can the risk be controlled or reduced?*** Designing in process safety focuses on this issue. Making the case for an *acceptable* risk requires that the methods supporting the design basis be technically sound and defensible, clearly documented, and accurate.
- ***What is the risk taker's past experience?*** Uncertainty regarding the impact of the risk influences the risk taker's level of acceptance. For example, the average person understands and accepts the risk of driving an automobile but is uncertain about the risk of nuclear power generation.

Companies that have successfully established risk criteria focus on gaining consistency in their decisions about risk (Post, Hendershot, and Kers 2001). These criteria typically represent levels of risk that the company believes will minimize impacts to continued operations. Risk criteria should also fit with a company's philosophy and culture and match the type of analysis its engineers normally conduct in the design stage. The selection of appropriate risk criteria is a corporate responsibility and requires the involvement and support of senior management, given that it establishes the levels and types of risks the company will accept.

Once a company has established specific risk criteria, these can be used to check outcomes throughout the design process, at Steps 3, 5, and 8 of the approach outlined earlier. This iterative approach builds consistency into the process and increases the likelihood of making risk-based choices early in design—where they are often most cost effective.

Risk-Acceptability Criteria

The following criteria were presented at the Fifth Biennial Process Plant Safety Symposium sponsored by the American Institute of Chemical Engineers (Post, Hendershot, and Kers 2001).

Release limits address the acceptability of potential release consequences by considering the amount of material that could be released. *Acceptable* quantities depend on the physical states and hazardous properties of released materials. A hypothetical release limit for gasoline, for example, might be as much as 5000 pounds, whereas for chlorine, it would be only 200 pounds (Post, Hendershot, and Kers 2001).

Threshold-impact criteria for fence or property line employ standard damage criteria, such as toxicity, thermal radiation, or blast overpressure, together with consequence modeling to determine whether potential impact at the facility's fence or property line exceeds an acceptable threshold.

Single versus multiple component failure criteria provide a qualitative approach to how many component failures will be accepted. For example, a company might choose to accept event scenarios that require three independent component failures, to conduct further analysis of event scenarios triggered by two failures, and not to accept events arising from single failures. *Independent component failures* refers to scenarios where components that fail are not linked to the failure-sequence conditions but fail independent of those conditions.

Critical event frequency addresses event scenarios with a defined high-consequence impact. Examples of such impacts would be a severe injury, a fatality, critical damage to the facility, or impacts on the surrounding community.

Risk-matrix criteria use qualitative and semiquantitative frequency and severity categories to estimate the risk of an event. Events with a low-risk ranking are considered acceptable.

Individual risk criteria consider the frequency of the event or events to which an individual might be exposed, the severity of the exposure, and the amount of time for which the individual is at risk.

Societal risk criteria are risks that can affect the local community. These risks explicitly address both events with a high frequency and minimal consequences and events with a low frequency and serious consequences. This class of criteria can be useful to companies that have recently experienced an adverse event.

Risk matrix and cost thresholds can account for the risk-reduction level provided by a design enhancement and its cost. In cases where the benefit of a risk-reduction step is large, and its cost is small, the way forward is obvious. In more complex situations, a risk matrix and cost threshold with definite "rules" can help clarify decision making.

Cost-benefit criteria are used to determine how much money the company is willing to spend to avert a risk. These criteria help define the amount of risk reduction expected for each dollar expended. They can be developed in conjunction with quantitative estimates of risk. In some cases, companies might use two thresholds—one for the dollars needed to achieve an acceptable risk level and another for any further reduction beyond that level.

Quantitative Analysis

A systematic approach does not necessarily mean a quantitative one. Quantitative analysis is most time- and cost-effective when it is used selectively. In many simple design situations, qualitative approaches are sufficient for selecting the basis of process-safety system design. More complex design cases may occasionally require quantitative risk analysis. But even then, quantitative methods should be used only up to the point where a decision can be made.

For example, consider a company that has toxic-impact criteria limiting off-site vapor cloud concentrations to a specific, quantified level. By performing vapor-cloud dispersion modeling, the company can determine whether specific loss-of-containment scenarios associated with specific failures exceed the toxic-impact acceptability criteria. If the scenario consequences do not exceed the criteria, then there is no need to continue with an analysis of event likelihood or further risk quantification. Specific quantitative analysis methods are discussed later in this text.

Design Solutions: Making the Right Decision

The best decisions about safety and risk reduction in process design bring together technical sophistication and clear business objectives. Decisions about risk should provide definite business value and fit into the business context: What is the business plan for this facility or process? The decisions should reflect consistent thinking and standards for risk-acceptability levels. And they need to be in line with an appropriate cost structure for the safety component of a process.

Understanding the primary types of design choices for safety can help engineers rank their options and introduce modifications where they can do the most good for the least cost. Most design solutions for reducing risk fall into one of these categories (CCPS 2000):

- *Inherently safer*—eliminates or mitigates identified hazards by substituting less hazardous materials and process conditions. Inherently safer solutions tend to require relatively high capital costs, offset by relatively low operating costs. Examples include substituting water for a flammable solvent and reducing large inventories of hazardous "intermediates."
- *Passive*—offers high reliability by operating without active devices that sense or respond to process variables. Like inherently safer design choices, passive systems often require a relatively high initial investment offset by relatively low operating costs. Examples include compatible hose couplings for compatible substances, equipment designed to withstand high-pressure hazards, and dikes that contain hazardous inventories.
- *Active*—uses devices that monitor process variables and trigger mitigation and control systems. Active systems can be less reliable than inherently safer or passive systems because they require more maintenance and more detailed operating procedures. They typically require moderate capital costs, followed by somewhat greater operating costs. Examples include check valves and regulators, pressure safety valves or rupture disks that prevent vessel overpressure, and high-level sensing devices that interlock with inlet valves and pump motors to prevent overfilling.
- *Procedural*—avoids hazards by requiring someone to take action. The capital cost of a procedural system is generally low, but operating costs, including staffing and training, can be high. Reliability, which rests on human variables such as company safety culture and the correct use and handling of mechanical devices, tends to be low. Following procedures also depends on the level of training provided to support procedure knowledge. Without training procedures, how to operate the equipment properly will likely not be well known or understood. Examples of procedural approaches include manually closing a valve after an alarm sounds or carrying out preventive maintenance to reduce the likelihood of equipment failure. Wearing proper personal protective equipment for a particular task would be another example of procedural safeguard.

Incorporating systematic risk assessment in process-safety design is sometimes viewed as an expensive way to achieve greater risk reduction. The reality, however, is that when risk assessment is left out of the

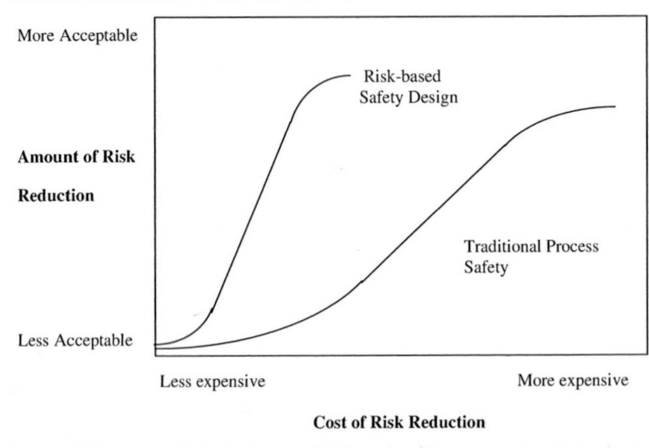

FIGURE 4. General representation of the cost of risk reduction (*Source:* CCPS 2000)

design process, two problems are likely to occur. The system may be overdesigned, with safety protection costing more than it needs to, or the facility may be unprotected from significant, unidentified risks.

Systematic risk-based design helps companies to more fully identify significant risks, rank the risks, and prioritize steps to address them. The result is that capital expenditures, operating expenses, staffing, and other resources are better allocated to risks, enabling companies to buy more risk reduction at a cost that is the same as or less than shown in Figure 4 (CCPS 2000).

When deciding from among the hierarchy of risk-mitigation options, designers should avoid the "project mentality" pitfall, which promotes focusing only on minimizing capital cost. Nor can they simply select the most reliable approach. The key to successful risk-reduction choices is to exploit the detailed technical information about risks and hazards that a systematic design process offers to judge the actual merits and disadvantages of each plausible solution. It is also important to examine the life-cycle costs of each option before making decisions, as shown in Figure 5 (CCPS 2000).

For example, a company was handling a very reactive substance. After several incidents involving the substance, the company reviewed two options for reducing the risk posed by the substance. The first option included total containment of the substance in a vessel rated to withstand a maximum pressure level of 1200 pounds per square inch (psi), which was an inherently safer approach. However, the cost of this vessel was very high, and using it meant having the vessel sit continuously within the facility at a very high pressure, a hazard in and of itself.

The second option was to construct a catch system and allow the reactor to activate an emergency pressure-relief system. This required a reactor vessel with a lower pressure rating and a large vessel to be used as a catch/quench tank. This approach was less expensive, but it required the facility to deal with the potential of a hazardous effluent and to address the reliability of the relief system. At the time, the pressure relief/catch system was found to provide an acceptable risk level overall. The company chose to take advantage of this option's lower cost and to implement mitigation measures that helped attain an acceptable level of risk.

Meeting Stakeholder Needs

Safe design has long been a priority in the energy, chemical, and petrochemical process industries. Today, process-industry companies need to be certain that

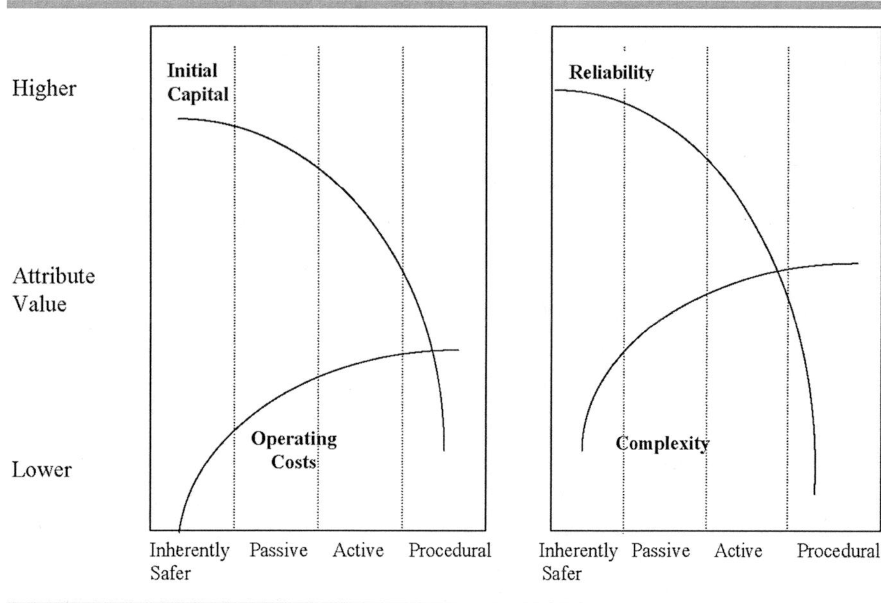

FIGURE 5. Life cycles of each cost option (*Source:* CCPS 2000)

their stakeholders trust how they manage the environmental, health, and safety implications of industrial activities. A safe and documented design basis, along with a formal safety-management system and safety practices, procedures, and training, is critical for providing the level of confidence required for risk management.

In recent years, regulations and industrial standards for acceptable risk have become increasingly stringent. This trend reflects a convergence of public opinion, government regulations, and industry initiatives. The momentum for controlling and reducing risk is likely to continue, with leading companies in process industries setting standards that go well beyond what is required.

At the same time, risk managers and safety environmental managers face unremitting pressure to run their activities "lean and mean" and control and justify costs. Risk-based design can be a key piece in a successful company's toolkit for reaching decisions about incorporating in the design process elements that integrate risk reduction and cost advantages without compromising safety. By communicating options clearly to all concerned stakeholders and by addressing the full life-cycle cost of different options, risk-based design enhances the business value of process-safety activities. Companies that are gaining the benefits of reduced risks and reduced risk-management costs find their competitive position strengthened by lower capital costs and by a more secure franchise to operate. In short, they are more competitive as a result of risk-based design (CCPS 2000).

The Tools and Techniques of System Safety Analysis

Analysis tools and techniques have been referred to earlier and different uses for various applications have been recommended. At this point, a closer look at these options is warranted. Analysis techniques presented in this chapter include the following: checklists, software fault tree analysis, event tree analysis, failure modes and effects analysis (FMEA), SoftTree analysis, hazard and operability (HAZOP) studies, time dependent Petri net analysis, functional flow analysis, information-flow analysis, software sneak analysis, nuclear safety cross-check analysis (NSCCA), real-time logic, and software code analysis. It is not the purpose of this chapter to explain each of these tools and techniques in great detail. However, an explanation is offered to provide a general understanding of each technique and its advantages and disadvantages.

Checklists

Checklists are the simplest and most cost-effective approach and are most often used in conjunction with other analysis techniques. They require the least amount of training to use and are often self-explanatory. Checklists reword the criteria in the form of a question with yes, no, or not applicable being an appropriate response. There is usually a comments section with each checklist item that is used to provide any special explanation regarding the environment in which the checklist was executed. A comments section can also describe why a particular item was marked "no" or "not applicable."

Fault Tree Analysis

A fault tree analysis can simply be described as an analytical tool, where an undesired state of a system is specified and analyzed in the context of its environment and operation. This is done to find all of the possible ways that the undesired event can occur. The fault tree is a graphic model using Boolean algebra symbols (shown in Figure 6) of the various parallel and sequential combinations of faults that will result in the occurrence of the predefined, undesired event. The faults, or top events (see an example of top events in Figure 7) can be events that are associated with component hardware failures, software faults, human errors, or any other pertinent events that can lead to an undesired event. A fault tree (shown in Figure 8) depicts the logical interrelationships of basic events that lead to an undesired event, which is the top event of the fault tree (Hammer 1989).

The fault tree is probably the most used analysis technique throughout system safety because of its inherent advantages (Rausand and Høyland 2004). Fault tree analysis is well understood by most system safety engineers, is well documented, and can be applied at

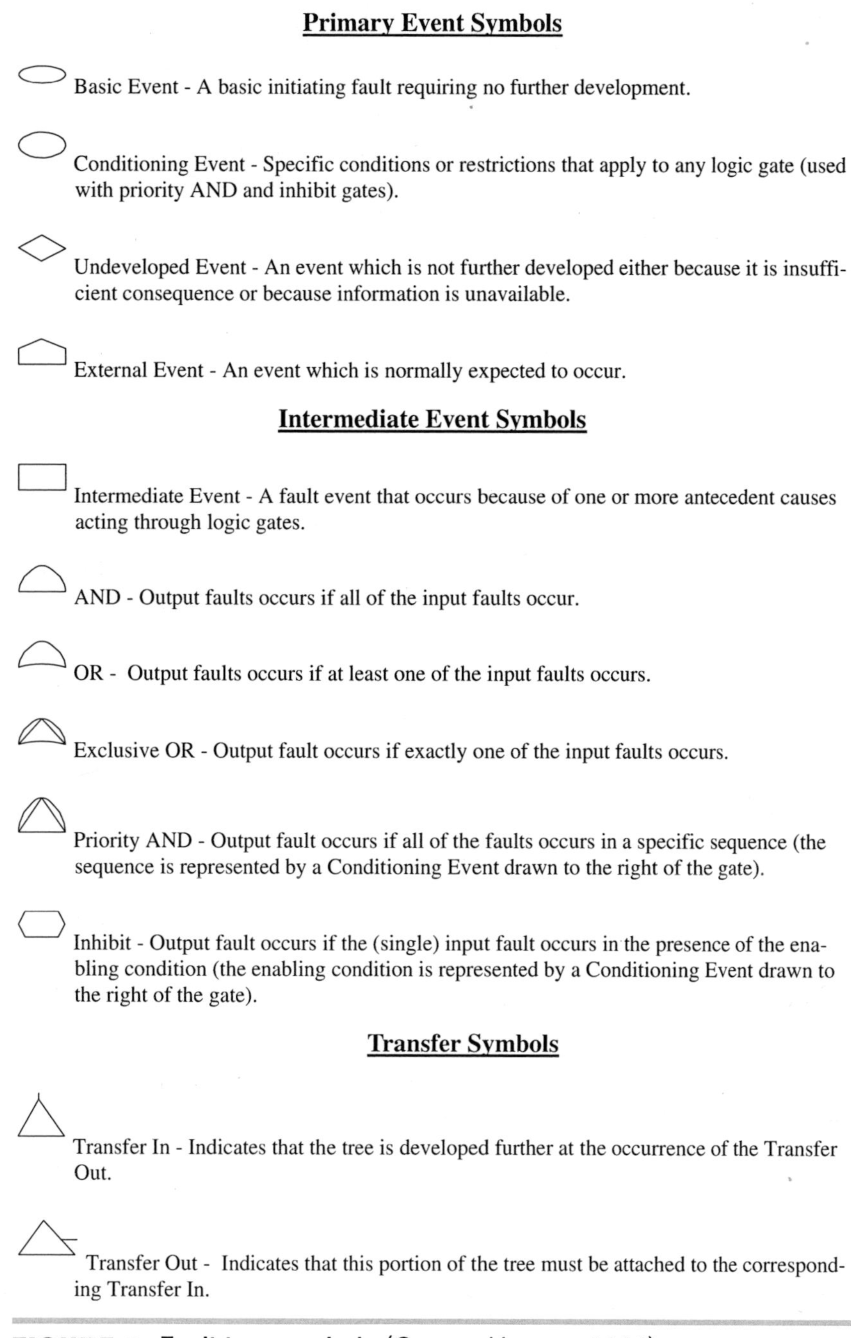

Primary Event Symbols
Basic Event - A basic initiating fault requiring no further development.
Conditioning Event - Specific conditions or restrictions that apply to any logic gate (used with priority AND and inhibit gates).
Undeveloped Event - An event which is not further developed either because it is insufficient consequence or because information is unavailable.
External Event - An event which is normally expected to occur.
Intermediate Event Symbols
Intermediate Event - A fault event that occurs because of one or more antecedent causes acting through logic gates.
AND - Output faults occurs if all of the input faults occur.
OR - Output faults occurs if at least one of the input faults occurs.
Exclusive OR - Output fault occurs if exactly one of the input faults occurs.
Priority AND - Output fault occurs if all of the faults occurs in a specific sequence (the sequence is represented by a Conditioning Event drawn to the right of the gate).
Inhibit - Output fault occurs if the (single) input fault occurs in the presence of the enabling condition (the enabling condition is represented by a Conditioning Event drawn to the right of the gate).
Transfer Symbols
Transfer In - Indicates that the tree is developed further at the occurrence of the Transfer Out.
Transfer Out - Indicates that this portion of the tree must be attached to the corresponding Transfer In.

FIGURE 6. Fault tree symbols (*Source:* Hammer 1989)

various levels of the system design (e.g., conceptual, design, and implementation). There are numerous automated tools that perform fault tree analysis. These tools use *standard* trees for logical statements. Boolean algebra is used to quantify probabilities of events based on the tree logic of combined symbols leading up to the event of interest. A few advantages of using fault trees include the following:

- Time is not wasted chasing dead-end events.
- Fault trees readily demonstrate the synergism of failures between related branches.
- Fault trees are easily adaptable to rapidly meet design changes and redesign.
- Fault trees are used to focus on specific safety-critical functions rather than the whole system.

- Fault trees can be used to analyze interfaces between inputs and outputs to and from internal and external systems and subsystems.

However, there are some inherent disadvantages of using fault trees. They are time-consuming and, as a result, expensive to perform. Even though fault trees can be used to determine relevant probabilities, they are not mathematically precise. Fault trees can be used to identify only sequential constructs, and they have no mechanism for handling parallel processes. Because parallel processing is becoming more of a norm in the computer industry, this is a serious shortcoming. When using timing constraints, fault trees become extremely cumbersome. There is no formalized way to ensure that human factors are evaluated in a consistent manner. Fault trees are very dependent on the expertise, judgment, and system knowledge of the analyst. Therefore, the results of the fault tree are only as good as the quality of the analyst. Fault trees were developed initially by Bell Telephone for analyzing electrical and electromechanical systems.

1. Injury to ________.
2. Radiation injury ________.
3. Inadvertent start of ________.
4. Equipment ________ activated inadvertently.
5. Accidental explosion of ________.
6. Loss of control of ________.
7. Rupture of ________.
8. Damage to ________.
9. Damage to ________ from ________.
10. Thermal damage to ________.
11. Failure of ________ to operate (stop, close, open).
12. Radiation damage to ________.
13. Loss of pressure in ________.
14. Overpressurization of ________.
15. Unscheduled release of ________.
16. Premature (delayed) release of ________.
17. Collapse of ________.
18. Overheating of ________.
19. Uncontrolled venting of ________ (toxic, flammable, or high-pressure gas).
20. (Operation to be named) inhibited by damage.

FIGURE 7. Example fault tree top events (*Source:* Hammer 1989)

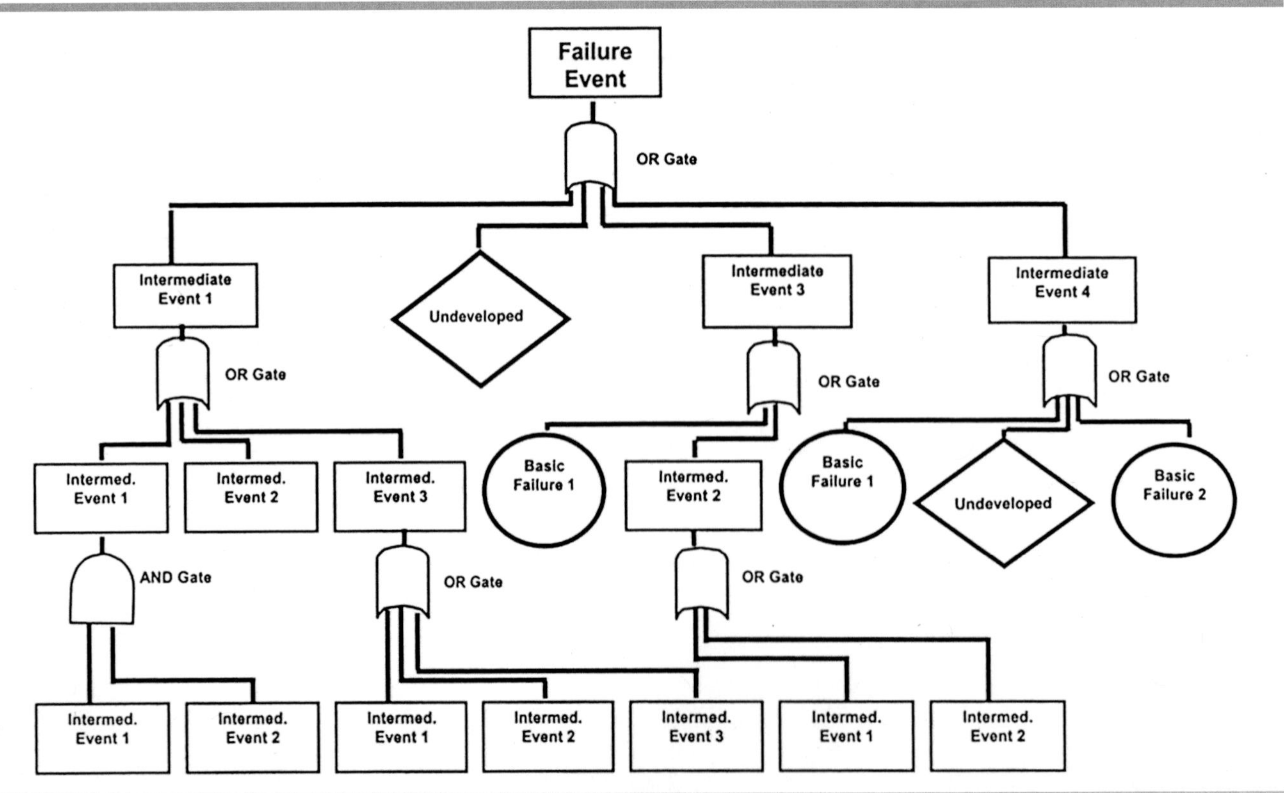

FIGURE 8. Example of fault tree (*Source:* Hammer 1989)

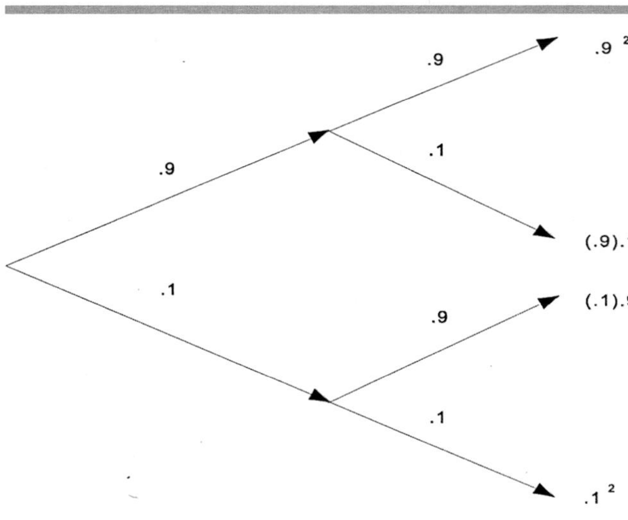

FIGURE 9. Example event tree
(*Source:* Clement 1987)

Events such as undesired missile launches are well suited for this analysis.

Event Tree Analysis

Event tree analysis is a bottom-up, deductive technique that explores different responses to challenges. This analysis appears to be a variation of a fault tree analysis. The event tree is developed from left to right, whereas the fault tree is developed top to bottom (as shown in Figure 9). The initiating, or challenge, event of the event tree is similar to the top event of a fault tree, even though gate logic or gates are not used in event trees. A primary difference is that fault trees tend to explore and list only factors that could lead to the failure, and event trees can be converted to fault trees. The procedures and formulae for quantifying each are similar (Clemens 2001).

Failure Modes and Effects Analysis (FMEA)

A FMEA is a reliability analysis technique that examines the effects of all failure modes of systems and subsystems. It is used to determine how long a piece of software or a component will operate satisfactorily and what the effects of any failure of individual components might be on the overall system performance (Hammer 1989). The hardware or software is decomposed all the way down to its lowest component level (e.g., modules). Each module is studied to determine how it could malfunction and cause downstream effects. Effects might result in error or fault propagation into other related software modules, perhaps causing the entire software program to fail. Failure rates for each module are identified and listed. The calculations are used to determine how long a module is expected to operate between failures and the overall probability it will operate for a specific length of time.

An FMEA has inherent advantages. It can be used without first identifying mishaps during any phase of system design. An FMEA helps to reveal unforeseen hazards and is good at helping the analyst identify potentially hazardous single-point failures. However, there are inherent disadvantages to using FMEAs. They are time-consuming and consequently expensive to perform. They are also very dependent on the expertise, judgment, and system knowledge of the analyst. FMEA results are only as good as the analyst (Clement 1987).

Hazard and Operability (HAZOP) Studies

Hazard and operability studies provide a quantitative and qualitative systematic approach to identifying hazards by generating questions ("What if...?") that consider effects of deviations in and from normal parameters of a particular chemical process. HAZOP studies are used to analyze steps during each chemical-process operating phase, operating limits, and safety and health considerations. Analysis of procedures for each operating phase (29 CFR 1910.119 and AIChE 1985) includes initial startup, normal operations, temporary operations, emergency operations, normal shutdown, and startup following a turnaround. Analysis of operating limits includes consequences of deviation, steps to correct or avoid deviation, and safety systems and their functions. Analysis of safety and health considerations includes properties of hazards, precautions necessary to prevent exposures, safety procedures, quality control, and any special or unique hazards (Stephans and Talso 1997). HAZOP studies consist of multidisciplinary teams that identify, analyze, and control hazards systematically. The HAZOP team traces the flow of the process, concentrating on specific study nodes. Parameters include normal temperature, pressure, flow, and medium type: gas and chemical. A node may be a vessel or a pipe between vessel 1 and vessel 2. Process parameters will generally define the size of the node. A set of guide words is used to determine types of deviations from prescribed parameters that could occur at each study node. The causes and consequences of the deviations are discussed with the aid of these guide words. Typical guide words and their meanings are shown in Figure 10.

A HAZOP study has inherent advantages. Because the guide words tend to describe failure modes, the HAZOP can be conducted in parallel with an FMEA and complement or perhaps even validate the results. A HAZOP may be used to conduct further analysis of critical items identified in an FMEA. This helps decrease the expense from spending too much time and money on an in-depth FMEA. A HAZOP tends to include human factors and operator errors, whereas other analyses tend to examine system-related failures.

A HAZOP analysis has inherent disadvantages as well. A HAZOP should be performed when the design is relatively firm (Stephans and Talso 1997). A HAZOP should be performed by the 35 percent complete design stage. Because system safety efforts should start as early as possible in the design phase, the HAZOP can be used only as an adjunct tool and not as a stand-alone tool.

Deviation	Meaning	Guide Word
NO	None	Pressure
LESS	Quantitative decrease	Temperature
MORE	Quantitative increase	Flow
PART OF	Qualitative decrease	
AS WELL AS	Qualitative increase	
REVERSE	Opposite of intended direction	
OTHER THAN	Substitution	

FIGURE 10. Example guide words

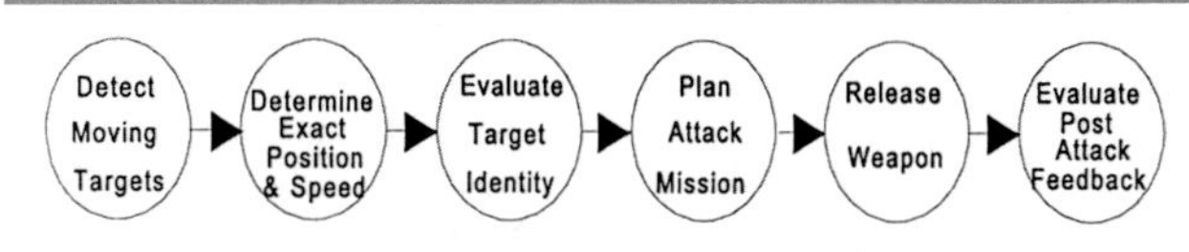

FIGURE 11. Functional and control flow analysis (*Source:* Leveson 2002)

Functional and Control Flow Analysis

Functional and control flow analysis is a static analysis technique. It requires the development of functional flow diagrams. Functional flow diagrams illustrate the flow of information through the system based on functions. This analysis is generally applied during the detailed design phase when functional flow diagrams have been completed. An example functional flow analysis is shown in Figure 11 (Leveson 2002).

Functional and control flow analysis has several advantages. It is applicable to all phases of system development. Functional flow diagrams are in various forms of completeness during the design phase and can be examined at any time. Functional flow analysis helps identify potential control problems between functions. As a result, it is a good tool to use for functional grouping and separation of safety-critical functions. It can be used to induce failures in design and to see how they may be propagated to other design elements. It can easily be related to safety-requirement analyses. Functional and control flow analysis has several disadvantages. The software designers usually use a different flow-analysis technique. As a result, the software flow analysis must be translated into intermediate or special language. It is dependent on the expertise of the analyst. Using it for medium-size systems at the detailed design level is complex. The synergistic effect of failures is not easily identified. It provides little benefit in analysis of safety-critical information flow. It requires separate safety analysis to identify safety-critical system states and functions. It is not a complete analysis of a system.

Information and Data Flow Analysis

Information and data flow analysis is also a static analysis of information or data flow through a system. It is generally applied during detailed design phase and requires development of information flow diagrams similar to functional and control flow analysis. An example information flow analysis is shown in Figure 12 (Leveson 2002).

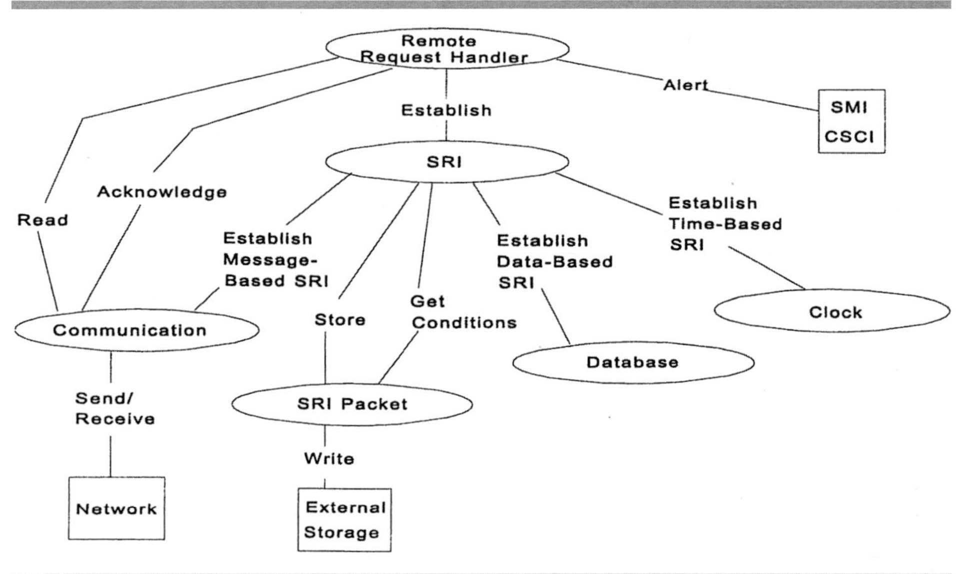

FIGURE 12. **Information and data flow analysis** (*Source:* Stephans 1997)

Information and data flow analysis has several advantages. It can be used to identify potential bottlenecks in information flow. Safety-critical information is easily tracked through the system. It complements functional flow analysis by coupling functional control with information flow. Information and data flow analysis has several disadvantages as well. It provides no benefit in control-intensive systems. The software designers usually use a different flow-analysis technique. As a result the software flow analysis must be translated into intermediate or special language. Its use is complex for medium to large systems. Again, it is dependent on the expertise of the analyst (Brown 1976).

Sneak Circuit Analysis

Sneak analysis is based on a sneak path, an unintended route, which can allow an undesired error or fault to occur, preventing desired functions from occurring, or which can adversely affect the timing of the functions. Sneak circuit analysis is performed to identify ways in which built-in design characteristics can either allow an undesired event to occur or prevent events from occurring. It is usually applied to electrical or software-hardware systems.

An important feature of sneak analysis is that the sneak paths being investigated are not a result of failures in the system. They are rather the result of the circuit design. A sneak analysis represents program paths as circuit diagrams. The sneak paths may show up only on rare occasions when the software is a unique configuration.

Sneak analysis is usually inductive and can be very difficult to perform without the aid of software tools. Proprietary sneak-analysis tools have been developed by Boeing, General Dynamics, Science Applications International Corporation (SAIC), and several others.

The most common approach to sneak analysis involves visual clues found by comparing circuits with the six basic topographs. The code topology patterns are shown in Figure 13, and the software sneak topology patterns are shown in Figure 14.

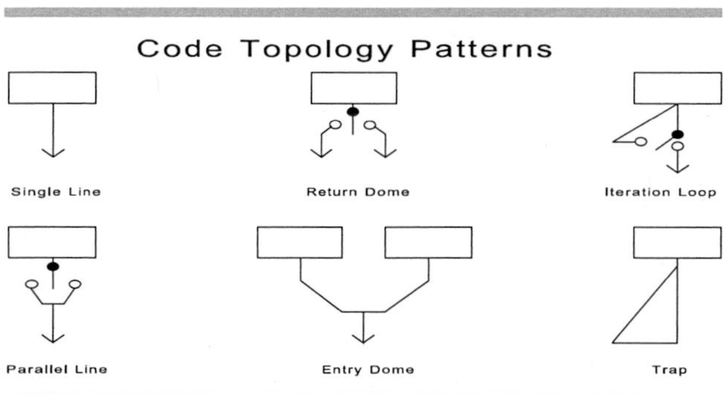

FIGURE 13. **Code topology patterns** (*Source:* AFISC/SESD)

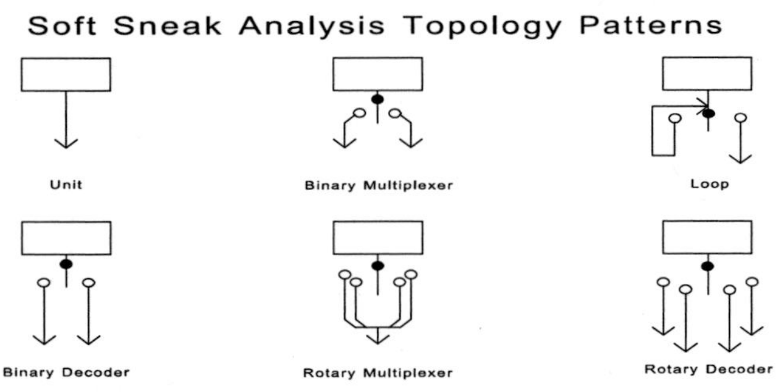

FIGURE 14. Software sneak topology patterns (*Source:* AFISC/SESD)

Nearly every circuit can be broken down into combinations of these topographs. The sneak conditions to be sought are as follows:

1. Sneak paths that can cause error or fault propagation to flow along an unexpected route
2. Incompatible logic sequences that can cause unwanted or inappropriate system responses (sneak timing)
3. Sneak conditions that can cause misleading, ambiguous, or false displays
4. Sneak labels that provide confusing or incorrect nomenclature or instructions on controls and that thus promote operator errors

A sneak analysis has several advantages. It provides an excellent documentation check. It is excellent in isolating alternate (sneak) paths in software. It is a thorough analysis of the source code such that logic errors are easily detected.

A sneak analysis has several disadvantages. It occurs after coding has been substantially completed. Therefore, fixing the problems requires changing code. It is primarily directed at logic errors rather than structural and design errors. As a result it does not validate software algorithms. It is directed at the whole system and does not concentrate on the most costly faults. It also does not consider environmental factors such as temperature, altitude, and radiation issues. Failure modes are handled as special cases. It is very dependent on *clue lists*. It is very labor-intensive and costly. It requires separate safety analysis to identify safety-critical system states and functions. Critical faults are easily lost in the mass of documentation errors (Stephenson 1991).

Hazard Analysis Worksheets and Hazard Reports

Preparation of Hazard Analysis Worksheets (HAWs)

The hazard analysis worksheet (HAW) is a tool used in system safety to analyze and document all hazard/energy sources and accident risk factors identified and evaluated during the various safety analyses performed on a system. The HAW is used to perform two functions: First, it promotes a systematic and thorough analysis of a hazard/energy source or risk factor; and second, it provides a permanent record of analyses performed.

The HAW differs from the hazard report in that it is a record of hazard/energy sources and risk factors evaluated. Typically, the hazard report documents only hazards with a initial risk severity code greater than IV and a frequency code greater than D (described in detail in the "Risk Assessment" section of this chapter). The HAW will generally be kept on file and incorporated in, or appended to, only the appropriate safety analysis documentation. The hazard report will be included in the formal documentation.

The HAW format selected should be formalized to the extent that a standard form and analysis methodology is adopted. The analysis can be handwritten (legibly) to minimize the administrative burden. If a HAW results in a hazard report being prepared, the HAW can be closed as long as reference is made to the hazard report that replaces it. A sample HAW format is shown in Figure 15. The form resembles the hazard-report format because the analysis methodology is similar. This facilitates the transfer of the HAW data to the hazard report. For the most part, the instructions for filling out this particular HAW format are the same as those for the hazard report. Some blocks that may differ from a hazard report are discussed in the paragraphs that follow.

HAZARD ANALYSIS WORKSHEET
SYSTEM ____________ SUBSYSTEM ____________ HAW NO. __________
EQUIPMENT/COMPONENT ________________ LOCATION ________________
HAZARD/ENERGY FACTOR ____
ORIGINATOR ________________ DATE _________ STATUS ____________
HAZARD REPORT SUBMITTED: YES _____ NO _____ HR NUMBER __________
SINGLE POINT FAILURE: YES ___ NO ___ HR DATE ____________ PHASE(S) OF
OPERATION: ________________
DRAWING/DOCUMENT NUMBER: ________________
REFERENCES:
EXISTING CONTROLS IN THE DESIGN:
ACCIDENT SCENARIO AND TRIGGERING EVENTS:
UNDESIRED EFFECTS: RISK CODES:
INITIAL RISK CODE:
RECOMMENDATIONS:
ORIGINATOR _____________ APPROVED ______________ DATE _________

FIGURE 15. Typical hazard analysis worksheet (*Source:* Hansen, 1993)

Status: The status block on a HAW will usually be *closed*. The HAW is closed if (1) the initial risk code is IV *or* D, and the reviewing and approving authority concurs with the recommendation that "no additional action is required" as shown, or (2) the HAW is coded higher than IV *and* D, and a hazard report is prepared. In this case the HAW must reference the hazard report number. The HAW will remain open if (1) the recommendations block states that additional analysis, study, research is required, or (2) the present risk of the HAW is coded IV or D, but the design is nevertheless in violation of a safety code or standard. In this case the recommendations block should provide recommended corrective actions required to bring the design into compliance.

Risk Code. The initial risk-code block may often contain a severity code of IV or a frequency code of D (described in detail in the "Risk Assessment" section of this chapter). Many companies use their own tailored version of risk codes to make them meaningful to their business. Examples are a laser printer that has been designed to comply with ANSI Z-136; a cathode ray tube that has been designed to eliminate the possibility of emitting ionizing radiation; lightning hazards properly controlled by a lightning protection system designed, installed, and verified as being in accordance with code; and a floor-loading analysis that shows that floor-loading limits are not exceeded. The risk code is one of the last items to be filled out by the analyst. The reason is that the risk code *cannot* be determined until the accident scenario and triggering events, undesired effects, and existing controls in the design have been determined.

Recommendations. The recommendations block will usually (but not always) contain one of four entries:

1. The hazard is adequately controlled by design features, and no additional actions are required (HAW closed).
2. Recommendations for actions necessary to bring the design into compliance with applicable standards (HAW open).
3. Recommendations for actions necessary to reduce the risk to an acceptable level (HAW closed, hazard report open).
4. Recommendation for studies, analyses, research, or other actions necessary to further qualify or quantify the hazard status (HAW open).

Originator—approved by. At a minimum, the analysis should be reviewed and approved by the safety manager or his supervisor if the system safety manager (SSM) is the HAW originator. This concurrence is the contractor's attestation that the design has an acceptable level of risk or that the corrective actions recommended will reduce the risk to an acceptable level.

Preparation of Hazard Report Forms

A typical hazard report (HR) form is shown in Figure 16. Hazard reports are used to document and guide the complete analysis and risk assessment of a hazard. Each reportable hazard, identified by analyses or other means, should be analyzed and documented on an HR form. The primary purposes of the hazard reports are (1) to document the hazard or accident risk factor, its cases, and the possible accident scenarios and undesired effects that can result from the hazard; (2) to document existing and recommended controls, present risk assessment, and other information pertinent to the assessment; and (3) to provide status tracking, verification, and a record of closure (or risk acceptance). The HR format is continuous to permit as much information as is available to fit in each block. The following paragraphs provide guidance and interpretation for completing each block of this typical hazard report form (Hansen 1993).

Conditions or hazards having an initial risk severity code of IV or a frequency code of D are not to be documented on an HR but are to be discussed and documented in the appropriate analysis and documented on an HAW. All other coded hazards should be documented on an HR.

A hazard report is prepared when approved and released drawings, or the actual physical configuration of the system, contains a hazard with an initial risk code of IIIC or higher. The safety manager is responsible for managing the hazard reports to include revising the HRs, monitoring the status of corrective actions, and reporting the status to program management, when required. The safety manager expeditiously advises program management when a hazard report is originated or revised. The hazard reports sections are described in detail in the following paragraphs.

Short title. A short phrase identifying the particular hazard. Keep it short but specific: not "thermal hazard" but "thermal hazard in [type, model] copier."

System/element. Enter the system or element to which the hazard being analyzed applies.

Rpt No. Hazard reports should be identified numerically by system or subsystem. For example, the first hazard report for a communications system should be COMM-001. This assists in tracking historical events of a particular hazard report.

Operation/Phase. Enter the operations or phases during which the hazard is applicable (e.g., testing,

Hazard Report Form

SHORT TITLE:		
SYSTEM/ELEMENT:		RPT. NO.
OPERATION/PHASE:	REV:	DATE:
EQUIPMENT:	LOCATION:	
ORIGINATOR (NAME):	ORGANIZATION:	DATE:
ACTION (NAME):	ORGANIZATION:	TELE:
SUSPENSE DATE (CLOSURE):		
HAZARD/ACCIDENT RISK FACTOR CODE:		
DESCRIPTION OF HAZARD:		
REQUIREMENTS:		
EXISTING CONTROLS	REFERENCE	
ACCIDENT SCENARIO:		
SINGLE POINT FAILURE: YES: NO:		
UNDESIRED EFFECTS	EFFECT RISK CODE	

FIGURE 16A. **Typical hazard report form** (*Source:* Hansen, 1993)

installation, operating, and maintenance (preventive or repair).

Revision and date. Enter the number of this revision (change or update) to the report and the date this revision was prepared. For the initial report enter Rev. 0 and the origination date.

Equipment. Identify the specific equipment or system that contains, or is impacted by, the hazard (e.g., laser printer model XX).

Location. State the location (building, module, room number, etc.) of the system or the equipment involved.

INITIAL RISK CODE CONSIDERING ACCIDENT SCENARIO & EXISTING CONTROLS:		
RECOMMENDED CORRECTIVE CONTROLS	REFERENCE	STATUS
ACTION(S) PLANNED/TAKEN:		
CURRENT RISK CODE BASED ON ACTIONS TAKEN AND VERIFIED:		
VERIFICATION METHODS	REFERENCE	STATUS
RESIDUAL RISK CODE:		
OTHER REFERENCES:		
SERVICE REPORT #:	DATE:	

FIGURE 16B. Typical hazard report form (*Source:* Hansen, 1993)

Originator, organization, and date. Enter the name and organization of the person originating the hazard report. Enter the date the HR on this hazard was first originated. This information (name, date) will not change regardless of subsequent revisions.

Action and organization. Enter the individual and agency (or office) responsible for implementing recommended corrective actions. Generally, this is *not* the safety manager or engineer because they usually do not have the responsibility, resources, or authority to order or implement design changes or equipment or facility modifications.

Suspense date. The latest required date for closure. This date should be prior to the implementation unless

ECP #: DATE:

DRAWING NUMBER(s):

Design Specification

OTHER:

RECOMMENDED CLOSURE: DATE:

CLOSURE CONCURRENCE:

SAFETY MANAGER: DATE:

MANAGER: DATE:

RISK ASSESSMENT CODE LEGEND:

RISK ACCEPTED:

		Probability Level			
		A	B	C	D
Severity Level	I	1	1	2	3
	II	1	2	3	4
	III	2	3	4	5
	IV	3	4	5	6

FIGURE 16C. Typical hazard report form (*Source:* Hansen, 1993)

approved workarounds are implemented that adequately control the hazard for the short term. These workarounds or other implemented controls should be explained in the "actions taken" block.

Hazard/risk factor code, description of hazard. Enter the risk factor from the risk-factor list in Table 1 and a description of the hazard. Only a single hazard or risk factor should be documented on each HR to reduce confusion and assure complete analysis of each hazard or risk factor. Each hazard or risk factor may have several applicable hazard reports to differentiate location of the hazard, different accident scenarios, different subcategories of the accident risk factor, and so on. The hazard should be stated as specifically as possible to facilitate complete and accurate analysis and risk assessment. For example, "Building exposed to damage from lightning strikes" is a specific hazard statement, whereas "bad weather" is too broad and vague for either accurate analysis (on one form) or control and closure. State the hazard locations, and list affected equipment, facilities, personnel, and so on. If several locations or items of equipment are impacted, then the accident scenario and the recommended corrective actions should be equally applicable to them all. If this is not the case, one or more separate hazard reports must be prepared.

Requirements. List all applicable codes, standards, specifications, and requirements that relate to the hazard being analyzed. Also include paragraph numbers that are applicable.

Existing controls and reference. List all *existing* controls that actually reduce the risk of the accident or undesired effects. Explain how each existing control specifically controls the hazard, accident scenario, accident risk factors (e.g., triggering events, necessary conditions, etc.), undesired effects, or risk. Explain the effectiveness of each existing control in reducing the risk. An *existing* control is one that is actually in effect and in some way mitigates the potential risk, severity, or frequency. Explain whether the control actually exists (i.e., is physically implemented), is designed but not yet implemented, is specified but not yet designed, or is procedural. In the "reference" block, list the drawing, specifications, procedure title or number, and other specific control documentation.

Accident scenario. Explain the credible accident scenario, including all causes, that can result from the hazard/accident risk factor being analyzed. Explain each step of each accident scenario in the cause-effect or chronological order in which it is likely to occur. The logic relationships (e.g., "and" versus "or") of the steps in the accident scenario must be determined to assure accurate risk coding based on the alternate paths to the undesired event and to assure all "or" paths are controlled. List and explain possible causes or triggering events that can propagate the hazard into an accident. Also explain each intermediate undesired effect and any special conditions that may be present to mitigate or worsen the severity or frequency of the undesired effects. Discuss simultaneous events that may cause other undesired effects. Discuss all accident scenarios that can result in the undesired effects listed in the "undesired effects" block below. A pictorial representation of the hazard/accident scenario flow is shown in Figure 17 (Hansen 1993).

The initial risk code is based on the hazard or accident risk factor being analyzed and the specific accident scenarios, including existing controls. Therefore, the discussion of the accident scenarios must be complete, factual, and thoroughly analyzed to support accurate risk coding and the development of effective recommended controls.

Single-point failure. A single-point failure is one in which the failure of a component or single action by an individual can cause an accident. If a single-point failure can result in an accident, this will be described in the accident scenario.

Undesired effects and effect risk code. List the potential undesired events or effects that can result from the hazard/accident risk factor just described. In the "effect risk code" block, enter the highest present risk code for *each* undesired effect (e.g., personnel II C, equipment III B). Again, these codes *cannot* be assigned until the accident scenario, undesired effects, and existing controls have been determined and analyzed. The highest effect risk code, as determined from Figure 16, is entered in the "initial hazard risk code" block.

Initial risk code. Enter the assessment of the initial risk—that is, the highest risk level arising from the hazard and its potential accident scenarios or effects, considering the effectiveness of any existing (in place) controls. The risk assessment and risk code assigned are based on the specific hazard statement, the possible undesired effects of the hazard and their severity, and the estimated frequency of occurrence of the accident scenarios described. The initial risk code *cannot* be assigned until the accident scenario, undesired effects, and existing controls have been determined and analyzed. The initial risk code is the highest-ranked effect risk code as determined from Figure 16.

Recommended corrective controls, reference, and status. List all recommended corrective controls that will reduce the initial risks. List and explain recommended design changes, specification changes, safety devices, procedures, and other controls that will elim-

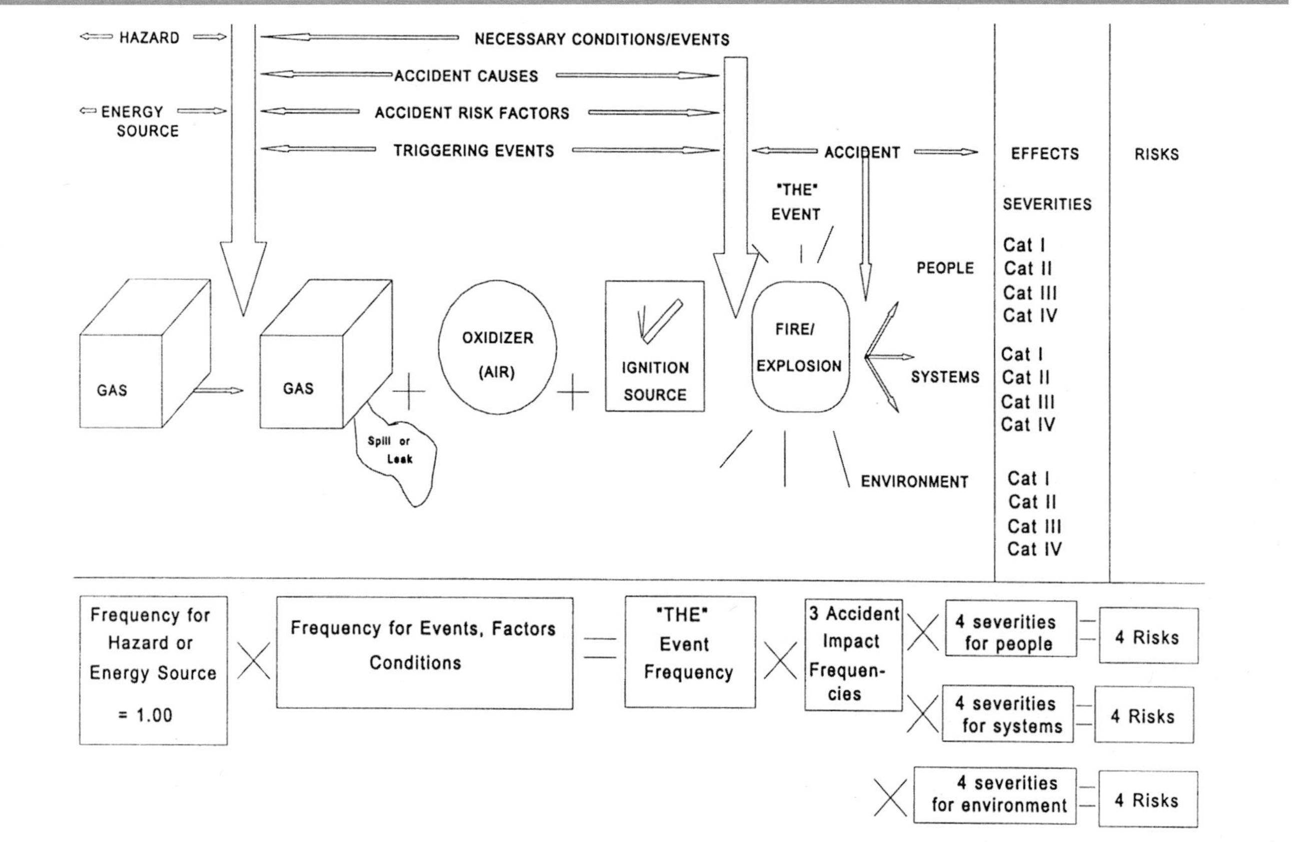

FIGURE 17. A pictorial representation of a hazard scenario (*Source:* Hansen 1993)

inate or mitigate the hazard, control or eliminate accident risk factors, decrease the severity of undesired effects, or reduce the frequency of occurrence of the possible accident scenarios. Recommendations to control undesired effects should be listed and explained. The system-safety precedence specified should be used in prioritizing recommended controls. If any of the recommended controls are alternative to other listed controls, so state. List the status, open or closed, of each recommended control. A control is not considered closed until it has been implemented and verified. For each recommended control, list applicable references (e.g., NFPA 12-1985, Paragraph 2). Recommended corrective actions must be closable and verifiable. As an example, "Personnel will be briefed periodically" cannot be closed and is therefore inappropriate. An appropriate recommendation would be as follows: "(1) A briefing will be prepared and approved by the safety office. (2) A procedure will be established to brief personnel annually and to document all the briefings."

Actions planned/taken. List and explain all actions planned or taken to mitigate the hazard/accident risk and their status (e.g., engineering change proposal, service report, etc.). Include dates of actual or planned completion of each action.

Current risk. The current risk is the initial risk code reassessed based on actions taken and verified as of the date of the HR revision.

Verification methods, reference, and status. List the verification methods (e.g., demonstration, analysis, inspection, test) for each existing and recommended control together with the person or agency that will physically do the verifications. List the status of each verification (i.e., "open" if not verified, "closed" if verified). For each verification listed, also list applicable references (e.g., analysis/test report number, date of inspection). If an item is closed by inspection, include the name of the person who had conducted the inspection as well as the date of the inspection.

Residual risk code. Enter the risk code for the highest remaining risk if all of the recommended controls are implemented. Keep in mind that few operations are risk-free; therefore, it may not be practical or possible to reduce the residual risk to a IV or D category. The residual risk code will be reevaluated, and changed as necessary, based on actions planned or taken.

Other references. List correspondence and other pertinent documentation relating to this hazard. Also list the service report number, drawing numbers, and the ECP number if they are applicable.

Recommended closure and date. The manager (action person) responsible for correcting the hazard signs and dates the report when, in the manager's professional judgment, the required actions have been implemented and verified and the degree of risk has been reduced to an acceptable level.

Closure concurrence and date. The SSM signs and dates the report when he or she concurs with closure of this hazard report. Closure of any hazard report should not be recommended until the residual risk is considered acceptable, and the controls have been verified as being in place and adequate. This signature is the SSM's attestation that the system can be operated safely.

Manager and date. The manager signs and dates when he or she concurs with closure of this hazard report. This signature constitutes the certification that the hazard is adequately controlled and the systems can be operated safely.

Safety manager and date. The SSM signs and dates the report when the SSM concurs with closure of this hazard report.

Residual risk accepted. This signifies the remaining (residual) risk accepted for this particular hazard. This officially closes the hazard report.

Summary

System safety is a discipline in and of itself within all the other safety disciplines. Its applicability is broad and can be applied to virtually every workplace situation to eliminate and control hazards to an acceptable level. There are many approaches and tools. It provides a systematic framework to identify, analyze, eliminate, and control hazards in all types of systems. Whether the system is simple or complex, system-safety techniques can be used to characterize the system. It is certainly a tool worthy of consideration by a safety professional for addressing workplace hazards.

Important Terms

Safety: Freedom from injury, damage, or loss of resources or system availability. Resources include not only people but also time, equipment, and money.

Reliability: The chance that an item can perform its required function for a specified time under specified conditions.

[Safety and reliability are two different concepts. They do, however, overlap. This happens when a safety-critical system fails to work properly (such as a life-support system or fire-alarm system) or when a component failure could result in injury, damage, or loss (such as the failure of a pipe coupling or allowing toxic gas to escape). Not all safety problems are reliability problems and vice versa.]

System: A collection of "things" that work together to achieve a common goal. The things may be people, equipment, facilities, software, tools, raw materials, procedures, organizations, and so on.

System safety: Involves the application of engineering and management principles and techniques to optimize safety. The system should be as safe as possible, given other constraints such as operational effectiveness, time, and cost. System safety covers all phases of the system life cycle.

System analysis: Separating the system into subsystems and subsystems into components, examining each subsystem and component and their interactions. It also involves documenting the results. Analysis is done to identify hazards and to present options for corrective action to decision makers.

Mishap: An unexpected, unforeseen, or unintended event that causes injury, loss, or damage to personnel, equipment, or mission accomplishment.

Hazard: A condition or event that can result from a mishap if it is uncontrolled. The mishap would be the effect of the hazard.

Hazard cause: A condition that contributes to a hazard. It could be unsafe design, environmental factors, failure, human error, and so on.

Hazard controls: Measures that are taken to eliminate a hazard or reduce the severity or probability of its potential effect.

Risk: The combination of severity and probability of a hazard effect.

REFERENCES

Air Force Inspection and Safety Center/ Space Electronic Security Division (AFISC/SESD). n.d. *Software Safety Handbook* (Draft). Norton Air Force Base, CA.

American Institute of Chemical Engineers (AIChE). 1985. *Guidelines for Hazard Evaluation Procedures*. New York: AIChE/Battelle Columbus Division.

______. 2000. *Guidelines for Process Safety in Outsourced Manufacturing Operations*. New York: AIChE.

Brown, D. B. 1976. *Systems Analysis and Design for Safety*. New Jersey: Prentice Hall.

Center for Chemical Process Safety (CCPS). 1992. *Guidelines for Implementing Process Safety Management Systems*. New York: CCPS.

Churchman, C. W. 1981. *The Systems Approach*. New York: Dell.

Clemens, P. L. 2001. *A Charlatan's Guide to Quickly Acquired Quackery: The Trouble with System Safety*. Houston: NASA Training Center.

Hammer, W. 1989. *Occupational Safety Management and Engineering*. 4th ed. Englewood Cliffs, NJ: Prentice Hall.

Hansen, M. D. 1993. "CSOC Integrated System Safety Program Plan." United States Air Force Space Command, Loral Command & Control Systems, Colorado Springs Division. December 31, 1993.

Hassl, D. E., N. H. Roberts, W. E. Vesely, and F. F. Goldberg. 1980. *Fault Tree Handbook* (NUREG 0492). Washington, D.C.: U.S. Nuclear Regulatory Commission, Office of Nuclear Research, Division of Systems and Reliability Research.

Leveson, N. G. 2002. "System Safety Engineering: Back to the Future, Aeronautics and Astronautics" (unpublished). Boston: Massachusetts Institute of Technology.

Lowrance, W. W. 1976. *Of Acceptable Risk*. Los Angeles: Kaufman.

Malasky, S. W. 1974. *System Safety: Planning, Engineering, and Management*. Rochelle Park, NJ: Hayden Books.

McGraw Hill. 1982. *Concise Encyclopedia of Science and Technology*. New York: McGraw Hill.

Post, R. L., D. C. Hendershot, and P. Kers. 2001. "Safety and Reliability: A Synergetic Design Approach." 5th Biennial Process Plant Safety Symposium, American Institute of Chemical Engineers, 2001 Spring National Meeting, April 22–26 2001, George R. Brown Convention Center, Houston, TX.

Rausand, M., and A. Høyland. *System Reliability Theory: Models, Statistical Methods and Applications*. 2d ed. New York: Wiley.

Roland, H. E. 1986. "The Fault Tree: Why and How of Quantification, Hazard Prevention." *Journal of the System Safety Society* May–June, pp. 28–31.

Roland, H. E., and B. Moriarty. 1983. *System Safety Engineering and Management*. New York: Wiley.

Stephans, R. A., and W. W. Talso. 1997. *System Safety Analysis Handbook*. 2d ed. Unionville, VA: System Safety Society.

Stephenson, J. 1991. *System Safety 2000: A Practical Guide for Planning, Managing, and Conducting System Safety Programs*. New York: Van Nostrand Reinhold.

Swain, A. D. 1974. *The Human Element in System Safety: A Guide for Modern Management, Industrial and Commercial Techniques*. London: Swain.

U.S. Department of Defense (DOD). 1990. DoD Directive 3150.2, *Safety Studies and Reviews of Nuclear Weapon Systems*. Washington, D.C.: DOD.

______. 2000. MIL-STD-882D, *Standard Practice for System Safety*. Washington, D.C.: DOD.

Additional Resources

Allocco, M. 2010. *Safety Analyses of Complex Systems: Considerations of Software, Firmware, Hardware, Human, and the Environment*. Hoboken, NJ: John Wiley & Sons.

American National Standards Institute /Government Electronics and Information Technology Association (ANSI/GEIA). 2009. ANSI/GEIA-STD-0010-2009, *Standard Best Practices for System Safety Program Development and Execution*. Washington, D.C.: ANSI/GEIA.

Clemens, P. L., and R. L. Simmons. 1998. NIOSH Instruction Module, "System Safety and Risk Management." Washington, D.C.: U.S. Department of Health and Human Services (DHHS), Centers for Disease Control and Prevention (CDC).

Ericson, Clifton A. 2005. *Hazard Analysis Techniques for System Safety*. John Wiley & Sons.

______. 2011. *Concise Encyclopedia of System Safety: Definition of Terms and Concepts*. New York: John Wiley & Sons.

Federal Aviation Administration (FAA). 2000. *System Safety Handbook*. Washington, D.C.: FAA.

______. 2005. Advisory Circular (AC) 431.35-2A, *Reusable Launch Vehicle System Safety Process*. Washington, D.C.: FAA.

Goldberg, B. E. et al. 1994. NASA Reference Publication 1358, *System Engineering Toolbox for Design-Oriented Engineers*. Washington, D.C.: NASA.

Hardy, T. L."Challenges in Qualitative Risk Assessments of Space Systems." Presented at the 4th International Association for the Advancement of System Safety Conference, Huntsville, AL, May 19–21, 2010.

______. "Using Cost of Quality Approaches to Improve Commercial Space Transportation Safety." Presented at the 24th International System Safety Conference (IAASS), Albuquerque, NM, July 31–August 4, 2006.

______. "Lessons Learned in the Safety Verification Process." Presented at the 29th International System Safety Conference, Las Vegas, NV, August 8–12, 2011.

______. "Using Accident Reports to Improve the Hazard Identification Process." Presented at the 28th International System Safety Conference, Minneapolis, MN, August 30–Sept. 3, 2010.

______. "Using Lessons Learned to Promote a Healthy Skepticism in System Safety." Presented at the 28th International System Safety Conference, Minneapolis, MN, August 30–Sept. 3, 2010.

Leveson, N. G. 1995. *Safeware: System Safety and Computers*. New York: Addison-Wesley.

Murray, D., and Hardy, T. L. "Developing Safety-Critical Software Requirements for Commercial Reusable Launch Vehicles." Presented at the 2nd International Association for the Advancement of System Safety Conference, Chicago, IL, May 14–16, 2007.

Myers, G., T. Badgett, T. Thomas, and C. Sandler. 2004. *The Art of Software Testing*. NY: John Wiley & Sons.

National Aeronautics and Space Administration (NASA). 1998. NASA-STD-8719.7, *Facility System Safety Guidebook*. Washington, D.C.: NASA.

______. 2004. *NASA Software Safety Guidebook*. Technical Standard. Washington, D.C.: NASA.

______. 2004. GB-8719.13B, *Software Safety Guidebook*. Washington, D.C.: NASA.

______. 2004. NASA-STD-8719.13B, *Software Safety Standard*. Washington, D.C.: NASA.

Raheja, D., and M. Allocco. 2006. *Assurance Technologies Principles and Practices: A Product, Process, and System Safety Perspective*. 2d ed. New York: Wiley-Interscience.

Society of Automotive Engineers (SAE). 1996. ARP4761, *Guidelines and Methods for Conducting the Safety Assessment Process on Civil Airborne Systems and Equipment*. Wahsington, D.C.: SAE.

Stephans, R. A. 2004. *System Safety for the 21st Century*. New York: John Wiley & Sons.

United States Air Force (USAF). 2000. *Air Force System Safety Handbook*. Kirtland, New Mexico: Air Force Safety Agency, Kirtland AFB.

U.S. Department of Defense (DOD). 2000. MIL-STD-882DF, *Standard Practice for System Safety*. Washington, D.C.: DOD.

______. 2010. *Joint Software Systems Safety Engineering Handbook*. Washington, D.C.: DOD.

Vincoli, J. W. 1997. *Basic Guide to System Safety*. New York: John Wiley & Sons

______. 2006. *Basic Guide to System Safety*. 2d ed. New York: John Wiley & Sons.

ELECTRICAL SAFETY

3

Steven J. Owen

LEARNING OBJECTIVES

The following objectives apply to working on or near energized electrical conductors and equipment operating at 50 volts or more to ground.

- Understand the hazards involved in such work.
- Know which rules and standards apply to electrical safety for personnel.
- Understand and be able to apply safety-related work practices.
- Be able to properly select and use personal protective equipment, including flame-resistant clothing, for electrical work.
- Be able to ensure proper training and the qualification of personnel performing electrical work.
- Understand the changes to NFPA 70E-2004 and 70E-2009, reflected in NFPA 70E-2012.
- Utilize safe switching procedures for personnel safety.
- Understand the need for temporary protective grounding for personnel.

ELECTRICITY HAS BECOME an essential part of modern life, both at home and on the job. Some employees, such as electricians, work directly with electricity; other employees work with wiring associated with overhead lines, cable harnesses, or circuit assemblies. Still others, such as office workers and salespeople, work with electricity indirectly. As a source of power, electricity is accepted without much thought about the hazards encountered. Perhaps because it has become such a familiar part of our daily surroundings, often it is not treated with the respect it deserves.

This chapter has been adapted from the book *Electrical Safety—Procedures and Practices* (Owen 1997). For purposes of discussion, the hazards associated with electricity are broken down into three types: (1) shock, (2) arc flash, and (3) arc blast.

HOW DOES ELECTRICITY ACT?

To handle electricity safely, it is necessary to understand how it acts, how it can be directed, and how parts of the human body react to it. For this purpose, it is helpful to compare the flow of electricity with the flow of water.

Operating an electric switch may be considered analogous to turning on a water faucet. Behind the faucet or switch there must be a source of water or electricity with something to transport it and with pressure to make it flow. In the case of water, the source is the reservoir or pumping station, the transportation is through pipes, and the force to make it flow is the pressure provided by a pump. With electricity, the source is the power-generating station. Current travels through electric conductors in the form of wires and by pressure, measured in volts, provided by a generator.

Resistance to the flow of electricity is measured in ohms and varies widely. It is determined by three factors: the nature of the substance itself, the length and cross-sectional area of the substance, and the temperature of the substance.

Some substances, such as metals, offer very little resistance to the flow of electric current and are called conductors. Other substances, such as Bakelite, porcelain, and dry wood, offer such high resistance that they can be used to prevent the flow of electric current and are called insulators. The relationship between resistance, current, and voltage is called Ohm's Law and is represented as follows:

Voltage = Current times Resistance

$$E = I \times R \tag{1}$$

Current = Voltage divided by Resistance

$$I = E/R \tag{2}$$

Resistance = Voltage divided by Current

$$R = E/I \tag{3}$$

A *volt* is the unit used to measure the electrical pressure causing the current to flow.

An *ampere* is the unit used to measure current, which is the net transfer of electric charge per unit time (e.g., conduction current in a wire).

An *ohm* is the unit used to measure the resistance of a conductor such that a constant current of one ampere in it produces a voltage of one volt between its ends (Owen 1997).

Shock

Electricity travels in closed circuits. The preferred, normal route is through a conductor. Shock occurs when the body becomes a part of the electric circuit. The current enters the body at one point and leaves at one or more other points. Shock normally occurs in one of three ways, as the person being shocked comes into contact with

- both wires of the electric circuit
- one wire of the electric circuit and the ground
- a metallic part that has become energized by being in contact with an energized wire while the person is also in contact with the ground or a grounded surface.

To better understand the harm done by electrical shock, one needs to understand something about the physiology of certain body parts, including the skin, heart, and muscles.

The Skin

Skin covers the body and is made up of three layers. The most important layer, as far as electric shock is concerned, is the outer layer of dead cells referred to as the horny layer. This layer is composed mostly of a protein called keratin. It is the keratin that provides the largest percentage of the body's electrical resistance. When it is dry, the outer layer of skin may have a resistance of several thousand ohms, but when it is moist, there is a radical drop in resistance, as is also the case if there is a cut or abrasion piercing the horny layer. The amount of resistance provided by the skin will vary widely from individual to individual. The resistance will also vary widely at different parts of the body. For instance, the workman with high-resistance hands may have low resistance on the back of his calf.

The skin, like any insulator, has a breakdown voltage at which it ceases to act as a resistor and is simply punctured, leaving only the lower-resistance body tissue to impede the flow of current in the body. This voltage will vary with the individual, but is in the area of 600 volts. Because most industrial power distribution systems are 480 volts or higher, people working at these levels need to develop a special awareness of the shock potential.

The Heart

The heart is the pump that sends life-sustaining blood to all parts of the body. The blood flow is caused by the contractions of the heart muscles, which are controlled by electrical impulses. The electrical impulses are delivered by a highly complicated, intricate system of nerve tissue with built-in timing mechanisms. A current, measured in milliamperes, can upset the rhythmic coordinated beating of the heart by disturbing the nerve impulses.

When this happens, the heart is said to be in fibrillation—that is, pumping action stops. Death will occur quickly if the normal coordinated rhythmic beating is not restored. Remarkable as it may seem, what is needed to defibrillate the heart is a shock of an even higher intensity.

Muscle

The other muscles of the body are also controlled by electrical impulses delivered by nerves. Electric shock can cause loss of muscular control, resulting in the inability to let go of an electrical conductor. Electric shock can indirectly cause other injuries because of involuntarily muscle reactions from the electric shock, which can cause bruises, fractures, and even death resulting from collisions or falls. The current from the contact with the energized conductor or equipment disrupts the normal electrical impulses, which causes the unexpected action from the muscles.

The Severity of Shock

The severity of shock received when a person becomes a part of an electric circuit is affected by three primary factors:

1. The amount of current flowing through the body, measured in amperes
2. The path of the current through the body
3. The length of time the body is in contact with the circuit

Other factors that may affect the severity of the shock are the frequency of the current, the phase of the heart cycle when shock occurs, and the general health of the person prior to the shock. Effects can range from a barely perceptible tingle to immediate cardiac arrest. There are no absolute limits or known values that show an exact injury at any given amperage range.

A severe shock can cause considerably more damage to the body than is visible. For example, a person may suffer internal hemorrhages and destruction of tissues, nerves, and muscle. In addition, shock is often only the beginning in a chain of events. The final injury may well be from a fall, cuts, burns, or broken bones.

The most common shock-related injury is a burn. Burns suffered in electrical accidents may be of three types—electrical burns, arc burns, and thermal contact burns. Electrical burns are the result of the electric current flowing through the tissues or bones. Heat generated by the current flow through the body causes tissue damage. Electrical burns are among the most serious injuries one can receive and should be given immediate attention. Because the most severe burning is likely to be on the inside, what may at first appear to be a small surface wound could, in fact, be an indication of severe internal burns. Arc and contact burns are discussed in the following sections.

Arc Flash

Arc burns make up a substantial portion of the injuries from electrical malfunction and may cause serious injury or death to workers. At the initiation of an arc fault, tremendous energy can be released in a very brief time as substantial electrical currents are passing through the air. Metal conductor parts can vaporize, resulting in hot vapors and hot metal being violently spewed. Through direct exposure or by igniting the worker's clothing, the thermal energy can result in severe burns to workers. A large portion (some estimates are as high as 80 percent) of all electrical injuries are a result of an arc flash igniting flammable clothing worn by personnel exposed to an arc flash.

Arc Blast

The third source of possible hazard is the blast associated with an electric arc. This blast comes from the pressure developed by the near-instantaneous heating of the air surrounding the arc and from the expansion of the metal as it is vaporized. The rapid thermal escalation of the air and vaporization of metal can create a very loud explosion and create tremendous pressures. These high sound levels can rupture eardrums. This is why NFPA 70E-2012 requires hearing protection in the form of inserts with no specific decibel rating for those working on or near electrical equipment classified as Risk/Hazard Category 0 and higher. Hearing protection is now required for all hazard/risk category levels 0 through 4.

These high pressures associated with the arc blast can cause collapsed lungs and result in forces that can cause workers to lose balance [i.e., the required safe working position required by the Occupational Safety and Health Administration (OSHA) and NFPA 70E (2012)]. During an arc blast, copper vapor expands to 67,000 times the volume of solid copper (copper expands by a factor in excess of 67,000 times when boiling). The air in the arc stream expands when heating from the ambient temperature to that of the arc, which is approximately 35,000 °F. Examples of this vaporization of metal may involve a noninsulated metallic screwdriver blade, a metal fish tape, or other noninsulated tools or parts coming in contact with energized parts as phase-to-phase or phase-to-ground faults. These pressures can be great enough to hurl people, parts, and equipment considerable distances.

Phase-to-phase faults, also referred as bolted faults, happen when an accidental contact is made between two or more energized ungrounded conductors simultaneously, resulting in the release of a tremendous amount of energy. An example of a phase-to-phase fault would be if a large tree limb fell across energized overhead lines, contacting two or more lines simultaneously. Another example would be if a noninsulated screwdriver or other tool, or a metal flashlight, was dropped or left lying across two or more exposed energized bus bars simultaneously.

Phase-to-ground faults happen when contact is made between an energized ungrounded conductor and a grounded conductor or grounded surface. An example of a phase-to-ground fault would be if a noninsulated screwdriver was dropped or somehow wedged between an exposed energized bus bar or conductor and a grounded metal surface or grounded conductor.

Other hazards associated with the arc and blast include spewing of molten metal droplets with temperatures as high as 1800° F, which can cause contact burns and associated damage, as well as being inhaled into the person's lungs (as when a startled person gasps for air). Another negative effect of an explosion caused by an arc blast is projectiles (for example, parts of the molded case, other metallic or nonmetallic parts of a circuit breaker, or the ferrule of a fuse traveling through air) that impact workers and other equipment. One possible result of the arc blast is that it can hurl or push a person who is near the arc blast away from the arc, as well as reduce the time a worker is exposed to the arc-flash temperatures (which can be as high as 35,000 degrees).

The total force exerted on a worker's body due to an arcing fault blast is dependent on the body surface exposed to the blast wave. The potential health risk to a worker resulting from the total forces exerted on his or her body depends on the worker's position when the blast contacted the worker. A worker standing on the floor would most likely be able to safely withstand more pressure than a worker on a ladder. A worker on a ladder, or working from a scaffold or bucket, who is subjected to an arc flash and arc blast has an increased chance of injury from a fall.

Under certain conditions (e.g., when misapplied and subjected to fault currents well above their rating), it is possible for objects such as overcurrent devices to disintegrate (blow up) and reach speeds as high as 700 miles per hour and pass through the body of a person who is standing in the path of the object (Cooper Bussman 1998). This is why qualified persons are trained to stand off to the side of switches, circuit breakers, and disconnects, and to use safe electrical switching procedures when operating the switches, circuit breakers, and disconnects. Nonqualified persons should not be performing electrical switching operations nor resetting circuit breakers that have tripped due to fault conditions.

Safety-Related Work Practices

General Requirements for Safety-Related Work Practices

The safety-related work practices of OSHA 29 CFR 1910, Sections 1910.331–335, and NFPA 70E-2012, Articles 110, 120, and 130, apply to work by both qualified persons (those who have training in recognition and avoidance of electrical hazards of working on or near exposed energized parts) and unqualified persons (those with little or no training). The rules apply to the following installations:

- premises wiring installations of electrical conductors and equipment within or on buildings or other structures

- wiring for connection to supply installations of conductors that connect to a supply of electricity
- other wiring installations of other outside conductors on the premises
- optical fiber cable installations of optical fiber cable, where such installations are made along with electrical conductors

Establishing Safe Work Conditions and Determining Safe Working Distances

Over the years, analytical tools have been developed to better assess the hazards created from arcing faults. Because of injuries and deaths, NFPA 70E-2012, *Standard for Electrical Safety in the Workplace*, adopted formulas to define the safe working distance from a potential arc. These formulas are used to determine the type of protective clothing and equipment a worker needs to use when working on energized electrical equipment. The formulas for this calculation are based on the work and a technical paper by Ralph Lee (1982).

Lee showed temperature and time thresholds for incurable and just-curable burns. At a distance of 3 feet, 0 inches, from the source of the arc, the arc energy required to produce these temperatures was determined to be 23 MW and 17 MW for incurable and just-curable burns, respectively. Lee also found that the maximum arc energy occurred when it represented 50 percent of the available three-phase bolted fault (bf). For example, the arc from a 46 MVA (million volt-amps) available source for 0.1 second could cause an incurable burn at a distance of 3 feet, 0 inches. The arc from a 34 MVA (34 million volt-amps) available fault for 0.1 second at 3 feet, 0 inches, would result in a just-curable burn. The following formulas, developed by Lee, were incorporated into NFPA 70E-2012:

$$Dc = (2.65 \times \text{MVA bf} \times t)^{1/2} \quad (4)$$

$$Df = (1.96 \times \text{MVA bf} \times t)^{1/2} \quad (5)$$

Dc = distance in feet for a just-curable burn

Df = distance in feet for an incurable burn

MVA bf = bolted three-phases MVA at point of short circuit = 1.73 × voltage L – L × available short-circuit current × 10^{-6}

t = time of exposure in seconds

Example 1: Assume an available 40,896-ampere bolted three-phase fault on a 480-volt system, protected with a noncurrent-limiting fuse with a clearing time of six cycles (0.1 second). Find the distance in feet for a just-curable burn.

$$Dc = (2.65 \times \text{MVA bf} \times t)^{1/2}$$
$$Dc = (2.65 \times 1.732 \times 480 \times 40{,}896 \times 10^{-6} \times 0.1)^{1/2}$$
$$Dc = (9.00)^{1/2}$$
$$Dc = 3 \text{ ft}$$

This means that any exposed skin closer than 3 feet, 0 inches, to this available fault for 0.1 second or longer may not be curable should an arcing fault occur. If employees must work on this equipment where parts of their bodies would be closer than 3 feet, 0 inches, from the possible arc, suitable protective equipment must be utilized so that the possibility of employee injury is minimized. See OSHA 29 CFR 1910, Section 1910.335(a)(1), and NFPA 70E-2012, Section 130.7(A).

Example 2: Assume an available 40,896-ampere bolted three-phase fault on a 480-volt system, protected by Class J, 200-amp, current-limiting fuses. The opening time is assumed at 1/4 cycle (0.004 seconds), and the equivalent root mean square (RMS) let-through current (as read from the fuse manufacturer's chart) is 6000 amperes.

$$Dc = (2.65 \times \text{MVA bf} \times t)^{1/2}$$
$$Dc = (2.65 \times 1.732 \times 480 \times 6000 \times 10^{-6} \times 0.004)^{1/2}$$
$$Dc = (0.0528)^{1/2}$$
$$Dc = 0.229 \text{ ft (or 2.75 inches)}$$

Thus, the flash protection boundary was significantly decreased, from 3 feet, 0 inches (36 inches) in Example 1 to 0.23 feet (2.75 inches) in Example 2, by the use of current-limiting fuses, which limited the short-circuit current from 40,896 amperes to 6000 amperes let-through and reduced the exposure time from 6 cycles to 1/4 cycle.

Employees must wear, and be trained in the use of, appropriate protective equipment for the possible electrical hazards with which they are faced. Examples of this personal protective equipment include head, face, neck, chin, eye, ear, body, and extremity protection as required. Electrical protective equipment selected for the job task, based on the Hazard/Risk Assessment from Table 130.7(C)(9)(a), and selected from Table 130.7(C)(10), must also meet the minimum arc thermal protective value (ATPV) ratings of Table 130.7(C)(10) of NFPA 70E-2012.

In Example 2, a person is doing a voltage test on a 600-volt bus in the back side of a 600-volt class switchgear by opening a hinged door to gain access to the bus. Opening the hinged door to gain access to the energized bus is considered a Hazard/Risk Category 2 according to Table 130.7(C)(15). Performing the voltage test would also be considered a Hazard/Risk Category 2 from the same table for this example. The appropriate protective clothing and PPE is found in Table 130.7(C)(10). Best practices for this example would be to choose category 2 as the appropriate hazard category level and to select the PPE from the category-2 level for this example. In Hazard/Risk Category 2, the minimum arc rating of 8 cal/cm^2 is required for this example. Required PPE for voltage testing at 480 vac consists of the following:

- arc-rated, long-sleeved shirt
- arc-rated pants (arc-rated coveralls may be used in lieu of the arc-rated shirt and pants)
- arc-rated flash suit hood (or a balaclava (sock hood) and arc-rated face shield
- hard hat (nonconductive)
- safety glasses or goggles
- hearing protection
- leather gloves (with insulting liners for shock protection of Class 00, with a minimum rating of 500 volts
- leather work shoes

Also careful consideration should be given to undergarments, such as underwear, tee-shirts, and socks. Cotton is generally a good choice because cotton (a natural fiber) is considered a material referenced as Hazard/Risk Category 0 in Table 130.7(c)(10). Over the years (before flame-resistant materials), cotton was considered a good choice for electrical work garments. Best practices call for cotton as an undergarment.

Note that there is no requirement in Table 130.7(C)(15) for foot protection for falling objects, nor does it require an electrical insulated shoe, even though both may be good ideas and are required by many employers.

The hazard/risk category is a determination of the relative danger of a given job task, which is based in part on the incident energy available, the distance from exposed energized parts, and the distance in which an arc flash could reach a person who may be injured by burns not exceeding second degree, or 1.2 cal/cm^2, which are considered to be just curable.

Personal protective equipment, sufficient for protection against an electrical flash, would be required for any part of the body within 3 feet, 0 inches, of the fault in Example 1. Such equipment would include a switching hood (nonconductive hard hat, arc-rated face shield, and flame-resistant head, neck, and face protection), hearing protectors, flame-resistant clothing that meets the minimum requirements of Table 130.7(C)(11), voltage-rated gloves, and leather footwear.

Significantly less personal protective equipment would be required for Example 2 because the flash zone is within 0.23 feet (2.75 inches) and the incident energy available is calculated to be 0.17 cal/cm^2. In this case, the required personal protective equipment might be reduced to a nonconductive hard hat, safety glasses, flame-resistant shirt, flame-resistant pants or blue jeans (minimum 12-ounce fabric weight), voltage-rated gloves, and leather footwear—which is equivalent to Hazard/Risk Category 1—and possibly treated as Hazard/Risk Category 0 (from Table 130.7(C)(11) Protective Clothing Characteristics), which requires no flame-resistant clothing.

In an actual case where an electrical worker is to work on energized equipment, the safe working distance must be determined by making calculations over the full range of possible currents and estimation of exposure time. The worker is required to wear protective clothing and gear for the worst-case condition. The possible currents would encompass the range of currents up to the maximum available current that could arise if a mishap occurred. The exposure time is dependent on reasonable reaction time and is situational. For example, a worker standing in front of a switchgear might reasonably be expected to get out of the way of a blast in one second. The normal human reaction time (to detect the condition and to move out of the path) has been estimated to be one-fourth of a second, whereas an arc fault may develop into an arc blast in one-sixth of a second. A worker on his or her knees might be exposed for two to three seconds or longer. A worker lying on the ground might be there for three to five seconds or longer. However, a worker in a bucket truck might be exposed to this hazard for many seconds or minutes. These times can be utilized with the time-current curves to determine the maximum amount of current at those times where the overcurrent protective device does not open in that reaction or movement time. With that information the hazard can be calculated for the worst-case condition.

Work Permits

A summary of the sources for the topics discussed in this section is presented in the chapter appendix. Readers are advised to consult the full text of the standards for recommended procedures and practices.

Live parts to which an employee might be exposed should be put into an electrically safe work condition before an employee works on or near them, unless the employer can demonstrate that de-energizing introduces additional or increased hazards or is infeasible due to equipment design or operational limitations. Caution should be taken when considering what is *infeasible* versus what is *inconvenient*; the difference is significant. In some cases, an employer may treat the terms interchangeably. What may be inconvenient cannot serve to justify work on or near exposed live parts. When work is performed on or near exposed energized circuits and parts, the employer must be able to document that the work task meets the criteria for one of the acceptable reasons for executing the work with the circuit or part energized.

Energized parts that operate at less than 50 volts to ground are not required to be de-energized if there will be no increased exposure to electrical burns or to explosion due to electric arcs.

Where the work to be performed will be on energized parts, the electrical work must be performed by written permit only. The energized electrical work permit should include, but not be limited to, the following items (see Figure 1):

- a description of the circuit and equipment to be worked on and the location
- justification as to need for the work to be performed in an energized condition
- a description of the safe work practices that will be employed
- results of the shock hazard analysis
- determination of shock protection boundaries
- results of the flash hazard analysis
- the flash protection boundary
- the necessary personal protective equipment to safely perform the assigned task
- means employed to restrict the access of unqualified persons from the work area
- evidence of completion of a job briefing, including a discussion of any job-specific hazards
- energized work approval (authorizing or responsible management, safety officer, owner, etc.) signature(s).

Exemptions to Work Permit

Work performed on or near live parts by qualified persons related to tasks such as testing, troubleshooting, voltage measuring, and so on, is permitted without an energized electrical work permit, provided appropriate safe work practices and personal protective equipment are provided and used.

Approach Boundaries

NFPA 70E-2012, Section 130.5, provides a basis for determining the flash protection boundary. For systems that operate at 600 volts or less, the flash protection boundary shall be 4 feet, 0 inches, based on the product of clearing times of 2 cycles (0.033 second) and an available bolted fault current of 50 kA or any combination not exceeding 100 kA cycles (1667 amperes per second). This is the *default value*.

At voltage levels above 600 volts, it is necessary to calculate the flash protection boundary. The *flash protection boundary* is the distance at which the incident energy equals 5 J/cm^2 (1.2 cal/cm^2).

Flash Hazard Analysis

Flash hazard analysis should be done before a person approaches any exposed electrical conductor circuit

ENERGIZED ELECTRICAL WORK PERMIT

Part I: To Be Completed by the Person or Organization Requesting Permit

Name of person/organization requesting permit: ______________________________

____

Today's date: ______________________________

Date for work to be performed: ______________________________

Job number/work order number: ______________________________

Part II: To Be Completed by Qualified Person(s) Performing Work on Energized Circuits and Parts

(1)(a) Description of circuit/equipment to be worked on: ______________________________

____

____

(1)(b) Location of circuit/equipment to be worked on: ______________________________

____

(2) Description of work to be performed: ______________________________

____

____

____

(3) Justification for performing work on energized circuits and parts. Why this work cannot be performed on de-energized circuits and parts:

____

____

____

(4) A description of the safe work practices to be employed: ______________________________

____

____

(5) Results of the shock hazard analysis: ______________________________

____

____

(6) Determination of the shock protection boundaries: ______________________________

____

(7) Results of the flash hazard analysis: ______________________________

____

____

(8) Determination of the flash protection boundary: ______________________________

____

FIGURE 1. Sample energized work permit (Adapted from NFPA 70E-2012, Annex J)

ENERGIZED ELECTRICAL WORK PERMIT (cont.)

(9) Determination of personal protective equipment necessary to perform job task safely: ______________________

____

____

(10) Evidence of completion of job briefing: ______________________

____

____

____

Part III: Approval(s) To Perform Work on Energized Circuits and Parts

(1) Signatures of authorizing person(s). Sign only if you are in agreement that work can be performed safely. If not in agreement, leave unsigned and return to requester.

(a)(1) Electrical-qualified person to perform work or supervise work:

____

Signature Date: ______________________

(a)(2) Electrical-qualified person to perform work or supervise work:

____

Signature Date: ______________________

(a)(3) Electrical-qualified person to perform work or supervise work

____

Signature Date: ______________________

(b)(1) Responsible management authority and title

____

Signature Date: ______________________

(b)(2) Responsible management authority and title

____

Signature Date: ______________________

(b)(3) Responsible management authority and title

____

Signature Date: ______________________

Add more names as necessary.

FIGURE 1. Sample energized work permit (Adapted from NFPA 70E-2012, Annex J)

part that has not been placed in an electrically safe work condition.

The incident energy exposure determined by the flash hazard analysis should be used to select protective clothing and personal protective equipment for job-specific tasks. The clothing should be flame-resistant. Clothing made from flammable synthetic materials that melt at temperatures below 315° C (600° F), such as acetate, acrylic, nylon, polyester, polyethylene, polypropylene, and spandex, either alone or in blends with cotton, should not be worn. The suggestion is to avoid wearing materials that may melt against the skin.

Employees working in areas where there are electrical hazards should be provided with and use protective equipment that is designed and constructed for the specific part of the body to be protected and for the work to be performed. This is taken from the *OSHA General Industry Standard*, 29 CFR 1910, Section 1910.335(a)(1).

Hazard/Risk Analysis

(Adapted in part from Cooper Bussman, *Handbook for Electrical Safety*, 2d ed., 2004.)

Hazard/risk analysis is a process that is used to do the following:

- evaluate circuit information drawings—eletrical distribution one-line and other appropriate drawings
- determine the degree and extent of hazards
- provide job planning as necessary to safely perform tasks
- determine approach-boundary requirements
- evaluate flash-protection-boundary requirements
- evaluate personnel qualifications
- determine appropriate personal protective equipment based on the potential hazards present

To engineer additional safety into electrical systems to protect personnel from arc flash and arc blast, engineering options may include the following: replacing existing switchgear with arc-resistant switchgear; installing a secondary main relay that can trip a primary circuit breaker; installing zone interlocking in switchgear (i.e., a signal from a downstream circuit breaker blocks an upstream circuit breaker from tripping); changing overcurrent device type to current-limiting device; installing differential relays; installing provisions for remote racking and remote operation; using a racking wrench or similar device that has a long or extra-long handle to increase working distance; changing the sequence of switching operations to reduce the time when exposure is high (Cooper Bussman 2004a).

Training and Qualification of All Personnel

The training requirements that are contained in NFPA 70E-2012, Section 110.2, and OSHA 29 CFR 1910, Section 1910.332(a), standards apply to all employees who face a risk of electrical shock or injury when they are working on or near exposed energized parts or parts that may become energized. If this training has not been completed, then a person cannot be considered qualified.

OSHA defined a qualified person as "one who is familiar with the construction and operation of the equipment and the hazards involved" (OSHA 2006). The term *qualified person* is intended to apply to a person who has knowledge of the construction and operation of the equipment and has received safety training to recognize and avoid the electrical hazards that might be present.

OSHA revised the definition of qualified person in Final Rule 72, effective August 13, 2007. A qualified person is "one who has received training in and has demonstrated skills and knowledge in the construction and operation of electric equipment and installations and the hazards involved" (OSHA 2007).

NFPA 70E-2012 gives the following definition:

> A qualified person shall be trained and knowledgeable of the construction and operation of equipment or a specific work method, and shall be trained to recognize and avoid the electrical hazards that might be present with respect to that equipment or work method.
>
> (a) Such persons shall also be familiar with the proper use of special precautionary techniques, personal

> protective equipment, including arc-flash, insulating and shielding materials, and insulated tools and test equipment.
>
> A person can be considered qualified with respect to certain equipment and methods but still be unqualified for others.
>
> (b) An employee who is undergoing on-the-job training and who in the course of such training has demonstrated an ability to perform duties safely at his or her level of training and who is under the direct supervision of a qualified person shall be considered to be a qualified person for the performance of those duties.
>
> (c) Such persons shall be permitted to work within the Limited Approach Boundary of exposed live parts operating at 50 volts or more shall, at minimum, be additionally trained in all of the following:***
>
> (d) Tasks that are performed less often than once per year shall require retraining before the performance of the work practices involved.
>
> Employees shall be trained to select an appropriate voltage detector and shall *demonstrate* how to use a device to verify the absence of voltage, including interpreting indications provided by the device. The training shall include information that enables the employee to understand all limitations of each specific voltage detector that may be used. [Emphasis added.]

Whether an employee is considered a qualified person depends on various circumstances in the workplace. It is possible for an individual to be considered qualified with regard to certain equipment in the workplace, but unqualified as to other equipment.

For example, an employee may have received the necessary training to be considered qualified to work on a particular piece of equipment. However, if that same employee were to work on other types of equipment for which he or she had not received the necessary training, he or she would be considered unqualified for that equipment.

In order to be considered qualified (permitted to work on or near exposed energized parts), employees, at a minimum, must be trained in and familiar with the following:

- the skills and techniques necessary to distinguish exposed live parts from other parts of electrical equipment
- the skills and techniques necessary to determine the nominal voltage of exposed live parts
- the clearance distances specified in OSHA 29 CFR 1910, Section 1910.333(c), Table 130.4; NFPA 70E-2012; and the corresponding voltages to which the qualified person will be exposed
- the decision-making process necessary to determine the degree and extent of the hazard and the personal protective equipment and job planning necessary to perform the task safely
- the safety-related work practices required by OSHA 29 CFR 1910, Section 1910.331-335, and Article 130 of NFPA 70E-2012 that pertain to their respective job assignments
- any electrically related safety practices not specifically addressed by OSHA CFR 1910, Section 1910.331-335 and Article 130 of NFPA 70E-2012 that are necessary for their safety

The training may be on the job, in a classroom setting, or both. All personnel should have training appropriate for their tasks, including safety training. This is required by the new definition of "qualified person" in NFPA 70-2011, *National Electrical Code* (NFPA 2011). NFPA 70E-2012 is more detailed in the definition of a qualified person (NFPA 2012).

Where does the term qualified person fit in? Who uses this term? The definition found in the *OSHA General Industry Standard*, 29 CFR 1910, Section 1910.399, is "one familiar with the construction and operation of the equipment and the hazards involved." This definition ties into the requirements of Section 1910.332 related to training. The *OSHA Construction Standard*, 29 CFR 1926, Section 1926.32, defines a qualified person as follows: "'Qualified' means one who, by possession of a recognized degree, certificate, or professional standing, or who by extensive knowledge, training, and experience, has successfully demonstrated his ability to solve or resolve problems relating to the subject matter, the work, or the project."

The *National Electrical Code* revised the definition of qualified person (NFPA 2011). The revised definition reads as follows: "one who has the skills and knowledge related to the construction and operation of the electrical equipment and installations and has received safety training on the hazards involved" (NFPA 2011).

No matter what the job task is and no matter which trade is involved, personnel need the appropriate level of training to perform a job task safely and efficiently. OSHA standard 29 CFR 1926, Section 1926.20, covering general safety and health provisions, is written as follows: "The employer shall permit only those employees qualified by training or experience to operate equipment and machinery" (OSHA 2006). This is merely the first of a number of requirements dictating training for employees. Why are references to training stressed? A person cannot be considered competent or qualified without having received the appropriate training that is required by the sections mentioned here.

There are advantages to providing the training to meet the definition of *qualified*. The number one priority is always safety. Only those persons qualified by training are allowed to work on or near exposed energized electrical circuits, conductors, or parts operating at 50 volts or more to ground. The benefits include a safer workplace and greater efficiency, along with improved employee morale and possibly lower insurance rates.

Use of Equipment

Test Instruments and Equipment

Test instruments, equipment, and their accessories should be rated for circuits and equipment to which they will be connected. Test instruments, equipment, and their accessories should be designed for the environment to which they will be exposed, and for the manner in which they will be used. Test instruments and equipment and all associated test leads, cables, power cords, probes, and connectors should be visually inspected for external defects and damage before the equipment is used on any shift.

If there is a defect or evidence of damage that might expose an employee to injury, the defective or damaged item should be removed from service and no employee should use it until necessary repairs and tests rendering the equipment safe have been made.

Because the use of test instruments can expose employees to live parts of electric circuits, testing on energized electric circuits or equipment should be performed only by qualified persons.

Visual Inspection

To prevent injuries to employees resulting from exposed conductors or defects in the test equipment, a visual inspection of all test equipment is required before it is used. If any defects are found or suspected, the damaged equipment must be taken out of service, and employees must not be allowed to use the defective damaged equipment until it has been repaired.

Using test equipment in improper environments or on circuits with voltages or currents higher than the rating of the equipment can cause equipment failure. Verification of voltage on an incorrect scale or value other than voltage (e.g., ohms or current) has led to meters being damaged and personnel being injured.

Hazards can be exceedingly greater for an incident in a high-energy circuit than one in a low-energy circuit. The same misapplication that results in a blown fuse and a puff of smoke in a low-energy circuit could result in a violent explosion and injury in a high-energy circuit.

Because employees can be injured as a result of this failure, test equipment must be used within its rating and to be suitable for the environment in which it is to be used.

Portable Electric Equipment

Grounded Tools

Portable electrical hand tools are widely used by those in general industry and on construction sites. Because they are so widely used, they are also often abused. Tools that are faulty or damaged can become a source of electrical shock to the user.

It is very important that all tools (unless double-insulated) contain an equipment grounding conductor that is connected to the tool frame and through the supply cord back to the service-entrance enclosure.

If a ground fault occurs in a defective tool, the grounding conductor must carry enough current to immediately trip the circuit breaker or blow the fuse. This requires that the ground-fault path have low impedance. All electrical power tools should be listed by a nationally recognized testing laboratory (NRTL), such as Underwriters Laboratories (UL) or an equivalent. Tools and their cords must be inspected before each and every use. If defects are found, the tool should be either marked and taken out of service until repaired or destroyed. Periodic ground-continuity and insulation-resistance testing should be performed to ensure that the tool can be operated safely.

Handling

Portable electric hand tools should always be handled in a manner that will not damage the tool. Flexible cords that are connected to the tool should not be used as a means of raising and lowering the tool. Flexible cords should never be fastened with staples or otherwise hung in any way that might damage the outer jacket or insulation.

Visual Inspection of Tools and Cords

Each shift, before portable electric tools and extension cords are used, they must be inspected for external defects (such as loose parts, deformed or missing pins, or damage to outer jacket or insulation) and for evidence of internal damage (such as pinched or crushed outer jacket). Cord-and-plug-connected equipment and extension cords that remain connected once they are put into place and are not exposed to damage need not be visually inspected until they are relocated.

If there is a defect or evidence of damage that might expose an employee to injury, the defective tool or cord must be marked and taken out of service and must not be used until the defect or damage has been repaired and tests have been made to ensure the safety of the tool.

When an attachment plug is to be connected to a receptacle (including a cord set), the relationship of the plug and receptacle contacts should first be checked to ensure they have the proper mating configuration. All extension cords that are used with grounding-type tools should contain an equipment-grounding conductor. These attachment plugs and receptacles must not be connected or altered in any way that would prevent continuity of the equipment-grounding conductor. Any adapter that will interrupt the continuity of the equipment-grounding conductor should not be used.

Quick Checklist for Tools

1. Visually check the tool and its cord for cracks or defects in the cord or the tool.
2. Check all cord-and-plug-connected electrical connectors for defects, broken or missing pins, and exposed insulation at connectors on electrical power tools.
3. Visually check extension cords for cracks, defects, broken or missing pins in the connectors, or exposed insulation at connectors.
4. Check handles to ensure they are in good condition, are of the proper type for the tool or equipment to which they attach, and are properly installed.
5. If any defect or damage is found, immediately remove from service, tag properly, repair and retest before using, or destroy.

Personal Protective Equipment and Other Equipment

Safeguards for Personnel Protection

Under 29 CFR 1910, Section 1910.335, OSHA specifies that employees working in areas where there are potential electrical hazards should be provided with, and use, electrical protective equipment that is appropriate for the specific parts of the body to be protected and for the work to be performed (OSHA 2006).

All electrical workers, at some time during the performance of their duties, will be exposed to energized circuits or equipment. There are two important considerations. Consideration number one is the use of flame-resistant clothing—that is, institute a flame-resistant clothing and equipment program. NFPA 70E-2012 goes into detail about how to comply with this requirement (NFPA 2012).

Where an employee is working within the flash protection boundary established by NFPA 70E-2012, Section 130.5, he or she should wear protective clothing and other personal protective equipment in accordance with the tables or the calculation provided in NFPA 70E-2012, Section 130.5 (NFPA 2012).

To protect the body, employees should wear flame-resistant clothing wherever there is possible exposure to an electric arc flash above the threshold incident-energy level for a second-degree burn (1.2 cal/cm^2). Clothing and equipment that provide worker protection from shock and arc-flash hazards should be utilized. Clothing and equipment required for the degree of exposure should be worn alone or integrated with flammable, nonmelting apparel. Where flame-resistant clothing is required, it should cover associated parts of the body as well as all flammable apparel, while allowing for movement and visibility. NFPA 70E-2012 provides tables that help with the hazard/risk assessment, the selection of flame-resistant clothing and other personal protective equipment, and the proper arc ratings of flame-resistant clothing and equipment. This information is found in Table 130.7(C)(15) and 130.7(C)(16).

A second consideration is the use of insulated rubber liners (gloves) with the proper voltage rating for the circuits or equipment being worked on. Specifications and in-service care of insulating gloves can be found in the manufacturer's instructions as well as in ASTM D120-02 and F496 (ASTM 2006a, 2006c).

Rubber Insulating Liners—Various Classes

ASTM D120-02, *Standard Specifications for Insulating Gloves* (2006a), has designated a specific color coding for the classification of rubber protective equipment. The following is the color, classification, and system voltage rating (ASTM 2002a):

Class 00	Beige	500 volts
Class 0	Red	1000 volts
Class 1	White	7500 volts
Class 2	Yellow	17,000 volts
Class 3	Green	26,500 volts
Class 4	Orange	36,000 volts

Inspection of Protective Equipment

Before rubber protective equipment can be worn by personnel in the field, all equipment must have a current test date stenciled on it and must be inspected by the user. Before insulating rubber liners (gloves) can be worn, they must be visually inspected and air-tested each day or work shift before they are used by the user. They must also be tested during the work shift if their insulating value is ever in question. Because rubber protective equipment is used for personal protection, and serious injury could result from its misuse or failure, it is important than an adequate safety factor be provided between the voltage on which it is being used and the voltage at which it was tested.

Gloves, sleeves, and other rubber protective equipment can be damaged by many different chemicals, especially petroleum-based products such as oils, gasoline, hydraulic fluid, inhibitors, hand creams, pastes, and salves. If contact is made with these or other petroleum-based products, the contaminant should be wiped off immediately. If any signs of physical damage or chemical deterioration are found (e.g., swelling, softness, hardening, stickiness, ozone deterioration, or sun-checking), the protective equipment must not be used. Rings, watches, jewelry, and sharp objects should not be worn on the hands or arms when one is wearing rubber gloves or sleeves.

Inspection Methods

Gloves and sleeves can be inspected by rolling the outside and inside of the protective equipment between the hands. This can be done by squeezing together the inside of the gloves or sleeves to bend the outside area and create enough stress to the inside surface to expose any cracks, cuts, or other defects. When the entire surface has been checked in this manner, the equipment is then turned inside out, and the procedure is repeated.

To check rubber blankets, place the blanket on a flat surface, roll the blanket from one corner, and then roll the blanket toward the opposite corner. If there are any irregularities in the rubber, this method will expose them. After the blanket has been rolled from each corner, it should then be turned over and the procedure repeated.

Holes and other small defects can be detected by inflating the protective equipment. This can be done by rolling the cuff of the glove closed and holding the glove close to the ear and face to detect any air leakage. Gloves and sleeves can also be inspected by using mechanical inflaters.

Storage of Insulating Equipment

Once the protective equipment has been properly cleaned, inspected, and tested, it must be properly stored. It should be stored in a cool, dry, dark place that is free from ozone, chemicals, oils, solvents, or other materials that could damage the equipment. Such storage should not be in the vicinity of hot pipes or direct sunlight. Gloves and sleeves should be stored in their natural shape and should be kept in a bag or box inside of their protectors. They should be stored, undistorted, right side out, and unfolded. Blankets may be stored rolled in containers that are designed for this use with the inside diameter of the roll being at least two inches.

Leather Protectors

Proper-fitting leather protector gloves must be worn over the rubber gloves whenever possible; these protectors must meet the specifications of ASTM F696-02 (ASTM 2006d). This is to prevent damage to the rubber glove from sharp objects and mechanical injury and to reduce ozone cutting. Leather protectors provide only mechanical protection for rubber insulating gloves and when used alone do not provide any protection against serious injury, death, or other potential injuries from electrical shocks and burns. Leather protectors provide protection from arc flash, which is important, because the rubber liners provided for shock protection could melt if subjected to an arc flash. If the leather protector gloves have been used for any other purpose, they must not be used for the protection of rubber gloves.

If work is being performed on small equipment where unusually high finger dexterity is required, the protector gloves for Class 00 (per manufacturer's instructions) and Class 0 insulating gloves may be omitted if the employer can demonstrate that the possibility of physical damage to the gloves is small, and if the class of glove is one class higher than that required for the voltage involved, in accordance with OSHA 29 CFR 1910, Section 1910.137(b). This should only be considered when the likelihood of damage to the glove is low. Rubber gloves being used without a protector must not be used again until they have been properly inspected and electrically tested per the requirements of Section 1910.137(b)(2)(viii) and (ix), 29 CFR 1910. NFPA 70E-2012 addresses the use of a rubber insulating glove without a protector (only where necessary) in Section 130.7(C)(7)(a)(EX) and does require that the requirements of ASTM F496, *Standard Specification for In-Service Care of Insulating Glove and Sleeves*, shall be followed (NFPA 2012).

Protector gloves must not be used if they have holes or tears. Care should be taken to protect the gloves from damage and from grease, oils, and other chemicals that could cause damage to the insulating glove. Whenever the insulating gloves are inspected, the protector gloves should also be inspected inside and out for sharp objects that could damage the insulating gloves. Workers are allowed to wear cloth gloves to keep hands warm in cold weather and to absorb perspiration in hot weather.

Inspection and Testing of Insulating Equipment

Before rubber protective equipment is placed into service, it must be cleaned, inspected, and electrically tested. Gloves and sleeves should be cleaned and washed using a mild detergent and warm water. After they have been cleaned, they should be thoroughly rinsed to remove all the soap and detergent. This cleaning can be done by utilizing a commercial tumble-dry washing machine. After the equipment has been cleaned and properly dried, the equipment must be inspected for any defects (see Table 1).

It is very important that the facility utilized for the electrical testing be approved and designed to protect the operator. Electrical tests should be performed only by individuals who have been given the proper training and instruction to perform these tests.

NFPA 70E-2012, Article 250, *Personal Safety and Protective Equipment*, lists fourteen items that shall be maintained in safe working condition. The items are as follows:

1. grounding equipment
2. hot sticks
3. rubber gloves, sleeves, and leather protectors
4. voltage test indicators
5. blanket and similar insulating equipment
6. insulating mats and similar insulating equipment
7. protective barriers
8. external circuit breaker rack-out devices
9. portable lighting units
10. safety grounding equipment
11. dielectric footwear
12. protective clothing
13. bypass jumpers
14. insulated and insulating hand tools

The insulation of protective equipment and protective tools, such as items (1) through (14), shall be verified by the appropriate test and visual inspection to ascertain that the insulating capability has been retained before initial use and thereafter, as service conditions and applicable standards and instruction require, but not to exceed three years, unless otherwise specified by the respective ASTM standards (NFPA 2012).

Insulating Equipment Failing to Pass Inspections

Insulating equipment failing to pass inspections or electrical tests may not be used by employees, except as follows:

- Rubber insulating line hose may be used in shorter lengths with the defective portion cut off.
- Rubber insulating blankets may be repaired using a compatible patch that results in physical and electrical properties equal to those of the blanket.
- Rubber insulating blankets may be salvaged by severing the defective area from the undamaged portion of the blanket. The resulting undamaged area should not be smaller than 22 inches by 22 inches (560 mm by 560 mm) for Class 1, 2, 3, and 4 blankets.

TABLE 1

Rubber Insulating Equipment Test Intervals

Type of Equipment	When to Test
Rubber insulating line hose	Upon indication that insulating value is suspect
Rubber insulating covers	Upon indication that insulating value is suspect
Rubber insulating blankets	Before first issue and every twelve months thereafter*
Rubber insulating gloves	Before first issue and every six months thereafter*
Rubber insulating sleeves	Before first issue and every twelve months thereafter*

*If the insulating equipment has been electrically tested, but not issued for service, it may not be placed into service unless it has been electrically tested within the previous twelve months.

(Adapted from OSHA 29 CFR 1910, Section 1910.137, Table I–6) (OSHA 2006)

- Rubber insulating gloves and sleeves with minor physical defects, such as small cuts, tears, or punctures, may be repaired by the application of a compatible patch. Also, rubber insulating gloves and sleeves with minor surface blemishes may be repaired with a compatible liquid compound. The patched area should have electrical and physical properties equal to those of the surrounding material. Repairs to gloves are permitted only in the gauntlet area.
- Repaired insulating equipment should be retested before employees can use it.

Rubber Insulating Line Hose and Covers

There are no in-service retest requirements for line hose and covers; however, frequent field inspections should be made. If the line hose and cover being used is type 1, it should not be left in service or on energized lines longer than necessary. Line hose and covers should be inspected inside and out for cuts, corona cutting, scratches, holes, and tears. If damage is found, and it extends beyond one-quarter the wall thickness of the hose, the line hose and cover should be removed from service. Line hose and covers should be wiped clean of any petroleum-based products that could damage the hose. All line hose and covers that appear to be suspect must be taken out of service and electrically tested in accordance with ASTM F478,

Standard Specification for In-Service Care of Insulating Line Hose and Covers (2007a).

Head Protection

Whenever employees are working in the vicinity of exposed energized parts, and there is a possibility of head injury due to contact, nonconductive head protection meeting the requirements of ANSI Z89.1, *Requirement for Protective Headwear for Industrial Workers* (2003), should be worn.

Insulated Tools

Whenever employees are working near any exposed energized parts, they must use insulated tools. The tools must be insulated for a voltage not less than that of the conductors and circuit parts on which they will be used, and they must be suitable for the environment in which they will be used and for the conditions of use. Insulated tools provide protection against flashover, shock, and burns. Note that ordinary plastic-dipped tools are not designed for this purpose, and applying electrical tape over the exposed metal parts of tools is not acceptable.

All approved double-insulated tools used on circuits and equipment operating at 1000 volts or less should bear the international 1000-volt symbol. These tools must meet the requirements of ASTM 1505, *Standard Specification for Insulated and Insulating Hand Tools* (2001). Insulated tools should be inspected prior to each use for cracks, cuts, or other damage. For example, should the inside (red) insulation become visible through the colored (orange) outer layer, the tool should be removed from service immediately, as it is no longer safe to use on energized circuits and parts.

Insulated tools used at other voltages should have a voltage rating appropriate for the voltage on which they are used. These tools are to be used as secondary protection and are not meant to be used in lieu of appropriate personal protective equipment. Rubber liners and leather protectors are still required to protect the hands when voltage testing, troubleshooting, or performing any task where the operating voltage is 50 volts or more to ground.

Protective shields, protective barriers, or insulating materials must be used to prevent injury from shock, burns, or other electrically related injuries while employees are working near exposed energized parts that might be accidentally contacted, or where dangerous electric heating or arcing might occur. When normally enclosed live parts are exposed, for maintenance or repair, they must be guarded to protect unqualified persons from contact with the live parts.

Double-Insulated Tools

Double-insulated tools and equipment generally do not have an equipment-grounding conductor. Protection from shock depends on the dielectric properties of the internal protective insulation and the external housing to insulate the user from the electric parts. External metal parts, such as chuck and saw blades, are generally insulated from the electrical system.

All users of double-insulated power tools should be aware of some precautions in their use. These include the following:

- Double-insulated tools are designed so that the inner electrical parts are isolated physically and electrically from the outer housing. The housing is nonconductive. Particles of dirt and other foreign matter from drilling and grinding operations may enter the housing through the cooling vents and become lodged between the two shells, thereby voiding the required insulation properties.
- Double insulation does not protect against defects in the cord, plug, and receptacle. Continuous inspection and maintenance are required.
- A product with dielectric housing—for example, plastic—protects the user from shock if interior wiring contacts the housing. Immersion in water, however, can allow a leakage path that may be either high- or low-resistance.
- Double-insulated tools and equipment should be inspected and tested as well as all other electrical equipment and should not be used in highly conductive, wet, or damp locations

without also using a ground-fault circuit interrupter (GFCI).

Equipment Use in Conductive Work Locations

All portable electric equipment that is used in highly conductive locations such as wet or damp locations must be listed and approved for use in such locations. While working in wet or damp locations, employees' hands often become wet. This can be a hazard to the employee while plugging and unplugging flexible cords and cord-and-plug-connected tools. Energized connections should be handled only with the proper insulating protective equipment in wet or damp conditions. It is also recommended that GFCIs (Class A) be utilized under these circumstances.

Equipment Used to Alert Personnel

Whenever energized parts are exposed, and there is a possibility of contact by other employees, alerting techniques to warn and protect employees and other personnel from hazards that could cause injury due to electric shock, burns, or failure of electric equipment parts must be used. These techniques include manual signaling and use of tags, signs, and barriers.

Safety Signs and Tags

Safety signs, safety symbols, or accident-prevention tags should be used where necessary to warn employees about electrical hazards that may endanger them. Such signs and tags should meet the requirements of ANSI Standard Z535, *Series of Standards for Safety Signs and Tags*, (2006–2007).

Barricades

Barricades shall be used in conjunction with safety signs where it is necessary to prevent or limit employee access to work areas containing energized conductors or circuit parts. Conductive barricades shall not be used where they might cause an electrical hazard. Barricades shall be placed no closer than the limited approach boundary established in Table 130.4(C) of NFPA 70E-2012 (NFPA 2012).

Alternate Alerting Techniques

When work areas are such that signs and barricades do not provide adequate warning of and protection from electrical hazards, manual signaling and alerting should be used to warn and protect employees. The primary duty and responsibility of an attendant providing manual signaling and alerting shall be to keep unqualified employees outside of a work area where such unqualified employees might be exposed to electrical hazards (OSHA 2006). He or she should remain in the area as long as employees are exposed to electrical hazards.

Vehicular and Mechanical Equipment

Any vehicle or equipment that is capable of contacting overhead lines must be operated so that it at no time comes closer than 10 feet to the overhead lines operating at 50 kilovolts (kV) or less. This would include vehicles capable of being elevated, such as trash trucks, concrete (pumper) trucks, rubber-tired and track cranes, backhoes, dump trucks, and vehicles transporting high loads.

However, under any of the following conditions, the clearance may be reduced:

- If the vehicle is in transit, with its structure lowered, it may come within 4 feet of energized lines. However, if the voltage is above 50 kV, the distance must be increased 4 inches for each 10 kV over 50 kV.
- If insulating barriers are installed that will prevent contact with the line.
- If the equipment is an aerial lift, the boom is insulated for the voltage involved, and the aerial lift is being operated and work is performed by a qualified person.

Whenever vehicles or mechanical equipment are being operated near overhead lines, and the lines have not been de-energized and grounded, no person standing on the ground may approach or contact the vehicle or equipment unless:

- the person is using protective equipment rated for the voltage

- the equipment is located so that no uninsulated part of its structure can come closer to the line than permitted, which is 10 feet maximum

If any vehicle or mechanical equipment capable of having parts of its structure elevated near energized overhead lines is intentionally grounded, employees working on the ground near the point of grounding may not stand at the grounding location whenever there is a possibility of contact with overhead lines. Additional precautions, such as the use of barricades or insulation, should be taken to protect employees from hazardous ground potentials, depending on earth resistivity and fault currents, which can develop within the first few feet of, or more outward from, the grounding point (step potential).

Step potential is caused by the flow of fault current through the earth, which creates a voltage drop at the earth's surface. A person standing with his or her feet apart bridges a portion of this drop, and this places a potential difference from foot to foot. This is the reason that all personnel and the public should be positioned at a safe distance from the driven ground rod.

Illumination

Whenever employees are working in the vicinity of exposed live parts, it is important to provide enough illumination to ensure that employees can see well enough to avoid contacting exposed live parts.

Where the lack of illumination or an obstruction precludes observation of the work to be performed, employees may not perform tasks near exposed energized parts. Employees should not reach blindly into areas that may contain energized parts. The intent is to eliminate the possibility of shock, burn, or electrocution because the worker was not able to clearly see the energized parts and avoid them.

OSHA provides Table 1926.56 in the construction standard 29 CFR 1926 to assist in the determination of the minimum illumination intensities in foot-candles for specific locations. NFPA 70E-2012 addresses illumination in 130.6(C), which instructs employees not to enter spaces containing electrical equipment or parts unless illumination is provided that enables the employees to perform the work safely (NFPA 2012).

Conductive Apparel

Conductive articles of jewelry and clothing (such as watchbands, bracelets, rings, key chains, necklaces, metalized aprons, cloth with conductive thread, or metal headgear) may not be worn where they present an electrical contact hazard with exposed live parts. Because such apparel could provide a conductive path for current flow between adjacent energized parts, which generally results in severe burns to the individual wearing such apparel, all conductive apparel must be removed or rendered nonconductive. This recognizes the use of gloves or wrapping of the conductive apparel with insulating tape as an alternative to removing the items. Be aware that some manufacturers require that no jewelry be worn underneath rubber insulating liners. The best approach is always to require that employees remove such jewelry.

Selection and Use of Work Practices

Whenever work is to be performed on or near exposed energized parts, safety-related work practices should be employed to prevent electric shock or other injuries resulting from either direct or indirect electrical contact. The specific safety-related work practices must be consistent with the nature and extent of the associated electrical hazards. The basic intent is to require that employers use one of three options to protect employees working on electric circuits and equipment:

1. De-energize the equipment involved and lock out its disconnecting means.
2. De-energize the equipment and tag the disconnecting means if the employer can demonstrate that tagging is as safe as locking.
3. Work the equipment energized if the employer can demonstrate that it is not feasible to de-energize it.

Work on De-Energized Parts

A *de-energized* part is obviously safer than an energized part. Because the next best method of protecting an employee working on exposed parts of electrical equipment—the use of personal protective equipment—would continue to expose that employee to a risk of injury from electrical shock, OSHA 29 CFR 1910, Section 1910.333, and NFPA 70E-2012, Section 120.1, suggest that equipment de-energizing should be the primary method of protecting employees (OSHA 2006, NFPA 2012).

Obviously there have been no electrical shock or arc-flash fatalities caused by de-energized circuits, though some fatalities have involved circuits that were thought to be de-energized. For this reason, OSHA has not accepted the argument that a qualified employee can work on energized circuits as safely as he or she can work on de-energized circuits. Therefore, OSHA is not leaving it up to the employer's discretion whether to de-energize electric circuits on the basis of convenience, custom, or expediency.

OSHA requires that all live parts to which an employee may be exposed be de-energized before the employee works on or near them, unless the employer can demonstrate that de-energizing introduces additional or increased hazards or is infeasible due to equipment design or operational limitations (OSHA 2006). However, live parts that operate at less than 50 volts to ground need not be de-energized if there will be no increased exposure to electrical burns or to explosion due to electric arcs. Examples of increased or additional hazards include the following:

- interruption of life-support equipment
- deactivation of emergency alarm systems
- shutdown of hazardous location ventilation equipment
- removal of illumination for an area

Examples of work that may be performed on or near energized circuit parts because of infeasibility of de-energizing due to equipment design or operation limitations include the following:

- Testing, troubleshooting, voltage measuring, and so on, of electrical circuits that can only be performed with the circuit energized. This could also include infrared scanning of equipment. When performing these tasks, additional steps such as selecting and using the appropriate personal protective equipment or isolating other energized parts by use of insulating materials may be used. However, after the testing, troubleshooting, measurement, or adjustment is completed, any repairs or additional preventive maintenance would have to be performed with the circuit de-energized.
- Work on circuits and parts that operate at less than 50 volts to ground need not be de-energized if there will be no increased exposure to electrical burns or to explosion due to electric arcs.

When the wording *additional or increased hazards* is used, it applies to instances where de-energization would be a threat to human life, and not merely to the equipment or process. Removal of illumination from an area is an example of a circumstance that might introduce additional or greater hazards. This would suggest that only in those instances where de-energizing a lighting circuit would present danger to personnel is it permissible to deviate from the basic requirement for de-energizing. If such de-energizing is simply an inconvenience, it should not be interpreted to be an additional or increased hazard.

The determination of what would constitute additional or increased hazards should not be applied without serious consideration. Elimination of the need for de-energizing prior to working on or near any equipment or circuit is permitted only where the employer can demonstrate that such de-energization would result in greater hazards or is impractical. This places the burden of proof on the employer. If an accident were to occur where the circuit was not de-energized, the decision not to de-energize would definitely come under scrutiny by an OSHA compliance officer, an insurance representative, or an expert in this type of accident investigation.

There are other instances where de-energizing is not required. Testing, troubleshooting, and making measurements and adjustments that can only be performed while the circuit is energized are exempt from OSHA and NFPA requirements of de-energizing if additional steps such as selecting and using the appropriate personal protective equipment or isolating the energized part(s) by use of insulating materials are used. However, after the testing, troubleshooting, measurement, or adjustment is completed, any repairs or additional preventive maintenance would have to be performed with the circuit de-energized.

One should be cautious when applying the term *infeasible* with respect to electrical work on or near energized conductors or parts. The term infeasible, as defined in *Webster's Dictionary*, is "not capable of being done or accomplished; impracticable." This is not the same as *inconvenient* and should not be confused with the term inconvenient.

Work on Energized Parts

If the exposed live parts are not de-energized because of increased or additional hazards or because it is infeasible to de-energize them, other safety-related work practices should be used to protect those who may be exposed to the electrical hazards involved. These work practices, such as selecting and using the appropriate personal protective equipment or isolating the energized part(s) by use of insulating materials, should directly protect employees against contact between energized parts and any part of their body, or indirectly through the use of some other conductive object. The work practices developed should be suitable for the work to be performed and for the voltage level of the exposed conductors or circuit parts.

Working on or Near De-Energized Parts

Conductors and parts of electric equipment that have been de-energized but have not been locked out or tagged should be considered and treated as energized, if employees are working on or near enough to them to expose them to any electrical hazard they present. This means that, even though the equipment or circuit has been de-energized, the PPE that the qualified person is wearing cannot be removed because the equipment or circuit has not been put into an electrically safe working condition. The circuit or equipment could possibly be re-energized without the knowledge of the qualified person who de-energized the circuit or equipment.

Lockout/Tagout (LOTO) Procedures

All employers who allow employees to perform work under activities requiring LOTO are required to establish a written LOTO procedure and also to establish procedures for enforcement of such a program. The LOTO procedure is intended to protect personnel from injury during servicing and maintenance of machines and equipment. LOTO is not intended to cover normal production operations. In order to have a safe and reliable LOTO program, the procedure must describe the scope, purpose, authorization, rules, responsibilities, and techniques needed to control all hazardous energy sources.

Work on cord-and-plug-connected electrical equipment does not require LOTO where the equipment is unplugged and where the plug is under the exclusive control of the employee who is performing the servicing and maintenance on the equipment.

In general, the kinds of activities covered under LOTO are lubrication, cleaning, unjamming or servicing of machines or equipment, and making adjustments or tool changes. However, activities that are normal production operations—such as minor tool changes and adjustments—are not covered if they are routine, repetitive, and integral to the use of the equipment for production, and the work is performed using methods that provide effective employee protection.

Lockout/Tagout

OSHA has determined (from experience in the field, including accident investigations and record keeping) that lockout is, by far, the most effective means of providing employee protection and is preferred over tagout. However, if the energy-isolating device is not capable of being locked out, a tagout program may be used, provided that the tagout program will provide the same level of safety as a lockout program. Additional means beyond those necessary for lockout are required. These means include the following:

- removal of an isolating circuit element
- blocking of a controlling switch
- opening of an extra disconnecting device
- removal of a valve handle to reduce the likelihood of an inadvertent energization

If the energy-isolating equipment is capable of being locked out, the employer must utilize a lockout program, unless it can be demonstrated that the tagout program will provide the same level of safety.

The energy-isolating devices for all equipment that has been replaced, repaired, renovated, or modified since October 31, 1989, must be designed to accept a lockout device.

Energy-Control Procedure

A written procedure must be developed and enforced for all employees who may be injured by the unexpected startup or re-energization of machines and equipment during service and maintenance. However, if all of the following elements are met for a particular machine or piece of equipment, the employer does not have to document the procedure:

- The machine or equipment has no potential for stored or residual use.
- The machine or equipment has a single source of energy, which can be readily identified and isolated.
- The isolation and locking out of the energy source will completely de-energize and deactivate the machine or equipment.
- The machine or equipment is isolated from the energy source and locked out during servicing or maintenance.
- A single lockout device will achieve a lockedout condition.
- The lockout device is under the exclusive control of the authorized employee performing the servicing and maintenance of the equipment.
- The servicing and maintenance of the equipment does not create a hazard for other employees.
- If this exception is used, the employer must not have had any accidents involving unexpected activation or re-energization of the machine or equipment.

In this written procedure, the employer must clearly and specifically outline the scope, purpose, authorization, rules, and techniques that will be utilized for the control of hazardous energy. Included should be the administrative responsibilities for implementation of the program, training, compliance, and the following:

- intended use of procedure
- steps for shutting down, isolating, blocking, and securing machines or equipment
- steps for placement, removal, and transfer of lockout/tagout devices and the responsibility for them
- requirements for testing a machine or piece of equipment to determine the effectiveness of the lockout/tagout

Interlocks

Where interlocks must be defeated to gain access to enclosures or other areas containing exposed live parts, only qualified persons may disable the interlocks. Because interlocks may be defeated only temporarily, anytime the qualified person working on the equipment leaves the equipment unattended, for whatever reason, the interlocks must be restored. Additionally, when the work is completed, the interlock should be returned to its operable condition.

Electric Power and Lighting Circuits

All disconnecting means that are used for opening, reversing, or closing the circuits under load conditions should be load-rated devices. Pieces of equipment, such as isolating switches, are intended for isolating an electric circuit from the source of power. Cable connectors not of the load-break type, fuses, terminal lugs, and cable splice connections may not be used for these purposes, except for emergencies.

Reclosing Circuits after Protective Device Operation

Anytime a circuit has been de-energized by the operation of a protective device (such as a fuse or circuit breaker), the circuit must be checked by a qualified person to determine if it can be re-energized safely. Under fault conditions, protective devices such as breakers can be damaged. Without such a check, it is possible for an employee to be injured in case of failure of the protective device. The repetitive manual reclosing of circuit breakers or re-energizing through replaced fuses is prohibited per OSHA 29 CFR 1910, Section 1910.334(b)(2), and NFPA 70E-2012, Section 130.6.

When it can be determined from the design of a circuit that the automatic operation of a protective device was caused by an overload rather than a fault condition, no examination of the circuit or connected equipment is required before the circuit is re-energized.

Overcurrent Protection Modification

Overcurrent protection of circuits and conductors may not be modified, even on a temporary basis. This provision prevents the use of a fuse or circuit breaker with a rating too high to protect the equipment or conductors involved. This is also intended to prevent the temporary bypassing of protective devices, which could lead to shock and fire hazard.

Lockout/Tagout Devices

The employer is required to furnish locks, tags, chains, and other hardware used for the isolation of hazardous energy sources. These devices must be uniquely identified and used for no other purpose and must meet the following requirements:

- standardized, using one or more of the following:
  - color
  - shape
  - size
  - type
  - format
- clearly visible and distinctive
- designed so that all essential information necessary for the application is provided
- designed in such a manner as to deter accidental or unauthorized removal and substantial enough to prevent removal without the use of excessive force or unusual techniques
- designed for the conditions of the environment in which they are installed
- capable of withstanding the environment to which they will be exposed for the maximum time that exposure is expected

Tagout devices and their attachment means must be substantial and durable enough to prevent accidental or inadvertent removal and must have the following characteristics:

- nonreusable attachment means
- attachable by hand
- self-locking
- unlocking strength of no less than 50 pounds
- at least equivalent, in general design, to a one-piece, all-environment-tolerant nylon cable tie

Identification on LOTO Devices

All lockout and tagout devices must have a means of identifying the person applying the lockout/tagout devices, and the tagout device must warn against hazardous conditions if the equipment is re-energized. The device should include at least one of the following warnings:

- Do not start.
- Do not open.
- Do not close.
- Do not energize.
- Do not operate.

Periodic Inspections

At least annually, an authorized employee, other than the ones utilizing the lockout/tagout procedure, must inspect and verify the effectiveness of the lockout/tagout procedure. These inspections must provide for a demonstration of the procedure and be implemented through random audits and planned visual observations. The inspections are intended to ensure that the lockout/tagout procedures are being properly implemented and to correct any deviations or inadequacies observed.

If the lockout/tagout procedures are used less than once a year, they only need inspecting when used. The periodic inspection must provide for and ensure effective correction of identified deficiencies. These periodic inspections must be documented and include the identity of the machine or equipment on which the lockout/tagout was applied, the date of inspections, the employees included in the inspection, and the person performing the inspection.

Training and Communication

Before lockout/tagout can take place, the employer must ensure that all employees are trained in the purpose and function of the lockout/tagout procedure. The employer must ensure that all employees understand and have the knowledge and skills required for the safe application, usage, and removal of energy controls. OSHA 29 CFR 1910, Section 1910.147, recognizes three types of employees: authorized, affected, and other.

Different levels of training are required for each type of employee based on the roles of each employee in lockout/tagout and the level of knowledge they must have to accomplish tasks and to ensure the safety of their fellow workers.

Authorized Employee: Any employee who is allowed to lock out or implement a tagout procedure on a machine or piece of equipment to perform servicing or maintenance. These employees must receive training in the recognition of hazardous energy sources and the methods and means necessary for the control of the hazardous energy.

Affected Employee: An employee whose job requires him or her to operate or use a machine or piece of equipment that is being serviced or maintained under a lockout/tagout, or who is working in an area in which the lockout/tagout procedure is being performed. These employees must receive training in the purpose and use of the lockout/tagout procedure.

Other Employees: All other employees who work around the area or are in the area where lockout/tagout is utilized must receive training about the procedure and about the serious consequences relating to the attempts to restart or re-energize the equipment.

Minimum Training Requirements

Each training program must cover at a minimum the following three areas:

1. The energy-control program
2. The elements of the energy-control procedures relevant to the employees' duties
3. The pertinent requirements of the OSHA lockout/tagout standard, 29 CFR 1910, Section 1910.147, as well as the lockout/tagout requirements in Section 1910.333

Retraining

Retraining for authorized and affected employees must be done under the following conditions:

- whenever there is a change in job assignments
- whenever there is a new hazard introduced due to a change in machines, equipment, or process
- whenever there is a change in the lockout/tagout procedure itself
- whenever the required or other periodic inspections by the employer reveal inadequacies in the company procedures or a lack of knowledge of the employees

Certification of Training

All training that has been completed must be documented, and this documentation must be kept on file and be up to date. The documentation must include the employee's name, the dates of training completion, and the name of the instructor.

Isolation of Electric Circuits and Equipment–Preplanning

Preplanning the safe manner in which equipment or circuits are going to be de-energized must be done. Before the machine, equipment, or circuits are de-energized, the authorized employee must have knowledge of the type of hazardous energy and the methods to control it. For example, preplanning stages would include determining the following:

- types and amount of energy involved
- the individual machine involved
- the processing machine with stored energy involved
- verification of energy-isolating devices

Before machines and equipment are shut down and de-energized, all affected employees must be notified. These notifications must take place before the controls are applied and after they are removed from the equipment. Only an authorized employee can implement the lockout/tagout controls. The methods for disconnecting electric circuits and equipment must include the following procedures:

- The circuits and equipment are required to be disconnected from all energy sources.
- Disconnecting is done only by personnel authorized by the employer.
- The sole disconnecting means must not be a control circuit device such as push buttons, selector switches, or electrical interlocks that de-energize electric power circuits indirectly through contractors or controllers.
- The sole disconnecting means is not allowed to be an electrically operated disconnecting device such as a panic button operating a shunt trip on a large power circuit breaker.
- The authorized employee who turns off a machine or equipment must have knowledge of the type and the magnitude of the energy, the hazards involved, and the methods or means to control the energy.
- An orderly shutdown must be utilized to avoid any additional hazards.

Applying Lockout/Tagout Devices

The lockout/tagout procedure for applying locks or tags, or both, to disconnected circuits and equipment, from all sources of energy, must be included in the written procedure. Where these requirements in the procedure are applied, they will prevent re-energizing of the circuits and equipment. These lockout/tagout devices must be applied only by an authorized employee. Tags are utilized to supplement the locks. A tag is a warning to indicate that the energy-isolated device, and the electrical equipment being controlled, cannot be operated until the lockout/tagout devices have been removed. The basic rule is that only the authorized employee placing the lockout/tagout device is allowed to remove it. This requirement prohibits an unauthorized person from removing the lockout/tagout device and energizing the circuit or equipment, which could cause serious injury to an employee working on the equipment. Many electrical shocks and other injuries are due to an unauthorized person removing a lockout/ tagout device and re-energizing the circuit or equipment. The authorized person who places the lockout/tagout device or an energy-isolating device is required to list the following on the tag:

- name of the authorized person applying the lockout/tagout device
- date of application

Applying Locks Only

Where work to be performed involves only a simple circuit and can be completed in a short time, a lock can be used safely without a tag. 29 CFR 1910.333 limits the use of this procedure to one circuit or single piece of equipment that involves a lockout period of no longer that one work shift. Additionally, affected employees are required to be trained in and familiar with this procedure to avoid confusion over the purpose of the lock on the energy-isolating device.

The procedure pertaining to using only a lock must provide a level of safety that is equal to both locks and tags. To use a lock without a tag, the following conditions must be met:

- Only one circuit or piece of equipment is involved in the lockout.
- The lockout period does not extend beyond the work shift.
- Employees exposed to the hazards associated with re-energization of the circuit or equipment are familiar with this procedure.

Applying Tags Only

Tags are allowed to be used without locks where locks cannot be applied to an energy-isolating device because of design limitations, or when the employer demonstrates that tagging alone will provide safety that is equivalent to applying a lock. However, because a person could operate the disconnecting means before reading or seeing the tag, one additional safety measure must be provided. These safety measures include the following:

- removal of a fuse or fuses for a circuit

- removal of a draw-out circuit breaker from a switchboard or switchgear, or a bucket from a motor control center, for example
- placement of a blocking mechanism over the operating handle of a disconnecting means; the handle must be blocked from being placed in the closed position
- the opening of a switch or disconnecting means that opens the circuit between the source of power and the exposed circuits and parts
- the opening of a switch for a control circuit that operates a disconnect and disables the system
- grounding the circuit where work is to be done

The additional safety measures are necessary because tagging alone is considered less safe than locking out. A disconnecting means without a lock can be closed by an employer who has failed to recognize the purpose of the tag. The disconnect is also capable of being accidentally closed by an employee who thinks it controls his or her equipment.

Tags should comply with these requirements:

- be marked distinctively
- have a standardized design
- clearly prohibit energizing the energy-isolating device

Stored Energy Release

All stored or mechanical energy that might endanger personnel is required to be released or restrained. Stored energy, such as from capacitors, must be discharged through either the motor windings or other effective means. High-capacitance elements are required to be short-circuited and grounded before the electrical equipment or components are worked on. If the possibility for reaccummulation of this energy to a hazardous level exists, verification of a safe condition must be continued until the work is complete. Mechanical energy, such as springs, must be released or restrained to immobilize the springs. This procedure of containing stored energy of all types will prevent unexpected power or energizing of devices that could cause injury to employees. Methods that can be used to release or restrain mechanical energy are:

- slide gate
- slip blind
- line valve and block
- grounding

Verifying that Equipment Cannot Be Restarted

Only authorized qualified personnel are allowed to operate the equipment operating controls or otherwise verify that the equipment cannot be restarted or re-energized. Where present, the following devices must be activated to verify that it is impossible to restart the equipment by energizing the circuits and parts:

- push buttons
- selector switches
- electrical interlocks
- opening the switch for a control circuit that operates a disconnect and disables the system
- grounding the circuit on which work will be done

Verifying that Circuits and Equipment Are De-Energized

Circuits and equipment must be tested by qualified employees using appropriate test equipment to verify that the circuits and equipment are de-energized. Verification that the circuit elements and equipment parts have been de-energized to ensure that employees will not be subject to live circuits and energized parts is mandatory. The test must also determine whether any inadvertently induced voltage or unrelated voltage backfeed, through specific parts of the circuit, are present on the electrical system. Where the circuit to be tested is over 600 volts, the test equipment is required to be checked for proper operation immediately before and immediately after the circuit to be worked on has been tested. One way to determine whether a circuit has been opened is to operate the controls for the equipment supplied by the circuit to verify that the equipment cannot be restarted. This method of testing has the advantage of not exposing employees to possible live circuits and parts. However, operating the equipment controls is not always reliable in that the circuit has been completely de-energized. It is possible to interrupt a portion of the circuit, while the rest of the circuit to the equipment may still be energized. A suggestion for enhanced safety would be to require further testing, such as a voltage test, to verify that the system is, in fact, de-energized.

Those who will perform a voltage check to verify the absence of voltage must be qualified. They must have received training in and demonstrate skills and knowledge in the construction and operation of electrical equipment and installations and the hazards involved per OSHA Final Rule 72.

Also, persons who are qualified shall be trained to select an appropriate voltage detector and shall demonstrate how to use a device to verify the absence of voltage, including interpreting indications provided by the device. The training shall include information that enables the employee to understand all limitations of each specific voltage detector that may be used. This is found in NFPA 70E-2012, Section 110.2(D)(1)(e) (NFPA 2012).

Inspection of Machines or Equipment

The work area must be inspected to ensure that all nonessential items have been removed and that all machines or equipment components are operationally intact.

Verifying that Employees Are Clear of Circuits and Equipment

Before disconnects are closed and power restored to circuits and equipment, all affected employees in the work area who are near or working on the circuits or equipment must be warned. A check is to be made to ensure all employees have been safely positioned or removed and are clear of circuits, parts, and equipment. After a visual check to verify all employees are indeed clear, the power can be restored.

Lockout/Tagout Device Removal

A lockout/tagout device is to be removed only by the authorized employee who applied it. However, if the employee who applied the lockout/tagout devices is absent from the workplace, the locks and tags can be removed by another authorized employee. In this case, the following rules should be followed:

- The employer must ensure that the employee who applied the lockout/tagout is absent from the workplace, and all reasonable efforts have been made to contact the employee to inform him/her that the lockout/tagout has been removed.
- The employee must be notified of the removal of the lockout/tagout before he or she resumes work at the facility.
- There must be unique operating conditions involving complex systems present.
- The employer must demonstrate that it is infeasible to do otherwise.

Release for Energizing

When circuits and equipment are deemed ready to be re-energized, employees should be available to assist in any way necessary to ensure that circuits and equipment can be safely energized. Employees who are responsible for operating the equipment or process should be notified that the system is ready to be energized.

Testing or Positioning of Machines and Equipment

Whenever contractors and their employees are utilized, they must follow the lockout/tagout procedure that is in place at the work site. If the contractor's personnel have not been properly trained in the lockout/tagout procedure, the employer must provide an authorized employee to implement lockout/tagout of the energy-isolating devices.

Section 110.1 of NFPA 70E-2012 requires that the on-site employer and the outside servicing personnel (contractor) have a documented meeting to coordinate the safety efforts of the owner and outside servicing personnel. Items to be discussed and coordinated include personal protective equipment/clothing requirements, safe work practices and procedures, emergency/

evacuation procedures, and existing hazards (NFPA 2012).

Group Lockout/Tagout

If more than one individual, craft, crew, or department is required to lock out or tag out equipment or processes, the lockout/tagout procedure should afford the same level of protection for the group as that provided by personal locks and tags. The group lockout/tagout should be used in accordance with, but not limited to, the following procedures:

- Primary responsibility for the group lockout/tagout is delegated to one authorized employee for a set number of employees working under the protection of a group lockout/tagout.
- Provisions have been made for the authorized employee to ascertain the exposure status of individual group members with regard to the lockout/tagout.
- When more than one crew, craft, or department is involved, an authorized employee has been assigned overall responsibility for the group lockout/tagout to coordinate affected work forces and ensure continuity of protection.
- Each authorized employee must place his or her own personal lockout/tagout devices in the group lockout/tagout device, group lockbox, or comparable mechanism before they begin work. These devices must be removed by each employee when the employees are done working on the machine or equipment.

Release from the group lockout/tagout must be accomplished by the following steps:

1. The machine or equipment area must be cleared of nonessential items to prevent malfunctions that would result in employee injuries.
2. All authorized employees must remove their respective locks or tags from the energy-isolating devices or from the group lockbox following procedures established by the company.
3. In all cases the lockout/tagout procedure must provide a system that identifies each authorized employee involved in the servicing and maintenance operation.
4. Before re-energization, all employees in the area must be safely positioned or removed from the area, and all affected employees must be notified that the lockout/tagout devices have been removed.

During all group lockout/tagout operations where the release of hazardous energy is possible, each authorized employee must be protected by his or her personal lockout/tagout device and by the company procedure. A master danger tag used for group lockout/tagout can be used as a personnel tagout device if each employee personally signs on and signs off on it and if the tag clearly identifies each authorized employee who is being protected by it.

Procedures for Shift Changes

The lockout/tagout procedure must ensure continuity of protection if the lockout/tagout is going to extend beyond the shift change or personnel changes. The procedure must make provisions for the orderly transfer of the lockout/tagout devices between off-going and on-coming employees.

Confined or Enclosed Work Spaces

Some installations of electric equipment provide limited working space for maintenance employees. Such cramped conditions can lead to employees backing or moving into exposed live parts. Areas such as manholes and vaults are examples. To prevent accidental contact from energized parts, precautions must be taken to assure that accidental contact does not occur. For example, protective blanks of the insulating type or the arc-blast type could be used to shield some of the live parts, or portions of the electrical installation could be de-energized. Safe work practices are required when the circuit(s) or part(s) are not de-energized.

OSHA 29 CFR 1910, Section 1910.333(c)(5), also requires that doors and panels be secured if they could swing into employees and cause them to contact exposed energized parts.

Overhead Lines

If work is to be performed in the vicinity of overhead lines, before this work can take place, the lines must be de-energized and grounded, or other protective measures should be used before the work is started.

If power lines are to be de-energized, arrangements must be made with the organization that operates and controls the electric circuits involved, in order to de-energize and properly ground the electric circuits. If protective measures are to be used, the measures should include guarding, isolating, and insulating.

Whichever protective measure is used, it must prevent employees from contacting such lines directly with any part of their body or indirectly through conductive materials, tools, or equipment.

When an *unqualified person* is working near overhead lines, in an elevated position, such as from an aerial device, the person and the longest conductive object with which he or she may be able to contact the line must not be able to come within the following distances:

- for voltages to ground 50 kV or below: 10 feet, 0 inches
- for voltages to ground over 50 kV: 10 feet, 0 inches, plus 4 inches for every 10 kV above 50 kV

When unqualified persons are working on the ground in the vicinity of overhead lines, the above distances still apply.

When *qualified persons* are working in the vicinity of overhead lines, whether in an elevated position or from the ground, the qualified persons may not approach or take any conductive object closer to the exposed lines than the distances shown in Table 2.

A qualified person may work closer to exposed energized overhead lines if one of the following protective measures has been taken:

- The qualified person is insulated from the energized parts (e.g., gloves, with sleeves if necessary, rated for the voltage involved, are considered to be insulation of the person from the energized part on which work is performed).
- The energized part is insulated both from all other conductive objects at a different potential and from the other persons.
- The person is insulated from all conductive objects and is at a potential different from that of the energized part.

TABLE 2

Approach Distances for Qualified Employees—Alternating Current

Voltage Range (Phase to Phase)	Minimum Approach Distance
300V and less	Avoid contact
Over 300V, but not over 750V	1 ft 0 in (30.5 cm)
Over 750V, but not over 2kV	1 ft 6 in (46 cm)
Over 2kV, but not over 15kV	2 ft 0 in (61 cm)
Over 15kV, but not over 37kV	3 ft 0 in (91 cm)
Over 37kV, but not over 87.5kV	3 ft 6 in (107cm)
Over 87.5kV, but not over 121kV	4 ft 0 in (122 cm)
Over 121kV, but not over 140kV	4 ft 6 in (137 cm)

(Adapted from OSHA 29 CFR 1910, Section 1910.333(c), Table S-5)

Because the installation of this type of protective equipment would require the person to be closer than 10 feet to the line, the person must be qualified. The persons performing this type of work must have the specialized training (generally provided by the employer) related to overhead line work necessary to perform this work safely (see qualified person, i.e., training). This is consistent with NFPA 70E-2012, Table 130.4 (NFPA 2012).

Electrical Switching Operations

Major causes of personnel injury at industrial plants are the malfunctions that occur during the closing or opening of some types of switches and circuit breakers (Owen 1997). Some of these are due to the inadequacy of the switch; many switches and breakers do not have sufficient capability to withstand possible fault currents, especially with supply systems increasing in fault capacity. In particular, when a switch is to be closed after work has been performed on its load circuit, there is a possibility of switch failure. Such failure frequently initiates a phase-to-phase or ground fault, which either burns through the cover or blasts open the cover or door of the switch, injuring or burning the person who operated the switch. See NFPA 70E-2012, Table 130.7(C)(9)(a), for Hazard/Risk category and Table 130.7(C)(10) for the selection of personal protective equipment, including flame-resistant clothing, required for this task (NFPA 2012).

Failure of a fuse with insufficient fault-interrupting capability upon switch closure can likewise initiate a fault within the enclosure with similar results.

A well-defined method of closing switches and circuit breakers can, in general, go far toward eliminating personnel hazards involving this operation. Steps in this procedure include:

1. Wear appropriate flame-resistant clothing and other appropriate clothing where necessary.
2. Wear gauntlet-type gloves and other appropriate personal protective equipment.
3. Check NFPA 70E-2012, Tables 130.7(C)(9)(a), 130.7(C)(10), and 130.7(C)(11), or calculate incident energy available and select flame-resistant clothing and equipment from Table 130.7(C)(10) and other PPE from Table 130.7 (C)(10) (NFPA 2012).
4. Stand to one side of the switch, not directly in front of it, facing the wall or structure on which the switch is mounted and as close to it as possible (hug the wall).
5. Use the hand nearest the switch to operate the handle; if standing to the right side of the switch, operate the handle with the left hand.
6. As the switch is operated, turn your face the opposite way (if at the left of the switch, look to the left, and vice versa).
7. Keep other personnel away from the front of the switch and at least 1.2 meters (approximately 47 inches) to either side.
8. Selection of the side to stand at will depend on the proximity of the handle to one side or the other, on ease of operations of the handle, or on the side of the enclosure more remote from the line terminals. The hinges are as likely to rupture from the internal pressure as the latch is to bust.
9. Firm and smart operation is desirable. Never indecisively operate (tease) the switch.

Grounding and Bonding Notes

Electrical systems are solidly grounded to limit the voltage to ground during normal operation and to prevent excessive voltages due to lightning, line surges, or unintentional contact with higher-voltage lines and to stabilize the voltage to ground during normal operation. This protects people and prevents fires.

Electrical connections are made to any available grounding electrodes (such as metal water piping systems, effectively grounded structural metal members, concrete-encased electrodes, and ground rings) that are present at buildings or structures. Where necessary, install grounding electrodes (ground rings, "ufer" grounds, ground rods) per *National Electrical Code* requirements found in Article 250 (NFPA 2011). To enhance this system, equipment-grounding conductors are bonded to the system-grounded conductor to provide a low-impedance path for fault current that will facilitate the operation of overcurrent devices under ground-fault conditions. The goal of the ground-fault current path is to provide a permanent and adequate path of low impedance so that enough current will flow in the circuit to cause an overcurrent device to operate.

Install equipment-grounding conductors for this current to flow on. Install bonding jumpers where required to help make an effective path for the fault current to flow on and over. Bonding by definition is the permanent joining of metallic parts to form an electrically conductive path that will ensure electrical continuity and the capacity to safely conduct any current likely to be imposed on it. This is a function of the grounding system. It is a part of the grounding system.

Ground systems for safety. Use personal protective grounding to protect individuals while they perform work on electrical systems. With respect to static electricity, ground and bond equipment in order to prevent a static spark from igniting a hazardous (explosive) atmosphere, which could cause an explosion.

Personal Protective Grounding

The primary use of personal protective grounds is to provide maximum safety for personnel while they are working on or near de-energized lines, buses, or equipment (Owen 1997). This is accomplished by reducing voltage differences at the work site (voltage across the worker) to the lowest practical value in case the equipment or line being worked on is accidentally energized. Another function of personal protective grounds is to protect against induced voltage from adjacent parallel, energized lines.

Proper protective grounding results in a safer working environment. Low-resistance ground cables will limit the voltage drop in the work area to acceptable levels. Personal protective grounds must be designed, assembled, and installed in a manner that satisfies the following basic criteria:

- The personal protective grounding cable to be applied must be capable of conducting the maximum available fault current that could occur if the isolated line or equipment becomes energized from any source.
- The grounding cable must be able to carry the maximum available fault current for a sufficient length of time to permit protective relays and circuit breakers to clear the fault.
- The grounding cable must be terminated with clamps of adequate capacity and strength to withstand all electrical and mechanical forces present under maximum fault conditions.
- The grounding cable must meet the following requirements: it must be easy to apply, it must satisfy the requirements of field conditions, and it must adapt to a wide range of conductor, structural steel, and ground rod/wire sizes.
- Cable length should be as short as possible for the specific task being performed. The greater the length, the longer the time it takes to clear faults.

Grounding Cables and Hardware

The American Society for Testing and Materials (ASTM) Committee F-18, Electrical Protective Equipment for Workers, has developed a consensus standard for protective grounds. The ASTM designation is ASTM F855, *Standard Specification for Temporary Protective Grounds to Be Used on De-Energized Electric Power Lines and Equipment* (ASTM 2004) (see Table 3).

All grounding cables, clamps, and ferrules used to construct grounding cables must meet the requirements of ASTM F855. Aluminum cables must not be used for personal grounds (ASTM 2004).

Personal protective grounding cables consist of appropriate lengths of suitable copper grounding cable with electrically and mechanically compatible ferrules and clamps at each end. In addition, appropriate hot sticks are required for installing and removing the conductor-end clamps to the conductors. Hot sticks are required for attaching ground-end clamps if the grounded system and worker are at different potentials (ASTM 2004).

NFPA 70E-2012, Table 130.7(C)(9)(a), has established hazard/risk categories for application of safety grounds (after voltage test to ensure that the circuit is de-energized prior to application of safety grounds). The hazard/risk category determined from Table 130.7(C)(9)(a) may then be used to determine the appropriate personal protective equipment (PPE) and flame-resistant clothing from Table 130.7(C)(10). One important piece of information to take from this section is that even when the circuit has been determined to be de-energized (through voltage-sensing

TABLE 3

Approach Distances for Qualified Employees—Alternating Current

Maximum Fault-Current Capability for Grounding Cables

Cable Size (AWG)	Fault Time (cycles)	RMS Amperes (copper)
1/0	15	21,000
	30	15,000
2/0	15	27,000
	30	20,000
3/0	15	36,000
	30	25,000
4/0	15	43,000
	30	30,000

(Adapted from ASTM F-855, *Standard Specification for Temporary Protective Grounds to Be Used on De-Energized Electric Power Lines and Equipment*, 2004)

equipment), PPE and flame-resistant clothing must still be worn when installing the protective safety grounds (Owen 1997).

Note: These current values are the "withstand rating" currents for grounding cables taken from Table 5, ASTM F855, *Standard Specification for Temporary Protective Grounds to Be Used on De-Energized Electric Power Lines and Equipment* (ASTM 2004). These values are about 70 percent of the fusing (melting) currents for new copper conductors. They represent a current that a cable should conduct without being damaged sufficiently to prevent reuse.

Size of Grounding Cable

The size of the grounding cable must be selected to handle the maximum calculated fault current of the power system or specific portion. The minimum size of cable allowed by ASTM is #2 American Wire Gage (AWG); however, the maximum available fault current may require larger cables. If larger cables are not available, parallel cables may be used. Most manufacturers and suppliers of grounding cables publish tables to assist the user in selecting the proper cable size for a given fault current (Owen 1997).

Jackets

Cables are normally insulated at 600 volts. When used as grounding cable, the insulation or jacket serves primarily for mechanical protection of the conductor. The flexible elastomer or thermoplastic jackets are manufactured, applied, and tested according to ASTM standards. Black, red, and yellow jackets are usually neoprene rubber compounds, whereas clear jackets are ultraviolet-inhibited polyvinyl chloride (PVC).

All jackets must have the AWG size stamped or printed repeatedly along the length of the cable. The clear jacket allows easy visual inspection of the conductor for strand breakage, but becomes stiff and hard to handle at low temperatures. The clear jacket will split or shatter at low temperatures (Owen 1997).

Ferrules

Ferrules should be of a type specified by ASTM F855 (2004). Ferrules should have the filler-compound vent hole at the bottom of the cable, so that employees can visually check that the cable is fully inserted into the ferrule. Compound should be used with crimped ferrules.

The ferrules should be crimped with the ferrule manufacturer's recommended die. The press must have enough pressure to completely close the die. Heat shrink tubing should be installed over a portion of the ferrule to minimize strand breakage caused by bonding. In all cases, the manufacturer's recommendations should be followed (Owen 1997).

Grounding Cable Length

Excessive cable lengths should be avoided; for example, do not use a 100-foot cable where a 50-foot cable will be sufficient. The greater the length, the longer the time for clearing a fault. Therefore, similar to lightning protection, the shortest possible length is desirable. Slack in the installed cables should be minimal to reduce possible injury to workers. Resistance in the cable increases with cable length, and excessive length will exceed the tolerable voltage drop. Longer-than-necessary cables also tend to twist or coil, which reduces the current-carrying capacity of the cable (Owen 1997).

Grounding Clamps

Grounding clamps are normally made of copper or aluminum alloys. Grounding clamps are sized to meet or exceed the current-carrying capacity of the cable and are designed to provide a strong mechanical connection to the conductor, metal structure, or ground wire/rod. Clamps are furnished in, but not limited to, four types, according to their function and methods of installation:

1. Type I clamps, for installation on de-energized conductors, are equipped with eyes for installation with removable hot sticks.
2. Type II clamps, for installation on de-energized conductors, have permanently mounted hot sticks.
3. Type III clamps, for installation on permanently grounded conductors or metal structures, have T-handles, eyes, and/or square or hexagon hand screws.

4. Other types of special clamps are designed for specific applications, such as cluster grounds, underground equipment grounding, and so on.

Application of Personal Protective Grounds

Prior to installation, each cable must be visually inspected for mechanical damage. Suspect cables must not be used. Grounds should be placed at the work site.

Before coming within the minimum work distances of high-voltage lines or equipment, workers must isolate, de-energize, test, and properly configure those parts that are required. All conductors and equipment must be treated as energized until tested and properly grounded.

The ground-end clamp of each grounding cable should always be the first connection made and the last to be removed. The phase connections should be made on the closest phase of the system first, and then each succeeding phase in order of closeness.

When removing the grounding cable, reverse the order by which the clamps were applied.

Always use appropriate personal protective apparel and equipment when applying and removing personal protective grounds (Owen 1997).

Safety-Related Maintenance Requirements

Qualified persons. Only persons who are considered qualified should be permitted to perform maintenance on electrical equipment.

Single-line diagram. Where single-line diagrams are provided, they should be maintained. It is important to keep drawings accurate and up to date.

Spaces around electrical equipment. All working space and clearances required should be maintained.

Grounding and bonding. Equipment, raceway, cable tray, and enclosure bonding and grounding should be maintained to ensure electrical continuity.

Guarding of live parts. Enclosures should be maintained to guard against accidental contact with live parts and other electrical hazards.

Safety equipment. Locks, interlocks, and other safety equipment should be maintained in proper working condition to accomplish the control purpose.

Clear spaces. Access to the working space and escape passages should be kept clear and unobstructed.

Identification of components. Identification of components, where required, and safety-related instructions (operating or maintenance), if posted, should be securely attached and kept in legible condition.

Warning signs. Warning signs, where required, should be visible, securely attached, and maintained in legible condition.

Identification of circuits. Circuit or voltage identification should be securely affixed and maintained in updated and legible condition.

Single and multiple conductors and cables. Electrical cables and single and multiple conductors should be maintained free of damage, shorts, and ground that would present a hazard to employees.

Flexible cords and cables. Flexible cords and cables should be maintained to avoid strain and damage.

- Damaged cords and cables: Cords and cables should not have worn, frayed, or damaged areas that present an electrical hazard to employees.
- Strain relief: Strain relief of cords and cables should be maintained to prevent pull from being transmitted directly to joints or terminals.

Testing and visual inspections are required for protective equipment, protective tools, safety grounding equipment, and PPE. Generally, all equipment needs to be visually checked before each use on any job site.

Employer's Electrical Safety Program

A plan should be designed so that neither workplace conditions nor the actions of people expose personnel unnecessarily to electrical hazards. Objectives of an employer's electrical safety program would include:

- Make personnel aware of rules, responsibilities, and procedures for working safely in an electrical environment.
- Demonstrate compliance with federal law (including appropriate safety standards).

- Provide documentation of general requirements and guidelines for providing electrically safe facilities.
- Provide documentation of general requirements and guidelines that direct the activities of personnel who may be exposed to electrical hazards.
- Encourage and make it easy for each employee to be responsible for his or her own electrical safety self-discipline. Address the safety needs of all employees, as well as contractors and visitors.

The content of the electrical safety program should include the following:

- management commitment
- organizational support
- electrical safety policies
- training and qualification of personnel
- use of protective equipment, tools, and protective methods
- use of electrical equipment
- documentation
- oversight and auditing
- technical support
- emergency preparedness

Responsibilities of the Employer's Electrical Safety Authority

- Assume responsibility of the electrical safety program.
- Develop and revise company electrical safety standards.
- Provide interpretations of nationally recognized codes and standards.
- Provide guidance for facility management.
- Resolve NFPA 70 (NEC), NFPA 70E, NFPA 70B, NFPA 79, and OSHA issues and questions.
- Establish and document effective safe work practices.
- Provide technical input for OSHA interpretations.
- Provide guidance for electrical training programs.
- Provide guidance for procedure preparation.
- Provide consultation services to management.
- Review electrical safety incidents and participate in investigations.
- Issue summaries and lessons-learned about electrical safety incidents.
- Evaluate nonlisted electrical equipment.
- Develop a program for documentation of standards, practices, procedures, and guidelines; accurate drawings; equipment manuals, inspection records, and histories; findings from audits; and completed training records.

Methods of Achieving Electrically Safe Work Conditions

To provide and maintain electrically safe facilities:

- Design electrical systems with safety in mind.
- Ensure that all electrical installations are code-compliant.
- Inspect new facilities, existing facilities, and renovated or modified facilities.
- Provide for maintenance—predictive and preventive.
- Ensure management and employee familiarity with recognized standards.
- Perform safety audits of workplace conditions.
- Provide appropriate training for personnel.
- Provide a technical authority with the knowledge and experience to respond to questions about design, installation, and maintenance.
- Provide the organizational structure to accomplish electrically safe work conditions.

New Ideas for Safe Work Practices

If at all possible, avoid work on energized electrical equipment. Work on or near exposed live parts should be prohibited, except under approved, controlled, and justified circumstances. If work must be done on energized circuits and parts, require work authorization. NFPA 70E-2012, Section 130.1, refers to this as a "Justification for Work" permit. Make sure that every authorized and qualified person performing work on or near energized electrical circuits and parts is properly trained to recognize and avoid electrical hazards and is able to select and use the appropriate personal protective clothing and equipment, as well as being familiar with the construction and operation of the electrical equipment and the appropriate safe work practices for the job or task. This is a reference to a qualified person. Ensure that the employer has established written safe practices and procedures and that employees understand the importance of following the written practices, as well as the consequences if the written practices are not followed.

Employers are required to provide safety training for all employees who are authorized, affected, and other persons with respect to lockout/tagout, as well as those who will be considered qualified to work on or near exposed energized conductors, circuits, or parts (NFPA 70E-2012, Section 110.2; OSHA 29 CFR 1910, Section 1910.332[a]). One of the benefits of providing safety training is to assist in the process of determining which employees will be considered qualified to work on or near exposed energized electrical conductors, circuits, and parts. Employers need to perform safety audits and make careful assessments of personnel activities. Best practices would encourage employers to solicit and use oversight groups to ensure the success of their safety programs. Employers need to establish a technical authority to respond to questions regarding safe work practices.

Final Notes and Suggestions

Fatal and survivable electrical accidents suggest that the majority of workplace events are related to work processes and practices. Therefore, it is important that companies have and use effective work practices and that appropriate protective equipment is supplied by the employer and used by the employee. Appropriate personal protective equipment can greatly reduce the chances of receiving flash burns, as well as burns resulting from a direct contact with energized parts. It should be noted that appropriate personal protective equipment provides minimal protection from shrapnel expelled and the explosive pressure exerted. This dictates the need for an effective training program.

The following is a list of suggestions for improved electrical safety, adapted from *Handbook for Electrical Safety* (Cooper-Bussman 2004a).

- Use finger-safe electrical components when possible. This can reduce the chance that an arc fault will occur.
- Specify the use of an insulated bus for equipment such as motor control centers, switchgears, switchboards, and so on. This will reduce the chance that an arc fault will occur. In addition, it has been found that it increases the probability that an arc fault will self-extinguish.
- Use current-limiting overcurrent protective devices such as current-limiting fuses and current-limiting circuit breakers. Obtain verifiable engineering data on the current-limiting ability of the overcurrent protective devices. Specify the most current-limiting devices available where possible; the greater the degree of current limitation, the less will be the arc-fault energy released (when the fault current is in the current-limiting range of the overcurrent protective device).
- Size current-limiting, branch-circuit overcurrent protective devices as low as possible. Typically, the lower the ampere rating, the greater degree of current limitation. Limit the ampere-rating size of main and feeders where possible. Where possible, split large feeders into smaller, parallel feeders; for example, rather than one 1600-ampere motor control center, specify two 800-ampere motor control centers. This will reduce short-circuit current and possibly reduce flame-resistant clothing requirements. Also, reduced ampere ratings may allow for lower overcurrent-device ratings (which is a result of the ability of the current-limiting overcurrent devices to clear faults more quickly than noncurrent-limiting overcurrent devices) and allow less fault-current let-through in the process of clearing the fault. Less let-through means less explosive energy potentially available to develop into an arc blast or arc flash.
- For motor starter (controller) protection, specify Type 2 protection that uses protective device combinations that have been tested for Type 2 protection.

- If noncurrent-limiting overcurrent protective devices are used, utilize high-impedance circuit components to try to limit the arc-fault current potentially available. Do not use circuit breakers with short time delays. It has been well documented that arc-fault incident energy is directly proportional to the time the fault is permitted to persist. Permitting an arcing fault to intentionally flow for 6, 12, or 30 cycles dramatically increases the hazards to electrical workers. If selective coordination of overcurrent protection is the objective, then use current-limiting fuses that can be selectively coordinated simply by adhering to minimum ampere-rating ratios between main feeder fuses or feeder and branch-circuit fuses.

Use NFPA 70E-2012, as a primary reference guide in conjunction with the OSHA standards for compliance with OSHA requirements for electrical safety for employees in the workplace.

References

American Society for Testing Materials. 1999. ASTM F1958, *Standard Test Method for Determining the Ignitability of Non-Flame-Resistant Materials for Clothing by Electric Arc Exposure Method Using Mannequins*. West Conshohocken, PA: ASTM.

______. 2001. ASTM F1505, *Standard Specification for Insulated and Insulating Hand Tools*. West Conshohocken, PA: ASTM.

______. 2002a. ASTM D1049, *Standard Specification for Rubber Covers*. West Conshohocken, PA: ASTM.

______. 2002b. ASTM D1051-02, *Standard Specification for Rubber Insulating Sleeves*. West Conshohocken, PA: ASTM.

______. 2002c. ASTM F1506-02, *Standard Performance Specification for Textile Material for Wearing Apparel for Use by Electrical Workers Exposed to Momentary Electric Arc and Related Thermal Hazards*. West Conshohocken, PA: ASTM.

______. 2004. ASTM F855, *Standard Specification for Temporary Protective Grounds to Be Used on De-Energized Electric Power Lines and Equipment*. West Conshohocken, PA: ASTM.

______. 2005. ASTM D1048, *Standard Specification for Rubber Insulating Blankets*. West Conshohocken, PA: ASTM.

______. 2006a. ASTM D120-02, *Standard Specification for Rubber Insulating Gloves*. West Conshohocken, PA: ASTM.

______. 2006b. ASTM F479, *Standard Specification for In-Service Care of Insulating Blankets*. West Conshohocken, PA: ASTM.

______. 2006c. ASTM F496-02, *Standard Specification for In-Service Care of Insulating Gloves and Sleeves*. West Conshohocken, PA: ASTM.

______. 2006d. ASTM F696-02, *Standard Specification for Leather Protectors for Rubber Insulating Gloves and Mittens*. West Conshohocken, PA: ASTM.

______. 2006e. ASTM F1959, *Standard Performance Specification for Determining the Arc Thermal Performance Value of Materials for Clothing*. West Conshohocken, PA: ASTM.

______. 2006f. ASTM F2178-02, *Standard Test Method for Determining Arc Rating of Face Protective Products*. West Conshohocken, PA: ASTM.

______. 2007a. ASTM F478, *Standard Specification for In-Service Care of Insulating Line Hoses and Covers*. West Conshohocken, PA: ASTM.

______. 2007b. ASTM D1236-01, *Standard Guide for Visual Inspection for Electrical Protective Rubber Products*. West Conshohocken, PA: ASTM.

Cooper Bussman, Inc. 2004a. *Handbook for Electrical Safety*. 2d ed. Saint Louis, MO: Cooper Bussman, Inc.

______. 2004b. *Safety BASICs—Bussman Awareness of Safety Issues Campaign*. PowerPoint slides. Distributed by Cooper Bussman, Saint Louis, MO.

Lee, R. 1982. "The Other Electrical Hazard: Electrical Arc Flash Burns." *IEEE Transactions on Industry Applications* 1A-18(3) (May/June):246.

______. 1987. "Pressures Developed by Arcs." *IEEE Transactions on Industry Applications* 1A-23:760–764.

National Fire Protection Association. 2011. NFPA 70, *National Electrical Code 2011 edition*. Quincy, MA: NFPA.

______. 2012. NFPA 70E, *Standard for Electrical Safety Requirements for Employee Workplaces*. Quincy, MA: NFPA.

Occupational Safety and Health Administration. 2006. *OSHA General Industry Regulations*. 29 CFR 1910, Subpart S Electrical, 1910.301–399. Washington, D.C.: U.S. Department of Labor.

______. 2006. *OSHA Construction Industry Regulations*. 29 CFR 1926, Subpart K Electrical, 1926.400–449. Washington, D.C.: U.S. Department of Labor.

Owen, S. J. 1997. *Electrical Safety—Procedures and Practices*. Pelham, AL: S. J. Owen.

Appendix: Electrical Safety Topics and Referenced Sources

Chapter Topic	Adapted From
Justification for Work–Work-Related Permits	NFPA 70E-2012, Section 130.1
Exemptions from Work Permit	NFPA 70E-2012, Section 130.1(A)
Approach Boundaries	NFPA 70E-2012, Section 130.3(A)
Flash Hazard Analysis	NFPA 70E-2012, Section 130.3(A)
Training and Qualification of All Personnel	OSHA 29 CFR 1910, Section 1910.332; NFPA 70E-2012, Section 110.6
Visual Inspection	OSHA 29 CFR 1910, Section 1910.334(a)(2)
Portable Electrical Equipment	OSHA 29 CFR 1910, Section 1910.334(a)(2); NFPA 70E-2012, Section 110.6
Handling	OSHA 29 CFR 1910, Section 1910.334(a)(1)
Visual Inspection of Tools and Costs	OSHA 29 CFR 1910, Section 1910.334(a)(2); NFPA 70E-2012, Section 110.9(b)(3)
Safeguards for Personnel Protection	OSHA 29 CFR 1910, Section 1910.335; NFPA 70E-2012, Section 130.6
Rubber Insulating Liners–Various Classes	ASTM D 120-02, Standard Specifications for Insulating Gloves, 2006
Inspection of Protective Equipment	OSHA 29 CFR 1910 Section 1910.137(b)
Inspection Methods	OSHA 29 CFR 1910, Section 1910.137(b)
Storage of Insulating Equipment	OSHA 29 CFR 1910, Section 1910.137(b)
Leather Protectors	OSHA 29 CFR 1910, Section 1910.137(b)
Inspection and Testing of Insulating Equipment	OSHA 29 CFR 1910, Section 1910.137(b)
Insulating Equipment Failing to Pass Inspections	OSHA 29 CFR 1910, Section 1910.137(b)
Rubber Insulating Line Hose and Covers	OSHA 29 CFR 1910, Section 1910.137(b)
Insulated Tools	OSHA 29 CFR 1910, Section 1910.335(a)(2)
Conductive Work Locations	OSHA 29 CFR 1910, Section 1910.334(a)(4)
Alerting Techniques	OSHA 29 CFR 1910, Section 1910.335(b)
Safety Signs and Tags	OSHA 29 CFR 1910, Section 1910.335(b)
Barricades	OSHA 29 CFR 1910, Section 1910.335(b)
Alternate Alerting Techniques	OSHA 29 CFR 1910, Section 1910.335(b)
Vehicular and Mechanical Equipment	OSHA 29 CFR 1910, Section 1910.333(c)
Illumination	OSHA 29 CFR 1910, Section 1910.333(c)(4) and 29 CFR 1926, Section 1926.56
Conductive Apparel	OSHA 29 CFR 1910, Section 1910.333(c)(8)
Selection and Use of Work Practices	OSHA 29 CFR 1910, Section 1910.333
Work on De-energized Parts	OSHA 29 CFR 1910, Section 1910.333(A)(1); NFPA 70E-2012, Section 120.1–2
Energized Parts	OSHA 29 CFR 1910, Section 1910.333(a)
Working on or Near De-energized Parts	OSHA 29 CFR 1910, Section 1910.333(b)
Lockout/Tagout (LOTO) Procedures	OSHA 29 CFR 1910, Sections 1910.147 and 1910.333
Lockout/Tagout	OSHA 29 CFR 1910, Sections 1910.333(b) and 1910.147

Energy-Control Procedure	OSHA 29 CFR 1910, Section 1910.147(c)(4)
Interlocks	OSHA 29 CFR 1910, Section 1910.333(c)(10)
Electric Power and Lighting Circuits	OSHA 29 CFR 1910, Section 1910.334(b)
Reclosing Circuits After Protective Device Operation	OSHA 29 CFR 1910, Section 1910.334(b)(2); NFPA 70E-2012 Section 130.6(K)
Overcurrent Protection Modification	OSHA 29 CFR 1910, Section 1910.334(b)(3)
Lockout/Tagout Devices	OSHA 29 CFR 1910, Section 1910.147(c)(5)
Identification	OSHA 29 CFR 1910, Section 1910.147(c)(5)(D)
Periodic Inspections	OSHA 29 CFR 1910, Section 1910.147(c)(6)
Training and Communication	OSHA 29 CFR 1910, Section 1910.147(c)(7)
Authorized Employee	OSHA 29 CFR 1910, Section 1910.147(c)(7)
Affected Employee	OSHA 29 CFR 1910, Section 1910.147(c)(7)
Other Employees	OSHA 29 CFR 1910, Section 1910.147(c)(7)
Minimum Training Requirements	OSHA 29 CFR 1910, Section 1910.147(c)(7)
Retraining	OSHA 29 CFR 1910, Section 1910.147(c)(7)
Certification of Training	OSHA 29 CFR 1910, Section 1910.147(c)(7)
Isolation of Electric Circuits and Equipment–Preplanning	OSHA 29 CFR 1910, Section 1910.147(c)(8)
Lockout/Tagout Device Application	OSHA 29 CFR 1910, Section 1910.147(d)(4)
Applying Locks Only	OSHA 29 CFR 1910, Section 1910.333(b)(2)(iii)(E)
Applying Tags Only	OSHA 29 CFR 1910, Section 1910.333(b)(2)(iii)(D)
Stored Energy Release	OSHA 29 CFR 1910, Section 1910.147(d)(5)
Verify That Equipment Cannot Be Restarted	OSHA 29 CFR 1910, Section 1910.147(d)(6)
Verify That Circuit and Equipment Are De-energized	OSHA 29 CFR 1910, Section 1910.333(b)(2)(iv)
Inspection of Machines or Equipment	OSHA 29 CFR 1910, Section 1910.147(e)(1)
Verify Employees Are Clear of Circuits and Equipment	OSHA 29 CFR 1910, Section 1910.147(e)(2)
Lockout/Tagout Device Removal	OSHA 29 CFR 1910, Section 1910.147(e)(3)
Release for Energizing	OSHA 29 CFR 1910, Section 1910.147(e)(3)
Testing or Positioning of Machines and Equipment	OSHA 29 CFR 1910, Section 1910.147(f)(1)
Group Lockout/Tagout	OSHA 29 CFR 1910, Section 1910.147(f)(3)
Procedures for Shift Changes	OSHA 29 CFR 1910, Section 1910.147(f)(4)
Confined or Enclosed Work Spaces	OSHA 29 CFR 1910, Section 1910.333(c)(5)]
Overhead Lines	OSHA 29 CFR 1910, Section 1910.333(c)(3)
Unqualified Persons	OSHA 29 CFR 1910, Section 1910.333(c)(3)(i)
Qualified Persons	OSHA 29 CFR 1910, Section 1910.333(c)(3)(ii)
Grounding Clamps	ASTM F855, Standard Specification for Temporary Protective Grounds to Be Used on De-Energized Electric Power Lines and Equipment, 2004
Safety-Related Maintenance Requirements	NFPA 70E-2012, Article 2005
Employers Electrical Safety Program	NFPA 70E-2012, Section 110.7

4

Permit-to-Work Systems

David Dodge

Learning Objectives

- Learn to identify the kind of tasks that need to be controlled by a permit-to-work system.
- Learn what steps must be taken after a task is identified as requiring a work permit so that the task can be performed safely.
- Ensure that only qualified persons issue permits and perform work under a permit.
- Understand the definition of a *qualified person*.
- Be able to take the concepts in this chapter and apply them to unique facilities and operations in order to identify tasks that require permits.

A PERMIT-TO-WORK SYSTEM is a managerial safety technique that enables everyone involved with a particular task to be sure that the procedure associated with the task is safe for its intended purpose. The permit to work is essentially a control document used to apply for permission to do work. Normally the permit-to-work system is used for nonroutine tasks that are performed infrequently and that need specialized equipment and/or training to perform safely. A permit-to-work system provides a formal control system that allows the unusual task to receive special attention by those who are knowledgeable in the techniques necessary to accomplish the task safely. The nonroutine task is not normally familiar to the worker, and therefore may present unique hazards that come from unfamiliarity. The permit, or request for permission, triggers a risk assessment and hazard-control analysis that will provide detailed, step-by-step procedures for the job as well as the safeguards and monitoring techniques needed.

As the first step in developing a permit-to-work system, each facility, building, or operation must be reviewed and inspected to determine which tasks performed must be subjected to the permission and review of a permit-to-work system. This chapter discusses seven tasks which, because of their nonroutine and potentially hazardous nature, normally fall under a permit-to-work system. However, you may find that your operation has others. Individual management teams must evaluate their operations by risk-assessment means to determine whether they may need permit-to-work systems.

No matter what the other tasks might be, the general approach taken in this chapter can be used to apply the permit-to-work system to them. Remember that a permit is normally required to perform nonroutine, unique tasks that can expose workers to hazards or hazardous conditions if not properly performed.

Once the tasks that require permits to perform them are identified, they should be catalogued. Any changes within the facility or operation that exclude or add similar tasks must be monitored and the catalog updated. For example, a building addition might add a confined space or a laboratory might add a new chemical or storage facility. Each of these changes must be reviewed by a person who is knowledgeable in that particular operation and who can perform a thorough risk assessment of the change. Once a list is made of all tasks to which the permit-to-work system applies, it must be conveyed to workers who might be involved so that they know which jobs will require permission to perform. Many facilities, understanding the importance of the permit system, provide signs in areas where tasks are performed that indicate that a permit is required. Still others merely inform supervisors of the permit-necessary tasks and provide them with a list. However it is accomplished, all those who might be involved must be informed that there is a permit-to-work system and which tasks require a permit.

Modern technology can help tremendously in the implementation of a permit system. For example, equipment and equipment components may be provided with individual bar codes that, when scanned, will provide the user of a hand-held computer with the lockout/tagout procedure for that equipment. All data, including permits, procedures, and equipment history, may be kept on a central computer, and all of that material may be accessed by way of hand-held computers (personal digital assistants or PDAs). Similarly, confined spaces and electrical equipment may be provided with individual bar codes that will provide permitting and safety-procedure documentation for the scanned space or equipment. The central computer may then be used to store historical maintenance and to access data for future reference.

A word of caution is in order on this subject. The technology is available to shut off or isolate equipment and components remotely by using computer technology. If equipment is secured in this way, the permitting system and safe work procedures must require that the securing method be manually verified.

At this point, it is well to define several terms that will be used frequently in this chapter. A *qualified person* (as defined in the American National Standards, *Safety Regulations for Confined Spaces*, ANSI Z117.1-2009) is one who by reason of training, education, and experience is knowledgeable in the operation to be performed and is qualified to judge the hazards involved and specify controls and/or protective measures. An *approving authority* is one who is assigned the responsibility of approving, by signature, the permit to work. The approving authority may or may not be a qualified person, and if not, he or she must require the input of a qualified person in order to approve the permit (ANSI 2009). A *risk assessment* (as defined in the American National Standard, ANSI Z244.1, *Control of Hazardous Energy Lockout/Tagout and Alternative Methods*, is a comprehensive evaluation of the probability and the degree of the possible injury or damage to health in a hazardous situation in order to select appropriate safeguarding (ANSI/ASSE 2008).

Once the tasks that come under the permit-to-work system are identified, a document that serves as the permit should be devised. The permit should be clear and concise, which increases the likelihood that it will be used; however, it should provide enough detail that the approval authority will have enough information to perform a proper risk assessment. When formulating a permit, keep in mind that a worker is asking permission and assistance in performing a duty that he or she does not perform very often. The permit, before approval, details exactly how the job is to be accomplished. Figure 1 is an example of a permit that can be used for several tasks discussed in this chapter.

Normally, the sequence of events within a permit-to-work system are as follows. A worker is assigned a task for which a permit to work is required. The worker then goes to a supervisor or other designated authority to obtain a permit. The worker then fills out the permit and returns it to the supervisor. The permit is assigned a unique number for identification purposes. The permit form must detail the duration for which it is issued, the issue date and time, and the exact location of the job. At this point, a qualified person must do a risk assessment of the task to stipulate the hazard control measures necessary to perform the task safely. American National Standard, ANSI Z244.1, *Control of Hazardous Energy Lockout/Tagout and Alternative Methods*

Permit Number ______________________

Location of work (building/Room No.) _______ Contact Name ______________________

Summary of work to be done

SAFETY PROCEDURES: To be implemented prior to commencement of work

1. The following processes are to be suspended during the course of the work:
2. The following equipment is to be withdrawn from service during the course of the work:
3. All users have been made aware of this suspension withdrawal Y/N
4. Safety Warning Notices have been posted where required Y/N
5. The following steps have been taken to eliminate, control, or contain hazards.

APPROVAL

Signed ______________________

CONTROL OF RISKS ARISING FROM THE WORK

1. Isolation of services: (please check as appropriate)

   _____ water _____ electrical power _____ fuel lines _____ compressed gases _____ other (specify)
2. Are there safety implications resulting from the isolation? Y/N
3. Lock-out required Y/N Location ______________________
4. Air monitoring required Y/N
5. Are there hazards associated with the work? Y/N
6. If yes, what safety precautions are required to control the risks?

Authorization

NAME: (Print) ______________________

Company/Department: ______________________

Signed: ______________________ Date: ____________ Time: ________

Permit Validity Period:

From: Date ___/___/___ Time: ________ To: Date ___/___/___ Time: ________

Completion of Work

I confirm that the work has been completed in accordance with this permit. Services have been restored and the work area is ready for inspection.

Signed: ______________________ Date: ____________ Time: ________

FIGURE 1. Sample permit-to-work permit

(ANSI/ASSE 2008), Annex A, is an example of a risk-assessment technique. The supervisor can be the approving authority, however, a qualified person might have to be consulted in order to obtain the best possible risk assessment. Depending on the complexity of the task and the number of times it has been performed in the past, the worker might have sufficient information already detailed on the permit form indicating the safeguards necessary. The qualified person must still review the hazards and the proposed safeguards to make sure that the best possible safety measures are used. For well-known permit-required tasks, such as confined space entry or asbestos removal, a preestablished job safety procedure should already have been formulated.

The following list outlines the steps that the permit-to-work system should require:

- type of permit (confined space, hot work, etc.)
- unique permit number
- names of the workers and/or contractors
- location of task
- details of the task to be performed
- identification of hazards
- risk assessment of task and hazards
- safeguards required
- personal protective equipment required
- authorization to begin the task
- permit time period
- extension of time period, if necessary
- completion date and time

Once the permit has been reviewed, approved, and signed by the approval authority, a copy of the completed permit should be made available to all involved in the task. This is normally accomplished by posting the permit in the area of the job.

When the work is completed, the permit is returned to the approval authority for cancellation and filing. The approval authority should assure himself or herself that the job site is free of hazards upon completion of the job.

Contractors and subcontractors must be held to the same high safety standards to which host managers, supervisors, and workers are held. Therefore, permits to work must be required of all outside firms who are asked to perform duties for which a permit is normally required. Most of these duties involve operations that affect other workers or operations. The prudent manager will want to be able to assess and monitor the contractor's presence and activities within the facility or operation. A contractor can provide its own qualified person, risk assessment, and hazard control measures, but the facility management will provide the permit approval authority so that oversight authority can be maintained.

The first specific permit-to-work system that is discussed in this chapter is for confined spaces, because it is more detailed due to the complexity of the hazards and safeguards involved, and because its concepts can be used in devising permits to work for any task or operation.

Permit to Work–Confined Spaces

Confined Space Survey

The first step in establishing a confined space permit-to-work system within any facility or operation is to perform a survey to establish a documented inventory of all areas that are to be considered confined spaces (ANSI 2009, section 3.1). A confined space is defined by the American National Standards Institute standard Z117.1-2009 as "an enclosed area that is large enough and so configured that an employee can bodily enter and has the following characteristics: its primary function is something other than human occupancy; and has restricted entry and exit" (ANSI 2009). The Occupational Safety and Health Administration (OSHA) standard 29 CFR 1910.146(b) uses a similar definition.

A survey must be performed by a qualified person or persons who have sufficient expertise to define a confined space. The goal, at this point, is simply to establish a list of the spaces that are, by definition, confined spaces. Keep in mind that confined spaces are not only limited to the interior of buildings or obvious external tanks, but can also be hidden in remote locations, be underground, and can be smaller than room size.

A blueprint of the facility is a handy reference tool when conducting the survey, as is a list of all maintenance tasks to be performed on a regularly scheduled basis. Many not-so-obvious confined spaces are those that are accessed infrequently for painting or cleaning and, as a result, might be missed. Further, the inventory of confined spaces should include mobile and abandoned or obsolete confined spaces.

In addition, each building, process, or equipment modification or addition must be reviewed by safety personnel or a qualified person to determine whether the changes create a confined space that must then be added to the inventory. The confined space survey must provide the following information:

- the confined space number
- the date of the survey
- the location of the space
- a description of the space
- the number of entry points
- the frequency of entry
- who usually enters the space
- reasons for entering the space
- if the space can be entered by a human
- if there is a hazardous atmosphere
- if there is limited or restricted entry
- if the space is designed for human occupancy
- other safety hazards
- possible atmospheric hazards such as oxygen deficiency, flammable materials, toxic materials
- identification of the specific hazards for flammable and/or toxic materials and their exposure levels
- possible hazardous contents of the space, such as past contents, current contents, and dust
- potential energy sources, such as electrical, hydraulic, pneumatic, and mechanical
- potential hazards of the space itself, such as slippery surfaces, high or low temperatures, and high noise levels
- hazards presented from the configuration of the space

It is not enough to create a list of confined spaces and file the list away where those who need its information most cannot find it. Once a confined space is identified, it must be physically labeled as such at all entry points. The labeling must indicate that the area is a confined space and that it can be entered only after a written confined space permit is obtained from the proper authority listed on the label. Identification labels are available from commercial suppliers.

Hazard Identification

The definition of a confined space does not require that there is a hazard present. The confined space survey might detect confined spaces that are free of hazards and, as a result, can be entered without a permit. These spaces are called "nonpermit confined spaces" by both ANSI Z117.1-2009 and OSHA 1910.146(b) and will not be further addressed in this chapter.

The permit-to-work system is concerned with those confined spaces that contain known or potential hazards and, therefore, require special permission and safeguards to enter. It must be noted that the concern is that *known* or *potential* hazards might exist. While a confined space might, at the time of entry, be deemed free of hazards other than those inherent to the space, there can be the *potential* for the creation of a hazard after work has commenced, whether by the nature of the work itself, or by the introduction of a hazardous material through piping or other entry means. Therefore, the hazard identification performed must take into consideration future as well as existing hazards within the confined space. Such future hazards can include the introduction of material through a pipe or other opening into the space, heat generated by the task being performed, or toxic materials generated by the task being performed.

Note that there are entities that do not regard underground sewage systems and their associated manholes, collection basins, and piping as confined spaces. For the purposes of this reference, such spaces fit all the criteria of a confined space and, thus, are considered confined spaces. Every portion of an underground, enclosed area that contains potentially hazardous material and has the potential for oxygen depletion must be considered a confined space and be subject to the permitting process.

The hazard identification process must be accomplished by a qualified person and must take into consideration several criteria during the identification process. First, the configuration of the confined space must be noted to determine means and ease of entry and exit. Many confined spaces require some means of assistance, such as a mechanical lifting device, to get workers in and out. If so, all necessary equipment is a requirement of the permit system. The point of entry and exit must be identified and examined to ensure that it does not interact with other operations in the area. If, for example, a worker within a confined space must exit within a fork-truck travelway, appropriate signage and barricades must be provided in order to redirect fork-truck travel.

Second, the hazard identification process should consider all uses, past and present, of the confined space. Past uses are important due to the fact that residues can be left behind that might interact with the work progress, such as cleaning chemicals used or hot work performed. Material Safety Data Sheets (MSDSs) should be used to determine hazards presented by whatever was in the space before the entry by workers, and to determine how those materials might interact with the process that made the entry necessary.

At this point, a documented list of confined spaces has been established and each space has been surveyed for its physical characteristics and its past and current uses. Next, the confined space evaluation process should determine the *existing* or *potential* hazards unique to each confined space. This process, too, should be documented so that everyone involved, no matter how far in the future, will have access to the information. It is extremely critical that the hazards be identified by a qualified person who might not necessarily be the same person who identified the confined spaces. The work can require different expertise, and it is very important that the present hazards and *potential* hazards are identified. The assistance of an industrial hygienist or someone of similar training and experience might be necessary.

During this phase of the confined space evaluation, the hazards to be assessed include oxygen depletion, oxygen enrichment, flammable and explosive atmosphere, and toxic materials in the confined space (ANSI 2009, section 3.2). The evaluator must understand that the work that is being performed within the confined space after the permitting process might contribute its own hazard. For example, an internal combustion engine used within the space will, if not properly exhausted, fill the space with carbon monoxide, or a chemical cleaning agent can, if not properly ventilated, fill the space with toxic materials. Each potential hazard must be identified and documented in preparation for a complete permit-to-work system.

Other hazards to be considered are biological hazards, mechanical hazards from any machinery that might be in the space or used in the operation, and physical hazards. Physical hazards include electrical exposures within the space, heat stress possibilities from process sources or an improperly ventilated space, and engulfment by solid or liquid materials that might inadvertently enter the space by way of unsecured entry pipes or chutes.

Hazard Evaluation

Now that the confined spaces have been identified and the hazards to which each might be subjected have been cataloged, the hazard presented must be evaluated (ANSI 2009, section 3.3). The evaluation determines the extent and breadth of the hazard as well as the consequences of exposure. At this point in the establishment of the confined space permitting system, the qualified person must determine what is the likelihood of worker exposure to the hazard and, if exposed, what is the likely extent of that exposure. This information will aid in determining what safeguards must be used to make and keep the confined space hazard-free while work is being performed inside. As in every step along the identification and evaluation process, any possibility of changes in the conditions within the confined space while workers could be exposed should be assessed.

At this point, the evaluator must consider how the identified hazards will be safeguarded. The logical risk evaluation must lead one to engineering safeguards that eliminate the hazard before personal protective equipment is considered. In order to best determine the most effective engineering safeguards, the evaluator must have knowledge of and access to updated data such as threshold limit values (TLVs) set by the American Conference of Governmental Industrial Hygienists (ACGIH), 29 CFR 1910, subpart Z, and

MSDSs. For safeguards of mechanical and physical hazards, consult the other chapters in this section of the handbook; OSHA 29 CFR 1910 and its referenced publications provide a good resource.

Whatever safeguards are determined to be appropriate must now be documented along with the corresponding confined space and listed hazards. Keep in mind that any one confined space can subject those entering it to more than one hazard, and each must be addressed if the ultimate goal of performing a safety task is to be realized.

Once the method of control for each of the identified hazards is ascertained, an emergency response plan must be formulated in the event that the established safeguards fail (ANSI 2009, section 14). Careful consideration must be given to exactly how it will be determined that a safeguard has failed and, next, how to get the workers out of the confined space in the safest, most efficient manner. All of these procedures must be documented, because they will eventually be part of the confined-space-entry permitting system. Then all involved will know exactly what to do, not only when the system is working well, but also when it is not. The permitting documentation will eventually state that, when emergency evacuation equipment is deemed necessary, it will be present and ready to use at the confined space entrance at all times when workers are inside the space.

The Written Confined-Space-Entry Permit Program

After performing the identification survey of the confined spaces within the operation or facility, identifying the hazards associated with each space, and evaluating those hazards, one is ready to formulate a written confined-space-entry program. Remembering that the permit-to-work system provides a systematic, disciplined, and documented approach to assessing the risks of a job and specifies the precautions to be taken when performing work in a confined space, a permit must be established that will lead the user through the proper steps to perform the required task safely.

Once it has been determined that work must be performed in a confined space, the supervisor can then go to the inventory list of confined spaces to determine what hazards are involved and the specified controls for each hazard. Now a permit system must be established that will:

- specify the work to be done and the equipment to be used
- specify the precautions to be taken when performing the task
- give permission for work to start
- provide a check to ensure that all safety considerations have been taken into account
- provide a check of the completed work

To this end, a permit must be established that will communicate all necessary information to all involved and provide for an approval process for the confined space entry. The permit should contain at least the following information:

- the name of the person controlling the confined space, and the date and time of entry
- the name of the person authorizing the entry
- the location of the confined space
- a description of the work to be performed
- the names of all workers required to enter the confined space as well as the names of all attendants
- the names of any outside contractors who will enter the confined space
- a list of all hazards to be controlled before entry and the controlling method of each
- a list of all safety equipment that will be necessary to control the identified hazards
- the type of atmospheric tests required, the expected results of those tests, and the type of equipment necessary to carry out the tests. In addition, the frequency of atmospheric testing must be stipulated
- the type of emergency rescue equipment necessary, including emergency communication equipment
- the type and number of communication devices present on the job, and to whom they will be assigned
- the duration of the permit

Confined Space Entry Permit

Date and Time Issued: ____________________ Date and Time Expired: ____________________

Job Site/Space I.D.: ____________________ Job Supervisor: ____________________

Equipment to be worked on: ____________________ Work to be performed: ____________________

Stand-by personnel: ____

1. Atmospheric checks: Time: __________

   Oxygen __________%

   Explosive __________% L.F.L.

   Toxic __________ PPM

2. Tester's signature ____

3. Source isolation (No Entry):	N/A	Yes	No
Pumps or lines blinded,	( )	( )	( )
disconnected or blocked	( )	( )	( )

4. Ventilation Modification	N/A	Yes	No
Mechanical	( )	( )	( )
Natural Ventilation only	( )	( )	( )

5. Atmospheric check after

   Isolation and Ventilation:

Oxygen __________%	>	19.5	%
Explosive __________ % L.F.L.	<	10	%
Toxic __________ PPM	<	10	PPM H(2)S

   Time __________

   Tester's signature: ____

6. Communication procedures: ____

____

7. Rescue procedures: ____

____

____

8. Entry, standby, and backup persons:	Yes	No
Successfully completed required training		
Is it current?	( )	( )

9. Equipment:	NA	Yes	No
Direct reading gas monitor–tested	( )	( )	( )
Safety harnesses and lifelines for			
entry and standby persons	( )	( )	( )
Hoisting equipment	( )	( )	( )
Powered communications	( )	( )	( )
SCBAs for entry and standby persons	( )	( )	( )
Protective clothing	( )	( )	( )
All electric equipment, listed Class I,			
Division I, Group D and			
Nonsparking tools	( )	( )	( )

FIGURE 2. Sample confined-space-entry permit

Confined Space Entry Permit (cont)

10. Periodic atmospheric tests

Oxygen	____%	Time _____	Oxygen	____%	Time _____
Oxygen	____%	Time _____	Oxygen	____%	Time _____
Explosive	____%	Time _____	Explosive	____%	Time _____
Explosive	____%	Time _____	Explosive	____%	Time _____
Toxic	____%	Time _____	Toxic	____%	Time _____
Toxic	____%	Time _____	Toxic	____%	Time _____

We have reviewed the work authorized by this permit and the information contained herein. Written instructions and safety procedures have been received and are understood. Entry cannot be approved if any squares are marked in the "No" column. This permit is not valid unless all appropriate items are completed.

Permit Prepared By:

(Supervisor) ________________________________

Approved by

(Unit Supervisor) ________________________________

Reviewed By:

(CS Operations Personnel): ________________________________

____

(signature)

____

(printed name)

This permit to be kept at the job site. Return job-site copy to Safety Office following job completion.

Copies: White Original (Safety Office)
Yellow (Unit Supervisor)
Hard (Job site)

FIGURE 2. Sample confined-space-entry permit

Figure 2 is an example of a confined-space-entry permit.

Personnel

Once the permit-to-work permit has been established, the qualifications of those involved in the confined space entry must be established. It has already been determined that a qualified person is one who is trained and knowledgeable in the operation and is qualified to judge the hazards involved and any specific control measures. Such a person was asked to identify confined spaces and identify and evaluate the hazards. However, there may be an entirely different group of workers who are involved in the actual confined space entry. There are generally five groups of personnel who are involved: the entry supervisor, the entrants, the standby attendants, atmospheric monitoring personnel, and emergency response personnel (ANSI 2009).

The entry supervisor is the person in charge of the permitting process and should be trained in and have knowledge of all aspects of the confined-space-entry permit. The entry supervisor is responsible for determining that all requirements of the permitting system have been filled before he or she signs the permit allowing confined space entry. In addition, he or she should ensure that all conditions of the safe work procedure, as detailed in the work permit, are followed for the entire duration of the task. These conditions include atmospheric monitoring and the presence of rescue apparatus and personnel.

An entrant is the one who actually enters the confined space and who should be trained in, and maintain familiarity with, the confined-space-entry permit system and the individual permit in use at the time of entry. The entrant should use only the equipment specified in the work permit, and should be informed of the symptoms that can be expected if exposure to atmospheric hazards elevates beyond acceptable levels. Further, the entrant should be trained in self-evacuation methods and proper communication techniques between the entrant and the standby attendant. The entrant and the standby attendant should be provided with communication equipment so that they can remain in constant communication throughout time spent within the confined space.

The standby attendant is the one who is stationed outside of the confined space at all times when the space is occupied, and who is responsible for assisting with entry and exit to the confined space. Most importantly, the standby attendant is not, under any circumstances, to enter the confined space so that he or she will be available to communicate evacuation procedures to the entrants. In the event of any deviation from the permit requirements, the standby attendant will be provided with a direct communication link to the rescue team and will not attempt rescue unless he or she is specifically trained in rescue techniques and acts as part of the rescue team. The standby attendant should remain outside of the entrance to the confined space at all times unless relieved by a trained attendant or until all workers have vacated the confined space.

Atmospheric monitoring personnel monitor the atmosphere of a confined space when the risk assessment has stipulated that such testing is necessary. Continuous monitoring/alerting devices, both personal and area, can be used. No person should enter the confined space to conduct monitoring except as provided by written authority. Results of any monitoring should be recorded on the confined-space-entry permit.

Rescue personnel are those who are trained and qualified in general rescue techniques and who are knowledgeable of the particular techniques involved in the specific confined space. Rescue personnel should also be trained in first-aid and cardiopulmonary resuscitation (CPR) or chest-compression techniques. Rescue personnel training should include an actual rehearsal of a rescue using all necessary apparatus and equipment.

Each of these categories of personnel and their duties are vital to the safety of the entrants. Therefore, they should be trained, knowledgeable, and dedicated. A list must be maintained of the names of each qualified person in each category, and the list must contain information concerning training dates and designation.

Work in the Confined Space

Once a permit has been issued for work to be performed within a known and labeled confined space, testing must then take place to assure all of those involved that the space is, indeed, safe to enter. All atmospheric testing within the confined space should be performed from outside of the space, and the atmosphere should be made safe for unprotected work before entry. However, there are times when this is impractical or impossible, and under these circumstances entrants must be protected by personal protective equipment. These events and the proper protective equipment must have been previously identified and evaluated and therefore are part of the completed confined space work permit.

The atmosphere within a confined space must be tested for (in this order) oxygen levels, flammability, and exposure levels of any hazardous materials that might be present, and all testing must be performed by a qualified person. The atmosphere within the confined space must be tested in a manner that will ensure that all levels and all areas within the space are free from hazard. To accomplish this, testing must take place at all vertical levels within the space and all areas that might trap contaminants. All areas within a confined space that access work areas must be tested, even though work might not be scheduled in all parts of the space. Flammable and toxic vapors migrate from place to place, as do workers. All testing equipment used should be listed for its intended purpose and should be calibrated at the frequency recommended by its manufacturer. A list shall be established and maintained that documents the calibration and service dates of all testing equipment (ANSI 2009, section 6).

Initial atmospheric testing within the confined space must be accomplished with any temporary or permanent ventilation systems shut down. If it is determined that ventilation is required, the atmosphere must be retested with the ventilation system functioning to determine the quality of the outside air drawn into the confined space. Care should be taken to make sure that ventilation intake equipment is well away from contamination sources, such as engine exhaust or operations that emit toxic vapors. Atmospheric testing with the ventilation system functioning will determine the proper location of the ventilation intake.

Because circumstances surrounding and within a confined space can change rapidly, the consideration should be taken under the risk assessment performed during the confined space evaluation for continuous atmospheric monitoring whenever workers are within the confined space. The risk assessment performed during the evaluation of the confined space and its hazards will have already determined the length of time that the entrants can be out of the confined space before retesting is required prior to reentry. Such an assessment must include the hazardous materials involved and their possible reentry mode, the possibility of oxygen depletion while the entrants were out of the space, the type of ventilation, and whether the work performed before departure from the space might have changed the oxygen level or the flammability and/or toxicity of the atmosphere.

The acceptable limits of atmospheric hazards within the confined space will have been determined during the hazard identification and evaluation phase of the permit-to-work system establishment and therefore will be prominently listed on the permit issued to those on the confined-space-entry team. The oxygen level will be set at between 19.5 percent and 23.5 percent for all confined spaces.

The flammability and toxicity will change for each space, depending upon the involved hazardous materials. The National Fire Protection Association (NFPA) has established flammability ranges for most chemicals in its publication, *Fire Protection Guide to Hazardous Materials* (NFPA 2010). If a reference source other than the NFPA is used, care must be taken to ensure that the provided data is reliable and accurate. The flammability of the atmosphere within a confined space must be reduced to less than 10 percent of the lower explosive limit (LEL), or below the lower flammable limit (LFL), before an entrant is allowed to enter a confined space. If the flammability of a space is to be lowered using ventilation, great caution must be taken in directing the exhaust of the ventilation system away from any surrounding sources of ignition. The hazard evaluation and risk assessment must also take into consideration the fact that a flammable atmosphere that is above the allowed explosive limit, meaning that it is too rich to ignite, carries another set of hazards that must be addressed, such as the toxicity of the material and the lowering of the flammable levels to within the flammable range during the work process.

The allowable toxicity of the atmosphere within the confined space will have been established during the hazard evaluation, and will be prominently listed on the approved confined-space-entry permit. The qualified person who evaluates and establishes the acceptable toxic limits has several reference sources available in which predetermined acceptable toxic levels for various materials are listed: The American Conference of Governmental Industrial Hygienists (ACGIH) Threshold Limit Values Document, Material Safety Data Sheets (MSDSs), and 29 CFR 1910, subpart Z, are reference sources that are widely used in industry. Any other reference sources used must be reviewed carefully and their accuracy verified.

When either the oxygen level is improper, the flammability of the atmosphere is unsuitable, or the toxicity levels are too high, or any combination of these hazardous conditions has been detected by testing, entry should not take place until the hazardous condition is corrected to acceptable levels or appropriate personal protective equipment is used as detailed in the confined space work permit. The first priority should be to eliminate the identified hazard within the confined space by engineering means. Using personal protective equipment to eliminate the hazard should be the last resort.

The risk evaluation and assessment might have determined that ventilation (either forced or natural) is required to provide an atmosphere in which persons can work and, when it has, the work permit should detail the amount of pre-entry purge ventilation time and the frequency of atmospheric testing once entry has been made. Of consideration as well is whether forced ventilation is necessary at all times that the space is occupied. It normally is. If it is determined that natural ventilation is an acceptable means of safeguard, care should be taken not to decrease the size of the air entry and exit points with the placement of tools, equipment, or other apparatus at openings.

Isolation of the Confined Space

Before work can be allowed in the identified confined space, care must be taken to make sure that no hazardous materials enter the space once it has been purged and work commenced (ANSI 2009, section 8). The permit to work will have detailed possible modes of entry and methods to isolate the confined space. Because the permit-to-work system has already evaluated the space and its hazards, the physical methods that must be taken to prevent unwanted entry of hazardous materials into the space will be detailed on the work permit. Each potential entry point or hazard source should be evaluated as a separate entity, and the best possible means of isolation or deactivation provided.

One method of entry of toxic or flammable materials into the space is by way of pipelines that lead into the space from other known and previously evaluated sources. Pipelines leading into the confined space must be drained, flushed, and cleaned of hazardous materials before entry, and the pipeline secured in an effective manner to prevent flow. The pipe can be provided with a blank, taken apart and misaligned at a flange, or isolated by valves if so provided. If valves are used, more than one valve should be used with a bleed valve in between. If piping must be left open during work within the confined space, a qualified person must assess the risk of exposure and provide other precautions as needed, such as personal protective equipment (ANSI 2009, section 8).

Entry of a hazardous material into the confined space is not the only hazard to address. Other sources can include electrical, mechanical, hydraulic, pneumatic, chemical, thermal, and radioactive hazards, and falling objects. Each of these potential hazards must be evaluated for its ability to injure workers just as they would outside of the confined space, and appropriate safeguards used and detailed on the work permit.

If it is determined during the hazard evaluation and risk assessment that a hazard must be controlled using either lockout or tagout methods, a program developed in accordance with ANSI Z244.1-2008 (ANSI 2008) and OSHA 29 CFR 1910.147 (OSHA 1996a) should be used. Such a requirement will be listed as part of the approved work permit.

Emergency Response in a Confined Space

A documented emergency response procedure should be developed that details the exact method by which rescue will take place, the type of personnel and training involved, and the equipment necessary to perform the rescue (ANSI 2009, section 14). Although some confined spaces are similar and may use the same personnel, equipment, and techniques, many will be dissimilar, therefore requiring a different plan and procedure. When assessing and devising the emergency response procedure, one must consider the area and configuration of the confined space and the distance away from an exit point a disabled worker or workers might be. The number of likely disabled workers will have a profound effect on the number of rescue personnel required and the type of equipment necessary. The entrance opening to and from the confined space will affect the type of equipment rescue workers wear and carry when entering the space. The site of the exit in relation to the size and weight of those to be rescued, as well as the type of entrance, must be considered. If an entrance and exit portal is provided with a ladder, the rescue method will have to provide a harness and mechanical lifting device to lift a disabled worker out of the space. Both the rescue procedures and the risk assessment from which they are derived must be reviewed before a rescue is required, and the safest rescue operation for all involved, including the rescue personnel, must be provided.

Understanding that a rescue is necessitated by a problem within the confined space, the first priority is to attempt to formulate a rescue plan that makes entry by rescuers into the confined space unnecessary. One way this can be accomplished is by fitting the entrants with body harnesses and lanyards prior to entry.

Establishing a predetermined method by which entrants can perform their own rescue is another rescue method that does not expose emergency personnel to hazards within the confined space. This method normally requires a warning of impending hazard, usually by way of continuous monitoring.

All rescue methods must be predetermined and documented in an emergency response procedure, and all those who are involved with the rescue must be trained in its implementation. Also, they must have practiced the rescue procedure in its entirety.

A rescue procedure is initiated by a standby attendant who, as established by the confined space permit system, has been stationed at the entry point of the confined space with the express duty of monitoring conditions within the confined space and initiating emergency procedures if necessary. The attendant must be warned that his or her first and most important duty in the event of an emergency is to contact rescue personnel as quickly as possible. The attendant must be advised that he or she is never to enter the space to attempt a rescue unless part of a designated, trained rescue team. If the attendant is a member of such a team, no rescue attempt inside of the confined space will be attempted until the entire rescue team is assembled at the confined space entry point. Someone must be left outside of the confined space during the rescue operation.

Outside Contractors

Outside contractors can be hired to perform work in confined spaces over which the plant or facility owner or operator has control. However, the owner or operator might have no direct control over those who actually perform the tasks. In this instance, the owner or operator and the contractor should act as a team to ensure the safety of all involved.

The facility owner or operator should accept no less degree of safety for the contractor's workers than it would for its own. That means the confined space entry must be made under the procedure developed by a well-thought-out permit-to-work system. The contractor should get information concerning the space and what is necessary to enter the space safely from the facility owner or operator (ANSI 2009, section 17).

The facility owner or operator must have performed an inventory of its confined spaces and labeled them as such before the confined space can be entered. In this way, both the contractor and the owner or operator know that the space does, in fact, fit the definition of a confined space. Also, the owner or operator will have identified hazards, evaluated them, and stipulated control and monitoring methods.

These duties must be performed before any confined space entry is made, no matter whose employees are entering. Normally, the owner or user of the space will accomplish this task. These duties can be performed by a contracted party, but the owner or operator must stipulate that they are performed in compliance with this chapter and accepted industry standards.

The owner or operator of the confined space must inform the hired contractor of all information concerning the space that has been discovered during the evaluation, such as the size and exit points of the space, the hazards discovered, the hazard safeguards, and rescue methods. The contractor will then have all of the information necessary to perform work safely within the confined space. A work permit must still be issued and approved before entry, even though a contracted party is used. The parties involved must understand that the facility owner will be responsible for the permit to work and its approval. The designation and training of personnel, including rescue personnel, and atmospheric monitoring procedures and equipment can be the responsibility of the contractor. Whoever is designated to perform these duties, responsibilities should be distilled to a document and signed by both parties so that all involved know who is responsible for each phase of the entry.

PERMIT TO WORK–HOT WORK

Hot work is work that involves temperatures that have the potential to create a source of ignition. These operations include grinding, welding, thermal or oxygen cutting or heating, and other related heat-producing or spark-producing operations. As discussed earlier in this chapter, the risk-assessment and hazard-control aspects of the confined space permit system can be used to develop a permit-to-work system for other operations where it is determined to be appropriate.

Just as is true for a confined space permit system, the permit for hot work must specify:

- the work to be done and equipment to be used
- the precautions to be taken when performing the task
- the clearance zone for flammable materials
- the location, date, and time of the task
- the type of firefighting equipment that must be available while the work is being performed
- an inspection of the area before beginning the work
- the assignment of a fire watch at the completion of the job, including the duration of the watch
- the type of communication devices to be provided to the parties involved
- an authorization from the approval authority to start the job
- the area around the operation is to be cleared of combustible and flammable materials

Hot Work Permit

DATE ISSUED: ____________________ VALID UNTIL: ____________________

BUILDING: ____________________ BUILDING # ____________ PROJECT # ____________

LOCATION OF WORK ____

CONTACT PHONE NO. ____

The following precautions must be taken before work is started:

–Cutting and/or welding equipment must be thoroughly inspected and found to be in good repair, free of damage or defects.

–At least one fire-alarm pull station or means of contacting the fire department (i.e., site telephone) must be available and accessible to person(s) conducting the cutting/welding operation.

–A multipurpose, dry chemical, portable fire extinguisher must be located such that it is immediately available to the work and is fully charged and ready for use.

–Floor areas under and at least 35 feet around the cutting/welding operation must be swept clean of combustible and flammable materials.

–All construction equipment fueling activities and fuel storage must be relocated at least 35 feet away from the cutting/welding operation.

Where applicable, the following precautions will also be taken before the work begins:

–Fire-resistant shields (fire-retardant plywood, flameproof tarpaulins, metal, etc.) must be put in place.

–Containers in or on which cutting/welding will take place must be purged of flammable vapors.

The following precautions will be taken during and after the work:

–Person(s) must be assigned to a fire watch during, and for at least 30 minutes after, all cutting/welding.

–Fire-watch person(s) are to be supplied with multipurpose, dry chemical, portable fire extinguishers and trained in their use.

FIGURE 3. Sample permit for hot work

The permit to work for hot work must include space (and prompting text) for the user to completely answer the above questions. Unlike a confined space permit system, the location of the work area is not predetermined. However, most of the safeguards for hot work are well known, and the permit is a mechanism that leads the user to ask the proper questions to assess the risks of the job, and then to provide the proper hazard control measures. Both the assessment and control methods must be reviewed and approved by a qualified person. Figure 3 shows an example of a permit for hot work.

The process for a job to commence under a hot-work permit system (and for most permitted work systems) is that a worker determines that hot work has to be performed. The worker then goes to the appropriate designated supervisor or other authority to request permission to perform such work and to obtain a blank permit-to-work form. (In order for the system to function properly, the worker must have been trained in at least the rudimentary aspects of the permit-to-work system so that he or she understands that a task involving hot work requires permission by way of a permit.)

Once the authority determines that a permit is required, the worker is issued a blank permit and is required to fill it out with all necessary information. Many times the worker requires assistance in determining the appropriate safeguards and assigning the fire watch.

When the permit form is completed, the approval authority determines whether the worker is properly trained to perform the job safely, and whether or not the safeguards are adequate. Upon approval, the worker proceeds to the job site and inspects it for hazards such as combustible or flammable materials in the area, and that the job site is provided with the extinguishing equipment as specified on the permit.

When the hot work is completed and the work area cleaned up, some form of fire watch must be assigned. This can range from requiring the worker or one of the work party to stay at the job site for a period of time (30 minutes) to ensure that there is no possibility of fire, to requiring several inspectors for an extended period of time. The extent of the fire watch is to be determined by the risk assessment performed before the job is started. Whatever fire watch remains after the job is completed (and there should be one no matter how small the job), it should be provided with appropriate fire-extinguishing apparatus and knowledge and training in its use.

Once the fire watch has ended, the work-permit document is returned to the authorizing person so the end of the job can be logged and the permit filed.

A permit should be issued for no longer than one work shift. If it becomes necessary for new personnel to take over the hot-work job, a new permit should be issued to ensure that the workers involved are properly trained.

Permit to Work–Roof Work

Work on roofs normally involves the risk of working at elevations, with the associated hazard of falls from the work area. Therefore, it is well for job rules to be established before the hazardous work is undertaken so that all involved know exactly how to perform the required duties in the safest possible manner.

If the entity for which one works is in the business of doing roof work, no permit-to-work system is required because the work is not out of the ordinary for the workers, and it is expected that all of the proper training and safeguarding will be in place before each day's activities. However, for the organization that only occasionally has to assign its workers job duties on building roofs, it is understood that those workers will not be as well-versed in roof work and the safeguarding necessary. For this reason, occasional roof work must be attempted only as part of a permit-to-work system that will ensure that those undertaking the tasks are trained, and that the job has been subjected to a formal risk assessment and, as a result, hazard controls have been implemented.

The permit document will be one that provides the date and location (building) of the work to be performed, and the exact location of the task upon the roof area. The exact location is necessary for the determination of the personal protection and fall arrest equipment that must be provided. For example, if work is to take place on the edge of a roof without a parapet (within ten feet of the edge), some form of fall protection, such as a lanyard safety system or edge protection, will be required. However, if the roof is large and all work will take place more than ten feet from the unprotected edges, fall protection might not be required. A risk assessment must be performed by a qualified person before each job that requires a roof-work permit in order to determine the exact method of hazard (fall) control.

One of the hazards to be considered during the risk assessment is whether roof work is to be performed in high winds and/or rain. High winds greatly affect the safety of personnel working with sheet material, and rain affects the coefficient of friction of roofing material and therefore its slipperiness. Another hazard to be addressed during a roof-work risk assessment is the effect that the additional weight of workers, repair equipment, and any additional equipment being installed on the roof may have on the roof's structural components. All roofs should be designed to accept additional weight applied during ordinary maintenance, but to the extent that the maintenance becomes extraordinary (such as in combination with a heavy snow load), the risk assessment must take this into consideration. In addition, the effect of the weight of any equipment left on the roof must be considered.

Taking all of this into consideration, the permit document must contain information that will allow the person who must authorize the work to determine the adequacy of the training of those undertaking the job. Roof work can be hazardous and should be performed only by those trained to avoid its risks.

A checklist can be developed that will assist all of those involved in determining the hazards in the roof work and the safeguards necessary to perform the task safely. The checklist should encompass at least the following:

- the location of the work
- expected weather conditions
- roof-loading restrictions
- fall protection equipment necessary
- perimeter or barrier guarding
- communication means
- coordination of crane operation
- adequacy of roof-access means (ladders, hoists)
- inspection of ladders
- protection of workers or equipment below
- chimney/fume hood discharge or steam discharge
- overhead electrical wire protection (insulation, distance)

Roofing contractors should be required by contract or written agreement to perform their tasks in compliance with industry safety practices and in a manner that will not adversely affect others within or surrounding the facility on which the work is to be performed. The contractor must apply for permission to work on the facility's roof by way of a permit to work, so that the facility manager will know what is taking place on the roof.

The sequence of events leading up to the authorization of a permit to perform roof work is similar to that for hot work. The permit must be issued for no longer than one day due to the large effect weather has on the safety of roof workers, therefore necessitating evaluation of the job on at least a daily basis. Weather changes during a 24-hour period might necessitate the revocation of a work permit. The permit to work shown in Figure 1 can be used as a guideline.

Not all elevated work takes place on a roof. There can be times within a facility or operation when nonroutine work is required at heights that demand special knowledge and safeguards. A permit should be required before such work is performed. Many of the hazards involved are similar to those involved in roof work; therefore the roof-work hazard checklist and permit system can be used.

Work performed from a ladder by maintenance workers is usually routine and so does not require a permit. If jobs other than roof work must be performed at heights, careful consideration should be given to providing the workers with simple, protected work platforms, such as aerial platforms or scaffolding with proper guarding of their open sides and proper access points (see the section "Permit to Work—Scaffolding" later in this chapter). If such a protected work platform cannot be provided, fall protection safeguards must be provided.

PERMIT TO WORK–EXCAVATIONS

Excavating is a task that is not often undertaken by a facilities maintenance department, and can be an extremely hazardous duty if not properly safeguarded. Therefore, a permit to work must be applied for and approved before any excavation is begun.

The permit itself should be designed as a tool to aid the person who applies for the permit to do the job, and the person who ultimately authorizes the permit, to ensure that all foreseeable hazards are discovered and addressed.

The process of excavating is not a new one, and to those who do it on a daily basis, the hazards associated with it might be commonplace. However, to the occasional excavator, the risks might not be readily apparent. The permit-to-work system provides the vehicle that allows them to recognize potential problems and leads to the proper safeguards. The permit system is meant to serve as a guide to allow all involved to perform a proper risk assessment and to develop adequate safeguards.

A checklist can be developed that will assist those involved in the permitting process to discover hazards and determine safeguards. The checklist should include at least the following:

- the type of soil into which the excavation will be made
- the type of wall protection required (shoring, sloping, trench box)
- type of access (ladder, lift)
- utilities in the areas, such as underground water, sewer, electrical, stream, piping
- the depth of the excavation
- the location of the spoils
- protection of the public
- inspection frequency while work is being performed
- weather, such as rain, that might affect side stability
- positioning of any excavating equipment, such as trucks and backhoes
- stability of adjacent structures and their foundations
- groundwater levels

Excavation can be a hazardous operation if not accomplished with the proper safeguards for the soil conditions. Therefore, the risk assessment should be undertaken with the input of a person who is trained, experienced, and competent in the safeguarding of excavations.

The permit-to-work system must require an approved permit for all excavations. For shallow or spot excavations, the permit might only be required to locate underground utilities or other underground installations with no other safeguards required. However, the location of these underground facilities is important enough to mandate the initiation of a permit. The permit, therefore, must lead the applicant to locate all underground installations such as sewer, water, fuel, and electrical lines before ground is broken, and any that are discovered shall be protected from damage or displacement. Utility companies shall be contacted to mark the actual locations of these installations. Contact numbers for "Dig Safe" or other similar programs should be available on the permit.

The permit must require that all excavation work within or near a public way, such as a road or pedestrian walkway, be safeguarded so as to protect both vehicular and pedestrian traffic. Any necessary barricades or diversion devices must be listed on the permit before approval.

The completed permit must also address all necessary shoring materials if the risk assessment of the excavation determines that it is needed. Alternative safeguards, such as sloping of the sides of the excavation or relying upon the consistency of the excavated material to prevent collapse, may be used. However, they must be stipulated on the work permit and ultimately approved by a qualified person. If the excavation process lasts for more than one day, or less because of weather conditions that might affect the collapse safeguarding technique, it must be inspected by a qualified person daily or after the weather incident.

The permit must require that the placement of excavated material be in a safe place. A diagram is often helpful to enable the approval authority to better understand exactly where the material will be placed. The approval authority must require that the permit be specific as to exact safeguarding and material placement.

General, vague statements about safety must not be accepted.

If the excavation is to be left unattended or left overnight, the permit applicant must be required to detail what precautions will be taken to prevent inadvertent interaction with the excavation by pedestrians or vehicles. If mobile equipment is to be used adjacent to the excavation, the method of keeping it a safe distance from the sides of the excavation must be stipulated.

The permit must require that the number and means of exit and entry points out of and into the excavation be indicated. Once again, a diagram is extremely helpful. If ladders are required, they should be inspected before use.

If there is any possibility that the excavation might have either insufficient oxygen or hazardous vapors, a confined space permit to work must be applied for as well. The method of job completion, such as backfilling and compacting, must be detailed. Any pedestrian or vehicular pathways disturbed during the excavation must be returned to safe, usable condition.

Lastly, the permit must list all personnel involved in the excavation project so that the approval authority can determine whether or not they are properly trained. As with all work permits, the permit itself must be returned to the approval authority when the job is complete and kept on file.

If a contractor is hired to perform excavation work, the contractor must be required to obtain a permit to work so that the facilities manager can share information concerning the location of underground utilities and equipment, and so that work affecting a public or private travelway can be properly addressed.

Permit to Work–Electrical

Electrical work, on either high- (above 600V to ground) or low-voltage (50 V to ground or above) electrical systems that are nonroutine in nature, must be performed only with the permission acquired through the permit-to-work system. While the permit to work must be obtained to start work, and will dictate the location, time, and extent of the electrical work to be performed, all electrical work must be accomplished in conjunction with a sound lockout/tagout system that has been established in compliance with OSHA regulations (1910.147) and with ANSI's *Standard for the Control of Hazardous Energy—Lockout/Tagout and Alternative Methods* (ANSI Z244-2008). The control of hazardous electrical energy through a lockout or tagout system or other alternative method is provided through the establishment of "... requirements and performance objectives for procedures, techniques, designs and methods that protect personnel where injury can occur as a result of the unexpected release of hazardous energy." (ANSI 2008, section 1.2)

Although unexpected energy release can come in many forms, electrical energy control activation is one of the most common hazards within any industrial setting. The primary method of electrical energy control is through a documented lockout/tagout program (ANSI 2008, section 1.2). The establishment of a lockout/tagout program is addressed in the previous chapter in this Handbook, "Applied Science and Engineering: Electrical Safety" by Steven J. Owen. This entails the systematic survey of an electrical control circuit to identify control devices and then demands the application of a means to secure the control device in the off position before any work is attempted on the system. The control device can be secured with a hasp and padlock for which only a designated worker has keys. If several workers are involved with the circuit, there may be several locks on the hasp. In the case of electrical work that requires a permit, the lockout/tagout procedure does not replace a permit to work, but might be required as part of the permitting process (see Figure 1).

However, there may be times when work on or near electrical systems must be performed when the systems cannot be de-energized by way of a lockout/tagout program and, therefore, must be maintained while in an energized state. In this case a permit that requests permission to do the work is essential so that the work may be completed in the safest possible manner. Keep in mind that a hazard exists not only when work is being performed on live electrical components, but also when work is being performed within certain preestablished safeguarding distances from those components. Those distances may be established with the help of the NFPA's 70E, *Standard for Electrical Safety in the Workplace* (NFPA 2012), and OSHA 1910.333.

Work on high-voltage electrical systems can be extremely hazardous, and requires specialized training and tools to perform it safely. Therefore, unless a facility employs workers with such specialized training, one might want to limit the activities of the staff to working only on low-voltage electrical equipment and hire contractors to work on the high-voltage equipment.

Even though a contractor might be hired to work on high-voltage electrical systems, a permit to work should still be required so that the authorizing personnel can understand the scope of the job and how it might affect not only the safety of surrounding employees, but also other facility operations.

If the facilities personnel are required to work within an electrical substation or in the area of high-voltage electrical systems or equipment, a permit to work must still be requested and approved so that the approving authority can have a clear understanding of the extent and location of the work. In this way the possible exposures can be determined by way of a risk assessment and, as a result, the proper safeguards applied. Also, the facility will want to know, through its approving authority, what influence the work will have on the remainder of the facility.

The electrical work-permitting system should be accompanied by a documented risk and hazard analysis, which should determine:

- the system on which or near where the work is to be performed and its voltage
- why the system cannot be "locked out" by a procedure compliant with ANSI Z244 and OSHA
- whether company personnel have the proper qualifications and training to safely perform the task; if not, a qualified contractor must be hired

Once the determination is made that employees will perform the task, a work permit should be completed. Only properly trained workers, whether the company's or an outside contractor's, should be allowed to work on energized electrical systems or equipment carrying 50 volts or more.

The electrical work permit should contain, at a minimum, the following information (Figure 1 can be used as a general outline for the electrical work permit):

- the date, time, and location of the work to be performed
- a description of the system and equipment on which the work is to be performed, including the voltage and existing safeguards, such as overcurrent protection, and physical barriers, such as isolation within a room or closet
- the personnel involved in the work and their qualifications
- a detailed, step-by-step procedure by which the task is to be accomplished
- a determination of the hazards to which all workers will be subjected (examples include exposure to uninsulated electrical components, electrical arcing, wet or moist conditions)
- a determination of the safe work distances from exposed electrical components as a function of the voltage of the system (reference NFPA 70E-2012)
- a determination of the personal protective equipment (PPE) that must be used as a function of the hazards, the voltage of the system, and the safeguard distance encroachment, if any [if a worker must work within the established safe distance, PPE that is manufactured and rated for the hazard (such as arcing, flash, or shock) must be used]
- the method of eliminating access by those not involved with the task [examples include a physical barrier or physical isolation (within a locked room); warning signs alone are not enough of a safeguard]
- the work permit must be reviewed and signed as authorization to perform the task

After the work permit is completed and the work is authorized, a pretask meeting should be held at which the permit is reviewed by all involved parties and the step-by-step job procedure is reviewed so that everyone has a thorough understanding of the task, the procedure, and the safeguards. While electric shock from contact with exposed, energized electrical conductors is a significant hazard and therefore must be addressed by a permitting system, arc flash (blast) must also be addressed. Arc flash is the bright, fiery burst of light and energy that takes place when high-voltage conductors (those over 120 volts) arc; it is the most common cause of injury when electrical work is performed. An arc-flash protection boundary can be established by performing a flash hazard analysis so that a defined area may be established within which there is a risk of injury if an arc flash does take place. If one is asked to perform a task within the circulated boundary, properly designated personal protective equipment (PPE) must be worn. The arc-flash hazard analysis will determine the amount of energy available—a function of the size of the conductors, the capacity of the source, and the overcurrent devices used—and will determine the protective boundary and the type of PPE required. The arc-flash hazard analysis must be performed by a qualified person. NFPA 70E will provide important guidance (NFPA 2012).

Work on hazardous, energized, and exposed electrical systems or components is extremely hazardous and should be allowed only as a last resort when it has been determined that the system cannot be "locked out" and completely de-energized before any work takes place. The permit to work is an application for permission to perform electrical work and will detail exact safety procedures necessary to accomplish the task without damaging person or property. In the case of electrical work, the permit to work might well encompass other permits to work, such as a confined space permit or the lockout/tagout system.

Permit to Work–Scaffolding

Erecting and working from scaffolding presents workers with risks that are not commonly encountered or well defined, and therefore requires a system that ensures worker safety. A permit-to-work system will accomplish this task by establishing standards for building scaffolding or similar work platforms, and by establishing a system of communication that will allow all involved with the scaffold to determine whether or not it is available for use.

Because a scaffold serves as an elevated work area, its proper erection is essential to the safety of the workers who use it. Thus, the ultimate approval of the permit demands that the person responsible for erecting the scaffold is a qualified person. This can mean that an outside party is hired to oversee this important function or, in the case of a contractor, the credentials of the contractor's qualified person are checked. This check is especially important if your employees will be working from a scaffold erected by someone over whom you have no control.

No matter who erects the scaffolding, the permit to work must stipulate that it be erected in compliance with OSHA regulations (1926, subpart L) and with reference to the ANSI standard *Safety Requirements for Scaffolding* (ANSI A10.8). Both the OSHA and ANSI standards require that the scaffolding be erected and inspected by a competent person who is ". . . capable of identifying existing and predictable hazards . . ." (ANSI 2001, sections 3.15, 4.44, 4.45; OSHA 1996b).

The competent person will need to maintain an inspection checklist that includes, at the very minimum:

- proper designer credentials
- proper placement of scaffolding tags
- proper placement of guard rails, mid rails and toe boards
- proper footing
- placement of safety netting, if required
- secure scaffolding plank
- safe scaffold access (ladder, stairway, etc.)
- proper attachment to the building or other structure, if necessary
- proper distance of scaffolding platform from the building
- scaffolding that is not overloaded (consider weight of workers, supplies, machinery, materials on the scaffolding, and the scaffolding components)
- the use of only scaffold-grade wooden components
- the protection of nearby electrical conductors
- weather conditions, such as high wind, snow, and rain that might affect the safety of the workers
- inspection of any support ropes for abrasion and corrosion

- the stability of freestanding scaffold systems
- protection from nearby vehicles

Scaffolding presents a hazard both during its use and during its erection, modification, and dismantling. However, the permit to work can be used for each phase. The person who undertakes the task of erecting the scaffold must request permission to do so by way of the permit system, which will establish not only the standards to which it will be built, but also the safeguards necessary to build the structure of the scaffold safely. During the erection phase, the proper fall protection must be detailed on the permit. The workers involved must be listed so that the proper training requirements can be established. Therefore, training requirements must be established before the permit to work is requested and a list of authorized workers developed.

The permit-to-work document must list the date of erection, the projected date of erection completion, and the length of time that the scaffold will be available for use. The permit must also establish inspection frequency criteria for the scaffold. Usually, because scaffolding can be subjected to extreme work and weather conditions, a scaffold is inspected for damage or displacement at the beginning of each shift.

The permit-to-work system must also establish a means to notify potential users as to the exact state of the scaffolding; that is, whether it is safe to use, or still in the process of erection or dismantling. Such a communication system will also serve to inform potential scaffolding workers of what type of work can be performed from the scaffold and any weight limitations that apply. Appendix E of the ANSI A10.8 safety standard details a Scaffolding Tagging Program, in which various colored tags are placed at the entranceways to the scaffold, informing workers of the status (complete or incomplete) of the scaffold (ANSI 2001). Any system that communicates this vital information to workers can be used and implemented as a necessary portion of the approved scaffold permit to work.

Permit to Work–Laboratory

Educational institutions have had research and testing laboratories for a long time, but these are now appearing more and more in manufacturing facilities. Each laboratory, depending upon the work performed and the materials stored, presents its own unique hazards. Maintenance workers or others who are asked to perform nonroutine tasks for which safety procedures are not already developed can be exposed to safety hazards that must be subjected to a risk-assessment process before the task commences in order to discover and detail the best and safest method to perform the task. This is the purpose for which a permit-to-work system was created. The most likely qualified person to at least assist in implementing the laboratory permit-to-work system will work within the laboratory itself. He or she should be well versed in all aspects of the safe handling of the materials used and stored within the laboratory, and have direct access to up-to-date safety literature.

The permit to work is an application for permission to work within the laboratory. It must stipulate exactly which system within the laboratory will be affected and what, if any, stored material might be in the area. A permit to work should be required for even minor tasks (such as replacing light bulbs, general building maintenance, and window cleaning) that demand general access to the laboratory.

With the permit request, the worker who is asked to enter the laboratory will have access to information concerning laboratory activities that might, if disrupted, create an unsafe condition. This is also true for contractors hired to work within the laboratory. Therefore, they should request permission for entry to the laboratory through the permit-to-work system.

In order to obtain approval, the permit to work should detail all necessary safeguards as determined by a risk assessment. Many permits to work within a laboratory are accompanied by a hot-work permit if flammable gases might be released. In addition, biological or radiological hazards might be encountered, and laboratory personnel are most probably the best source of reference for safeguarding measures.

As with all permits to work, location, date, and time of the work to be done should be listed, along with the duration of the permit. Most permits should expire after one day so that any changes within the laboratory can be assessed. The permit should list the qualified person within the laboratory, and provide in detail the safety measures that will be taken. The work permit should not be approved by the laboratory's qualified person, but rather by someone who can review the safeguarding methods with an impartial viewpoint.

Any work performed on the wastewater or waste disposal systems within the laboratory, up to the first external manhole from the laboratory, should be subjected to the critical review provided by the permit-to-work system so that a risk assessment of the potential hazards of accumulated hazardous materials within the system can be completed. The confined space permit system's criteria will serve as a good resource for risk assessment, atmospheric testing, and personal protective equipment requirements, even if the waste system is not determined to be a confined space.

Permit to Work–Asbestos

"Asbestos is a problem because, as a toxic substance and a known carcinogen, it can cause several serious diseases in humans. Symptoms of these diseases typically develop over a period of years following asbestos exposure" (EPA 2005).

Because of the hazards outlined in this statement, all work with asbestos materials shall be performed in compliance with current federal and state regulations. All work involving the removal of asbestos-containing materials must be undertaken by contractors licensed for asbestos removal. However, some maintenance or facilities workers might come into contact with asbestos-containing materials while performing their daily activities. Such a scenario is the type of activity that should be addressed by a permit-to-work system.

The permit system will be of benefit only if all asbestos-containing material within the facility has been identified before the work has begun so that all those involved with the permit-to-work system will be able to adequately assess the risk. Once permission is requested to perform work and the material to be disturbed indicated, the approving authority should confirm, by referring to the previously compiled asbestos inventory, whether or not the material does contain asbestos. If the material is not on the list, and there is any question whatsoever that the material might contain asbestos, the material should be tested before any work is performed. If testing confirms that asbestos is present, it should then be added to the asbestos materials list for future reference.

Once the permit document is received by the approving authority, he or she should then determine whether the task can be performed by in-house staff or by a contractor, because the ultimate goal is to prevent atmospheric contamination and the hazard it creates to both workers involved in the task and those who are not involved but who might be exposed.

The Occupational Safety and Health Act carries very specific regulations concerning work with asbestos (OSHA 1910.1001) and the permit-approving authority will have to assess whether in-house workers are capable of performing the task safely. The facilities management will want to monitor the job carefully through the permit-to-work system, no matter who performs the work. To this end, the permit must accurately locate the work area and note the time and date of the work. The exact nature of the work to be performed should be provided in detail so the approval authority and the qualified person can assess the risk and extent of possible contamination. Safety measures should be listed in detail, including personal protective equipment required, confinement methods, air-monitoring procedures, emergency procedures, decontamination, and waste disposal. Because of the risks presented by asbestos contamination, a similarly detailed permit to work must be presented and approved before any work is started by either a licensed contractor or in-house personnel.

A qualified person should be assigned to inspect the work area setup and its safety, control, and monitoring measures after those measures have been put in place, but before any work takes place. A qualified person should inspect the work area after the work is completed, but before any containment structure is removed, to make sure that the area is ready for release. At this time, atmospheric monitoring should indicate that the asbestos fiber count is within the preestablished limits.

References

American National Standards Institute (ANSI). 2001. ANSI/ASSE A10.8-2001. *Scaffolding Safety Requirements*. New York: ANSI.

______. 2008. ANSI/ASSE Z244.1-2008. *Control of Hazardous Energy—Lockout/Tagout and Alternative Methods.* New York: ANSI.

______. 2009. ANSI/ASSE Z117.1-2009. *Safety Requirements for Confined Spaces*. New York: ANSI.

Colonna, Guy R., ed. 2010. *Fire Protection Guide to Hazardous Materials*. Quincy, MA: NFPA.

Environmental Protection Agency (EPA). 2005. *Asbestos and Vermiculite* (retrieved November 1, 2007). www.epa.gov/asbestos/pubs/asbreg.html

National Fire Protection Association (NFPA). 2012. NFPA 70E, *Standard for Electrical Safety in the Workplace.* Quincy, MA: NFPA.

Occupational Safety and Health Administration (OSHA). 1996a. OSHA 29 CFR 1910.147. *The Control of Hazardous Energy (Lockout/Tagout)* (retrieved November 1, 2007). www.osha.gov/pls/oshaweb/owadisp.show_document?p_id=9804&p_table=STANDARDS

______. 1996b. OSHA 29 CFR 1926.451 (a)(3). *General Requirements* (retrieved November 1, 2007). www.osha.gov/pls/oshaweb/owadisp.show_document?p_table=standards&p_id=10752

______. 2008. 29 CFR 1910, Subpart S, Electrical (accessed March 21, 2011). www.osha.gov/pls/oshaweb/owadisp.show_document?p_table=STANDARDS&p_id=10135

5

Basic Safety Engineering

John Mroszczyk

Learning Objectives

- Become familiar with *designing for safety*—the thought process involved in identifying hazards and using the design-for-safety hierarchy. From top priority to lowest priority, the hierarchy helps management eliminate the hazard or reduce the risk to an acceptable level by engineering design, providing a safety device, or providing warnings, instructions, and special operating procedures.
- Know the basic areas of safety engineering: noise control, walking-working surfaces, industrial/commercial ventilation, lockout/tagout, power tools, machine safeguarding, and material handling.
- Recognize the hazards involved in each of these basic areas and the role that designing for safety plays in each area.

A *HAZARD* IS the potential to cause injury or damage. *Risk* is the product of the probability of an occurrence and the severity of the injury or damage. A *safe* design is a design in which all hazards have been eliminated, or the associated risk reduced to an acceptable level. A *defective* design is one in which there is little or no attempt to eliminate or control hazards.

It is most effective to eliminate or control hazards during the design phase. All too often this is not what happens. Risks are frequently managed after the design has been released. The notion of addressing hazards during the design phase dates as far back as 1946 (NSC 1946). *Designing for safety* is a formal process that incorporates hazard analysis at the beginning of the design. Safety methodology should be applied to the design of products, equipment, machines, facilities, buildings, and job tasks.

NIOSH has since embarked on a national initiative called *Prevention Through Design* (PTD), which takes a broader view of designing for safety. Schulte (2008) defines the process as:

> the practice of anticipating and "designing out" potential occupational safety and health hazards and risks associated with new processes, structures, equipment, or tools, and organizing work, such that it takes into consideration the construction, maintenance, decommissioning, and disposal/recycling of waste material, and recognizing the business and social benefits of doing so.

Designing for Safety: The Process

Once a preliminary design concept has been proposed, the first step in designing for safety is to identify the hazards. All available background information should be collected, reviewed, and analyzed. Important background information would include, for example, the foreseeable use and misuse, the environment, and the capabilities and behaviors of the user. The injury history can be useful in assessing what the uses and misuses are. In the workplace, the injury history can be obtained from injury records within the plant or related industries, from Occupational Safety and Health Administration (OSHA) statistics (www.osha.gov), or National Institute of Occupational Safety and Health (NIOSH) statistics (www.cdc.gov/niosh/). The injury history for a product can be obtained by contacting the National Injury Information Clearinghouse.

Information on human capability and behavior can be found in references on ergonomics and human factors, such as Woodson (1992), Hammer (1972), Salvendy (2006), Cott (1963), the National Safety Council (NSC 1988), or Plog (2002). Examples of human behavior as it relates to product and equipment design within the corresponding design approach (Woodson 1992) are:

1. Adults often avoid reading instructions. Products and equipment should be designed as nearly as possible to be understandable without reading special instructions.
2. Adults are absent-minded, easily distracted, or may be in a hurry. Products and equipment should have protective features in the event that the user forgets to press a button, turn a knob, follow prescribed steps, or is in a hurry.
3. Adults tend to believe they are smart enough to take shortcuts. During design, potential hazards due to taking short cuts should be eliminated.
4. Many adults are willing to take risks. Products and equipment should be designed so that they can only be operated in a safe manner.
5. Children are extremely curious. They investigate, examine, and try to play with many things.
6. Small children investigate by touching things, putting their fingers or hands into openings, and putting things into their mouths. Holes should be small enough in diameter so that a child's finger will not fit. Product finishes should be nontoxic. Products should be designed so that parts that are small enough to be swallowed do not come off.
7. Children like to climb or reach for things on surfaces that they cannot see. Products, such as stoves, should be designed so that children cannot reach the controls or the burners.
8. Children will always use a toy in a different manner. Toys should be strong enough that they do not come apart or break. There should be no sharp edges, corners, or projections.
9. Children are unsteady on their feet. Products, equipment, or other objects that will be used around children should be designed with the consideration that a child may fall on it. There should be no sharp edges, corners, projections, or breakable materials.

Industry standards and regulations also should be reviewed. Some of the organizations that write standards include the American National Standards Institute (ANSI), Underwriter's Laboratories (UL), the American Society for Testing and Materials (ASTM), the Society of Automotive Engineers (SAE), and the National Fire Protection Association (NFPA). However, it should be noted that standards generally have serious limitations that the designer needs to be aware of. There are a number of reasons why deficiencies may exist. A standard cannot address every possible design situation that may be encountered. The standard-writing process (negotiation and compromise) can severely weaken the safety content of a standard. There may be hazards that are not addressed, or a standard for a particular product or piece of equipment may not even exist. Federal regulations (OSHA, Environmental Protection Agency, Department of Transportation, and U.S. Consumer Product Safety Commission) and building codes are other sources of information.

Many hazards can be readily identified. *Kinematic* hazards occur whenever moving parts create cutting, pinching, or crushing points. Any mechanical component that rotates, reciprocates, or moves transversely should be examined for kinematic hazards. Any product or piece of equipment that vibrates or emits noise should be checked for high noise or vibration levels. Hot surfaces and hot substances should be checked to ensure that the temperature will not cause scalding or burn injuries. The uncontrolled release of energy from energy storage devices, such as springs, capacitors, and compressed gas storage cylinders, is hazardous. Electrical circuits, toxic materials, and flammable materials, are some other potential hazards.

There can be hidden hazards. One approach for identifying hidden hazards is a "what if" analysis. Using this method, a series of questions is posed focusing on each component, including manufacturing processes, materials, maintenance, wear and tear, operator error, and operator capabilities. Typical questions might be: "What if component A does not operate as intended?" "What if the user forgets to perform routine maintenance?" "What if the user does not follow the step-by-step instructions?" or "What if part X wears out?"

Once all the hazards have been identified, the first priority is to eliminate or reduce the risk to an acceptable level. Examples of eliminating a hazard by engineering design include using a ramp in place of a single step, placing a guard over critical switches to prevent an inadvertent activation, using an irregular bolt pattern so that a critical bracket cannot be installed upside down, and making components of a child's toy large enough so that they are not a choking hazard. If a design alternative does not eliminate the hazard or provide adequate risk reduction, then a safety device should be considered. Examples of safety devices include *dead-man controls* on lawn mowers and snow throwers, guards on table saws, obstruction detection sensors on automatic garage door openers, and chain brakes on chain saws. A dead-man-type control is a control that requires continuing operator contact for the machine to operate. The machine stops when the operator lets go of the control.

In some cases it is not possible to achieve adequate risk reduction by a design change or by providing a suitable safety device. Under these circumstances, warnings and/or written instructions should be provided. A warning can be either an audible or visual alarm, such as a back-up alarm on a construction vehicle, or a warning label. Examples of residual and latent hazards that would require a warning label are not using a grinding wheel in excess of the rated speed, not using a flammable liquid near an open flame, or exposure to radiation hazards. A warning should never be used in place of an alternative design or safety device.

A warning label or sign should alert the user to the specific hazard, the seriousness of the hazard, the consequences of interaction with the hazard, and the ways to avoid the hazard. The ANSI Z535 series of standards sets forth a simple and straightforward format for designing warning labels and signs (ANSI 2006b–c, 2007a–d). A warning sign or label should consist of a signal word panel, a message panel, and an optional symbol panel (see Figure 1). The label can be in a horizontal or a vertical format.

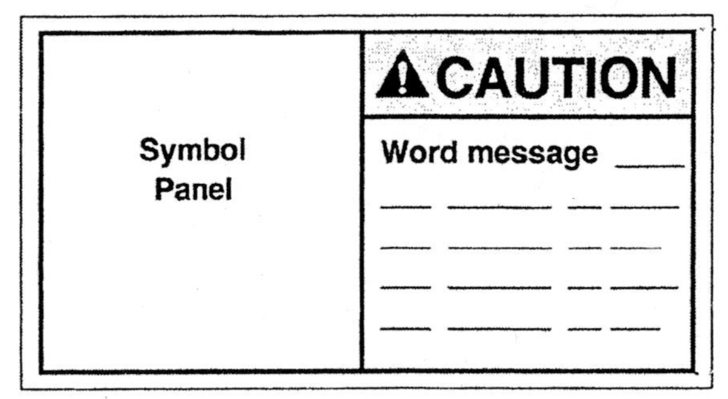

FIGURE 1. Warning label, horizontal format
(*Source:* ANSI 2007c)

Colors should conform to ANSI Z535.1, *Safety Color Code* (ANSI 2006b). This standard establishes uniformity for colors used in safety signs, safety labels, and other areas where warnings are required. The specifications are in terms of the Munsell Notation System, a system of specifications based on hue, value (lightness), and chroma (IES 2003). The hue scale consists of 100 steps in a circle containing five principal and five intermediate hues. The value scale contains ten steps from black to white (0 to 10). The chroma scale contains steps from neutral gray to highly saturated. For example, standard safety red has a Munsell hue of 7.5R and a Munsell value/chroma of 4.0/14. Standard safety green has a Munsell hue of 7.5G and a Munsell value/chroma of 4.0/9. The Munsell notation for safety white is N9.0 and safety black is N1.5 (ANSI 2006b).

The signal word panel contains the signal word. A safety alert symbol should also be included for personal injury hazards. The three-tiered hierarchy of signal words are DANGER, WARNING, and CAUTION. DANGER with the safety alert symbol indicates an imminently hazardous situation which, if not avoided, will result in death or serious injury. This signal word should be used only in the most extreme situations. The word DANGER shall be safety white on a safety red background. WARNING with the safety alert symbol indicates a potentially hazardous situation which, if not avoided, could result in death or serious injury.

The word WARNING shall be safety black on a safety orange background. CAUTION with the safety alert symbol indicates a potentially hazardous situation which, if not avoided, may result in minor or moderate injury. The word CAUTION shall be safety black on a safety yellow background. CAUTION without the safety alert symbol indicates a potentially hazardous situation that may result in property damage.

The message panel should describe the hazard, the consequences of not avoiding the hazard, and ways to avoid the hazard. The lettering should be black on a white background or white on a black background. The message should be written in action sentences rather than passive ones (ANSI 2007c). For example, "Keep hands away from rotating blade" should be used rather than "Your hand must be kept away from rotating blade," or "Lockout power before servicing equipment" should be used instead of "Power must be locked out before servicing equipment." Use wording such as "Turn off power if jam occurs" instead of "Turn off power in the event a jam occurs."

The optional safety symbol is a graphic to convey the hazard without words. ANSI Z535.3 lists criteria for the design of safety symbols (ANSI 2007b). The user population for a proposed symbol should be carefully studied. A symbol that is to be used in a multilingual environment should be evaluated with a multilingual audience focus group. Figure 2 shows several safety symbols that have passed the ANSI Z535.3 criteria for acceptance: (a) an entanglement hazard—hand and gears, and (b) a person falling on a surface (ANSI 2007b).

A warning should be durable and placed in an area where it will be visible. The warning label should last as long as the product itself. A label that has faded or fallen off is of no use. Multilanguage labels may be required depending on the users.

FIGURE 2. Examples of acceptable safety symbols (*Source:* ANSI 2007b)

In many instances, instructions telling the user how to use the product or machine will be required. It would be preferable to place the instructions directly on the product or machine. When this is not possible, an instruction/operation manual should accompany the product or equipment. The instruction manual should provide directions on the proper use, installation, assembly, and maintenance of the product or piece of equipment. Instructions should be clear, concise, and worded using positive language, which tells the user what to do. Installation/assembly instructions should note the proper installation/assembly sequence and be logical and easily understood. There should be warnings of the consequences of not following the proper installation or assembly procedure. The instruction manual should include a duplication of the warning labels that are on the product or piece of equipment.

Administrative procedures, such as training and/or special operating procedures, should be implemented when warnings are not suitable. End users should develop and implement training programs based on the proper use, installation, assembly, and maintenance procedures outlined in the manual provided by the manufacturer. For example, forklift drivers need to be trained in the proper use of forklift trucks. Lockout/tagout is an example of a special operating procedure implemented by the end user when machinery or equipment is serviced.

Once a product or piece of equipment becomes operational, its use should be monitored so that the safety can be improved. This requires anticipating, identifying, and evaluating current hazards as well as new hazards, and monitoring field data. The analysis and investigation of incidents in the field can be used to improve current or future designs.

Walking and Working Surfaces

Falls are one of the leading causes of injury and death (Marpet and Sapienza 2003). Many factors may contribute to a fall besides walking-surface hazards. These include mental impairments, physical impairments, age, attentiveness, fatigue, and footwear. Engineers

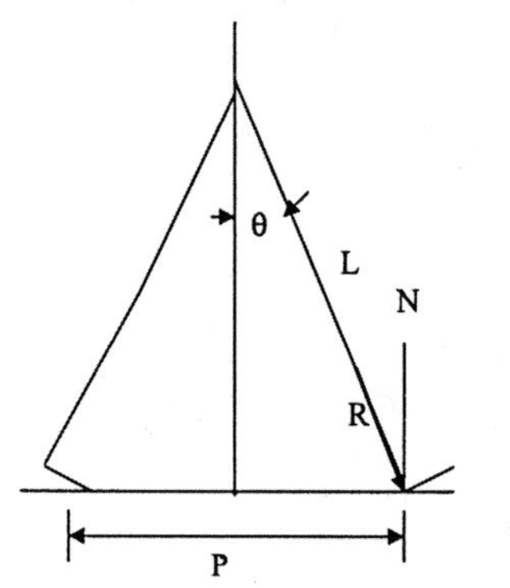

FIGURE 3. Walking on a level surface

can design safety features into walking surfaces to accommodate humans, such as handrails, skid resistance, proper stairway tread and risers, ramps with an appropriate incline, and color contrast to provide depth of field.

An understanding of the biomechanics of walking provides insight into the causes of falls (Chapman 2008, Rosen 2000, Templer 1994). The normal gait cycle on a level surface starts with pushing off with the ball and then the big toe of the rear foot. The other leg swings forward while bent at the hip, knee, and ankle. The bending of the leg allows it to clear the ground. The swinging leg straightens at the knee as the heel strikes the ground. The body weight is momentarily supported by the ball/big toe of the rear foot and the heel of the forward foot. The weight then shifts forward as the point of contact on the forward foot shifts from the heel, to the arch, to the ball, then to the big toe. The forward foot then becomes the rear foot, pushing off as the other foot is now swung forward and the cycle repeats.

Walking occurs automatically. We do not consciously think about each foot's placement as we walk. People fall when their normal gait is suddenly interrupted. The body cannot adjust in time, their center of gravity moves outside of the base provided by their feet, and they fall. Typically this occurs when one foot slips or is blocked from moving forward.

Pedestrians generally slip and fall when the force applied to the floor by the feet during walking overcomes the resisting force at the floor/shoe interface. Under dry conditions the resisting force, or traction, is related to the *coefficient of friction* (COF) between heel and floor. The COF is defined as the force required to move one surface over another divided by the force pressing the two surfaces together. The traction provided by a floor surface can be affected by humidity, precipitation, oil, dust, dirt, debris, or any other foreign materials that may be on the floor.

There is some controversy as to whether the static or dynamic COF is most relevant in walking. The difference between the two can be illustrated by the classic high-school physics experiment. Consider a block resting on a horizontal surface. The *static* coefficient is the horizontal force that must be applied to the block to start the block moving, divided by the weight of the block. The *dynamic* coefficient is the horizontal force that must be applied to keep the block moving, divided by the weight of the block (Templer 1994). The static coefficient is usually higher than the dynamic coefficient (Sotter 1995). The advocates for static friction argue that no motion is observed between the shoe and the floor during walking. Advocates for dynamic friction argue that the shoe does not stop moving during walking. In the United States, the *static coefficient of friction* (SCOF) is used to rate walking surfaces (Templer 1994, Sotter 1995).

A theoretical model (Templer 1994, Meserlian 1995) used for analyzing walking on a level surface is shown in Figure 3. The angle θ is the angle that the forward leg makes with the vertical. The force R is the force applied to the heel. The forces H and N are the components of the resultant force R and at an angle θ to the walking surface. The length L is the length of the leg from hip to heel and P is the pace (step length). The required SCOF ($\mu = H/N$) is:

$$\mu = \frac{H}{N} = \frac{R \sin \theta}{R \cos \theta} = \tan \theta \text{ and } \sin \theta = \frac{P}{2L} \quad (1)$$

For example, a person with a leg length of 32 inches and a pace of about 21 inches:

$$\sin \theta = \frac{21}{(2)(32)} \text{ or } \theta = 19.16 \quad (2)$$

then

$$\mu = \tan 19.16 = 0.35.$$

The pace and leg length vary in the general population depending on sex and size of the person. The pace can also vary with walking speed. For example, tests done on human subjects (Meserlian 1995) found the range in calculated SCOF to be 0.30 to 0.46 as the walking speed was varied from very slow (69 steps per minute) to very fast (138 steps per minute).

Foreign substances such as liquid, grease, and oil on a walking surface can make an otherwise safe floor slippery. Usually, an unexpected wet, oily, or greasy spot on an otherwise safe floor creates the problem. As the heel touches down, the liquid or substance cannot move out of the way quickly enough. The heel is momentarily supported by the liquid film, not the floor's surface. This phenomenon (hydroplaning) is familiar to anybody who has ever driven too fast on a wet road (Sotter 1995). The presence of the intermediate material makes the SCOF of the bare floor surface irrelevant. Under these circumstances it is more appropriate to use the term *slip resistance* of the surface in place of SCOF. It should be noted that in some of the literature, the term SCOF is used interchangeably with slip resistance.

Slip resistance with foreign substances can be increased by imparting roughness to the surface. Typically this is done by grinding or sanding the surface, applying coatings that contain abrasive particles, or broom-finishing in the case of concrete. The roughness should be deep enough and sharp enough to penetrate the film or contaminant. A small representative area should be tested before the entire floor is treated.

Building and fire codes generally require that floor surfaces be *slip resistant* without specifying any particular surface or a numerical value. Historically, a SCOF of 0.50 or higher has been considered adequate for most pedestrian safety (Kohr 1994). A more recent guideline, ANSI A1264.2, reaffirms the 0.50 threshold for safety (ANSI 2006a). Since the traction requirement is the same, regardless of what the person is walking on, the 0.50 safety threshold is also used to evaluate surfaces where foreign substances may be present.

There are many factors that must be considered when selecting a surface material or maintaining a walking surface. There is no design standard that can control shoe material. Therefore, any recommendation for flooring material should assume that pedestrians may be wearing slippery shoes. Other factors to be considered include people walking fast, running, or turning, the age and physical capability of the users, and foreign substances. An office area on an upper floor could be assumed to be dry, while a ground floor entrance lobby is probably going to be wet during inclement weather. Other areas where foreign substances will likely be found on the floor are produce areas, cafeterias, repair garages, machine shops, and restaurants. Under some circumstances a slip resistance greater than 0.50 may be required.

Table 1 lists the SCOF for a representative sample of flooring materials (Templer 1994). Note that many floor materials such as quarry tile, brick pavers, exposed aggregate, and granite are unsafe with leather soles, using the 0.50 guideline.

TABLE 1

Coefficient of Friction for Selected Dry Materials

Material	Leather Shoe	Neolite Shoe
Brushed concrete, new, against grain	0.75	0.90
Asphalt tile, waxed, heavy-use area	0.56	0.47
Smooth steel, rusted slightly	0.54	0.49
Asphalt, old, in parking lot	0.53	0.64
Steel checker plate, rusted moderately	0.50	0.64
Quarry tile, unglazed	0.49	0.60
Thermoplastic, old, on crosswalk	0.45	0.86
Brick pavers, new, on stair	0.43	0.73
Exposed aggregate, pea gravel	0.41	0.57
Granite stairs, old exterior	0.40	0.66
Plywood "A" side, unfinished, with grain	0.39	0.75
Plywood "A" side, unfinished, against grain	0.39	0.75

(*Source:* Templer 1994)

TABLE 2

Slip Resistance of Floor and Tread Finishes

Material	Dry, Unpolished	Wet
Clay tiles (Carborundum finish)	> 0.75	> 0.75
Carpet	> 0.75	0.40 to < 0.75
Clay tiles (textured)	> 0.75	0.40 to < 0.75
Cork tiles	> 0.75	0.40 to < 0.75
PVC (with nonslip granules)	> 0.75	0.40 to < 0.75
PVC	> 0.75	0.20 to < 0.40
Rubber (sheets or tiles)	> 0.75	< 0.20
Mastic asphalt	0.40 to < 0.75	0.40 to < 0.75
Vinyl asbestos tiles	0.40 to < 0.75	< 0.40
Linoleum	0.40 to < 0.75	0.20 to < 0.40
Concrete	0.40 to < 0.75	0.20 to < 0.40
Granolithic	0.40 to < 0.75	0.20 to < 0.40
Cast iron	0.40 to < 0.75	0.20 to < 0.40
Clay tiles	0.40 to < 0.75	0.20 to < 0.40
Terrazzo	0.40 to < 0.75	0.20 to < 0.40

(*Source:* Templer 1994)

Table 2 lists the slip resistance of some flooring materials (Templer 1994). In particular, linoleum, clay tiles, concrete, and terrazzo are unsafe when wet.

The control of slipping hazards may not end with the design and specification of a flooring material. For example, cleaning and maintenance can degrade the slip resistance of many floor materials. Inadequate rinsing of cleaning compounds, inappropriate floor finishes, wax residue, and spilled liquids can create an unsafe condition. Administrative measures (floor safety programs) may therefore be required in some commercial and workplace establishments to deal with these foreseeable events.

A floor safety program should include regular inspections. For some establishments it may be necessary to measure the slip resistance several times during the year. The slip resistance should be checked after the floor is cleaned and/or a new finish is applied. Supermarkets, in particular, should do periodic walk-arounds to check for foreign substances on the floor. The frequency of these inspections may need to be every 15 to 30 minutes, depending on the area. Employees should be trained to clean up foreign substances as soon as they are found. A warning sign or a warning cone should be placed in the area, particularly if an employee cannot remain to warn customers. Extra janitorial service should be employed during inclement weather.

Drag sleds are one class of devices for measuring the SCOF of dry surfaces. A drag-sled test device consists of a known weight, which is drawn across a surface. The force required to overcome the initial friction divided by the weight is the SCOF. ASTM F609-05, *Standard Test Method for Using a Horizontal Pull Slip Meter (HPS)*, standardizes drag-sled devices (ASTM 2005). These devices should only be used on dry surfaces. The susceptibility to sticktion, operator-induced variables, and an inability to mimic the dynamics of a human foot striking a surface severely limit the usefulness of drag sleds. Sticktion is the temporary bond created from water being squeezed out of the interface between the test foot and the surface. Sticktion produces unrealistically high readings on wet surfaces (DiPilla and Vidal 2002).

Articulated inclinable testers are another class of instruments for measuring surface traction. These devices use the striking angle at the onset of slipping to determine the slip resistance. The English XL uses a footpad that is thrust out onto the surface, just as the heel does during walking, by actuating a force cylinder. The force cylinder is attached to a mast. The angle of the mast is varied with an adjustment wheel. The inclination of the mast at the onset of slipping provides a direct reading of the slip resistance or slip index (the slip index is simply the tangent of the angle). The English XL can be used on dry and wet surfaces.

The Brungraber Mark II is another articulated inclinable tester that is approved for dry and wet testing. This device uses a 10-pound weight on an inclinable frame. The angle of the frame is adjusted after each time the weight is released until a slip occurs. The English XL and the Brungraber Mark II produce comparable slip-resistance readings under both dry and wet conditions, provided the Mark II is used with a grooved test foot (Grieser et al. 2002).

A *ramp* is an inclined walking surface. Walking on a ramped surface is similar to walking on a flat surface. However, people tend to lean forward when ascending a ramp and backward when descending. Most building codes, including the Americans with Disabilities Act (ADA), limit the maximum slope to 1 in 12 (8.3 percent).

Figure 4 shows the same theoretical model as Figure 3, except the person is walking on a ramp with slope α. It is assumed that the pace (P) is the same as on a level surface. The SCOF ($\mu = H/N$) is:

$$\mu_{\text{ramp}} = \frac{H}{N} = \frac{R\sin(\alpha + \theta)}{R\cos(\alpha + \theta)} = \tan(\alpha + \theta) = \frac{\tan\alpha + \tan\theta}{1 - (\tan\alpha)(\tan\theta)} \tag{3}$$

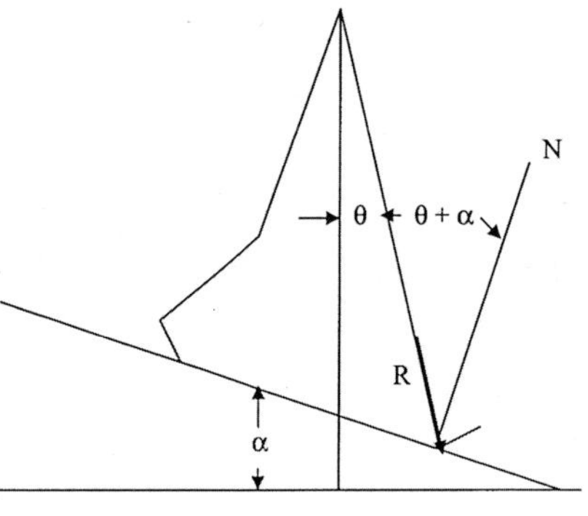

FIGURE 4. Walking on a sloped surface

TABLE 3

SCOF for Level and Ramped Walking Surfaces

Level	1:20	1:18	1:16	1:14	1:12	1:10	1:8	1:6	1:4
0.80	0.89	0.90	0.91	0.92	0.95	0.98	1.03	1.12	1.31
0.75	0.83	0.84	0.85	0.87	0.89	0.92	0.97	1.05	1.23
0.70	0.78	0.79	0.80	0.81	0.83	0.86	0.90	0.98	1.15
0.65	0.72	0.73	0.74	0.76	0.78	0.80	0.84	0.92	1.07
0.60	0.67	0.68	0.69	0.70	0.72	0.74	0.78	0.85	1.00
0.55	0.62	0.62	0.63	0.65	0.66	0.69	0.72	0.79	0.93
0.50	0.56	0.57	0.58	0.59	0.61	0.63	0.67	0.73	0.86
0.45	0.51	0.52	0.53	0.54	0.55	0.58	0.61	0.67	0.79
0.40	0.46	0.47	0.47	0.49	0.50	0.52	0.53	0.61	0.72
0.35	0.41	0.41	0.42	0.43	0.45	0.47	0.50	0.55	0.66
0.30	0.36	0.36	0.37	0.38	0.39	0.41	0.44	0.49	0.59

(*Source:* Templer 1994)

The tan θ term is the SCOF for a flat walking surface, so that Equation 3 can be rewritten as:

$$\mu_{\text{ramp}} = \frac{\tan \alpha + \mu_{\text{flat}}}{1 - \mu_{\text{flat}} \tan \alpha} \qquad (4)$$

Equation 4 indicates that sloped surfaces require a higher SCOF than flat surfaces. Table 3 shows a tabulation using the mathematical expression for μ_{ramp}. The column on the left lists the SCOF on a level surface. The remaining numbers list the required SCOF necessary to maintain the same level-surface SCOF for each slope.

It is interesting to note that for a ramp slope of 1 in 12 (1:12), a SCOF of 0.61 is required to maintain an equivalent 0.50 level-surface SCOF.

A trip and fall usually occurs when one foot becomes caught or is blocked from moving forward. Recognized tripping hazards include extension cords, mats and runners, walking-surface hardware, torn or loose carpeting, merchandise left on the floor, speed bumps, and wheel stops. Mats and runners should have beveled edges. The underside should have a suction design or be secured so that the mat or runner does not slide. Speed bumps should be clearly marked with a contrasting color according to ANSI Z535.1 (2006b). Wheel stops should also be marked with contrasting color and should not be placed in pedestrian walkways. Tripping hazards in the workplace include tools, pipes, debris, wood, and other objects that are left on walking/working surfaces.

Abrupt changes in elevation are also tripping hazards. Research on the effect of step height on gait dynamics (Gray 1990) established a maximum allowable step height of 6.7 mm (about 0.25 inch). Safety standards, such as ASTM F1637 (2009) limit a vertical change in elevation in a walking surface to less than 0.25 inch. Height changes between 0.25 and 0.50 inch should be beveled with a slope no greater than 1:2. Height changes greater than 0.50 inch should be transitioned by a ramped walking surface.

Low-level objects can also create a tripping hazard. These hazards are usually found in mercantile establishments. Customers may not see a low-level object in their immediate vicinity as they move about the sales floor. Examples of such tripping hazards are merchandise displays, pallets, baskets, boxes, bags, stools, pails, and flatbed trucks. Merchandise displays and any other objects placed on the sales floor should be at least 36 inches high so they will be readily visible.

The gait cycle on stairs is different from walking on level surfaces (Templer 1994). In descent, the lead foot swings forward and stops directly over the nosing. At the same time, the heel of the rear foot lifts off the previous tread; the body is supported by the forward foot. The rear foot then begins to swing forward, and the cycle is repeated. In ascent, the leading foot moves forward and is lowered on the tread, well forward of the nosing. The rear foot then rises tiptoe, lifting the body upward and forward. The rear leg is then raised and swings forward to the next step. The human mind automatically controls the foot placement on subsequent steps based on the initial step geometry. This results in walking up and down stairs without a lot of conscious thought.

Falls on stairways can be attributed to slippery treads, tripping hazards, poor visual contrast, different tread/riser dimensions, and poor geometry. Slip-resistant surfaces are an important factor for safe stairs. The nosing area is most critical because this is the area that the foot contacts during descent. Surfaces with a low SCOF, such as smooth concrete, marble, terrazzo, ceramic tile, and polished surfaces, should be avoided. Abrasive strips, slip-resistant nosings, or inlaid abrasive material are some of the measures that can be taken to improve the slip resistance of stair treads.

Anything on the stair treads that can snag or block a foot is a tripping hazard. Tripping hazards on stairways include loose or frayed carpeting and loose or raised leading edges. Raised nails or screws are also common tripping hazards on stairways. Carpeting should be tightly fitted. Stair treads should be flat and planar.

Poor visual contrast can also lead to falls on stairs, especially during descent. This situation usually arises with concrete stairs and carpeted stairs. The lack of visual contrast makes the stair treads appear to blend together. If the leading edge of the tread is not clearly defined, cognitive misinformation can lead to improper foot placement. Overstepping or understepping due to such misleading information can lead to falls. Color contrast provided at the leading edge and step illumination are some of the measures that can be taken to improve the delineation of stair treads. Step illumination can be small lights along the sidewalls or in the risers that illuminate the steps. Illuminated strips embedded in the step nosings can also be used to illuminate steps in dark environments.

Safe stairs are also related to tread-riser geometry (Templer 1994). Risers between 6.3 and 8.9 inches create fewer missteps during ascent. When descending, treads between 11.5 and 14.2 inches and risers between 4.6 and 7.2 inches result in the fewest missteps. OSHA (1910.24) permits tread-riser combinations that result in a rise angle between 30°35′ (approximately 6.5-inch riser/11-inch tread) and 49°54′ (approximately 9.5-inch riser/8-inch tread). Most commercial building codes and the NFPA 101, *Life Safety Code*, require risers between 4 and 7 inches and treads greater than 11 inches (NFPA 2009). The *International Residential Code* limits the maximum riser to 7.75 inches and the minimum tread depth to 10 inches (ICC 2006a). Local and state-adopted building codes should be referred to when designing or building stairs. Risers in the range of 7 inches, and treads in the range of 11 inches, are important factors in reducing falls on stairways (Cohen 2009).

Dimensional irregularities between risers and treads on a stairway are also important factors in stairway safety. When risers and treads vary, a person must unknowingly adjust his or her gait, leading to imbalance. Irregularities as little as 0.25 inches between adjacent treads and risers can disrupt a person's gait, leading to a fall (Cohen 2009).

An important stairway safety feature is a handrail. A handrail offers support for the user and provides a means to arrest a fall, regardless of the cause of the fall. The required handrail height may vary with local building codes. The *International Residential Code* requires a handrail height of 34 to 38 inches (ICC 2006a). Commercial codes permit a handrail height between 34 and 38 inches. OSHA (1910.23) requires a handrail height of 30 to 34 inches. More than one handrail may be required depending on the width of the stairway. Most building codes require intermediate handrails so that all portions of a stairway width are within 30 inches of a handrail.

Handrail assemblies should be able to resist a single concentrated load of 200 pounds applied in any direction and should have attachment devices and supporting structure to transfer this load to the appropriate structural elements of the building. Handrails should also be graspable. Circular cross-sections should have an outside diameter of at least 1.25 inches and not greater than 2 inches. If the handrail is not circular, it should have a perimeter dimension of at least 4 inches and not greater than 6.25 inches, with a maximum cross-section of 2.25 inches (ICC 2006b). Recent research has found that symmetric handrail shapes that are between 1.25 and 2.75 inches wide, with a height above the widest portion of the profile not exceeding 0.75 inches, are graspable as handrails in arresting falls (Dusenberry et al 2008).

Short flights of stairs (one or two risers) are extremely dangerous and should be avoided whenever possible. The reason is that the small change in elevation is so slight that it is not readily apparent. There are several safety measures that can be taken to reduce the risk of a fall for existing short-flight stairs or in cases where they cannot be avoided (NFPA 2006). The safety measures include prominent handrails, contrasting colors, step illumination, contrasting nosings, and warning signs. These measures make the steps more readily apparent to users; however, they do not eliminate the hazard.

Industrial/Commercial Ventilation

Industrial/commercial ventilation systems are mechanical systems designed to supply and exhaust air from an occupied space to reduce or eliminate airborne substances. Safety engineers design ventilation systems to control health hazards (cigarette smoke, dusts, toxic fumes, heat disorders), fire/explosion hazards (flammable vapors, dusts), and other hazards caused by airborne contaminants. Ventilation systems may also be used, for example, to prevent woodworking equipment from clogging by removing the sawdust from the cutting area.

Ventilation systems reduce the risk of a health or explosion hazard by lowering the concentration of the substance below maximum allowable limits. For example, the *threshold limit value* (TLV) of a substance is the concentration at which workers may be exposed on a regular basis without experiencing adverse health effects. OSHA 29 CFR 1910.1000 lists TLVs for many airborne contaminants. In the case of fire/explosion hazards, the lower explosion limit is the important threshold. The *lower explosive limit* (LEL) is the lower limit of flammability or explosibility of a gas or vapor at ambient temperature expressed as a percent of the gas or vapor in air by volume. The *NFPA Fire Protection Handbook* lists the fire-hazard properties of many liquids, gases, and volatile solids (NFPA 2008). In the case of heat control, the amount of ventilation should be such that the net effect of body metabolism, external work performed, evaporative heat losses, convective heat exchanges, and radiative heat exchanges do not produce excessive heat gain, potentially resulting in adverse health problems. OSHA regulations, NFPA standards, ANSI standards, and local and state building and fire prevention codes should be referred to in order to assess the amount of ventilation that may be required in a particular situation.

Industrial/commercial ventilation systems consist of fans, blowers, ducts, air-cleaning devices, and hoods. Fans and blowers generate airflow by creating a pressure difference in the system. Air-cleaning devices include electrostatic precipitators, fabric collectors, dust collectors, and filters. Exhaust hoods provide an entry point to capture the air. Ducts transport the air between the inlet, the fan or blower, and the exhaust.

A well-designed ventilation system consists of supply and exhaust. The supply system provides makeup air to replace the air that is exhausted. In most cases the supply air is tempered to suit the space. The amount of supply air should be approximately equal to the amount of air that is exhausted. Air should be discharged outdoors at a point where it will not cause a nuisance and where it cannot be drawn in by a ventilating system. Air should not be discharged into an attic or crawl space. Air-intake openings should be located a minimum of 10 feet from any hazardous or noxious contaminant, such as vents, chimneys, plumbing vents, streets, alleys, and loading docks (ICC 2006c).

There are two types of exhaust ventilation systems. *General ventilation* systems dilute the contaminated air with uncontaminated air. These systems are also known as *dilution ventilation* systems. General ventilation systems are most effective when the air contaminants are gases or vapors, are evenly dispersed, and do not pose a high health risk. These systems should be monitored carefully because the level of exposure is controlled by the amount of dilution air.

Local ventilation systems control the contaminants directly at the source. These systems are most effective when there are several large, fixed sources. In many circumstances, a local ventilation system is the only choice, as in the case of a contaminant source located directly in a worker's breathing area.

There are several basic principles of fluid mechanics that are used in the design of a ventilation system. The *static pressure* (SP) in a moving fluid is the pressure that would be exerted upon a surface moving with the velocity of the fluid. In ventilation ducts, the static pressure is the pressure that tends to burst (or collapse) the duct. The *velocity pressure* (VP) or *dynamic pressure* is the pressure that results from the kinetic energy of the moving fluid. The *total pressure* (TP) or *stagnation pressure* is the sum of the static pressure and the velocity pressure. In the design of ventilation systems, it is customary to express the pressure in inches of water (w.g.). The pressure under a 1-inch column of water is 0.036 psi. The relationship between the total pressure (TP), velocity pressure (VP), and static pressure (SP) is:

$$TP = SP + VP \tag{5}$$

where

$VP = 1/2\ \rho V^2$
ρ = mass density of the air
V = velocity of the air stream

The total pressure (TP), static pressure (SP), and velocity pressure (VP) can be illustrated in the manometer arrangement in Figure 5. In the first manometer, the total fluid pressure consists of the static pressure and the velocity pressure that impinges on the tube. The second manometer only reads the pressure acting on the duct wall, which is the static pressure. The third manometer reads the difference between the total pressure and the static pressure, which is the velocity pressure.

Another fluid mechanics principle is the conservation of mass, which requires that the flow that enters a duct must be the same as the flow that exits the duct. The principle of conversion of energy states that all the energy must be accounted for as the air goes from one point in the system to another. If "1" corresponds to some upstream condition and "2" corresponds to a downstream condition, the conservation of mass and energy can be stated mathematically (ACGIH 2010):

$$\text{conservation of mass: } \rho_1 V_1 A_1 = \rho_2 V_2 A_2 \quad (6)$$

$$\text{conservation of energy: } TP_1 = TP_2 + H_L \quad (7)$$

or

$$SP_1 + VP_1 = SP_2 + VP_2 + H_L$$

where

A = duct area
H_L = energy losses (gains)
ρ = fluid mass density

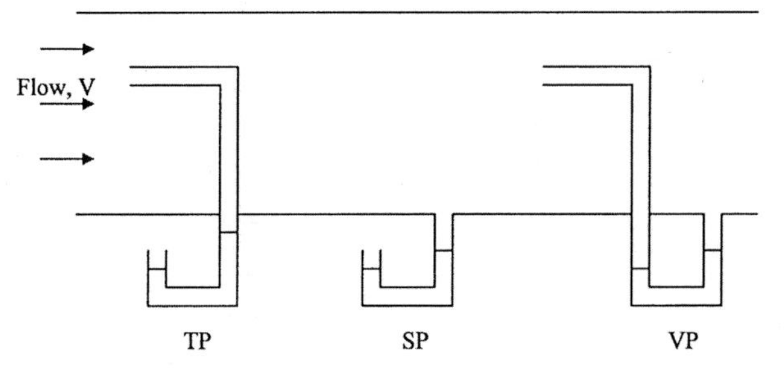

FIGURE 5. Total pressure (TP), static pressure (SP) and velocity pressure (VP) in a pressurized duct

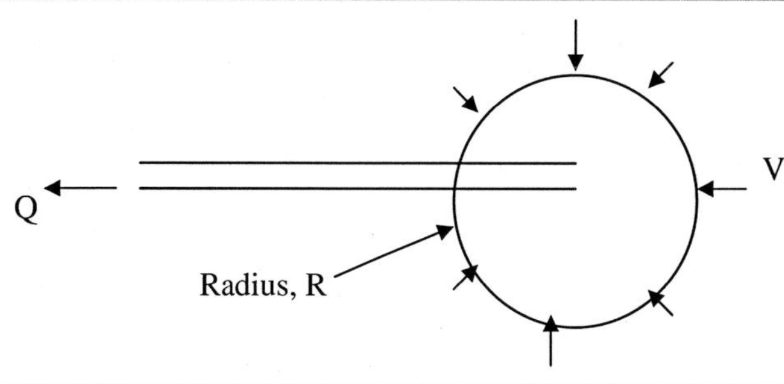

FIGURE 6. Point suction source

The energy losses, H_L, are usually expressed as the product of a loss coefficient and the velocity pressure. Loss coefficients depend on the particular loss mechanism. They can be found in a number of references (ACGIH 2010, Burton 1995) or may be provided by the equipment manufacturer.

The *capture velocity* is the minimum induced air velocity that is required to capture and convey the contaminant. This can be best illustrated by considering a point suction source, as shown in Figure 6. Using the principle of conservation of mass, with constant density, the induced velocity over a sphere of radius R is:

$$Q = V(4\pi R^3) \quad (8)$$

where

Q = volume suction flow rate
V = velocity at radius R

In order to entrain a particular contaminant located at a radius R, the suction flow, Q (cfm), must be equal to or greater than the capture velocity times the area of capture for that contaminant. Typical capture velocities are listed in Table 4. The velocity contour entering a typical hood is actually quite different from the point suction source depicted in Figure 6. Velocity contours for hoods are generally determined experimentally or provided by the vendor. Some velocity contours for basic hoods can be found in the literature (ACGIH 2010).

Once the contaminant has been drawn into the hood, the velocity in the duct must be such that the contaminant does not settle. The transport velocity is the minimum velocity that will move a particular

TABLE 4

Range of Capture Velocities

Dispersion of Contaminant	Contaminant	Capture Velocity (fpm)
Little motion	Evaporation from tanks, degreasing, etc.	75-100
Average motion	Intermittent container filling, low-speed conveyor transfers, welding, plating, pickling	100-200
High motion	Barrel filling, conveyor loading, crushers	200-500
Very high motion	Grinding, abrasive blasting, tumbling	500-2000

(*Source:* ACGIH 2010)

TABLE 5

Typical Transport Velocities

Contaminant	Example	Transport Velocity (fpm)
Vapors, gases, smoke	Vapors, gases, smoke	1000-2000.
Fumes	Welding	2000-2500
Very fine light dusts	Cotton lint, wood flour	2500-3000
Dry dusts and powders	Rubber dust, leather shavings, Bakelite molding power dust	3000-4000
Average industrial dusts	Grinding dust, limestone dust	3500-4000
Heavy dusts	Sawdust, metal turnings, lead dust	4000-4500
Heavy and moist	Lead dusts with small chips, moist cement dust, buffing lint, quick-lime dust	4500 and up

(*Source:* ACGIH 2010)

contaminant without settling. Typical values for the transport velocity are listed in Table 5.

The amount of ventilation required to reduce vapor concentrations is also important. The ventilation rate required to reduce steady-state vapor concentrations to acceptable levels can be calculated from Equation 9 (ACGIH 2004).

$$Q = \frac{G}{CK} \tag{9}$$

where

Q = ventilation rate (cfm)
G = vapor-generation rate (cfm)
C = acceptable concentration
K = a factor to allow for incomplete mixing

The rate of vapor generation for liquid solvents is expressed as

$$Q = \frac{\text{CONSTANT} \times \text{SG} \times \text{ER}}{\text{MV}} \tag{10}$$

where

CONSTANT is the volume in cubic feet that 1 pint of liquid will occupy at STP (70° and 29.2 in Hg) when vaporized
SG = specific gravity of the liquid
ER = evaporation rate of liquid
MV= molecular weight of liquid

The rate of vapor generation of a certain process can be calculated if the evaporation rate is known. The ventilation rate required to reduce the concentration can then be calculated.

In designing a ventilation system, the required ventilation rate in cfm may be specified by the equipment manufacturer (in the case of woodworking machines), building codes, the required capture velocity, the required transport velocity, or the vapor-generation rate. Once the flow enters the duct, there will be losses in static pressure. The fan or blower must supply enough pressure difference to pull the air through the ventilation system.

Losses arise from duct friction, turbulence in elbows, contractions, entries, and expansions. There are also hood-entry losses and equipment losses. The losses due to duct friction are a function of velocity, duct diameter, air density, air viscosity, and duct surface roughness. The Reynolds number (Re) and the relative roughness (e/D), both dimensionless quantities, characterize these parameters. The friction factor can be determined from the Moody diagram once the Reynolds number and the relative roughness have been determined. The Moody diagram is a plot of friction factor versus Reynolds number for various relative roughness values. The Moody diagram can be found in any basic text on fluid mechanics, ventilation design, or the *NFPA Fire Protection Handbook* chapter on hydraulics (NFPA 2008).

$$\text{Reynolds number: } \text{Re} = \frac{\rho VD}{\mu} \tag{11}$$

$$\text{Relative roughness} = \frac{e}{D} \tag{12}$$

where

e = absolute roughness
D = duct diameter (ft)
V = duct velocity (ft/sec)
ρ = air density (lbm/ft^3)
μ = air viscosity (lb-sec/ft^2)

Typical values for absolute roughness, e, are listed in Table 6. Once the friction factor has been determined from the Moody diagram, the duct friction loss, H_L, can be calculated from the following relationship:

$$H_L = f\left(\frac{L}{D}\right)VP \tag{13}$$

where

f = friction factor
D = duct diameter (ft)
L = duct length (ft)
VP = velocity pressure (psf)

There are many computer solutions, nomographs, and tabulations that make the computation of duct friction loss less tedious.

There are two components of losses associated with hoods. The first component occurs when the fluid is accelerated from still air into the hood. If "1" in the conservation of energy equation is still air, the static pressure (SP_1) and the velocity pressure (VP_1) are zero (or close to zero), so that $SP_2 = -VP_2$. This says that the static pressure drop due to acceleration of the air into the hood is equal to the velocity pressure.

The other component of losses associated with hoods is due to flow separation in the hood, which causes the flow to contract through a smaller diameter. Entry loss factors have been determined and are tabulated in a number of references (ACGIH or ASHRAE) or can be obtained from the manufacturer. For example, entry loss factors (H_h) can range from 0.93 for a plain inlet to 0.04 for a bellmouth inlet. The total loss associated with a hood, SP_{hood}, is

$$SP_{hood} = VP + (H_h \times VP) \tag{14}$$

where

VP = velocity pressure (psf)
H_h = hood-entry loss factor

TABLE 6

Absolute Roughness

Duct Material	Surface Roughness (ft)
PVC, ABS plastic	0.0001
Aluminum, stainless steel	0.0003
Rolled galvanized steel, spiral wound duct	0.0004
Galvanized steel, longitudinal seams	0.0005
Fiberglass reinforced plastic (strands showing)	0.003
Riveted steel, concrete	0.01

(*Source:* Burton 1995)

Most ventilation systems are complex, with many hoods and branches connecting to one main trunk line. Each branch in the system must be balanced to achieve the desired flow. The total flow entering the main trunk line from the branches must be accurate so that the fan or blower can be sized properly.

There are two methods for designing a ventilation system. One method is the blast-gate method, which relies on the adjustment of blast gates after the system is installed to balance the flow in each branch. The main drawback to the blast-gate method is that loss factors can vary greatly depending on the degree to which the blast gate is closed. Also, in the case of dusts, for example, particles can be trapped by the blast gate, building up to the point that the duct becomes clogged.

The second method, the static pressure balance method, starts with the entry requirements at the farthest hood. The duct is sized to achieve the required transport velocity. The velocity pressure usually does not change significantly within the ventilation system. Under this condition, the energy equation states that losses will appear as a reduction in static pressure. The static pressure drop is then calculated based on all the loss mechanisms in the system. At each junction, the branches are balanced analytically by redesigning each branch entering a junction so that the static pressure is the same at the point of entry to the junction. Physics states that the air flow distributes itself based on the losses in each branch; the static pressure at a junction can have only one value.

A typical junction is depicted in Figure 7. The static pressure loss for branch "1" is SP_1 entering the

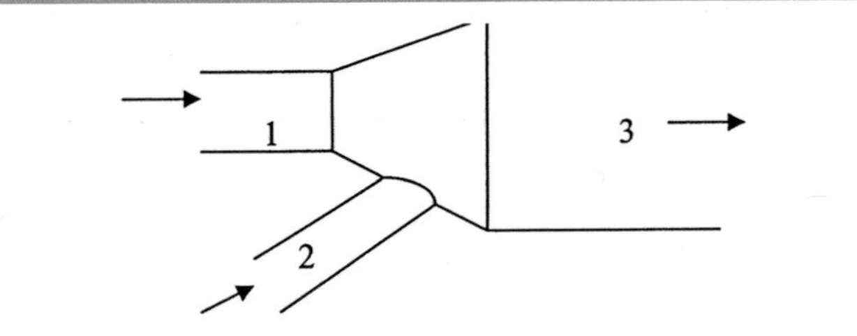

FIGURE 7. **Balancing of two branches at a junction, $Q_3 = Q_1 + Q_2$**

junction, and the static pressure loss for branch "2" is SP_2. Both branches enter the junction and mix together in branch "3," $Q_3 = Q_1 + Q_2$. In the design process, the branch with the lower static pressure must be redesigned by adjusting duct size, elbows, flow, or other parameters until the static pressure drop matches that of the higher branch. This iterative procedure can be systematically done by adjusting the components in that branch using a corrected flow for that branch, given by

$$Q_{corrected} = Q_{design} = \sqrt{\frac{SP_{governing}}{SP_{duct}}} \quad (15)$$

where

$SP_{governing}$ = desired SP at the junction

SP_{duct} = original calculated SP for the duct being redesigned

Q_{design} = original calculated flow for the duct

This design method proceeds branch by branch, junction by junction, up to the fan.

Figure 8 depicts a hypothetical junction ventilation system for a welding operation. The BC branch consists of a tapered hood and 25 feet of flexible duct. The exhaust rate into the tapered hood is chosen as 1000 cfm for adequate capture velocity. The AC branch consists of a plain duct end, a 90° elbow, and 25 feet of galvanized duct. The exhaust rate into the plain duct end is chosen as 1335 cfm for adequate capture velocity. The BC and AC branches meet at junction C. At C, both branches combine into 40 feet of galvanized duct. The minimum transport velocity for welding fumes is 2500 fpm (from Table 5).

An 8-inch diameter duct is chosen for the BC branch. The actual duct velocity for a 1000 cfm exhaust rate is 2865 fpm, which is above the minimum 2500 fpm transport velocity. Using properties for standard air, the velocity pressure is 0.512 inches. The energy loss coefficients for the duct entry and branch entry are obtained from references (ACGIH 2010). The duct friction calculation will use the Moody diagram directly for the purposes of illustration. In practice, there are many useful approximations that make this computation less tedious.

The absolute roughness for flexible duct with wires covered is 0.003 feet (from Table 6), so *e/D* is 0.0045. The Reynolds number is 202,948. The *f* value of 0.030 is read off the Moody diagram for an *e/D* of 0.0045 and a Reynolds number of 202,948. The friction loss (per VP), equal to *f*(*L/D*), is 1.15. The total loss (per VP) for the BC branch is the summation of 0.25, 1.0, 0.28, and 1.15, or 2.68. The total energy loss is then 2.68 times the velocity pressure, or 1.372 inches (see Table 7). The same calculation procedure is applied to the AC branch.

The BC and AC branches meet at junction C. In reality, the static pressure at C must be the same for both branches. The AC branch in this case governs, since it has a higher static pressure than BC. The flow in the BC branch is corrected as 1000(1.676/1.372), or 1104 cfm. The static pressure is then calculated for the BC branch using a 1104 cfm exhaust rate. The resultant total energy loss, 1.669 inches, is very close to the AC value of 1.676 inches, so no further adjustment is necessary.

Both branches join at C. Using conservation of mass, the total flow in the CD branch is 2439 cfm. The static pressure calculation for the CD branch is as follows. The cumulative pressure loss at the fan is

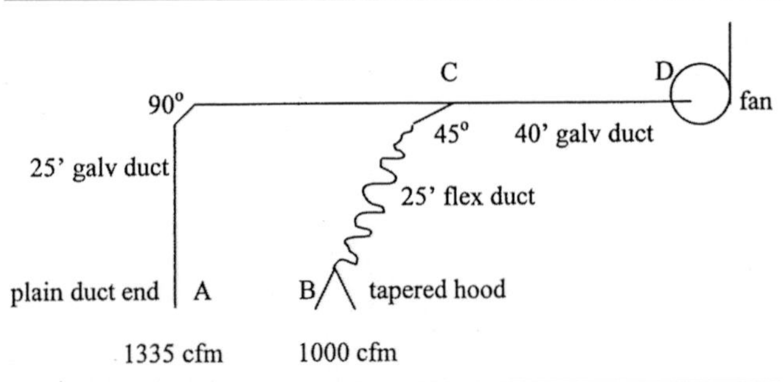

FIGURE 8. **Local exhaust junctioned system example**

TABLE 7

Static Pressure Calculation, Example Figure 8

	BC	AC	BC redesign	CD
Volumetric flow rate (cfm)	1000	1335	1104	2439
Minimum transport velocity (fpm)	2500	2500	2500	2500
Duct diameter (in.)	8	9	8	12
Duct area (sq ft.)	0.349	0 .441	0.349	0.785
Actual duct velocity (fpm)	2865	3027	3162	3107
Duct velocity pressure (VP) (in. w.g.)	0.512	0.571	0.623	0.601
Energy loss coefficients:				
Duct entry (ACGIH, Table 6–6)	0.25	0.93	0.25	--
Acceleration	1.0	1.0	1.0	--
90° elbows (ACGIH, Fig. 9–e)	--	0.33	--	--
Branch entry (ACGIH, Fig. 9–f)	0.28	--	0.28	--
Duct friction				
e/D	(0.0045)	(0.00066)	(0.0045)	(0.0005)
$\mathrm{Re} = \rho VD/\mu$	(202,948)	(241,227)	(223,986)	(330,136)
f (Moody Diagram)	(.030)	(.020)	(.030)	(.018)
$f(L/D)$	1.15	0.675	1.15	0.754
Total:	2.68	2.94	2.68	0.754
Total Energy Loss (in. w.g.)	1.372	1.676	1.669	0.453
Governing?	No	Yes	--	--
Cumulative Energy Loss (in. w.g.)	--	--	--	2.112

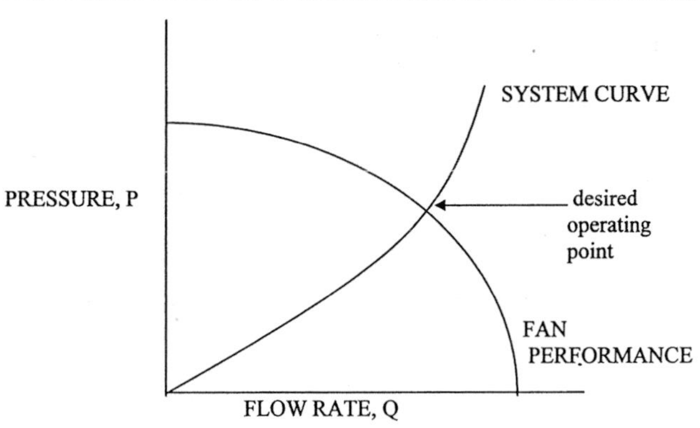

FIGURE 9. Intersection of system curve and fan performance curve

the sum of the static pressures at C (1.669 inches) plus the additional loss in the CD branch (.453 inches), or 2.112 inches.

The design of the ventilation system yields one flow (Q) and one static pressure. This point—the desired system operating point—can be plotted on a pressure versus flow graph (see Figure 9). Using the example in Figure 8, the desired operating point would be 2439 cfm at 2.112 inches static pressure. A system curve can be generated by plotting the desired system operating point with other static pressure/flow system values. The curve will be quadratic, since the change in static pressures is proportional to the square of the change in flow.

The fan performance curve, usually obtained from the manufacturer, is then overlaid on the system curve. There may be a number of performance curves corresponding to fan speed, efficiency, horsepower, and diameter. The resulting operating point will be where the system curve and the performance curve intersect. The best fan or blower will be the one that results in the desired operating point. There may be tradeoffs. The most efficient operating points are usually on the flat part of the fan performance curve. The most stable operating points are on the steep part of the curve, where large changes in static pressure result in small changes in flow.

The following fan laws can be used to estimate system changes

$$Q_2/Q_1 = (\mathrm{RPM}_2/\mathrm{RPM}_1) \quad (16)$$

$$Q_2/Q_1 = (\mathrm{SIZE}_2/\mathrm{SIZE}_1)^3(\mathrm{RPM}_2/\mathrm{RPM}_1) \quad (17)$$

$$\mathrm{SP}_2/\mathrm{SP}_1 = (\mathrm{RPM}_2/\mathrm{RPM}_1)^2 \quad (18)$$

$$\mathrm{PWR}_2/\mathrm{PWR}_1 = (\mathrm{RPM}_2/\mathrm{RPM}_1)^3 \quad (19)$$

where

Q = flow
RPM = fan RPM
SP = static pressure
PWR = power
SIZE = size of the fan

The subscripts refer to conditions before and after the change.

Noise Control

Noise is unwanted sound, such as the sound produced by a honking horn, machinery, or a jack-hammer. *Sound* is the pressure wave that travels in air, giving rise to the sensation of hearing. A pressure wave is created when a mechanical disturbance causes air molecules to move one way and then back. This produces areas where the air molecules are spread apart and areas where they are compressed together. A sound wave has wavelength λ, velocity c, and frequency f. The velocity of sound at 70° F is 1128 feet per second. The wavelength, velocity, and frequency are related by $c = f\lambda$.

Noise generally contains many sound waves with different frequencies, amplitudes, and durations that make it difficult to measure. A more useful quantity is the time average or mean-squared pressure for approximating the magnitude of the sound. It is customary to report sound-pressure levels, Lp, as a quantity that varies linearly as the logarithm of the mean-squared pressure. This quantity, having units of *decibels* (dB), is defined as

$$Lp = 10 \log \left(\frac{p^2_{\text{ave}}}{p^2_{\text{ref}}} \right) \tag{20}$$

The p^2_{ave} quantity is the mean-squared sound pressure and can be that of the total sound-pressure level, one frequency component, or a band of frequencies. The reference pressure (p_{ref}) is 20 micropascals, the threshold of human hearing. Sound-pressure levels for some typical sources (Pierce 1981) are listed in Table 8.

Sound is produced by changes in force, pressure, or velocity. For example, there is no sound if you stand still on a hardwood floor because the force acting on the floor is constant. But if you jump up and down, the force acting on the floor changes and sound (noise) is produced. A balloon full of air does not produce sound because the pressure is constant. If the air is released, then pressure changes and noise are produced. An ordinary house fan produces noise because the air flowing through the fan undergoes rapid changes in velocity.

In the workplace, noise is produced by any number of machines. Pieces of equipment with moving parts, such as belt drives, gear boxes, and motors, produce noise, especially if they cause a nearby panel to vibrate and radiate sound. Production machinery, including punch presses, saws, grinders, planers, and mills, produces noise. Processes that release high-pressure fluids or compressed air, will produce noise. The noise exposure can be continuous, intermittent, or from a sudden impact.

TABLE 8

Typical Sound Pressure Levels

Source	Level (dB)
Jet engine	140
Threshold of pain	130
Rock concert	120
Accelerating motorcycle	110
Pneumatic hammer	100
Noisy factory	90
Vacuum cleaner	80
Busy traffic	70
Two-person conversation	60
Quiet restaurant	50
Residential area at night	40
Empty movie house	30
Rustling of leaves	20
Human breathing	10
Hearing threshold	0

(*Source:* Pierce 1981)

The human ear is a complex device that permits us to hear sound. The outer ear acts like a funnel to direct sound-pressure waves traveling through the air to the eardrum. The eardrum is simply a membrane that vibrates in response to the pressure waves. The mechanical vibration is transmitted to the middle ear. The middle ear consists of three tiny bones—the hammer, the anvil, and the stirrup. These bones transmit mechanical vibration to the fluid-filled inner ear.

The inner ear includes three semicircular canals and the cochlea. The mechanical vibration input from the stirrup is transmitted to fluid vibrations in the inner ear. The cochlea is lined with thousands of hair cells, which are tuned to different frequencies. As the fluid vibrations excite the appropriate hair cells, nerve endings in the cochlea send electrical impulses along the auditory nerve to the brain.

The human ear can detect sounds from frequencies of 20 Hz to 20,000 Hz. It is most sensitive in the middle and high frequencies. The human ear cannot perceive a change in sound level less than 3 dB (Woodson 1992). A change of 5 dB is noticeable. A change of 10 dB is perceived as twice as loud (or soft). A sound is perceived as much louder (or softer) if the difference is 20 dB.

Long-term exposure to hazardous noise levels will cause permanent changes in the cochlea, resulting in permanent, noise-induced hearing loss. This usually starts with a reduction in hearing at 4000 Hz and may extend to the speech frequency range with continued exposure. The onset and extent of hearing loss depends on the level and the exposure duration. It is pervasive and painless, except in extreme situations, such as an explosion.

A hand-held sound-level meter or a noise dosimeter is adequate for assessing most occupational and environmental noise exposures. A frequency analyzer or other instruments may by used when more detailed measurements are needed, such as determining the exact frequency content of the noise emitted by a particular machine. A sound-level meter is suitable for a fixed location and when the noise levels are continuous. A noise dosimeter is more appropriate when the noise level varies or when the employee moves around.

A sound-level meter is a hand-held instrument, consisting of a microphone, a frequency selective amplifier, and an indicator. Most sound-level meters are equipped to make A-weighted, B-weighted, and C-weighted measurements (see Figure 10). A-weighed measurements (dBA) correct direct noise to match how the human ear hears sound. The human ear is less sensitive at low audio frequencies. Figure 10 shows the A-weighted correction that should be made to an unweighted sound-level measurement as a function of frequency. Other scales, such as B-weighting and C-weighting, emphasize the low frequencies. The main difference between sound-level meters is the accuracy. ANSI S1.4 specifies three accuracy levels for sound-level meters: precision (Type 1), general purpose (Type 2), and survey (Type 3) (ANSI 2006e). OSHA recommends that either Type 1 or Type 2 be used for OSHA noise surveys.

The choice of the meter response depends on the noise being measured, the use of the measurements, and applicable standards. The response of sound-level meters is generally based on either FAST or SLOW averaging. The FAST response corresponds to a 125-millisecond time constant, while the SLOW response corresponds to a 1-second time constant. That is, the meter will reach 63 percent of the final steady-state value within 1 second.

The employer's legal obligation for occupational noise exposure is specified in 29 CFR 1910.95 (General Industry) and 29 CFR 1926.52 (Construction). There are two action levels that are required by OSHA, corresponding to noise doses of 50 percent and 100 percent. The first action level requires that a hearing conservation program be implemented whenever the 8-hour continuous exposure exceeds 85 dBA (a dose of 50 percent). The second action level requires administrative or engineering controls if the 8-hour continuous exposure exceeds 90 dBA (a dose of 100 percent). If controls are not feasible, then personal protective equipment shall be provided. Appendix B of 29 CFR 1910.95 describes the methodology for determining the adequacy of hearing protection. The noise reduction rating (NRR) is usually written on the hearing protector package. For example, when an employee's A-weighted, time-weighted average (TWA) is obtained using a sound-level meter, subtract 7 dB from the NRR, and then subtract the remainder from the A-weighted TWA to obtain the estimated A-weighted TWA with the ear protector.

The permissible noise exposures for other sound levels are listed in Table G-16 of 29 CFR 1910.95 and

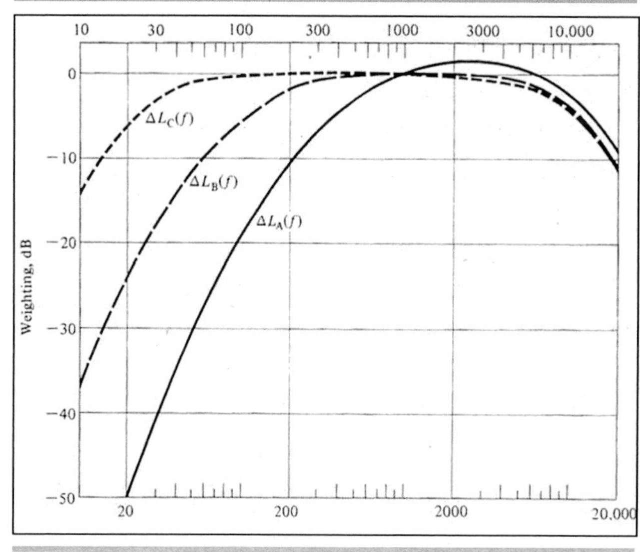

FIGURE 10. A, B, and C sound-weighting versus frequency

Table D-2 of 29 CFR 1926.52. These values are replicated in Table 9. When the noise exposure is comprised of more than one period of noise and difference levels, the noise dose is given by

$$D = 100(C_1/T_1 + C_2/T_2 + C_3/T_3 + \ldots C_n/T_n) \quad (21)$$

where C_n is the exposure time at a specific noise level and T_n is the reference permissible duration for that level. The equivalent continuous 8-hour exposure, the 8-hour *time-weighted average* (TWA) noise level, in decibels is

$$\text{TWA} = 16.61 \log10 (D/100) + 90 \quad (22)$$

For example, if a worker operates a machine for 5 hours at 92 dBA, is exposed to 95 dBA for 2 hours, and has 1 hour in an area where the noise level is 75 dBA. The noise dose is

$$D = 100[0 + (5/6) + (2/4)] = 133.33\% \quad (23)$$

$$\begin{aligned}\text{TWA} &= 16.61 \log10 (133.33/100) + 90 \\ &= 106.7 \text{ dB}\end{aligned} \quad (24)$$

If the worker operates a machine for 5 hours at 85 dBA, is exposed to 92 dBA for 3 hours, and has 1 hour quiet time, the noise dose is

$$D = 100[0 + (3/6) + 0] = 50.0\% \quad (25)$$

$$\text{TWA} = 16.61 \log 10 (50.0/100) + 90 = 85.0 \text{ dB} \quad (26)$$

In the first example, the noise exposure exceeds a TWA of 90 dBA, or 100 percent, and requires administrative controls, engineering controls, or personal protective equipment. A hearing conservation program would also be required if the engineering controls did not lower the TWA to below 85 dBA. The second example requires a hearing conservation program.

A noise survey should be done to determine the employee 8-hour exposure. The instruments used to measure the noise levels should be regularly calibrated. The survey should begin with a preliminary survey. The purpose of the preliminary survey is to identify areas where hazardous noise levels may exist and to determine if special equipment is needed. For example, measurements might be taken at the center of each work area. If the maximum level does not exceed 80 dBA, then detailed measurements in this area may not be necessary. However, if the maximum noise levels exceed 80 dBA, more detailed measurements should be taken. Areas where it is difficult to communicate with a normal voice level or where workers complain of ringing in their ears should be noted for further investigation.

TABLE 9

Permissible Noise Exposures

Duration per Day (hrs)	Sound Level (dBA) Slow Response
8	90
6	92
4	95
3	97
2	100
1.5	102
1	105
0.5	110
0.25 or less	115

Note: Exposure to impact noise should not exceed 140 dB peak (*Source:* Knowles 2003)

A detailed survey should then be done to determine the noise levels that exist at each workstation, areas employees may occupy, and any hazardous areas that were identified in the preliminary survey. These results will then be used to define the guidelines for engineering controls, to identify areas where hearing protection is required, and to identify areas where audiometric testing may be required. The survey should be repeated on one or more days to account for potential day-to-day variations. The employer shall notify each employee of the results of the monitoring and the employee (or representative) shall have the opportunity to observe the noise measurements.

For accurate measurements, the sound-level meter should be placed 6 inches to 1 foot from the operator's ear. Care should be taken to ensure that the sound field is not altered. There should be no objects, including the operator, between the noise source and the meter. Objects that could reflect the sound should also be avoided (Thuman and Miller 1986).

If a particular job requires an employee to move in more than one area during the day, or if the noise levels vary above and below 85 dBA, it may be desirable to have the employee wear a dosimeter. A noise dosimeter is basically a sound-level meter with storage and/or computational capability and a clip-on microphone. The instrument stores the readings during the exposure time and computes the percent dose, or TWA. The placement location can significantly influence the measurement. For example, a microphone placed on the right side of the body will not accurately measure the noise level from a machine located on the left side of the body. Other factors that affect the accuracy include the type of sound field, the angle of incidence of the sound, the frequency of the sound, and the sound absorption of the person's clothing. For most industrial applications, the microphone should be mounted on the shoulder, collar, hat, or helmet. Dosimeter measurements should be checked with previous measurements to rule out employee sabotage (Harris 1991).

A hearing conservation program should be implemented whenever the employee 8-hour, time-weighted, average sound level (TWA) equals or exceeds 85 dBA. The hearing conservation program should include monitoring, employee notification, observation of monitoring, audiometric testing, hearing protection, training, and record keeping. Employees shall be provided with hearing protection when the 8-hour time-weighted average exceeds 85 dBA.

A baseline audiogram should be taken within 6 months of an employee's first exposure. Audiograms should be done annually thereafter. If there is a 10-dB shift at 2000 Hz, 3000 Hz, or 4000 Hz between the annual audiogram and the baseline, then follow-up steps need to be taken. These steps may include fitting the employee with hearing protection, upgrading the hearing protection, and a clinical audiological evaluation.

The employee training program should include the effects of noise on hearing, the purpose of hearing protection, and the purpose of audiometric testing. The training should be repeated annually. The employer should maintain records of the exposure measurements and audiometric testing. Noise-exposure measurement records should be retained for two years. Audiometric test records should be retained for the duration of the employee's employment.

If the 8-hour continuous exposure exceeds 100 percent, then the employer should implement administrative or engineering controls. If these controls fail to reduce sound levels, then personal protective equipment should be provided for the employees.

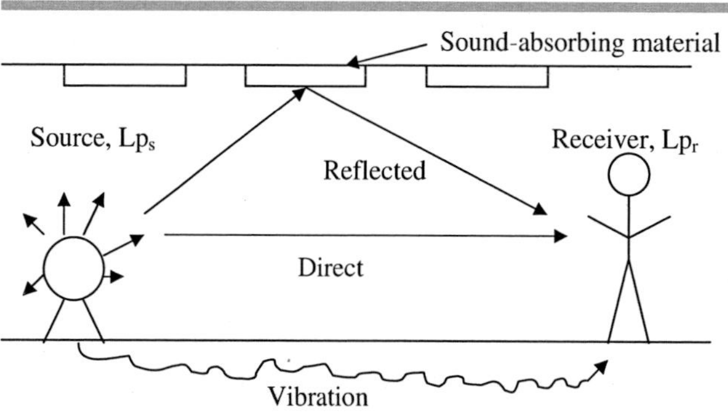

FIGURE 11. Noise source, transmission path, and receiver in a room

In designing for safety, the first priority in controlling hazardous noise is elimination or isolation of the noise by engineering design. There are three areas where noise control can be effective: at the source of the noise, in the transmission path between the source and the receiver, and at the receiver (see Figure 11). The transmission path includes direct sound, reflected sound, and vibration.

Engineering controls that can be taken at the source include reducing the noise output of the source and/or enclosing the source. Reducing the noise output requires an understanding of how the source produces noise (changes in force, pressure, or velocity). Information about the frequency content can also be very useful. For example, any rotating component will produce noise at its rotation rate or multiples of the rotation rate. Noise that has a strong frequency content at 100 Hz could be caused by a bent shaft rotating at 6000 rpm. A 36-tooth gear rotating at 1500 rpm can generate noise at a frequency of $36 \times 1500/60 = 900$ Hz. Corrective measures that can be taken to reduce noise generated by rotating equipment include balancing, replacing bent shafts, replacing worn bearings, lubricating moving parts, or changing the rotation rate.

Machine covers are sometimes made with thin sheet-metal panels that can vibrate and radiate sound. This usually occurs when the driving frequency is close to the natural frequency of the panel. Increasing the thickness of the panel or adding stiffening ribs will change the natural frequency and thereby reduce the noise. Sheet-damping material can be added to dampen the vibration. These sheets are made of visco-elastic material with a self-adhesive backing and can be attached directly to the panel.

The application of engineering controls to reduce the noise output at the source is illustrated in the following examples (Knowles 2003):

1. A control panel mounted to a hydraulic system is determined to be the source of radiated noise. The noise level is reduced by detaching the control panel from the system.
2. In another case, a solid metal cover on a belt drive is found to be radiating noise. A wire mesh cover reduces the vibration so that there is less radiated noise.
3. A urethane rubber coating is clamped to a circular saw blade to reduce noise.
4. Fan noise is reduced by moving the control vanes farther upstream so that the flow entering the fan is less turbulent.
5. A low-frequency resonance in an engine room produces a very loud noise near the walls. The noise is eliminated by changing the revolution speed.
6. Low-frequency noise is produced by a wide belt drive. The wide belt is replaced with several narrow belts.
7. Building vibrations are found to be caused by an elevator. Isolating the elevator drive from the building reduces the noise.

If the noise output of the source cannot be reduced by any appreciable means, then enclosing the source should be considered (see Figure 12). The enclosure should be designed with a dense material, such as sheet metal or plasterboard, on the outside. Sound-absorbing material should be used on the inside. The *transmission loss* (TL) is the logarithmic ratio of the sound-power incident on one side of the enclosure wall to the sound power transmitted to the other side. A good rule of thumb (Harris 1991) for enclosures with partial absorption is that the transmission loss of the wall material should be greater than the required noise reduction (NR) plus 15 dB. If the enclosure has complete absorption, then the transmission loss of the wall material should be greater than the required noise reduction plus 10 dB. Install mufflers on cooling air openings. Access panels should also be incorporated for maintenance and service. A well-designed enclosure should reduce the noise by as much as 30 dB.

There are several paths that noise can travel from the source to the receiver. Direct sound is a straight-line propagation of sound waves from the sound source. Moving the receiver farther from the source will reduce the direct sound noise. If the source is nondirectional and is located near the center of a wall or floor in a room, the relationship (Hirschorn 1989) between the source-sound power level (L_w) and sound-pressure level at the receiver (Lp_r) located R feet from the source is

$$Lp_r = L_w - 20 \log R + 2.3 \quad (27)$$

In Equation 27, doubling the distance will reduce the sound-pressure level at the receiver by approximately 6 dB.

Sound rarely reaches the receiver by a direct path alone. Repeated reflections within the room provide another transmission path from source to receiver. Available methods to reduce reflected noise are to absorb the sound energy and/or to reflect it away from the receiver. Sound-absorbing materials fall into three categories. Sound energy can be converted to heat by internal friction within the sound-absorbing material. Glass fiber is a common absorbing material. Sound energy can also be converted to mechanical energy, such as lead sheets with mass and stiffness that are designed to vibrate. The third option is sound-absorbing cavities in which the sound waves are reflected back

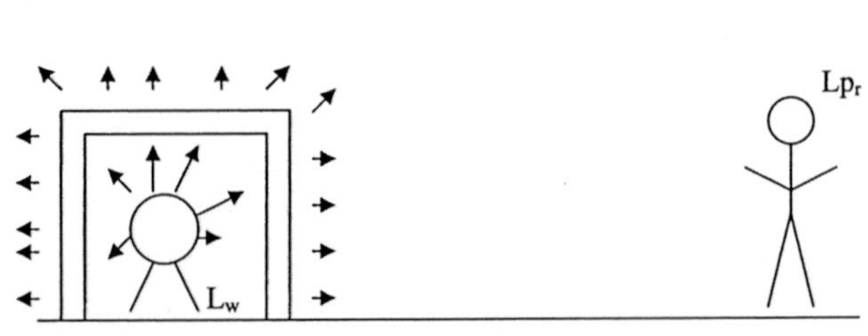

FIGURE 12. Enclosing a noise source to reduce noise at the receiver

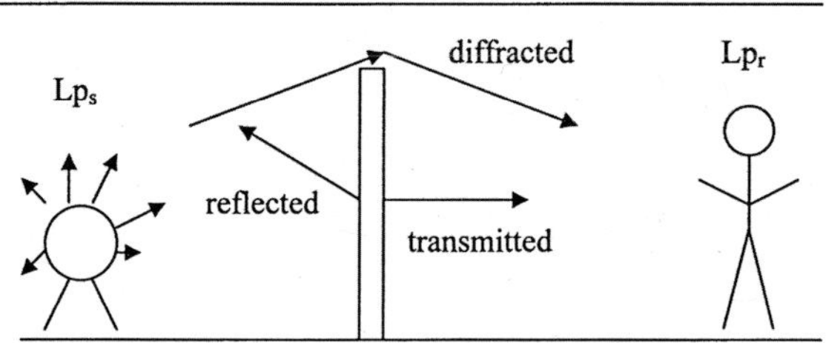

FIGURE 13. Installing a barrier between the source and the receiver

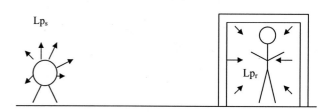

FIGURE 14. Noise reduction by enclosing the receiver

and forth until they are dissipated. Hollow concrete blocks are specially designed for this purpose.

If the reflected sound field is uniform within the room (diffuse), the sound-pressure level at the receiver (Lp_r) due to a source with sound-power level L_w is (Harris 1991)

$$Lp_r = L_w - 10 \log A + 16.3 \quad (28)$$

where A is the total room absorption in sabins. The total room absorption can be calculated by adding up the product of the area of each absorbing surface times the absorption coefficient for the entire room.

Another noise-control measure is the installation of a barrier between the source and the receiver (Figure 13). The barrier creates an obstacle to the sound waves. Some of the sound waves will be reflected back toward the source, some will be transmitted through the barrier, and some will be diffracted around the barrier. The amount of sound that is reflected depends on the sound absorption of the barrier. The transmitted sound depends on the transmission loss of the barrier. The diffracted sound will vary with the height of the barrier. Rules of thumb (Harris 1991) for the design of barriers include placing the barrier as close to the source as possible without touching the source, extending the barrier beyond the line of sight of the source by one-quarter wavelength of the lowest noise frequency, and using a solid barrier that has a transmission loss at least 10 dB higher than the required attenuation.

Noise can also be transmitted through other paths, such as floor vibration. For example, a machine may cause a floor to vibrate. The vibration may be transmitted through the floor to a worker standing on the floor. Isolating the machine from the floor in this case can reduce noise at the receiver by eliminating or lowering the vibration transmitted through the floor.

A sound-absorbing control room or office can be built to reduce the noise at the receiver (see Figure 14). The room should have adequate ventilation and air conditioning. The control room walls and ceiling should have a high TL and good sealing around the doors and windows. The absorptive treatment on the walls and ceiling are important because the sound transmitted through the walls and ceiling will be reinforced by reflected sound waves within the room. If the source is located in a highly reverberant area and the receiver room walls and ceiling are treated with a material that has a high sound absorption, the noise reduction (NR) will be nearly equal to the transmission loss (TL) of the receiver room. If the receiver room is highly reflective, the noise reduction can be as much as 20 dB. In general (Hirschorn 1989),

$$NR \approx TL + 10 \log (\alpha A/S) \quad (29)$$

where

α = average sound-absorption coefficient of the receiver room

A = total area of the receiver room

S = surface area separating the source room and receiver room

Case studies where engineering controls have been effective (with quantified results) can be found in Jensen et al. (1978). Several of these case studies are summarized below.

1. An 800-ton blanking press was mounted on four footings set on concrete piers. Noise levels

were 120 dB on impact, 105 dB at quasi-peak, and 94.5 dB at the operator position located 4 feet in front of the press. Isolating pads were added. The pads cost about $3000, including labor. The isolator pads reduced the noise level at the operator's station from 94.5 dB to 88 dB.

2. In the folding carton industry, pieces of paper scrap striking the sides of a conveyor caused high noise levels. Sound levels in excess of 90 dB were measured at the operator's platform. A layer of lead damping sheeting was glued to the ducts and other equipment. The sound levels were reduced to the range of 88 to 90 dB.
3. A worker was exposed to high noise levels while operating a metal cut-off saw. The solution was to enclose the saw. The work pieces were transferred through slots in the enclosure. The noise levels were reduced by 13 dB.
4. The sound level at the operating station of a 200-ton punch press was measured as 104 dB. An enclosure was built around the machine. The enclosure included a heat exhaust system and access doors. The sound level for the operator was reduced to 83 dB.

Lockout/Tagout (LOTO)

Lockout/tagout (LOTO) is an administrative procedure for protecting employees from the unexpected start-up of equipment and machines or the release of energy while the equipment is being serviced or repaired. The general industry regulation, 29 CFR 1910.147, *The Control of Hazardous Energy*, sets forth procedures for lockout/tagout. The regulation requires an employer to implement a program to ensure that machines and equipment are rendered inoperable and isolated from energy sources when equipment is serviced. The program shall consist of energy control procedures, employee training, and periodic inspections.

Electrical power to the equipment is the obvious energy source that should be locked out. There are other sources of energy in a typical industrial facility. These include gas, pressurized air, steam, electrical capacitors, hydraulic lines, raised loads, and compressed springs. It is the latent build-up of energy that can be released even when the power is locked out that typically goes unnoticed.

Lockout is a procedure in which locking devices are placed on energy-isolating devices so that the equipment cannot be operated until the locking device is removed. An *energy-isolating device* is a mechanical device that physically prevents the transmission of energy. Examples of energy-isolating devices are manually operated electric circuit breakers, disconnect switches, and line valves. There are a number of different lockout devices. Electrical plug boxes work by inserting the disconnected plug into a small box and locking it. This prevents plug connection during maintenance. Multiple lockout devices can hold up to six padlocks. This is important when several people may be working on a machine. Figure 15 shows a multiple lockout device.

If an energy-isolating device is not capable of being locked out then a tagout system shall be used. *Tagout* is the placement of a tag to indicate that the energy-isolating device and the equipment should not be operated until the tag is removed. Tags warn of specific hazards, such as "Do Not Operate" or "Do Not Start." It should be noted that these tags are warning devices; they do not provide positive restraint as

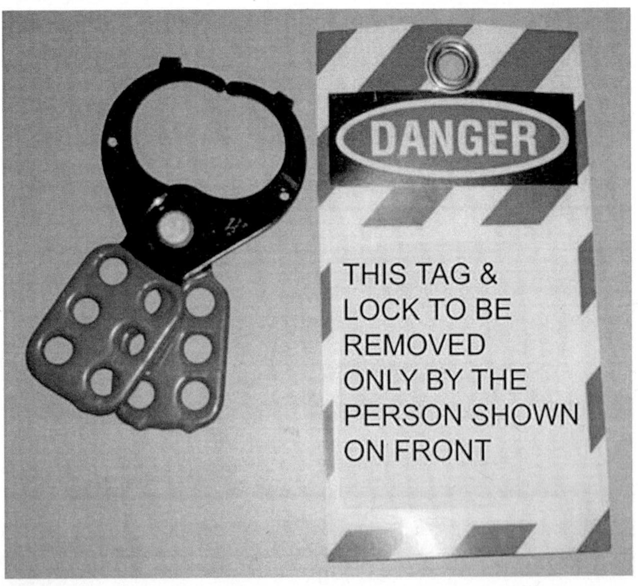

FIGURE 15. Example of a multiple lockout device and tag

lockout devices do. Figure 15 shows an example of a tag.

There are several pointers to putting together a LOTO program. Simply locking the power does not necessarily mean the equipment is safe to work on. Check for trapped air, gas, springs, raised loads, or other sources of residual energy. For example, bleed air from pneumatic lines so there can be no unexpected release of compressed air or unexpected actuation of an air cylinder. Be careful of multiple workers performing maintenance. Miscommunication can occur, for example, during shift changes. A complete check should be done before the equipment is restarted. Check that all safeguards have been put back in place and that all tools have been removed. The person who applies the lockout device should be the one to remove it. Make sure that all employees are at a safe distance before the equipment is started.

A LOTO program should include the following steps:

1. ***Prepare for shutdown:*** The authorized person should refer to the written company procedure. The authorized person should be trained on the piece of equipment, including the sources of energy, the hazards, and the means to control the energy.
2. ***Shutdown:*** An orderly shutdown should be done. The machine or equipment should be turned off.
3. ***Energy isolation:*** All energy-isolating devices should be located and operated to isolate the machine or equipment from energy sources.
4. ***Lockout or tagout devices applied:*** The authorized employee should apply lockout and/or tagout devices.
5. ***Check for stored energy:*** Residual energy must be restrained, dissipated, or otherwise made safe.
6. ***Verify equipment:*** The authorized employee must verify the isolation and de-energization of the equipment. This usually involves pressing the push buttons to be sure the equipment will not start.
7. ***Prepare for release from LOTO:*** The equipment should be checked to be sure that all safeguards have been put back in place, the equipment is intact, and all tools have been removed. All workers should be at a safe distance.
8. ***Lockout and/or tagout devices removed:*** Each lockout and/or tagout device should be removed *only* by the person who applied it.

OSHA lockout/tagout requirements for some specific types of equipment are listed below:

1. ***Powered Industrial Trucks:*** Disconnect battery before making repairs to the electrical system (1910.178(q)(4)).
2. ***Overhead and Gantry Cranes:*** The power supply to the runway conductors shall be controlled by a switch or circuit breaker located on a fixed structure, accessible from the floor, and arranged to be locked in an open position (1910.179(g)(5)). The main or emergency switch shall be open and locked in the open position. If other cranes are operating on the same runway, rail stops shall be installed to prevent the operating crane from interfering with the crane being serviced. (1910.179(l)(2)).
3. ***Woodworking Machinery:*** All power-driven woodworking machines should be equipped with a lockable disconnect (1910.213(a)(10)). Controls on machines operated by electric motors should be rendered inoperable (1910.213(b)(5)).
4. ***Mechanical Power Presses:*** The power-press control system should be equipped with a main disconnect that can be locked in the off position (1910.217(b)(8)(i)). The die setter should use safety blocks during die adjustment or repairing the dies in the press (1910.217(d)(9)(iv)).
5. ***Forging Hammers:*** Means shall be provided for disconnecting the power and for locking out or rendering cycling controls inoperable (1910.218(a)(2)(iii)). The ram shall be blocked when the dies are changed or work is being done on the hammer (1910.218(a)(2)(iv)).

Steam hammers should be equipped with a quick-closing emergency valve in the admission piping. The valve should be closed and locked while the equipment is being serviced (1910.218(b)(2)).

6. ***Welding, Cutting, and Brazing:*** Resistance welding machines should be equipped with a safety disconnect switch, circuit breaker, or circuit interrupter so that the power can be turned off during servicing (1910.255(a)(1)).
7. ***Pulp, Paper, and Paperboard Mills:*** The main power disconnect and valves for the equipment should be locked out or blocked off when the equipment is being serviced (1910.261(b)(1)). The valve lines leading to the digester should be locked out and tagged when inspecting or repairing the digester (1910.261(g)(15)(i)). The control valves leading to the pulpers should be locked out and tagged out, or blanked off and tagged before a worker enters the pulper (1910.261(j)(5)(iii). All drives should be equipped with a power switch lockout device (1910.261.(k)(2)(ii)).
8. ***Bakery Equipment:*** The main switch should be locked in the open position prior to servicing an oven or electrical equipment (1910.263(l)(3)(b)).
9. ***Sawmills:*** The hydraulic equipment must be rendered safe prior to servicing (1910.265(c)(13)). The main control switches to the mechanical stackers must be designed so that they can be locked in the open position (1910.265(c)(26)).
10. ***Grain Handling:*** Auger and grain transfer equipment must be de-energized, locked out, and tagged out (1910.272(h)).

Power Tools

Power tools are inherently dangerous for the simple reason that any tool that is powered by electricity, air, powder, or gasoline for the purpose of cutting through wood, metal, concrete, or other materials can easily cut through bone and tissue. The hazards associated with power tools include contact with moving parts, contact with the power source (electricity), losing control of the tool, flying debris, harmful dust and fumes, excessive noise, vibration, and being struck by the work piece. Other factors, such as a less-than-ideal working environment (uneven construction site versus a clean, level shop) or momentary inattentiveness by the user, can further increase the risk of an injury.

In designing for safety, the first priority is to eliminate the hazard or provide a safety device to reduce the risk to an acceptable level. There are a number of basic safeguards and design features for reducing the risk of an injury from a power tool. All hazardous moving parts of a power tool should be guarded to the greatest extent possible. This would include belts, gears, shafts, pulleys, sprockets, spindles, chains, blades, reciprocating parts, and rotating parts. OSHA 1910.243 addresses the guarding of portable power tools. Refer to the "Machine Guarding" section of this chapter for guarding mechanical hazards.

One of the main hazards with electric-powered tools is electrical shock. An electrical shock can result in injury or death, or cause the user to fall off a ladder or scaffold. To protect the user from electrical shock, the tool should have a three-prong grounding plug that mates to a three-hole receptacle, or be double insulated. In the case of a grounded tool, any current resulting from a defect or short inside the tool will be conducted through the ground wire and not through the operator's body. When an adapter is used to accommodate a two-hole receptacle, the adapter wire must be connected to a known ground. The third prong should never be removed from the plug. Double-insulated tools have an internal protective layer of insulation that isolates the housing. This eliminates the possibility of current flowing through the housing to the operator.

In the case of hand power tools, the handles should be properly designed so that the operator can control the tool. Handles should be located where they allow the operator to balance the tool and apply force in the direction that is needed. Tools with rotating components may need a second handle so that the operator can resist the torque.

Power switches should be conveniently located in such a manner that the operator does not have to relinquish control (grip) of the tool to activate the switch.

A power switch should be protected from inadvertent activation. Lock-on switches, switches that remain engaged without having to keep your finger on them, are used in many hand power tools. However, these switches are generally not recommended, especially for heavy-duty tools, because the power will not shut off if the operator loses control of the tool.

There are a number of general precautions that should be observed by operators of power tools. A power tool should never be carried by the cord or hose. Cords and hoses should be kept away from heat, oil, and sharp edges. Never yank a cord or hose to disconnect the tool. Always disconnect the tool when it is not in use, when changing accessories, or when servicing it. Secure the work piece so that both hands can be used to operate the tool. Do not operate power tools when wearing loose clothing, ties, jewelry, or other apparel that can be caught in moving parts.

Personal protective equipment should be used when operating a power tool. Always wear eye protection with side shields when using power tools. A face shield should be used when large flying particles may be present. Many power tools produce dangerous noise levels. Wear hearing protection with noisy tools. A dust mask or respirator should be worn if there are dusts or harmful fumes present.

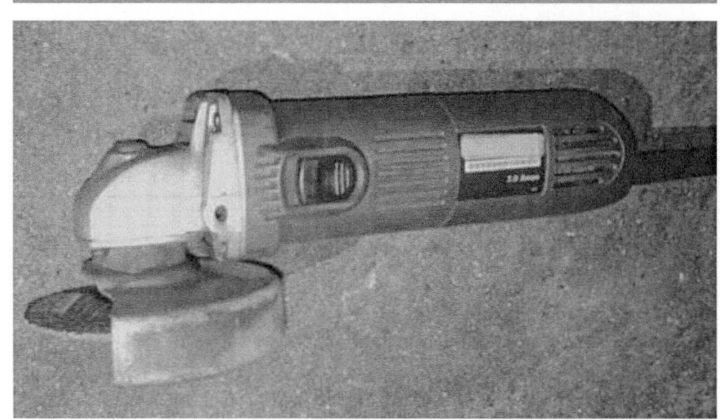

FIGURE 16. A typical hand-held grinder

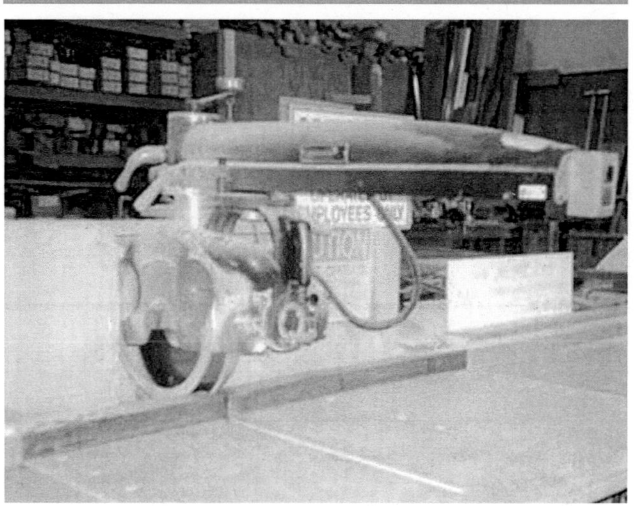

FIGURE 17. Example of a radial saw

Hand-Held Grinders

Injuries from hand-held grinders occur from particles being thrown into the operator's eye, kickback, and disk fracturing. Although it is impractical to guard the entire disk, the portion between the disk and the operator should be guarded to deflect broken pieces away from the operator. A heavy-duty grinder should have a second handle so the operator can maintain control of the tool. Figure 16 shows a photograph of a typical hand-held grinder.

There are a number of safety precautions that should be followed to prevent fracture of the disk. Only approved flanges should be used to mount the disk. The motor speed must not exceed the safe operating speed on the disk. The disk should be inspected for cracks or chips before using. A disk should not be used if it has been dropped on a hard surface. A grinder should never be used as a cutting tool. This imposes high stresses on the disk.

Radial Saws

Radial saws are powered circular saws. These saws have features that make them more versatile than table saws. For example, the saw arm can be raised, lowered, or swung from side to side to adjust the depth and angle of the cut. The blade can also be replaced with cutters, disks, drum sanders, or other accessories. Figure 17 shows an example of a radial saw.

As with most saws, injuries are the result of contact with the blade (Hagan et al. 2009). To reduce the risk of injury the upper half of the blade, from the top down to the end of the arbor, should be guarded. The lower half of the blade should have a self-adjusting, floating guard that adjusts to the thickness of the stock. The saw should have a limit chain or other positive stop to prevent the blade from traveling beyond the front of the table. There should be a device that will automatically return the saw to the back of the table when it is released at any point in the travel.

Additional precautions should be taken when ripping. A spreader should be used to prevent internal stresses in the wood from causing the wood to bind the blade and cause kickback. Antikickback pawls should also be used. The stock should be fed against the direction of rotation of the blade from the nose of the guard; the side of the guard where the blade rotates upward should be toward the operator. Feeding from the wrong side can cause the operator's hand to be drawn into the blade. To prevent an operator from ripping from the wrong side, the direction of rotation should be marked on the hood. Also, a standard warning label should be affixed to both sides of the rear of the hood stating, "Do not rip from this end."

Hand-Held Circular Power Saws

Hand-held circular power saws are one of the most widely used power tools. Figure 18 shows a photo of a typical hand-held circular power saw. Most injuries with hand-held circular saws are the result of contact with the blade. To reduce the risk of injury, these saws should have guards above and below the faceplate. The lower guard must retract as the material is cut and maintain contact with the material. The guard should be frequently checked to be sure that it operates properly and covers the blade teeth when not in use. Other safety features include a trigger switch that must be depressed to power the saw.

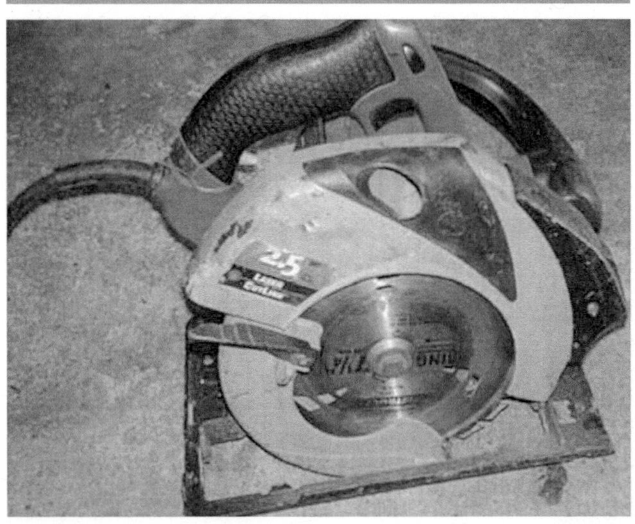

FIGURE 18. Example of a hand-held circular saw

Many injuries with hand-held circular saws are caused by kickback. Kickback is a sudden reaction that occurs when the blade is pinched. The reaction forces the tool out of the cut and toward the operator. If this occurs quickly enough, the lower portion of the blade may contact the operator before the guard retracts. Since this is a hazard that cannot be designed out, the operator should follow some very basic operating procedures to reduce the likelihood of a kickback event and possible injury. These procedures, along with warnings concerning the kickback hazard and the consequences of not following procedures, should be in the manual.

To reduce the likelihood of the blade binding or pinching, never use dull, bent, warped, or broken blades. Avoid cutting wet wood as the wet wood chips can bind the blade and may also bind the guard. Waiting for the blade to stop rotating before removing the saw from the cut will also reduce the chance of kickback. If the blade does bind, releasing the switch immediately can reduce the extent of the kickback. Standing to the side of the cut will put the operator out of the trajectory of the saw if a kickback does occur.

Table Saws

Table saws are used for a variety of tasks, such as ripping, crosscutting, grooving, rabbetting, and dadoing. Most injuries with table saws occur from contact with the saw blade. This can happen if the operator's hands are held too close to the blade, if the operator's hands slip off the stock as it is being pushed through the saw, or when removing scrap or finished pieces from the table. Injuries can also occur during ripping operations when the board being cut can be thrown violently backward toward the operator (kickback). A typical table saw is depicted in Figure 19.

Since table saws are used for a multitude of tasks, it is difficult from an engineering design prospective to design a single guard that covers all foreseeable uses of the saw. All table saws should be designed with a guard that protects the operator for most cutting operations. The top part of the blade, the part that projects above the table, should be guarded with a hood guard. The guard should adjust automatically to the thickness of the work piece, and should remain in contact as the piece is being cut. One chronic problem with hood guards is that users tend to remove them. The exposed part of the saw blade under the table should also be guarded.

The table saw should have a splitter and antikickback devices for ripping. These devices are usually built into the hood guard. Antikickback pawls, along with the spreader, act to reduce kickback. The rip fence should also be parallel to the blade so that the work piece does not bind.

A number of tasks may require special procedures (Hagan et al. 2009). An auxiliary fence and push block should be used for ripping pieces less than 2 inches wide. A push stick should be used when ripping pieces from 2 to 6 inches wide. For other operations (grooving, rabbetting, dadoing) it is impossible to use the spreader and may be impractical to use the hood guard. These tasks will require special jigs to keep the operator's hands away from the blade or cutting head.

FIGURE 19. Example of a typical table saw

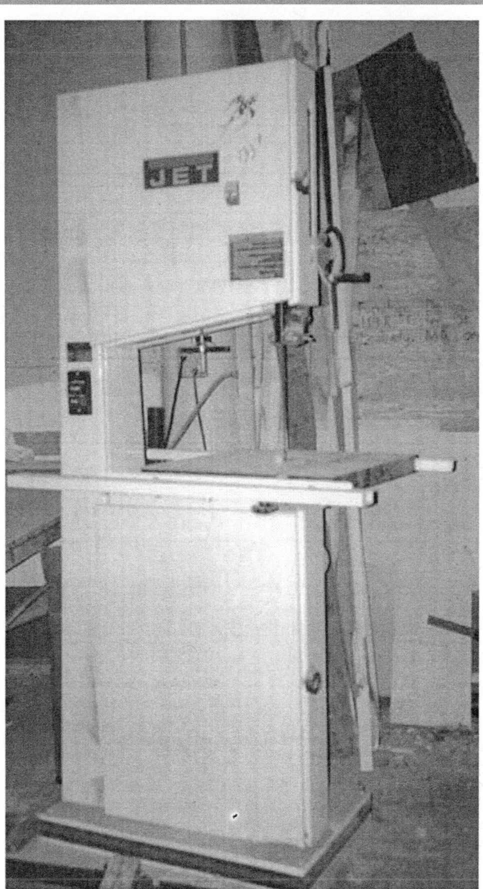

FIGURE 20. Example of a typical industrial band saw

Band Saws

Band saws are used for cutting curves, miter cuts, and ripping. Injuries from band saws are generally less than from table saws. Figure 20 shows a photo of a typical industrial band saw. Most injuries with band saws occur from contact with the blade. Like many power saws, the point of operation cannot be completely guarded. The wheels of the band saw should be guarded. An adjustable guard should provide protection from contact with the front and right side of the blade above the blade guides.

A band saw should have a tension-control device to indicate the proper blade tension. Other safety devices include an automatic blade-tension device to prevent breakage of blades, and a device that prevents the motor from starting if the blade tension is too tight or too loose.

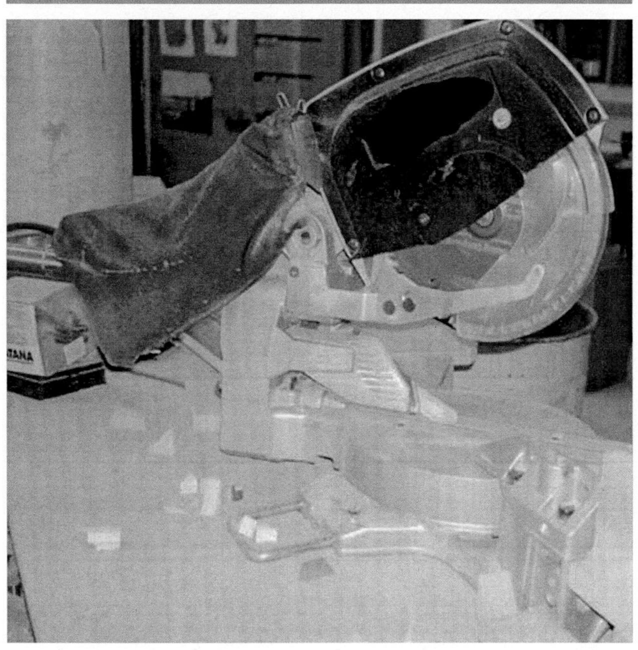

FIGURE 21. Miter saw with a linkage-activated guard

Miter Saws

Miter saws are stationary tools used for crosscutting, mitering, and beveling. These saws consist of a saw head (circular saw blade, arbor, electric motor) mounted to a pivot arm. The pivot arm is supported on a carriage that can be rotated left and right. The work piece is mounted on a horizontal table. The cut is made by swinging the saw head in a downward motion and depressing the trigger. The pivot arm is spring loaded so that the saw head returns to the upright position when it is released. Figure 21 shows a photo of a typical miter saw.

The saw blade should be guarded to protect the operator. Many miter saws use a contact-type of guard. This guard covers the sides of the blade, but is open around the periphery. As the saw head is brought down to make the cut, the guard contacts the work piece and retracts. When the saw head is raised back up, the guard returns to its original position. These guards provide some measure of protection, but an operator can still be injured from inadvertent contact with the guard. Body contact with the guard will cause it to retract since the guard cannot distinguish between contact with the work piece and contact with a body part. Many injuries occur when a worker brushes against the guard, exposing the blade, while drawing a board from left to right across the table to make the next cut.

A linkage-driven guard, a guard that retracts and returns to place as the arm is lowered and raised, is a safer design. These guards cover both sides of the blade and the periphery. As the saw head is brought down, a linkage mechanism connected to the pivot arm retracts the guard. The guard cannot be inadvertently displaced. The guard retracts as the pivot arm is drawn down to make the cut and goes back into position as the arm is brought up.

Miter saws should also have a brake that stops the rotation of the blade when the trigger is released. All safety features (guard and brake) should be checked before using the saw to ensure they are operating properly. The operator's hands should be kept away from the cutting plane of the blade when the saw head is lowered.

Chain Saws

Chain saws are another labor-saving tool used for cutting downed trees, branches, large logs, or pieces of wood. However, there is an increased risk of injury because the operator is exposed to a high-speed, powered chain that is sharp and unguarded. Serious injuries or death can occur if an operator falls while carrying the saw, even if it is not running. Injuries can also occur if an operator lowers the saw to his side while the chain is still moving. Figure 22 shows a photo of a typical gas-powered chain saw.

Since it is impractical to guard the chain, the operator should be thoroughly trained in the hazards and

FIGURE 22. A typical gas-powered chain saw

use of a chain saw. There are a number or procedures that should be followed to reduce the likelihood of a chain-saw injury. The chain brake should be engaged when starting the saw so that the chain will not be powered during start-up. Keeping the work area clear, maintaining a firm footing, and turning the engine off when carrying the saw will reduce the likelihood of falling or stumbling onto a powered or stationary chain. Holding the saw with both hands provides optimum control when making a cut.

Aside from being exposed to the sharp chain, the next biggest cause of chain-saw injuries is kickback. Kickback is a sudden and violent upward and/or backward movement of the saw toward the operator. It is caused when the motion of the chain is suddenly stopped. This can occur if the chain near the nose or tip of the guide bar contacts an object, such as a log or branch. Kickback can also occur when the wood pinches the chain in the cut. Any interference with the moving chain transfers its energy (either gasoline or electric motor) into movement of the entire saw.

There are design safeguards to reduce the likelihood of kickback. Antikickback safety features include a safety nose, a safety chain, and chain brakes. A safety nose is effective is preventing nose-tip kickback. Safety chains use a lower profile, different cutting pitch, and fewer links, thereby reducing the tendency of the chain to get caught. A chain brake stops the chain when kickback occurs. A common method to activate the brake is by a mechanical switch located at the front hand guard. When the saw is propelled backward, the lead hand pushes on the hand guard, activating the brake. It should be noted that these safety devices only reduce the probability of kickback and contact with a moving chain if kickback occurs. They do not prevent kickback.

Pneumatic Nail Guns

Nail guns (pneumatic nailers) are pneumatically powered tools that drive nails into wood (see Figure 23). Small nailers are used for finish work, while larger framing nailers can drive a three-inch framing nail into wood or even concrete. These tools significantly increase work production, but not without an increased risk of injury. Nail guns deserve the same respect as firearms. Nails can be driven into the human body if the gun fires before the operator is ready, if the nail completely penetrates the work piece and comes out the other side, or if the gun is directed at something other than the work piece.

Pneumatic nail guns work with compressed air generated by an air compressor. The *hammer* portion of the gun is a piston that drives a long blade. A trigger mechanism opens a valve that allows compressed air into the chamber at the top of the piston, driving it down and propelling the nail at speeds as high as 1400 feet per second. When the valve closes, the air is directed to the return chamber below the piston, pushing it back up. Safety requirements for compressed air-fastener driving tools are addressed in ANSI SNT-101, *Portable, Compressed-Air-Actuated Fastener Driving Tools* (ANSI 2002).

Injuries include nails driven into the extremities (hands, feet) to more serious injuries and death from nails driven into heads, eyes, and major organs. For example, a worker shot a nail into his wrist when his wrist brushed against the nail discharge area of the gun. In another case, two workers were positioned on a roof, one above the other. The top worker slipped, the nail gun moved across his body, and the gun

FIGURE 23. A typical pneumatic nail gun

activated. The gun shot a nail into the bottom man's head. Nails have penetrated drywall and struck workers on the other side. Workers have also been injured when a driven nail ricocheted off another nail.

Various engineering designs have been implemented by manufacturers to reduce the risk of injury from unintentional firing. Most nail guns have two separate firing triggers. One trigger is finger-activated and located under the handle, similar to most hand power tools. The other trigger, the nose trigger, is located at the nail discharge (nose). The nose trigger is activated by pressing the nose of the gun against the work piece. In order to fire the gun, both triggers must be depressed.

There are two types of trigger systems. In the *contact-trip* or *bounce-firing* system, the operator depresses the finger trigger and bounces the nose against the work to fire the gun. This method can be very fast and efficient. However, this system is still dangerous because it allows the operator to fire nails in rapid succession by keeping the finger trigger depressed while quickly bouncing the nose of the gun. Workers can still be injured from double fires that can occur during rapid bouncing of the gun. Injuries can also occur if the nose contacts something other than the work piece while the finger trigger is held.

The *sequential-trip* firing system requires that the nose be engaged against the work piece before the trigger finger is depressed. This system is safer because only one nail can be fired per finger-trigger activation. It eliminates injuries from double firing and from brushing the nose against an object while the finger trigger is depressed. Many nail guns can be converted from sequential mode to bounce mode and vice versa.

The *single-shot* system is a compromise between the bounce-firing system and the sequential-trip system (Arnold 2002). The single-shot mode can fire a nail in one of two ways. One way is with the nose guard pressed against the work and the trigger pulled and held. The other way is by depressing the trigger first, then bouncing the nose guard. Either way, the gun will not fire if the trigger is held down and the nose guard is lifted and pressed again. However, if the nose is held against the work piece and dragged to the next nailing spot, and the trigger is released and depressed, the gun will fire again. Nail guns also come equipped with anti-double-firing mechanisms.

There are also nail guns with a *brain* (Arnold 2002). A computer chip senses the prior firing mode, either bounce or sequential. In the sequential-trip mode, the operator has two seconds to pull the trigger before the nose guard has to be reset. In the bounce-fire mode, the operator has one second between shots before the trigger has to be released and pulled again.

Machine Safeguarding

Safeguarding is any means of preventing a worker or user from contacting a dangerous part of a machine, product, or other device. There are three areas where mechanical hazards requiring safeguarding are typically found. Any part that moves while the machine is operating should be safeguarded. Power-transmission apparatus components (e.g., pulleys, belts, chains, cranks, shafts, and spindles) should be safeguarded. The *point of operation*, the area where moving parts bend, shape, or cut material, should also be safeguarded. In the workplace, machines that typically require attention include power presses, press brakes, mills, calendars, shears, grinders, and printing machines. Examples of consumer products where safeguarding should be considered include food processors, lawn mowers, power tools, and snow throwers.

Following the designing for safety hierarchy, the first priority is to eliminate the hazard altogether. If this is not possible, there are a number of safeguarding methods that can be considered. A *guard* is a physical barrier that prevents any body part from contacting the hazard. A guard may be fixed or adjustable. A *fixed guard* is one that is permanently attached to the machine, and special tools are required to remove it. *Adjustable guards* are used in cases where openings in the guard, such as for feeding stock, vary from operation to operation. There are a number of design criteria to be considered when designing a guard:

1. The guard must prevent a body part from contacting dangerous parts of a machine.
2. A well-designed guard does not reduce a worker's productivity. A guard that impedes

a worker from doing his job might be discarded.

3. The guard must be strong enough so that it does not break under the loads that will be applied to it.
4. The guard must be rigid enough so that it does not vibrate or deflect, causing it to come into contact with other machine parts.
5. The guard must contain flying particles, liquids, or fractured tools.
6. The guard must allow visibility in the working area.
7. The guard must not create additional hazards.

In some cases, it may be necessary to have an opening in the guard to feed material. An opening of 3/8 of an inch or less is generally considered to be safe. However, this opening may be too small to pass material. In these cases, the guard must be designed so that material can be fed in, yet the hand is prevented from reaching the nip point. One formula that is used when the distance from the guard to the danger zone is less than 12 inches is the following (Hagan et al. 2001):

Maximum Safe Opening = 1/4 in + 1/8 in × distance from guard to danger zone (30)

ANSI B11.1 (ANSI 2009) provides "opening versus guard distance" data, which is tabulated in Table 10. For example, if a 0.625-inch opening is required in a guard for feeding material, then the guard must be 3.5 to 6.5 inches from the point of operation. This will

TABLE 10

Opening Versus Guard Distance

Distance of Opening from Point of Operation (inches)	Maximum Width of Opening (inches)
< 1/2	Not permitted
1/2 to 2 1/2	1/4
2 1/2 to 3 1/2	3/8
3 1/2 to 6 1/2	5/8
6 1/2 to 17 1/2	1 1/4
17 1/2 to 36	1 7/8
> 36	5

(*Source:* ANSI B11.1 2009)

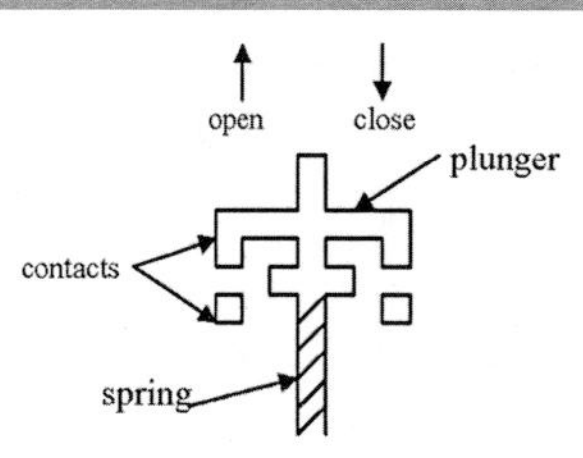

FIGURE 24. Spring-loaded switch

minimize the chances that an operator's fingertips will reach the danger area.

An *interlocked guard* is required when the operator must enter the point of operation to add material, remove material, or perform maintenance. A safety interlock switch or device prevents the machine from operating or from being started if the guard is not in place. There are many different types of interlocks. Many food processors, for example, have a spring-loaded plunger, which prevents the processor from starting unless the cover is locked into place. In general, an interlock should operate reliably, be designed so that it is not easily defeated, have positively driven contacts, and should not fail in a closed position.

Figure 24 shows a common spring-loaded switch to illustrate the safety issues involved in designing an interlock. It should be noted that the switch shown in Figure 24 should not be used as an *interlock switch*. The switch consists of a spring-loaded plunger and electrical contacts. When the door is opened, the spring pushes the plunger up and the contacts are opened. When the door is closed, the plunger is pushed down and the contacts are closed. The switch is easily defeated since the plunger can be taped down. Also, the operator may inadvertently lean on the plunger while performing maintenance. The contacts are not positively driven. Opening the contacts depends solely on spring pressure. Opening the door does not directly pull the contacts apart. The switch does not fail in the open position. If the contacts become stuck or welded, or if the spring fails, the contacts remain closed. Lastly, the switch has no redundancy.

There are two types of interlocking systems. In a *power interlocking system*, the removal of the guard directly disrupts the power source. The most common system is a *control interlocking system*. In this system, the power source is interrupted by the switching of a circuit that controls the power-switching device. Interlocking systems can become very complicated. For example, in most cases not only do you want to prevent machine activation if the guard is removed, but you also want to prevent the operator from entering the area until the machine stops moving. In these cases, it may be necessary to incorporate a guard-locking device so that the guard cannot be opened until the machine has stopped.

In some cases, it is not possible to design a fixed or adjustable guard. For example, in some machines such as metal shears or pizza dough-rolling machines, the operator must hand feed the material into the point of operation. In these cases, an *awareness guard* may be the only alternative. An awareness guard alerts an operator that he is entering a dangerous area of a machine rather than preventing the entering as a properly designed barrier guard would. Typically, an awareness guard consists of a series of heavy rollers placed across the feed area. As the operator feeds the material, the weight of the rollers on the operator's hands provides a tactile cue that there is an impending hazard.

Another method to keep the operator's hands out of the point of operation is a *two-hand control*. A two-hand control usually consists of two palm buttons. To activate the machine, the operator must use both hands, one on each button. The buttons should be spaced far enough apart that the operator cannot activate both controls with, for example, a hand and an elbow, leaving the other hand free. The two-hand control should be located far enough from the point of operation so that the operator cannot reach into the danger area after the machine is activated. A two-hand control only protects the operator; it does not protect other workers who may be in the area.

There are also *presence-sensing devices* that can be used in place of a physical barrier. Light curtains are one such device. These devices work by sending an array of synchronized, parallel infrared light beams to a receiver. If a hand or body part breaks the beam, the control logic sends a signal to stop the machine. Capacitive sensing devices use an electromagnetic field generated by an antenna. A change in the field caused by a hand or body part sends a signal to the control unit, which stops the machine.

Safety mats are another type of presence-sensing device. A safety mat is basically a large switch. It consists of two metal plates separated by bumpers. When a person steps on the mat, contact is made, sending a control signal to stop the machine. Safety mats are usually used where perimeter guarding is required, such as around robotic workstations and automated equipment. Trip cords, body bars, and trip bars are other types of presence-sensing devices. When a hand or other part of the body contacts these devices, the machine is stopped.

Presence-sensing devices should be installed in such a manner that the worker cannot reach over, under, or around the device. The overall presence-sensing system, including the control circuitry and the braking mechanism, must be able to stop the machine before the worker penetrates the protected area and reaches the point of operation. There are several formulas for calculating the minimum safe distance for the placement of presence-sensing devices (see Figures 25 and 26). The formula presented in ANSI B11.1 (ANSI 2009) is

$$D_s = K(T_s + T_c + T_r + T_{spm}) + D_{pf} \tag{31}$$

where

D_s = minimum safe distance in inches between the light curtain or the outside edge of the safety mat and the nearest hazard

K = maximum speed at which the operator can approach the hazard in inches per second

T_s = total time in seconds that it takes for the hazardous motion to stop

T_c = time in seconds that it takes for the machine control system to activate the machine's brake

T_r = response time of the presence-sensing device in seconds

T_{spm} = additional stopping time in seconds that is allowed by the stopping-performance monitor

D_{pf} = added distance, in inches, due to the depth penetration factor. For light curtains this is related to how far an object can move through the sensing field before the light curtain reacts. For a safety mat this distance is 48 inches.

Safeguarding of specific classes of machines can be found in the following ANSI standards:

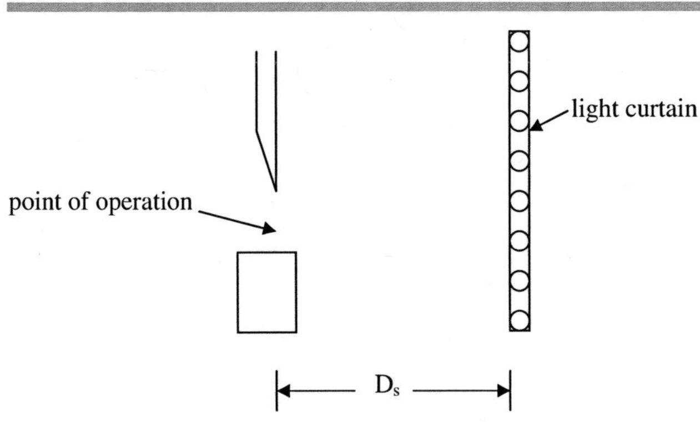

FIGURE 25. Minimum safe distance (D_s) for a light curtain

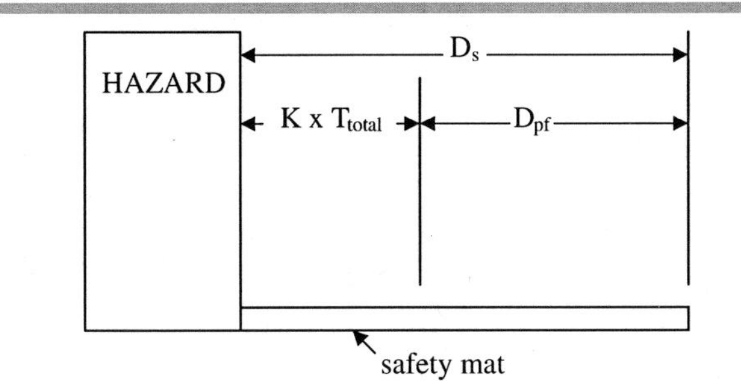

FIGURE 26. Minimum safe distance (D_s) for a safety mat

B7.5	Abrasives
B11	Machine Tools
B15.1	Power Transmission Apparatus
B65	Printing Equipment
B71.1	Garden Equipment
B154.1	Rivet Setting Equipment
B155.1	Packaging Equipment
B173	Hand Tools
B165	Power Tools
B186.1	Portable Air Tools
B209	Hand Tools
B208.1	Pipe Threading Machines
B01.1	Woodworking Machinery
R15.06	Robots
Z245.5	Baling Equipment

Laser Machining

According to ANSI B11.21, laser machining presents a new set of problems when it comes to machine guarding (ANSI 2006d). Mechanical damage to the protective housing, the laser itself, or the beam delivery system can cause the laser to be aimed at an operator or the viewing window. Electrical hazards include high voltages, stored energy, and high current capability. There can also be thermal hazards. Poorly designed interlock switches, switch assemblies, interlock circuits, gas lines, and gas valves can create hazardous conditions. Radiation hazards can exist in the form of X-rays from plasmas and UV radiation. Potentially hazardous material by-products may be emitted, depending on the material being cut.

ANSI B11.21 (ANSI 2006d) lists safety requirements for laser machine tools. The emergency stop shall deactivate laser-beam generation, automatically position the laser-beam stop, stop all hazardous motion, and eliminate or control all stored energy. There should be a means to conduct exhaust effluent out of the machine tool. Personnel need to be protected from laser radiation. This can be accomplished by floor mats or light curtains that prohibit entrance into a hazard zone.

Material Handling

Conveyors

Conveyors are used in almost every industry. Thousands of miles of conveyors are used to transport materials every day. These devices have many hazardous areas that need to be safeguarded. The number of operating and maintenance injuries from conveyor systems is in the range of 10,000 per year (Schultz 2000, Schultz 2004). Most injuries occur when workers clean or maintain the conveyor, reach into the conveyor to remove objects, tools, or clothing caught there, or fall or reach into a pinch point. Hazardous areas include power transmission, nip points, shear points, pinch points, spill points, exposed edges, areas under the conveyor, and transfer mechanisms.

There are many types of conveyors. Gravity-driven conveyors can have either wheels or rollers that transport the loads. Runaway loads and material falling off the conveyor are some of the hazards associated with gravity conveyors. Powered roller conveyors use powered rollers to move the loads. A belt conveyor uses a moving belt to transport loads. These conveyors consist of the belt, the idlers that support the belt, the pulleys that move the belt, the drive systems, and the supporting structure. Belt conveyor hazards include pinch points, moving parts, attempting repairs to a moving conveyor, and attempting to cross over a moving belt. A chain conveyor uses a series of slats attached to a chain. Other conveyor types include overhead, vertical reciprocating, harpoon, screw, vibrating, and bucket elevator conveyors.

Designing for safety should be applied to the design, installation, and maintenance of conveyor systems. ANSI B20.1, *Safety Standard for Conveyors and Related Equipment*, sets forth minimum safety standards for conveyors (ANSI/ASME 2009). All exposed moving parts that present a hazard should be guarded. When it is not possible to install a guard, such as in cases where the guard would render the conveyor unusable, prominent warnings should be provided. Nip and shear points should be guarded. Antirunaway, brake, or backstop devices should be provided on inclined and vertical conveyors. Openings to hoppers and chutes should be guarded to prevent personnel from falling into them (ANSI/ASME 2003).

There are a number of additional safety issues that should be addressed when selecting a conveyor system. First, on–off controls should be provided near operator stations. The controls should be located where the operator can see as much of the conveyor as possible. Emergency stop controls, such as emergency cables, should be installed in areas where there are exposed moving parts. Warning signs should be provided to alert personnel about standing on conveyors, removing guards, bypassing safety devices, and any hidden hazards.

Railings should be installed in areas where materials can be knocked off the conveyor. Usually this happens when an object protrudes over the edge and gets caught on another object. This can also happen if objects become backed up. Nets or other guards should be installed in areas where a conveyor passes over a pedestrian walkway. Steps or bridges should be installed in areas where workers may need to cross over the conveyor. This would discourage workers from walking on the conveyor. Gates or pull stops should be located in areas where a person could enter a dangerous area after falling onto a conveyor. Select operator stations should be ergonomically designed, including the proper height and reach to avoid worker injuries.

Robots

A *robot* is a programmable material-handling mechanism that is capable of automatic position control for orienting materials, work pieces, tools, or devices. Figure 27 shows industrial robots in an automotive assembly line. Robots are more hazardous than conventional machines in that robots are programmed, and they do not always follow a continuous, regular cycle of operation. A worker may be tempted to enter the work area thinking the robot is idle or continuing with the same pattern. For example, if a robot happens to be motionless, it should not be assumed that it will remain that way. The program may have a delay where the robot remains idle before taking up the next task. If a robot repeats a particular pattern, it should not be assumed that it will continue to repeat the same pattern.

FIGURE 27. Industrial robots on an automotive assembly line (Courtesy of Kuka Robotics Corporation 2007)

Computers can automatically modify the pattern that the robot was following.

Injuries associated with robotic systems include being struck by the robot, being entrapped between the moving parts of the robot and a fixed object, and being struck by objects that are being handled by the robot. Many injuries involving robots are the result of inadequate safeguarding. A study of 32 robotic injuries (Gainer and Jiang 1987) uncovered the following breakdown:

- operator in work area while robot in operation
- operator in work area while robot stopped, but put in operation by worker inadvertently hitting start button
- operator entered work area with robot stopped by compressed air trapped in line
- operator placed work piece on conveyor during setup, and a conveyor sensor activated robot
- adjacent work area within robot work area
- robot reached over fence
- worker performed task while robot held the work piece
- maintenance worker in robot area, and colleague started robot
- maintenance worker in robot area performing test-run after maintenance
- maintenance worker entered robot area to perform maintenance while robot was in operation

Sometimes robots are programmed by being physically guided through the desired tasks by the operator using a *teaching pendant*. The robot *learns* by storing feedback from its position sensors. Teaching pendants should contain an emergency stop button or dead-man switch so the operator can stop the robot. The rate of movement should be limited to 6 inches per second or less when in the teach mode. The robot should be programmed so that the operator cannot put it into automatic cycle using the teaching pendant.

Many of the safeguards that are used for machine safeguarding, such as safety mats and light curtains, can be used to safeguard a robot. Safeguards should prevent entry into the robot's operating area or envelope. The operating envelope is the entire volume swept by all possible motions of the robot. Fences or fixed guards should be placed around the perimeter of the robot operating area. Care should be taken not to make these barriers rigid in areas close to the robot as to avoid entrapment. Fences should not be easy to climb over. Access gates should be interlocked. The interlock should incorporate a blocking device to prevent opening until the robot is shut down. A deliberate manual action should be required to restart the robot. There should be ample clearance between the robot's operational area and any fixed objects, such as columns, posts, or poles. Warning signs should be placed in the area and at the access gates. An amber light on the robot will make it more conspicuous and alert nearby workers that the robot is energized.

The following list (Russell 1982) provides additional factors to consider for the design, installation, operation, and maintenance of a robot system:

1. The robot should be positioned to prevent unintentional access. This may require barriers with interlocked gates and/or presence-sensing devices, such as light curtains and safety mats.
2. The control panel for the robot should be located outside the danger area.
3. A "power on" light should be installed so that it is clear to everybody that the robot is energized, even if it isn't moving.
4. The robot should not automatically reactivate if the electricity is interrupted.
5. If the robot stops suddenly, it should not lose its grip on the part it is handling.
6. Consideration should be given to equipping the robot arm with a pressure-sensitive switch that will shut it down if it strikes someone or something.
7. Emergency stop switches and/or trip wires should be installed around the perimeter of the robot's working area.
8. Computer software programs should include preprogrammed reach limits.
9. Fixed mechanical stops should be used to limit the reach of the robot arm.

10. Teaching pendants should have an emergency stop button. The robot should be operated at a reduced speed when in the teaching mode.
11. The robot system should be properly locked out during maintenance.

Powered Industrial Trucks

A powered industrial truck (PIT) is a powered vehicle that is used to transport, stack, and lift material. They travel up to 10 mph. There are many types of powered industrial trucks. Low-lift trucks transport loads 4 to 6 inches from the floor and do not raise the load for stacking. Some low-lift trucks are battery-powered and allow a rider to stand on the equipment. High-lift trucks can transport and lift loads very high. Counterbalance rider trucks are the most common PIT used in industry. These trucks consist of adjustable forks, a tilt mast, and a counterweight. The counterweight acts to balance the truck when the load is lifted. These trucks are powered by electricity, gasoline, liquefied natural gas (LNG), liquefied petroleum gas (LPG), or diesel fuel. Narrow-aisle trucks are designed for material handling in narrow aisles. The operator stands on the operator's platform while working the controls. Order-picking trucks are another form of narrow-aisle truck, except the operator's platform rides up with the forks.

The improper operation of PITs continues to be responsible for worker and pedestrian injuries. Tables 11 and 12 list incident statistics (Swartz 2001). Collisions with fixed objects, such as doors, walls, posts, beams, sprinklers, pipes, racking, electrical boxes, fencing, machinery, and other trucks, can cause operator injuries. Pedestrians are also at risk. Injury to the operator and/or pedestrians can result from a falling load or a truck tipover. Rearward travel (forks trailing) is a common factor with narrow-aisle truck accidents, accounting for over 90 percent of collisions with racking, walls, posts, and other objects.

TABLE 11

Collision Details of Narrow-Aisle Truck

Incident	Rate
Collisions with racking	33%
Collisions with walls	21%
Collisions with posts	18%
Collisions with other stationary objects	16%
Collision with other forklifts	12%

(*Source:* Swartz 2001, 26)

TABLE 12

Percentage of Forklift Fatalities

Incident	Rate
Tip over	25.3%
Struck by PIT	18.8%
Struck by falling load	14.4%
Elevated employee on truck	12.2%
Ran off dock or other surface	7.0%
Improper maintenance	6.1%
Lost control of truck	4.4%
Employees overcome by CO or propane fuel	4.4%
Faulty PIT	3.1%
Unloading unchocked trailer	3.1%
Employee fell from vehicle	3.1%
Improper use of vehicle	2.6%
Electrocutions	1.0%

(*Source:* Swartz 2001, 26)

The risk of injuries can be reduced by a number of PIT design features. PITs that are capable of elevating loads should be equipped with an overhead guard to prevent falling objects from striking the operator. The guard should provide good visibility. PITs should have an audible warning device under the operator's control that can be heard above the ambient noise levels. Flashing lights are another warning device that can alert employees or pedestrians that a truck is approaching. If feasible, a back-up alarm should operate when the truck is backing up. The controls should be confined to the operator's station. The operator should not have to reach outside this area where a body part could be pinched between the truck and a fixed object. There should be a dead-man control; the truck should stop if the operator leaves the operator's station. ANSI B56.1 lists other specifications for steering, braking, and controls (ANSI 2005a).

There are also design measures that can be implemented in the operating area. Barriers, such as horizontal guardrails or vertical posts, should be installed to protect offices, doors, stairs, electrical boxes, gas meters, racking, beams, and pedestrian walkways. Highlighting posts and beams with yellow paint makes them readily conspicuous compared to the surroundings. Highlighted cushions around fixed objects, such as steel columns, not only make them conspicuous, but also reduce the force of impact as well. Mirrors should be installed at intersections. Pedestrian walkways should be highlighted. Adequate ventilation should be provided in operating areas to prevent the build-up of carbon monoxide.

Injuries with PITs cannot be reduced by design measures alone. Operators need to be trained. An industrial truck training program involves selecting, training, and testing the operator. The applicant should have a valid motor-vehicle license and a good driving record. The operator should be mature, must be able to see well, judge distances, and have good hand and eye coordination. The training program should include classroom instruction, hands-on instruction, a driving test, and a written examination. Each trainee should have the operator's manual for the truck he/she will be operating. The operator training program should be specific to the type of trucks to be used, the company's policies, and the operating conditions. New operators and experienced operators who may be new to the particular facility need to be trained. All operators should receive a periodic refresher course. Any operator who has been involved in an accident while driving a PIT should be retrained before returning to work as an operator. There should be written documentation of the training.

Hands-on training is important, even if the operator has a valid driver's license. There are many differences between driving an automobile and driving a PIT. A PIT has a higher center of gravity and a shorter wheelbase than an automobile. Also, a PIT typically has three points of stability—two front wheels and the center of the rear axle—while an automobile has four. A PIT usually has only two braking wheels instead of four.

Hands-on training should be done in a planned practice area. The practice area should allow sufficient room for maneuvering a truck. The trainer should demonstrate each maneuver; then the trainee should perform the same maneuver. Each operator should successfully pass a written test and a driving skills test before being allowed to drive an industrial truck unsupervised.

Operators should keep their hands, legs, and other body parts inside the operating station of the truck and/or guard. Passengers should never be allowed to ride on the truck. Operators should sound the horn when approaching pedestrians and should never drive near a pedestrian who is standing in front of a fixed object. Operators should stop and sound the horn at blind corners and before going through doorways.

Automated Guided Vehicles (AGVs)

Unlike conventional powered industrial trucks (PITs), automated guided vehicles (AGVs) are driverless vehicles with automatic guidance systems capable of following prescribed paths. In automated factories and facilities, AGVs move pallets and containers. In offices they may be used to deliver and pick up the mail. Figure 28 shows a photo of an AGV.

FIGURE 28. An AGV system (Courtesy of FMC Technologies)

Until about 10 years ago, most AGVs followed electromagnetic wires buried in a floor. Then laser-guided systems came onto the market. These navigation systems allowed the AGV to determine its position in the plant based on the location of reflectors within the area. In-plant global positioning systems may be in the future.

From a safety standpoint, AGVs can reduce injuries due to driver inattention, driving too fast, or personnel not paying attention. However, AGV systems introduce a whole new set of safety concerns. There should be a reliable obstacle detection system so the AGVs do not strike an object or a person in its path. The AGV travel and turning paths need to be clearly marked so that personnel know what areas to stay clear of. Workers need to be trained in the risks associated with AGVs.

The AGV system should include a carefully designed traffic control system to prevent collisions between the AGVs and any towed vehicles. One of the oldest forms of traffic control systems is in-floor zone blocking. With this system, the guide path is divided into zones. Vehicles are allowed to enter a zone only when that zone is completely clear. Sensors in the floor at the zone boundaries detect vehicles as they pass. Vehicles can be released into the zone by having the path energized (Miller 1987)

All areas where there is pedestrian travel or interaction with workers should have a minimum clearance of 18 inches between the AGV and its load and any fixed object. This clearance allows a person to stand while the AGV and its load passes without presenting a safety hazard (Miller 1987).

ANSI B56.5 defines the safety requirements for guided industrial vehicles and automated functions of manned industrial vehicles (ANSI 2005b). There are separate responsibilities for the user and for the manufacturer. User responsibilities include load stabilization, marking the travel path on the floor, including turning and maneuvering clearances, and preventive maintenance. The manufacturer is responsible for guidance, travel performance, braking emergency controls and devices, and object detection.

Obstacle detection systems have largely consisted of mechanical bumpers—giant emergency stops (E-stops) that stop the AGV if it contacts a person or obstacle. This low-cost method to prevent contact has a number of drawbacks. A contact-sensitive mechanical bumper has only two states: on or off. Once the contact has been made, additional time is required to stop the vehicle. The stopping time varies with the speed of the vehicle. From a productivity standpoint, the vehicles must operate at lower speeds and the E-stop must be reset after the obstacle is cleared. Mechanical bumpers are also sensitive to vibration and wear, require regular maintenance, and may not be totally effective when an AGV contacts an object when turning.

There are human-factors issues related to contact-sensitive obstacle detection systems. Workers may be uncomfortable with the fact that they have to be hit by the AGV before it will stop. Workers may also be injured trying to beat the AGV, thinking that they can get past the vehicle and a fixed object.

New advanced virtual bumpers using proximity laser scanner and laser scanner interface (PLS/LSI) technology are a significant improvement over contact-sensitive systems. A proximity laser scanner (PLS) creates a sensing field with a pulsed light that is reflected off of a rotating mirror so that it is transmitted in a 180-degree pattern. When an object enters the sensing field, the light is reflected back to the PLS. The distance to the object is computed using the time interval between the transmitted pulse and the reflected pulse and the angle of the rotating mirror. The sensing field is divided into three areas: safety zone, warning zone, and surveyed zone. The surveyed area is the maximum radius surveyed by the PLS. When the PLS determines that an object is in the safety zone, hazardous motion is stopped. When an object is detected in the warning zone, it initiates a warning or an avoidance maneuver.

A laser scanner interface (LSI) is essentially a computer that interprets information and acts on it. The LSI can interpret data from up to four PLSs. When the PLS and LSI are combined in this way, the PLS acts as the *eyes* and the LSI acts as the *brain*. The LSI can also tell the PLS to change its view depending on the location within the plant. For example, if the LSI gets input from the navigation system that the AGV is near a corner, the PLS view can be changed to go around the corner. The PLS also has a self-checking feature.

The exit window is continuously checked for signal loss by an internal sensing array. Systems approved for AGV use should be able to detect a black vertical object with a diameter of 70 mm and a height of 400 mm (representing a leg in black trousers) anywhere in the AGV route.

There are a number of safety and productivity advantages with virtual bumpers. Speed can be controlled as the vehicle approaches an object and the configuration of the warning and safety zones can be flexible. For example, the vehicle slows down as it approaches an object. Also, a warning can be sounded if an object enters the warning zone. This advanced system permits increased speed and productivity because the size and shape of the stopping/slow-down/warning zones can be adjusted in real time depending on speed and the load. The protective area can be automatically extended on the sides of the vehicle when turning corners. Vehicle speeds can be increased in straight, unobstructed paths for improved productivity. Response times are as low as 60 milliseconds, depending on the system.

Consideration should be given to load size and tuggers when marking travel paths. Although a travel path may be adequate for the AGV, it may not be adequate if the AGV is towing a tugger or carrying a wide load. The travel path should be kept clear of material. Employees should be trained not to ride the AGVs. Training should also include instructing personnel to stay clear of an approaching AGV. The training program should also include contractors that may come into a plant or warehouse to perform work. A safety procedure should be put in place when work has to be done in an area where AGVs are operating. For example, weighted cones or other portable obstacles can be placed where workers may be working on or near an AGV travel path.

References

American Conference of Governmental Industrial Hygienists (ACGIH). 2010. *Industrial Ventilation*. 27th ed. Cincinnati, Ohio: ACGIH.

American National Standards Institute (ANSI). 2002. SNT 101, *Portable, Compressed-Air-Actuated, Fastener Driver Tools-Safety Requirements For*. New York: ANSI.

______. 2005a. B56.1, *Standard for Low Lift and High Lift Trucks*. New York: ANSI.

______. 2005b. B56.5 2005, *Safety Standard for Guided Industrial Vehicles and Automated Functions of Manned Industrial Vehicles*. New York: ANSI.

______. 2006a. A1264.2, *Standard for the Provision of Slip Resistance on Walking/Working Surfaces*. New York: ANSI.

———. 2006b. Z535.1, *Safety Color Code*. New York: ANSI.

———. 2006c. Z535.6, *Product Safety Information in Product Manuals, Instructions, and Other Collateral Materials*. New York, ANSI.

______. 2006d. B11.21, *Safety Requirements for Machine Tools Using a Laser for Processing Materials*. New York: ANSI.

———. 2006e. S1.4, *Specification for Sound Level Meters*. New York: ANSI.

———. 2007a. Z535.2, *Environmental and Facility Safety Signs*. New York: ANSI.

———. 2007b. Z535.3, *Criteria for Safety Symbols*. New York: ANSI.

———. 2007c. Z535.4, *Product Safety Signs and Labels*. New York: ANSI.

———. 2007d. Z535.5, *Safety Tags and Barricade Tapes*. New York: ANSI.

———. 2009. B11.1, *Safety Requirements for Mechanical Power Presses*. New York: ANSI.

American National Standards Institute and American Society of Mechanical Engineers (ANSI/ASME). 2009. B20.1, *Standard for Conveyors and Related Equipment*. New York: ANSI.

American Society for Testing and Materials (ASTM). 2005. F609-05, *Standard Test Method for Using a Horizontal Pull Meter*. West Conshohocken, PA: ASTM.

———. 2009. F1637, *Standard Practice for Safe Walking Surfaces*. West Conshohocken, PA: ASTM.

Arnold, R. 2002. "Choosing a Framing Nailer." *Fine Homebuilding* (Feb/March), pp. 68–75.

Burton, D. 1995. *Industrial Ventilation Workbook*. Bountiful, Utah: IVE, Inc.

Chapman, A. 2008. *Biomechanical Analysis of Fundamental Human Movements*. Champaign, IL: Human Kinetics.

Cohen, J., C. LaRue, and H. Cohen. 2009. "Stairway Falls: An Ergonomic Analysis of 80 Cases." *Professional Safety* (January), pp. 27–32.

Cott, H., and R. Kinkade. 1972. *Human Engineering Guide Equipment Design*. New York, NY: McGraw-Hill.

DiPilla, S. and K. Vidal. 2002. "State of the Art in Slip Resistance Measurement." *Professional Safety* (June), pp. 37–42.

Dusenberry, D., H. Simpson, and S. DelloRusso. 2008. "Effect of Handrail Shape on Graspability." *Applied Ergonomics* (October), pp. 1–13).

Gainer, C. G., and B. Jiang. 1987. *A Cause and Effect Analysis of Industrial Robot Accidents from Four Countries*. Dearborn, MI: Society of Manufacturing Engineers.

Gray, B. 1990. *Slips, Stumbles, and Falls*. Philadelphia: ASTM.

Grieser, B., T. Rhoades, and R. Shah. 2002. "Slip Resistance Field Measurements Using Two Modern Slipmeters." *Professional Safety* (June), pp. 43–48.

Hagan, Philip, et al., eds. 2009. *Accident Prevention Manual for Business and Industry Engineering & Technology*. 13th ed. Itasca, IL: NSC.

Hammer, Willie. 1972. *Handbook of System and Product Safety*. Englewood Cliffs, NJ: Prentice-Hall.

Harris, C. 1991. *Handbook of Acoustical Measurements and Noise Control*. New York: McGraw-Hill.

Hirschorn, Mark. 1989. *Noise Control Reference Handbook*. New York: Industrial Acoustics Company.

International Code Council (ICC). 2006a. *International Residential Code for One- and Two-Family Dwellings*. Country Club Hills, IL: ICC.

______. 2006b. *International Building Code*. Country Club Hills, IL: ICC.

______. 2006c. *International Mechanical Code*. County Club Hills, IL: ICC.

Jensen, P., C. Jokel, and L. Miller. 1978. NIOSH Publication No 79-117, *Industrial Noise Control Manual*. Washington, DC: NIOSH.

Knowles, E., ed. 2003. *Noise Control*. Des Plaines, IL: ASSE.

Kohr, Robert. 1994. "A New Focus on Slip and Fall Accidents." *Professional Safety* (January), pp. 32–36.

Marpet, Mark, and Michael Sapienza, eds. 2003. *Pedestrian Locomotion and Slip Resistance*. West Conshohocken, PA: ASTM.

Meserlian, Donald. 1995. "Effect of Walking Cadence on Static Coefficient of Friction Required by the Elderly." *Professional Safety* (November), pp. 24–29.

Miller, Richard. 1987. *Automated Guided Vehicles and Automated Manufacturing*. Dearborn: Society of Manufacturing Engineers (SME).

National Fire Protection Association (NFPA). 2008. *Fire Protection Handbook*. Quincy, MA: NFPA.

______. 2009. NFPA 101, *Life Safety Code*. Quincy, MA: NFPA.

National Safety Council (NSC). 1946. *Accident Prevention Manual for Industrial Operations*. Chicago: NSC.

______. 1988. *Making the Job Easier—An Ergonomics Idea Book*. Itasca, IL: NSC.

Pierce, Alan. 1981. *Acoustics: An Introduction to its Physical Principles and Applications*. New York: McGraw-Hill.

Plog, B., ed. 2002. *Fundamentals of Industrial Hygiene*. 5th ed. Itasca, IL: NSC.

Rosen, Stephen. 2000. *The Slip and Fall Handbook*. 8th ed. Del Mar, CA: Hanrow Press.

Russell, John. 1982. "Robot Safety Considerations . . . a Checklist." *Professional Safety* (December), pp. 36–37.

Salvendy, G., ed. 2006. *Handbook of Human Factors and Ergonomics*. Hoboken, NJ: John Wiley & Sons.

Schulte, P., R. Rinehart, A. Okun, C. Geraci, and D. Heide. 2008. "National Prevention Through (PtD) Initiative." *Journal of Safety Research*, 39:2, pp. 115-121.

Schultz, George. 2000. *Conveyor Safety*. Des Plaines, IL: ASSE.

______. 2004. "Conveyor Safety." *Professional Safety* (August), pp. 24–27.

Sotter, George. 1995. "Friction Underfoot." *Occupational Safety and Health* (March), pp. 28–34.

Swartz, George. 2001. "When PITs Strike People & Objects." *Professional Safety* (March), pp. 25–30.

Templer, John. 1994. *The Staircase*. Cambridge, MA: The MIT Press.

Thuman, A, and R. Miller. 1986. *Fundamentals of Noise Control Engineering*. Englewood Cliffs, NJ: Prentice-Hall.

Woodson, Wesley, et al. 1992. *Human Factors Design Handbook*, 2d ed. New York: McGraw-Hill, Inc.

Appendix: Recommended Reading

American Society of Heating, Refrigerating and Air-Conditioning Engineers (ASHRAE). 1999. *HVAC Applications*. Atlanta: ASHRAE.

______. 1997. *Fundamentals*. Atlanta: ASHRAE.

Baggs, J., et al. 2001. "Pneumatic Nailer Injuries." *Professional Safety* (January), pp. 33–38.

Beohm, Richard. 1998. "Designing Safety into Machines." *Professional Safety* (September), pp. 20–26.

Binder, Raymond. 1973. *Fluid Mechanics*. Englewood Cliffs, NJ: Prentice-Hall.

Constance, John. 1998. "Understanding Industrial Exhaust Systems." *Professional Safety* (April), pp. 26–28.

Etherton, John. 1988. *Safe Maintenance Guide for Robotic Workstations*. Washington, D.C.: NIOSH.

Gallagher, V. 1990. "Guarding by Location: A Dangerous Concept." *Professional Safety* (September), pp. 34–40.

Gierzak, J. 2003. "Duct Liner Materials and Acoustics." *ASHRAE Journal* (December), pp. 46–51.

Guckelberger, D. 2000. "Controlling Noise from Large Rooftop Units." *ASHRAE Journal* (May), pp. 55–62.

Guenther, F. 1998. "Solving Noise Control Problems." *ASHRAE Journal* (February), pp. 34–40.

Hagan, Philip, et al., eds. 2009. *Accident Prevention Manual for Business and Industry Administration & Programs*. 13th ed. Itasca, IL: NSC.

Howard, G. 1982. "Reduce Chain Saw Accidents." *Professional Safety* (December), pp. 15–18.

Hynes, G. 1981. "Occupational Noise Exposure." *Professional Safety* (September), pp. 13–18.

Illuminating Engineering Society (IES). 2003. *IESNA Lighting Ready Reference*. New York: Illuminating Engineering Society of North America.

Jones, Robert. 2003. "Controlling Noise from HVAC Systems." *ASHRAE Journal* (September), pp. 28–34.

Katz, Gary. 2006. "Avoiding Accidents on the Tablesaw." *Fine Homebuilding* (June), pp. 86–92.

Lilly, J. 2000. "Noise in the Classroom." *ASHRAE Journal* (February), pp. 21–29.

Marshall, Gilbert. 2000. *Safety Engineering*. 3d ed. Richard T. Beohm, ed. Des Plaines, IL: ASSE.

McConnell, Steven. 2004. "Machine Safeguarding: Building a Successful Program." *Professional Safety* (January), pp. 18–27.

Moisseev, N. 2003. "Predicting HVAC Noise Outdoors." *ASHRAE Journal* (April), pp. 28–34.

Moore, M., and G. Rennell. 1991. "Kickback Hazard: Do Manufacturer Warnings and Instructions Help Saw Users Understand the Risks." *Professional Safety* (April), pp. 31–34.

Mutawe, A., et al. 2002. "OSHA's Lockout/Tagout Standards: A Review of Key Requirements." *Professional Safety* (February), pp. 20–24.

National Safety Council (NSC). 1993. *Safeguarding Concepts Illustrated*. Itasca, IL: NSC.

______. 1991. *Falls on Floors*. Itasca, IL: NSC.

Occupational Safety and Health Administration (OSHA). 1980. 3027, *Concepts and Techniques of Machine Safeguarding*. Washington, D.C.: OSHA.

Parker, Jerald. 1988. *Heating, Ventilating and Air Conditioning*. New York: John Wiley & Sons.

Parks, R. 1996. "The Basics of Industrial Ventilation Design." *ASHRAE Journal* (November), pp. 29–34.

Roughton, James. 1995. "Lockout/Tagout Standard Revisited." *Professional Safety* (April), pp. 33–37.

Stalnaker, K. 2002. "Making the Transition from Startup to Normal Operation." *Professional Safety* (November), pp. 14–15.

Swartz, George. 1997. *Forklift Safety*. Rockville, MD: Government Institutes.

______. 1998. "Forklift Tipover: A Detailed Analysis." *Professional Safety* (January), pp. 20–24.

Turek, Mark.1991. "Lockout/Tagout Maintaining Machines Safely." *Professional Safety* (November), pp. 33–36.

Winchester, S. 1995. "Safety Fixtures for Table Saws and Shapers." *Fine Homebuilding* (December), pp. 78–80.

Pressure Vessel Safety

6

Mohammad A. Malek

LEARNING OBJECTIVES

- Learn about the fundamentals and various types of fired and unfired pressure vessels that are commonly used in industries.
- Recognize the potential hazards and the causes and severity of accidents involving pressure vessels, and learn about the government safety regulations to prevent such accidents.
- Become familiar with the process of design, fabrication, inspection, code stamping, and certification of new pressure vessels in accordance with the American Society of Mechanical Engineers (ASME) Code.
- Compare the pressure vessel construction codes of ASME, the American Petroleum Institute, and the Tubular Exchanger Manufacturers Association.
- Be able to determine the corrosion rate, remaining life, and maximum allowable working pressure of existing pressure vessels.
- Understand the importance of establishing a pressure vessel hazard-control program and list the elements of such a program.

A PRESSURE VESSEL is a closed container designed to withstand pressure, whether internal or external. The pressure may be imposed by an external source, by the application of heat from a direct or indirect source, or by any combination thereof. The pressure vessels are usually subjected to an internal or external operating pressure greater than 15 psig (103 kPa).

Internal pressure in a vessel is developed from the fluid in process application. External pressure on a vessel may be imposed by an internal vacuum or by pressure of the fluid between an outer jacket and the vessel wall. The components of a vessel may fail, causing dangerous accidents, if the vessel cannot withstand the internal or external pressure.

Pressure vessels are designed and constructed in various shapes. They may be cylindrical with heads, spherical, spheroidal, boxed, or lobed. Common types of pressure vessels include boilers, water heaters, expansion tanks, feedwater heaters, columns, towers, drums, reactors, heat exchangers, condensers, air coolers, oil coolers, accumulators, air tanks, gas cylinders, and refrigeration systems.

Pressure vessels contain fluids such as liquids, vapors, and gases at pressure levels greater than atmospheric pressure. Some of the fluids may be corrosive or toxic. All types of workplaces, from workshops and power generators to pulp and paper processors and large petrochemical refiners use pressure vessels. Small workshops use compressed air tanks. Petrochemical industries use hundreds of vessels that include towers, drums, and reactors for processing purposes. Depending upon the application, the vessels are constructed of either carbon steel or alloy steel.

Most pressure vessels are designed in accordance with the codes developed by the American Society of Mechanical Engineers (ASME) and the American Petroleum Institute (API). In addition to these codes, design engineers use engineering practices to make vessels safe. A pressure vessel bears the symbol stamping of the code under which it has been designed and constructed. Because a pressure vessel operates under pressure, safety is the main consideration during its design, construction, installation, operation, maintenance, inspection, and repair.

Figure 1 shows a diagram of a typical pressure vessel. The main components are the shell, the head, and the nozzles. This cylindrical vessel is horizontal and may be supported by steel columns, cylindrical plate skirts, or plate lugs attached to the shell. The vessel may be used for any type of industrial process application under internal pressure.

Like any other machine, a pressure vessel is comprised of many components and fitted with controls and safety devices. The major components of a pressure vessel are as follows:

Shell: The main component—the outer boundary metal of the vessel.

Head: The end closure of the shell. Heads may be spherical, conical, elliptical, or hemispherical.

Nozzle: A fitting to inlet and outlet connection pipes.

Types of Pressure Vessels

There are many types of pressure vessels, but they are generally classified into two basic categories:

1. Fired pressure vessels burn fuels to produce heat that in turn boils water to generate steam. Boilers and water heaters are fired pressure vessels.
2. Unfired pressure vessels store liquid, gas, or vapor at pressures greater than 15 psig (103 kPa) and include air tanks, heat exchangers, and towers.

This chapter will limit its discussion to unfired pressure vessels, and use of terminology should be assumed to reflect this throughout.

Most pressure vessels are cylindrical in shape. Spherical vessels may be used for extremely high-pressure operation. Vessels may range from a few hundred pounds per square inch (psi) up to 150,000 psi. The operating range of temperature may vary from –100°F to 900°F. The American Society of Mechanical Engineers (ASME), *Boiler and Pressure Vessel Code,* Section VIII—Division I (ASME 2011b) has exempted the following vessels from the definition of pressure vessel:

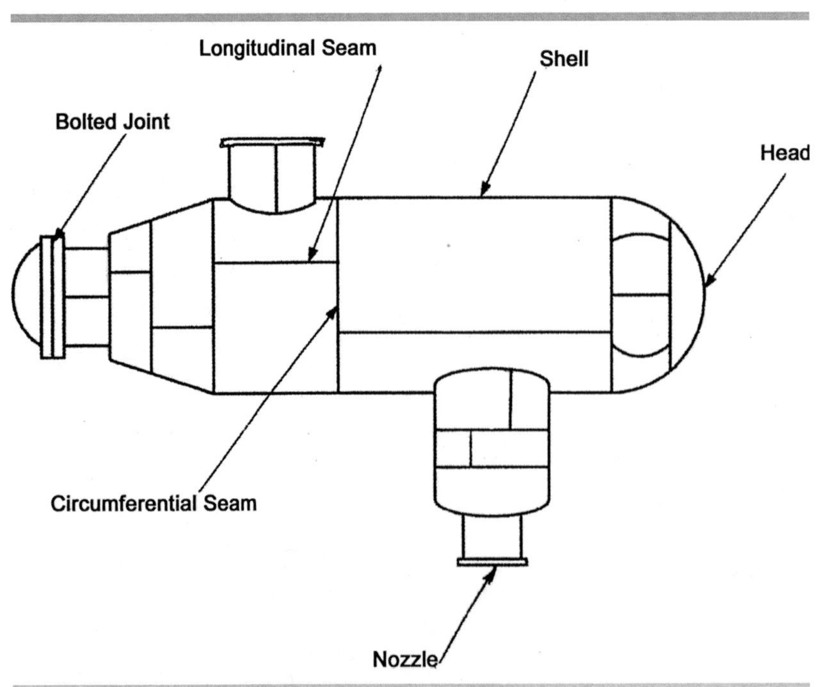

FIGURE 1. Pressure vessel

1. Pressure containers that are integral components of rotating or reciprocating mechanical devices, such as pumps, compressors, turbines, generators, and so on
2. Piping systems, components, flanges, gaskets, valves, expansion joints, and similar devices
3. Vessels for containing water under pressure, including those containing air compression to serve merely as a cushion, when neither of the following limitations are exceeded:
   a. design pressure of 300 psi
   b. design temperature of 210°F
4. Hot-water-supply storage tanks heated by steam or any other indirect means when none of the following limitations are exceeded:
   a. heat input of 200,000 Btu/hr
   b. water temperature of 210°F
   c. nominal water-containing capacity of 120 gal
5. Vessels having an internal or external operating pressure not exceeding 15 psi, regardless of size
6. Vessels having an inside diameter, width, height, or cross-section diagonal not exceeding 6 in, regardless of vessel length or pressure
7. Pressure vessels designed for human occupancy

Pressure Vessel Code

Pressure vessels are designed, constructed, inspected, and certified according to the ASME's *Boiler and Pressure Vessel Code* (ASME 2011a), the American Petroleum Institute (API) Code, and the Tubular Exchanger Manufacturers Association (TEMA) Code:

1. ASME Boiler and Pressure Vessel Code (2011a). ASME Code Section VIII is used internationally for construction of pressure vessels. This Code has three separate divisions—Division 1: *Pressure Vessels* (2011b), Division 2: *Alternative Rules* (2011c), and Division 3: *Alternative Rules for Construction of High Pressure Vessels* (2011d).

ASME Section VIII—Division 1: *Rules for Construction of Pressure Vessels* (2011b). These rules contain mandatory requirements, specific prohibitions, and nonmandatory guidance for pressure vessel materials, design, fabrication, examination, inspection, testing, certification, and pressure relief.

ASME Section VIII—Division 2: *Alternative Rules for Construction of Pressure Vessels* (2011c). These rules provide an alternative to the minimum construction requirements for the design, fabrication, inspection, and certification of pressure vessels with maximum allowable working pressure (MAWP) from 3000 to 10,000 psig.

ASME Section VIII—Division 3: *Alternative Rules for Construction of High Pressure Vessels* (2011d). These rules have to do with the design, construction, inspection, and overpressure protection of metallic pressure vessels with design pressure generally greater than 10,000 psi.

2. American Petroleum Institute (API) Code. API 510, *Pressure Vessel Inspection Code* (2006) is widely used in the petroleum and chemical process industries for maintenance inspection, rating, repair, and alteration of pressure vessels. This inspection code is only applicable to vessels that have been placed in service and that have been inspected by an authorized inspection agency or repaired by a repair organization defined in the code. The code has provisions by which to certify pressure vessel inspectors.

API RP 572, *Inspection of Pressure Vessels* (2009a) is a recommended practice (RP) standard for inspection of pressure vessels (towers, drums, reactors, heat exchangers, and condensers). The standard covers reasons for inspection, causes of deterioration, frequency and methods of inspection, methods of repair, and preparation of records and reports.

API 620, *Recommended Rules for Design and Construction of Large, Welded, Low-Pressure Storage Tanks* (2008) provides rules for the design and construction of large, welded, low-pressure carbon steel aboveground storage tanks. The tanks are designed for metal temperature not greater than 250°F and with pressures in their gas or vapor spaces of not more than 15 psig. These are low-pressure vessels that are not covered by ASME Section VIII—Division 1 Code (2011b).

API Standard 650, *Welded Steel Tanks for Oil Storage* (2007) covers materials, design, fabrication, erection, and testing requirements of aboveground, vertical, cylindrical, closed- and open-top, welded steel storage tanks in various sizes and capacities. This standard is applicable to tanks having internal pressures of approximately atmospheric pressure, but higher pressures are permitted when additional requirements are met.

ANSI/API Standard 660, *Shell-and-Tube Heat Exchangers for General Refinery Services* (2007a) defines the minimum requirements for the mechanical design, material selection, fabrication, inspection, testing, and preparation for shipment of shell-and-tube heat exchangers for general refinery services.

ANSI/API Standard 661, *Air-cooled Heat Exchangers for General Refinery Service, Petroleum and Natural Gas Industries* (2007b) covers the minimum requirements for the design, materials, fabrication, inspection, testing, and preparation for shipment of refinery process air-cooled heat exchangers.

3. Tubular Exchanger Manufacturers Association (TEMA) Standards. The *TEMA Standards* [9th ed. (2007)] covers nomenclature, fabrication tolerance, general fabrication, and performance information, installation, operation, maintenance, mechanical standard class RCB heat exchangers, flow-induced vibration, thermal relations, physical properties of fluids, and recommended good practices of shell-and-tube heat exchangers.

Potential Hazards

When a substance is stored under pressure, the potential for hazards exists. Improper vessel design and maintenance increase the risk of pressure vessel failure, posing a serious safety hazard. The risk increases when vessels contain toxic or gaseous substances. A pressure vessel is considered hazardous equipment.

Every year accidents occur to many pressure vessels that are in use in the industry. OSHA statistics indicate that 13 people were injured in 1999, 1 in 1998, 3 in 1997, and 9 in 1996 by pressure vessel accidents. A survey by the National Board of Boiler and Pressure Vessel Inspectors in 2002 shows 1663 accidents involving unfired pressure vessels that caused 5 fatalities and 22 injuries.

Pressure vessel accidents can be very serious. A serious accident takes human life, damages property, and increases costs for downtime production. Most accidents are caused by one of several things:

Slow rupture. A small crack can allow fluid to escape. The vessel typically remains intact, without fragments. The crack becomes larger over a period of time if not repaired early. Leak hazards are usually determined by the contents of the vessel. Fluid types, such as toxic gases, flammable vapors, and so on, determine the severity of leakage. High pressure inside the vessel may generate high-velocity gases that can create tremendous cutting or puncturing forces.

Rapid rupture. Sudden increases of internal pressure can cause total structural failure of the vessel. The container is rapidly destroyed, producing fragments and sometimes a shock wave. If the vessel releases toxic or flammable materials, this may increase the likelihood of injury, death, or property damage. Generally, rupture occurs when the internal pressure exceeds the design limits or when structural damage caused by normal wear and tear, corrosion, galvanic action, or acute accident reduces the strength of the vessel. Figure 2 is an example of an air-tank explosion caused by normal wear and tear.

FIGURE 2. Air-tank explosion

Negative pressure. Many vessels collapse under negative pressure. Vacuum breakers can protect structural integrity.

Explosion of reactive chemicals. Rapid chemical reactions in the vessel may produce a large volume of gas in a short period of time. The mixture of gas expands, rapidly producing high temperatures and a shock wave having substantial destructive potential.

Causes of Deterioration

A variety of conditions can cause deterioration in pressure vessels. Common conditions are described below:

Corrosion. Corrosion is the most frequent condition found in pressure vessels. Most common corrosions involve pitting, line corrosion, general corrosion, grooving, and galvanic corrosion.

- In *pitting*, a vessel is weakened by shallow, isolated, and scattered pitting over a small area. Pitting may eventually cause leakage.
- In *line corrosion*, pits are closely connected to each other in a narrow line. Line corrosion is frequently found near the intersection of the support skirt with the bottom of the vessel.
- *General corrosion* covers a considerable area of the vessel, reducing material thickness. Safe working pressure should be calculated based on the remaining material thickness.
- *Grooving* is caused by localized corrosion and may be accelerated by stress corrosion. Grooving is found adjacent to riveted lap joints or welds on flanged surfaces.
- In *galvanic corrosion*, two dissimilar metals contact each other and, with an electrolyte, constitute an electrolytic cell. The electric current flowing through the circuit may cause rapid corrosion of the less noble metal (the one having the greater electrode potential). The effects of galvanic corrosion are especially noticeable at rivets, welds, and flanged and bolted connections.

Fatigue. Many vessels are subjected to stress reversals such as cyclic loading. If stresses are high and reversals frequent, failure of components may occur as a result of fatigue. Fatigue failures may also result from cyclic temperature and pressure changes.

Creep. Creep may occur where vessels are subjected to temperatures above those for which they are designed. Because metals become weaker at high temperatures, such distortion may result in failure, especially at points of stress concentration.

Temperature. At subfreezing temperatures, water and certain chemicals inside a vessel may freeze, causing failure. A number of failures have been attributed to brittle fracture of steels exposed to temperatures below their transition temperature and pressures greater than 20 percent of the hydrostatic test pressure.

Temper embrittlement. This is a loss of ductility and notch toughness caused by postweld heat treatment or high-temperature service above 700°F. Low-alloy steels are prone to temper embrittlement.

Hydrogen embrittlement. This loss of strength and ductility in steels, caused by atomic hydrogen dissolved in steel, occurs at low temperatures but is occasionally encountered above 200°F. It is typically caused by hydrogen produced from aqueous corrosion reactions.

Stress-corrosion cracking. This cracking of metal is caused by the combined action of stress and a corrosive environment. Stress corrosion can only occur with specific metals in specific environments.

Causes of Accidents

There are many causes of pressure vessel accidents. After accidents, experts use various methods to ascertain causes, such as visual inspection, nondestructive testing, destructive testing, and metallurgical analysis. Causes and points of failure may be categorized as follows:

- Safety valves
- Limit controls
- Improper installation
- Improper repair
- Faulty design
- Faulty fabrication
- Operator error
- Poor maintenance
- Irregular inspection

TABLE 1

Accidents, Injuries, and Deaths Involving Unfired Pressure Vessels

Year	Accidents	Injuries	Deaths
1993	261	24	6
1994	387	19	5
1995	245	65	6
1996	319	22	6
1997	292	41	13
1998	153	12	9
1999	145	73	6
2000	221	3	6
2001	201	18	4
2002	176	22	5

Accident Data

Historical data collected by the National Board shows that more people have died because of accidents involving unfired pressure vessels than because of those associated with fired pressure vessels (such as boilers). Table 1 shows the accidents, injuries, and deaths involving unfired pressure vessels that occurred in a recent ten-year period.

Accident Severity

Any pressure vessel accident can be severe, damaging lives and properties. Such an accident can also cause loss of production time and business, as well as employee layoff and fear. The severity of an accident depends on the pressure, temperature, and type of fluid inside the vessel involved. Vessel size is also important; the bigger the size, the vaster the heating surface exposed to explosive power.

Every accident costs money. For the purpose of cost analysis, work accidents can be classified in two general categories: (1) accidents causing work injuries and (2) accidents causing property damage or interfering with production. Furthermore, there are two types of costs: insured and uninsured.

Each company paying insurance premiums recognizes such expense as part of the cost of accidents. In some cases, medical expenses are covered by insurance. Insurance costs can be obtained directly from the insurance company.

Uninsured costs, sometimes referred to as "hidden costs," include the following:

- Wages paid for time lost by workers who were not injured
- Damage to material and equipment
- Wages paid for time lost by the injured worker, other than compensation payments
- Overtime pay rates necessitated by the accident
- Wages paid supervisors for time required for activities necessitated by the accident
- The effect of the decreased output of the injured worker upon return to work
- The effect of the training period for a new worker
- Uninsured medical costs borne by the company

The following example demonstrates the severity of a pressure vessel accident. At about 3:40 P.M. on April 13, 1994, pulp digester #15 at the Stone Container Corporation in Panama City, Florida, exploded (OSHA Accident: 170670616, Report ID: 0419700). The wood-chip pulp digester ruptured and the release of pressure blew the digester through the roof, exposing workers to flying debris and hot wood pulp. The explosion killed three workers and injured five others, including one worker who had third-degree burns over 25 percent of her body. Nearly 600 workers were laid off during the closure. The company's insurance covered property damage and business interruption claims for an undisclosed amount.

Because the state of Florida has no pressure vessel law, the digester was never inspected and certified by the Florida Boiler Safety Program. The condition of the digester before the explosion was unknown. OSHA investigated the accident and proposed an initial penalty of $1 million. After negotiation, the Stone Container Corporation agreed to pay OSHA $690,000 in penalties and to implement improvements at the facility. The corporation agreed to carry out new inspections, maintenance, repairs, and alterations to its digesters in accordance with national codes.

Safety Regulations

Codes and standards have no legal standing; they become mandatory only when adopted by jurisdictions having authority over the locations where the pressure vessels are installed. A jurisdiction is defined as a government authority, such as municipality, county, state, or province.

Adoption of codes and standards is accomplished through legislative action requiring that pressure vessels for use within a jurisdiction must comply with the ASME, API, or other code rules. Designated officials, such as chief boiler and pressure vessel inspectors and their staffs, enforce the legal requirements of the jurisdictions. Legal requirements of pressure vessels vary from jurisdiction to jurisdiction.

Federal Government

The federal requirements of pressure vessels are covered under the Occupational Safety and Health Act of 1970. The federal government has practically handed over pressure vessel safety to the state governments. The U.S. Department of Labor has issued the following guidelines for pressure vessel safety:

1. *OSHA Technical Manual* (OTM), Section IV, Chapter 3, "Pressure Vessel Guidelines" (OSHA undated) contains an introduction and descriptions of recent instances of cracking under pressure, deals with nondestructive examination methods, and gives information to aid safety assessment (OSHA undated).
2. OSHA Publication 8-1.5, *Guidelines for Pressure Vessel Safety Assessment* (1989) presents a technical overview of, and information concerning, metallic pressure-containment vessels and tanks. The scope is limited to general industrial application vessels and tanks constructed of carbon or low-alloy steels and used at temperatures between –100 and 600°F. Information on design codes, materials, fabrication processes, inspection, and testing that is applicable to these vessels and tanks are presented.

State Governments

Most states have pressure vessel safety laws, rules, and regulations. Pressure vessel safety bills are introduced by legislators, passed by houses and senates, and signed by governors, becoming laws. Rules and regulations are introduced by departments that have adopted pressure vessel safety programs. Codes and standards are adopted under rules and regulations.

Presently the following states enforce pressure vessel laws, rules, and regulations: Alabama, Alaska, Arkansas, California, Colorado, Delaware, Georgia, Hawaii, Illinois, Indiana, Iowa, Kansas, Kentucky, Maine, Maryland, Massachusetts, Minnesota, Mississippi, Missouri, Nebraska, Nevada, New Hampshire, New Jersey, New York, North Carolina, North Dakota, Ohio, Oklahoma, Oregon, Pennsylvania, Rhode Island, Tennessee, Utah, Vermont, Virginia, Washington, Wisconsin, and Wyoming.

The following states, however, are without pressure vessel laws: Arizona, Connecticut, Florida, Louisiana, Michigan, Montana, New Mexico, South Carolina, South Dakota, Texas, and West Virginia.

County Governments

Some counties have pressure vessel laws and rules, including Jefferson Parish (Louisiana) and Miami–Dade County (Florida).

City Governments

Many cities have their own pressure vessel laws and rules. The following cities enforce pressure vessel laws: Buffalo (New York), Chicago (Illinois), Denver (Colorado), Detroit (Michigan), Los Angeles (California), Milwaukee (Wisconsin), New Orleans (Louisiana), New York (New York), Omaha (Nebraska), Seattle (Washington), Spokane (Washington), St. Louis (Missouri), and Washington, D.C.

Certificates

The jurisdictional authorities, abiding by pressure vessel laws and rules, issue certificates to authorized inspectors and to pressure vessels. Certificates issued to inspectors, whether by a state or an insurance company, are called *certificates of competency*. On the other hand, certificates issued to pressure vessels for operation of those vessels are called *certificates of compliance*.

Certificate of competency. An authorized inspector must have a valid certificate of competency for performing inspections in a jurisdiction. The certificate, or commission, is issued by the pressure vessel program of the jurisdiction. This certificate usually expires December 31st yearly, irrespective of date of issue. The certificate indicates the inspector's identification (ID) number, the date of certificate issue, and the certificate expiration date, in addition to the inspector's name and address. A work card usually accompanies the certificate that can be carried in an inspector's wallet.

Certificate of compliance. Each pressure vessel must have a valid certificate of compliance in order to operate the pressure vessel. The pressure vessel program of the jurisdiction issues this certificate, also called the *certificate of operation*. This certificate is valid for 2 to 3 years, depending on the type of pressure vessel. A certificate of compliance is shown in Figure 3.

CONSTRUCTION OF NEW VESSELS

ASME *Boiler and Pressure Vessel Code,* Section VIII (2011a) establishes design rules for the vessels and their components. The code delineates the responsibilities of the various organizations involved with the design and fabrication of components. It is the responsibility of the purchaser of a vessel to specify sufficient design information for manufacturers to design and fabricate vessels for the intended service. Users are responsible for providing manufacturers with information, including the intended operating pressure and temperature, as well as any other information relative to any special circumstances (such as lethal or other corrosion problems anticipated, or secondary loadings

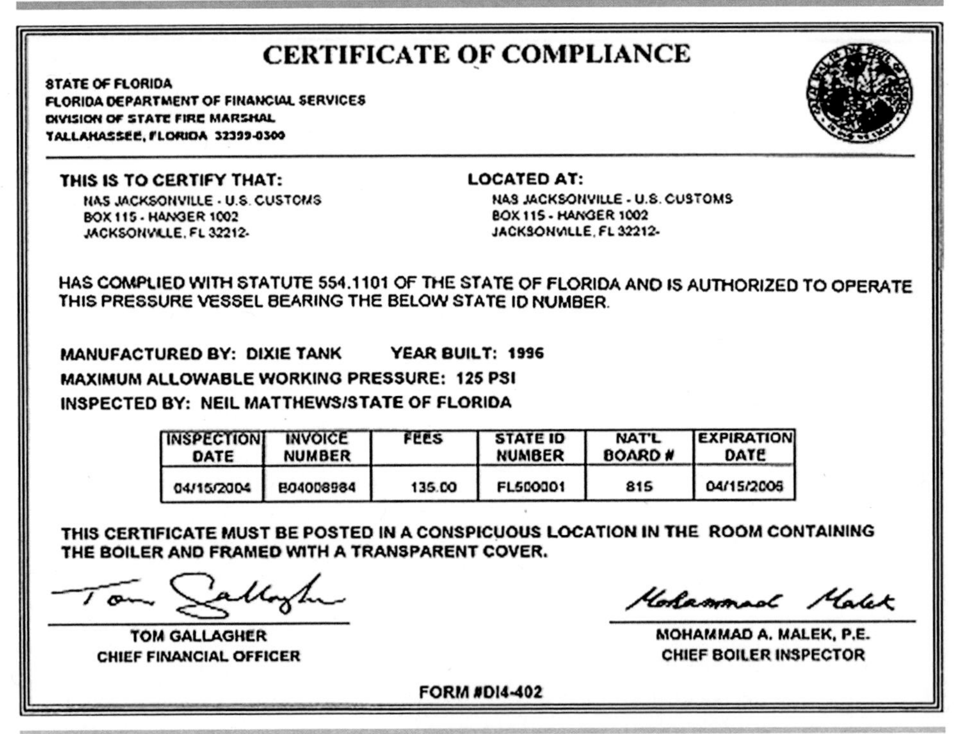

CERTIFICATE OF COMPLIANCE

STATE OF FLORIDA
FLORIDA DEPARTMENT OF FINANCIAL SERVICES
DIVISION OF STATE FIRE MARSHAL
TALLAHASSEE, FLORIDA 32399-0300

THIS IS TO CERTIFY THAT:
NAS JACKSONVILLE - U.S. CUSTOMS
BOX 115 - HANGER 1002
JACKSONVILLE, FL 32212-

LOCATED AT:
NAS JACKSONVILLE - U.S. CUSTOMS
BOX 115 - HANGER 1002
JACKSONVILLE, FL 32212-

HAS COMPLIED WITH STATUTE 554.1101 OF THE STATE OF FLORIDA AND IS AUTHORIZED TO OPERATE THIS PRESSURE VESSEL BEARING THE BELOW STATE ID NUMBER.

MANUFACTURED BY: DIXIE TANK YEAR BUILT: 1996
MAXIMUM ALLOWABLE WORKING PRESSURE: 125 PSI
INSPECTED BY: NEIL MATTHEWS/STATE OF FLORIDA

INSPECTION DATE	INVOICE NUMBER	FEES	STATE ID NUMBER	NAT'L BOARD #	EXPIRATION DATE
04/15/2004	B04008984	135.00	FL500001	815	04/15/2006

THIS CERTIFICATE MUST BE POSTED IN A CONSPICUOUS LOCATION IN THE ROOM CONTAINING THE BOILER AND FRAMED WITH A TRANSPARENT COVER.

TOM GALLAGHER
CHIEF FINANCIAL OFFICER

MOHAMMAD A. MALEK, P.E.
CHIEF BOILER INSPECTOR

FORM #DI4-402

FIGURE 3. Certificate of compliance (*Source:* State of Florida, Florida Department of Financial Services, Division of State Fire Marshal.)

such as earthquakes). In turn, vessel manufacturers are responsible for assuring that designs comply with all applicable requirements of the code.

A pressure vessel is always designed by taking the safety factor into account. The vessel should withstand the operating conditions and function safely during its service life. Each and every component is designed carefully by using engineering judgment in addition to the code requirements, which are considered minimum requirements. The design engineer must determine all design parameters such as service, design temperature, design pressure, loadings, corrosion, materials, joint category, extent of nondestructive testing, extent of heat treatment, welding process to be used, and maximum allowable stress values.

Calculation of loads is very important in the design of a pressure vessel. The loadings are internal and/or external pressures, dead weight, local loads, cyclic loading, wind and earthquake loads, thermal stresses, and impact and shock loads.

Once the calculations, drawings, and specifications are completed, a vessel is ready for construction. The following design for components is based on ASME Section VIII—Division 1 (2011b).

Cylindrical Shells under Internal Pressure

The minimum required thickness or maximum allowable working pressure of cylindrical shells shall be the greater thickness or lower pressure as given by formulas (1) or (2). The following symbols have been used in the formulas:

t = minimum required thickness of shell (in)
P = internal design pressure (psi)
R = internal radius of the shell course (in)
S = maximum allowable stress values (psi)
E = joint efficiency

(a) Circumferential Stress (Longitudinal Joints). When the thickness does not exceed one-half of the inside radius, or P does not exceed $0.385SE$, the following formula (Section VIII—Division 1) is applicable:

$$t = \frac{PR}{SE - 0.6P} \text{ or } P = \frac{SEt}{R + 0.6t} \tag{1}$$

(b) Longitudinal Stress (Circumferential Joints). When the thickness does not exceed one-half of the inside radius, or P does not exceed $1.25SE$, the following formula [Section VIII—Division 1 (2011b)] is applicable:

$$t = \frac{PR}{2SE + 0.4P} \quad \text{or} \quad P = \frac{2SEt}{R - 0.4t} \tag{2}$$

Example: What is the MAWP of a cylindrical pressure vessel shell having a thickness of 1.125 inches and a type-2 longitudinal joint with RT 3 examination? The outside diameter of the vessel is 36 inches. The material is SA-515 Gr65 and the vessel design temperature is 800°F.

Solution:

OD = 36 in
t = 1.125 in

$$R = \frac{36 - 1.125 \times 2}{2} = 16.875 \text{ in}$$

S = 11,400 psi [from ASME *Boiler and Pressure Code,* Section II, Part D, Stress Table (2011e)]
E = 0.8 [from Table UW-12 of ASME Section VIII—Division 1 (2011b)]

Use formula 1 above:

$$P = \frac{SEt}{R + 0.6t}$$

$$= \frac{11{,}400 \times (0.8 \times 1.125)}{16.875 + (0.6 \times 1.125)}$$

$$= \frac{10{,}260}{17.55}$$

$$= 584.62$$

$$\approx 590 \text{ psig}$$

Therefore, MAWP of the cylindrical shell is 590 psig.

Formed Heads

Heads are used as enclosures for the shells. There are various types of dished heads used for pressure vessel construction. The most commonly used heads are ellipsoidal, torispherical, hemispherical, conical, or toriconical (cone head with knuckle). Sketches of these types of heads are shown in Figure 4. The following symbols have been used in the formulas of Paragraph UG-32 [Section VIII—Division 1 (2011b)] and Figure 4:

t = minimum thickness of head after forming (in)
P = internal design pressure (psi)
D = inside diameter of the head skirt (in)
D_i = inside diameter of the conical portion (in) $= D - 2r(1 - \cos\alpha)$
r = inside knuckle radius (in)
S = maximum allowable stress values in tension as given in the tables referenced in UG-23 (psi)
E = lowest efficiency of any joint in the head
L = inside spherical or crown radius (in)

(a) Ellipsoidal Heads. The required thickness of a dished head of semiellipsoidal form, in which half the minor axis equals one-fourth of the inside diameter of the head skirt is calculated by the following formulas:

$$t = \frac{PD}{2SE - 0.2P} \quad \text{or} \quad P = \frac{2SEt}{D + 0.2t} \tag{3}$$

An acceptable approximation of a 2:00 ellipsoidal head is one with a knuckle radius of 0.17D and a spherical radius of 0.90D.

(b) Torispherical Heads. The required thickness of a torispherical head when the knuckle radius is 6 percent of the inside crown radius and the inside

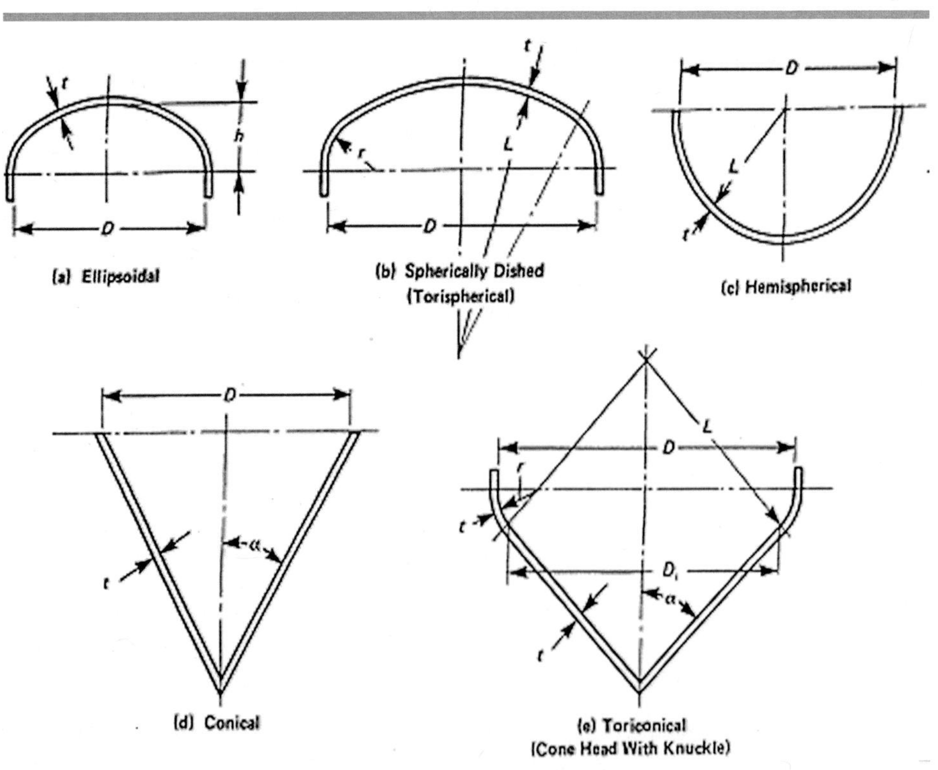

FIGURE 4. Formed heads (*Source:* ASME 2011a)

crown radius equals the outside diameter of the skirt is calculated by the following formulas:

$$t = \frac{0.885PL}{SE - 0.1P} \text{ or } P = \frac{SEt}{0.885L + 0.1t} \quad (4)$$

Torispherical heads made of materials having a specified tensile strength exceeding 70,000 psi are designed using a value of S equal to 20,000 psi at room temperature and reduced in portion to the reduction in maximum allowable stress values at temperatures for the material.

(c) Hemispherical Heads. When the thickness of a hemispherical head does not exceed 0.356L, or P does not exceed 0.665SE, the following formulas are applicable:

$$t = \frac{PL}{2SE - 0.2P} \text{ or } P = \frac{2SEt}{L + 0.2t} \quad (5)$$

(d) Conical Heads and Sections (Without Transition Knuckle). The required thicknesses of conical heads or conical shell sections that have a half apex angle (α) not greater than 30 degrees are determined by the following formula:

$$t = \frac{PD}{2\cos\alpha(SE - 0.6P)}$$

or

$$P = \frac{2SEt\cos\alpha}{D + 1.2t\cos\alpha} \quad (6)$$

(e) Toriconical Heads and Sections. The required thickness of the conical portion, in which the knuckle radius is neither less than 6 percent of the outside diameter of the head skirt nor less than 3 times the knuckle thickness is determined by formula 6, using D_i in place of D. The required thickness of the knuckle is determined by formula 5 in which

$$L = \frac{D_i}{2\cos\alpha} \quad (7)$$

Toriconical heads or sections may be used when the angle α is less than 30 degrees and are mandatory for conical head designs when the angle α exceeds 30 degrees.

Example: Determine the maximum allowable working pressure of a seamless ellipsoidal head with a 96-inch inside diameter and that is 0.25 inches thick. Stress value is 20,000 psi for SA-515 Gr70 at 500°F.

Solution:

D = 96 in
E = 1.0 (for seamless head)
S = 20,000 psi for SA-515 Gr70 at 500°F
Maximum Allowable Working Pressure formula:

$$P = \frac{2SEt}{D + 0.2t}$$

$$P = \frac{2 \times 20{,}000 \times 1.0 \times 0.250}{96 + (0.2 \times 0.25)}$$

$$P = \frac{10{,}000}{96.05}$$

P = 104.11
~ 110 psig

Therefore, maximum working pressure for the head is 110 psig.

Pressure Parts

In addition to shells and heads, prefabricated or preformed pressure parts may be used as components for pressure vessels that are subjected to allowable stresses caused by internal or external pressure. Pressure parts such as pipe fittings, flanges, nozzles, welding necks, welding caps, manhole frames, and covers may be formed by casting, forging, rolling, or die forming. No calculations are required for these parts.

Materials

Pressure-vessel-quality materials are used for the fabrication of pressure vessels. Great care is taken to assure quality of materials. The term *pressure vessel quality* requires that materials withstand the pressure, high temperature, corrosive environment, and other operating conditions for which pressure vessels are designed.

The specifications of pressure-vessel-quality materials, which are subject to stress caused by pressure, are described in ASME Code, *Materials,* Parts A, B, C, and D (2011e). Most of the materials are covered in

Section II; those not so addressed are not permitted for construction uses. Materials for nonpressure parts, such as skirts, supports, baffles, lugs, and clips, need not conform to the specifications to which they are attached. If they are attached by welding, then these parts should be of weldable quality. Material specifications are not limited by production methods or countries of origin. The specifications of materials for major components are given below.

Plate Materials	
SA-285 Grade B	Carbon steel plate
SA-515 Grade 60	Carbon steel plate
SA-516 Grade 70	Carbon steel plate
SA-542 Grade B	2¼ Cr-1Mo plate

Pipe and Tubes	
SA-178 Grade A	Carbon steel welded tube
SA-106 Grade A	Carbon steel seamless pipe
SA-335 Grade P2	¼ Cr-¼ Mo seamless pipe
SA-556 Grade C2	Carbon steel seamless tube

Pressure parts	
SA-105	Carbon steel forgings
SA-234 Grade WPB	Seamless and welded fittings
SA-281	Carbon steel forgings
SA-352 Grade LCA	Carbon steel castings

Fabrication

A pressure vessel is fabricated according to the drawings, design, and calculations. The fabrication may be performed partly or wholly in the manufacturer's shop or in the field. Most of the fabrication is done by welding in accordance with ASME Code, Section IX, *Welding and Brazing* (2011f). The fabrication procedures are required to comply with ASME Section VIII.

Shop Inspection

A pressure vessel is inspected and tested in the fabrication shop or field during its construction by an authorized inspector. The manufacturer is responsible for design, construction, and quality control in accordance with ASME Code, Section VIII (2011a). The authorized inspector is responsible for the inspection and testing of a pressure vessel for code compliance.

Authorized Inspectors. The authorized inspector (AI) is the person responsible for inspection of pressure vessels and their parts during and after construction. An authorized inspector acts as a third party to make sure that all the code requirements are met.

The authorized inspector is assigned the following responsibilities:

1. Checking the validity of the manufacturer's certificate of authorization
2. Ensuring that the manufacturer follows the quality control system accepted by the ASME
3. Reviewing design calculations, drawings, specifications, procedures, records, and test results
4. Checking material to ensure that it complies with code requirements
5. Checking all welding and brazing procedures to ensure that these are up to standards
6. Checking the qualification of welders, welding operators, brazers, and brazing operators
7. Visually inspecting the transfer of material identification
8. Witnessing the proof tests
9. Inspecting each pressure vessel during and after construction
10. Verifying the stamping and nameplate information and attachment
11. Signing Manufacturer Data Reports.

The authorized inspector ensures that all necessary inspections have been performed to certify that the pressure vessels have been designed and constructed in accordance with Section VIII and that the code's symbol stamp can be applied (ASME 2011a).

Many pressure vessels, especially large ones, are constructed partly in the shop and partly in the field. The authorized inspector is also responsible for inspection in the field if the manufacturer performs construction there. The field inspection is similar to a shop inspection except that inspection procedures are carried out at the site.

Stamping and Data Reports

Each pressure vessel designed according to the rules of Section VIII is required to be stamped with the appropriate code symbol stamp. The stamping is done after the hydrostatic test and in the presence of the authorized inspector. Once the stamping has been applied, the manufacturer completes the data reports and the authorized inspector signs them (ASME 2011a).

Stamp Holders

The construction of pressure vessels may be performed either in the shop or in the field. In both cases, a manufacturer or stamp holder is required to have a certificate of authorization to fabricate and stamp pressure vessels in accordance with the provisions of Section VIII Code (ASME 2011a).

An organization interested in fabricating pressure vessels may apply to ASME for a certificate of authorization in accordance with Paragraph UG-105 of Section VIII. The prescribed forms are available from the Secretary of the Boiler and Pressure Vessel Committee. The applicant is required to complete the form specifying the ASME stamp required and the scope of activities to be performed. The Secretary issues a certificate of authorization for each plant.

If authorization is granted after receiving a recommendation from the joint review team, and the proper administrative fee is paid, an organization is granted a certificate of authorization giving permission to use the ASME symbol stamp for a period of three years. A copy of the certificate of authorization for ASME Code symbol "U" is shown in Appendix A.

The certificates of authorization and the symbol stamps are the property of ASME. The stamp-holder organization must use them in accordance with the rules and regulations of the society. The organization must not use the stamp when a certificate expires and shall not allow any other organization to use it. The certificates of authorization and stamps are required to be returned to the society on demand. A stamp holder is required to apply for renewal six months prior to the expiration date of the certificate. The society has the right to cancel or renew certificates of authorization.

Quality Control System

A manufacturer applying for a certificate of authorization to use a code's symbol stamp must have a quality control system in place. The quality control system is a written document describing all code requirements, including materials, design, fabrication, and testing by the manufacturer, as well as inspection criteria of pressure vessels and their components to be assessed by the authorized inspector.

A joint review team visits the manufacturer's shop facilities to determine whether the quality control system is adequate to manufacture pressure vessels and their parts. The team consists of a representative of the authorized inspection agency and an ASME designee, who is leader of the team. The ASME designee is selected by the legal jurisdiction. In some cases, a representative of the legal jurisdiction can act as a team leader. The joint review team evaluates the quality control system and its implementation. The manufacturer is required to demonstrate administrative and fabrication functions to show the ability to produce code items according to the description of the quality control system. The demonstration may include a model vessel or part showing fabrication functions.

The joint review team submits its written recommendations to the society. The Subcommittee on Boiler and Pressure Vessel Accreditation reviews the report, and a certificate of authorization is issued if the recommendation is satisfactory.

The quality control system, which is presented in a document called the *Quality Control Manual*, is a very important document for the manufacturer. The manufacturer, the inspector, and the joint review team use this manual to perform all code activities. The manufacturer must describe the system suitable for the manufacturer's own circumstances. Description of the quality control system is required to meet the requirements of the Mandatory Appendix A-10 of Section VIII—Division 1 (ASME 2011b). An outline of the features of the quality control system are:

1. Authority and responsibility
2. Organization
3. Drawings, design calculations, and specification control
4. Material control
5. Examination and inspection program
6. Correction of nonconformities
7. Welding
8. Nondestructive examination
9. Heat treatment
10. Calibration of measurement and test equipment
11. Records retention
12. Sample forms
13. Inspection of pressure vessels and parts
14. Inspection of safety and safety relief devices

The *Quality Control Manual* may contain other noncode activities of the manufacturer. The code activities in the shop and the field must be described clearly.

Code Symbol Stamps

The American Society of Mechanical Engineers (ASME) Code uses six symbol stamps—U, UM, U2, U3, UV, and UD, either individually or in combination—for the design, construction, and assembly of pressure vessels and their parts in accordance with Section VIII (ASME 2011a):

U: Code symbol for vessels designed under Section VIII—Division 1 (2011b)

UM: Code symbol for miniature vessels designed under Section VIII—Division 1 (2011b) (See Figure 5.)

FIGURE 5. ASME Code symbol stamp for pressure vessels designed under Section VIII—Division 1 (*Source:* ASME 2011b)

U2: Code symbol for vessels designed under Section VIII—Division 2 (2011c)

U3: Code symbol for vessel designed under Section VIII—Division 3 (2011d)

UV: Code symbol stamp for pressure relief valve

UV3: Code symbol stamp for pressure relief valve, as required by Section VIII—Division 3 (2011d)

UD: Code symbol stamp for rupture disk devices

Required Marking

Data marking. Each pressure vessel, after fabrication, shall be marked with the following data:

1. The official code symbol stamp
2. The name of the manufacturer of the pressure vessel
3. The maximum allowable working pressure: _________ psi at _________ °F
4. The minimum design metal temperature of _________ °F at _________ psi

TABLE 2

Marking for Type of Construction

Type of Construction	Letters
Arc or gas welded	W
Pressure welded (except resistance)	P
Brazed	B
Resistance welded	RES

5. The manufacturer's serial number
6. The year it was built

Type of Construction. The type of construction used for the vessel shall be indicated under the code symbol stamp by applying the appropriate letter(s) as shown in Table 2.

Vessels employing combination types of construction must be marked with all applicable construction letters.

Method of Marking

A manufacturer is required to stamp each pressure vessel after the hydrostatic test. The stamping is done in the presence of the authorized inspector either in the shop or the field. The stamping consists of the appropriate code symbol stamp and data items with letters and figures at least 5/16 of an inch (8 mm) high. An example of the form of stamping is shown in Figure 6.

If the stamping is so located that it is not visible from the operating floor, the manufacturer is required to provide a metallic nameplate on which all data are stamped. The letters and figures on the nameplate should not be less than 5/32 of an inch (4 mm) high.

Manufacturer's Data Reports

A Manufacturer Data Report is similar to a birth certificate. During and after fabrication of a pressure vessel in the shop or field, principal data of the pressure vessel and its components are recorded. The data report provides certain important information regarding manufacturer, purchaser, location, and identification number. The data report also provides summary information about construction details, materials, dimensions, design pressures, hydrostatic test pressures, and maximum designed steaming capacity. This information is used in making decisions about future repairs and alterations of pressure vessels.

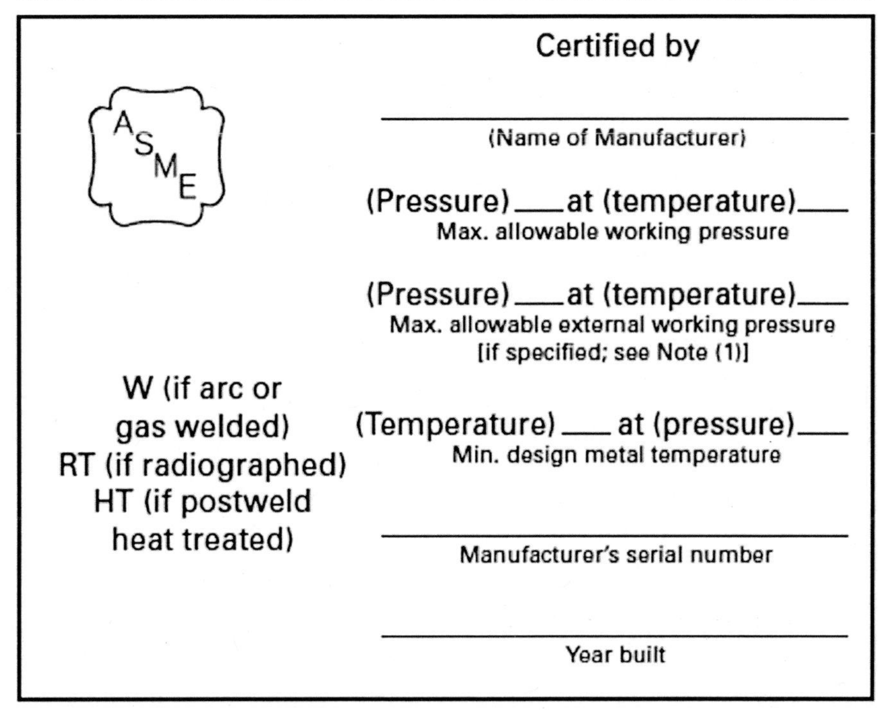

FIGURE 6. Data plate stamping (*Source:* ASME Code, Section VIII–Division 1 2011b)

There are twelve different Manufacturer Data Reports for the pressure vessels constructed in accordance with the requirements of Section VIII (ASME 2011a). These data reports are recorded on forms published by the ASME. The Manufacturer Data Report Forms are:

1. Form U-1, Manufacturer's Data Report for Pressure Vessels as required by Section VIII—Division 1 (Appendix B) (ASME 2011b)
2. Form U-1A, Manufacturer's Data Report for Pressure Vessels (alternative form for single-chamber, completely shop-fabricated vessel only) as required by Section VIII—Division 1 (ASME 2011b)
3. Form U-2, Manufacturer's Partial Data Report as required by Section VIII—Division 1 (ASME 2011b)
4. Form U-2A, Manufacturer's Partial Data Report (alternative form) as required by Section VIII—Division 1 (ASME 2011b)
5. Form U-3, Manufacturer's Certificate of Compliance for Pressure Vessels with UM symbol as required by Section VIII—Division 1 (ASME 2011b)
6. Form U-4, Manufacturer's Data Report Supplementary Sheet as required by Section VIII—Division 1 (ASME 2011b)
7. Form A-1, Manufacturer's Data Report for Pressure Vessels Constructed under Section VIII—Division 2 (ASME 2011c)
8. Form A-2, Manufacturer's Partial Data Report as required under Section VIII—Division 2 (ASME 2011c)
9. Form A–3, Manufacturer's Data Report Supplementary Sheet as required under Section VIII—Division 2 (ASME 2011c)
10. Form K-1, Manufacturer's Data Report for High Pressure Vessels as required by Section VIII—Division 3 (ASME 2011d)
11. Form K-2, Manufacturer's Partial Data Report for High Pressure Vessels as required by Section VIII—Division 3 (ASME 2011d)
12. Form K-3, Manufacturer's Data Report Supplementary Sheet as required by Section VIII—Division 3 (ASME 2011d)

Safety Devices

Pressure sources in a vessel are limited to the maximum allowable working pressure of the lowest system component. Pressure relief devices are used in case the internal pressure exceeds the maximum allowable working pressure. Common relief devices include pressure relief valves and rupture disks.

A *conventional pressure relief valve* is a direct, spring-loaded pressure relief valve with operating characteristics that are directly affected by changes in the back pressure. This type of valve is used for vessels designed for Section VIII Code (ASME 2011a). A spring-loaded pressure relief valve is shown in Figure 7.

The capacity of a safety relief valve in terms of a gas or vapor other than the medium for which the valve was officially rated may be determined by the following formulas:

For steam:

$$W_s = 51.5\ KAP \quad (8)$$

For any gas or vapor:

$$W = CKAP\sqrt{\frac{M}{T}} \quad (9)$$

where

W = flow of any gas or vapor (lb/hr)
W_s = rated capacity (lb/hr of steam)
C = constant for gas or vapor, which is a function of the ratio of specific heats, $k = C_p/C_v$
K = coefficient of discharge [Para. UG-131(d) and (e) of ASME Section VIII—Division 1 (ASME 2011b)]
A = actual discharge area of the safety relief valve (in^2)
P = (set pressure × 1.10) + atmospheric pressure (psia)
M = molecular weight
T = absolute temperature at inlet (°F + 460)

Example: A safety valve is required to relieve 5000 pounds of propane per hour at a temperature of 125°F. The safety valve is rated at 3000 pounds of steam per hour at the same pressure setting. Will this valve provide the required relieving capacity in propane service on this vessel?

Solution:

W_p = 5000 lb/hr
W_s = 3000 lb/hr

Molecular weight of propane = 44.09
C = 315
T = 125 + 460 = 585

$$W_p = CKAP\sqrt{\frac{M}{T}}$$

Transpose for KAP:

$$KAP = \frac{W_p}{C\sqrt{\frac{M}{T}}}$$

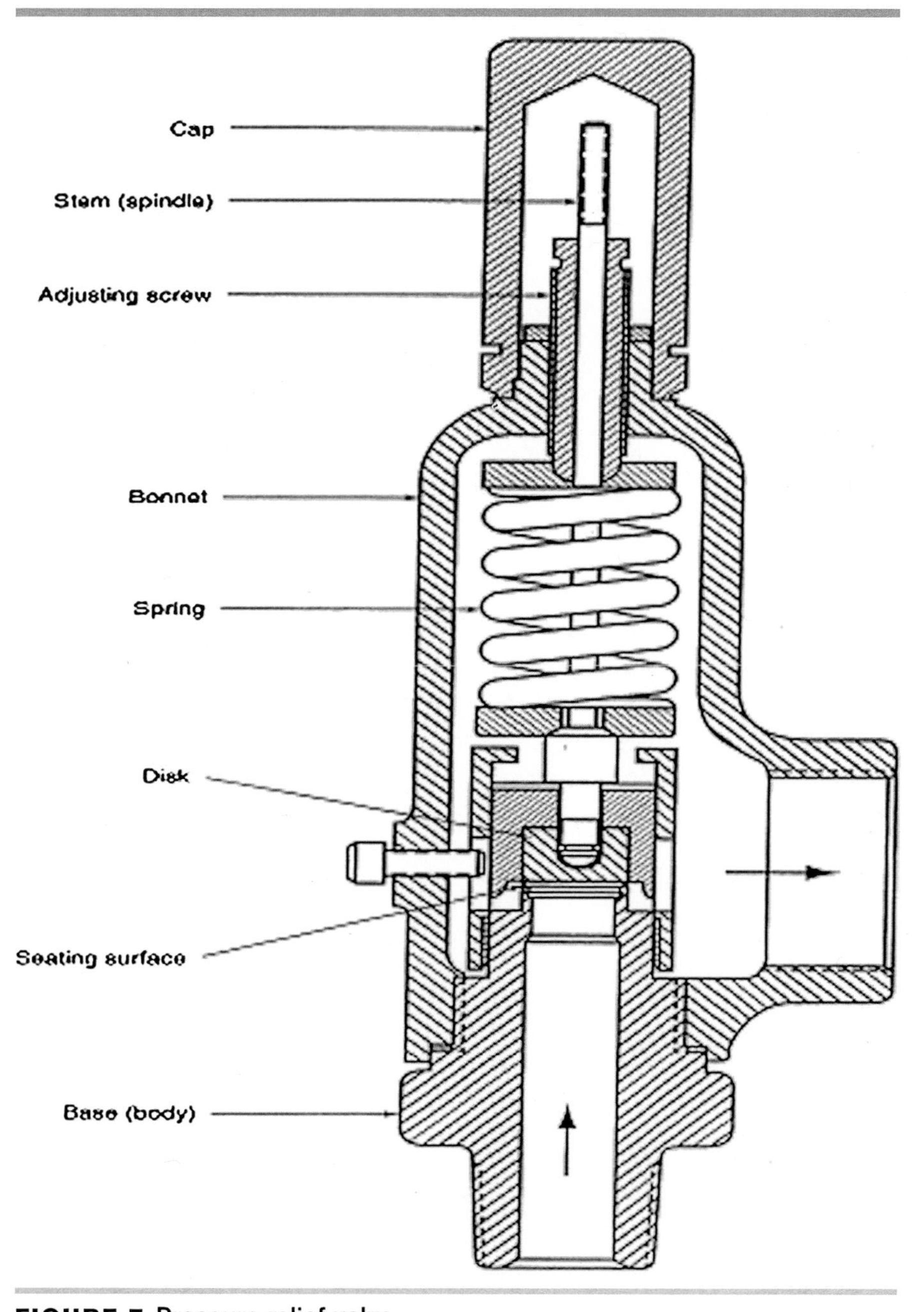

FIGURE 7. Pressure relief valve

$$KAP = \frac{5000}{315\sqrt{\frac{44.09}{585}}}$$

KAP = 57.81857

For steam W_s = 51.5KAP

W_s = 51.5 × 57.81857

W_s = 2,977.65627 ~ 2,978 lb/hr

The safety-relieving capacity required is 2,978 lb/hr and the capacity provided is 3000 lb/hr.

Therefore, the valve will provide required capacity in propane on this vessel.

A *rupture disk* is designed to rupture at a predetermined burst rating when installed in a piping system. Rupture disks protect equipment from the effects of overpressurization in static and dynamic pressurized systems. A rupture disk should have a specified bursting pressure at a specified temperature. The manufacturer of a rupture disk should guarantee that the disk will burst within ±5 percent of the specified bursting pressure.

Risk Assessment of Existing Vessels

It is extremely important to assess the safety and hazard implications of pressure vessels in service. The equipment data and current information should be made available to a technical expert for evaluation of safety and risk.

Corrosion Rate Determination

Corrosion rate is defined as loss of metal thickness, in inches (or millimeters) per year. An inspection should determine the vessel's probable corrosion rate.

The corrosion rate of a pressure vessel may be determined by one of the following methods:

1. A corrosion rate may be calculated from data collected by the owner on pressure vessels in the same or similar service.
2. A corrosion rate may be estimated from the owner's experience or from published data on vessels used for comparable service.
3. A corrosion rate may be determined from on stream after 1000 hours of service by using corrosion-monitoring devices or actual thickness measurements of the vessel.

During inspection, a thorough examination should be performed using ultrasonic thickness measurements or other appropriate means to measure thickness for assessing the integrity of the metal. A representative number of thickness measurements should be taken on all major components such as shells, heads, cone sections, and nozzles. The number and location of thickness measurements should be decided based on previous experience. Once thickness is known, corrosion rate may be calculated by the following formula:

$$Corrosion\ rate = \frac{t_{previous} - t_{actual}}{years\ between\ t_{previous}\ and\ t_{actual}} \tag{10}$$

where the corrosion rate is measured in inches (or millimeters) per year and equals t_{actual} (the thickness in inches or millimeters), recorded at the time of inspection for a given location or component, minus $t_{previous}$ (the thickness in inches or millimeters) at the same location as measured during a previous inspection, divided by the lapse in years.

Example: During the in-service inspection of a pressure vessel, an ultrasonic thickness of a cylindrical shell was measured at 2.75 inches. The vessel, when installed 5 years prior, was 3 inches thick. The vessel has a MAWP of 2900 psig and an inside diameter of 24 inches. What is the corrosion rate if the vessel is used for ammonia service?

Solution:

t_{actual} = 2.75 in
$t_{previous}$ = 3 in
Years between t_{actual} and $t_{previous}$ = 5

$$Corrosion\ rate = \frac{3-2.75}{5} = 0.05 \text{ in}$$

The corrosion rate of the vessel is 0.05 inches (1.27 mm) per year.

Statistical data may be maintained for corrosion rate calculations for the pressure vessel components.

This statistical approach may be utilized to assess inspection types or to determine inspection intervals.

Remaining Life Determination

Remaining life refers to the number of years a pressure vessel is expected to last in service. This life expectancy is a very important consideration when making decisions regarding pressure vessel replacement, plant production capacity, and an appropriate inspection interval.

The period between internal or on-stream inspections shall not exceed half the estimated remaining life of the vessel based on the corrosion rate, or 10 years, whichever is less. In cases where the remaining safe operating life is estimated to be less than 4 years, the inspection interval may be the full remaining safe operating life up to a maximum of 2 years.

For pressure vessels in noncontinuous service that are isolated from process fluids, leaving them unexposed to corrosive environments (such as inert gas purged or filled with noncorrosive hydrocarbons), the 10 years shall be the 10 years of actual exposed life.

The remaining life of the pressure vessel can be calculated from the following formula:

$$\text{Remaining life(years)} = \frac{t_{actual} - t_{minimum}}{Corrosion\ rate} \quad (11)$$

where $t_{minimum}$ equals the minimum allowable thickness in inches (or millimeters), for a given location or component, divided by the yearly corrosion rate in inches (or millimeters).

Example: During the in-service inspection of a pressure vessel, an ultrasonic thickness of a cylinder shell was measured at 2.8 inches. The vessel, when installed 5 years prior, was 3 inches thick. The vessel has a MAWP of 2500 psig and an inside diameter of 30 inches. The vessel is used for propane service and a minimum thickness of 2.5 inches can be allowed for the shell. What is the remaining life of the vessel?

Solution:

$t_{actual} = 2.8$ in

$t_{previous} = 3$ in

$t_{minimum} = 2.5$ in

Years between t_{actual} and $t_{previous} = 5$

$$Corrosion\ rate = \frac{3-2.80}{5} = 0.04 \text{ in. } (1.106 \text{ mm}) \text{ yearly}$$

$$\text{Remaining life(years)} = \frac{t_{actual} - t_{minimum}}{Corrosion\ rate}$$

$$\text{Remaining life} = \frac{2.80-2.50}{0.04} = 7.5 \text{ years}$$

Therefore, the remaining life of the vessel is 7.5 years.

Statistical data should be kept of remaining life calculations for pressure vessel components. This statistical approach may be used to assess inspection types or to determine inspection intervals.

Maximum Allowable Working Pressure Determination

The *maximum allowable working pressure* for a pressure vessel in service may be determined using the formulas of ASME Code, Section VIII—Division 1 (ASME 2011b). For a pressure vessel in service, it is recommended that the original ASME Code edition or construction code (for non-ASME designed vessels) should be used. The calculated maximum allowable working pressure should not be greater than the original maximum allowable working pressure.

Maximum allowable working pressure calculations require detailed information used in the original code of construction. Details include design data for all the major components, material specifications, allowable stresses, weld efficiencies, inspection criteria, and service conditions. The wall thickness used in the calculations shall be the actual thickness determined by nondestructive examination at the time of inspection. This actual thickness shall not be greater than the thickness reported in the manufacturer's data report. An example of determining maximum allowable working pressure for an existing pressure vessel in service is given below:

Example: During in-service inspection of a pressure vessel, an ultrasonic measurement taken of a cylindrical shell recorded a thickness of 0.595 inches. The vessel has a MAWP of 1300 psig at 650°F and an outside diameter of 12.75 inches. The vessel is fabricated from SA-106 Gr B, 0.688-inch nominal thick pipe with an allowable stress of 15,000 psi. Based on this information, may the vessel be allowed to continue in operation as-is, or will repairs be required?

Solution:

P = 1300 psig at 650°F
D_o = 12.75 in
R_o = 6.375 in
$t_{measured}$ = 0.595 in
S = 15,000 psi
Seamless pipe, no radiography, E = 0.85

The formula for minimum required thickness is:

$$t = \frac{PR_o}{SE - 0.6P} \tag{12}$$

$$t = \frac{1300 \times 6.375}{(15{,}000 \times 0.85) - (0.6 \times 1300)}$$

$$t = \frac{8287.5}{11{,}970}$$

t = 0.692 in
(Section VIII—Division 1, 2011b)

Because the measured thickness of 0.595 inches is less than the calculated minimum thickness of 0.692 inches, it does not comply with the code. Therefore, the vessel may not be allowed to continue in operation as-is. A repair is required to build up the minimum required thickness at that location.

In-Service Inspection

In-service inspection plays a vital role in assessment of pressure vessel safety. In selecting the type of inspection, both the condition of the vessel and the environment in which it operates should be taken into consideration. For example, internal inspection is not required for a newly installed pressure vessel, but external inspection is required to verify that installation has taken place according to the code.

An authorized inspector determines the type of inspection to be performed on a particular vessel. The inspection may include various inspection methods such as visual inspection, pressure test, and nondestructive examinations. The appropriate inspection method should provide the information necessary to determine that all components of the vessel are safe to operate until the next scheduled inspection.

Internal inspection. The *internal inspection*, which may be a visual inspection or a combination of visual and nondestructive examination, is used for assessing the internal condition. Defects such as corrosion, erosion, and cracks are generally revealed as the result of internal inspection. The authorized inspector may replace internal inspection with on-stream inspection. The period between internal or on-stream inspections should not exceed half the remaining life of the vessel (projected by corrosion rate) or 10 years, whichever is less.

On-stream inspection. The *on-stream inspection* is conducted either while the vessel is out of service, while it is depressurized, or while it is on stream and under pressure. When an on-stream inspection is conducted in lieu of an internal inspection, a thorough examination should be performed using ultrasonic thickness measurements, radiography, or other appropriate means of nondestructive examination (NDE) to measure metal thickness. The authorized inspector should have sufficient access to all parts of the vessels so that an accurate assessment can be made of the vessel's condition.

External inspection. Each pressure vessel should be inspected externally when the vessel is under operation. The interval between consecutive external inspections should be 5 years or the same interval as between required internal or on-stream inspections, whichever is less. Such inspection should reveal the condition of insulation and supports, allowance for expansion, evidence of leakage, and general alignment of the vessel on its supports. The authorized inspector may wish to observe conditions under the insulation, but the condition of the insulating system and outer jacketing (such as of the cold box) should also be inspected no less frequently than every 5 years.

Pressure test. A *pressure test* is necessary when certain repairs and alterations are made to a pressure vessel. The pressure test must also be done if the authorized inspector believes that a pressure test is necessary to assess the mechanical integrity of the vessel. Pneumatic testing may be applied when hydrostatic testing is impractical because of temperature, foundation, refractory lining, or process reasons.

Risk-Based Inspection

A *risk-based inspection* (RBI) is a system of combining the assessment of the likelihood of failure and the consequence of failure. When an owner chooses to conduct an RBI assessment, it includes a systematic evaluation of both the likelihood of failure and the associated consequence of failure.

The assessment of likelihood of failure must be based on all the possible degradation that could reasonably be expected to affect a vessel. The degradation mechanism in pressure vessels includes metal loss because of corrosion, cracking (including hydrogen and stress-corrosion cracking), any further forms of corrosion, erosion, fatigue, embrittlement, creep, and mechanical degradation. The likelihood of failure assessment should be repeated each time the equipment or process changes.

The consequence assessment should consider the potential incidents that may occur because of failures. Such incidents may include fluid release, explosion, fire, toxic exposure, environmental impact, and other health effects.

The American Petroleum Institute (API) has developed an RBI approach. API RP 580, *Risk-Based Inspection* (2009b), is used in the petroleum industry to focus inspections and resources on equipment items that have the greatest likelihood or consequence of failure.

Vessel Records

Owners and users shall maintain records throughout the service life of each pressure vessel. The records should be regularly updated to reflect new information regarding operation, inspection, maintenance, alteration, and repair. These records should be evaluated by a technical expert to assess the safety of the pressure vessel.

Pressure vessel records should contain five types of information pertinent to mechanical integrity:

1. The *vessel identification record* indicates general information about the vessel.
2. The *design and construction information* identifies the design conditions and all codes and standards used for design and construction.
3. The *operating history* reflects the operating conditions of the vessel.
4. The *inspection history* provides information on past inspections, verifying that the condition of the vessel is indeed monitored as required.
5. The *repair record* indicates all repairs or modifications to the vessel.

HAZARD CONTROL

The management should employ good engineering principles to reduce the potential hazards from pressure vessels. Plants and facilities should be operated and maintained to protect the environment, as well as the safety and health of employees. The management should also advise employees, customers, and the public of significant pressure vessel–related safety, health, and environmental hazards.

A survey was undertaken to determine all of the probable causes of unsafe conditions and to make safety assessments for preventing pressure vessel accidents. The survey questionnaire was sent to 100 pressure vessel manufacturers, repairers, and users. Table 3 indicates common causes for pressure vessel accidents according to the survey responses:

TABLE 3

Causes of Pressure Valve Accidents

Causes	Percentage of Accidents
Operator error	29%
Poor maintenance	27%
Controls and safety-device failure	10%
Faulty design	9%
Faulty construction	8%
Improper installation	6%
Irregular inspection	5%
Improper repair	4%
Unknown	2%

In order to control pressure vessel hazards, the management should give serious consideration to the following safety practices.

Design Vessels According to Code

The design of a pressure vessel according to the code is the first step in ensuring that vessel structure is safe. The study in Table 3 shows that 9 percent of accidents occur as a result of faulty design.

The safest code for designing pressure vessels is ASME *Boiler and Pressure Vessel Code,* Section VIII—Pressure Vessels (ASME 2011a). It is the responsibility of the owner and user to provide sufficient information to design engineers. In addition to the ASME Code, design engineers must comply with the jurisdictional requirements of locations where vessels are going to be installed. The American Petroleum Institute's codes and standards should be used for designing pressure vessels for petrochemical industry uses.

Construct Vessels According to Code

The manufacturer is responsible for construction of pressure vessels. Construction includes fabrication, provision of materials, inspection and tests during fabrication, and stamping of pressure vessels. The study in Table 3 shows that 8 percent of the accidents occur because of faulty construction.

A pressure vessel is fabricated according to the design, drawings, and calculations done by a design engineer or professional engineer. In addition to the ASME Code, Section VIII (2011a), the manufacturer must use ASME Section IX (2011f) and V (2011g) codes. Again, the manufacturer must comply with the API codes and standards for fabrication of pressure vessels to be used in petrochemical industries. The manufacturer must have a certificate of authority from the American Society of Mechanical Engineers to use code symbol stamps (U, U2, and U3). The shop inspection during construction should be performed by an authorized inspector to ensure that the manufacturer complies with all of the code requirements.

Install Vessels Properly

Pressure vessels are installed according to manufacturers' recommendations and the requirements of the local jurisdiction. The proper installation is key to controlling hazards from long-term use of pressure vessels. The survey in Table 3 shows that 6 percent of the pressure vessels fail because of improper installation.

Generally, a mechanical contractor installs pressure vessels in equipment rooms or at outdoor locations. The contractor is responsible for obtaining necessary permits from the jurisdictions involved prior to installation and startup. The owner must ensure that the contractor has applied proper codes and the manufacturer's recommendations for installation. When the job is completed, the owner or owner's representative must inspect the entire pressure vessel system. If a violation of the local code is found, an authorized inspector must affirm that the violation has been corrected.

Take Care of Controls and Safety Devices

Controls and safety devices are used on pressure vessels for efficient and safe plant management. The survey in Table 3 shows that 10 percent of the pressure vessel accidents occur as a result of control and safety-device failure.

These controls and safety devices are very sophisticated instruments specially designed by control engineers. The types of controls and safety devices depend on the application of pressure vessels, but, once installed, they are supposed to function smoothly without any problem. Owners and users must ensure their proper operation by checking and testing devices at regular intervals. It is advisable to follow manufacturers' recommendations and local jurisdictional requirements for installation, operation, maintenance, and repair of these devices.

Engage Qualified Operators

The survey in Table 3 shows that 29 percent of all the pressure vessel accidents occur because of operator error. It is essential that the management hire, train, and maintain qualified engineers and operators to operate pressure vessel systems.

Operators in process plants make crucial decisions at times. Because most jurisdictions do not have regulations for qualifying operators, the owner and user are responsible for giving proper training to the operating personnel. An operator must be familiar with all operating conditions including hazardous conditions related to pressure vessels. There should be written procedures, including emergency procedures, for each pressure vessel and its associated system. The operators should have detailed knowledge of startup, shutdown, process upsets, or other unusual conditions.

Maintain Vessels Properly

According to the study in Table 3, 27 percent of pressure vessel accidents occur because of poor maintenance. It is very important that management establish a maintenance program for all types of maintenance on pressurized systems.

In addition to preventing accidents, maintenance is performed on pressure vessels to increase efficiency, ensure safety, and prevent unscheduled shutdowns. The maintenance department should have a separate program for routine, preventive, shutdown and overhaul maintenance. Every pressure vessel should have a maintenance log sheet, recording any maintenance done on the equipment in detail. The maintenance department is also responsible for readying the pressure vessel for inspection by an authorized inspector.

Inspect Vessels Regularly

Inspection is necessary to ensure that pressure vessels are fit for service. The study in Table 3 shows that 5 percent of failures occur because of noninspection or irregular inspection.

The objectives of inspection are the evaluation of the operational integrity of pressure vessels in service and the issuing of certificates in accordance with jurisdictional laws and rules. An authorized inspector, qualified by the jurisdictional authority, conducts in-service inspection. In large industrial complexes, the owner may establish an inspection department staffed with inspectors qualified by the jurisdictional authority. The owner's inspectors must inspect the equipment according to jurisdictional laws and rules. The management should implement the authorized inspectors' recommendations for controlling plant hazards.

Repair Vessels Properly

Repair work is done to restore a pressure vessel to safe and satisfactory operating conditions. The survey in Table 3 shows that 4 percent of the pressure vessel accidents occur because of improper repair.

Management should engage qualified repair firms to undertake all types of repairs. The various forms of repairs are major repair, minor repair, alteration, rerating, and modification. While undertaking any type of repair, the repair organization must follow the original code of construction. Approval from the authorized inspector is required before and after the repair. Vessels should be tested hydrostatically if required by the inspector. The repair organization must submit a repair report duly signed by the authorized inspector for repair work done. A pressure vessel repair report on Form R-1 is shown in Appendix C.

Investigate Unknown Factors

It may be difficult to determine the cause of an accident in some cases. Every effort should be made to determine possible causes to avoid repetition of such accidents in the future. Thorough investigation should be made to find out if the accident is related to terrorism, sabotage, or natural disaster. Operating personnel should be questioned to avoid missing any possible clues or links to outsiders.

Maintain Records

The management must ensure that proper records are maintained for each piece of equipment. These records include vessel identification, design and construction information, operation history, inspection history, and repair records.

In addition to the above records, the management should document training programs, qualification records, statistical analyses, and any reports by technical experts. The latest editions of all codes and standards related to pressure vessels should be available.

Comply with Jurisdictional Regulations

The management must comply with all local, state, and federal laws, rules, and regulations applicable to locations where pressure vessels are installed. Penalties or other consequences may occur when such regulations are not followed.

Many jurisdictional laws require that pressure vessels be offered for internal and external inspection at regular intervals. An inspector authorized by the jurisdiction performs such inspections and issues a certificate of compliance. The law requires that the certificate of compliance be posted in the equipment room. The owner is also responsible for informing the jurisdiction of all accidents.

Conclusion

An unsafe act, an unsafe condition, a pressure vessel accident—all are symptoms of something wrong in the safety management system. Safety should be managed as any other company function. The management should direct safety effectively by setting achievable goals and by planning, organizing, and controlling in order to achieve them. An effective safety management program should be established to minimize pressure vessel hazards.

In order to achieve pressure vessel safety, management should establish an effective pressure vessel safety program. Typical components of a safety program are:

- Management's statement of policy
- Safety rules
- Authority and responsibility
- Training of employees
- Inspections
- Investigations
- Obtaining services from experts
- Record keeping

Each component of the safety program should be designed with the objective of reducing the number of pressure vessel accidents. Top management must support, and middle management must participate in, such a program. The industrial safety survey in Table 3 shows that a safety manager's role is crucial to the success of a safety program. A safety manager must structure, program, investigate, and analyze safety functions to ensure proper functioning.

Pressure vessel safety programs determine and define causes that allow accidents to occur by (1) searching for root causes of accidents and (2) controlling the variables related to root causes. The highest risk is mostly associated with a small percentage of pressure vessels in a plant. Risk-based inspection (RBI) based on ranking of equipment, experience, and engineering judgment may be established to help carry out pressure vessel safety functions. ANSI/API RP-580, *Risk-Based Inspection* (2009b) may be used for setting up a risk-based inspection program.

The use of risk-based inspection procedures and good engineering practices reduces the number of catastrophic pressure vessel failures. Management should include pressure vessel safety management as an element of production in order to control hazards. Only by safety management can the health and welfare of employees be ensured and the environment protected from the effects of dangerous pressure vessel explosions.

References

American National Standards Institute (ANSI)/Amercan Petroleum Institute (API). 2006. Standard 661, *Air Cooled Heat Exchangers for General Refinery Service Petroleum and Natural Gas Industries.* Washington, D.C.: API.

______. 2007. Standard 660, *Shell-and-Tube Heat Exchangers.* Washington, D.C.: API.

American Petroleum Institute (API). 2006. API 510, *Pressure Vessel Inspection Code: In-Service Inspection, Rating, Repair, and Alteration.* 9th ed. Washington, D.C.: API.

______. 2007. API 650, *Welded Steel Tanks for Oil Storage.* 11th ed. Washington, D.C.: API.

______. 2008. STD 620, *Recommended Rules for Design and Construction of Large, Welded, Low-Pressure Storage Tanks.* 11th ed. Washington, D.C.: API.

______. 2009a. RP 572, *Inspection of Pressure Vessels.* 3d ed. Washington, D.C.: API.

______. 2009b. RP 580, *Risk-Based Inspection.* Washington, D.C.: API.

American Society of Mechanical Engineers (ASME). 2011a. *Boiler and Pressure Vessel Code*, Section VIII. New York: ASME International.

______. 2011b. *Boiler and Pressure Vessel Code*, Section VIII, Division 1—Rules for Construction of Pressure Vessels. New York: ASME International.

______. 2011c. *Boiler and Pressure Vessel Code,* Section VIII, Division 2—Alternative Rules. New York: ASME International.

______. 2011d. *Boiler and Pressure Vessel Code,* Section VIII, Division 3—Rules for Construction of High Pressure Vessels. New York: ASME International.

______. 2011e. *Boiler and Pressure Vessel Code,* Section II, Materials—Parts A–D. New York: ASME International.

______. 2011f. *Boiler and Pressure Vessel Code,* Section IX—Welding and Brazing. New York: ASME International.

______. 2011g. *Boiler and Pressure Vessel Code,* Section V—Nondestructive Examination. New York: ASME International.

National Board of Boiler and Pressure Vessel Inspectors. 2002. "Pressure Vessel Safety Survey." www.nationalboard.org

Occupational Safety and Health Administration (OSHA). 1989. Publication 8-1.5, *Guidelines for Pressure Vessel Safety Assessment.* Washington, D.C.: OSHA.

______. 1999. *OSHA Technical Manual.* www.osha.gov/dts/osta/otm/otm-iv/otm-iv-3/html

Tubular Exchanger Manufacturing Association (TEMA). 2007. *TEMA Standards.* 9th ed. Tarrytown, NY: TEMA.

Appendix A

(*Courtesy:* ASME International.)

The American Society of Mechanical Engineers

CERTIFICATE OF AUTHORIZATION

This certificate accredits the named company as authorized to use the indicated symbol of the American Society of Mechanical Engineers (ASME) for the scope of activity shown below in accordance with the applicable rules of the ASME Boiler and Pressure Vessel Code. The use of the Code symbol and the authority granted by this Certificate of Authorization are subject to the provisions of the agreement set forth in the application. Any construction stamped with this symbol shall have been built strictly in accordance with the provisions of the ASME Boiler and Pressure Vessel Code.

COMPANY:

AEREX INDUSTRIES, INC.
3504 INDUSTRIAL 27TH STREET
FORT PIERCE, FLORIDA 34946

SCOPE:

MANUFACTURE OF PRESSURE VESSELS AT THE ABOVE LOCATION AND FIELD SITES CONTROLLED BY THE ABOVE LOCATION

AUTHORIZED:	SEPTEMBER 24, 2003
EXPIRES:	DECEMBER 1, 2006
CERTIFICATE NUMBER:	29,984

Chairman of The Boiler
And Pressure Vessel Committee

Director, Accreditation and Certification

Appendix B

(*Courtesy:* ASME International.)

FORM U-1 MANUFACTURER'S DATA REPORT FOR PRESSURE VESSELS
As Required by the Provisions of the ASME Boiler and Pressure Vessel Code Rules, Section VIII, Division 1

1. Manufactured and certified by ________ ① (Name and address of Manufacturer)
2. Manufactured for ________ ② (Name and address of Purchaser)
3. Location of installation ________ ③ (Name and address)
4. Type ________ ④ (Horizontal, vertical, or sphere) ________ ⑤ (Tank, separator, jkt. vessel, heat exch., etc.) ________ ⑧ (Manufacturer's serial number)
________ ⑨ (CRN) ________ ⑩ (Drawing number) ________ ⑫ (National Board number) ________ (Year built)
5. ASME Code, Section VIII, Div. 1 ________ ⑬ [Edition and Addenda, if applicable (date)] ________ ⑭ (Code Case number) ________ ⑮ [Special service per UG-120(d)]

Items 6–11 incl. to be completed for single wall vessels, jackets of jacketed vessels, shell of heat exchangers, or chamber of multichamber vessels.

6. Shell: (a) Number of course(s) ________ ⑯ (b) Overall length ________ ⑰

Course(s)			Material	Thickness		Long. Joint (Cat. A)			Circum. Joint (Cat. A, B & C)			Heat Treatment	
No.	Diameter	Length	Spec./Grade or Type	Nom.	Corr.	Type	Full, Spot, None	Eff.	Type	Full, Spot, None	Eff.	Temp.	Time
	⑱	⑲	⑳	㉑	㉒	㉓	㉔		㉕	㉖		㉗	

7. Heads: (a) ________ ⑳ (Material spec. number, grade or type) ㉗ (H.T. — time and temp.) (b) ________ (Material spec. number, grade or type) (H.T. — time and temp.)

	Location (Top, Bottom, Ends)	Thickness		Radius		Elliptical Ratio	Conical Apex Angle	Hemispherical Radius	Flat Diameter	Side to Pressure		Category A		
		Min.	Corr.	Crown	Knuckle					Convex	Concave	Type	Full, Spot, None	Eff.
(a)		㉘	㉒	㉙	㉚								㉛	
(b)														

If removable, bolts used (describe other fastening) ________ ㉜ (Material spec. number, grade, size, number)

8. Type of jacket ________ ㉝ Jacket closure ________ ㉞ (Describe as ogee and weld, bar, etc.)

If bar, give dimensions ________ If bolted, describe or sketch.

9. MAWP ㉟ (Internal) ________ (External) at max. temp. ㊱ (Internal) ________ (External) Min. design metal temp. ________ ㊲ at ________.
10. Impact test ________ ㊳ [Indicate *yes* or *no* and the component(s) impact tested] at test temperature of ________ ㊳.
11. Hydro., pneu., or comb. test pressure ________ ㊴ Proof test ________ ㊵

Items 12 and 13 to be completed for tube sections.

12. Tubesheet ⑳ [Stationary (material spec. no.)] ⑱ [Diameter (subject to press.)] ㉑ (Nominal thickness) ㉒ (Corr. allow.) [Attachment (welded or bolted)]
⑳ [Floating (material spec. no.)] ⑱ (Diameter) ㉑ (Nominal thickness) ㉒ (Corr. allow.) (Attachment)
13. Tubes ⑳ (Material spec. no., grade or type) ________ (O.D.) ________ (Nominal thickness) ________ (Number) ________ [Type (straight or U)]

Items 14–18 incl. to be completed for inner chambers of jacketed vessels or channels of heat exchangers.

14. Shell: (a) No. of course(s) ________ (b) Overall length ________

Course(s)			Material	Thickness		Long. Joint (Cat. A)			Circum. Joint (Cat. A, B & C)			Heat Treatment	
No.	Diameter	Length	Spec./Grade or Type	Nom.	Corr.	Type	Full, Spot, None	Eff.	Type	Full, Spot, None	Eff.	Temp.	Time

15. Heads: (a) ________ (Material spec. number, grade or type) (H.T. — time and temp.) (b) ________ (Material spec. number, grade or type) (H.T. — time and temp.)

	Location (Top, Bottom, Ends)	Thickness		Radius		Elliptical Ratio	Conical Apex Angle	Hemispherical Radius	Flat Diameter	Side to Pressure		Category A		
		Min.	Corr.	Crown	Knuckle					Convex	Concave	Type	Full, Spot, None	Eff.
(a)														
(b)														

If removable, bolts used (describe other fastening) ________ (Material spec. number, grade, size, number)

APPENDIX B (continued)

(*Courtesy:* ASME International.)

FORM U-1 (Back)

16. MAWP ________ (Internal) ________ (External) at max. temp. ________ (Internal) ________ (External) Min. design metal temp. ________ at ________ .

17. Impact test ________ [Indicate yes or no and the component(s) impact tested] at test temperature of ⑶⑻ ________ .

18. Hydro., pneu., or comb. test pressure ⑶⑼ ________ Proof test ⑷⑽ ________

19. Nozzles, inspection, and safety valve openings:

Purpose (Inlet, Outlet, Drain, etc.)	No.	Diameter or Size	Type	Material		Nozzle Thickness		Reinforcement Material	Attachment Details		Location (Insp. Open.)
				Nozzle	Flange	Nom.	Corr.		Nozzle	Flange	
				(20)	(20)						
(41)		(42)	(43)	(44)	(45)	(46)		(47)	(48) (49)	(48) (49)	(50)

20. Supports: Skirt (51) (Yes or no) Lugs (51) (Number) Legs (51) (Number) Others (51) (Describe) Attached (51) (Where and how)

21. Manufacturer's Partial Data Reports properly identified and signed by Commissioned Inspectors have been furnished for the following items of the report (list the name of part, item number, Manufacturer's name, and identifying number): (52)

22. Remarks ________ (53)

(58) **CERTIFICATE OF SHOP COMPLIANCE**

We certify that the statements in this report are correct and that all details of design, material, construction, and workmanship of this vessel conform to the ASME BOILER AND PRESSURE VESSEL CODE, Section VIII, Division 1.

U Certificate of Authorization Number ________ Expires ________

Date ________ Name ________ (Manufacturer) Signed ________ (Representative)

(60) **CERTIFICATE OF SHOP INSPECTION**

I, the undersigned, holding a valid commission issued by the National Board of Boiler and Pressure Vessel Inspectors and/or the State or Province of (61) ________ and employed by ________ of ________ have inspected the pressure vessel described in this Manufacturer's Data Report on ________ , and state that, to the best of my knowledge and belief, the Manufacturer has constructed this pressure vessel in accordance with ASME BOILER AND PRESSURE VESSEL CODE, Section VIII, Division 1. By signing this certificate neither the Inspector nor his/her employer makes any warranty, expressed or implied, concerning the pressure vessel described in this Manufacturer's Data Report. Furthermore, neither the Inspector nor his/her employer shall be liable in any manner for any personal injury or property damage or a loss of any kind arising from or connected with this inspection.

Date ________ Signed ________ (Authorized Inspector) Commissions (62) ________ [National Board (incl. endorsements), State, Province, and number]

(64) **CERTIFICATE OF FIELD ASSEMBLY COMPLIANCE**

We certify that the statements in this report are correct and that the field assembly construction of all parts of this vessel conforms with the requirements of ASME BOILER AND PRESSURE VESSEL CODE, Section VIII, Division 1. U Certificate of Authorization Number ________ Expires ________ .

Date ________ Name ________ (Assembler) Signed ________ (Representative)

(65) **CERTIFICATE OF FIELD ASSEMBLY INSPECTION**

I, the undersigned, holding a valid commission issued by the National Board of Boiler and Pressure Vessel Inspectors and/or the State or Province of ________ and employed by ________ of ________ , have compared the statements in this Manufacturer's Data Report with the described pressure vessel and state that parts referred to as data items (66) ________ , not included in the certificate of shop inspection, have been inspected by me and to the best of my knowledge and belief, the Manufacturer has constructed and assembled this pressure vessel in accordance with the ASME BOILER AND PRESSURE VESSEL CODE, Section VIII, Division 1. The described vessel was inspected and subjected to a hydrostatic test of ________. By signing this certificate neither the Inspector nor his/her employer makes any warranty, expressed or implied, concerning the pressure vessel described in this Manufacturer's Data Report. Furthermore, neither the Inspector nor his/her employer shall be liable in any manner for any personal injury or property damage or a loss of any kind arising from or connected with this inspection.

Date ________ Signed ________ (Authorized Inspector) Commissions (62) ________ [National Board (incl. endorsements), State, Province, and number]

Appendix C

FORM R-1 REPORT OF REPAIR

in accordance with provisions of the National Board Inspection Code

1. Work performed by Paul Mueller Company (name of repair organization) (Form R. No.)

1600 W. Phelps PO Box 828 Springfield MO 65801 (address) (P.O. No. Job No. etc.)

2. Owner Tropicana Products, Inc. (name)

P.O. Box 338 Bradenton FL 33506 (address)

3. Location of installation Tropicana Products, Inc. (name)

6500 Glades Cut Off Road Fort Pierce FL 34981 (address)

4. Unit identification Press. Vessel (boiler, pressure vessel) Name of original manufacturer Stainless Fabrication Inc

5. Identifying nos.: 2019-2A (mfg serial no.) 68 (National Board No.) (jurisdiction no.) DDM0263 (other) 1980 (year built)

6. NBIC Edition / Addenda 2001 (edition) A03 (addenda)

Original Code of Construction for Item: ASME SEC VIII DIV 1 (name/section/division) 1980 (edition/addenda)

Construction Code Used for Repair Performed: ASME SEC VIII DIV 1 (name/section/division) 2001 A03 (edition/addenda)

7. Repair Type: [X] Welded [ ] Graphite Pressure Equipment [ ] FRP Pressure Equipment

8. Description of work: Paul Mueller Company repaired a leak in shell temp-plate. Hydro (use supplemental sheet, Form R-4, if necessary) test was performed after repair.

Pressure Test, if applied 225 psi MAWP 150 psi

9. Replacement Parts. Attached are Manufacturer's Partial Data Reports or Form R-3s properly completed for the following items of this report.

(name of part, item number, data report type, mfr's. name and identifying stamp)

10. Remarks

CERTIFICATE OF COMPLIANCE

I, [signature], certify that to the best of my knowledge and belief the statements in this report are correct and that all material, construction, and workmanship on this Repair conforms to the National Board Inspection Code.

National Board "R" Certificate of Authorization No. 2957 expires on Oct. 27, 2004

Date 6/15/04 Paul Mueller Company (name of repair organization) Signed [signature] (authorized representative)

CERTIFICATE OF INSPECTION

I, RODNEY SENN, holding a valid Commission issued by The National Board of Boiler and Pressure Vessel Inspectors and certificate of competency issued by the jurisdiction of FLORIDA and employed by HSBCT of Hartford, CT have inspected the work described in this report on 8/11/04 and state that to the best of my knowledge and belief this work complies with the applicable requirements of the National Board Inspection Code.

By signing this certificate, neither the undersigned nor my employer makes any warranty expressed or implied, concerning the work described in this report. Furthermore, neither the undersigned nor my employer shall be liable in any manner for any personal injury, property damage or loss of any kind arising from or connected with this inspection.

Date 8/11/04 Signed [signature] (inspector) Commissions NB12603A, FL445 (National Board and jurisdiction, and no.)

7

Cost Analysis and Budgeting

Mark Friend

LEARNING OBJECTIVES

- Understand the rationale for cost analysis and budgeting from a safety management perspective.
- Be able to explain the mechanics of the budgeting process.
- Learn the definitions of key budgeting and financial analysis terms.
- Be able to identify methods of loss control.
- Outline the methods of simple cost determination.

ACCORDING TO renowned economist Milton Friedman (Davis 2005), "The business of business is business." Management expert Peter Drucker, who has years of experience working with top American corporations, gives us a new perspective on safety when he says (Drucker 1986): "It is the first duty of business to survive. The guiding principle is not the maximization of profits but the minimization of loss." The bottom line in most business decisions is strictly business. Safety managers may have difficulty with this concept, because they tend to focus on compliance or some of the technical or human aspects of safety. These issues are what they know best, and sometimes it might be difficult for them to comprehend the importance of the financial aspects of safety.

The rising costs of health care (Ginsberg 2004, 1593), workers' compensation, equipment repair and replacement, insurance, and litigation arising from safety problems should make every safety professional aware that the job of the safety professional is increasingly mired in the business of business. There must be a marrying of the missions between management and the safety function (Pope 1985). The business of both is business.

Safety managers may not receive the support from management they believe they deserve. Executive management supports the areas management believes will provide the greatest returns. In spite of personal desires or the best of intentions, business decisions are often—and, in fact, must be—made based purely on financial considerations. How much profit or how much cost savings will result?

Safety managers and the whole management team face difficult decisions involving allocation of resources to various projects.

Their decisions must be pragmatic and cost effective to best serve the owners of the business they represent. If the decision regarding making the workplace safer costs anything, that cost must be weighed against the cost benefit of the decision, as well as against the costs of other opportunities the business may forego as a result of making the workplace safer.

The safety function competes with every other function in the organization for resources. Funds spent on safety translate into equivalent amounts not being spent for new product development, employee raises, capital improvements, or dividends to investors or stockholders (Ferry 1985). In most organizations, a manager looks at the request from the safety department and compares that request to others he or she receives. The request perceived to provide the greatest benefit, typically in terms of financial gain, is funded, although sometimes that gain is expressed in terms of good will, positive employee attitude, or other assets not necessarily directly associated with company profit and loss statements. Generally, management is seeking a clear contribution to the profitability of the company.

Either way, managers will knowingly or intuitively build consideration of both approaches into their decision-making processes. Both ultimately involve money. When building a business case for any safety program, it is the responsibility of the safety manager to bring to the table the cost and the value of any item requiring funds beyond the normal allocated safety budget. When making plans within the budget, financial considerations must be paramount to ensure maximum use of resources by the firm. For example, a safety department has analyzed its records and found that, during the previous three years, there have been four injuries resulting from contact with rotating saw blades. A safety technician has researched the problem and determined it can be corrected by replacing current equipment with new equipment containing soft-tissue sensors that will stop a rotating saw blade on contact with hands, fingers, or other body parts. The cost of replacement is compared to the total cost of injuries over a specified period of time. The dollar savings provides a return comparable to the return on other opportunities presented to management for use of the funds. In addition to the monetary return, management may also consider the value of the reduction of human loss and suffering, providing psychic benefits to decision makers and those potentially affected by the decision. All are ultimately weighed against the dollar costs involved less the potential dollar return.

Ultimately, the responsibility for the safety function rests not with the safety professional, but with line management (Morris 1985), because line management is ultimately held accountable for the financial decisions and the profitability of the organization. The role of the safety professional is to monitor safety and advise management on the steps it must take to improve or maximize safety for the employees.

The language of business is that of accounting and finance. The successful safety professional, seeking the support of top management, will learn to speak in the terms used by executive management. These terms include those typically found on corporate financial statements and the standards by which those items are measured. "Return on investment," "tax benefit," and "capital" versus "budget expenditures" become relevant vocabúlary terms. According to William Pope (Friend 1986, 51), the safety professional will realize that anything done regarding safety is done because management wants it to be done. Management only wants things done that have a positive financial impact on the organization (Pope 1983).

Budgeting

The task of budgeting should be familiar to any safety professional. Most businesses and government entities operate on budgets, as do their subunits. Corporate and government budgets are usually developed on an annual or more frequent basis in a number of ways.

Budgets tend to be based on expenditures from previous periods. The assumption is that performance will continue much as it has in the past, and that budgets will be similar this year to what they were in the past. Often a percentage growth factor is built in, depending on the profitability and trends within the organization. For example, if growth for the company tends to be around 5 percent per year, then each line for the next planned budget may be increased by 5 percent. Exceptions may be made for special projects

General Corporation
Safety Department Budget
For the Year 2011

Personnel wages and benefits		$216,000
Operating expenses		
Equipment purchases	113,221	
Materials	36,414	
Supplies	19,652	
Total operating expenses		169,287
Total estimated safety department expenses for 2011		$385,287

FIGURE 1. Sample budget
(*Source:* Horngren, Sundem, and Stratton 2002)

or for capital expenditures requiring additional funds beyond the normal budget.

The budget often resembles an income or profit and loss statement. When the amount to work with is known, it is shown in the first line; otherwise, only expenses required to operate are listed. Figure 1 is an example of a typical budget.

The budget is developed for a specific period of time, as noted in the figure's title. This particular budget simply lists items for which funds are expected to be needed. Normal protocol suggests that items are listed from more durable to less durable; thus, equipment is listed before materials, which is listed before supplies. Subcategories are indented, with totals appearing opposite the last item in the list or as a total of the list in the final column. Subtotal amounts are always indented one column. Subtotals of subtotals are indented two columns. Budgets may be developed for one year, six months, a quarter, or any period desired.

A budget may also be built for a particular project. It may include items as outlined above. There may be separate columns for maximum/minimum estimates, quotes, and final project amounts. Contingency amounts may also be included to cover unexpected costs.

Zero-based budgets are those requiring justification in each new period for each expenditure (Investopedia 2005). Instead of basing the budget for the coming year on the budget from last year, the budget manager is asked to deliver a budget proposal for the forthcoming year, with justification for each line item. In essence, cost estimates are built from scratch or from zero. In reality, most managers usually ask for more than they want, hoping to get a percentage of it and thereby winding up with the actual amount desired.

Normal practice suggests that the budget manager prepares three budgets. The first represents the optimum amount with all the wants and desires built in, just in case there happens to be more than enough money to spread around. The second budget represents the very least amount the manager needs to survive during the coming year. Any negotiations may permit cutting to this point, but no lower. The last budget is an actual, realistic budget that accurately reflects the goals of the planning period. An appropriate approach in some situations is to present top management with this budget, with optimistic and pessimistic figures in mind for each line item.

Fixed and Variable Costs

Costs involved in any budget fall into two major categories: fixed and variable. *Fixed costs* are operating costs that exist regardless of activity or level of production (Kiger, Loeb, and May 1987, 888). For example, in a manufacturing operation, a fixed cost is the cost of the real estate and buildings in which the operation is run. *Variable costs* are those incremental costs that vary according to production levels (Kiger, Loeb, and May 1987, 889). Materials or component parts are examples of variable costs.

Consideration is often given to fixed and variable costs in the budget because management is particularly attuned to the additional costs involved in adding a new program. Ongoing costs, such as safety staff salaries, utility costs for the offices, and apportioned lease costs on the office space, may not be considered when new budgets are proposed. Management may make budgetary decisions based only on the variable costs introduced for new projects or programs.

Before a budget is assembled, a determination of expected costs to be included is made. Additional variable costs are always included, but some ongoing, fixed costs may also have to be added so that a fully informed decision can be made by management. Many companies simply apply a standard overhead rate to all budgets to account for the fixed costs. This saves time, in that they do not have to be calculated every time a budget or proposal is prepared.

Calculating how much a project will cost or how much a department will spend is the easy part of the task. The difficult part is justifying the expenditures.

Risk and Loss Exposure

Risk describes the expected value of potential: both the probability and the severity of a loss event (Roland and Moriarty 1990, 303). All companies face risk, and often embrace it. Of course, risk implies an exposure to the potential for loss. There are two types of loss exposure: speculative and pure. *Speculative* loss offers the opportunity for gain as well as loss exposures (Williams et al. 1981, 5). The purchase of a lottery ticket, the investment in a new product, or the move to a new location could all provide positive cash flows or loss of profits. Most companies engaged in marketing, investment, or other business ventures face speculative exposures; they are not within the realm of risk management.

On the other hand, *pure* loss exposures are those that only allow for the possibility of loss (Williams et al. 1981, 6). The most that can be hoped for is to break even. Fires, thefts, natural disasters, and other accidents can cause loss of profits but do not provide the business with opportunity for gain. These are within the purview of the risk manager. Risk management deals only with pure loss exposures by identifying, analyzing, and minimizing risk through cost-effective means. Risk management is a responsibility of the safety manager.

Organizations and their employees are subject to risk on a regular and ongoing basis. They are always exposed to potential losses, so the possibility of loss from various threats is always present. This loss exposure has three elements (Williams et al. 1981, 4–6):

1. the item that might be lost or suffer damage
2. the perils or agents that might cause the loss
3. the adverse reaction, which usually comes in the form of financial impact

Intervention measures can minimize loss from any of these elements, and all should be considered in any risk-management problem.

Organizations and their employees are always at risk from various perils. These may be controllable or completely uncontrollable. Any level of risk exposure over a long enough period of time will result in loss. Any item exposed to any peril enough times will suffer loss. Obviously, the more often an item is exposed to a peril, the more likely it is to suffer loss.

It is impossible to eliminate all accidents and resulting losses because it is impossible to eliminate all risk. Any exposure to any risk lends itself to the possibility of an accident, and thus a loss. For example, consider a hypothetical company engaging in one activity and having only one risk. The company is able to nearly eliminate the risk by reducing it to one-tenth of one percent (0.1 percent or 0.001). In other words, every time the company engages in the activity there is a chance of loss of only one in a thousand. In one exposure, the risk is very low, and the probability of an accident resulting is so miniscule as to be virtually nonexistent. It could happen, but it is highly improbable that it will happen. That is the ideal place for all probability of accidents to be.

What if the company repeated its procedure 1000 times per day? In one day, the probability of an accident is $1 - (1 - 0.001)^{1000}$, or 0.73. If the procedure is repeated 200 days per year, with 1000 exposures per day, an accident is almost a certainty. There is a 0.73 probability of having an accident on any given day, and the probability of having an accident over the course of a year is so high that multiple accidents are nearly a certainty: $1 - (1 - 0.001)^{260{,}000}$ (assuming 260 workdays per year). This certainty is the result of the law of large numbers at work. As the number of exposures is increased, the predictability of the accident becomes more certain. In this case, the company will likely have an accident at least seven days out of ten. Reducing the probability lower than it already is may be an impossibility, depending on the complexity of the system at work.

At one time, it was believed that if enough money and manpower were spent on a problematic safety situation, the situation could be resolved. The *Challenger* and *Columbia* disasters proved this was not true. Although NASA benefited from huge budgets to finance the shuttle program (AAAS 2006), each of the two shuttles failed, killing the occupants, destroying the craft, and delaying the space program for months. Even though the probability of failure of any one part may have been extremely low, the large number of parts and complex systems, combined with the political realities at NASA, made disaster inevitable. NASA was under tremendous pressure to succeed, and to keep the launches on schedule. Repeating risk eventually leads to loss. Repeating the space shuttle launches ultimately resulted in disastrous consequences. The probabilities of failure were not and could not have been reduced to zero. Unfortunately, they were not kept low enough to preclude disastrous failure twice in less than 100 exposures (NASA 2006).

Eliminating Loss

There are companies with goals of zero losses and zero accidents. The philosophy pervading these entities is that safety is of paramount importance, and therefore the organization should do whatever it takes to eliminate the accident problem. This is an impossible goal that cannot be sustained. Attempts to do so may lead to falsified reports, sandbagged claims, and hidden information.

A more likely goal is one of continuous improvement in terms of fewer accidents and incidents. Worthwhile targets might be expressed in terms of lower insurance or workers' compensation premiums. Emphasizing working more safely, improving processes, or eliminating hazards potentially leading to accidents may be more beneficial than trying to reach goals not reachable on a large-scale basis. Although zero accidents and the resultant zero losses are not likely, there are certain steps that can be taken to minimize or avoid exposure to loss. These techniques are collectively referred to as *managing risk* or *risk management*.

Risk Management

Managing risk consists of certain systematic steps that apply the resources of the organization to lower the probability of loss by ameliorating exposures, events, or results of incidents. The steps involved include:

- systematically identifying significant exposures and analyzing those exposures in terms of loss-producing potential and probability
- identifying and implementing the most cost-effective method of reducing or eliminating the probability of the loss or lessening the effects of the loss
- periodically and systematically analyzing the system to ensure that overall system loss reduction is maximized in terms of the item, the perils, and any adverse reactions that can be reasonably anticipated

When problems are found or loss exposures exist, an effort is made not only to correct the problem, but to correct any fault in the management system that permitted or even encouraged the problem to exist. For example, if there have been reports of injuries that could have or should have been avoided through the use of appropriate personal protective equipment (PPE), why did these problems exist? If the appropriate PPE program was not in place, or if a significant portion of the PPE program was overlooked, why did that occur? Was the original PPE analysis not thorough enough? Were changes made after the PPE program was put into place and, if so, why were they not incorporated? In other words, what is wrong with the management system that it did not respond to change? If the problem was with employees not wearing PPE because they chose not to do so, the same type of analysis must be made. Why did employees perceive they could ignore the program and proceed with their job without wearing appropriate PPE? Do not just fix the problem; fix whatever deeper problem existed in the management system to allow or encourage the surface problem to exist. Always look for problems in the management system that can and should be corrected.

Identifying and Analyzing Exposure

There are many ways to identify personnel and property subject to loss. Most approaches involve determining hazards and the effects of unattended exposure of people or property. Typical approaches to simple hazard determination are as follows:

- ***Record analysis.*** The first approach most companies take is to analyze past records. The OSHA 300 log, workers' compensation, first aid, and insurance records may all be used to point to problem areas. Multiple injuries of the same type or in the same area merit the highest levels of concern. Not only should the equipment, procedure, or person causing the problem be addressed, but the deeper management-system fault also must be corrected.
- ***Inspection forms.*** Inspection forms can be obtained from OSHA, insurance companies, or safety textbooks. OSHA has checklists for specific types of businesses and operations, as well as generic checklists for general safety problems. With experience in an operation, a safety professional may prefer to develop an in-house form appropriate to the specific enterprise. The enterprise is simply evaluated against the checklist to aid in finding hazards. An example of a typical checklist appears in Figure 2.
- ***Production flow analysis.*** A common approach to identifying hazards is to follow a product through the production cycle, from receipt of raw materials through assembly or processing to shipment of finished goods. Evaluate each step in the production cycle and identify the hazards associated with it. Any hands or equipment touching the product must be considered as potential recipients and providers of hazards.
- ***Financial statement review.*** A line-by-line review of each item on the financial statement, such as a balance sheet or income statement, can reveal areas where the company may be vulnerable financially. This goes beyond the typical inspection to review potential liability items in terms of litigation or legal obligation. This type of review tends to focus more scrutiny on business activities, as opposed to the tasks revealed in the production flow.
- ***Employee interviews.*** Time spent with employees to determine what hazards they note can be invaluable. Typical interviews include asking employees what near-misses they have observed, trouble spots they have noted or foresee, and loss-producing events they know about. Periodic discussions with production employees and their supervisors will sometimes reveal areas they are reluctant to write up.
- ***Incident and near-miss reports.*** Forms can be completed and turned in by employees any time they want to give insight into near-misses that might otherwise go unnoticed. These should only be used in conjunction with formal incident reports, similar to those required by the OSHA 301 form. The goal of any subsequent investigation is to determine fault in the management system so that corrections can be made. Investigations creating the impression that the intent is to point the blame at an individual or group have a diminished probability of having a valid conclusion.

All of the above methods are used to determine loss exposures or areas where loss might occur. Unfortunately, these methods may not be able to uncover all potential loss exposures. Even though a manager has access to previous OSHA 301 forms and the written description of the incident or accident, he or she may still not be aware of the real cause. Such phrases as "operator error" or "employee mistake" only serve to cover the true cause of the incident. Sometimes more sophisticated techniques will help reveal the actual cause or causes of an incident or accident.

FAULT TREE ANALYSIS (FTA)

Identifying the loss-producing hazard is not always a straightforward task. It may involve investigation into the cause of a particular incident or accident. *Fault tree analysis* may be useful in a number of situations. Widely used in system reliability studies, it offers the ability to focus on an event of importance, such as a highly critical safety issue. Fault tree analyses

Responsibility, Authority, and Accountability Checklist

In order to accomplish anything in the workplace, supervision must have the tools of the trade available. For the supervisor, the essential tools are the assignment of responsibility for a function or activity, the authority to do the job, and accountability to senior management to see that it is done. Using the following checklist, supervisors can determine if, in fact, they do have the tools necessary to do their job in safety. For self-directive work teams, the team must decide these issues.

Typically, these tasks are the responsibility of the supervisor for which he/she has complete authority and for which they are held accountable. They should also agree that these are of key importance to safety and health. Where check marks fall outside the "Yes" or "Complete authority" boxed, the recommended action is for the supervisor to discuss the situation with senior management and agree on steps necessary to assume appropriate responsibility, authority, and accountability. Note however, it is acceptable to delegate some of these items to assigned employees. This is part of the empowering process.

Is this your responsibility? ... *Yes!*	Is this your responsibility? ... *No!*	Do you have COMPLETE authority?	Do you have the authority to DECIDE; BUT TELL?	Is your authority limited to DECIDE; BUT CHECK FIRST?	Do you have NO authority?	Are you measured for accountability? ... *Yes!*	Are you measured for accountability? ... *No!*	Is this issue of key importance? ... *Yes!*	Is this issue of key importance? ... *No!*	
										Ensure equipment, materials, facilities, and conditions are safe.
										Provide for safety and health training
										Require employee compliance with safety requirements and rules.
										Recognize and reinforce safe behaviors.
										Make safety and health part of job standards and procedures.
										Request safety and health technical assistance.
										Obtain safe work permits
										Investigate accidents and take appropriate corrective action.
										Conduct inspections, audits and surveys.
										Establish emergency procedures for area.
										Hold safety meetings and workshops
										Correct unsafe conditions and behaviors.
										Stop production for safety reasons.
										Delegate authority for safety to others.

FIGURE 2. Sample responsibility, authority, and accountability checklist (*Source:* OSHA 2007)

are performed using a top-down approach. Begin by determining a top-level event, such as an accident, and then work down to evaluate all the contributing events that may ultimately lead to the occurrence of the top-level event. Probability can be used in fault tree analysis to determine the likelihood of the top-level event in any number of scenarios.

The fault tree diagram is a graphical representation of the chain of events in the system or process, built using events and logical gate configurations (Relex 2004). It can be used to:

- identify potential system reliability or safety problems during the design phase of an operation
- assess reliability or safety of a system during operation
- identify components that may need testing or more rigorous quality-assurance scrutiny

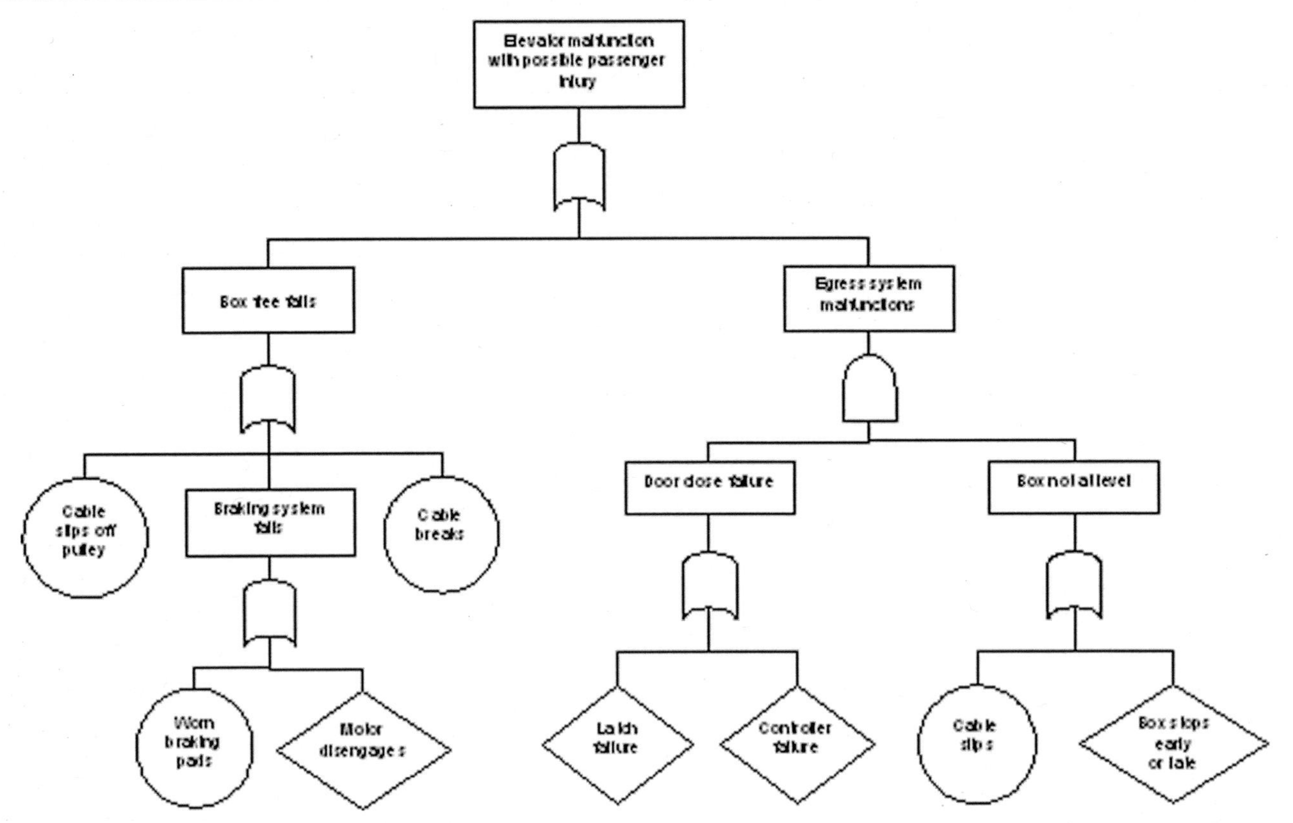

FIGURE 3. Sample fault tree analysis (Courtesy of Dr. Clarence Rodrigues, Embry-Riddle Aeronautical University)

- identify root causes of equipment failures, accidents, or incidents

The analysis may also be combined with probabilities to determine mathematical risk (the fault tree shown in Figure 3 does not use the assignment of probabilities). The fault tree analysis is conducted using the following basic steps:

1. Determine the head event or the event to be analyzed.
2. Determine the next-level event or events that caused the head event to occur.
3. Determine the relationship between or among causal events using the terms "and" and "or."
4. Continue the process through lower-level events until all possibilities are exhausted.
5. Assign probabilities to lowest-level events and systematically convert them to probabilities upward through the system.

Figure 4 defines the symbols that are used in fault tree analysis diagrams.

Determining Severity and Quantifying Risk

Once the potential loss exposures have been identified, the exposures must then be analyzed in terms of severity. MIL-STD-882, *System Safety Program*

Symbol	Name	Description
	Rectangle	Any event in the system
	Circle	Primary fault with no further development
	Diamond	Secondary fault with no further development. These are usually expected to happen
	AND Gate	All outcomes connected with an AND gate must occur in order for the next higher-level event to happen
	OR Gate	Any outcome connected with an OR gate must occur in order for the next higher-level event to occur

FIGURE 4. Fault tree diagram symbols

Requirements, identifies severity categories as catastrophic, critical, marginal, and negligible. It lists frequency of occurrence as frequent, probable, occasional, remote, and improbable. The resulting hazard-assessment matrix can guide the safety professional in combining the two categories to help determine overall risk.

The following matrix is derived from MIL-STD-882D, *Standard Practice for System Safety* (DoD 2000). It provides one systematic method for assigning a hazard level, based upon severity and frequency.

The hazard level consists of one number and one letter. The number represents the severity of the event. The numbers represent:

(1) Death, system loss, or irreversible environmental damage
(2) Severe injury, occupational illness, major system damage, or reversible severe environmental damage
(3) Injury requiring medical attention, illness, system damage, or mitigable environmental damage
(4) Possible minor injury, minor system damage, or minimal environmental damage

The letter assigned to the hazard level represents the frequency of occurrence. The letters represent:

(A) Expected to occur frequently
(B) Will occur several times in the life of an item
(C) Likely to occur sometime in the life of an item
(D) Unlikely, but possible to occur in the life of an item
(E) So unlikely, it can be assumed occurrence may not be experienced

As can be seen from Figure 5, each hazard level is associated with a risk category. Risk categories assist risk managers in differentiating credible, high-hazard threats that may result in loss of life and property from less probable risks, therefore aiding management in risk versus cost decisions.

The risk-assessment matrix is useful in determining overall risk and assigning resources to alleviate risk.

Frequency of Occurrence	Severity			
	(1) Catastrophic	(2) Critical	(3) Marginal	(4) Negligible
(A) Frequent	1A	2A	3A	4A
(B) Probable	1B	2B	3B	4B
(C) Occasional	1C	2C	3C	4C
(D) Remote	1D	2D	3D	4D
(E) Improbable	1E	2E	3E	4E

Risk Categories: High, Serious, Medium, Low

FIGURE 5. Risk-assessment matrix (*Source:* Safety Management Services, Inc. 2010)

Figure 5 can be useful in determining overall risk, and thereby ensuring that resources are allocated to the most pressing need. Exposures are assigned to a position on the figure by determining where they fall relative to frequency of occurrence and severity. Items falling in the upper-left portion of the figure deserve immediate attention and maximum application of resources. Those appearing in the lower-right part of the figure deserve little or no attention. Those in the middle category are addressed only after the more pressing needs are attended.

Identifying and Implementing Loss-Control Techniques

Reducing or controlling losses typically involves using engineering or administrative techniques or personal protective equipment (PPE). There are numerous control measures available for dealing with loss exposures or risk. These can be categorized as loss-control techniques and financing techniques (Williams et al. 1981, 53–100). Loss-control techniques attempt to reduce loss by intervening in the process. They include engineering techniques, administrative techniques, or PPE to deal with potential loss-producing exposures. For hazards potentially affecting personnel, engineering techniques are the first line of defense, followed by administrative techniques and PPE. Engineering approaches may not be cost effective or feasible; thus, less-effective approaches may be considered. In certain operations, loss is inevitable, and a better approach may be to avoid it or to transfer it to another party.

Risk Avoidance

A large sporting goods manufacturer might have among its products helmets and pads for football players. Over a period of years, the company finds itself suffering from an increasing number of lawsuits alleging that the helmets are defective. Rather than continue producing helmets, the company may choose to withdraw altogether and purchase helmets from an outside vendor. Employers engage in this type of risk avoidance regularly when they refuse to participate in a certain type of activity due to the risk.

An alternate strategy may be to contract with a third party to pursue the activity and then possibly transfer the risk to them. As long as the company continues to manufacture the helmet or retain the risk, it should be aware of the risk and periodically evaluate it in terms of cost, severity, and the resulting potential losses.

Lease

Contracting or subcontracting is not the only method of transferring risk. Another common vehicle for transferring risk is through the use of a lease. A lease can be used to transfer risk from the occupier of property to another party. For example, Company A builds a building for its own use, sells it to Landlord B, and rents it back. Depending on the terms of the lease, certain responsibilities and risks may also transfer to the landlord. The landlord may be responsible for damages and upkeep. Certainly, market risk or the risk that the value of the real estate will decline transfers to Landlord B. The contract and common law will spell out many of the relationships.

Disclaimer

Disclaimers may also be used in an attempt to transfer risk. For example, a parking-lot owner assumes no risk to vehicles parked there, as stated on the parking ticket and on signs. A renter of snow skis or jet skis may be requested to sign a statement releasing the owner of the equipment from liability in the event of injury.

The fact that a vehicle owner or an equipment renter accepts a statement refusing liability on the part of the premise or equipment owner does not necessarily release the owner from that liability. The owner may still be sued, and a judge or jury will determine whether liability on the owner's part exists. The decision may rest upon whether or not the owner was negligent, as well as on the reasonableness of the claim. Simply refusing to accept liability does not release the owner from it. For example, a passenger on a common carrier such as a bus, taxi, or airline expects to be delivered safely to his or her destination. If a taxi driver operates the taxi in a reckless manner and injures the passenger, the taxi driver and the owner of the taxi would reasonably expect to pay damages, regardless of any claims to the contrary on receipts or signs.

Attempting to transfer risk to another party without the benefit of insurance carries many potential pitfalls. A claim against any party assumes that the party has the wherewithal to cover the cost of losses and/or litigation. If not, the original transferor of the liability may ultimately be held responsible anyway. Any ambiguities in the contract may be construed against the originating party, so care must be taken in carefully outlining responsibilities. Insurance may be the best defense when all else fails.

Insurance

Insurance is purchased when all or part of the risk-producing process is retained. It provides a last-resort safety net when all else fails. The results of purchasing insurance are multifold:

- The insurer may assume all or part of the risk. The value of the insurer's assumption varies with the premium paid. Typically, it is less expensive for the insurer to cover the last dollar rather than the first dollar of the loss. In other words, it is less expensive to pay for a policy with high dollar limits on it and a high deductible than it is to pay for one with relatively low limits and little or no deductible.
- The insurance company may provide risk-management services designed to aid the insured in minimizing or controlling losses. The insurance company may employ loss-control specialists whose job it is to help clients identify and rectify potential loss-producing situations. These services may be included as part of the benefits package purchased with the premium.

- Due to the nature of insurance and insurance companies, as few as one loss may result in a policy cancellation. The insurance company may only be willing to cover the loss one time before refusing to renew. If the insurer continues coverage for more than one loss, the premium will reflect the loss experience.
- Insurance companies must not only cover the value of the loss, but also overhead and profits for those insurance companies with stockholders. Obviously, the stockholders, who actually own the company, expect a return on their investment from the stock of the insurance company, paid in the form of a dividend. A dividend is a payment of a portion of the profits to the company owners.

  Insurance companies owned by the policyholders return the profits or dividends to them. These companies are known as mutual companies. Although dividends may be higher when paid to a mutual company, standard wisdom holds that long-term premiums are actually lower, due to the fact that no profits are paid to outsiders.
- A major benefit of owning an insurance policy may be the legal representation provided by the insurer in the event of a major claim.The insurance company, as the entity paying the benefit, may find it advantageous to contest payment of benefits in court. If they do so, they pay for legal counsel and other related fees, thus transferring the cost of counsel from the insured to the insurer.

Self-Insurance

Many companies choose to maintain a certain level of risk themselves and not purchase insurance. They may even have a plan to cover the losses if they do occur. The primary result of not purchasing insurance or retaining the risk is that the company self-insures. Self-insurance is no insurance. The company assumes the cost of all losses and all legal fees associated with any litigation. This may be referred to as a calculated risk, but in many cases, it is simply risk.

Self-insurance plans may be limited or restricted by law. This is particularly true of plans designed to cover the costs of workers' injuries or deaths. The state department of labor and/or workers' compensation bureau should be contacted before implementing any self-insurance plan designed to compensate injured workers or survivors of fatalities.

An alternate plan is to purchase a very high-dollar deductible policy. In the event of a loss, the company will pay the first dollar amount and the insurance company picks up the loss after that. For example, a company may purchase a policy to insure it for losses up to $100 million or more, with a $1 million deductible. The deductible is high, but the insurance may be relatively inexpensive, due to the fact that losses rarely ever exceed $1 million. In the event of a catastrophic loss, even though the company will not like paying the first $1 million, the insurance policy may save the company from bankruptcy by paying any losses over $1 million, up to the $100 million of coverage.

Small insurance companies often do the same and hedge their own risks by purchasing insurance policies to cover huge losses that exceed a certain dollar amount. Although the risk is low, the potential severity is high, so they pay the premiums in order to ameliorate their risks.

Another way to help alleviate the pain of losses is to establish a sinking fund, whereby monies are set aside periodically to offset the cost of any losses due to certain events. For example, a large shipping company may decide against paying a $5 million dollar annual premium on one of its ships, but instead places that amount of money in the bank each year. In the event of a loss, that fund will be tapped to cover the loss. The risk, of course, is that enough funds will not be available at the time of the loss or that multiple losses could wipe out the fund in a short period of time. Purchasing an insurance policy in the early years, until the sinking fund is adequate to handle the losses, may offset this risk.

In addition, a high-dollar deductible insurance policy may be maintained.

The absolute worst approach to take with any risk or potential loss-producing situation is to ignore it and call it a "calculated risk."

Time Value of Money

Calculating the present value of future benefits is useful when considering alternative projects on a limited budget. Present-value calculations compare the cost of implementation against the dollar value of the benefit. For example, a safety manager is considering committing $10,000 to a project that will save approximately $17,000. However, the savings will not be realized for five years. Should the company commit? Can the safety manager convince management that this is a worthwhile investment? If financial considerations are a primary concern, it must be determined whether the benefit the company will receive later will be greater than the investment. This question is easily answered by using the following formula to determine present value (PV) of a dollar:

$$PV = 1/(1 + I)^n \quad (1)$$

In this formula, I equals the discount rate used and n equals the number of years that will elapse until funds are received. The discount rate is determined by considering alternative uses for the funds at similar risk. If management believes it can receive a return of 10 percent by investing in a venture of similar risk, the discount rate to be used is 10 percent.

Substitute these figures into the equation and solve for PV. The answer is for $1, and it must be multiplied by the number of dollars saved. In this case, solve for the present value by substituting as follows:

$$PV = 1/(1 + 0.10)^n \quad (2)$$

Alternatives to this formula include using a financial calculator or the present-value table (see Table 1). To use this table, determine the number of years until the return is received. For this example, it is 5 years. Find 5 in the "Period" column on the left, and go across the row to the figure listed under the designated discount rate. The factor for this problem is 0.621, which means that every dollar to be received 5 years from now, at a discount rate of 10 percent, is worth $0.621 today. Multiply $0.621 by $17,000 to determine the current value of the amount to be received in 5 years. The answer is $10,557.

At the 10 percent discount rate, this proposal will provide slightly better than a break-even return. The total dollar benefit is $557. If a 12 percent or higher discount rate were used, the proposal would no longer be cost-beneficial. If the applicable discount rate decreases to below 10 percent, the proposal becomes increasingly beneficial.

Table 1 is used to determine the value of $1 to be received at n periods in the future, assuming a given interest or discount rate.

TABLE 1

Present Value of $1

Present value interest factor of $1 per period at i% for n periods, PVIF(i,n).

Period	1%	2%	3%	4%	5%	6%	7%	8%	9%	10%	11%	12%	13%	14%	15%	16%	17%	18%	19%	20%
1	0.990	0.980	0.971	0.962	0.952	0.943	0.935	0.926	0.917	0.909	0.901	0.893	0.885	0.877	0.870	0.862	0.855	0.847	0.840	0.833
2	0.980	0.961	0.943	0.925	0.907	0.890	0.873	0.857	0.842	0.826	0.812	0.797	0.783	0.769	0.756	0.743	0.731	0.718	0.706	0.694
3	0.971	0.942	0.915	0.889	0.864	0.840	0.816	0.794	0.772	0.751	0.731	0.712	0.693	0.675	0.658	0.641	0.624	0.609	0.593	0.579
4	0.961	0.924	0.888	0.855	0.823	0.792	0.763	0.735	0.708	0.683	0.659	0.636	0.613	0.592	0.572	0.552	0.534	0.516	0.499	0.482
5	0.951	0.906	0.863	0.822	0.784	0.747	0.713	0.681	0.650	0.621	0.593	0.567	0.543	0.519	0.497	0.476	0.456	0.437	0.419	0.402
6	0.942	0.888	0.837	0.790	0.746	0.705	0.666	0.630	0.596	0.564	0.535	0.507	0.480	0.456	0.432	0.410	0.390	0.370	0.352	0.335
7	0.933	0.871	0.813	0.760	0.711	0.665	0.623	0.583	0.547	0.513	0.482	0.452	0.425	0.400	0.376	0.354	0.333	0.314	0.296	0.279
8	0.923	0.853	0.789	0.731	0.677	0.627	0.582	0.540	0.502	0.467	0.434	0.404	0.376	0.351	0.327	0.305	0.285	0.266	0.249	0.233
9	0.914	0.837	0.766	0.703	0.645	0.592	0.544	0.500	0.460	0.424	0.391	0.361	0.333	0.308	0.284	0.263	0.243	0.225	0.209	0.194
10	0.905	0.820	0.744	0.676	0.614	0.558	0.508	0.463	0.422	0.386	0.352	0.322	0.295	0.270	0.247	0.227	0.208	0.191	0.176	0.162
11	0.896	0.804	0.722	0.650	0.585	0.527	0.475	0.429	0.388	0.350	0.317	0.287	0.261	0.237	0.215	0.195	0.178	0.162	0.148	0.135
12	0.887	0.788	0.701	0.625	0.557	0.497	0.444	0.397	0.356	0.319	0.286	0.257	0.231	0.208	0.187	0.168	0.152	0.137	0.124	0.112
13	0.879	0.773	0.681	0.601	0.530	0.469	0.415	0.368	0.326	0.290	0.258	0.229	0.204	0.182	0.163	0.145	0.130	0.116	0.104	0.093
14	0.870	0.758	0.661	0.577	0.505	0.442	0.388	0.340	0.299	0.263	0.232	0.205	0.181	0.160	0.141	0.125	0.111	0.099	0.088	0.078
15	0.861	0.743	0.642	0.555	0.481	0.417	0.362	0.315	0.275	0.239	0.209	0.183	0.160	0.140	0.123	0.108	0.095	0.084	0.074	0.065
16	0.853	0.728	0.623	0.534	0.458	0.394	0.339	0.292	0.252	0.218	0.188	0.163	0.141	0.123	0.107	0.093	0.081	0.071	0.062	0.054
17	0.844	0.714	0.605	0.513	0.436	0.371	0.317	0.270	0.231	0.198	0.170	0.146	0.125	0.108	0.093	0.080	0.069	0.060	0.052	0.045
18	0.836	0.700	0.587	0.494	0.416	0.350	0.296	0.250	0.212	0.180	0.153	0.130	0.111	0.095	0.081	0.069	0.059	0.051	0.044	0.038
19	0.828	0.686	0.570	0.475	0.396	0.331	0.277	0.232	0.194	0.164	0.138	0.116	0.098	0.083	0.070	0.060	0.051	0.043	0.037	0.031
20	0.820	0.673	0.554	0.456	0.377	0.312	0.258	0.215	0.178	0.149	0.124	0.104	0.087	0.073	0.061	0.051	0.043	0.037	0.031	0.026
25	0.780	0.610	0.478	0.375	0.295	0.233	0.184	0.146	0.116	0.092	0.074	0.059	0.047	0.038	0.030	0.024	0.020	0.016	0.013	0.010
30	0.742	0.552	0.412	0.308	0.231	0.174	0.131	0.099	0.075	0.057	0.044	0.033	0.026	0.020	0.015	0.012	0.009	0.007	0.005	0.004
35	0.706	0.500	0.355	0.253	0.181	0.130	0.094	0.068	0.049	0.036	0.026	0.019	0.014	0.010	0.008	0.006	0.004	0.003	0.002	0.002
40	0.672	0.453	0.307	0.208	0.142	0.097	0.067	0.046	0.032	0.022	0.015	0.011	0.008	0.005	0.004	0.003	0.002	0.001	0.001	0.001
50	0.608	0.372	0.228	0.141	0.087	0.054	0.034	0.021	0.013	0.009	0.005	0.003	0.002	0.001	0.001	0.001	0.000	0.000	0.000	0.000

Calculating Project Savings

It is evident that potential dollar savings to be realized are attractive or unattractive based upon prevailing returns of other investments. However, the typical safety project provides a return over a period of years, as opposed to a one-time return. To calculate the savings gained from this project, the present value of an annuity formula is used:

$$\mathrm{PVA} = \sum_{n=1}^{n} \frac{1}{(1+I)^n} \qquad (3)$$

For example, if a project provides a return of $2000 per year for the next 7 years at the discount rate of 10 percent, present value is determined by substituting 7 for *n* and 0.10 for *I*.

The present value of an annuity table can also be used to determine project savings (see Table 2). To use this table, determine the number of years over which savings will be received—for this example, 7 years. Then, find the 7 in the "Period" column on the left. Go across the row to the figure listed under the designated discount rate. The factor for this problem is 4.868. If $1 is received each year over the next 7 years at a discount rate of 10 percent, the total amount received is worth $4.87 today.

Table 2 is used to determine the value of $1 to be received at the end of each of *n* periods in the future, assuming a given interest or discount rate.

Multiply $4.87 by the $2000 that will be saved each year to determine current value of the total savings over 7 years. The answer is $9736. In this case, based strictly on dollar savings, this project would not be cost-beneficial. However, if the prevailing return or discount rate was only 9 percent, the return would be worth $10,066, making this a sound project in which to invest.

As is evidenced by the numbers, the higher the dollar saving potentially realized or the lower the potential return with alternatives, the greater the attractiveness of investing in any given safety project.

When considering the total value of potential savings of any project, it is tempting to factor in related costs, such as the associated time spent by the personnel department interviewing temporary replacement help, or the time spent investigating an accident. Management often views these costs as part of overhead and may refer to them as "utilization of idle time." To maintain a convincing argument, it is essential to point out costs that arise only as a result of not implementing the new program or developing the proposed project.

Expected Value Technique

The expected value technique, combined with these other methods, increases the ability to make sound

TABLE 2

Present Value of an Annuity

Present value interest factor of an (ordinary) annuity of $1 per period at i% for n periods, PVIFA(i,n).

Period	1%	2%	3%	4%	5%	6%	7%	8%	9%	10%	11%	12%	13%	14%	15%	16%	17%	18%	19%	20%
1	0.990	0.980	0.971	0.962	0.952	0.943	0.935	0.926	0.917	0.909	0.901	0.893	0.885	0.877	0.870	0.862	0.855	0.847	0.840	0.833
2	1.970	1.942	1.913	1.886	1.859	1.833	1.808	1.783	1.759	1.736	1.713	1.690	1.668	1.647	1.626	1.605	1.585	1.566	1.547	1.528
3	2.941	2.884	2.829	2.775	2.723	2.673	2.624	2.577	2.531	2.487	2.444	2.402	2.361	2.322	2.283	2.246	2.210	2.174	2.140	2.106
4	3.902	3.808	3.717	3.630	3.546	3.465	3.387	3.312	3.240	3.170	3.102	3.037	2.974	2.914	2.855	2.798	2.743	2.690	2.639	2.589
5	4.853	4.713	4.580	4.452	4.329	4.212	4.100	3.993	3.890	3.791	3.696	3.605	3.517	3.433	3.352	3.274	3.199	3.127	3.058	2.991
6	5.795	5.601	5.417	5.242	5.076	4.917	4.767	4.623	4.486	4.355	4.231	4.111	3.998	3.889	3.784	3.685	3.589	3.498	3.410	3.326
7	6.728	6.472	6.230	6.002	5.786	5.582	5.389	5.206	5.033	4.868	4.712	4.564	4.423	4.288	4.160	4.039	3.922	3.812	3.706	3.605
8	7.652	7.325	7.020	6.733	6.463	6.210	5.971	5.747	5.535	5.335	5.146	4.968	4.799	4.639	4.487	4.344	4.207	4.078	3.954	3.837
9	8.566	8.162	7.786	7.435	7.108	6.802	6.515	6.247	5.995	5.759	5.537	5.328	5.132	4.946	4.772	4.607	4.451	4.303	4.163	4.031
10	9.471	8.983	8.530	8.111	7.722	7.360	7.024	6.710	6.418	6.145	5.889	5.650	5.426	5.216	5.019	4.833	4.659	4.494	4.339	4.192
11	10.368	9.787	9.253	8.760	8.306	7.887	7.499	7.139	6.805	6.495	6.207	5.938	5.687	5.453	5.234	5.029	4.836	4.656	4.486	4.327
12	11.255	10.575	9.954	9.385	8.863	8.384	7.943	7.536	7.161	6.814	6.492	6.194	5.918	5.660	5.421	5.197	4.988	4.793	4.611	4.439
13	12.134	11.348	10.635	9.986	9.394	8.853	8.358	7.904	7.487	7.103	6.750	6.424	6.122	5.842	5.583	5.342	5.118	4.910	4.715	4.533
14	13.004	12.106	11.296	10.563	9.899	9.295	8.745	8.244	7.786	7.367	6.982	6.628	6.302	6.002	5.724	5.468	5.229	5.008	4.802	4.611
15	13.865	12.849	11.938	11.118	10.380	9.712	9.108	8.559	8.061	7.606	7.191	6.811	6.462	6.142	5.847	5.575	5.324	5.092	4.876	4.675
16	14.718	13.578	12.561	11.652	10.838	10.106	9.447	8.851	8.313	7.824	7.379	6.974	6.604	6.265	5.954	5.668	5.405	5.162	4.938	4.730
17	15.562	14.292	13.166	12.166	11.274	10.477	9.763	9.122	8.544	8.022	7.549	7.120	6.729	6.373	6.047	5.749	5.475	5.222	4.990	4.775
18	16.398	14.992	13.754	12.659	11.690	10.828	10.059	9.372	8.756	8.201	7.702	7.250	6.840	6.467	6.128	5.818	5.534	5.273	5.033	4.812
19	17.226	15.678	14.324	13.134	12.085	11.158	10.336	9.604	8.950	8.365	7.839	7.366	6.938	6.550	6.198	5.877	5.584	5.316	5.070	4.843
20	18.046	16.351	14.877	13.590	12.462	11.470	10.594	9.818	9.129	8.514	7.963	7.469	7.025	6.623	6.259	5.929	5.628	5.353	5.101	4.870
25	22.023	19.523	17.413	15.622	14.094	12.783	11.654	10.675	9.823	9.077	8.422	7.843	7.330	6.873	6.464	6.097	5.766	5.467	5.195	4.948
30	25.808	22.396	19.600	17.292	15.372	13.765	12.409	11.258	10.274	9.427	8.694	8.055	7.496	7.003	6.566	6.177	5.829	5.517	5.235	4.979
35	29.409	24.999	21.487	18.665	16.374	14.498	12.948	11.655	10.567	9.644	8.855	8.176	7.586	7.070	6.617	6.215	5.858	5.539	5.251	4.992
40	32.835	27.355	23.115	19.793	17.159	15.046	13.332	11.925	10.757	9.779	8.951	8.244	7.634	7.105	6.642	6.233	5.871	5.548	5.258	4.997
50	39.196	31.424	25.730	21.482	18.256	15.762	13.801	12.233	10.962	9.915	9.042	8.304	7.675	7.133	6.661	6.246	5.880	5.554	5.262	4.999

decisions about where to spend budget dollars. It also is an additional tool for convincing management of the fiscal soundness of a proposal. When attempting to prioritize the placement of resources, this technique combines educated assessment of the situation with simple arithmetic to help determine greatest need.

For example, management is considering undertaking three major safety programs; each will be a considerable investment. Which ones should be pursued, and in which order? The following step-by-step approach may be useful.

Step One: Determine the probability of loss for each problem area if the course of action is not pursued. Probabilities can be determined by examining past company records or records of similar organizations in similar situations. Many times, an insurance carrier can also provide useful data.

One example would be considering a program to counteract the effects of a flood. The probability of a flood occurring can be determined by reviewing experience from previous years and applying it to current years. If a company is located in an area that has experienced a damage-producing flood twice in the last 50 years (and no effective countermeasures have been taken), it appears the probability of such a flood occurring in any given year would be about 2 in 50, or 4 percent.

The same technique can be applied to fire, theft, or any other loss-producing event. Percentages can range from virtually zero for a remote probability (for example, damage from a volcanic eruption in the midwestern United States) to 100 percent for fire and theft. While the probability is only an estimate, it should be as accurate as practicable.

CASE STUDY

Acme Widget Company

Acme Widget Co. has limited funds to spend on a major project during the coming year. All company departments, including the safety department, are vying for these funds. Management's decision will be based on its perception of where the highest rate of return can be earned without excessive risk.

The safety manager is considering submitting a proposal asking for funds to alleviate problems in one of three target areas.

Process A on the production line has experienced four injuries in the last 5 years. The average cost of each injury accident was calculated at $15,000. Probability of loss is 4/5 = 0.80.

Process B has experienced 22 injuries in the last 5 years. The average cost of each injury accident was calculated at $2500. Since the company is experiencing multiple losses per year, the likely number of losses in a given year is 22/5 = 4.40.

Process C has only been online for 3 years. Two injuries have occurred in that time. The average cost of each injury accident was calculated at $14,000. Probability of loss is 2/3 = 0.67.

From a cost standpoint, which problem is the highest priority? Calculate expected value for each as follows:

$$EV_A = \$15,000 \times 0.80 = \$12,000 \quad (6)$$
$$EV_B = \$2500 \times 4.40 = \$11,000$$
$$EV_C = \$14,000 \times 0.67 = \$9380$$

Process A has the highest expected value and would, therefore, receive highest priority. Expected savings from correcting these problems would be $12,000 annually. Expected savings from correcting Process B problems would be $11,000 and for Process C would be $9380.

Process A will be completely overhauled at the end of 6 years. How much would correcting the problems in this process be worth today? The company would save $12,000 annually for 6 years, a total of $72,000. The present value of that savings is based on the rate of return management expects on alternative investments of low risk–in this case, 12 percent. By using the present value of annuity table, the value of $1 to be received at the end of each year for 6 years at 12 percent is $4.111; therefore, multiply 4.111 by $12,000 to learn that total savings is equivalent to $49,332. If correcting Process A cost Acme Widget Co. $20,000, total savings in today's dollars will be $29,332.

The assumption in using this table is that all returns are gained at the end of each year. In application, however, it will not likely work this way. Therefore, a slight math error makes actual returns higher than they appear.

Savings realized on a permanent basis would typically be capped at no more than 10 years. Otherwise, it would be infinitely profitable to invest in any venture with a positive rate of return. With business uncertainties and the potential for new technology to eliminate any process that might be corrected, it may be impractical to project dollar savings beyond a 10-year period. The decision as to whether to limit the number of years to consider in present value is a judgment based on the individual business.

As any safety manager knows, safety budgets are always competing with other investment-returning projects within the organization. The safety manager must be able to use the same tools as other departments to formulate and present convincing arguments to management for increases in budgets and project funding.

Step Two: Estimate expected dollar loss from all such events during an entire year. This can be accomplished by estimating from past records or by enlisting the help of the company's insurance carrier. Contacts through professional associations may also be helpful.

Step Three: Multiply the expected annual loss in a category by the probability of a loss occurring. The resulting figure is the expected value, which can be compared to expected values determined for other categories.

For example, after reviewing company records, it is determined that fire losses have occurred four times in the last ten years. Employment records indicate that the workforce has been stable during that time, and that no major changes have occurred in the facility that would have significantly impacted the loss record. Thus, these figures should be representative of future figures. If it appears this is not a representative figure, adjust it accordingly. (The safety manager must use his/her best judgment in this area if no objective evidence is available.)

Obviously, basing the estimate on data from a longer time period enhances the probability that the figures are representative. In this case, the probability of a loss occurring in one year is the number of times a loss occurred over the 10-year period divided by the number of years in the period (Annual Probability of Loss = Number of Losses ÷ Number of Years) or

$$\text{Probability} = 4/10 = 40\% \qquad (4)$$

Step Four: Calculate the total dollar cost of each loss by reviewing records. Losses from ten years ago will obviously not reflect current dollar costs. These amounts can be adjusted, however, by using an index (such as a consumer price index) to update them to current dollar figures.

Assume that the average fire loss is estimated to cost a company approximately $19,000. Multiply this average loss by the probability of a loss occurring in a given year to obtain the expected value:

$$\text{Expected Value} = \$19{,}000 \times 40\% = \$7{,}600 \qquad (5)$$

This expected value represents the amount a company can expect to lose from fire losses in any one year. It can be compared to insurance coverage costs, other expected losses, or the cost of investing in a fire prevention program. When comparing such figures for three different projects, the highest priority is that with the highest expected value. Always consider tax implications when making comparisons of this nature.

For those unwilling to manually process the data concerning return on investment (ROI) and the future financial impact of implementation of safety systems, a number of packages designed to aid in the financial investment process may prove useful in performing calculations. These can be found on other Web sites, which are quickly apparent through an Internet search.

International Standards and Budgeting

As companies move toward international markets, questions arise concerning the role of international standards on safety and safety decisions. The economic and social constraints placed on companies vary from country to country, as do the relationships existing between companies and the local governing bodies. For example, the financial constraints on a decision may be completely different in Sweden than in Mexico.

An international safety and health standard was discussed at the International Organization for Standardization (ISO) meeting in Geneva, Switzerland in 1996, but it was generally agreed that it was not feasible. A majority of the participants failed to support any standard, as did the American National Standards Institute (ANSI). Much of the lack of support was due to cultural and labor law differences. The benefits and economic impacts also affected the decision (Swartz 2000, 290).

Conclusion

Effective handling of budgetary matters on the part of the safety manager requires a knowledge and use of fundamental accounting techniques. The safety practitioner should be able to identify costs associated with hazard exposure, as well as those associated with amelioration of the exposures. Safety program decisions are ultimately made by line management, so presentation of potential costs as well as those of remediation are critical to the decision-making process. In order to be effective, the safety manager must also be aware of alternate techniques or methods to solve the risk problem. These may range from risk avoidance to insurance. Long-term cost savings may also result in long-term benefits. The value of savings over time can be instrumental in persuading management of the soundness of a safety proposal. Consideration must also be given to the costs and benefits of operating in overseas environments for a company doing business on a multinational basis.

References

American Society for the Advancement of Science (AAAS). 2006. *NASA R&D Gains, But Steep Cuts Loom for Research* (retrieved November 1, 2006). www.aaas.org/spp/rd/nasa07p.pdf

Davis, Ian. 2005. *What is the Business of Business?* www.mckinseyquarterly.com/article_page.aspx?ar=1638&L2=21&L3=3

Department of Defense (DoD). 2000. MIL-STD-882D, *Standard Practice for System Safety*. www.safetycenter.navy.mil/instructions/osh/milstd882d.pdf

Drucker, Peter. 1986. *The Practice of Management*. New York: Harper Collins.

Ferry, Theodore S. Interview by Mark A. Friend, August 1985.

Friend, Mark A. "Safety Management Philosophies of Seven Major Contributors to Safety Management." PhD diss., West Virginia University, 1986.

Ginsberg, Paul B. 2004. "Controlling Health Care Costs." *New England Journal of Medicine* (October 14) 351:1591–1593.

Horngren, Charles T., Gary L. Sundem, and William O. Stratton. 2002. *Introduction to Management Accounting*. Upper Saddle River, NJ: Prentice Hall.

Investopedia. 2005. *Zero-Based Budgeting – ZBB* (retrieved December 21, 2005). www.investopedia.com/terms/z/zbb.asp

Kiger, Jack E., Stephen E. Loeb, and Gordon S. May. 1987. *Accounting Principles*. 2d ed. New York: Random House.

Money-zine Magazine. "Return on Investment Calculator" (retrieved May 25, 2011). www.money-zine.com/Calculators/Investment-Calculators/Return-on-Investment-Calculator

Morris, Julius. Interview by Mark A. Friend, August 1985.

National Aeronautics and Space Administration (NASA). 2006. *Volume 3 Space Shuttle Mission Chronology 2005–2006* (retrieved December 19, 2005). www.pao.ksc.nasa.gov/kscpao/nasafact/pdf/SSChronologyVolume3.pdf

Occupational Safety and Health Administration (OSHA). 2007. *Responsibility, Authority and Accountability Checklist*. www.osha.gov/SLTC/etools/safetyhealth/mod4_tools_checklist.html

Pope, William C. Interview by Mark A. Friend, August 1985.

______. 1983. *Principles of Organization and Management of Risk Control 2-A-3-4*. Alexandria, VA: Safety Management Systems, Inc.

Relex Software Corporation. 2004. *Fault Tree/Event Tree* (retrieved October 25, 2004). www.relexsoftware.com/products/ftaeta.asp

Roland, Harold E., and Brian Moriarty. 1990. *System Safety Engineering and Management*. New York: John Wiley & Sons.

Safety Management Services. 2002. MIL-STD-882B *Hazard Risk Assessment Matrix* (retrieved October 22, 2004). www.smsink.com/services_pha_matrix.html

Swartz, George. 2000. *Safety Culture and Effective Safety Management*. Chicago, IL: National Safety Council Press.

Washington State Department of Labor & Industries. *Self-Insurance* (retrieved May 23, 2011). www.lni/wa.gov/claimsins/insurance/selfinsure

Williams, C. Arthur, George L. Head, Ronald C. Horn, and G. William Glendenning. 1981. *Principles of Risk Management and Insurance*. 2d ed. vol 1. Malvern, PA: American Institute for Property and Liability Insurance.

BENCHMARKING AND PERFORMANCE CRITERIA

8

Brooks Carder and Patrick Ragan

LEARNING OBJECTIVES

- Understand the concepts of reliability and validity and how they are critical to the evaluation of any measurement process.
- Be able to apply these concepts to performance measurement.
- Conduct better performance measurements based on an understanding of research that evaluates the reliability and validity of incident-based measures, audits, and surveys.
- Understand the limitations of performance measurement and the hazards of incentives for performance that can lead to manipulating the results.
- Be able to identify instances of manipulation of results.
- Develop the ability to design, conduct, and evaluate a productive benchmarking study.

PERFORMANCE MEASUREMENT is a fundamental step in risk assessment. In a stable system, performance will remain the same until the underlying process changes, so a measure of current performance constitutes an assessment of future risk (Deming 1982, 1993). Performance measurement and benchmarking are both methods that can assist in hazard control by revealing opportunities for process improvement.

THE RELATIONSHIP BETWEEN PERFORMANCE MEASUREMENT AND BENCHMARKING

Performance measurement and benchmarking are obviously intertwined. Merriam Webster's online dictionary (www.m-w.com) defines *benchmarking* as "the study of a competitor's product or business practices in order to improve the performance of one's own company." However, the term derives from the noun *benchmark*. The definition of a benchmark includes "a point of reference from which measurements may be made" and "something that serves as a standard by which others may be measured or judged." Performance measurement is usually not very meaningful unless there is a benchmark for comparison. If you are asked how fast someone is going, and you get an answer of 100 miles per hour, you would think that was extremely fast on a bicycle, fast in a car, not very fast in a racing car, and extremely slow in a jet plane. To the extent that performance measurement is evaluative, there must be an explicit or implied benchmark. The benchmark is needed even if it is only the benchmark of change for the measure from its previous position(s).

On the other hand, to the extent that benchmarking represents an attempt to improve performance, it is necessary to find benchmarking partners that have excellent processes and excellent performance (Camp 1995). The objective is to identify and implement the processes that lead to superior performance in other companies. Thus, benchmarking cannot be done effectively in the absence of good performance measurement. Keeping these interrelationships in mind, the chapter first addresses performance measurement and then benchmarking.

Performance Appraisal

Defining Performance Appraisal

On the face of it, performance appraisal in safety should be very simple. One can simply count injuries, deaths, and property loss. In reality, however, the appraisal is very difficult. The following problems arise:

- Some industries and activities are inherently more hazardous than others.
- Over a short period of time or with a relatively small population, the inherent variability of these counts is high, making judgment based on the numbers very inaccurate.
- In an environment where a major disaster could occur, such as with an airline, a chemical plant, or a refinery, assessing the likelihood of a major event should be a top priority. These are so rare that, thankfully, at most sites, there is nothing to count, even though the danger may be high.

Dictionary.com defines *safety* as freedom from danger, risk, or injury. Conditions are easily conceived in which there is no history of injury but great risk of future injury. Of course this appears to be the case with shuttle flights up to the time of the Challenger and Columbia disasters. Although there was no history of injury, the engineers working on the flights estimated the probability of the loss of a vehicle in the range of 1 in 100 (Feynman 1999). In fact, hindsight suggests that this is a very good estimate, with 2 vehicles lost in 130 flights as of February 8, 2010.

Ideally, a measure of performance would tell us the level of freedom from danger, risk, and injury. The measure would not be a picture in the rearview mirror, but rather an accurate forecast of future expectations, so long as the system is not changed. Many readers may believe that incident counts are indeed an accurate forecast of overall safety. But the available evidence indicates that this is not the case. Part of the problem lies in the lack of reliability of incident counts because the standards for OSHA-recordable events can vary from company to company, and even from day to day in the same company (Carder and Ragan 2004). An article in *Professional Safety* describes how recordable counts can be altered through "medical management of injuries" (Rosier 1997). While legitimate and widespread, this practice introduces a great deal of variability and places a significant limitation on the reliability of accident counts (Carder and Ragan 2004). Adding to the problem is that accident counts have proven to be poor predictors of catastrophic events (Manuele 2003, Petersen 2000, Wolf and Berniker 1999). Rosenthal and his colleagues (Elliott et al, 2008) have addressed the problem of predicting major accidents for a number of years, and have done the most exhaustive study of the relationship between incident rates and the occurrence of what they call "low probability-high consequence" (LP-HC) events. For incident rates they used OSHA recordables, and for LC-HC events they used events reportable to the EPA under the Risk Management Program of the Clean Air Act. In fact, the facilities with the lowest rates of LP-HC events tended to have the highest recordable rates. However, this was because facilities such as chemical plants and refineries tend to have low incident rates but high risk, while facilities like poultry processors have high incident rates, but low risk of LP-HC events. When they controlled for this risk, they found a trend toward a positive relationship between incident rates and HP-HC events, but it was "far from statistical significance."

While the reader will not be left without some notions of a solution to the problem of performance measurement, the problem of assessing the ability of the safety management system to prevent major events remains unsolved However, it does appear clear that achieving a low indicent rate should not lead to confidence that the system is effective at preventing LP-HC events. Elliott et. al. point out that in the Texas City refinery explosion, which killed 15 workers, BP had achieved a low incident rate. The Baker Panel Report (Baker et al 2007) went so far as to suggest that reliance on injury rates might even mask or distract an organization from measures and actions that would identify and avoid these LP-HC incidents. They note that BP had emphasized personal safety but not process safety and "mistakenly interpreted improving personal injury rates as an indication of acceptable process safety performance at its US refineries."

Objectives of Performance Appraisal

An important objective of performance appraisal is to provide information to guide improvement efforts. Another is to track the effectiveness of improvements that are implemented. This is the plan-do-study-act cycle described by Deming (1982). Closely related to this is the need to evaluate the performance of managers and to provide guidance for establishing reward systems.

Hazards of Performance Appraisal

The first question to be asked is whether an accurate, meaningful assessment can really be made. This chapter suggests that one can indeed make a useful assessment of the safety performance of an organization or subunit. The second question is, whose performance is being appraised? A safety manager in a plant is part of a system. He or she usually has very limited control over the larger system. The system includes such practices as hiring policies, education and training, manpower decisions, budgets, capital expenditures, and much more. All of the things mentioned have an impact on safety. Although one can measure the performance of the system, it is much more difficult to measure the performance of individuals working in that system. Deming (1982) argues continuously and eloquently that attempting to evaluate the performance of individuals working in a complex system is a waste of time. Nevertheless, it is unlikely that business will move away from this anytime soon. However, the reader should be aware of the limitations of such evaluations when they are used.

Consider the following actual case study: Many years ago a marketing company had a young man in sales who was very bright and energetic. However, his performance in sales was continuously disappointing to his superiors. He was labeled an underachiever and, in private conversations, much worse. He constantly asked his managers to be allowed to sell in a different way and was constantly told that the company had a system of proven success and that he should sell exactly as he was told. The sales rep wanted to uncover marketing problems that confronted the customer and return to his office to prepare a solution. The solution would be presented to the customer on a subsequent visit. He was told that he needed to present a solution and close the order on the initial visit, like all of his successful colleagues. One day the management system changed, and his new manager told him to go out and sell in the way he wanted. Within a year he was the company's top salesperson and a leader in the industry. Up to this time, the company had considered a \$10,000 order to be very large. After the system change, this rep wrote orders as large as \$500,000, at higher margins. Changing the system dramatically changed his performance. At best, one can measure only the interaction between an individual and the system in which he or she works (Deming 1982).

One of the worst risks of conducting a performance appraisal is that when rewards are based on that appraisal, it can provide an incentive to game the system. Levitt and Dubner's recent book (2005), *Freakonomics*, describes, in considerable detail, a number of cases of how reward systems lead to cheating. This is not an accusation that managers commit fraud in order to secure bonuses. Although this has happened, as evidenced by the accounting fraud convictions in the cases of Enron and World Com, it is hopefully rare. However, there is an inherent conflict of interest in basing the pay of a person who is measuring something on the result of that measurement process. An example of this kind of manipulation is seen in Figure 1 (Carder and Ragan 2004).

Figure 1 shows a control chart of recordable accidents for Group 2, one of several manufacturing units in a large plant. Each point on the *x*-axis represents

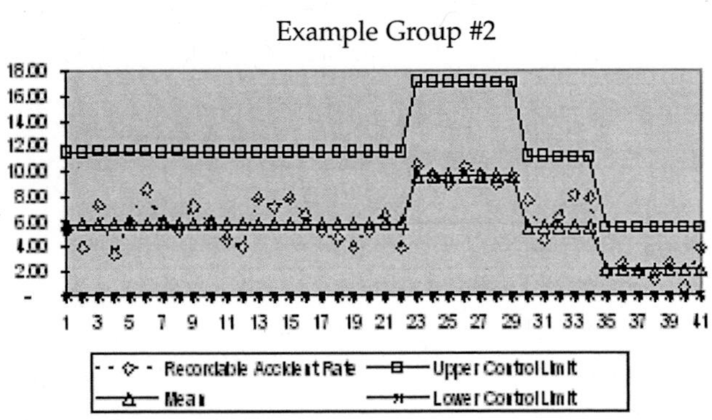

FIGURE 1. Control chart of accidents by month, showing process shifts

one month. The *y*-axis is the rate of recordable accidents. There is an upward shift around months 23 to 28. This shift illustrates a process shift in the wrong direction with seven consecutive points above the previous mean. For rules of interpreting control charts, the reader can refer to Nelson (1984). Although the output of a stable process will vary, certain patterns in the variation indicate that the process has changed, indicating a special cause. Special causes need to be investigated. Some special causes indicate that there is something wrong with the measurement process. On closer examination, the next series of points is very close to the new mean. According to the rules of control charts (Nelson 1984), a special cause requires the finding of fifteen points within one standard deviation of the mean. In this case, this condition is not met because there is another process shift at month 30. However, the points between months 23 and 29 are much closer to the mean than one standard deviation, suggesting the presence of a special cause. Upon investigation, it was found that because of the upward shift in the incident rate, managers in Group 2 put extreme pressure on the group to hold down the accident rates. In their zeal to turn the trend, they did not realize they had gotten exactly what they asked for. People stopped reporting accidents. Accidents happened at the rate expected for the process; they simply did not report those they could hide or classify as not being recordable. As the number of accidents in the month increased, pressure to not report also increased. Part of the reason the rates did not drop farther was that some accidents were just too serious to hide. This actual case is a clear illustration of manipulating the data to achieve an outcome and shows the value of using effective measurement tools to identify when this happens. Here the safety managers knew that the existence of nonrandom patterns indicated that something was wrong with the measurement process. Such patterns are frequently an indication that someone is manipulating the data (Deming 1982). The safety managers used that understanding to focus attention on the causes of the statistical anomaly and acted to correct it. This type of anomalous condition is sometimes referred to as "chopping the peaks." This is an example of why it is important for any manager, especially one responsible for the safety of others, to have a good basic understanding of statistics. While there are unintentional examples of gaming the numbers, there are also cases of knowingly *adjusting* input to get desired results. The old saying that figures don't lie but liars do figure applies when safety results are a basis for performance reviews.

In order to guard against the risks involved in assessing performance, one must have an understanding of the principles of measurement. Application of these principles is critical to a meaningful assessment of performance. Incidentally, the application of these principles to Enron, World Com, and Health South would probably have revealed the problems early in the game. For example, Banstetter (2002) points out that several analysts who looked carefully at a variety of measures of Enron's performance were able to foresee serious problems. While revenues were growing, net margins were shrinking. Potential risks were obscured by keeping them off the balance sheet. Also, senior management was dumping a lot of stock.

Principles of Measurement

The quality of a measure is determined by its reliability and validity. No measure is perfect, and all measures have limitations on their reliability and validity (Deming 1982). Deming frequently illustrates this point by referring to measurements of the speed of light, which is an important constant in physics. He charted the variation of this measurement over time. Because the speed of light is assumed to be constant, the chart shows the variation in the measurement. Another illustration he used is variation in the census, depending on the method used. He noted that there is "no true value of anything. There is a measurement method and a result." If the method changes, it is likely the result will change.

Reliability of a Measurement

Essentially, *reliability* refers to the repeatability of a measure. For example, there is a particular golf course in central California at which the yardage markers appear to be unreliable. The markers that signify 150 yards to the green appear to be out of place on the eighth and ninth holes, reflecting a distance of closer to 160 yards. This may be explained by the assertion of one of the course employees that the persons who put in the markers used a 150-yard rope to make the measurements. The rope was nylon and got wet as they proceeded. The wet rope stretched, yielding longer distances on the later holes.

One could use many methods to measure the course, ranging from pacing off the distance to using a steel cable, laser, or global positioning system. Measuring a distance repeatedly with each method, would likely yield a spread of numbers around an average in each case. This is called *spread variation*. Variation is quantified by computing the standard deviation. The standard deviation is a statistical estimate that quantifies the variability of a measure. The greater the standard deviation, the greater the variability of the measure. The variability of measurements from the laser, presuming it was working properly, would be much smaller than the others. The wet nylon rope would very likely have the most variation. One would conclude that the laser was more reliable. There is no such thing as a perfectly reliable measure. All measures will show variation.

In some cases reliability is assessed by looking at the variation between observers. For example, audits are scored based on the judgment of an auditor or audit team. To judge the reliability, ask whether a different audit team, unaware of the initial team's evaluation, would give the same or a similar score. In practice, have two auditors conduct audits of a number of sites. Each auditor would be unaware of the scores given by the other. Then compute a correlation coefficient between the scores given by the two auditors. A correlation coefficient assesses the degree to which one measure predicts another. In this case one is assessing whether the score assigned by one team predicts the score of the other. A high value, meaning that the scores of one team are good predictors of the scores of the other, would indicate good reliability. A very low or even negative correlation would mean that the process has no reliability at all, in this particular test. It is still possible that one of the auditors is very accurate. However, there are two problems with this: (1) one can't know which auditor was correct, and (2) even if that could be determined, the process would be dependent on one person's judgment. In this case the measure is neither reliable nor useful. In order to develop a reliable and useful measure, one might attempt to clarify and better define the criteria and methods, retrain the auditors, and test again for reliability on a different set of plants.

No matter how reliable a measure might be, it will still have variation. If two auditors consistently report exactly the same score for the audit of a plant, management should question whether they are really operating independently. As mentioned previously, anomalies in variation often signal a problem with the measurement process. If a measure has no variation at all, one is not looking closely enough, the gauge is broken, or the numbers are being manipulated by the observer.

Reliability is not a property of the instruments, but of the entire measurement process. This includes the tools, the instruments, the procedures, and the people. Subjective judgment can be very reliable in some cases, and measurement with the finest instruments can be unreliable if the process that uses these instruments is flawed.

To repeat, any measure will vary. If the measure does not vary, or if the pattern of variation is not normal, an investigation is warranted. Assuming there are no anomalies in the variation, then the less the variation, the higher the reliability. For any particular purpose, there is a level of reliability that is acceptable for the task. When carpeting a room, one can use a tape measure, but not one that is elastic. When measuring length in order to construct a complex optical system, the laser might be required.

In the safety area of a business, it must be realized that all measures have reliability limitations and that all measures are subject to manipulation. It is important to understand the limitations of each measure and to take these limitations into account when making decisions based on the measurements.

It is important to realize also that a measure with high reliability may still be worthless if it does not convey anything useful about what one is trying to measure. Just because a measure is reliable does not mean it will help management take effective action. This leads to the concept of validity. Audits are good tools to confirm compliance to specific actions, such as regulations or essential high reliability of procedural steps. They work well in the *verify* aspect of "trust but verify" management. They are extremely difficult to use as a culture or system measurement tool.

Validity of a Measurement

Validity relates to whether one is measuring what he or she wants to measure. When measuring the width of a room, the question of validity usually does not arise. When measuring a complex process such as aptitude to perform well in college, or the ability of the safety management system in a plant to prevent future loss, validity becomes a serious question. Scientists (Cronbach and Meehl 1955) generally define three categories of validity: content-related validity, criterion-related validity, and construct-related validity.

CONTENT-RELATED VALIDITY

Often called *face validity*, content-related validity asks whether the content of the measurement process is, on its face, related to the purpose of the measurement. A good example is found in safety audits. If a question asks whether employees use personal protective equipment on the factory floor, that question has face validity. If one asks whether employees go out for beer together after work, that lacks face validity because nothing in the content appears to have anything to do with safety. However, the question might have criterion-related validity and construct-related validity. It could turn out that when employees have close personal relationships the plant is safer, and that going out for a beer (or bowling, or to church, etc.) after work is evidence of such relationships. Of course, this is not an assertion that this is actually the case.

CRITERION-RELATED VALIDITY

This is sometimes called *predictive validity*. It deals with whether one measure correlates with other measures that could be called criteria. For example, the SAT test is an attempt to measure the likelihood that a student will succeed in college. Obviously the criterion here is college performance. Yale University has used the SAT for many years. Although they admit it is not a very good predictor, they also say that it is the best they have. This is because different high schools have very different criteria for grading, so that an A in one might be equivalent to a C in another. Over the years, the Pearson correlation between SAT scores and Yale grades has run in the range of 0.2–0.3. This is statistically significant, meaning that the SAT does indeed have criterion-related validity. However, this level of correlation means that, at best, what is measured by the SAT is accounting for no more than 9 percent of the variation in college grades. (Squaring the correlation coefficient of 0.3 gives us the percent of variation accounted for, 0.09.) The other 91 percent is presumably accounted for by other things, such as motivation, the quality of the student's secondary education, the difficulty of the courses chosen at Yale, luck, or any number of other variables each student must face and overcome to "make the grade" at the university.

When dealing with large populations, it may make good economic sense to use measures such as the SAT, which have relatively low criterion-related validity. However, individuals who are negatively affected by such measures will always have a pretty good argument that the measurement was unfair to them.

It is also important to realize that the criterion is arbitrary. After all, the success of a Yale career should not be measured by grades. Yale and most other universities are interested in producing good, productive citizens and leaders. Does the SAT predict that?

In the safety field, injuries and monetary losses are certainly useful criteria against which to test other measurements. However, they are not the only possible criteria, and they may not be the best criteria. Ultimately, one would like to know the ability of the safety management system to prevent future accidents and losses. Although a burned finger may be of some concern in a chemical plant, it is trivial in comparison with the release of a toxic chemical that could injure or kill many people. Because catastrophes are fortunately infrequent, they are inconvenient to use as criteria in a validation study. An ideal safety measure would enable the prevention of catastrophic events. While minor incidents (such as burned fingers) are associated with cost and suffering, they are neither equivalent nor significantly related to catastrophic events (Manuele 2003, Peterson 2000, Elliott et. al. 2008).

Because criteria are usually somewhat arbitrary, and because there is often no single, ultimate criterion, it is best to use several criteria when attempting to establish criterion-based validity. This not only will make it more likely that validity will be established, but also will likely increase understanding of the measure being tested and the results attained. This leads to the concept of construct-related validity.

CONSTRUCT-RELATED VALIDITY

Construct-related validity goes to the understanding of what is being measured. In the measurement of safety performance, there has been little work on construct validity. Carder and Ragan (2004) used a reliable and valid safety survey to measure performance. They found that the critical constructs measured by the survey were (1) management's demonstration of commitment to safety, (2) education and knowledge of the workforce, (3) quality of the safety supervisory process, and (4) employee involvement and commitment. Coyle, Sleeman, and Adams (1995), working with a different survey, identified a similar set of constructs.

Safety professionals have been inclined to take the measures they are using for granted as a result of their content-based validity. If their intuitive feeling is that the measure is valid, they use it. They look to the content of their measurements to determine exactly what is being measured. There is a serious limitation in this practice. The most obvious case is the way incidents are counted. A minor cut or burn is recorded and investigated. On the other hand, many more important events, such as a chemical reaction going temporarily out of control, are often neither recorded nor investigated. The assumption, based on faith rather than evidence, is that the burn and the control of the chemical process are the same thing. Although they may be related, given they are both outputs of the overall site culture and management system, the evidence indicates they are not the same thing (Wolf and Berniker 1999, Manuele 2003, Petersen 2000, Elliott et. al. 2008).

A better understanding of what is being measured, leads to better judgment of what management actions are suggested by the measurement (Carder and Ragan 2004).

Managers prefer measures they believe to be highly reliable, in spite of the lack of any evidence regarding the validity of those measures. Many managers believe that surveys and interviews are of doubtful reliability and that the measurement of incident rates is quite reliable. In fact the data show that surveys and interviews can be very reliable, whereas the recording of incidents is frequently unreliable. In a recent book (Carder and Ragan 2004), we describe numerous examples from our own personal experience of how incident rates can be unreliable. More important is the limited ability of incident rates as a measure to enable the prevention of future catastrophic loss (Wolf and Berniker 1999, Manuele 2003, Petersen 2000, Elliott et. al. 2008). This is an important limitation of the construct-based validity of incident-rate measures.

A measure with moderate reliability and high construct-related validity is much preferred over a measure with high reliability and little or no evidence of construct-related validity. The latter measure may be very accurate, but it does not provide anything useful to guide management actions. If it is used to guide action, the effort will likely be wasted. Because it has little construct validity, it tells very little about the process one is attempting to improve. It would be like using a map of Ohio to drive in Pennsylvania. A frequently uttered idea in business is that "What gets measured is what gets done." Of course this poses the risk that if the wrong thing is measured, the wrong thing will be done. One might be achieving improvement in a measure but in achieving that improvement, if the measure is not properly selected, the company may be taken in a wrong direction. If the measure is to reduce reported injuries, that may be exactly what is achieved. Less reporting of injuries, not fewer injuries.

Usability of a Measurement

Usability refers to the ease and cost of the following:

- collecting the data
- analyzing the data
- communicating measurement results
- using results to devise action plans

COLLECTING DATA

In 1994, a safety survey (Carder and Ragan 2003, 2004), which is discussed in detail later on, was developed. The survey was conducted in more than 50 plants of a major chemical manufacturer. In the previous year, the company had established a manufacturing strategy team (MST) to evaluate the quality of the management system in the same plants. When the plants' survey scores were compared with the MST scores, the correlation coefficient was –0.58. The correlation is negative because on the MST, lower scores indicated better performance, whereas with the safety survey, higher scores indicated better performance. This correlation indicates that the two processes were measuring many of the same things. However, the MST process required two to three highly trained and experienced staff members to conduct several days of interviews at each plant. The survey process required the employees to fill out a simple yes/no survey that took 20–30 minutes, usually during an already scheduled safety meeting. The scoring of the surveys was automated, and the analysis of the resulting data was relatively simple. Moreover, the survey had high reliability. The reliability of the MST process had not been evaluated. Thus, as a measure of performance, the survey was less expensive and simpler to implement than the MST process. It had much higher usability. Actually, the strong correlation between the survey and MST represented a validation of the MST process because the survey had been validated against other criteria as well.

An important lesson taken from this experience was that a good management system is likely to yield good safety performance. A tool that is used to measure the quality of the safety management (accident prevention) system also gives a good evaluation of the quality of the overall management system.[1] The survey was a simple, quick, and inexpensive tool that provided insight into how well a group was being managed. The alternative approaches to measuring the overall quality of the management system had a cost that was orders of magnitude higher, required much more effort, and produced less statistically supportable results. The survey tool is in the public domain, as are descriptions of how it can be used for measurement and for process improvement (Carder and Ragan 2003, 2004).

ANALYZING DATA

Managers often want to reduce performance evaluations to numerical data. This simplifies comparison between employees, plants, or other management units. It is relatively easy to accomplish with incident counts and surveys. It is more difficult with observational data and interviews. For example, developing a method to score an audit is a complex process because of the need to decide the proper weighting of various components. This is highlighted in the very extensive study of the audit process by Kuusisto (2000). To generate a numerical score, the investigation is broken into categories and subcategories. Each category must then be given a weight. Kuusisto shows that there is considerable variation in category weighting among different, widely used audit processes. The study also highlights the difficulty in establishing a reliable scoring process. This does not mean that interviews and observation should not be employed—because they can sometimes discover conditions that would not be revealed in a survey. However, it does mean that observation and interviews are at a disadvantage with respect to ease of data analysis.

COMMUNICATING MEASUREMENT RESULTS

Because performance evaluation is useful only to the extent that it can generate positive action or limit negative action, communicating measurement results to those who are impacted by it or who need to respond to it is critical. In the example being followed, processes such as the MST evaluation sometimes have a usability advantage. If a manager has a high degree of confidence in a staff member, then reports by the staff member are likely to generate action. Of course there is a problem with this, in that the usability of this kind of report is dependent on the relationship between the manager and the staff member. It may not always be possible to find the right staff member for a particular evaluation. With survey data, experience indicates that when the reliability and validity of the survey are carefully explained to the manager, action is usually generated (Carder and Ragan 2004). This should be done carefully and thoroughly by someone who has a good understanding of the survey process.

USING MEASUREMENT RESULTS

Measurement results should be used to devise effective action plans. This is the last consideration, but a critical one. For example, counting accidents tells one little about what to do. Often managers see an accident rate that is too high and tell their subordinates to try harder to be safe. This is not useful. Deming (1993) describes exactly this kind of event, and we have seen it ourselves many times. Deming recommends "looking into the process" that produced the accidents, rather than exhorting people to do better. A way of looking into the process is to find the true root causes of accidents using an effective investigation process. Then one can work to eliminate those causes, thereby reducing the potential for many future accidents.

If there are two methods with relatively equal reliability and validity, it makes sense to employ the one with the highest usability. However, although usability is important, remember that if a measure has very poor reliability or validity, the strong usability is worthless. It is like a man who is found one evening looking for his car keys on the street. A passerby questions him, finally asking if this is where the keys were lost. The man tells him he actually lost them in the middle of the block. The passerby asks why the man is looking for them on the corner. The searcher replies that he is searching at the corner because the light is better.

Effective Use of Available Measures for Performance Appraisal

The sections that follow examine some widely used types of measurement for reliability, validity, and usability, and ultimately for their value as measures of safety performance.

Incident-Based Measures

An almost universal measure of safety performance is based on incidents: the recording of accidents and the investigation of their causes. Since 1970 OSHA has required companies with eleven or more employees to maintain a record of accidents and injuries. Many other countries use incident-based measures with different incident definitions and different normalizing factors. In the United States the number is based on the number of incidents per 200,000 exposure hours. In Europe and many other countries the number of exposure hours used is 1,000,000.

The mere fact that accident counts are the fundamental method by which the government measures safety suggests that they can be measured very reliably. Although there are frequent and very articulate complaints that incident-based measures are not very helpful in process improvement (Petersen 1998), there is rarely a question about their reliability or validity. But, in fact, an examination of reliability and validity suggests that there are serious limitations to performance measures based on the counting of incidents. Many of these limitations are discussed in the following sections. For a more extensive treatment of this issue, see Carder and Ragan (2004).

Reliability of Incident Rates

There are two sources of limitation on the reliability of incident rates: variation in interpretation of the criteria for recording an incident and inherent variation in the statistic itself.

VARIATION IN RECORDING CRITERIA

Recording incidents is relatively complex. Studies of the reliability of classifying events as recordable or not recordable are lacking. However, there are many examples of stretching of the criteria:

1. Use of over-the-counter ibuprofen instead of prescription dosages. If the prescription is not used, then recording the incident is not required. Many doctors will cooperate with this approach. This cooperation is rationalized by the assumption that this is what the employee or employer wants, that it provides the same relief for the injured employee, and that it is less expensive than prescription medication.
2. First aid given for increasingly serious injuries that could have or, in some cases, should have warranted medical treatment. An article in *Professional Safety* (Rosier 1997) actually recommends setting up first-aid stations to "prevent the accident from falling into the OSHA recordable category."
3. Liberal interpretations of preexisting conditions are made to avoid recording an incident or to count a case as one case instead of two. Sometimes the first injury or illness case will have been in a different year, so even if the second is counted, the first incident is not included in the measures for the time being considered. It can be recorded with no negative effect because most companies do not factor in such historical changes.
4. Classification of more events as not being work-related. The pendulum swings from taking the employee's word for a case being work-related to requiring the employee to prove the case is work-related beyond any doubt.
5. Employees being offered full pay to work at home when their injuries prohibit their working at their normal workplace or traveling to and from their workplace. The requirement is that they go along with the story that the injury did not result in lost work.
6. Employee job definitions being used to define work relationship. In one case, an employee fell from a scaffold, breaking both wrists and suffering multiple other injuries. The injuries resulted in a hospital stay, but the case was initially not included on the injury log because it was argued that the employee was not doing his regular job. It seems this was an infrequent task that was not in his regular job description.
7. Manipulation of medical diagnosis. For example, an employee was cut and received fifteen stitches. After consulting with a physician, the employer argued that the stitches were "cosmetic," not "therapeutic," and therefore the case was not counted.

These are only a few of the many approaches used to avoid counting. It makes one feel there may be some truth in an old joke about an accident: An employee fell from a rooftop, and his scream drew the attention of his supervisor. It was lucky for the company that he screamed because it saved their twelve-year no-lost-day case record. It seems the supervisor was able to fire him for a safety violation before he hit the ground and was injured.

Although these might be extreme examples, they illustrate the difficulty in comparing the incident rates of two companies and being certain that the one with the lower rate truly has better safety performance. Petersen (1998) notes that accident rates do not discriminate between good and poor performers. Consider the plausible scenario where one company has a low accident rate because it underreports, and another company has a relatively high accident rate because it sees the reporting of accidents as an opportunity for investigation and improvement. The company with the higher reported record may actually have the better safety management system.

The problem noted here is not so much that employers are scofflaws and do everything they can to avoid the record-keeping rules out of contempt or malice. Frequently managers do not even know when "marginal" reporting is taking place. In almost every case of which we are aware, the companies involved went to great efforts to prevent unlawful practices and routinely disciplined those who knowingly committed these acts, including using termination in some cases.

A serious problem is that the events being measured are so complex that systems to define and count them must be elaborate and cumbersome. In addition, often strong incentives attached to the numbers can lead to manipulation of the count (Flanders and Lawrence 1999). The complexity provides more and more opportunity for errors or manipulation, intentional and unintended. Although the regulations may stand as an attempt to create a useful operational definition of a recordable accident, in practice, this has not been entirely successful. Petersen (1998) argues that accident data are not "useful for anything," although he concedes that some safety professionals disagree, and many executives object to the removal of these statistics. However, he argues, "it would be best for practitioners to wean their companies from dependency on such worthless figures."

VARIATION IN THE STATISTIC

Even if one determines that the recording process in a particular population could be reliable, the fact that the variability of incident rates is quite high for small groups or short periods of observation still remains. The appropriate statistic for computing the standard deviation of an accident rate is the *U* statistic, based on the Poisson distribution (Carder 1994): *U* = square root of (*R/N*), where *R* is the recordable rate, and *N* is the number of 200,000 work-hour exposure units. The OSHA-defined 200,000 hours is the expected annual work of 100 workers.

When computing control limits of a process that has an average OSHA recordable rate of 3, the range of the control limits increases greatly as the population decreases. For a plant with 25 workers, the standard deviation is *U* = square root of (3/0.4), or 2.74. The upper control limit is three standard deviations from the mean, or 3 + (3 × 2.74), or 11.22. This is based on one year of data. If the observation period shrinks to a month, then the units of exposure go from 0.4 to 0.033, and the upper control limit rises to 31.60. This looks high, but how many incidents can happen in a month for the measure to remain within control limits? The answer is that one accident in a month will yield a rate of 30.3 for that month, just inside the control limits. At this example site, two recordables in the month would exceed control limits. The point here is that comparing the recordable rates of small sites, or the rates of larger sites computed over short periods, is not very useful. If there are two plants with 40 employees, and if over a one-year period one has a rate of 8 and the other of 0, there is not a sound statistical basis for concluding that they are different. This difference is within the normal random variation of measure being used. The incident rate of 8 required only three recordable events.

Figure 2 shows how the control limits change as the plant population changes. The upper control limit (UCL) and lower control limit (LCL) are plotted on the *x*-axis, the group size on the *y*-axis. The mean recordable rate is 3. The control limits are for one year of data. Monthly control limits would be much wider.

The meaning of this is important. Safety managers would generally conclude that a recordable incident rate of 1 was good performance, an incident rate of 10 was not very good, and a rate of 30 was terrible. With a plant of 25 persons, an underlying rate of 3, and one year of observation, one might observe a rate of 1, or one might observe a rate of 10. In fact, one might see a monthly rate as high as 30! Any of these rates would be within the control limits and therefore would not signify that the process has changed. Remember that these observations are based on the

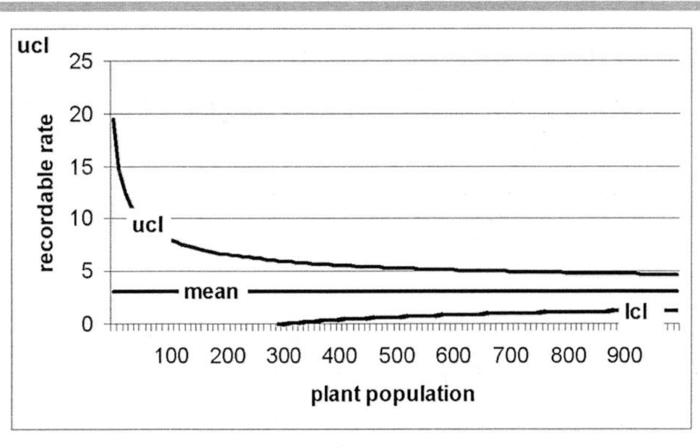

FIGURE 2. Control limits for accident rates as a function of plant size for a mean accident rate of 3

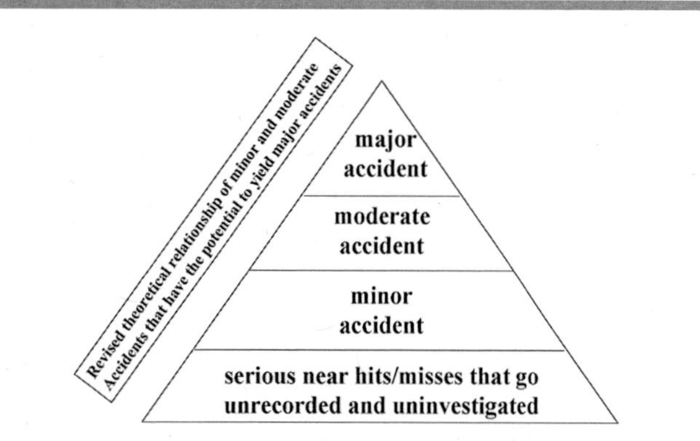

FIGURE 3. Revised version of Heinrich's accident triangle

same underlying safety process. Being aware of the statistical constraints, one will need several years of data to draw a definitive conclusion about the safety performance of this plant.

Validity of Incident Rates

Incidents are often used as a criterion for validation of other measures (see Carder and Ragan 2004). However, it is important to recognize that all measures have limitations on validity (Deming 1982). Moreover, a measure such as incident rates, which has low or, at best, moderate reliability, must, of necessity, have limited validity. It is important to discuss these limitations.

CONTENT-RELATED VALIDITY

Accident rates have obvious face validity as a measure of the safety process. After all, most recordable accidents are instances of something we are attempting to prevent. At the same time, a cut finger, on its face, is very different from the release of a large cloud of toxic gas. To the extent that one is concerned more about the release than about the cut finger, the cut finger may have little content-related validity. If the release does not result in an injury, in many current measurement schemes, the cut finger will receive higher importance and demand more resources be directed toward its prevention. It might be argued, as Heinrich essentially did, that the release and the cut finger are both instances of exactly the same thing and that "the severity of an incident is largely fortuitous." Therefore, cut fingers (incidents) are a measure that is valid in all respects. However, the available evidence indicates that this is not correct. Severe losses are associated with high energy, nonrepetitive work, and construction (which involves both high energy and nonrepetitive work) (Petersen 1998). In an environment in which resources are limited, the incidents that are related to potentially serious outcomes should be investigated first, whether they happen to be recordable or not.

Realize that the relationship between minor incidents and serious incidents is an empirical question, and no amount of argument or opinion can settle it in the absence of data. Figure 3 depicts an alternative look at Heinrich's (1959) assertion that minor incidents, moderate accidents, and major accidents are causally related (Carder and Ragan 2004). However, showing that the ratio of minor injuries to major injuries is 29:1, or something similar, does not in any way demonstrate that the injuries derive from the same process or that a reduction in minor injuries will lead to a reduction in major injuries. And even if a reduction of minor and major injuries is achieved, there may be no change in the probability of a major event.

The success of treating all events the same, and assuming that by recording minor incidents one proportionally estimates the likelihood of more serious incidents, is not supported by available evidence. This frequently draws attention and resources away from finding and correcting the system hazards that could produce very serious outcomes, such as the chemical release that may be overlooked because the company was too busy investigating steam tracer burns.

The Israeli Air Force provides a striking example of the potential importance of near-misses (Carder and Ragan 2004). In the early 1980s they were confronted with an unsustainable rate of major accidents. In 1980, they had over 30 class-5 accidents—accidents involving the loss of an aircraft, a pilot, or over $1 million in damage. Their approach was to report and thoroughly investigate all near-miss incidents. The result was a gradual decline in the rate of class-5 events, reaching near zero by the year 2001.

Of course, near-misses in aircraft operation are probably easier to define and identify than equivalent events in a chemical plant or a refinery, but it can certainly be done in any industry. Investigation of these events is likely to be far more fruitful than investigation of minor injuries.

CRITERION-RELATED VALIDITY

Accident rates themselves are frequently used as a criterion. However, safety is not necessarily the same as an absence of accidents. If safety is defined as freedom from danger, risk, and injury, then conditions are easily conceived in which there is no history of injury but great risk of future injury. Space shuttle flights, described previously, are an example of this. Although there was no history of injury prior to the Challenger flight, the engineers' estimates of the probability of loss of a vehicle indicated that shuttle flights were quite risky.

The work of Rosenthal and his colleagues (Elliott et. al. 2008), which failed to find a significant relationship between incident rates and major events, has already been described. Perrow (1984), in his theory of normal accidents, argued that what he called normal accidents—disruptions of the flow of complex processes—were related to potential catastrophic events. Most of these disruptions in flow would not be classified as recordable accidents. In fact, plants that present the most significant hazard to workers and the public are typically high-capital, nonlabor-intensive plants that are likely to have very low rates of recordable accidents (Wolf and Berniker 1999).

In a test of Perrow's theory, Wolf and Berniker (1999) studied data on hazardous releases at 36 refineries from 1992 to 1997. Their assumption was that reportable releases are instances of normal accidents. They also provided data on the total case rate and catastrophic incidents. There were three fatal accidents in the period. They argued from the data that the incident rate was a poor measure for prediction of catastrophic loss. Better predictors were the complexity of the system and the number of toxic releases. More complex, tightly coupled (continuous processing) systems have the highest danger, and the data showed that toxic releases were much better indicators of system problems than were recordable accidents. Although there was a small positive correlation between case rate and releases ($r = 0.23$, $n = 22$), it was far from statistical significance ($p = 0.30$, 2-tailed). The relationship between case rate and catastrophic accidents is not statistically significant, but the relationship between releases and catastrophic accidents is very significant ($p < 0.01$).

Incident measures certainly have some criterion-based validity. Because they represent injury and cost, they can be categorized as a criterion. They are not, however, the only important criterion, nor are they a substitute for measures of catastrophic loss or for measures that more accurately forecast the probability of such loss.

The suggestion from Wolf and Berniker's data is that releases may be a promising form of incident to use as the basis of safety performance measurement. At the time of this writing, there is insufficient data to suggest anything beyond the exploration of this possibility, however.

CONSTRUCT-BASED VALIDITY

To consider construct-based validity, one must address the question of what it is that accident counts are measuring. This leads to the consideration of accident causation. The logic is that accidents are providing information about a set of underlying processes, which are labeled as causes.

Heinrich (1959) suggested that in 85 to 93 percent of cases, the primary cause is a human cause, so that incident rates may provide us with a measure of unsafe behavior. In fact, it is likely that 100 percent of all accidents involving anything manmade or involving people in any way reflect a human element.[2] In some way a human decision, action, or inaction was a contributing cause of the accident. Drawing on the logic of the cause-and-effect diagram that is widely used in quality improvement (Scherkenbach 1990), The Center for Chemical Process Safety of the American Institute of Chemical Engineers has documented a system in which causes are divided into three major components: human, material, and organizational (AIChE 2002). The assumption of the process is that causes will exist in all three areas.

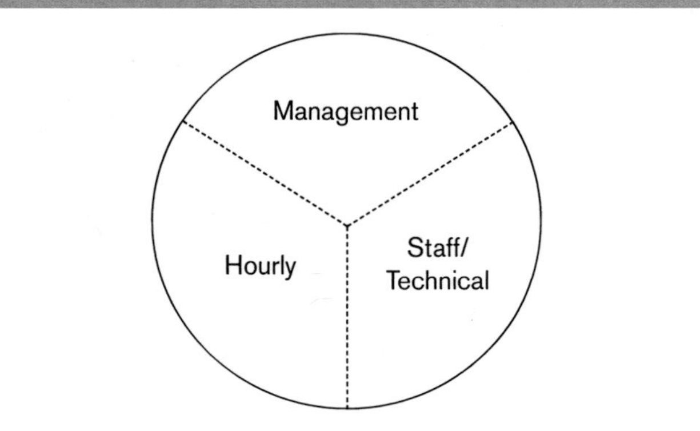

FIGURE 4. Division of sources of human causes

The human element consists of those actions or failures to act based on knowledge, beliefs, attitudes, physical abilities or capabilities, motivation, and so on. Usually the actions of operators are listed as a principal human cause. It is necessary to consider the entire community of humans who had influence on the event, including some who are no longer employees and some who might never have been employees.

The roles of people can be categorized as broken down in Figure 4. The internal lines are dotted because the distinctions are not necessarily sharp. Individuals can have both managerial and technical responsibility, for example. The staff/technical category includes the designers of the system, who may have departed from the company a long time ago or who may have never been employees. Other similar circles can be added for peripheral or indirect human-cause groups, such as agencies, customers, suppliers, family, and so on.

The material element consists of physical aspects such as oil on the floor, a failed relief valve, a plugged line, and so on. It includes the physical work environment, working conditions, equipment, supplies, and materials. Based on the work of Wolf and Berniker, the complexity of the physical environment could also be included, with increased complexity creating higher risk. Of course, the physical environment is mostly the result of human activity. But like culture, it has a life that is somewhat independent of the persons currently involved in the system and is therefore worthy of identification as a causative factor. Because 100 percent of all accidents involve a human element, an organizational element, and a material element, systems theory tells us that one element cannot be changed without affecting the others. Nor can one element cause an accident independently of the rest of the system.

An ***organizational element*** relates to the structure, practices, procedures, policies, and so on, in place in the organization, as well as its history. This would include hiring policies, compensation policies, policies for promotion, reporting structures, training practices, work standards, regulations, and enforcement practices. These include both the stated policies and practices and the actual policies and practices, referring to what is actually done as opposed to what is written or said.

The human, material, and organizational factors come together to form the ***cultural system of the organization***. The cultural system represents the attitudes, beliefs, and expectations of the people in the organization. These are the product of human experience over time with the organizational factors and the material. All events are interpreted through the lens of this culture. In spite of changes in emphasis, rules, procedures, incentives, and personnel, the culture is resistant to change (Deal and Kennedy 1982, Senge et al. 1994). For example, in organizations that have a history of short-lived initiatives that are soon replaced by new initiatives, employees come to expect the "flavor of the month" (an initiative that is in line with the current trend but likely to change soon). Thus, any new initiative is greeted with resistance (McConnell 1997). Change is stalled, and the expectation of short-lived initiatives becomes a self-fulfilling prophecy. Changing culture requires changing the experience of the people over time. An organization in which senior management has paid little real attention to safety cannot expect to see an immediate change when some attention is given. However, if the attention and involvement of senior management is maintained over a period of time, on the order of years not months, the culture will change.

This system of accident causation is diagrammed in Figure 5, with the three areas combining to create an organizational culture. This is presented as an example of how this problem can be approached. Many

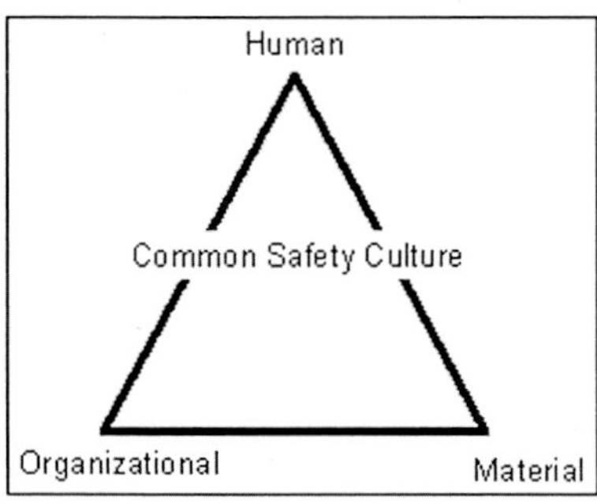

FIGURE 5. Three components create a common safety culture

ways of doing this can be productive, as long as the coverage of potential causal factors is comprehensive.

Attempting to summarize the issue of construct validity for incident-based measures, means measuring the performance of a very complex accident-producing process that includes people, the physical environment, and the organizational system. Some incidents may reveal problems with these processes that could produce catastrophic outcomes. Other incidents may offer no insight at all into such problems. To the extent that recordable accidents are what is to be prevented, this limited validity is not an issue. However, if the primary objective is to prevent major or catastrophic loss, then management needs to be very conscious of finding systemic causes and directing its actions first at the most serious hazards.

Of course, a frequent assumption of performance measurement is that what is really being measured is the performance of the manager who controls a particular system of human, material, and organizational elements. With senior management, this may be appropriate. With the manager of a small plant or a department head, this is a stretch. These lower-level managers often have far less than complete control over much of the material and organizational systems in which they work. The incident rates that are produced by that system are certainly related to the performance of the manager, but they are also related to important elements beyond the manager's control, including the existence of an established culture that the manager has not had time to change.

Proper Use of Accident Statistics

Incident rates should be plotted on a control chart. The purpose of this is to see if the process is changing over time. This enables the user to detect system problems that have developed if the rate goes up or to evaluate the effects of improvement efforts that should drive the rate down.

The first step is to *establish a process mean*, which would be the mean recordable rate over the past twelve months or so. The next step is to *calculate control limits*. The upper control limit is equal to the mean plus three standard deviation units as calculated by the *U* statistic.[3] The lower control limit is the mean minus three standard deviation units. Of course it cannot go below zero. The mean and control limits are laid out on a chart, and each month the recordable rate is plotted. The following events indicate the process has changed, either improving or getting worse (Nelson 1984):

- a single point above or below the control limits
- two out of three consecutive points in the upper third of the chart (more than two times *U* from the mean) or two of three consecutive points in the lower third
- seven consecutive points above the mean
- seven consecutive points below the mean
- six points in either ascending or descending order

Should any of these criteria be met, it is appropriate to try to find out what happened. If there is a run of points above or below the mean or several excursions outside of control limits, it is appropriate to compute a new mean and new control limits, going back to the time that the run started or that the first out-of-control point was observed.

As long as the process stays within limits, it is not useful to assume that the performance of the system has changed or to question what went wrong or what went right in a particular month. One is simply observing random variation. Trying to track down the cause would be like trying to find out why a roulette wheel came up on 17 on a particular spin or hit red four times in a row. On the other hand, if the wheel hit red eight times in a row, investigation might be worthwhile. That is the logic of the control chart. Look for the cause of a variation only when the process varies in a way that is extremely unlikely to have been a result of chance.

In fact, the control-chart interpretation rules are designed to identify nonrandom conditions in the data. No set of rules can cover all such conditions. If there is a clear and repeating pattern in the data, a special cause is likely present. For example, if points consistently alternate, one above the mean and one below the mean, there is likely a special cause. Special causes are indicated where the data are not random (Duncan 1986). A good example of a nonrandom pattern was presented by plotting a control chart of accidents for a particular pipeline company. A series of peaks, near but not beyond control limits, appeared to repeat on a 12-month cycle. Investigation revealed that these peaks occurred in summer. Each summer the company hired students to do landscaping and housekeeping chores. This group had a high rate of incidents. This special cause was dealt with by instituting safety training as part of the orientation of these students, and the peaks went away.

It is critical that normal fluctuations of the measure, within the control limits, not be treated as signs that the process has changed. Acting on these random fluctuations as though they represent process changes is called *tampering* (Deming 1982). Tampering not only wastes resources, but usually makes the performance of the system worse. An example of tampering would be to have a special safety meeting to figure out why so many accidents occurred in March when the number did not exceed control limits. There is nothing special about March. The focus should be on the causes of accidents, not on what happened in March.

Audits and Inspections

Audits and inspections are probably as widely used and accepted in safety as incident-based measures. Many companies use audit scores as a measure of performance.

The online *Merriam-Webster Dictionary* (2007) lists the following definitions for audit:

1 a : a formal examination of an organization's or individual's accounts or financial situation **b:** the final report of an audit

2 : a methodical examination and review.

Obviously, the second definition would apply to a safety audit. The word *audit* implies a standard. The purpose of the audit is to find out if the standard is being met. This could be a standard for the number and location of fire extinguishers, whether operators have met certain training requirements, whether the relief valves on pressure vessels have been tested in the time period required, or virtually anything else that management deems essential to safety. Audits can involve any or all of the following: physical inspections, interviews, and review of documents and records.

The basis of an audit is the assumption that the designer of the audit understands the process and has created an instrument to ensure that the process performs properly. Audits, then, derive their content from the theory of accidents held by the author of the audit. Depending on the author's point of view, the audit might emphasize unsafe conditions, unsafe acts, deficiencies in the safety management system, or any number of other personally held accident-causation philosophies.

Standardized Auditing Methods

There are a number of widely used and standardized audit systems. Kuusisto (2000) reviews some widely used systems, including a process developed by Diekemper and Spartz (D&S), the Complete Health and Safety Evaluation (CHASE I&II), the safety map, the OSHA VPP protocol, and the International Safety Rating System (ISRS), which appears to be the most widely used system.

All of the systems have a list of questions or areas of investigation, along with a method for scoring each question. Typically the audit involves interviews with site employees to obtain answers to the questions. The audit protocol lists various specific areas of investigation and describes the criteria for scoring the company's performance in that area. Table 1 shows a very brief section of a Diekemper and Spartz protocol as used by Kuusisto.

TABLE 1

Portion of Diekemper and Spartz Audit Protocol

Activity	Level 1 (Poor)	Level 2 (Fair)	Level 3 (Good)	Level 4 (Excellent)
1. Statement of policy responsibilities assigned	No statement of safety policy. Responsibility and accountability not assigned.	A general understanding of safety, responsibilities, accountability, but not in written form.	Safety policy and responsibilities written and distributed to supervisors.	In addition to the previous items, safety policy is reviewed annually. Responsibility and accountability is emphasized in supervisory performance evaluations.
2. Direct management involvement	No measurable activity.	Follow up on accident problems.	Active direction on safety measures. Management reviews all injury and property damage reports. and supervises the corrective measures.	Safety matters are treated the same way as other operational parameters (e.g., quality or production design). Management is personally involved in safety activities.

(*Source:* Kuusisto 2000)

It is apparent from this brief snapshot that this is not a simple process. For example, with regard to Activity 1, consider the problem of judging whether there is "a general understanding of safety." There is no operational definition here. An operational definition would very specifically outline how to make the judgment (Deming 1982). For example, the only way to really know if the understanding was *general* would be to interview a large number of employees. The operational definition might include "at least 63 percent of employees can describe the company's safety policy." Of course, that does not end the problem. What is the standard for deciding that their description is adequate? Lacking such definitions, there will be variation between auditors and diminished or nonexistent reliability.

A second issue is the fact that both questions have potentially equal weight in the final scoring. Are they equally important? That is an empirical question. To answer it one would want to see data relating the item score to some independent measure of the safety management system, such as injury rate, costs, and so on. We are not aware of any such published studies.

In fact, there is wide variation in the points of emphasis of the various standardized auditing systems. Kuusisto divides the areas of inquiry into four broad categories: (1) policy, organization, and administration; (2) hazard control and risk analysis; (3) motivation, leadership, and training; and (4) monitoring, statistics, and reporting. Which components are emphasized in the final score depends on the system. Kuusisto describes the differing emphases of three systems in Table 2: D&S, CHASE-II, and ISRS.

These differences are obviously quite substantial. Unfortunately, there is no published research which affords the most reliable and valid measurement of the safety management system.

Reliability of Audits

There is very little published work on the reliability of audit systems. Kuusisto (2000) conducted an extensive study on the reliability of auditing methods. His dissertation reviews the literature on this topic and reports an original study of the interobserver reliability of the D&S method and of an *improved* audit method labeled Method for Industrial Safety and Health Activity Assessment (MISHA). In an initial test, Kuusisto audited six companies in the United States using the D&S method. He compared the audit scores that he recorded with the scores of internal audits conducted by a company

TABLE 2

Factor Emphasis of Three Audit Systems

Category	D&S	Chase II	ISRS
1. Policy, organization, and administration	20%	35%	33%
2. Hazard control and risk analysis	40%	48%	19%
3. Motivation, leadership, and training	20%	6%	19%
4. Monitoring, statistics, and reporting	20%	11%	29%
TOTAL	100%	100%	100%

(*Source:* Kuusisto 2000)

employee who also used the D&S method. Statistical testing indicated that the reliability was "poor to moderate." In only one company did reliability reach the moderate level. Two companies reached the *fair* level, two reached the slight level, and one was *poor*.

In a second test of the D&S method, Kuusisto examined three Finnish companies and compared the scores he recorded with scores independently recorded by his students. Here the reliability ranged from fair to almost perfect. The company employees in the first test were generally more strict in their interpretation than Kuusisto. In explaining the difference, he points out that the company auditors, because they worked in the company, had much more knowledge about the company than he did, whereas the students were working from the same information he was.

In the study of the MISHA method, Kuusisto compared his scores on a Finnish company with the scores recorded by the company's personnel manager, safety director, safety manager, and safety representative. He found *fair* agreement between his scores and the scores recorded by the safety manager and safety director and only *slight* agreement between his scores and those of the other two observers.

A reasonable conclusion from Kuusisto's studies is that audits can be made relatively reliable if they are conducted by individuals with similar training who are working from the same information. The highest reliability was achieved by comparing Kuusisto with his students, who were working from the same information. An intermediate level of reliability was obtained when comparing Kuusisto's scores with those of other safety professionals who were employees of the company. The safety professionals had specialized safety training and experience but different information because they knew much more about the company. If audits are conducted by persons with different training and different information about the company, then reliability is very low. It must be pointed out that this was not a determination of whether the finding of the audit was an accurate representation of the performance of the safety management system. That is a question of validity. The test of reliability means that the results of the audit are reproducible. The auditors with more experience, training, and personal knowledge (company employees) gave scores that differed more from Kuusisto's scores than did the scores produced by his students. Whose scores provided the most accurate or valid representation of the system's performance is left to question. More recently, Huang and Brubaker (2006) used an audit based on OSHA's Performance Evaluation Profile administered by subject-matter experts from an insurance company. They tested reliability using both inter-rater reliability and internal consistency. The inter-rater reliability coefficient was 0.98—very high. However, the raters did not score the audits independently. Two auditors would do the examinations independently, but then jointly discuss the results with the site management before issuing a score. They also examined another method for testing reliability: internal consistency. Typically this is done by splitting the scores of individual components into random halves, and then looking at the correlation. They found a correlation of 0.7, indicating a *reasonable* level of reliability, though they were concerned that on two components, behavior and health management leadership and occupational health protection, the correlations were 0.51 and 0.47 respectively.

Overall, the limited published literature suggests that under the best conditions audits can be a reliable measure.

Content-Based Validity

Because safety audits are typically designed by safety professionals, they would be assumed to have content-based validity. Certainly the questions are those that are deemed by the designers to be the most important indicators of safety performance. The fact that, at least in some circumstances, reliable scores can be generated should satisfy us that the method has content-based validity. The presence of reliability indicates that several auditors are using similar definitions of the content, which provides a validation of that content.

Criterion-Based Validity

There are very few studies on criterion-based validity of audits. Bailey and Petersen (1989) and Polk (1987) describe an attempt to relate safety program characteristics with accident statistics and monetary losses

CASE STUDY

Safety Surveys

Some of the issues involving safety surveys can be illustrated by the following case study of a large chemical company. This company had grown in the previous several years through a set of acquisitions. It had over 6000 employees in the United States, distributed across more than 50 plants. Only two plants had more than 500 employees. Most had in the range of 25 to 50 employees.

This small plant size presented a problem for safety performance measurement. In 1993 the company was well along with the implementation of a total quality management (TQM) program. Based on the recent training in variation and the use of control charts, the safety managers had begun to use U-charts when looking at the incident-rate measures. The wide limits of variation encountered with small plant sizes convinced them that incident rates would not be particularly useful as a measure of performance in the company, at least for small sites and short time periods.

The safety director convened a high-level committee of safety professionals and plant managers to address the issue. Essentially, this was a process-improvement team focused on the problem of companywide safety measurement. The committee brought in consultants and industry experts for a series of seminars.

The most prominent survey at the time was the Minnesota Safety Perception Survey. This survey had been developed in the 1980s by a team that included safety professionals from the Association of American Railroads and scientists from the Army's Aberdeen Proving Ground (Bailey and Petersen 1989, Bailey 1997).

Bailey's team had designed and validated the Minnesota survey, which had subsequently been administered to over 100,000 employees in a number of companies. Bailey's database included survey results from six chemical companies, providing a good opportunity for benchmarking. Consequently, the company chose that survey. Chuck Bailey made a presentation to the team to explain how the survey had been constructed and how it could be used as a tool for improvement.

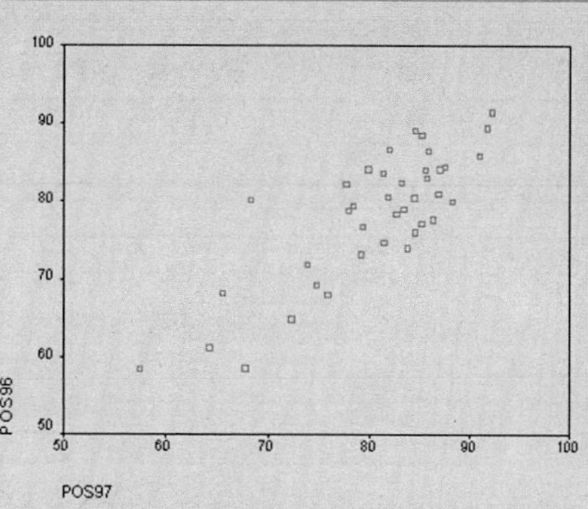

FIGURE 6. Scatterplot of scores for plants tested in two years
(*Source:* Carder and Ragan 2003)

To test the criterion-based validity of the survey, the group designed a pilot study. The basis of the study was the assumption that, if a question was valid, then a site with an effective safety program should have a higher proportion of positive answers on that question than would a site that had a weak safety program.

The survey that was tested consisted of the 74 questions from the Minnesota survey, along with 14 additional questions written by the team. The additional questions were written to cover some issues not covered in the original survey, but that were important to a chemical company, including process safety and emergency response. In addition, the team added some questions covering incident reporting and the use of drugs and alcohol. The plan was to conduct a pilot study and then roll out the survey to the entire company if the pilot study demonstrated validity.

Reliability

The pilot studies tested only the validity of the survey, under the assumption that if it was valid, it would have to have at least moderate reliability. Subsequently, reliability was quantified in two ways (Carder and Ragan 2003). One method utilized the split-half technique, in which a person's total response (percent of favorable answers) to one-half of the survey's items (randomly selected) are correlated with his or her total response to the other half. If a particular respondent has 67 percent favorable answers on one-half of the questions, you would expect a similar percent favorable from that person on the other half of the questions. Application of this method yielded reliability coefficients in the range of 0.9, indicating a high degree of reliability.

The second method for testing reliability was the test-retest method. This took advantage of the fact that the survey was repeated in most of the plants in several consecutive years.

Figure 6 is a scatterplot of scores for the same plants when tested in 1996 (POS96) and 1997 (POS97) using the same survey instrument. The correlation between the two test scores yielded a Pearson *r* of 0.82, indicating again a high degree of reliability. If you were studying the reliability of an IQ test, you might want a somewhat higher number, under the assumption that IQ does not change materially over time. You would not want a perfect correlation with the safety survey. It is assumed that the performance of plants can either improve or decline, based at least in part on the actions of management. It should be expected that some sites will do more than others to implement changes based on the survey and that the scores of these sites will improve in comparison to the scores of sites that do not take any significant action.

In addition, subsequent administrations of the survey included questions that asked whether the site had taken action on the previous year's survey. There was a positive correlation between the proportion of respondents saying that action was taken and the change in the survey score of the site. In one study of 23 sites for which there were scores from 1996 and 1997, the Pearson *r* correlation between the questions on the site's response to the survey and the change in the site's overall score from 1996 to 1997 was 0.51. The probability of this being a result of chance is 0.02.

Safety Surveys (cont.)

Content-Based Validity

The original Minnesota survey and the fourteen questions that were added were all written by teams of safety professionals. Because the judges of content-based validity were safety professionals, the questions had *de facto* content-based validity.

Some might argue that the survey was measuring only the perceptions of workers and that such perceptions may have no relationship to reality, and therefore, one should not assume content-based validity. The response is that if workers have the *perception* that safety is not a high priority for management, then the workers are less likely to follow safety procedures. It does not matter what management actually thinks. The worker is guided by his or her own belief. He or she cannot read the mind of the manager.

Criterion-Based Validity

In spite of arguments that incident rates are not an ultimate criterion, they offered an obvious and readily available criterion against which to assess the validity of the survey. In addition, the team used the judgment of safety professionals regarding the quality of the safety program at the site. Here there were two levels: strong and weak. It must be realized that these criteria are not truly independent. When a safety professional is aware that a particular plant has a high incident rate, it is unlikely that he or she would judge it to have a strong safety program. It is possible that he or she might judge a site with a low rate as weak. He or she may be aware of serious hazards that the site has not effectively dealt with and conclude that they have been lucky so far.

The validity of each question was assessed using a statistical test to ensure that sites with strong safety programs and better accident records had better scores than sites with weak programs and high accident rates. The methodology is described extensively elsewhere (Carder and Ragan 2004).

Some of the original questions from the Minnesota survey were not valid in this test environment, even though they had been validated using a similar procedure when the Minnesota survey was developed (Bailey, personal communication). Validation studies were subsequently conducted in another company (Carder and Ragan 2003). This second company manufactured copy machines. Ten questions from the original Minnesota survey were not valid in either company. They were subsequently dropped from the survey that had been developed by the team.

Although Bailey (personal communication) has reported that questions would be valid only when the scores of hourly workers were used for the validation test, the studies described here showed that most questions would also be valid when only the scores of managers were used. Although managers generally had a higher proportion of favorable answers, these scores usually showed the same pattern of strengths and weaknesses. When there are severe problems at a site, the scores of managers may actually be lower than those of hourly workers (Carder and Ragan 2004).

An alternative method of assessing criterion-based validity is to look at the correlation between scores on the entire survey and some criterion, such as incident rates. Table 3 depicts the average recordable accident/incident rate for 1992–93 (Aver RAIR) and the survey score (total % favorable) for each site (Pcpt). In addition, there is a column titled MST. This is the rating given each of the sites by the company's manufacturing strategy team based on their analysis of the quality of the management system in operation at the site. This was not an attempt to rate safety management, but to rate the quality of the management system for manufacturing in general. The higher the number, the weaker the management system was judged to be. Because these scores were available, they offered an additional criterion against which to evaluate the survey. Although the accident record is not independent of the safety professional's rating of the site, this MST score should be independent from both.

TABLE 3

Perception Survey Scores, Manufacturing Scores, Strategy Team Scores, and Recordable Rates for Thirteen Plants

Site #	Pcpt	MST	Aver RAIR
15	0.73	8	4.95
17	0.70	8	5.15
19	0.83	2	0.00
27	0.83	4	1.80
35	0.82	8	6.00
38	0.83	2	3.70
44	0.78	5	2.55
56	0.69	8	3.30
58	0.76	4	2.55
72	0.62	6	4.90
75	0.78	5	2.65
78	0.55	8	8.25
80	0.71	4	1.80

(*Source:* Carder and Ragan 2003)

Table 4 is a matrix of the Pearson correlation coefficients (RAIR = Aver RAIR, PCPT SVY = Pcpt, and MST = MST).

There is a negative correlation between the RAIR and the survey score, as you would expect. The more positive the survey score, the lower the RAIR should be. A correlation this strong would occur in random data only 19 times in 1000, so this correlation is statistically significant and provides further evidence for criterion-based validation.

It is very interesting to note that the MST rating is also correlated with both the survey score and the RAIR. The correlation between the survey score and MST is negative because a high survey score and a low MST score are both indicative of good performance.

TABLE 4

Matrix of Pearson Correlation Coefficients for Table 3

	RAIR	PCPT SVY	MST
RAIR	1.000		
PCPT SVY	−0.639 $p < 0.019$	1.000	
MST	0.756 $p < 0.003$	−0.577 $p < 0.039$	1.000

Safety Surveys (cont.)

The correlation between MST and RAIR is positive because the lower the MST and the lower the RAIR, the better the site. The difference in the strengths of these correlations may or may not be important. What is clearly important is that the existence of a correlation between all three measurements indicates that all three measures must involve some common factors. The fact that the MST rating, which is not based on safety, correlates strongly with two measures of safety suggests that both are dealing with some common characteristics of the plant.

One could argue from these data that quality and safety are fundamentally related and that the survey, in its most general sense, is a measure of the effectiveness of the management system and is not isolated to safety. The MST rating was an attempt to measure the quality of the management system. Although it is not surprising that this is a strong predictor of safety, it is the only statistical evidence that we are aware of that demonstrates the connection between safety and the quality of the overall management system. As discussed previously, the survey was a much less laborious process than the MST ratings. The survey may be a much more cost-effective method to evaluate the quality of the management system with regard to quality and productivity as well as safety. In fact, our personal experience indicates that when these questions are edited to remove the safety specificity, they can be an effective tool in helping understand the strengths and weaknesses of the overall management system.

To put the strength of these correlation coefficients into context, remember the example from another field–that the correlation between SAT scores and Yale grade-point average is in the range of 0.2 to 0.3. This means that the SAT, the best available predictor, can only account for about 10 percent of the variation in college GPA. In comparison with the SAT, the perception survey appears to be a much better predictor, accounting for 25 to 50 percent of the variation. It is also reasonable to suspect that the survey is a much more reliable measure than the MST rating, which represents the subjective judgments of a small staff group.

Costruct-Based Validity

The study of construct-based validity has been described extensively elsewhere (Carder and Ragan 2003). The original Minnesota survey purported to measure "20 factors influencing safety performance" based on an analysis by the survey's authors. An initial attempt to verify these twenty components measured the correlations between questions. More than one question is identified in each component. The logic of this is, if there are three questions that measure "goals for safety," the answers to these three questions should have a relatively strong correlation. It turned out that questions within one of the twenty components often correlated more strongly with questions in other components than with other questions in their own component.

A factor analysis was conducted to better understand what was being measured by the survey. This is a statistical process that segregates the questions into groups of factors. Each factor represents a construct measured by the survey. An extensive series of focus groups was then conducted, with both hourly employees and managers,, to determine what was being measured by each set of questions. Of course it is the respondents who know what they are telling the interviewers when they answer a question, not the designers of the questions. The basic design of the focus group was to present the group with a set of questions that represented one of the statistical factors. They were asked to explain what the set of questions was really getting at in a facilitated discussion, which ended with the group suggesting a name for the factor. Each focus-group session lasted from three to six hours.

The groups named the following seven factors measured by the survey:

1. *Management's demonstration of commitment to safety.* Do management's actions convey the message that safety is very important?
2. *Education and knowledge of the workforce.* Are workers properly trained to do their jobs, and do they receive proper safety training? Do they understand their jobs and how to work safely?
3. *Quality of the safety supervisory process.* Does the company have standards for work, and are these standards enforced?
4. *Employee involvement and commitment.* Are employees involved in the planning process, and are they sufficiently committed to cautioning co-workers about unsafe practices?
5. *Drugs and alcohol (fitness for duty).* Is drug and alcohol use prevalent and tolerated?
6. *Off-the-job safety.* Does the company have an effective off-the-job safety program?
7. *Emergency preparedness.* Are employees at the site properly prepared to respond to an emergency?

The first four factors appear to be relatively universal, being similar to the results of other attempts to identify the critical components of the management system. Table 5 (from Carder and Ragan 2003) depicts the factors derived from several sources: (1) factor analysis of a database from the application of a safety perception survey entitled the "Safety Barometer" developed by the National Safety Council (NSC, Carder and Ragan 2003); (2) a factor analysis conducted by Coyle et al. (1995) on data from a safety survey that he developed; and (3) the factors identified by a group of managers at Dow Chemical in the 1980s that formed the basis for the company's "self-assessment process."

The first four factors are present in all of the surveys except for the NSC safety barometer, where we found no "education and knowledge" component.

In a similar vein, OSHA, through their VPP Star program, has identified "four major elements of an effective safety program" (1989). These are (1) management commitment and employee involvement, (2) work-site analysis, (3) hazard prevention and control, and (4) safety and health training. Again, these overlap with our factors. According to OSHA,

Safety Surveys (cont.)

hazard prevention and control must include a "clearly communicated disciplinary system." This is similar to our "quality of supervisory process" factor. Taking this into account, the OSHA elements cover all of ours.

Usability

The largest hurdle to clear is to explain the reliability and validity of the process to managers who are likely to hold a bias that incident counts are concrete and directly reflect reality and that survey scores are highly contrived and subject to many more sources of error.

Experience suggests that this hurdle can be successfully overcome. After the survey had been in use for two years in our target company, we conducted a survey of plant managers. Figure 7 (from Carder and Ragan 2003) shows their appraisal of the usefulness of the survey.

On the *x*-axis are the ratings, ranging from 7, very beneficial, to 0, not beneficial at all. Each bar represents the number of managers giving that particular rating. The majority (17 of 22) thought it was a useful process. None of the 22 respondents thought it was not useful at all (G-1).

TABLE 5

Management System Factors from Four Sources

Carder/Ragan Survey	Safety Barometer	Coyle Survey	Dow Self-Assessment
Management's demonstration of commitment	Management's demonstration of commitment	Maintenance and management issues	Line management leadership
Education and knowledge	not present	Training and management attitudes	Training
Quality of supervisory process	Quality of supervisory process	Accountability	Operating discipline
Employee involvement and commitment	Employee involvement and commitment	Personal authority	Total employee involvement
Off-the-job safety	not present	not present	Off-the-job safety
Emergency preparedness	not present	Included in company policy	not present
Drugs and alcohol	not present	not present	not present

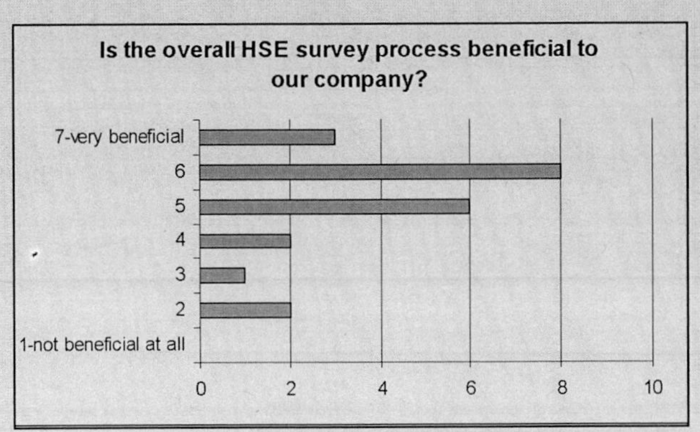

FIGURE 7. Plant managers rate the benefit of the survey process (Carder and Ragan 2003)

in a very large study of railroads. They surveyed eighteen railroads and scored them on the following areas of safety programs:

1. safety program content
2. equipment and facilities resources
3. monetary resources
4. reviews, audits, and inspections
5. procedures development, review, and modifications
6. corrective actions
7. accident reporting and analysis
8. safety training
9. motivational procedures
10. hazard-control technology
11. safety authority
12. program documentation

Only two program areas had the appropriate correlation with the measures of loss: monetary resources and hazard-control technology. Companies that spent more and employed more advanced hazard-control technology had fewer and less costly incidents. Those companies report that two areas had counterintuitive correlations (meaning the higher the score, the higher the accident rate): equipment and facilities resources and reviews, audits, and inspections. Thus, the finding is that the more extensive the audits, reviews, and inspections, the less effective the safety program. This could mean that the audits and inspections make matters worse, or it could mean that railroads with frequent incidents and greater monetary losses increased their use of reviews, audits, and inspections, perhaps as a remedial measure. Although this is not a direct test of validity, the finding at least suggests that the audits in this study had no criterion-related validity and, more importantly, that the auditing may have actually impaired safety performance.

The first positive evidence for criterion-based validation comes from a study by Ray et al. (2000) of 25 manufacturing plants in Alabama. They developed an audit on the maintenance function of these plants. The audits were conducted by outside auditors from the University of Alabama. Audit scores were correlated with the recordable rate. Using a rank-order correlation, they found a statistically significant negative correlation between the audit scores and the incident rate, meaning that the better the audit score, the lower the incident rate.

Although this may be called a pilot study, it is a strenuous test of validity. Because the 25 plants were from different industries and clearly had different levels of risk, there was huge variation in the incident rates. This "noise" vastly decreases the likelihood of finding the expected correlation. A significant limitation of the study is that it is confined to the maintenance function. Another limitation was that the authors did not test reliability. However, low reliability would create even more noise to interfere with validation. It is important to note that this study was limited to an audit of the maintenance function and cannot be generalized at this point to different audits of different functions. Huang and Brubaker (2006) also tested the criterion-based validity of their audit. The correlation between audit scores and injury rates was –0.28 (the lower the audit score, the higher the injury rate), indicating marginal but significant criterion-based validity.

Construct-Based Validity

There appears to be nothing in the literature regarding what underlying constructs might be measured by audits. They generally measure compliance with standards that the authors of the audit believe to be essential to safe performance. It is apparent from Kuusisto's work on emphasis that the experienced safety professionals who write audits can have very different opinions about what is most important.

Usability of Audits

It is necessary to distinguish between the use of audits and inspections to maintain safety standards and their use to measure safety performance. In the former case, current practices may be sufficient. However, if audits are to be used as a performance measure, careful attention must be given to establishing a reliable and valid process. Ensuring reliability requires standardization of the audit protocol, training of the auditors, and testing of the reliability. Testing of the reliability requires that at least two auditors evaluate a number of sites independently, meaning that no auditor is aware of the scores assigned by another auditor. Then the scores are compared. The degree of correlation is a measure of the reliability. Although it is not likely to be perfect, there should be a strong positive correlation.

The second issue to address is validation. Sites with high audit scores should have other evidence of safety excellence, such as low incident rates and low monetary losses. Again, validation is established by correlating some other performance criteria with audit scores. The only systematic study found in the literature that confirms a criterion-based validity, Ray et al. (2000), found a rank-order correlation of –0.336 between an injury-frequency index and audit scores on the maintenance function. This is statistically significant. Nevertheless, because the information is so limited, and the confirmation of validity is so narrow, anyone who wants to properly use audits as a performance measure has a long hill to climb in order to establish the reliability and validity of the process.

Summary of Performance Measurement

This chapter has discussed the most commonly used systematic measures of safety performance, incident rates, and audits. Surveys, which appear to have certain advantages over the other methods, have also been discussed. Many other measures might have been included, such as costs and severity measures. They are not sufficiently developed and standardized to include in this chapter. However, it is not time to close the book on the development of better measures. The development of the survey has been a systematic search for a better measure by safety professionals, scientists, and managers. As the understanding of safety continues to improve, new and better measures will appear. The most important function of the preceding discussion is to lay out the ground rules for the evaluation of a performance measure: It must have reliability and at least content-related and criterion-related validity. Ideally it would also have construct-related validity so that it could serve as a basis for prescribing improvement actions. In fact, it is unlikely that anyone will ever develop the *perfect* performance measure. Consequently, we agree with Petersen (2005) when he suggests that the "ideal strategy" would be to use a combination of measures, including incident-based measures, audits, and surveys. Of course we add the caveat that great care must be taken to ensure the reliability and validity of each measure. This is particularly difficult with audits, but the literature indicates that it can be achieved.

Benchmarking

Benchmarking is properly viewed as one method of collecting information to enable the development of a plan for process improvement. Logically, benchmarking is a part of the plan phase for a plan-do-study-act cycle as described by Shewhart and Deming (Deming 1993). The proper way to engage in the planning phase is to develop information in order to guide the plan. Of course this must include information on internal processes. Benchmarking is another important source of data. One way to look at it is as a form of reality testing. If one wants to know what would happen if a certain practice were implemented, he or she may be able to find a benchmarking partner that has already implemented the practice and can study that partner's results.

As defined here, benchmarking is the study of a competitor's product or business practices in order to improve the performance of one's own company. This is a very complex process. First, it requires identification of superior performance. Second, it requires identification of the particular processes or activities that are responsible for that performance. Third, it requires the implementation of those processes or practices in one's own company.

Although none of these is simple, the implementation phase may be the most difficult. As an example, the Israeli Air Force has developed remarkable[4] safety performance over the last 25 years, driving their incidence of class 5 accidents (loss of pilot, aircraft, or damage over $1 million) from over 30 per year in the early 1980s to near zero by 2001 (Carder and Ragan 2004). According to Mr. Itzhak Raz, who was deeply involved in this improvement process, a critical change was the understanding in the culture that when pilots fly in a safe way, according to regulations, they are actually better fighters than pilots who cut corners and take risks. This runs counter to the macho culture that tends to pervade many air forces. Implementation of this cultural change required years of commitment from the most senior commanders to be effective. It is often easy to see what lessons are to be learned from the success of these measures. Implementation, however, is another matter entirely.

According to the American Society for Quality (ASQ), the reasons to engage in benchmarking are as follows (Hill 2000):

- It avoids starting from scratch.
- It enables the transfer of tacit knowledge.
- It creates urgency and accelerates change.
- It identifies performance gaps.
- It helps develop performance goals.
- It helps develop realistic objectives.
- It encourages continuous innovation.
- It creates a better understanding of the industry.
- It establishes a process of continuous learning.

Against this backdrop of positive reasons, consider the following pitfalls.

- ***The Enron problem.*** As of February 2001, Enron had been ranked as the most innovative company by *Fortune* for six consecutive years and was ranked eighteenth on *Fortune*'s list of most admired companies. The measures of Enron's financial performance were, of course, quite flawed. One must be very careful about the performance measures that define outstanding companies. In safety, incident rates are not difficult to manipulate. Never select a benchmarking partner in safety merely on the basis of a low incident rate. It is critical that the benchmarking identify excellent processes rather than simply focusing on numerical results (DeToro 1995).

- ***The low-ceiling problem.*** Do not set ultimate targets based on the performance of others. The idea that the road to excellence is through imitation of superior performers already suggests that the company may be confined to second place. Even second place might be temporary. The company might discover processes and practices that will enhance its own performance, but the idea of trying to model one company after another is no guarantee of success. First, the company might set its sights too low and expend energy adopting processes that are soon to be obsolete. For many years GM was the target of Ford, in cost and product quality. Then along came Toyota and Honda, raising the bar by an order of magnitude. Table 6, published in 1990 (Womack, Jones, and Roos 1990), depicts the relative quality and cost parameters of GM and Toyota as of 1986. Fortunately for Ford, they had changed their target to Toyota by the early 1980s.

A second danger of copying is that the processes copied may not be compatible with the circumstances and culture of this particular company. If this is the case, it is possible these efforts do more harm than good (Stauffer 2003).

These cautions are not a reason to avoid benchmarking. However, anyone who develops a benchmarking project should keep them in mind. At any given time there will be strong performers and weak performers. Usually this changes over time. Do not look for "the player of the week"; look for superior processes that drive superior performance in the long term.

The ASQ offers the following four suggestions for successful benchmarking.

- Tie the benchmarking to the strategic initiatives of the organization. If this is not done, successful improvement efforts are unlikely, and those efforts will probably be wasted.
- Involve the process owners. First, their knowledge is critical to the company's benchmarking process. Second, their buy-in is necessary for any successful intervention.
- Understand one's own process. This is not as simple as it sounds. Discussions with managers in other companies in the course of benchmarking can assist in developing a better understanding of one's own process. Moreover, it is wrong to assume that the company will always find a better process than the one already in place. Even if it does, the company may determine that it would not be appropriate to implement in the firm (Stauffer 2003).
- Benchmark inside and outside. In any large company, there are likely to be units with excellent processes that may be as good as or better than anything one can find outside the company. An excellent process that already exists inside the company has one strong advantage: there is evidence that this process can succeed inside the culture and structure of this particular company.

TABLE 6

Comparison of GM and Toyota Productivity and Profit

	A Good System	A Better System
	GM	Toyota
Assembly hours/car	31	16
Assembly space/car	8.1	4.8
Parts inventory	2 wk	2 hr
Defects/100 cars	130	45

(*Source:* Womack et al. 1990)

Determining What Companies or Processes to Benchmark

On the surface, choosing the processes and companies to benchmark might appear to be a simple—find a company with the best performance, understand the processes that lead to this performance, and establish similar processes. Consider the application of this approach to baseball. The New York Yankees have had the one of the best performances over the past few years. One feature of their process has turned out to involve the expenditure of huge sums to hire star, free-agent players away from other teams.

This process seems to have been adopted by a few teams. In 2003 the Yankees had a payroll of $180 million. Seven teams spent over $100 million: the Mets, the Dodgers, the Red Sox, the Braves, the Cardinals, the Rangers, and the Giants. The average payroll was $80 million, and the average team won 81 games, so that the average win cost about $1 million, but the Yankees, who won 101 games, were spending $1.8 million for each win. The most interesting anomaly in the data is the Oakland As. They won 96 games with a payroll of $57 million, thus spending $0.59 million per win. Over the past several years, they have won nearly as many games as the Yankees with one-third the payroll.

Oakland's *process* has been eloquently described in the best-selling *Moneyball* by Michael Lewis (2003). Lewis described Oakland's use of statistical analysis of what player characteristics win baseball games; they look for players who will be undervalued in the marketplace, relative to their contribution to winning. For example, on-base percentage is more important than batting average. On-base percentage includes hits, walks, and being hit by a pitch. A player with a high batting average will be expensive, even if he rarely gets a walk. A player who has a relatively low batting average but who gets lots of walks and consequently has a higher on-base percentage will be much cheaper but also more valuable in terms of winning games.

The point of this is that benchmarking cannot be based simply on the identification of superior performance. Certainly, in 2003 the Yankees had superior performance and an effective process. However, attempts to copy it have not been entirely successful. Moreover, most teams cannot even try because their revenue is not sufficient to spend even $100 million on payroll.

The following criteria can assist in the selection of effective benchmarking partners:

- ***Excellent performance.*** It does not have to be the best, but it has to be very good. Consider how the performance is measured and by whom. If the company is using accident records, be certain that the company is using the same recording criteria as its competitors? Does the company place such a strong emphasis on numerical goals, giving one reason to suspect the numbers they produce?
- ***Excellent processes.*** There are many sources of information about this. What do experts say? What do industry colleagues say? What has been written about them, excluding self-serving PR efforts? What kind of emphasis do they put on education? Education is a powerful driver of innovation. What is the quality of their education and training?[5] Excellent processes require excellent education and training.
- ***Interest in a cooperative effort.*** Look for partners who will share information candidly in a give-and-take relationship. Fortunately, in safety it is not likely competitors will want to protect the secrecy of their processes. Although safety may indeed be a competitive advantage, it is in everyone's interest to have excellence across an industry. A disaster at one chemical plant or refinery will put an entire industry on the defensive. However, look for more than a passive partner. The company will succeed most with a partner who will view the relationship as a win-win situation and who will put energy into the sharing process.

How to Proceed with Benchmarking[6]

The following list should be helpful in approaching the benchmarking process.

1. Clearly define the safety objective. Improving safety performance might seem to be a sufficient objective, but more thought is required. For example, is the company able to devote more resources to safety? Does the safety manager have the ability to implement actions based on the findings? When setting out to improve the

processes of safety measurement, it is best to have the backing of senior management and a relatively large amount of control over the measurement process in the company. It is important to define an objective that is realistic, rather than setting out on a fishing expedition.

2. Understand one's own process, including the perception of its strengths and weaknesses. This actually goes hand in hand with the first objective. The study of one's own process will assist in defining the project. Most safety professionals have a pretty good intuitive idea of the strengths and weakness of their system.
3. Compare the company's performance with that of potential benchmarking partners. Use as many independent sources of information as possible. Examine the methods of measurement to understand reliability and validity. Include the subjective reports of professionals who have experience with the potential partners.
4. Select partners based on evidence of excellent performance, suitability for the company's strategic objectives, applicability to its processes, and the willingness of the potential partner to actively engage in the process.
5. Meet with the partners to develop a joint plan for the process. The plan should benefit both parties. It should be specific, but also sufficiently flexible so that unexpected discoveries can be followed up.
6. Engage in a thorough process of data collection. Use as many sources as possible, including interviews, site visits, reviews of documents, and reviews of whatever numerical data exist. One may want to construct surveys, although it is a good idea to have surveys reviewed by a professional so that the results will be meaningful. Another option is to use TQM methods for data collection, such as flow charts and fishbone diagrams. Follow the findings as the process proceeds, so that promising leads are not missed because they were not discovered until the data-collection process was completed.
7. Integrate the data collected from the company's benchmarking process with the data that was collected in order to develop the action plan.

A final word (or two) on benchmarking:

Professionals in the fields of safety, incident prevention, risk management, and so on are likely to have an advantage over most others when benchmarking. They have the luxury of working in a field in which professionals are usually willing to share successes and failures. Managers are less likely to provide information on successful processes in manufacturing, sales, and marketing when these processes represent their competitive advantages.

Benchmarking, properly done, is a valuable assessment and improvement tool. One word of caution, however: benchmarking involves comparing outside practices to existing practices, and sometimes existing practices are not what one should be looking at. Often even *best practices* are based on current concepts. Sometimes a company is looking for a paradigm shift. Looking at what is being done and doing it as well as possible is essentially an example of continuous improvement. Taking a new look at how to do something unconstrained from existing practice is a valuable approach when a company seems to have reached the limits of improvement using existing systems and processes.

The field of safety experienced a paradigm shift in the early 1900s when people such as Heinrich suggested that accidents were the results of linear systems (Heinrich's domino theory) and that through work on minor accidents, the occurrence of serious accidents would be reduced because there was a ratio of minor to serious events.[7] Professionals started to look at accident trends and events that foreshadowed the occurrence of accidents so that they might prevent more accidents. At the time, many accidents were caused by inadequate guarding or exposure to unsafe work environments. The obvious answers were guarding and using personal protective equipment (PPE). Major improvements were made.

Another major paradigm shift occurred when guarding and PPE began to reach the limits of their ability to reduce accidents. Behavioral safety became an important topic of discussion in the 1980s. This included the work of Petersen and his colleagues (1991) and Krause and his colleagues (1997). Although the two groups took very different approaches to the problem, they remained focused on the leverage that could be developed by focusing on behavior.

Much of what has been discussed in this chapter is an example of yet another shift—viewing accidents as being caused by an interconnected system. In the authors' experience, dividing this system into human causes, organizational causes, and causes in the work environment is an effective approach.

ENDNOTES

[1]This is the ability of the management system to manage important outcomes such as quality, cost, productivity, innovation, safety, and profit.

[2]The only accidents that do not have a human element are those that in no way involve humans. For example, lightning striking a tree and causing a fire could be an accident with no human element, unless of course the tree was planted by a person or someone cut down all of the surrounding trees, leaving this one as the highest and most vulnerable to lightning strikes. Only pure acts of nature appear to have no human element. Even then, the consequences are frequently affected by where humans build, remove, or otherwise alter the natural course of events. A tidal wave is an act of nature. The destruction of a coastal city has a human element because humans built there in the first place. Earthquakes are an act of nature, but the degree of damage is greatly dependent on where people built and the way they built their structures.

[3]The *U statistic* is based on the Poisson distribution. U = square root of (R/T) where R is the recordable rate and T is the number of 200,000-hour exposure units on which that rate calculation was based (Deming 1993, Carder 1994).

[4]In fiscal year 2002, the U.S. military had 97 class A aviation accidents, including 35 in the Air Force (see www.denix.osd.mil/denix/Public/ESPrograms/Force/Safety/Accidents/fy03_final.html).

[5]Deming has insisted on the differentiation of *education*, which is the teaching of theory, and *training*, which is the teaching of a skill. We agree with the distinction. The two are obviously related, and both are very important.

[6]This list is largely derived from Hill (2000).

[7]Heinrich suggested the accident triangle to illustrate this theory.

REFERENCES

American Institute of Chemical Engineers (AIChE). 2002. *Guidelines for Investigating Chemical Process Incidents*. New York: AIChE.

Bailey, C. 1997. "Managerial Factors Related to Safety Program Effectiveness: An Update on the Minnesota PerceptionSurvey." *Professional Safety* 8:33–35.

Bailey, C. W., and D. Petersen. 1989. "Using Safety Surveys to Assess Safety System Effectiveness." *Professional Safety* 2:22–26.

Baker, III, J. A. et. al. 2007 Report of the BP US Refineries Independent Safety Review Panel. Retrieved from www.aiche.org/uploadedfiles/ccps/resources/baker_panel_report.pdf

Banstetter, T. "Some Saw Through Enron's Ploys." *Fort Worth Star-Telegram*. February 10, 2002.

Camp, R. C. 1995. *Business Process Benchmarking: Finding and Implementing Best Practices*. Milwaukee: ASQC Quality Press.

Carder, B. 1994. "Quality Theory and the Measurement of Safety Systems." *Professional Safety* 39:23.

Carder, B., and P. T. Ragan. 2003. "A Survey-Based System for Safety Measurement and Improvement." *Journal of Safety Research* 34:157–165.

______. 2004. *Measurement Matters: How Effective Assessment Drives Business and Safety Performance*. Milwaukee: ASQ Quality Press.

Coyle, I. R., S. D. Sleeman, and N. Adams. 1995. "Safety Climate." *Journal of Safety Research* 26:247–254.

Cronbach, L. J., and P .E. Meehl. 1955. "Construct Validity in Psychological Tests." *Psychological Bulletin 52*, pp. 281–302.

Deal, T. E., and A. A. Kennedy. 1982. *Corporate Cultures: The Rites and Rituals of Corporate Life*. New York: Addison-Wesley.

Deming, W. E. 1982. *Out of the Crisis*. Cambridge, MA: MIT Center for Advanced Engineering Study.

______. 1993. *The New Economics for Industry, Government, Education*. Cambridge, MA: MIT Center for Advanced Engineering Study.

DeToro, I. 1995. "The 10 Pitfalls of Benchmarking." *Quality Progress* 28:61–63.

Duncan, A. J. 1986. *Quality Control and Industrial Statistics*. Homewood, IL: Irwin.

Elliott, M. R., P. R. Kleindorfer, J. J. Dubois, Y. Wang, and I. Rosenthal. 2008. "Linking OII and RMP Data: Does Everyday Safety Prevent Catastrophic Loss?" *International Journal of Risk Assessment and Management* 10:130–146.

Feynman, R. P. 1999. *The Pleasure of Finding Things Out*. Cambridge, MA: Perseus.

Flanders, M. E., and T. W. Lawrence. 1999. "Warning! Safety Incentive Programs Are Under OSHA Scrutiny." *Professional Safety* 44:29–31.

Heinrich, H. 1959. *Industrial Accident Prevention*. 4th ed. New York: McGraw Hill.

Hill, C. 2000. *Benchmarking and Best Practices*. American Society for Quality. www.ASQ.org

Huang, Y-H., and S. A. Brubaker. 2006. "Safety Auditing: Applying Research Methodology to Validate a Safety Audit Tool." *Professional Safety* 51:36–40.

Krause, T. R. 1997. *The Behavior-Based Safety Process: Managing Involvement for an Injury Free Culture*. 2d ed. New York: Van Nostrand Reinhold.

Kuusisto, A. 2000. "Safety Management Systems: Audit Tools and the Reliability of Auditing." Doctoral dissertation, Technical Research Center of Finland.

Levitt, S. J., and S. J. Dubner. 2005. *Freakonomics: A Rogue Economist Explores the Hidden Side of Everything*. New York: HarperCollins.

Lewis, M. 2003. *Moneyball*. New York: W. W. Norton.

Manuele, F. 2003. *On the Practice of Safety*. 3d ed. New York: Wiley.

McConnell, M. C. 1997. "Formula Management: In Search of Magic Solutions." *Health Care Supervisor* 16:65–78.

Merriam-Webster Online Dictionary (retrieved March 28, 2007). www.m-w.com

Nelson, L. S. 1984. "Shewhart Control Chart—Tests for Special Causes." *Journal of Quality Technology* 16:237–239.

Occupational Health and Safety Administration (OSHA). 1989. *Safety and Health Program Management Guidelines; Issuance of Voluntary Guidelines*. Federal Register 54:3904–3916.

Perrow, C. 1984. *Normal Accidents: Living with High Risk Technologies*. New York: Basic Books.

Petersen, D. 1998. "What Measures Should We Use and Why?" *Professional Safety* 43:37–41.

______. 2000. "Safety Management 2000: Our Strengths and Weaknesses." *Professional Safety* 45:16–19.

______. 2005. "Setting Goals, Measuring Safety Performance." *Professional Safety* 50:43–48.

Petersen, D. E., and J. Hillkirk. 1991. *A Better Idea: Redefining the Way American Companies Work*. Boston: Houghton Mifflin.

Polk, J. F. 1987. "Statistical Analysis of Railroad Safety Performance, 1977–1982." Final Report of Contract DTFR 53-82-X-0076, Federal Railroad Administration.

Ray, P. S., R. G. Batson, W. H. Weems, Q. Wan, G. S.Sorock, S. Matz, and J. Coynam. 2000. "Impact of Maintenance Function on Plant Safety." *Professional Safety* 45:45–49.

Rosier, G. A. 1997. "A Case for Change." *Professional Safety* 42:32–35.

Scherkenbach, W. W. 1990. *The Deming Route to Quality and Productivity: Roadmaps and Roadblocks*. Milwaukee: ASQ Quality Press.

Senge, P. M., C. Roberts, R. B. Ross, B. J. Smith, and A. Kleiner. 1994. *The Fifth Discipline Field Book*. New York: Doubleday.

Stauffer, D. 2003. "Is Your Benchmarking Doing the Right Work?" Harvard Management Update 8.

Wolf, F., and E. Berniker. 1999. *Validating Normal Accident Theory: Chemical Accidents, Fires and Explosions in Petroleum Refineries*. Retrieved from www.plu.edu/~bernike/NormAcc/Validating%20NAT.doc

Womack, J. P., D. T. Jones, and D. Roos. 1990. *The Machine that Changed the World: Based on the Massachusetts Institute of Technology 5-Million-Dollar 5-Year Study on the Future of the Automobile*. New York: Rawson Associates.

9

Best Practices

Stephen Wallace

Learning Objectives

- Learn about the various codes, standards, and strategies used to identify risks and how to ensure that necessary safeguards are in place to prevent incidents.
- Be able to identify best practices in process design, including installing active and passive controls.
- Explain hazard reviews and the steps necessary to make processes inherently safer.
- Know what equipment is related to fire control and suppression.
- Recognize the steps necessary to ensure that building occupants are safe and that maintenance is being performed in an effective manner.
- Understand the steps that must be taken to ensure that facilities remain secure from internal and external threats.
- Be able to discuss special material hazards, such as reactivity and asphyxiation.

Assessing risks and controlling hazards in chemical and manufacturing plants often involves the use of sophisticated tools to evaluate detailed engineering designs. As noted in this chapter, the areas that must be considered are broad and include aspects such as design of pressure-relief valves, electrical safety, and materials of construction. It may be difficult for the practitioner to be well versed in all aspects. Various evaluation tools may be used to determine whether the risk involved with certain processes is acceptable and what provisions need to be made to lower it. Such tools can be qualitative or more complex, such as fault trees.

Regulatory compliance alone does not guarantee that an organization will assess and control risks in the most effective manner. For example, OSHA 29 CFR 1910.119(d)(3)(ii) states that organizations must document that equipment complies with *recognized and generally accepted good engineering practices*, sometimes referred to as RAGAGEPs (OSHA 1996a). Fortunately, there are several sources available to aid practitioners in understanding good practices (sometimes referred to as *best practices*) in this area. To reflect the jargon used in the chemical and manufacturing industries, the terms "good practices" and "best practices" will be used interchangeably in this chapter.

Voluntary Guidelines, Codes, and Consensus Standards

Best practices for assessing and controlling risks go beyond regulatory compliance and come from a variety of sources. These practices are developed to provide specific guidance in the design, operation, and maintenance of equipment processing hazardous materials. Good practices can be voluntary guidelines, recommended practices, codes, and consensus standards. This chapter does not attempt to differentiate between the legalities of these different types; instead it presents the relevant information in the content of each.

Trade organizations with member companies often develop standards to assist their membership in assessing and controlling hazards. Some property and business insurance companies in the chemical and manufacturing industries develop guidelines for those they insure to follow to minimize the risk of loss. Even companies and individuals that are not members of these organizations can often obtain these guidelines, codes, and standards, generally for a fee.

Some good-practices organizations, such as the Center for Chemical Process Safety (CCPS), grew out of larger professional societies and were established to address the needs of members who desired more specific guidance on ways to ensure that their processes were designed, operated, and maintained in the safest manner. Individual practitioners or members of academia with expertise in a particular subject area may also publish and present their ideas and findings. Companies sometimes develop internal guidelines, although this information is often considered proprietary and is not always publicly available.

The last portion of this chapter provides a listing and description of some of the organizations that develop voluntary guidelines and consensus standards. Although this listing is not comprehensive, it does include organizations whose products are referenced frequently and cited throughout industry.

Best Practices in Risk Assessment and Hazard Control

As noted previously, the field of risk assessment and hazard control is very broad. Risks must be evaluated and controlled during all stages of process operation, including design, commissioning, operation, maintenance, and decommissioning. This section will address risk assessment during some of the most critical phases. A number of best practices resources will be referenced, and an explanation of these follows at the end of the chapter. It is important to note that the guidance provided in this chapter is not meant to replace any codes and standards but rather to make the practitioner aware of sources that exist and critical components of their contents. The guidance presented in this chapter is meant to distill some of the fundamental concepts and is not meant to be a comprehensive discussion of each area. Also, codes, standards, and good-practice guidelines are subject to revision, so users must ensure that they are using the most recent editions and the ones most applicable to their situations.

The information in this chapter has broad applicability to several industries. Although specific sectors such as refining and petrochemical processing are discussed, the lessons of hazard identification, inherently safer design, and adequate layers of protection are applicable to a variety of industries, including the defense and aerospace industries as well as manufacturers of pulp and paper, food, pharmaceuticals, and explosives. Also, many of the examples in this chapter are taken from the process-safety field, but the concepts are appropriate in a variety of settings, including evaluating occupational hazards. For example, adequate hazard identification and inherently safer design are useful concepts to apply whether an organizaton is trying to mitigate a chemical release or prevent injury to a worker using a complex machine with several moving parts.

Finally, requirements listed throughout this chapter are noted as good practices. Several factors determine whether a requirement is mandatory, such as determinations by the authority having jurisdiction (AHJ). Because of this, the handbook chapters generally do not specify legal requirements, except those noted specifically in OSHA regulations. This chapter lists good practices and specifically does not make "shall"-type statements. The practitioner is encouraged to consider all of these practices based on their merits. Specific codes and the AHJ should be consulted to determine which practices are mandatory and which are suggested.

Process Design

The most critical phase in identifying risks is the design phase. It is during this phase that errors can be corrected most easily. Flaws that exist after the design phase will require a larger expenditure of capital to correct. In other words, it is easier to make corrections *on paper* before the equipment is actually in place.

To effectively control risk, both the likelihood and the consequences of accidents must be reduced. It is during process design that the technology, process monitoring and control instrumentation, materials of construction, and mitigation equipment are chosen.

In *Guidelines for Engineering Design for Process Safety*, the Center for Chemical Process Safety (CCPS) notes that redundant levels of safeguards, often referred to as "layers of protection," should be built into processes. The CCPS recommends that designers minimize risks by making processes inherently safer, installing design features that do not need to actively function to be effective, and installing additional equipment that may be relied upon to function if needed to avoid process deviations (CCPS 1993, 6). The last step in protecting the safety of the process is implementing procedural safeguards, often referred to as *administrative safeguards*. Inherent safety is the most effective design strategy and is addressed first in this section.

Inherent Safety

The concept of *inherent safety* can be implemented most effectively during process design. The CCPS notes that during the early stages of design, the process engineer has maximum degrees of freedom to consider alternatives in technology, chemistry, and location of the plant (CCPS 1993, 5). Applying the concept of inherent safety means that the process designers use strategies of safer chemistry, rather than control systems and operator intervention, to prevent injuries and environmental and property damage. The elements involved in inherent safety include:

- ***intensification*** (using smaller quantities of hazardous materials)
- ***substitution*** (replacing materials with less-hazardous substances)
- ***attenuation*** (using less-hazardous conditions or a less-hazardous form of a material)
- ***limiting of effects*** (designing facilities that minimize the impact of releases)
- ***simplification/error tolerance*** (designing facilities that make operating errors less likely or less consequential).

The first three elements of inherent safety stated above involve using smaller quantities or less-hazardous materials. Generally, these issues are easily understood by practitioners, although at times it may be challenging to implement them. Designers should consider whether the operating unit can tolerate having smaller supplies of raw materials on hand. While a lower inventory of raw material may cause production concerns if there are upsets in the supply, it also means there is less material to be released in the event of a failure. However, caution must still be exercised when these principles are applied. For example, by decreasing the size of chlorine cylinders kept on site, more change-out of cylinders may be needed, which is a risk that must be managed. Designers should also consider whether less-hazardous materials can be used in the process, such as aqueous rather than anhydrous ammonia.

Limiting of effects involves designing facilities and equipment in such a way as to minimize the impact of releases. Separation distances should be adequate between hazardous material unloading, storage, and processing. Facilities should be designed to minimize the need for transportation of highly hazardous materials. Distances to sensitive receptors, such as residential communities, should be considered in the design. Adequate buffer spaces should exist between sensitive receptors and hazardous installations. Facilities should be located in proximity to utilities, emergency response support, and adequate water supplies.

Finally, equipment in facilities should be designed to minimize errors or make them less consequential. Equipment can be designed to ensure that flow rates are within safe limits by choosing pumps and sizing lines appropriately. Vessels should be designed for a full vacuum [–14.7 pounds per square inch gauge (psig)] if the possibility exists for pumping the materials out with the vents closed or if hot vapor may become trapped and condense. Reactors should be designed to be robust enough to withstand the maximum allowable pressure and eliminate the need for a large emergency relief system. Piping systems may be designed to eliminate components susceptible to leakage by using sight glasses, flexible connectors, and so on.

Protective Equipment–Passive and Active Safety Systems

Once inherent safety is considered and implemented to the extent possible, engineers should install equipment and devices to provide passive safety protection for workers and equipment. *Passive* safety measures, as opposed to *active* safety measures, have the advantage of being able to function with no additional operation or moving parts necessary. For example, pressure vessels typically contain relief valves that must open to relieve pressure in a vessel to prevent rupture. While safety relief valves generally are designed with high reliability, the valves still must operate to perform their function, but if a vessel is designed to withstand a higher pressure than can be generated in the process, the pressure rating of the vessel works in a *passive* manner to keep the vessel from rupturing.

Active devices include controls, interlocks, and shutdown systems that detect deviations from design intent and take action to correct the situation before a problem develops. As an example, Figure 1 shows a tank with redundant high-level alarms and interlocks to both trip the feed pump and close the block valve on the inlet line. Particularly hazardous systems generally are designed with multiple active devices to ensure that redundant layers of protection exist. For example, in a system that is likely to generate pressure, a pressure indicator is installed, which allows operations personnel to monitor the pressure. This device typically has high-pressure alarms (and high-high-pressure alarms) coded into it to warn of a pressure excursion (deviation from a normal path). A high-pressure shutdown will be designed to take action, such as opening a vent or closing a heating source. Ultimately, an emergency shutdown can be installed to take a number of actions, including stopping the flow of all feed material to the unit where the upset is detected. Such shutdown systems may be programmed to activate based on various types of inputs, including high pressure, temperature, and concentration of contamination.

When instrumentation is added to equipment during design, the designer must install sufficient levels of protection in the most economical manner. In ISA 84, *Safety Instrumented Systems for the Process Industry Sector*, the International Society of Automation (ISA) (formerly Instrumentation, Systems, and Automation Society) has guidelines for installing levels of protection based on how hazardous the material is and how critical the device should be (ISA 2004). A comprehensive discussion of the methods employed by the ISA is outside the scope of this chapter, but a device that is critical and operating in a hazardous service should have a high reliability rating, on the order of 99.99 percent reliable. (Stated another way, the safety system should have a high availability, on the order of 0.9999.) Generally, this level is not achieved by a single safety device but by including redundant devices.

Procedural Safeguards

The final safeguards at the facility level are often procedural or administrative. When active and passive safety devices fail to control an event, operations personnel must intervene and bring the system back to a stable state. This may involve correcting the situation, if possible, or instituting a controlled shutdown.

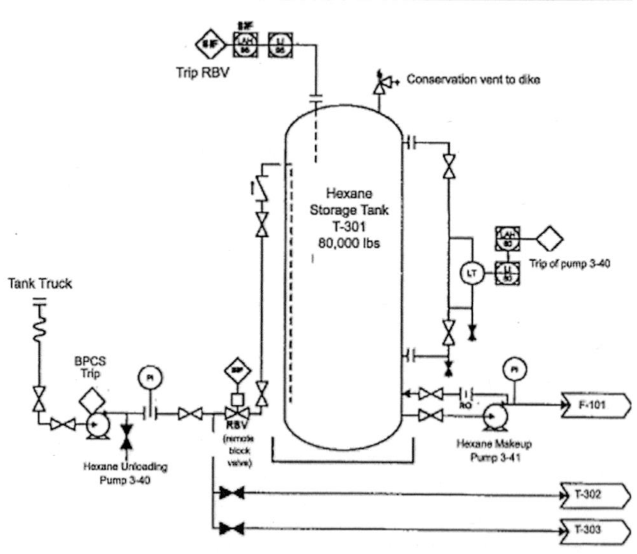

FIGURE 1. Example of a tank with redundant sensors, controls, and shutdowns (*Source:* CCPS 2001)

While this level of safeguard typically is not considered a *design* issue, the plant can be designed to make the job of operations personnel easier or more difficult. The facility must be designed with inputs to help personnel quickly diagnose a situation. Newer plants are likely to have computer-based systems monitoring process control. Critical parameters should be alarmed, and alarms should be prioritized. A temptation for designers is to add numerous alarms to a process. This can be done for the sake of safety; however, if a process is overalarmed, it can be difficult for operations personnel to determine the critical parameters during an emergency.

Control of ignition sources is often achieved by using procedural safeguards. Preparation for hot work—such as welding and cutting—and placement of vehicles that could be ignition sources, such as vacuum trucks, are best controlled by administrative safeguards. However, control of other ignition sources, such as the placement of furnaces, deflagration vents, and electrical equipment, is best addressed during design.

Hazard Reviews during Design

As mentioned previously, the design phase is the best time to make changes to improve the safety of a process. In *Guidelines for Engineering Design for Process Safety* (CCPS 1993, 5), the CCPS notes that the opportunity for ensuring maximum inherent safety occurs during the early design stages. If the process to be designed is a well-established technology, there may already be templates for equipment (including safety equipment) to be installed. However, if the process conceived is a new technology or a complete reapplication of an existing technology, the design phase can be extensive, lasting several months or even years. New technologies are often tested in smaller pilot plants before designs are scaled up to full production capacity.

The design phase itself consists of a number of iterative steps, including conceptual design, design review, and revisions. Of particular interest to safety practitioners is the design review stage. At this point, the general concept of the process is on paper, but many of the details may not have been completed. Early in the design phase, a simple review technique such as what-if may be sufficient to identify items that need to be included. As the design concept becomes more advanced, techniques such as hazard and operability analyses (HAZOPs) and layers of protection analysis (LOPA) probably are necessary to identify equipment needs.

Managing Changes during Design

Since the design process is by nature a dynamic one, it is easy for changes to be made that may not be widely communicated. If changes are not discussed, alterations may be made that could impact the safety of the process. Therefore, similar to the system used to evaluate changes once the process is running, it is important to have a system for managing changes during design. In *Loss Prevention in the Process Industries*, Frank Lees notes that such a system should include appropriate review, authorization, and communication of changes (Mannan 2005, 11.4). A thorough technical evaluation is also critical. Similar systems also must be in place for construction, commissioning, and operation.

Equipment Design

Process design should be undertaken only by knowledgeable persons who are familiar with all applicable codes and standards. Control and instrumentation should be available for critical parameters, such as pressure, temperature, level, and flammable and toxic concentrations. Alarms should alert operators to deviations, then interlocks should take automatic action if the situation is not corrected.

Below are some general design guidelines for specific equipment types. Detailed standards should be consulted for more specific information. Note that design standards for some equipment, such as pressure vessels and control systems, are addressed elsewhere in this handbook. Furthermore, fire protection is covered later in this section. General information is presented on storage vessels, piping systems, and reactors.

Storage Vessels

Storage tanks contain a variety of toxic, flammable, and corrosive materials. Since large quantities of materials are found in storage tanks, preventing a loss of containment is particularly important. Tanks should be provided with adequate pressure relief for the controlling case, which is generally an external fire in the case of tanks storing flammable materials. Design should also consider vacuum relief valves (sometimes called vaccuum breakers) for atmospheric tanks to avoid collapse of the tank wall (API 2008, 9-2). Fire protection, such as monitors, spray and foam applicators, along with flame arrestors, should be installed to prevent flames from entering the tank. Foundations and supporting structures should be capable of handling the weight of the vessel and the maximum amount of liquid that it will hold. Materials of construction and corrosion allowances should be appropriate for the material.

Low-pressure storage tanks should be designed to withstand a combination of gas pressure (or partial vacuum) and static liquid head (Figure 2). Tanks should be capable of handling the anticipated volume, and they should be provided with an overflow system that discharges to a safe location. Consideration should be given to providing an inerting blanket in the vapor space on tanks storing flammable material. A floating roof design can also be considered if the vapor pressure of the fluid is high or a cone roof when emissions should be minimized but do not need to be collected. As a guide, a fixed roof can be used for materials with vapor pressures below 1.5 pounds per square inch absolute (psia); for vapor pressures between 1.5 and 11 psia, a floating roof should be considered. For materials (such as ammonia) stored as pressurized liquid, pressure spheres are generally used. Horizontal tanks can be used for high-pressure storage. Walls of the tank should not have any pockets where gases may become trapped. The temperature of liquids, vapors, and gases in the tank should not exceed 250°F. Additional metal thickness must be provided as a corrosion allowance where corrosion is expected. API (American Petroleum Institute) 620, *Design and Construction of Large, Welded, Low-Pressure Storage Tanks*, should be consulted for additional information regarding minimum wall thickness, stress allowances, and other design issues (API 2008, 5-2).

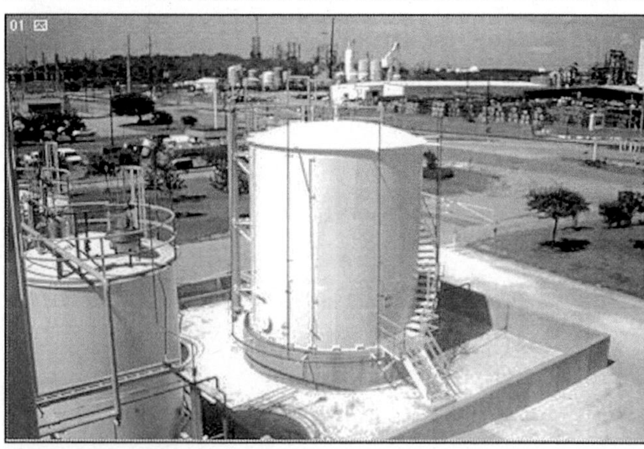

FIGURE 2. Example of a low-pressure tank
(Photo courtesy of Roy Sanders)

Piping Systems

Piping should be chosen based on the ranges of operating temperatures and pressures, properties of the fluids and materials, flow conditions such as two-phase flow, and any special valving needs. The American Society of Mechanical Engineers (ASME) B31.3 piping code lists a number of restrictions. Of note to the practitioner, cast iron shall not be used above ground within process unit boundaries in hydrocarbon or other flammable fluid service at temperatures above 300°F, and high silicon iron and lead, tin, and associated alloys shall not be used in flammable fluid services. Also, nonfireproof valves should be avoided. ASME B31.3 should be consulted for more details (ASME 2008).

Reactors

Chemical reactors are often the heart of a chemical plant, because it is in the reactors that reactants are turned into useful, salable product. The different types of reactors are *batch* and *continuous*; continuous reactors are further categorized as *continuous stirred tank reactors (CSTRs), tubular reactors, and fluidized bed reactors.*

The CCPS's *Guidelines for Engineering Design for Process Safety* provides good guidelines on loss prevention considerations for chemical reactors (CCPS 1993, 118–125). Reactors should have adequate pressure protection. Reactors should also have adequate cooling capabilities. The issue of adequate pressure relief and cooling is often dependent on the potential for a runaway reaction. This potential may mean that the relief protection needs to consider two-phase flow. Also, traditional pressure relief may not be adequate because of the need to relieve a runaway reaction. Multiple relief devices, placement lower on the vessel closer to the liquid level, and additional safeguards to prevent a runaway reaction may need to be considered. Also, because temperature and pressure can increase rapidly in a reactor, redundant instrumentation that monitors temperature and pressure—and actuates an alarm in advance of reaching critical setpoints—must be installed. Batch reactors must be designed to minimize the possibility of making sequencing mistakes (e.g., adding components in the wrong order or for the wrong amount of time). Where materials are added manually, operators need to have accurate measures of how much material has flowed into the vessel. Valve sequencing should be part of the control scheme to ensure that valves on reactants are not opened prematurely.

Fire Protection and Fire Mitigation Systems

Preventing the release of flammable and toxic materials is the best way to ensure that losses will not occur due to uncontrolled fires and explosions; therefore, the emphasis during design should be to avoid such situations. However, even though efforts are made to prevent releases and minimize ignition sources, fires and explosions can still occur in facilities processing flammable materials. Fire protection equipment is designed to minimize losses during such events and is more sophisticated than simple sprinkler systems. Fire protection equipment can be categorized much as process equipment is, with both active and passive systems.

Isolation Valves

Isolation valves should be placed in piping throughout the process to ensure that large inventories of flammables or toxics can be segregated and protected if there is a leak downstream in the process (see Figure 3). The locations of such valves depend on inventory, condition of the material, and ability to isolate the inventory by other means. Often such emergency isolation valves are located at the battery limits of the process to afford emergency access. Valves can be power-operated or manual, and controls can be local or remote. Automatic valves should be considered when the configuration of piping will not ensure that operators can access valves easily during a fire. For example, in piping leading from a vessel to the suction of a pump when the pump is located directly under the vessel, a pump seal fire may hinder efforts to reach and close manual valves on the bottom of the tank. Isolation valves should still function when utilities are lost. Manual valves should be placed in an accessible position. If the valve is elevated, a chain wheel should be provided. However, the chain should be secured in such a way that it is not a hazard to personnel walking or riding bicycles through the process

FIGURE 3. Isolation valve in a chemical plant (Photo courtesy of Roy Sanders)

area. Valves with fusible links are sometimes used to ensure that the valves will operate during a fire.

Approaches to Fighting Fires

For a fire to occur, three elements must be present: fuel, oxidant, and an ignition source. These three items collectively are known as the *fire triangle*. The CCPS notes that generally, fire protection systems involve removing one or more of the elements (CCPS 1993, 490). Fire protection often consists of a combination of systems that are activated automatically, based on exceeding some parameter and by responders activating systems. Responders may choose to extinguish a fire to prevent a large-scale loss. However, depending on the circumstances, it may be preferable to let the fire burn until all the fuel is exhausted, if extinguishing the fire causes unburned material to be released. The unburned material might be toxic, or it might contact an ignition source and result in an explosion. The National Fire Protection Association's *Fire Protection Handbook* is a good source for more information about the technology of fires and fire suppression/detection systems (Cote 2008).

If a fire is to be extinguished, this can be accomplished by exhausting the fuel source, manually fighting the fire, or by using fixed fire-fighting systems. Equipment to accomplish all three methods will be discussed below.

Detectors and Alarms

Effective fire protection starts with detection systems. A fire that is detected and extinguished in its incipient stage will not spread and result in a catastrophic incident. Therefore, fires or conditions that could result in fires need to be detected as soon as possible. Personnel cannot be available at all times to detect fires, so it is important to install automatic detectors in areas that process flammable and combustible materials. Detectors can trigger alarms, activate deluge systems, or both. Detectors that trigger alarms generally come in two categories: *combustible gas detectors* and *fire detectors*. The functioning of each type and some good practices are discussed below. Much of the information in the following sections on detectors can be found in *Guidelines for Engineering Design for Process Safety* (CCPS 1993, 491–515). The NFPA's *Fire Protection Handbook* is also an excellent source to provide additional information on this subject (Cote 2008).

Gas Detectors

Combustible gas detectors can detect vapors from a liquid release before a fire occurs. The detector senses the presence of potentially flammable mixtures of vapor in air before they reach an explosive limit. Such detectors are used in facilities where a potential leak source exists. These systems often have a warning alarm to indicate to personnel in the area that there is a problem and an automatic action alarm that is set at a higher level. The actions taken automatically can include shutting down processes or activating deluge systems.

Gas detectors should be located in such a way as to consider ignition sources, wind direction, and gas density. They can be located throughout an area to provide coverage or strategically be placed at potential flammable release points. Gas detectors should be maintained according to manufacturers' guidelines. It should also be noted that calibration of gas detectors can present a challenge, since calibration depends on the specific gas to be detected. Inaccuracies can result if a mixture of gases is released.

Some of the more common types of detectors are diffusion-head-type catalytic oxidation detectors, infrared sensors, metal oxide semiconductors, and thermal incineration flame cell sensors. *Catalytic oxidation detectors* work by oxidizing the gas and heating an internal element, which causes a measurable change in the resistance. *Infrared detectors* sense a change in radiation absorbed at specific wavelengths, with higher gas concentrations absorbing more infrared radiation. *Metal oxide semiconductors* respond to certain gases by experiencing a change in electrical current at a given voltage. *Thermal incineration flame cell sensors* operate as their name indicates. They pass the flammable gas through a constantly burning flame and measure the increase in heat.

Fire Detectors

Fire detectors differ from gas detectors because they identify changes in the atmosphere after a fire occurs by sensing either smoke, heat, or flame (radiant energy). *Radiant energy detectors* can be used if rapid response is critical.

The CCPS provides information on detectors. *Thermal detectors* are of two types: those that identify rises in heat by sensing the rate at which the temperature is increasing and those that sense when the temperature reaches a predetermined setpoint. A third type of thermal detector, known as a *rate-compensated fixed-temperature detector*, is a combination of the other two types. Because fixed-temperature detectors typically are set at high temperatures, a rate-compensated detector usually operates faster than a fixed-temperature detector. But rate-compensated detectors also have the advantage of being able to sense a slow-rising, gradual fire, which may not be detected by a rate-of-rise sensor. However, the distinction between these types disappears in modern *addressable heat detectors* because the heat sensor sends a continuous signal to a central microprocessor that can use a wide variety of signal-processing algorithms to monitor temperature variations from background ambient values (CCPS 1993, 494–496).

Fire detectors should be located in accordance with NFPA standards, particularly NFPA 72 (NFPA 2010c). Protection such as shielding should be installed on detectors that are outdoors so that they are not compromised by the elements. Detectors can be set up to sound an alarm locally and/or remotely. Heat detectors can also be used to close valves and stop a fuel source that may be feeding a fire. For example, plastic tubing, which can act as a crude heat detector, can shut air-operated valves if they are burned, causing a loss of air through the tube. More sophisticated, commercial spot and linear heat detectors (as well as other fire protection equipment) are tested and certified by organizations such as the Underwriters Laboratories (UL) and Factory Mutual (FM), and their counterparts in other countries.

Smoke Detectors

Smoke detectors work by detecting airborne combustion particulates. The two general types of smoke detectors are *ionization* and *photoelectric* detectors. The CCPS notes that ionization detectors have widespread use in industry (CCPS 1993, 495). Smoke detectors may give an alarm or can be set to automatically actuate fire suppression systems. In chemical and manufacturing facilities, false alarms may occur (for example, due to dirty environments), so it is often prudent to have voting logic for detectors so that a false positive from one will not result in an inadvertent trip of a suppression system. Smoke detectors are often used in areas such as offices, control rooms, and rooms with electrical and computer equipment (CCPS 1993, 495–496).

Radiant Energy Detectors

The other property besides a rise in temperature and combustion particulates that is measured by fire detectors is radiant heat emitted by a flame. *Ultraviolet* (UV) and *infrared* (IR) *radiation* detectors are the most common detectors of this type. Often, redundant and multiple-wavelength UV/IR or IR/IR detectors are used to decrease the chances of a false trip being set off by sunlight or devices such as welding arcs and flashing lamps. Since these devices sense optical signals through a lens, it is imperative to keep the lens clean. Some detectors are self-cleaning. Those that are not should be located where they can be maintained as needed. Of course, a balance must be struck in that the detectors should be located where routine, necessary maintenance can be performed, but also must be situated so that they will sense radiant heat and afford the maximum detection benefit (CCPS 1993, 496).

Manual Alarms

Even in facilities where there are automatic alarms and shutdowns, manual alarms are installed so that operations personnel can activate them if they observe problems. There are two common types of pull stations: *pull-lever* and *break-glass* design. These alarms generally require two distinct operations to avoid a false trip. Alarms should be located in areas with normal means of egress. Buildings and process areas should have as many manual stations as deemed appropriate by code and design engineers. There should be at least one station that is in clear view at all times, is accessible from any point in the building or area, and has a maximum distance to travel of no more than 200 feet. The activation of a manual alarm generally should also activate the main alarm system, alerting personnel in other parts of the facility of the situation so that they can respond appropriately or avoid the unit with the emergency (CCPS 1993, 496–497).

Fire Suppression and Mitigation Systems

In addition to detection systems, equipment must be in place to suppress and mitigate the effects of a large fire if one should occur. A comprehensive package of suppression and mitigation equipment consists not only of sprinkler or deluge systems, but also includes active and passive systems to aid in extinguishing the fire and protecting surrounding structures. Active systems must be activated to function, whereas passive systems provide protection by their mere existence (CCPS 1993, 497–515).

Portable Fire Extinguishers

The most basic suppression system is a portable fire extinguisher. Extinguishers should be used only on very small fires. If the fire grows and spreads beyond the incipient stage, the appropriate response for personnel using portable extinguishers is to withdraw and use fixed equipment that can be operated from a distance. The *Accident Prevention Manual for Business and Industry* provides additional information on fire extinguishers (NSC 2009).

Extinguishers come in four classes and are designed to be used on different types of fires:

- Class A: Used on ordinary combustible materials, such as wood, paper, cloth, rubber, and many plastics.
- Class B: Used on fires involving flammable liquids, greases, oils, tars, oil-base paints, lacquers, and similar materials.
- Class C: Used on fires in or near live electrical equipment, where the use of a nonconductive extinguishing agent is of first importance.
- Class D: Used on fires that occur in combustible metals, such as magnesium, lithium, and sodium.

Fixed Fire Suppression Systems

Fixed fire suppression systems generally consist of equipment in place to deliver water or some other agent to extinguish the fire. These systems are very important since mobile fire-fighting strategies result in delays (due to responders' need to collect and don protective equipment and execute a plan). Systems can be manual or automatic, and the number of units, size, capacity, and specifications of the system vary with the size of the building or facility and the amount of flammable material present (CCPS 1993, 497–499).

Fire-Water Supply

The CCPS notes that the two critical elements of fire protection equipment are adequacy and reliability (CCPS 1993, 497). The equipment needs to be of adequate capacity to extinguish the largest credible worst-case scenario fire a facility is likely to experience. The flow requirements for an anticipated fire typically range from two to four hours. The system must also be able to continue functioning after explosions, so redundancy in piping, pumps, and supply is important to ensure availability. Redundant equipment prevents single failures from impairing the entire system.

Redundant supply pumps should be installed with different sources of power. Diesel-engine pumps are generally more reliable, although electric pumps can be adequate if they have a reliable power source. Pumps should start automatically and have manual shutdown switches. A *makeup pump* (often called a *jockey pump*) is often installed and is triggered by the initial pressure drop due to the opening of sprinklers. An automatic switch can start the primary pump when the jockey pump no longer has the capacity to supply the equipment. Pumps should be located away from areas where hazards exist so that the pumps themselves will not be damaged, and as much fire-water piping as possible should be buried to protect it from explosions and direct fire exposures. Redundant pumping stations are also desirable in the event that shrapnel from an incident damages one. Installing piping in loops allows different sections to be used if some sections are damaged during an incident, and adequate valves must be installed to isolate damaged sections.

A good practice is to have the water dedicated to fire protection completely separate from the process water. Dedicated fire-water pumps and storage facilities should be installed. Combination systems should be avoided if possible because using fire water for process needs may diminish the supply of fire water; process-water equipment may not be designed for the pressures needed during a fire; and in combined process-/fire-water systems, water can be redirected from process needs that are critical during an emergency, such as cooling water. If supply tanks or outdoor reservoirs are shared, passive safeguards should be in place to ensure that enough fire water will be present during emergencies. Such safeguards include installing the takeoff from the process-water supply tank sufficiently high so that if the tank is drained down to that level, there will still be an adequate amount of fire water.

The supply system must deliver copious amounts of water to multiple areas simultaneously. For design purposes, consider the maximum demand, both instantaneous and continuous, and consider the maximum number of water sprays, deluge systems, and sprinklers that may have to operate at the same time. Also consider needs for manual fire fighting. Total demand can be as high as 10,000 gallons per minute (gpm) for process or storage areas. In *Guidelines for Engineering Design for Process Safety*, the CCPS recommends that the on-site, dedicated fire-water supply should be capable of being replenished within 24 hours after being used (CCPS 1993, 499).

Automatic Water Delivery Systems: Sprinklers, Water Sprays, and Deluge Systems

Automatic water delivery systems are commonplace throughout industry in commercial buildings and in various manufacturing settings. These fixed delivery systems include sprinklers, water sprays, and deluge systems. Several codes from the NFPA govern the design specifications for these fixed water delivery systems based on the application.

TYPES OF SPRINKLERS

There are various types of fixed automatic water delivery systems. According to the *Accident Prevention Manual,* the wet-pipe system is the most common type of sprinkler installed. It is referred to as *wet pipe* because piping in the system is filled with water that is under pressure. When one or more sprinkler heads actuate because of heat exposure, the water automatically sprays out of the open sprinkler heads (NSC 2009).

According to NFPA 13, pressure gauges shall be installed in each system riser and above and below each alarm check valve (NFPA 2010b). Relief valves of at least one-quarter inch are to be installed on every gridded system unless a pressure-absorbing air reservoir is present. The relief valve should be set to operate at 175 pounds per square inch (psi) or ten psi above the maximum system pressure. One caution about wet-pipe systems—because water is present at all times in the pipe, there is a constant concern with freezing in climates where freezing temperatures occur. NFPA 13 provides guidance on adding antifreezing agents to water in such services (NFPA 2010b). Wet-pipe systems can also supply auxiliary dry-pipe, preaction, or deluge systems if the water supply is adequate (NFPA 2010b, 7.1).

A *dry-pipe* system is one in which the piping contains pressurized air that holds the water in the system until a sprinkler opens. When the sprinkler opens, the air is released, and a *dry-pipe valve* that is holding the water back opens to allow water to flow into the risers. The dry-pipe valve is a critical device in these systems, and NFPA 13 lists several requirements to protect it, including specifications for the valve enclosures, supply, and protection against accumulated water above the clapper. Except under circumstances where the system is quick-acting, NFPA 13 recommends that each dry-pipe valve control no more than 750 gallons of water. Pressure gauges should be installed throughout the system, including on both sides of the dry-pipe valve (NFPA 2010b, 7.2).

Dry-pipe systems are often a better choice in areas where the piping is susceptible to freezing. The NSC notes that a good rule of thumb is to use dry-pipe systems when more than twenty sprinklers are involved. One caution regarding dry-pipe systems is that the action of depressuring the system and opening the valve to allow water flow results in a delay of actuation (NSC 2009). The NFPA recommends that quick-opening devices be installed on dry-pipe valves if they contain more than 500 gallons of water (NFPA 2010b, 7.2.4).

The pressure in the system can be supplied by either air or nitrogen, and must be maintained throughout the year. The pressure should be in accordance with the manufacturer's recommendations for the dry-pipe valve or twenty psi higher than the calculated trip pressure of the valve.

A *preaction system* is similar to a dry-pipe system; however, generally, it reacts faster. The preaction valve controls the water supply to the system's piping and is actuated either manually or by a fire detection system. An alarm generally is installed with such systems that annunciates when the valve opens and starts to allow water to flow. In a preaction system, water is released into the piping, but there is no discharge unless a sprinkler head actually has opened. One advantage of preaction systems is that sensors can send a signal to the control panel at the same time they send the signal to the valve, so that the fire may be extinguished before the sprinkler heads open, thus limiting water damage. This approach may be effective where valuable merchandise is stored and water damage (along with fire damage) is regarded as especially problematic. Some sources note that one disadvantage of preaction systems is that they are more complex and are considered less reliable than standard water-spray sprinkler systems. Often a combination dry-pipe and preaction system may be used in areas that are larger than one dry-pipe valve can accommodate. NFPA notes that when this combination is used, it should be designed such that the failure of the detection system shall not prevent the entire system from functioning as a conventional automatic dry-pipe system (NFPA 2010b, 7.4.2).

Deluge systems spray water into an entire area by allowing water to flow to sprinkler heads that are open at all times. The entire area receives water spray from all sprinklers. These systems are used to protect areas where the risk of a widespread fire is significant and it is believed that regular sprinklers would not act quickly enough over a large enough area. Some areas deluge systems may be chosen to protect include buildings that contain large quantities of flammable materials, explosives plants, and airplane hangars. The deluge valve can be actuated either manually or by thermal or flame detectors. Deluge systems may discharge 5000 gpm or more, and may require an on-site water supply in addition to municipal water systems.

FIGURE 4. Water spray system on a tank
(Photo courtesy of Roy Sanders)

Water spray systems protect specific hazards, such as tanks that contain flammable material, whereas sprinkler systems protect broader areas including buildings and structures (see Figure 4). Water spray systems are similar to deluge systems except that there are spray nozzles in the water spray systems (instead of the open sprinklers in the deluge systems.) NFPA 15, *Standard for Water Spray Fixed Systems for Fire Protection*, provides in-depth guidance on water spray systems (NFPA 2007a, ch. 7).

One additional type of water supply sprinkler is a *limited water supply system*. As the name indicates, this type of system is installed when facilities do not have access to a large supply of water. When this type of system is installed, great care must be taken to ensure that the fire-extinguishing needs of the facility are still being met adequately.

PURPOSE OF WATER SPRAY SYSTEMS

Most people know that water spray systems are used to extinguish fires and cool surrounding equipment, but spray systems are also used in some industries to prevent fires and explosions. The systems accomplish this through a variety of mechanisms. Water spray systems activate when they detect a release of material that may act as a fuel and act to dilute, disperse, and quench it. The activation of the spray may also induce air into the fuel and reduce the concentration below flammable limits. The water may also absorb some of the material if it is soluble, thereby lowering the amount of fuel available.

NFPA 15, *Standard for Water Spray Fixed Systems for Fire Protection*, provides limited information to help practitioners design a water spray system to prevent fires and explosions. Although the standard acknowledges that systems can be designed to accomplish this purpose, the guidance essentially states that application rates should be based on field experience or actual test data with the product (NFPA 2007a, 7.5). In *Guidelines for Fire Protection in Chemical, Petrochemical, and Hydrocarbon Processing Facilities*, the CCPS notes that the design model for water spray systems includes choosing scenarios, calculating the area of concern, determining dilution and/or absorption required, and determining water spray characteristics. Once these factors are known, the required flow rates can be determined. Practitioners who design spray systems should consider the limitations of the systems in preventing fires and explosions. Additional research is needed to determine under what circumstances these systems actually will prevent fires and explosions and how they should be designed to accomplish this task (CCPS 2003c, 133–136, 251–255).

WHERE TO INSTALL SPRINKLERS

Automatic sprinklers generally are installed for protection in buildings of combustible construction or occupancy. Such areas typically include laboratories and warehouses. NFPA 13 notes that sprinklers should be installed throughout the premises and discusses the spacing, location, and position of sprinklers (NFPA 2010b, 8.1). NFPA 30 provides specific sprinkler protection requirements for flammable liquid warehouses and processing facilities (NFPA 2008c, ch. 15 and 17).

SIZING OF SPRINKLERS

In years past, pipes in sprinkler systems were sized using the schedule system, which used tables and assumptions to calculate sizes. However, virtually all sprinkler, deluge, and water spray systems are now sized based on hydraulic calculations. This method involves a number of steps, and the calculations generally are facilitated using computer programs. In order to use the hydraulic calculation method to design sprinkler piping systems, several pieces of information must be known, including the minimum rate of water application, the area to be protected, information about the sprinkler system itself (such as coverage for each sprinkler and a discharge constant for each nozzle type), pipe sizes, friction losses, and required pressure at reference points. The hydraulic design procedure can be used to calculate pressure along branches, pressure at cross mains, and pressure in risers. Several reference books have application problems that can demonstrate this method (Lindeburg 1995, 38–39).

Maintenance and Inspection

The components of a fire protection system must be maintained and inspected periodically to ensure that the components will function properly when necessary. NFPA 25 provides guidance on inspecting, testing, and maintaining fire protection systems. It also addresses potential changes after initial design (NFPA 2008b). Building owners must perform an evaluation before changing the occupancy or processing, use, and storage of materials. The evaluation must consider items such as changing office space into storage, process or material changes, and revisions to the building (such as relocating walls).

Equipment must be inspected and tested periodically to ensure that it will be able to function when needed. Where possible, automatic supervision should be installed so that a monitoring system is in place to display the status and indicate abnormal conditions with equipment. It is critical to verify the condition of the equipment in the water supply system. The water temperature and heating system should be inspected daily during cold weather, or weekly if the system is supervised automatically. If the water level is part of a system that is not supervised automatically, it should be inspected monthly. The tank exterior should be inspected quarterly, and the interior should be inspected every three to five years. Temperature alarms should be tested quarterly, and high-temperature switches should

TABLE 1

Inspection, Testing, and Maintenance Frequencies for Selected Equipment

Equipment	NFPA Reference	Inspection	Testing	Maintenance
Water supply tank	25 Table 9.1	Internal: 3–5 yrs; External: quarterly	--	--
Piping	25 Table 11.1	Quarterly (for corrosion and damage)	Annually (water supply piping)	See individual components
Preaction/deluge valve	25 Chapter 12	Externally: monthly Internally: annually (every 5 years if the valve can be reset without removing faceplate.)	Annually (full flow)	Annually
Fire pump system	25 Table 8.1	Weekly	Weekly (no flow); Annually (flow)	Annually (motor)

(Adapted from NFPA 25, 2008)

be tested monthly during cold weather. Water-level alarms should be tested semiannually and level and pressure indicators every five years (see Table 1).

Manual Water-Based Protection Systems

Manual fire-fighting protection usually is provided by hydrants, monitor nozzles, fire trucks, and hose lines. Monitor nozzles can supply large amounts of cooling water to equipment exposed to fire. Unlike hydrants, monitors can be placed into service quickly and then operate unattended. Critical areas should be covered by at least two monitor nozzles. Remotely operated nozzles decrease the risk to personnel even further.

Fire truck pumps can supply as much as 1000 gpm. *Fire hydrants* generally are chosen from standard designs based on operating characteristics. Hydrants should have at least two 2.5-inch capped outlets. A 4- or 5-inch pumper connection can be used to supply water to a monitor or fire truck if necessary. Spacing for hydrants depends on a number of factors, including layout, hazards, and drainage. Due to limited hose lengths, hydrants should be located within 300 to 400 feet of the buildings they protect. Lindeburg notes that typical spacing is 300 feet for storage and distribution of petroleum oils and 400 feet for warehouses (Lindeburg 1995, 26). Spacing intervals between hydrants range from 250 to 400 feet. Hydrants should be installed close to paved roads for accessibility, and the pumper connections should face the street.

Chemical Extinguishing Systems

In addition to water distribution systems for extinguishing fire, special circumstances may call for fire-fighting foams and chemical and gaseous agents to be used. These systems are often installed to supplement, rather than replace, traditional sprinkler systems. The agents include foam, carbon dioxide, steam, hydrofluorocarbons, and inert gas systems (CCPS 1993, 502–506).

Foams

The CCPS discusses the different types of foams used in industry (CCPS 1993, 502–504). Several types can be effective extinguishing agents. They work partly by excluding oxygen from the fire by smothering and partly by absorbing the radiant heat flux from the flame to the burning liquid pool. Two types of foam that are widely used in industry are *synthetic* and *protein* foams. A popular type of synthetic foam is *aqueous film-forming foam* (AFFF), which works to extinguish a fire by forming a vapor seal on the surface of hydrocarbon liquid. Protein foams have a high burnback resistance and can be used to cover vertical surfaces as an insulating blanket to aid in confining fire. These foams are especially useful when foam must adhere to the hot side of a vessel. However, because higher concentrations of protein foams are required, larger quantities of material must be on hand, and they are more costly. Synthetic foams, like AFFF, have the advantage that they can be applied through fog or water spray nozzles as well as conventional foam nozzles. However, AFFF in particular has limited usefulness on petroleum fires since it cannot adhere to vertical surfaces.

Foam is rated based on the expansion rate when it is mixed with water and aerated. Low-expansion foams have an expansion ratio of 20 to 1. Medium-expansion foams can have expansion rates of up to 200 to 1, and high-expansion foams can have rates up to 1000 to 1. Medium- and high-expansion foams are often used to flood indoor areas and confined spaces. NFPA 16 provides guidance for the installation of foam-water sprays and sprinkler systems (NFPA 2007b, ch. 7).

NFPA 11 provides standards for foam systems. It notes, among other things, that the foam concentrates and equipment should be stored in an area where they are not exposed to the hazard they protect (NFPA 2010a, 4.3.2). Concentrate should be available in sufficient quantities to protect the largest single hazard or group of hazards. Different types of foam should not be mixed together and stored, but they can be applied to a fire either sequentially or simultaneously. Since foam works by being injected into water, the discharge pressure ratings of foam pumps must exceed the maximum water pressure available at the point of injection (NFPA 2010a, 4.3, 4.4, 4.6).

Piping in the hazard area should be constructed of steel or another alloy rated for the pressure and temperature involved. The NFPA specifically states that pipe carrying foam concentrate shall not be galvanized. All valves used for the water and foam solution should be of an indicator-type, such as a post indicator valve (PIV). The tank requiring the largest foam solution flow can serve as the basis for the capacity of the foam system.

Foam can be mixed with water and applied to fires, or it can be injected directly into tanks containing flammable material. For example, methods for protecting fixed-roof tanks include foam monitors, surface application with fixed discharge outlets, subsurface application, and semisubsurface injection methods. The NFPA provides design criteria for tanks containing hydrocarbons. Fixed-roof (cone) tanks containing hydrocarbon are a common type of vessel in which nozzles supply foam. When fixed foam-discharge outlets are used in this type of tank, good practice requires that minimum discharge times and application rates should be determined in the design. For example, for crude petroleum, the minimum application rate is 0.10 gpm (per ft^2), and the minimum discharge time for a type-II discharge outlet is 55 minutes. Similarly, subsurface foam injection systems can be used for liquid hydrocarbons in vertical fixed-roof atmospheric storage tanks. When these systems are used, the foam discharge outlets should be located at least one foot (0.3 m) above the highest water level to prevent destruction of the foam. Piping that is inside dikes can be buried to protect it against damage (NFPA 2010a).

Special requirements exist for medium- and high-expansion foams. They can be used on ordinary combustibles and flammable and combustible liquids and should be discharged to cover the hazard to a depth of at least two feet (0.6 meters) in two minutes (NFPA 2010a, 6.13.3). High-expansion foams should be used on liquefied natural gas vapor and fire control. Reserve supplies of foam must be on hand in order to put the system back into service after operation. Specifically, NFPA recommends maintaining enough high-expansion foam concentrate and water to permit continuous operation for 25 minutes or to generate four times the submergence volume (whichever is less) but at least enough for 15 minutes of full operation (NFPA 2010a, 6.12.9, 6.3).

Other Extinguishing Media

The CCPS discusses other common extinguishing media, including carbon dioxide and halon systems. Carbon dioxide extinguishes fires by excluding oxygen and smothering the fire. Carbon dioxide can be delivered by manual and fixed applicators and is often delivered through portable extinguishers. Carbon dioxide may be chosen to extinguish fires involving flammable liquids and electrical equipment. However, care must be exercised when using this extinguishing medium, as the flooding application needed for effectiveness is between 30 percent and 40 percent, and it becomes an asphyxiation hazard at these levels (CCPS 1993, 505–506). NFPA 12 can be referenced for good practices involving carbon dioxide systems (NFPA 2008a, Annex G).

Other common extinguishing media are halon and halon alternatives. Halon is used for both manual and fixed-system applications. Halon systems are often installed in control rooms and in sensitive areas such as switchgear and motor-control centers.

Halon becomes toxic to humans at higher concentrations, both because it is an asphyxiation hazard and because it emits toxic decomposition products. The production of halon gases has now been phased out and alternatives are being produced. For halon systems that are still functional, NFPA 12A provides guidance on designing and maintaining them (NFPA 2009b, ch. 5 and 6).

See Table 2 for a list of the major NFPA standards that offer guidance on fire-fighting equipment.

TABLE 2

Selected Listing of NFPA Standards Applicable to Fire-Fighting Equipment

NFPA Standard	Title
11	Standard for Low, Medium, and High-Expansion Foam
12	Carbon Dioxide Extinguishing Systems
13	Installation of Sprinkler Systems
14	Standard for the Installation of Standpipe and Hose Systems
15	Standard for Water Spray Fixed Systems for Fire Protection
16	Standard for the Installation of Foam-Water Sprinkler and Foam-Water Spray Systems
17	Standard for Dry Chemical Extinguishing Systems
17A	Standard for Wet Chemical Extinguishing Systems
20	Standard for the Installation of Stationary Pumps for Fire Protection
22	Standard for Water Tanks for Private Fire Protection
24	Standard for the Installation of Private Fire Service Mains and Their Appurtenances
25	Standard for the Inspection, Testing, and Maintenance of Water-Based Fire Protection Systems
30	Flammable and Combustible Liquids Code
58	Liquefied Petroleum Gas Code
69	Standard on Explosion Prevention Systems (addressing inerting and explosive venting)
86	Standard for Ovens and Furnaces (discusses steam used to extinguish fires in enclosures)
230	Standard for the Fire Protection of Storage
430	Liquid and Solid Oxidizers
484	Combustible Metals, Metal Powders, and Dusts
654	Fires and Dust Explosions from Combustible Particulate Solids
2001	Clean Agent Extinguishing Systems

Passive Protection

Similar to the philosophy applied to process equipment design, fire equipment can be active or passive. Previous sections discussed active equipment—equipment that requires an action (e.g., electrical, mechanical, or manual) in order to be effective. Such equipment includes deluge systems that actuate based on a signal from a flame detector. There is also equipment that, by its inherent nature, prevents incidents or mitigates consequences by simply existing—so-called *passive equipment*. Similar to passive process equipment, fire equipment of this nature is considered reliable because it does not need to have functioning components. However, this equipment should be inspected and maintained regularly in order to ensure that it does not deteriorate (CCPS 1993, 507).

Barriers

Barriers are put in place to minimize the consequences of fires by limiting their spread. Fire barriers typically are built from materials such as concrete or masonry. Such materials generally have a resistance rating that indicates how long the barrier can resist heat and flame. Ratings typically range from half an hour to four hours. Caution should be exercised, however, in considering ratings to be absolute. Ratings determined by simulating the heat from ordinary combustibles may not accurately represent the way the barrier will behave during fire fueled by a flammable liquid, and the actual resistance in process settings may be less than the specified value.

Two types of barriers include fire walls and fire partitions. Fire walls provide better protection than partitions. A standard fire wall has no openings, has a resistance rating of four hours or more, and is designed to remain standing even if the structure around it collapses. End walls should be provided if a fire can spread around fire walls. Openings in any barriers should be made with caution, and protections should be provided to maintain the barrier's integrity. If possible, penetrations should be avoided and conduit should be routed around fire barriers. Partitions provide less protection than fire walls (CCPS 1993, 507–509). The resistance rating is generally less for partitions, and they are not designed to continue standing independent of surrounding structures. Locations of barriers are based on several factors, including types of fire hazards and company and insurance requirements. In general, barriers should be considered between areas with high fire hazards and those that are occupied by personnel or that contain critical operations such as instrument rooms. CCPS provides additional examples of areas where barriers should be considered, such as between occupancy types (e.g., warehouse and production), and between separate unrelated processes (CCPS 1993, 508). Where barriers are used, they should be designed and constructed in accordance with local code requirements and engineering designs, such as those published by Underwriters Laboratory.

Fireproofing

Fireproofing is used in office buildings and warehouses, to provide insulation for steel structures, as steel can fail if it is exposed to an intense fire for a prolonged period of time. According to Lees, steel members should not reach a temperature greater than 1000°F. In a facility that contains flammable material, fireproofing serves to prevent the failure of equipment supports. Such a failure could result in additional releases of flammable material that could feed the fire. Fireproofing in the form of thermal insulation is also installed on equipment that contains flammable material to provide protection to the vessels in the event of a fire. This can be done in conjunction with, or instead of, water sprinkler systems. Care must be taken when choosing a method of protection, and experienced designers should be consulted.

Fireproofing comes in three basic types: *spray-on* or *coated systems*, *wrap systems*, and *box systems*. When using spray-on fireproofing material, the substrate surface must be prepared properly so that the material will adhere to it. The material should be clean and rust free before insulation is applied. Fireproofing must be sufficient to resist damage from normal plant activities and from water from fire hoses. Factors that need to be considered in the choice of fireproofing include the type and height of the structure and the degree of protection needed. Lees, quoting a 1967 study by Waldman, notes that the height above grade that fireproofing must be applied is variable, but it must be applied at least 35 feet above grade (Mannan 2005, 16.258). The CCPS adds that fireproofing must be applied not only above grade, but also above other objects where flammable liquids could pool. The CCPS further notes that consideration should be given to installing fireproofing within 15 to 25 feet of potential fires, including drainage paths for liquids (CCPS 1993, 511). Lees quotes Kayser as stating that fireproofing should keep the temperature of structural members below 1000°F for 1.5 hours (Mannan 2005, 16.258). In deciding the degree of fireproofing, consideration should also be given to existing fire protection systems, including water sprays. Care must be exercised in applying fireproofing to ensure it will adequately protect structures. In the report on the collapse of the World Trade Center Towers, the National Institute of Standards and Technology (NIST) determined that the Twin Towers withstood the impact of the aircraft during the attacks of 9/11 and would likely have remained standing were it not for dislodged fireproofing and subsequent multifloor fires (NIST 2005, xxxvii). In addition, NIST questioned the in-service inspections of the passive fire protection during the life of the building and found no technical basis for the properties of the sprayed fire-resistive material (NIST 2005, 198). As a result, NIST recommended, among other actions, developing criteria and standards for the in-service performance of fireproofing and ensuring that the as-installed condition of these materials is adequate (NIST 2005, 210).

Fireproofing should be inspected periodically for damage or deterioration. Insulation should be applied and maintained so that water cannot penetrate it and corrode the member underneath, because corrosion under insulation is difficult to detect. Insulation should also accommodate expansion and contraction of the underlying member.

Separation to Minimize Fire and Explosion Impacts and Allow Access

Using the principles of inherent safety, it is important to locate equipment in such a way as to minimize the impact of fires and explosions on surrounding vessels, piping, and structural supports (Wallace et al. 1994). One approach is to separate units and equipment within units so that the heat from a fire will not impact the surrounding area severely. Using this strategy can also minimize the impact of debris from explosions in a way that other fire-fighting strategies, such as sprinklers and fireproofing, cannot. Another consideration in the unit and equipment layout is to provide separation for access by emergency vehicles.

Separation distances can be determined in different ways. Combustible materials can be separated to decrease the intensity of a potential fire. Organizations can use separation charts developed by industry (including insurers) that provide guidelines for minimum distances between areas with hazardous materials and equipment. Another method is to apply a risk-ranking method and make decisions about spacing based on the results. A number of commercially available tools traditionally have been used to do this type of ranking. The developers generally caution, however, that the tools are meant only to provide a relative ranking of risks, and any separation distances yielded from the calculations should be considered in context.

A more sophisticated method of determining separation distances involves calculating the heat that may be received by objects and setting separation distances based on the results. While this method often yields smaller distances (and thus space can be used more efficiently), it requires a high level of expertise. Various computer programs can assist in this analysis (CCPS 1993, 512–513). This chapter will explore the traditional method of using spacing charts and general guidelines.

Insurance companies such as IRI (Industrial Risk Insurers, now a division of GE Insurance Solutions) have developed charts listing different types of equipment and proposed separation distances between them. The charts are revised periodically and are available for purchase. Previous versions of charts have been published publicly and are available in a number of places, such as *Guidelines for Engineering Design for Process Safety* (CCPS 1993, 70). These charts offer generally conservative estimates of safe distances and discuss spacing between units, equipment, and particular types of storage tanks. To effectively use such charts, one needs to judge whether a processing unit represents a moderate hazard, an intermediate hazard, or a high hazard. The minimum distance between units deemed to be of moderate hazard is given as 50 feet, whereas the minimum distance between high-hazard units is 200 feet. The minimum distance between control rooms and processes considered moderate, intermediate, and high hazard is given as 100, 200, and 300 feet, respectively. More information on designing control rooms is given in the section on building design.

Special consideration should be given to the spacing of storage tanks, since they often hold large inventories of hazardous material. Arranging storage tanks in groups allows for the common use of fire-fighting equipment. Although many sources advise practitioners to use common diking as well, caution must be exercised since a release from one tank directly affects other tanks in the same containment area. Storage tanks should be located remote from process areas to keep upsets in processes from endangering the inventories in storage. Lees quotes one source as indicating that the distance between storage and ignition sources for petroleum spirits and similar flammable liquids should not be less than 15 meters, or approximately 50 feet (Mannan 2005, 10.19). Regarding access for emergency vehicles, there should be access on all sides of a storage area, and access routes should be connected, so that if one route is affected by a fire, others will be available.

The NFPA also has tables on separation distances between storage tanks and public ways or important buildings on a site. NFPA 30 should be referenced directly for guidance on distances, as they vary depending on the stability of the liquid stored, the type and capacity of the tank, the protection provided, and the operating pressure of the tank (NFPA 2008c, 17.4.3). For example, a tank with a capacity of 100,000 gallons, stable emergency relief, and pressure less than 2.5 psig, should be separated from property lines by at least 80 feet or from important buildings by at least 25 feet, but these distances may be adjusted depending on the factors noted in the previous sentence.

The CCPS also provides guidance on spacing, which includes locating fired heaters away from units that could leak flammable materials. It also recommends not placing rotating equipment, such as pumps and compressors, in a single area and around vessels and vulnerable equipment because rotating equipment can often be the source of leaks (CCPS 1993, 71).

CHALLENGES WITH APPLYING A SEPARATION STRATEGY

While the benefits of maintaining separation distances have been explained, there are challenges in this approach of which practitioners should be aware. Land on which facilities are built can be limited by factors outside practitioners' control, which may make it difficult to adhere to ideal separation distances. Also, as plant expansions occur, distances between units and equipment within units decrease. Plant expansions are changes that must be managed with the same diligence that accompanies equipment changes in facilities. Practitioners must clearly define and maintain distances as much as possible during plant expansions and advocate for extra separation distances during design if future expansions are expected.

SEPARATION BETWEEN CHEMICAL FACILITIES AND SENSITIVE RECEPTORS

One sometimes-controversial aspect of layout considerations is where to site a chemical or manufacturing facility in relation to the community. Buffer spaces between facilities and sensitive community receptors tend to be governed by local rather than national codes. NFPA 30 provides some guidance regarding locating storage tanks close to public ways (NFPA 2008b, 17.6.1). Sensitive receptors include residential homes, community services such as hospitals and schools, and environmental receptors, such as waterways. The risk management plan mandated by the Clean Air Act Amendments of 1990, as required by the Environmental Protection Agency (EPA 1990), attempts to have facilities that handle or process highly hazardous materials determine the potential effects on the surrounding community and communicate those effects. Other environmental legislation, such as the Emergency Planning and Community Right-to-Know Act (EPCRA) (EPA 1986a) and the Superfund Amendments and Reauthorization Act of 1986 (SARA), Title III (EPA 1986b), previously fostered this concept.

A challenge with this aspect of applying separation distances is that it often does not lend itself to the hard science of conducting a risk assessment by determining the impact based on the properties and quantities of materials handled, but is often governed by the climate of the relationship between the facility and its neighbors. Also, sometimes a facility was actually in place before the residential community was. However, these realities do not relieve the company owners/operators from using science to determine, as best they can, the potential impact on the community from a release. Factors to consider include credible worst-case scenarios, population densities, and the ability to notify and control the movement of people in an emergency. Other aspects that companies need to address are their relationship to the community, their role in ensuring that community notification equipment and procedures are state of the art, and their partnerships with other industrial neighbors and emergency responders that could provide mutual aid in the event of a release. Since communities often grow up around chemical or manufacturing plants, causing community expansion toward the plant if there are not local codes prohibiting it, communication between the facility and its neighbors must be ongoing to be most effective.

Drainage

Drainage serves the purposes of containing flammable and toxic liquid spills and discharging runoff from water used to fight a fire. Drains should be designed to take liquids away from the area of the spill so they can be treated properly in a way that will not exacerbate a situation. Potential soil and groundwater contamination should be considered in the design of sewers. One of the primary aspects of designing such systems is to consider the volume of material that is likely to be released during a spill. Systems must be able to handle the largest accidental and anticipated release of material, as well as expected rainfall. Other factors that should be considered include type of surface, spacing of facilities, and possible interactions between chemicals that could lead to reactive chemical incidents. Special consideration must be given to providing drainage from storage areas. Flammable materials must not be allowed to collect at low points or flow to points in the facility where there are ignition sources.

Drainage systems must also be designed to be effective during a fire. The discharged water from a fire-fighting event must be controlled and contained; otherwise, the flammable materials may spread to other areas. The containment system can use a combination of curbing, grading, trenches, ditches, and diking. The system should safely handle burning liquid in areas that contain flammable liquids. Practitioners should consider whether drains can be left open or should be closed. Enclosed systems should contain traps or other means to prevent flames from entering the system. Systems should be designed to handle the combined flow of spray systems that will operate simultaneously, streams from hoses and monitors that may be used during a fire, the largest anticipated or accidental release of liquid, and rainwater. The containment system should be able to handle the flow of material for the expected duration of a fire unless authorities grant approval to handle the flow for a shorter period of time.

Inerting

Inerting prevents explosions by displacing oxygen and replacing it with inert gas. Nitrogen and carbon dioxide are common inerting agents. Inerting generally is used to pad the space above flammable liquid storage tanks. Inerting may also be used to sweep flammable materials out of equipment prior to maintenance.

Building Design

Of special concern to safety practitioners is the design and integrity of buildings in facilities. This is because personnel are particularly vulnerable in buildings when there is a fire, explosion, or toxic release. In some high-profile incidents, including Flixborough in Europe in the 1970s and Phillips in the United States in the late 1980s, the majority of the fatalities were personnel inside the control room. Temporary structures or trailers present particular problems, as illustrated by the explosion at the British Petroleum (BP) facility in Texas City in 2005 (CSB 2007). Unless buildings are located and/or designed in such a manner as to protect inhabitants, people inside can be impacted by the pressure wave and shrapnel if there is an explosion, toxic gases if there is a release, and the inability to escape if there is a fire.

Besides the requirement of protecting personnel inside buildings, another incentive to ensure that buildings are adequately protected is the ability to allow operators to continue to control the process in the early stages of an incident. By maintaining control, personnel and automatic control systems may decrease the chances that the incident will escalate into a catastrophic event. All on-site buildings can be of concern; however, of particular importance are control rooms. Large concentrations of employees may be gathered in these places, often located close to hazardous sources. Also, critical activities may need to be conducted from control rooms during emergencies, including shutting down processes. For these reasons, control rooms are given special attention in the following sections.

Location of Important Buildings and Service Functions

The location of important buildings, especially control rooms for process units, is critically important in keeping people safe. The desire from an operational standpoint to have the control room located close to the unit so that operations personnel have ready access to the equipment must be considered along with the desire to have people exposed to the smallest risk possible. Historical tables from IRI suggest the minimum distance from control rooms to process units with moderate, intermediate, and high hazards is 100, 200, and 300 feet, respectively (CCPS 1993, 70, referencing IRI 1991). Lees contains tables that recommend minimum distances from process units to control rooms in the range of 9 to 50 meters, or around 30 to 165 feet, depending on the hazard of the unit (Mannan 2005, 10.19). Distances may need to be increased based on the results of hazard studies.

Of equal importance to the location of the control room is the location of other important service functions. Control rooms often contain additional services, including laboratories, instrument shops, offices, meeting rooms, locker rooms, and break rooms. While it is convenient to have these functions located in the control room, placing them there means that more people may be exposed unnecessarily to hazards than if these service functions were placed in a location remote from the control room, and therefore farther from the process unit. Several sources advise practitioners to strongly consider the merits of securing control rooms so that the only functions contained in them are those that are essential for the control of the facility. Other functions can be moved farther from the process areas.

Also regarding service functions, control rooms should not function as emergency control centers, since operations will continue from them, and operational activities should not interfere with emergency response. Competition between process control during the critical phases of an incident and emergency control is undesirable.

Designing Buildings to Protect Against Explosions

One of the hazards for personnel in buildings during an event is the risk of an explosion that could impact the building. If a process unit contains substances that can explode, such as flammable or chemically reactive materials, this factor must be considered in the design and location of its building. The American Petroleum Institute's (API) RP 752 provides a framework for conducting building evaluations for permanent process-plant buildings (API 2009c). Although this organization primarily writes standards for the petrochemical industry, the guidelines are useful in the design of buildings in chemical and manufacturing facilities as well. Their suggested methodology in evaluating building design involves a three-step approach.

Building and Hazard Identification

The first step is to identify both the hazards and the buildings that are on site. The hazard-identification step includes an analysis to determine whether there is a potential for an explosion. All general sources that can cause explosions from vapor clouds, chemical decomposition, dust, boiling liquid–expanding vapors, or mechanical failures of vessels must be considered.

Once it is determined that an explosion can occur, the buildings must be evaluated. Building evaluation involves taking an inventory of buildings that exist or are planned for the site and then determining the occupancy load for each building. Once occupancy loads are determined, buildings can be compared to company standards to see whether they merit further quantitative evaluation or whether a simple checklist will be sufficient to determine risks (see "Checklists for Evaluating Buildings" later in this chapter for an example).

There are several aspects involved with determining the occupancy and establishing company standards for screening purposes. One aspect is the normal occupancy load for the building each week. *Load* in this case refers to the number of hours that people are expected to be inside the building. This is determined by calculating the collective number of hours that personnel spend in the building each week. Two other aspects of occupancy are the individual and peak occupancies. The *individual occupancy* is the percentage of time an individual typically spends in the building. *Peak occupancy* is the number of people who may be exposed at a given time. For example, meeting rooms, kitchens, and maintenance shops may have high numbers of personnel at peak times. Practitioners should realize that peak occupancy should be seriously considered when determining the actual risk posed to personnel. Determining the hours of occupancy only on an annualized (or some other normalized) basis will underestimate the actual risk to personnel in situations in which people gather on a temporary basis. Episodic events, such as regular meetings, represent times when large numbers of personnel may gather in buildings and be at risk, even if it is for a short period of time.

Since the concept of screening buildings is based on risks, it should be noted that the criteria used by companies varies. API 752 notes that building owners and operators may choose to establish a single risk criterion, expressed as individual risk, aggregate risk, or exceedance values. The current version of API 752 (2009c) does not list values for occupancy loads; however, the previous version of the RP noted that some organizations choose occupancy loads that range from 200 to 400 person-hours per week (API 2009c, 5). It should be noted, however, that any numbers are given as references only, and organizations must consider several factors in determining their own occupancy standards. For example, the occupancy load of 400 person-hours per week referenced above equates to ten people each working a full 40-hour work week in a building, and it may not be advisable for a company to accept this degree of risk.

Building Evaluation

Once it is determined that a hazard exists, and a list of occupied buildings has been developed, the buildings must be evaluated. Three assessment methods are discussed in API 752: a *consequence-based approach*, a *risk-based approach*, and *spacing tables* (API 2009c). The three methods are discussed briefly below.

CONSEQUENCE-BASED ANALYSIS

The *consequence-based approach* accounts for the impact of explosions, fires, and toxic releases. In this method, the practitioner considers maximum credible events associated with each of these three hazards and then determines what the consequences could be on the occupants of each building or the building itself. The vulnerability of the building is assessed, based on its blast load design, and the intensity and duration of fires, and flammable or toxic releases (API 2009c). A building that is designed to withstand the overpressure from an explosion is less vulnerable than one that is not; its occupant vulnerability and the potential building damage is also reduced.

In this method, release scenarios are chosen (generally from a process hazard-analysis-type of study), considering passive and active mitigation. Then, based on the quantity of material released and other factors related to the characterization of the facility, the potential overpressure that could be generated is calculated. A number of methods exist to perform these calculations, and opinions vary regarding which method is best, so each should be considered on its merits. Some widely used methods include the TNO multienergy, Baker-Strehlow-Tang, and the congested assessment method. Advanced blast simulation through computational fluid dynamics is also used, though less frequently (API 2009c, 14). These methods are complex and beyond the scope of this chapter; however, more detailed information can be found in these CCPS publications: *Guidelines for Evaluating the Characteristics of Vapor Cloud Explosions, Flash Fires, and BLEVEs* (1994) and *Guidelines for Evaluating Process Plant Buildings for External Explosions and Fires* (1996).

Buildings must be designed to withstand an overpressure in excess of that calculated so the occupants will be protected in case of an explosion. If the study is evaluating existing buildings, the calculated overpressure should be compared to the design rating of the building. Charts are used to predict potential building damage at various blast loads. If the charts are not appropriate (due to the building's structure differing from the available charts, for example), then a detailed structural analysis should be conducted on the building.

The practitioner can then use the damage assessment to estimate the potential vulnerability of the building occupants. There are tables that correlate occupant vulnerability to potential building damage, such as in the *Guidelines for Evaluating Process Plant Buildings for External Explosions and Fires* (CCPS 1996). The practitioner should always understand the basis for such tables to ensure their applicability. If the owner or operator determines that the building is not adequate to withstand potential overpressures that could be generated, then mitigation measures must be taken to ensure the safety of occupants.

It is also important to make a distinction between explosion-resistant and explosion-proof. *Explosion-resistant* means that a building is expected to withstand the effects of an explosion without collapsing and should therefore be able to protect personnel inside, although the building may suffer structural damage and need extensive repair prior to being placed back into service. In contrast, an *explosion-proof* building is one that is not expected to be damaged significantly in an explosion. Different levels of reinforcement affect the degree to which a building will be functional after an explosion. Generally, explosion-proof construction is significantly more expensive than explosion-resistant construction, which often makes it a less attractive alternative (CCPS 1993, 86).

SPACING-TABLES APPROACH

Building distances from hazards can be compared to spacing standards. In the *spacing-tables approach*, the practitioner attempts to apply distancing strategies and locate buildings away from hazards so that, if there are explosions, fires, or releases, the buildings will not be vulnerable. One caution the practitioner must consider is the basis of the tables. If the spacing is based on the effects of a fire, the tables will not be adequate tools to use in the event of explosions or toxic releases (API 2009c, 6). In this case, the building owners or operators may need to develop site-specific spacing distances based on the credible events that could occur at their site. The effects of explosions on buildings decrease as the distance from the process increases, so spacing guidelines can be used to determine whether the building is remote enough from the process.

RISK-BASED APPROACH

A third method, along with comparison to established standards and consequence assessment, is the *risk-based approach.* This method generally requires more time and effort than the methods previously mentioned. It is similar to consequence analysis, except that the frequency of potential explosions, toxic releases, or fires, is considered along with their consequences. Information on explosion frequencies may be limited, but a frequency for the unit being studied should be used if available. The CCPS provides a table of generic frequencies of major explosions for various types of petrochemical units, including a value of 4.3×10^{-4} as the frequency of explosions per year of operation as a value for all units (CCPS 1996, 23). (Stated another way, this represents the probability of one explosion in about 2300 years of operation.) Once the frequency is found, charts showing the *probability of fatality* are used to determine the risk to occupants based on the anticipated peak overpressure. An aggregate risk to all occupants is then determined and compared to the company's accepted criteria to determine whether additional evaluation is necessary.

COMPARISON TO INDUSTRY STANDARDS

Buildings can be compared to industry standards, such as the spacing standards discussed earlier in this section. The effects of explosions on buildings decrease as the distance from the process increases, so spacing guidelines can be used to determine whether the building is remote enough from the process to likely escape the major effects of an explosion.

STANDARDS FOR BUILDING DESIGN

There are also standards for building design. Lees's *Loss Prevention* series has used several sources to collect good practices for the design of control rooms, which are generally the most vulnerable buildings on site due to proximity to the unit, occupancy, and role in controlling the process (Mannan 2005, 10.29–30). As discussed previously, control rooms in hazardous areas should contain only necessary process-control functions, which limits occupancy in the event of an explosion. Control rooms generally should be located only one floor above the ground. The roof of a control room should not hold heavy machinery. There should be no tall structures (such as tall distillation columns) around the building that could fall on the control room during an explosion (Mannan 2005, 10.30). Its windows should be reinforced—or it could be windowless—to eliminate the possibility of shattering glass affecting personnel inside. Subsequent to an explosion, broken windows and perforations in buildings can serve as points of entry for toxic materials. However, the desire to minimize the effects of broken windows must be balanced against the operational advantages of being able to view the process directly from inside the control room, which makes reinforced glass a possible alternative. The control building should be constructed of ductile materials, such as steel and reinforced concrete, rather than brittle materials that collapse easily during an explosion, such as brick and masonry.

If the building is in a vulnerable location in proximity to the process, it should be reinforced to withstand an overpressure that the walls and ceiling are likely to experience during an explosion. This is a complex and evolving subject, and practitioners need to be aware of the newest codes and standards related to designing buildings to withstand explosions. Some guidance is derived from conducting an evaluation to determine the likely overpressure, and other guidelines present a minimum overpressure loading that the building should be designed to withstand. (These references are provided to allow comparison to historical standards. See the section on "Consequence-Based Analysis" for additional information on how to determine overpressure.)

Some sources provide a combination distance and overpressure loading, indicating that buildings are best protected by both placement and design. Other guidance, not accounting for distance from the process, tends to be more conservative in the design requirements. Various guidelines list a pressure that the building should be able to withstand for a certain period of time, typically between 20 and 100 milliseconds (ms). According to the guidance available, buildings should be designed to withstand pressures ranging from three to ten psi at a distance of 100 feet. For high-hazard areas, buildings may be designed to withstand ten to fifteen psi for a duration of 30 to 100 ms. Roofs generally can be designed to withstand less overpressure than walls, but they should still be designed to withstand between three and ten psi in high-hazard areas.

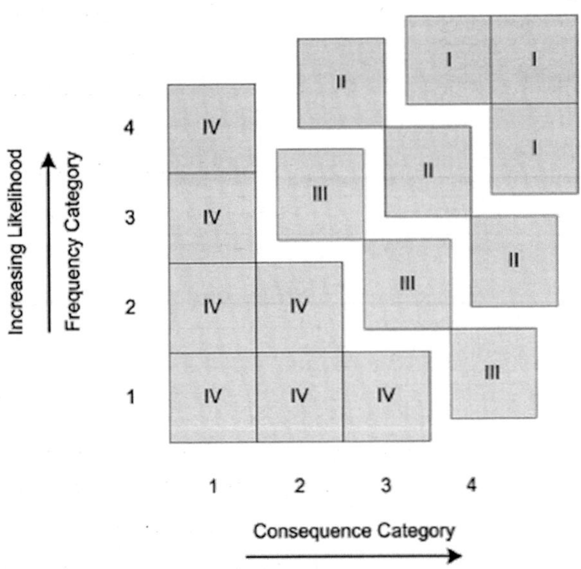

Example Risk Ranking Categories

Number	Category	Rank
I	Intolerable	Should be mitigated with engineering and/or administrative controls to a risk ranking of III or less within a specified time period, such as six months.
II	Undesirable	Should be mitigated with engineering and/or administrative controls to a risk ranking of III or less within a specified time period, such as 12 months.
III	Tolerable with controls	Should be verified that procedures or controls are in place.
IV	Tolerable as is	No mitigation required.

FIGURE 5. Example of a 4-by-4 matrix (*Source:* CCPS 1996)

Additional Evaluation for Buildings at Risk

Buildings that are shown to be of concern from earlier analyses should undergo a risk assessment, during which specific release events are identified and the overall potential risk to building occupants is determined. A ranking of the potential risks, based on frequency and severity, should be applied. The Center for Chemical Process Safety proposes that a four-by-four risk matrix plotting the consequence versus the frequency can be a useful tool to assist in qualitative risks decisions (CCPS 1996, 88) (see Figure 5). Scenarios that are of higher consequence and higher frequency will be ranked as a higher risk on the matrix. The risk for a particular building is then compared to a company's risk-acceptance criteria to determine whether mitigation measures should be applied or the building is within acceptable limits. CCPS cautions that, for events having major catastrophic potential, more quantitative methods may be appropriate.

The methods of conducting risk assessments of this type are complex, and the general outline is discussed here for exemplary purposes only. Detailed guidance can be found in CCPS, *Guidelines for Evaluating the Characteristics of Vapor Cloud Explosions, Flash Fires, and BLEVEs* (1994), *Guidelines for Evaluating Process Plant Buildings for External Explosions and Fires* (1996), and others. Such methods should be applied by someone knowledgeable in the field. Also, the acceptance criteria chosen by a company are important variables in determining whether further mitigation should be applied to buildings. Several issues must be considered when companies develop such criteria, including the hazard, factors of importance to those generating and regulating the risks, and public attitudes. In general, the field of quantitative risk assessment is more advanced in the nuclear field than in the chemical and petrochemical fields.

Risk-Reduction Measures for Buildings

If the series of building evaluations shows that a building is at risk, a number of options exist for reducing the risk, including taking additional measures to prevent incidents, altering the design, and changing the occupancy loading. Options for preventing explosions include applying inherently safer principles, such as reducing inventories of hazardous materials and changing conditions in the process to reduce the potential for runaway chemical reactions or releases due to corrosion. Additional engineering controls can be added, such as redundant instrumentation. Also, procedural safeguards can be enhanced. Inspection frequencies for piping and equipment can be increased. Stringent permit systems for line opening, hot work, and maintenance can be developed, implemented, and enforced.

A number of mitigation actions can be considered for buildings that are at risk. As mentioned previously, windows can be reinforced or eliminated (although the risk-reduction potential of eliminating windows must be balanced against the operational advantage of being able to see the unit from the control room.) Also, doorways can be strengthened. Modifications can be made to buildings to reinforce them structurally, or a new building with more robust supports and a sufficient distance from the hazard can be constructed.

A final remedy to buildings at risk may be to study the occupancy and reduce the hours personnel work inside the building. Companies should consider opportunities to relocate personnel who are not critical to the function of the unit to another location. Several good practices for building design and spacing were discussed above.

Building Design to Protect Against Fires

Fires pose a hazard to buildings and their occupants. Fires can result in additional hazards, such as explosions and toxic releases—which are covered elsewhere in the chapter—but this section presents good practices only meant to protect against the direct hazards of a fire. Types of process fires include pool fires, jet fires, flash fires, and fireballs (API 2009c, 18).

The degree of risk to which building occupants are exposed depends on a number of factors, including the materials the building is made of, the occupants' distance from likely fire hazards, and the effectiveness of fire suppression systems. A key aspect of preparing occupants for a fire is to ensure that emergency plans have appropriate measures for occupants to take regarding safe shutdown of the process, escape, and sheltering-in-place, as well as instructions to anyone who has responsibility for fighting incipient fires inside buildings. Escape routes should be clearly noted in emergency response plans, and personnel should be trained in advance on where and how to evacuate properly and where to assemble once they are out of the building.

The same practices that apply to reducing the potential for explosive incidents that were discussed above apply to reducing the potential for fires as well. Mitigation measures to protect occupants include locating buildings away from areas with fire hazards. Spacing considerations were discussed in the "Fire Protection and Fire Mitigation Systems" section. In addition, drainage outside of the building should direct spills of flammable and combustible materials away from the building. If buildings are in proximity to hazardous areas, they should be constructed with fire-resistant exteriors. Fire and smoke suppression systems should be installed, including water sprays inside the building and monitors outside the building. The ventilation system for the building should stop entry of outside air when products of combustion are detected.

Building Design to Protect against Toxic Releases

Toxic materials affect personnel inside buildings in different ways than flammable and explosive materials do. They impact personnel largely through inhalation, and even small amounts of some materials can affect people's ability to make critical judgments during an incident. Assessment of the potential risks to building occupants involves an analysis process to identify whether any toxic materials of concern are handled on site. If it is determined that a toxic material could enter a building (or buildings), the company must examine its mitigation and emergency response systems to determine whether they are adequate.

If it is deemed necessary to take remedial actions to protect occupants, the risk-reduction measures described above to prevent explosions will also be helpful in preventing toxic release incidents. If control rooms are susceptible to entry by toxic materials, they must be gas tight. Windows (if they are present) should be nonopening. Door and window frames should be designed to minimize gas entry. There should be no more than two entrances/exits, and they should contain air locks. Gas detectors should be used to warn of gas releases (Mannan 2005, 10.30–10.31). Emergency response plans should include instructions on sheltering-in-place and evacuating. Appropriate PPE should be provided. Self-contained breathing apparatuses (SCBAs) should be considered for personnel who normally will occupy the building. The building functions should be examined to determine whether the occupancy can be reduced. Pressurized ventilation systems should be seriously considered, and the building must be reviewed thoroughly to determine whether there are areas of vulnerability that must be sealed.

Consideration should be given to the location of buildings that may need to be used as emergency control centers. People who are part of incident command should not have to pass through a toxic cloud to access the facility (Mannan 2005, 10.31).

Ventilation in Process Buildings

Of special consideration in industrial or office buildings that may be exposed to toxic releases and smoke is the ventilation system. Ventilation systems must have detectors that indicate whether a contaminant has infiltrated the system, and the detectors should shut down the intake system so that additional contaminated air will not continue to be drawn into the building. These detectors should also activate an alarm in the control room to let occupants know of the change in atmosphere. Intake stacks should be elevated so that contaminants that are heavier than air will not be drawn into them, and stacks should have sensing devices that measure contaminant levels and trip or sound alarms when the level is too high (CCPS 1993, 87–88).

The entire heating, ventilation, and air conditioning (HVAC) system should be designed of material that will not corrode. The system (including the intake) should be inspected and maintained frequently so that the integrity of the entire system will not be compromised.

The occupants should be provided with a supply of air for a period of time. If the ventilation system needs to be shut off, which will cause the building to lose pressurization, this is an important protection against ingress of contaminants. As noted previously, SCBAs should be available for occupants. Alternatively, it may be possible to supply air from a clean source remote from the control building. If possible, positive pressure in the building should be maintained between 0.5 and 1.0 inches of water (gauge), which requires two to fifteen air changes per hour depending on building size and integrity (Mannan 2005, 10.31).

Trenches directly under or close to the control room should be tightly sealed or avoided if possible. Instrument sample lines for toxic materials should not be routed into the control room, as their leakage could expose occupants. The control room should have an indication of the wind direction and a water spray inside the building that can be activated automatically or manually. Such a system can provide additional protection against toxic ingress. A communication system in addition to the phone system should be installed in the control room to allow communication with a remote command center during an emergency (Mannan 2005, 10.31).

Building Design to Allow Egress and Functioning during an Emergency

A critical aspect of building design is ensuring that personnel will be able to escape quickly if necessary. The design of buildings is governed by a number of state, local, and insurance codes. In general, these codes are influenced to a great extent by NFPA publications such as NFPA 1, *Uniform Fire Code* (NFPA 2009a), NFPA 220, *Standard on Types of Building Construction* (2009d), and NFPA 101, *Life Safety Code* (NFPA 2009c), which governs building construction, means of egress, and fire protection. A few general requirements are noted below, and the NFPA codes and the *Fire Protection Handbook* (Cote 2008) should be referenced directly for more information.

Buildings should have at least two clearly illuminated escape routes, even during a power failure. Emergency lighting should be provided and maintained to ensure functionality. Exits should be free from obstacles, and designers must consider that they need to be accessible to personnel who may be partially incapacitated or wearing bulky breathing equipment. Exits can include doors, walkways, stairs, ramps, fire escapes, and ladders. There must be an effective means to notify occupants that an emergency has occurred and tell them the proper response to take. This can be accomplished by a combination of communication strategies (such as a public announcement system or alarm warning system) and training in advance of an incident. Locking or fastening devices on doors should not be permitted, as they could hinder the free escape of personnel inside the building. Fire alarms should be installed and maintained to function properly during an emergency. Initial construction and significant modifications must be reviewed by the AHJ to ensure that the intent of the codes is met. Equipment, devices, and systems intended to provide safety to occupants should be continually maintained to ensure their integrity during an emergency.

Exit doors and adjacent areas must be free of mirrors, which could confuse the direction of egress. Doors should be of the side-hinge or pivotal type and should swing out (in the direction of egress). Exits must discharge at a public way or at an exterior exit discharge. In order to facilitate emergency exiting, the means to communicate the direction of egress should be clearly understandable, noncontradictory, consistent with societal expectations, and in languages and symbols that can be clearly understood by the population occupying the building.

Portable Buildings

Portable buildings are convenient for housing personnel in a manufacturing facility. However, as the incident at the BP facility in Texas City in 2005 illustrated, these structures can present significant risks to occupants (CSB 2007). API recommended practice (RP) 753 provides relevant guidance. It notes that personnel should be located as far from the process areas as possible. Three questions that frame the decision on locating portable buildings near the process are:

1. Do personnel need to be located near a covered process area?
2. Do personnel need to occupy a portable building?
3. Can the building be placed further away from the covered process area? (API 2007, 3)

For explosion hazards, the RP provides a methodology for portable building placement based on the congested volume of the process and the design of the structure. The area around a process is separated into three zones, and portable buildings can be placed only in a zone that is a safe distance from the process. Figures provide appropriate spacing. For example, if the congested volume of the process is 300,000 cubic feet, a light wood trailer should be placed no closer than 1273 feet from the edge of the unit (API 2007, 15). RP 753 recommends that a building be designed as a shelter-in-place or that facility owners have a response plan directing occupants to such an area if a toxic release could result in an ERPG-3 level in the area (API 2007, 9).

Checklists for Evaluating Buildings

Even if buildings in process areas are deemed to be of low occupancy or are remote enough from the process to be less at risk, it is a good idea to complete a checklist to determine whether there are additional opportunities for risk reduction. While it is difficult to design a checklist for all situations, the following is a list of typical questions that should be asked:

1. Is the building located upwind of the hazard?
2. Is the building included in an emergency response plan for fire and toxic release? Are the occupants trained in emergency response procedures? Are evacuation instructions posted?
3. Are large pieces of office equipment or stacks of materials within the building adequately secured?
4. Are the lighting fixtures, ceilings, or wall-mounted equipment well supported? Are process controls mounted on interior walls?
5. Is there heavy material stored on the ground floor only?

6. Have all the exterior windows been assessed for potential injury to occupants?
7. Are there doors on the sides of the building opposite from an expected explosion or fire source?
8. Is there exterior and interior fire suppression equipment available to the building?
9. Is there a detection system within the building or in the fresh air intake to detect hydrocarbons, smoke, or toxic materials?
10. Is the air intake properly located?
11. Can the ventilation system prevent air ingress or air movement within the building? Are there hydrocarbon or toxic detectors that shut down the air intake? Does the building have a pressurization system?
12. Are there wind socks visible from all sides of the building?
13. Is there a building or facility alarm or communication system to warn building occupants of an emergency?
14. Is there sufficient bottled fresh air or fresh supplied air for the occupancy load?
15. Are all sewers connected to the building properly sealed to prevent ingress of vapors?

MAINTENANCE

Along with proper design and operation of a chemical or manufacturing facility, a third critical component is maintenance. Appropriate maintenance keeps equipment functioning properly and corrects malfunctioning equipment. This section discusses the different types of maintenance and best practices associated with different maintenance activities. Maintenance activities may be performed on specific pieces of equipment or parts or a process while the rest of the process is operational, or it may be performed on several pieces of equipment simultaneously, such as in the case of an entire unit shutdown or turnaround. Large-scale turnarounds are a tremendous undertaking in a large manufacturing operation, generally requiring the addition of many temporary workers to accomplish all the tasks. The length of time between turnarounds varies from process to process, but it can run anywhere from every few months to three to five years. Once a schedule for unit shutdowns and maintenance is established, it should be adhered to. Even with production pressures to continue operating, a general shutdown, which allows maintenance to be performed on a broad scale throughout the unit, should not be compromised or delayed without serious consideration of the potential consequences. Publications from a number of organizations were used in developing this section, including CCPS, API, and OSHA.

Types of Maintenance

This section explores the different types of maintenance, including planned and unplanned. Although some of the examples cited are of equipment in processing plants, all machines must be maintained at some point, so the concepts are broadly applicable throughout a variety of facilities. A section is also devoted to reliability-centered maintenance (CCPS 1995, 203).

Planned Maintenance

It is preferable to perform maintenance in advance of a breakdown so that problems can be prevented. This is accomplished by developing a list of equipment to maintain and specifying the appropriate activities to keep the equipment from breaking down (CCPS 1995, 205). Also, the frequency of such activities should be thoughtfully established. When maintenance is planned according to a schedule, then parts, materials, and trained personnel can be available. Conducting maintenance according to a routine plan can also ensure that equipment is emptied properly, purged, and isolated. In order for planned maintenance to be successful, management must be committed to the idea that shutting down a piece of equipment that is currently operating well is appropriate; however, planned maintenance can reduce equipment breakdowns and downtime and prove economically justified. Only equipment that is not critical to operations and safety, and thus can wait to be fixed if it breaks, does not need to be included in a planned maintenance program (CCPS 1995, 205–207).

Preventive Maintenance

Preventive maintenance involves the process of establishing fixed schedules for routine inspection, replacement, and service of equipment. In broad terms, it encompasses all planned maintenance activities from replacing seal oil in pumps to verifying the functionality of instrumentation systems to calibrating instruments and emptying, cleaning, and inspecting tanks. Preventive maintenance involves cleaning and servicing equipment while it is operating and dismantling and checking or inspecting equipment while it is shut down.

In *Guidelines for Safe Process Operations and Maintenance*, the CCPS notes that preventive maintenance should begin as soon as possible, even during the design phase of a project (CCPS 1995, 207). Equipment selected should be dependable and easy to maintain. For example, locating heat exchangers at the perimeter of a facility allows maintenance personnel to extract bundles without having to lift them over other equipment. Necessary activities and schedules should be established based on plant experience, codes and industry standards, and manufacturers' recommendations. First- and second-line maintenance and operations supervisors must be proactive in recognizing the need to establish preventive maintenance programs or in altering the activities or schedules of existing programs. The CCPS notes that they are also the ones who should recommend whether a piece of equipment should be placed into a predictive maintenance program, discussed in the next section (CCPS 1995, 207).

Predictive Maintenance

Predictive maintenance is similar in concept to preventive maintenance. The CCPS notes that while preventive maintenance operates according to a predetermined schedule, predictive maintenance takes into account real-time conditional variables. Parameters such as temperature, vibration, flow rates, and motor current are analyzed to determine whether service requirements have changed and should be adjusted (CCPS 1995, 207).

Critical equipment should be included in a predictive maintenance program. This type of program lends itself especially well to rotating equipment, pumps, and compressors, because of the types of information that can be collected on an ongoing basis (CCPS 1995, 207). Also, schedules for predictive maintenance on electronic equipment can be based on statistical failure information.

Unplanned Maintenance

Although all maintenance, even breakdown maintenance, involves some degree of planning, the term *unplanned maintenance* refers to activities that take place after a failure has occurred. If the failure involves equipment that is not critical to safety or operations, the process may not need be to be shut down, and maintenance may be performed during normal operations. However, if the equipment is critical to safety or operations, maintenance activities often must take place in an expeditious manner to keep the process running. Because of these pressures, unplanned maintenance of critical equipment carries additional risks to personnel and the process. Qualified personnel, tools, and the parts necessary to conduct unplanned maintenance activities may not be readily available (CCPS 1995, 212). An incident at a refinery in Martinez, California, killed four people when personnel cut into a line containing naphthalene before it was properly emptied. The maintenance was being performed while the unit was operating, and the hot surfaces of surrounding equipment may have acted as ignition sources (CSB 2001).

Even when unplanned maintenance must be performed on critical equipment, it is important that enough preparation be made so that the job can be performed safely. A good practice is to bring together a multidisciplinary team representing maintenance and operations to perform a hazard analysis in order to determine potential problems, as well as steps to ensure that any problems encountered can be addressed. Also, consideration should be given to problems with equipment preparation (e.g., draining and purging) so that maintenance personnel are not put at additional risks. In the incident mentioned in the previous paragraph, personnel had trouble draining equipment due to lines being plugged with corrosion products. Some good practices for the different activities involved with preparing for maintenance are discussed later in this section.

Reliability-Centered Maintenance (RCM)

One approach that is widely used in chemical and petrochemical facilities is *reliability-centered maintenance*, or RCM. As the name suggests, RCM is a method that is largely based on the reliability of equipment, often determined through an analysis process similar to a failure modes and effects analysis (FMEA). RCM begins by establishing the primary and secondary functions of equipment. Ways in which the equipment can fail to function are then determined. The effects of failures are evaluated, including so-called "hidden consequences," such as failures of relief devices that may go unannounced but may impede their functioning at critical times later. Finally, maintenance tasks that can eliminate or reduce failures and are considered feasible and effective are identified for each failure mode. If a specific preventive maintenance task is not identified for a failure mode, certain default actions are taken, which may include redesign, inspection, or no action if the risk is deemed to be low. RCM is a formal process, and a great deal of literature exists to assist in its implementation.

Developing Critical Equipment and Instrument Lists

The first step in an effective maintenance plan is to identify what equipment and instrumentation must be included in the mechanical integrity program (CCPS 1995, 203). This list includes equipment such as pressure vessels, storage tanks, piping, pressure-relief systems, pumps, alarms and interlocks, fire protection, and emergency shutdown devices. A key step is to determine which specific equipment should be included in the list of *critical* equipment and instrumentation—equipment that is essential to the safety, operation, and environmental functioning of the unit. A facility must establish a list of criteria for critical equipment and revisit it often to ensure that it reflects changes in equipment and operational modes.

The critical equipment list should include all equipment (including instrumentation) necessary for the continued safe operation of the plant, but caution should be exercised so that the list remains meaningful. This list can then be used to develop a preventive and predictive maintenance inventory so the service schedule for that equipment can be developed more accurately. Having a critical equipment and instrument list also allows supervisors to assign reasonable priorities when writing work orders.

Several considerations go into developing a list of critical equipment. Use of a modified hazard-analysis technique, augmented by discussions of operational reliability and criticality for each piece of equipment and instrument may be appropriate for determining which equipment requires greater scrutiny. When developing a list of critical instruments, the severity of the consequences if the instrument system fails should be a major consideration. Safety alarms and interlocks, fire protection, and equipment whose failure would result in an automatic and sudden shutdown of the process are typical candidates for the list. Instruments that protect against unplanned releases of flammable or toxic material are typically considered critical, especially in cases where there is limited redundancy and both the process control and safety functions rely on the same equipment (e.g., when level control, alarm, and shutdown are all on the same circuit and rely on the same sensor). Along with the functioning of the equipment, other factors to consider include availability of spare parts (e.g., presence of redundant pumps) and whether failures are likely to be announced, especially in the case of instrumentation and shutdown systems. Such devices must be readily availabile for the plant to continue to function safely.

Causes of Eventual Failures in Piping and Vessels

Corrosion and erosion that are allowed to progress in piping and vessels can result in failures in equipment and a release of material (CCPS 1995, 217–219). Vessels and piping designed to be used in corrosive services generally have additional thickness, referred to as a *corrosion allowance*. Monitoring strategies such as ultrasonic thickness (UT) testing allows maintenance personnel to determine whether areas of piping are thinning at an accelerated rate.

Corrosion can have the effect of thinning vessel and piping walls and also depositing products of corrosion that can plug equipment downstream. Corrosive systems, such as those containing sulfides and chlorides, must be monitored. Attention must be paid to temporary piping as well, since it may not be designed to withstand corrosion. Of particular concern to maintenance technicians is corrosion under insulation, in part because it is very difficult to detect visually. Such corrosion can remain hidden but eventually result in loss of containment. Intruding water can bring in corrosive elements and ultimately result in stress corrosion cracking. Representative sections of insulation should be stripped off periodically so that the piping can be inspected. Doing this is especially important if the temperature of carbon steel piping is between approximately 25°F and 250°F (or if austenitic stainless steel piping is between 150°F and 400°F), because at these temperatures water will not be driven off quickly. Areas of special concern include those where insulation is penetrated (such as at deadlegs) or damaged and at low points in the system.

Another type of corrosion, referred to as pitting corrosion, occurs when cavities are produced in the walls of piping and equipment. *Pitting* is a localized form of corrosion and is often more difficult to detect than uniform corrosion. It can be caused by localized damage to a protective coating or imperfections in the metal structure.

Erosion is another problem that can cause failures in equipment. Erosion can occur when liquid at high velocity wears down the walls of piping at injection points and elbows. Water hammer can occur when fluid flows through sharp turns. Particulates in fluid can also erode piping walls over time. Other potential causes of failure include wear (e.g., in pumps and valves) and intermittent operation. Intermittent operation can cause additional stress on equipment (including instrumentation) because the equipment is always in a state of flux.

Testing and Inspection

A common theme in maintenance programs for all types of equipment is to collect data—by testing or inspection—that may indicate a problem in advance. When discussing systems that act to maintain safety or operations, such as instrumentation loops or emergency shutdown systems, failures generally are detected by testing the system's functionality (CCPS 1995, 221–223), whereas with piping systems and vessels in which the failure generally is a breach of a vessel wall, or a pump in which a failure may be a blown seal, problems are identified by conducting inspections to determine the integrity of equipment. Piping inspection can be quite challenging and is not dealt with in this section.

Testing of Interlocks

Safety interlocks and process control loops are critical to the safe operation of a unit. It is important that these systems be reliable and available when needed. Because of the nature of some interlocks, they may not be activated until an emergency occurs. It is important that instrument failures be detected. Some instruments have a self-checking capability. But for many interlocks, testing for functionality, or *proof-testing*, is important. Instrument loops contain several parts, including sensors, transmitters, transducers, and actuators, and it is important that all of the parts work properly. Instrument loops are often tested as entire circuits. Frequency of proof-testing depends on the instrument and the service, but a typical schedule would be every six to twelve months. Proof-testing is accomplished according to certain procedures (CCPS 1995, 221–223). Two methods are an *actual test* and a *simulated test*. In the actual test, the process is brought to the trip point, and the functionality of the instrument circuit is observed. As the name suggests, a simulated test only simulates these conditions. A comprehensive functionality test of an interlock system involves inspecting the system from sensor to actuator to ensure it is not deteriorated at any point. This is more complex than simply ensuring that the interlock works.

Critical instruments are those that require greater scrutiny because their failure could result in serious safety consequences. These instruments should be maintained and calibrated according to an authorization system. The test frequency can be determined based on engineering judgment from maintenance studies. When establishing testing frequencies, facilities should consider the potential frequency of the failure. The test frequency must be at much smaller intervals than the process demands on the system. If an emergency shutdown device is tested annually, for example, it could potentially be in an unannounced failed state for an entire year. The process demands may require more frequent testing than that, indicating that the system may not work when necessary. Testing frequencies must consider the criticality of the system, which is why the development of a meaningful critical equipment and instrumentation list is important. When critical instrument lists are developed, the severity of the consequences if the instrument system fails should be a major consideration. Critical instruments should be tested more frequently than those that are not as critical.

Establishing Inspection Schedules

A number of sources can be consulted to establish inspection schedules. Various codes and standards provide guidance on external and internal inspections for different types of equipment. The API, with codes including API 570 (2009d), 576 (2009a), and 653 (2009b), is an excellent source even for facilities that are not units in a refinery. Where a corrosion rate is not known, a short inspection interval is recommended. Risk-based inspections use inspection strategies based on the likelihood and consequences of failures. Intervals between inspections should be established based on corrosion rates, the remaining life of the equipment, piping service classifications, the judgment of subject-matter experts (such as inspectors), and applicable jurisdictional requirements.

API 570 provides maximum inspection frequencies for different classes of piping. Class 1 is piping that has a high potential for an emergency if a leak were to occur, and includes flammable services (such as liquid propane) that may auto-refrigerate, leading to brittle fractures, and pressurized services that may vaporize rapidly, creating an explosive mixture. This class also includes piping over public throughways and over or adjacent to water, and pipes carrying material with a high concentration of hydrogen sulfide, anhydrous hydrogen chloride, or hydrofluoric acid. Class 2 involves much of the piping in petrochemical plants and includes materials such as hydrocarbons that do not vaporize rapidly, hydrogen fuel and natural gas, and strong acids and bases. Class 3 piping involves materials that are flammable but vaporize slowly upon release. Distillate and product lines to and from storage are also included in this class (API 2009d, 6.3.4).

TABLE 3

Recommended Maximum Inspection Intervals for Piping

Type of Circuit	Thickness Measurements	Visual External
Class 1	5 years	5 years
Class 2	10 years	10 years
Class 3	10 years	10 years
Class 4	Optional	Optional

(*Source:* API 2009c)

TABLE 4

Recommended Maximum Inspection Intervals for Buried Piping Without Effective Cathodic Protection

Soil Resistivity (Ohm-cm)	Inspection Interval
< 2000	5 years
2000 to 10,000	10 years
> 10,000	15 years

(*Source:* API 2009d)

Class 4 services involve nonflammable and nontoxic materials, such as nitrogen, air, and steam. Inspection frequencies for Class 4 piping are often based on reliability needs and business impact.

Table 3 shows recommended maximum inspection intervals for the various classes. Risk-based inspection is sometimes used to adjust schedules such as these, but caution should always be exercised when increasing the interval between inspections to ensure that the equipment will continue to be adequately protected.

Guidance on the frequency of inspections for buried piping depends on the soil resistivity. Table 4 provides some guidelines for piping without cathodic protection. (Cathodic protection applies a current and reduces the corrosion potential by bringing the metal to an immune state.)

The API notes that the inspection interval for pressure vessels should be based on operating experience, manufacturers' recommendations, recommendations of applicable regulatory bodies, and the performance of equipment in the particular service. API 576 also notes that the maximum interval between inspections of pressure-relief devices is ten years, unless qualified by a risk-based inspection assessment (API 2009a, 6.4.1).

This time frame, along with the other factors mentioned previously, may be used as one basis for equipment inspections. The inspection frequency for low-pressure storage tanks should be based on a number of factors, including the nature of the product stored, results of visual inspections, corrosion rates, changes in operating mode, and changes in service (API 2009b, 6.2.1). External visual inspections should be made at least every five years. When the corrosion rate is not known, external thickness measurements should be taken ultrasonically at least every five years (API 2009b, 6.3).

Establishing Inspection Methods

Inspection and surveillance methods usually fall into one of the following categories: internal visual, external visual, vibrating piping, and thickness measurement. Supplemental measurements can also be conducted as necessary. *Internal visual inspections*, while common with vessels, generally are not performed on piping unless it has a large diameter. Internal inspections of vessels should include the vessel shell, linings, and internal devices such as trays. *External visual inspections* determine the condition of the outside of vessels and piping. Painting and coating need to be observed, as well as the condition of the insulation system. Signs of leakage, vibration, corrosion, movement, or the misalignment of piping can also be observed. Any vibrating piping, or piping that has moved from its original location, should be reported for inspection.

Thickness measurements are taken at various locations along the vessel or pipe circuit and are used to determine the presence of localized corrosion. An average, or more conservatively, the thinnest reading, is used to calculate the rate of corrosion and the remaining life, along with the time for the next inspection. The number and the location of measuring points should be determined based on risks. A higher number of readings should be taken in areas where the consequences of failure are higher, where materials are deemed to be more prone to corrosion, and where there is a high number of fittings, branches, deadlegs, and other such configurations. For piping and vessels with low potential for safety and environmental consequences and those in relatively noncorrosive systems, fewer thickness readings are necessary. If the consequences are extremely low or if the service is noncorrosive, thickness readings may be eliminated.

The minimum thickness can be located by ultrasonic scanning or radiography. Ultrasonic scanning is the most accurate means for measuring thickness on piping with a nominal size greater than one inch, whereas radiographic techniques are better for piping with diameters of one inch or smaller. API 570 notes that radiographic profile techniques can be used to locate areas to be measured in insulated systems or areas where local corrosion is expected. Then ultrasonics can be used to determine actual thicknesses. Inspectors must correct measurement readings for temperature, especially at temperatures above 150°F (API 2009d).

These methods can be used when equipment is in operation. When equipment is not in service, thickness measurements can be taken directly with calipers. If there is pitting, special pit-depth measuring devices may also be used (API 2009c, 5.7).

Other nondestructive methods of measuring thickness discussed in literature include magnetic methods, liquid-penetrant methods, field metallographic replication, and acoustic emission examination. One other method of determining equipment integrity should be mentioned: hydraulic or pneumatic pressure-testing of piping systems, although this method is not normally conducted as part of a routine inspection. API 570 has more detailed information about conducting pressure tests (API 2009d, 5.7–5.8).

A unique challenge is inspection of underground piping. Because of inaccessibility and the fact that most of the piping is not visible, inspections are difficult. Techniques used include above-ground visual surveillance to detect changes that may indicate a leak, such as discoloration of soil, pool formation, and odors. The soil resistivity around piping may be tested to determine the likelihood of corrosion. Low resistivity indicates a more corrosive environment than high resistivity. A number of inspection methods exist, including intelligent pigging (passing a device through the line to determine the internal conditions), video cameras inserted into the piping, and excavation, which allows for an external inspection (API 2009d, 9.2).

Finally, personnel performing inspections must be properly trained and certified. The API issues certification to personnel who have demonstrated competency at the craft of inspection and interpretation of results. These certifications require completion of an exam to show that the requirements of API standards are well understood. There are also minimum education and experience requirements. Risk-based inspections (RBIs) should be performed by knowledgeable individuals or teams in accordance with API 580 (API 2009e).

Hazards of Maintenance Work and Preparation for Maintenance

Maintenance includes several functions, such as testing, inspecting, cleaning, calibrating, repairing, and installing replacement equipment. The nature of maintenance work brings with it inherent hazards. Technicians must perform work on machinery with moving parts and on systems that contain hazardous materials. Hazards faced by maintenance workers include entanglement, crushing, burns, exposure to toxic materials, electrocution, asphyxiation, and injury by impact. Also, since maintenance work can affect operations, improper restoration of the equipment after maintenance can result in hazards when the system is restarted. Such problems can include release of toxic and flammable materials or hazards due to improper guarding of equipment.

To address these issues, an effective work-permit system should be implemented. The purposes of such a system are to ensure that hazards of conducting work are considered and precautions are properly thought out and specified and to make sure that all of these issues are understood by the persons involved (Mannan 2005, 21.5). The system also facilitates communication, especially between operations personnel, who generally prepare equipment for maintenance and start it up after maintenance, and maintenance personnel, who conduct the work (see Figure 6). Permit systems allow the coordination of work, as maintenance jobs can be large in scope and involve several people. A clear system of handover is a critical part of the permitting process. The permitting system should ensure that everyone involved with the job understands the hazards and how to comply with safe codes of practice. Permit forms vary from company to company, but in general permits include a description of the work, its location, precaution requirements, potential hazards, authorization, personal protective equipment required, an acceptance of conditions, and the acknowledgement of completion (Mannan 2005, 21.15). Refer to the "Permit to Work" chapter of this handbook for additional details on the permitting system and the various hazards of maintenance.

Tasks that should be permitted prior to commencing work include those on equipment where toxic, flammable, or corrosive substances are present, especially when equipment needs to be opened for servicing and/or cleaning. Such tasks include:

- work on equipment that is pressurized or that operates at extreme temperatures
- maintenance requiring hot work or evacuation
- work that requires entry into confined spaces or areas where there is a potential for oxygen deficiency or enrichment
- work on machinery, especially machines with moving parts, such as conveyors, hoists, and lifts, and includes work requiring heavy equipment to be lifted, such as with a crane.

First- and second-line supervisors are a critical key to an effective permitting process. They are responsible for making sure that maintenance work is properly authorized and controlled. Checklists are often used in the process to prompt personnel about potential hazards of the process. Also, provisions must be made to stop work if the requirements of the safe preparation of equipment, such as draining and isolation, cannot be met (Wallace et al. 2003, 214–215). A reasonable approach if such a situation occurs is to stop the work and bring together a multidisciplinary team to plan a strategy for safely accomplishing the job. As mentioned previously, a serious incident occurred in Martinez, California, when personnel cut into a line containing flammable material before it had been properly evacuated (CSB 2001, 11).

Communication is another function of the permit process. Since equipment that may be dangerous or contain hazardous material is being handed off

Hot Work / IGNITION SOURCE Permit

Issue Date:________	Start Time: AM PM	End Time: AM PM	Welding, Burning, Open Flame Ignition Source
Unit / Location:			
Permit Issued To:			
Detailed Description of Job/Including Tools and equipment:			

Operations / Equipment Owner (Permit Issuer)

LEL/O_2	Required	Not Required	Calibration Date:____________
	Initial Result/Time	Revalidation Result/Time	Chemical Name(s)
Oxygen (19.5-23.5%)			
LEL (0%)			

	YES	N/A
1. Can material to be worked on be removed to a shop area?		
2. Has process equipment been cleared of all flammable material?		
3. Have all control points been identified, locked & or blinded? Spools removed?		
4. Is a water hose or a proper fire extinguisher on site and in working order?		
5. Is a fire watch required?		
6. Have Flammable/Combustible materials in the vicinity or on lower floor levels been removed or protected?		
7. Have all drains, sewers, cracks, and openings been covered or shielded to prevent sparks or hot slag from entering?		
8. Have combustible materials been removed from the hot work area or shielded with fire retardant material such as fire blankets?		
9. Have precautions been taken to prevent heat transfer from object of hot work to other combustible materials?		
10. For overhead work, has the work area(s) below been properly barricaded or Fire Watch posted?		
11. Have conveyors and ducts been shut down or protected to prevent sparks from traveling?		

Maintenance Foreman / Construction Foreman

1. Has job been reviewed with workers (Special Precautions & JSI)?		
2. Has the Fire Watch been advised of his/her duties?		
3. Has appropriate PPE been assigned for the task?		

I have verified the work area to be clear and approve this permit. (Signature and Phone/Pager)

WBOF - Equipment Owner/Supervisor:	
WBOF - Maintenance/Construction Foreman:	
Ignition Source - Operations Representative:	

Please Notify Permit Issuer Upon Completion or Changes in Conditions.

FIGURE 6. Example of a permit for hot work (*Source:* CCPS 1996)

from one department to another, it is imperative that the departments communicate. Operations personnel must communicate with maintenance personnel and vice versa. For critical jobs, a prejob conference between operations and maintenance departments at the job site should be conducted. Supervisors, operators, and craftspersons who will be performing the work should all attend the conference. Safety precautions and potential problems must be discussed and action items must be developed to resolve any potential issues. The equipment that requires maintenance must be clearly identified on the permit, and operations personnel should consider having a discussion with maintenance personnel at the job site if maintenance personnel are unfamiliar with the equipment—or if the equipment to be maintained is in a confusing maze of piping and other equipment—to decrease the chances of the wrong equipment being opened. Personnel should be available to ensure communication throughout the job, similar to the concept of a fire watch when hot work is being performed. Also, it is vital that communication occur from shift to shift if the job extends beyond one shift. In some cases, if safety testing (such as testing for flammables) is not being done continuously, it should be redone when a new shift comes on.

Supervision and training are important elements in a maintenance preparation and execution system. While permit systems may establish authority, appropriate supervision must continue throughout the execution of critical work. Also, maintenance personnel should be trained adequately in their craft, in safe preparation tasks such as isolation, and in the permitting system. Refresher training and continuing education must be included for all crafts. All maintenance personnel, whether employees or contractors, must be trained in the general hazards at the facility and the hazards of the specific chemicals used there (Wallace et al. 2003, 213).

Line Breaking, Equipment Opening, and Isolation

Because maintenance often requires dismantling equipment that processes hazardous material, properly evacuating that material and purging the system should preface any job where equipment will be opened. As mentioned previously, identification of the correct equipment is vitally important. Use of a mini-conference at the job site should be considered if the job is particularly hazardous, if personnel performing the work are new or unfamiliar with the hazard, or if equipment is in a confusing maze or adjacent to other similar equipment. Tagging is also important, especially on flanges that must be opened.

After the correct equipment is identified, the general steps for opening equipment containing hazardous liquids and gases are depressuring, cooling, isolating, emptying liquids (and solids), purging, and cleaning. Liquids and gases may be conveyed to a different part of the unit or to a scrubber or flare system. Material should not be vented to the atmosphere unless it can be proven that doing so is safe and the material is benign. For processes that operate at elevated temperatures, the equipment should be cooled prior to opening. Caution should be exercised, however, because equipment that contains hot material that is cooled prior to maintenance may be at risk for vacuum. To protect against this hazard, equipment should be properly vented during cooldown. Inert gas may be injected to ensure that the vapor space continues to be occupied.

Prior to opening, the equipment must be isolated from process fluids and high-pressure and temperature sources. Machinery and automatic valves must be isolated from sources of power and energy. Methods of isolating vessels and piping include, in order of effectiveness, closing block and isolation valves, double-blocking and bleeding (DBB) the piping, installing blinds, and disconnecting the equipment. Closing valves is the least effective method because valves leak. DBB is more effective because it involves closing two valves and opening a bleed between them, which keeps material from accumulating and pressure from building up between the valves. Installation of blinds and physical disconnection are the best methods for isolation; however, care must be taken to use blinds that are of appropriate thickness to withstand the highest pressure to which they may be exposed. Also, caution must be exercised when the piping system is separated to install a blind, as residual material may be present and maintenance technicians may be at risk. When lines are physically disconnected, a blank should be installed so that the end of the piping is not exposed to the atmosphere. In the event of a breech of isolation upstream, a blank will prevent material from being released. Physical disconnection is the preferred method if personnel are entering confined spaces and for relief and vent lines, due to the various connections that may be involved. The system of isolation should guarantee that blinds are uninstalled after work is completed and that physically disconnected piping is reconnected prior to restarting the process.

Machines and other devices that operate from an energy source must be isolated from their sources of power, including electrical, hydraulic, and pneumatic, to ensure that there is no unexpected energization. A lockout/tagout system consistent with the requirements in OSHA 1910.147 (1996b) should address these concerns. *Lockout* refers to installing locks on circuit breakers, switches, and flanges or valves so those devices cannot be opened while equipment is being maintained. Everyone involved with the job, from operations to maintenance to electricians, typically will add a lock to the equipment so that it cannot be operated until all locks are removed. *Tagout* involves the use of tags instead of locks, and this method should be used only if it can be proven to be as effective as lockout. Although typically thought of in conjunction with electrical equipment, a lockout/tagout system should be used with equipment whenever premature use could result in injury or a release of material. Electrical sources may be isolated by removing the fuses or locking off the isolator. Refer to the "Permit to Work" section of this handbook for more information.

Once the equipment is isolated, the next step is to remove residual hazardous materials from the equipment to be serviced. If it is liquid, it can be pumped to a different location or drained if it is not hazardous. Then any vapor must be evacuated from the equipment by ventilation, flushing with water, purging, or steaming. *Purging* involves replacing a toxic or flammable gas with an inert gas and then with air. It is important that an inert gas, such as nitrogen, be used initially so that flammable material and air do not form a flammable mixture. Also, it is important that an air purge follow the inert gas purge before personnel enter the equipment; otherwise, there is a risk of asphyxiation. The sequence of shutdown steps is very important, especially during the purge phase. In the case of flammable gas, it is during the purge phase that the material in the vessel is likely to pass through the flammable range. Inert gas or steam is often used to control this hazard.

Under no circumstances should a vessel or piping be opened unless operations and maintenance personnel can be certain of the conditions inside the equipment. Personnel must be able to verify that the system is free of pressure, high temperature, and the presence of flammable, toxic, or reacting material (Wallace et al. 2003, 213). Gauges and analyzers should be used where available, and must be included in the design of the process. Indirect measures, such as analysis of the material on exit from the equipment and purge time and rate can be used if necessary, but they are not the preferred method. However, even when gauges are present and are used, personnel should be aware of conditions inside equipment that may render gauges useless. As an example, in Augusta, Georgia, three operators died during an incident in which they were opening a vessel that contained what they believed to be fully reacted polymer. A portion of the polymer in the core of the vessel was still unreacted and, due to the buildup of pressure inside the vessel, exploded when bolts on the vessel cover were loosened. The polymer had plugged the lone pressure gauge on the vent line, and no other effective means existed to ensure that there was no pressure inside the vessel. This case speaks to the need for redundancy of gauges and instrumentation to monitor conditions in process equipment (CSB 2002b, 47).

The final step in preparing a vessel for entering is often cleaning. Methods of cleaning equipment prior to entering include flushing with water, chemical cleaning, steaming, and manual cleaning. The method chosen will depend on the type of facility and nature of the material present in the equipment.

Welding, Cutting, and Other Hot Work

A number of maintenance jobs require some type of hot work to remove or repair equipment. Hot work brings a source of ignition into a potentially flammable or toxic atmosphere, so protections must be in place to minimize the hazard. The first step is to conduct a job analysis to determine whether hot work is required or there is a lower-risk way to accomplish the work. The analysis should be completed by competent personnel. If it is determined that hot work is required, then the hazards must be determined and appropriate precautions taken.

Many of the precautions that must be taken prior to hot work, such as isolation and purging, are standard steps that must be taken in conjunction with most permitted work (API 2002, 13). Some of the specific requirements for hot work include ventilation, testing for hazards, and fire watches. Note that some references state that welding should be confined to manual electric-arc methods.

VENTILATION

Ventilation is required in a variety of circumstances, including those in which hot work is performed in areas with limited air movement (API 2002b, 14). The intent of ventilation is to prevent worker exposure to hazardous fumes by removing contaminated air and adding fresh air to the environment. *Air-movers* are mechanical devices that facilitate ventilation. They should direct fumes and vapors away from working personnel. Air-movers should be bonded so they are less likely to generate static electricity. Local ventilation may also be an alternative in some applications. With this approach, a high velocity of airflow (e.g., 100 cfm) is directed at, or close to, the hot work.

FLAMMABILITY TESTS

A competent person must perform flammability tests in the area before hot work commences, and the detector must be calibrated and maintained appropriately. Hydrocarbons that may be in the liquid phase (not detectable by gas monitoring) must be found and removed before hot work is started. Testing should be conducted after purging with steam and inert gases has occurred, but testing personnel must be aware that steam vapors can affect detector results. The surrounding area should be thoroughly tested as well to ensure that no flammable vapors are present. Low points and confined areas must be included in the testing. Tests must be conducted at multiple locations on runs of piping. If there is any detectable reading of flammable vapor, work should be stopped or not allowed to begin until the source is found and eliminated.

Consideration should be given to the frequency of testing. One-time testing conducted only before the work begins has limitations. Conditions can change during the course of work, and continuous monitoring rather than initial testing is often necessary to ensure that any change in flammable conditions is detected. During an incident in Delaware City, Delaware, a flammables test was conducted at the beginning of a maintenance shift prior to the commencement of welding on a walkway around tanks containing flammable material. During the course of the day, conditions changed, and flammable vapor that had leaked out of a hole in a tank was apparently blown in the direction of the welding operation, which resulted in an explosion, causing a fatality and resulting in a large release of acid to a river (CSB 2002a).

FIRE WATCHES

According to OSHA 1910.252, *Welding, Cutting, and Brazing* (1998b), fire-watch personnel are required any time there is a permit for performing hot work. The purpose of the fire watch is to provide constant surveillance in the area. Fire-watch personnel look for sparking and potential fires. They extinguish fires only if they are able to do so with a fire extinguisher or a water hose. If the fire watch cannot extinguish a fire, he or she should sound a fire alarm. OSHA 1910.252 also notes that the fire watch should keep vigil for at least 30 minutes after completion of hot work (OSHA 1998b). As a precaution, fire blankets should be used to protect other equipment in the area from sparks. The fire watch should make sure these precautions are in place and that general safety is maintained in the area.

Hot Tapping

Hot tapping is the procedure of fitting a branch onto a pipe or vessel that is in service and then cutting a hole in the attached fitting. Hot taps allow modifications to be made without shutting the plant down, but there are several potential hazards associated with the procedure. In addition to the usual welding hazards, a leak may occur during the operation, the fluid in the pipe may decompose explosively due to the heat applied during welding, and the modified equipment may fail at some point later. Because of these hazards, hot tapping should be avoided whenever possible.

If hot tapping is necessary, it requires careful preparation and consideration of the process fluid, operating conditions, materials of construction and their dimensions, and requirements of the specific job. API 2201, *Procedures for Welding or Hot Tapping on Equipment in Service*, provides good guidance on performing such activities (API 2003):

- The pressure should be reduced as much as possible so the hazard is reduced.
- The material of construction and the thickness of the pipe or vessel wall should be thoroughly checked.
- Welding must not take place if the shell has deteriorated to the point that it is unsafe.
- To prevent burn-through (a condition in which the unmelted area beneath the weld cannot support the pressure), API 2201 recommends using a 3/32-inch (or smaller) welding electrode for piping less than 1/4-inch thick. For pipe walls greater than 1/2 inch, larger diameter electrodes can be used (API 2003, 2).

- Flow through pipes during hot tapping generally helps to dissipate heat and prevent burn-through; however, a balance must be maintained because high flow rates can increase the cooling rate and increase the risk of cracking. Therefore, a minimum flow should be maintained but high flow should be avoided.
- A minimum wall thickness of 3/16 inch is recommended for most hot-tapping applications.
- Hot tapping close to connections and seams must be avoided, and it should not be conducted within eighteen inches of a flanged or threaded connection or within three inches of a welded seam.
- If a hot tap is performed on a tank, it should be performed at least three feet below the top of the liquid level at the point of the cut to ensure that the cut is not being made into the vapor space.
- Hot taps should be avoided on vapor and oxygen mixtures that are close to their flammable range. They should also be avoided on hydrogen systems (unless a special engineering review approves it) and on systems containing chemicals that are likely to decompose on heating, including unsaturated hydrocarbons such as ethylene that may experience decomposition upon heating (API 2003, 4).

Confined Space Entry

Entry into a confined space poses unique hazards, as personnel are particularly vulnerable to the atmosphere inside and have limited mobility. The hazards personnel are likely to face include flammables, toxic substances, oxygen deficiency, and oxygen enrichment. Entry into a confined space should be avoided if at all possible.

OSHA 1910.146 (1998a) lays out regulations for confined spaces:

- Vessels having held flammable or toxic material must be cleaned thoroughly before entry.
- Personnel must ensure that all sources of flammables are positively isolated from the vessel.
- The use of only a single valve for isolation is not recommended. Physical disconnection is the recommended isolation strategy.
- If an oxygen-deficient environment is expected, personnel must use a respirator, either self-contained or with an air line and a reliable source of oxygen.
- The atmosphere should be tested for flammables, toxics, and oxygen concentration. If possible the tests should be conducted without entering the vessel. The tests should continue as necessary to verify that the space is still safe for entrants.
- Ventilation must be provided to ensure that the space remains nonhazardous.
- Lighting should be sufficient to allow personnel inside the vessel to see to work and escape if necessary.
- A plan of rescue should be developed prior to personnel entering a vessel. The plan should consider the configuration inside the vessel, as many reactors and columns contain trays and supports that can hinder rescue. Personnel should wear a safety line to facilitate rescue if necessary.
- An attendant must stand watch to monitor workers in confined spaces.
- A system of communication must be set up so that personnel in a confined space can quickly alert personnel outside of any problems.

Quality-Control and Documentation Program

Even the best maintenance organizations can have serious problems unless a comprehensive quality-assurance program is in place. Such a program will ensure that proper construction materials are used in design and replacement, that installation and inspection procedures are effective, and that the system for spare parts and service products (such as gaskets, packing, and lubrication) are of the correct type. The system should also ensure that inspections and preventive maintenance activities occur on schedule, and that the action items resulting from those activities are addressed promptly. Data on equipment failure, repair, and availability should be readily at hand. Records of maintenance on safety-critical and protective devices are particularly important and should be accurately kept. Protective devices include relief valves, vents, safety interlocks and shutdowns, and fire protection equipment. In such a record-keeping system, as-built drawings, certifications of compliance with codes and standards for equipment, and verification of materials of construction are documented in such a way that they can be easily referenced. Audits of equipment suppliers that have occurred (or are planned), along with documentation, should also be part of the system.

Replacement parts should be inventoried and stored in a warehouse. Keeping critical parts in inventory is a significant purpose of any quality-control and documentation system. The inventory may be used to determine when parts are likely to run out and need to be reordered. A proactive system considers usage, criticality, lead time, and costs in making decisions on inventories. The system controls equipment that is checked out to ensure that the correct parts are selected for installation in the field. Many organizations have adopted the standards set forth by the International Organization for Standardization (ISO), such as ISO 9000 or ISO 14000. While these programs may still have errors and should be audited occasionally by the end user, participation in ISO generally means that documentation is kept and the programs are easier to audit. Finally, particular attention should be paid when equipment is reused. The integrity of the equipment should be checked and the intended use should be verified. Mixing reconditioned parts with new parts is not advised. The fitness of each piece of used equipment must be considered before putting it into service.

Contractor Safety

Recent trends in industry have been to use contractors for more work, not only in construction activities, but also on more routine tasks (Mannan 2005, 21.5). OSHA 1910.119 requires facilities that fall under the jurisdiction of the process safety management program (PSM) standard to evaluate contractors' safety performance, inform contractors of hazards, and explain emergency procedures to them. The owner/operator of the facility is also required to develop procedures to control contractor entrance and exit into hazardous areas and maintain an injury/illness log for contractors (OSHA 1996).

The obligation of evaluating contractors' safety performance begins before a contracting organization is hired. A contractor's recent injury and illness logs, as well as incident reports from significant injuries, can be reviewed. Employers seeking contractors should ensure that the contractors have the appropriate skills, certifications, and knowledge to perform the jobs they will be assigned. Past experience with the particular process or chemicals can prove to be useful. The owner or operator must train contractors on any known material or process hazards. This training must be in a language and manner that is understandable to contract employees. The safety of contract workers should also be monitored and evaluated throughout a job. Close interaction between facility employees and contractors is essential. Contractor companies must ensure that their employees are trained in the work practices necessary to perform the tasks they are likely to be assigned. They should ensure that their personnel have received training on hazards and must document that it was understood and that contract employees follow the safety rules of the facility. Contractors must advise owners/operators of hazards created by their work and any hazards found during their work.

Material Handling

There are a number of safety aspects related to the handling of materials, much of which includes lifting and moving material either manually or with mechanical equipment. These activities can result in numerous types of occupational injuries, such as back strains. This section addresses only those aspects of material handling that are related to process safety issues, such as knowing the inherent properties of the materials and reducing sources of ignition. Readers should refer to the "Ergonomics" section in this handbook for additional information on the ergonomic issues of material handling.

In *Guidelines for Engineering Design for Process Safety*, the CCPS states that to safely handle materials, facilities must thoroughly understand their physical and chemical properties. CCPS notes that the general properties, such as boiling point, vapor pressure, and critical pressure and temperature, should be determined and their application thoroughly understood. Other important properties include reactivity, flammability, toxicity, and stability. Once these properties are determined, safe-handling procedures should be developed (CCPS 1993, 56–61).

Of special concern in material handling is avoiding ignition sources. Such sources should be avoided during the design of the facility as much as possible and controlled through the permitting system. However, additional protections are needed to prevent the buildup of static electricity. It can occur due to product flow in piping, particulates passing through conveyors, filling operations in containers, and personnel wearing nonconductive shoes. Personnel grounding and the use of antistatic footwear should be considered where appropriate. Equipment should be grounded, and facilities should be aware that static can accumulate in various media, such as plastic-lined pipes. Another strategy for avoiding static discharge is allowing relaxation time for charge bleed-off. A study should be conducted to determine whether static electricity is a hazard in a particular process. Brush discharges should be avoided, as should splash-filling into barrels and tanks. Caution should be exercised during handling of solids, as small particles may ignite.

Facility Security

Since the terrorist attacks of September 11, 2001, federal and state governments have been concerned about installations that potentially could become targets for those wishing to harm U.S. citizens. Chemical and manufacturing facilities qualify as such facilities because they often contain hazardous materials that can impact workers on site and the surrounding community if the materials are released through acts of sabotage (CCPS 2003b, 1). This concern is prevalent in all sectors of the chemical, petrochemical, manufacturing, transportation, and storage industries. A study of vulnerabilities should be conducted at all chemical, paper production, weapons production, waste and water treatment, and pharmaceutical facilities, as well as at any other installation that contains material or equipment that could be used for malevolent purposes by an adversary. In 2006, the federal government established a requirement that certain chemical facilities must conduct vulnerability assessments. The Department of Homeland Security (DHS) has promulgated regulations that certain chemical facilities must conduct vulnerability assessments (DHS 2007).

Often, facility security is equated with the physical security at the perimeter of the building or unit, which is designed to keep persons without a need from entering the processing units. However, a comprehensive security-vulnerability analysis involves a number of steps, including assessing the threat, vulnerability, target attractiveness, likelihood of adversary success, countermeasures, and emergency response in the event that an event does occur. Good practices guidelines are available from a number of sources. Most of the guidance presented in this section comes from the American Chemistry Council (ACC) and the Center for Chemical Process Safety (CCPS) and deals largely with the threat of terrorism. However, the techniques that are used to analyze this threat can be used to address other security issues. Excellent guidance is also available from organizations such as the National Safety Council (NSC), which notes that security issues include prevention of drugs in the workplace, fraud, liability, theft, and violence. As this subject continues to be an evolving aspect of safety, practitioners should stay abreast of updates in the concept of plant security and in mandates from federal, state, and local governments.

Facility Characterization

Facility characterization involves determining assets, hazards, and potential consequences for a particular installation This information can be developed as a separate step in the analysis or in conjunction with the threat and vulnerability assessments (CCPS 2003b, 43).

Critical Assets Identification

The team analyzing security vulnerability should identify assets for the installation (CCPS 2003b, 49). Assets include both material and nonmaterial items that allow a facility to operate and could be used for malevolent purposes by adversaries. Examples of critical assets include:

- chemicals that are processed, stored, generated, or transported

- storage tanks, process vessels, and interconnected piping
- the process-control system
- operating personnel
- sophisticated machinery that can be used for multiple purposes
- raw materials and finished product
- utilities and waste treatment facilities
- business information and management systems
- community and customer relations.

Hazard Identification

The security-analysis team must identify and understand the hazards of the assets at the facility (CCPS 2003b, 50). Development of a potential target list should include the following items:

- *Highly hazardous chemicals:* These materials include all raw, intermediate, and finished materials. The team must document not only the presence of such materials, but also the locations, concentrations, and states of the chemicals. Also, any particular hazards associated with a chemical—such as the ability to be a chemical weapon's precursor of an inhalation poison—should be noted. Lists of highly hazardous chemicals, such as those in OSHA 29 CFR 1910.119 (1996), EPA 40 CFR Part 68 (2004), DHS 6 CFR Part 27 (2007), and on the U.S. Chemical Weapons Convention Web site (www.cwc.gov) can be referenced to determine whether there are chemicals of concern at the site. Additionally, all flammables, corrosives, environmental damagers, carcinogens, and explosives must be included.
- *Safety information:* All information on the assets of the facility, such as the design basis for equipment, plot plans, flow diagrams, and hazard studies, should be collected for the evaluation. Information on the population and sensitive environmental receptors in the surrounding community should be included as well.

Consequence Analysis

Similar to the way a hazard evaluation for accidental events focuses on the potential consequences, a security-vulnerability analysis must identify the potential consequences of a successful attack on the assets of an installation. Different scenarios must be considered to accurately identify consequences. Scenarios developed in conjunction with the EPA Risk Management Plan (EPA 2004) can be used for guidance on the release of material. For instance, in the case of the release of a toxic chemical into the atmosphere, the atmospheric concentrations of concern can be estimated at various distances downwind. Also, the potential consequences to a neighboring population or the environment must be assessed. If the situation has to do with the release and subsequent ignition of an explosive material, potential effects of overpressure and radiant heat must be estimated. If the scenario of concern is the theft of a chemical or piece of sophisticated machinery, the consequences to others from future misuse must be considered. If the problem of a cyber-attack is to be evaluated, the consequences would include loss of production or the sudden shutdown of a process.

Attractiveness of the Target

One of the important considerations in assessing the threat to an installation is how attractive the target is to adversaries. Examples of considerations include the proximity of the installation to a symbolic target such as a national landmark, a high corporate profile among terrorists, and proximity to large populations (CCPS 2003b, 54).

Layers of Protection

To develop reasonable recommendations for countermeasures, the analysis team must determine the safeguards already in place to prevent an incident. These include physical security, cyber-security, administrative controls, and other safeguards (CCPS 2003b, 55).

The information collected during the facility-characterization phase can be used during the subsequent steps to identify a list of specific potential targets and the vulnerability of each.

Threat Identification

An assessment of the threats to a facility includes identifying potential sources of threats, types of threats, and their likelihood. This step involves identifying adversaries and investigating their intentions and capabilities. The information collected during the facility-characterization step will help to inform the analysis team during this phase (CCPS 2003b, 55–60).

The list of potential threats to industrial facilities includes:

- release of hazardous materials to cause a fire, explosion, or dispersion of toxins
- theft of hazardous chemicals or confidential information
- damage to the infrastructure of the installation
- contamination of products
- vandalism of equipment
- cyber-attack
- disabling of safety and security systems

These acts may be carried out by internal or external adversaries who can be terrorists (foreign or domestic), criminals, violent activists, or disgruntled employees. All of these groups represent threats that must be evaluated and addressed. However, the major threat to consider is external adversaries, such as terrorists, who intend to inflict a large number of casualties. This threat should be considered first. An especially dangerous situation is one in which someone with inside knowledge of all the materials and processes on site is working in collusion with external terrorists.

The information collected during this phase, along with the information collected during the facility-characterization phase, will allow a facility to assess the threat to its installation. Such information includes a list of all possible adversaries; assessment of their capabilities; information about the materials on site, including their quantities, toxicities, and locations; and information about existing security measures.

Vulnerability Analysis

There are two approaches to assessing the vulnerability of a facility—the *asset-based approach* and the *scenario-based approach*. One advantage of the asset-based approach is that it is generally less labor intensive than the scenario-based method.

In the asset-based approach, a list of critical assets, or potential targets, is developed. This may be accomplished by breaking the facility down into zones and considering the assets in each zone. The critical assets may include material that is released or systems that will affect the operation of a company, such as computer systems or irreplaceable equipment. Much of this information may already have been gathered during the threat-assessment and consequence-analysis steps of the process. Then the organization considers what the worst-case scenario is for the loss or damage of each asset, along with protective layers in place to prevent loss or damage of the asset. Such layers include security, lighting, and barriers. Where layers are not deemed sufficient to prevent an attack, the target may be considered vulnerable, and the team should develop a list of such targets. Targets can then be characterized as very high, moderate, or very low risk by using tools such as a three-by-three matrix that considers both severity and likelihood. Of particular concern are high-value targets that are vulnerable. These so-called high-value, high-payoff targets are listed on the priority scale as very high.

The other approach is the scenario-based method of vulnerability analysis. While this approach generally requires more time and effort, it has the advantage of producing recommendations for countermeasures that are more cost effective, since they are tailored to the scenarios that are developed. The analysis team collects information from on-site inspections and interviews to develop a list of potential targets. The analysis for this method is similar to the asset-based method in that the assets are identified and potential consequences are determined. However, in the scenario-based approach, the analysis is carried further to determine how a target might be attacked. For example, the team considers the possibility that material in a storage tank can be released, but also considers how an attacker may accomplish this task, such as driving a truck into the tank. Once the list of scenarios is developed, protective layers to prevent each scenario are considered, and the team rates the likelihood of the success of an attack as high, medium, or low. The team reviews all scenarios and then determines which ones are representative and should be analyzed further (CCPS 2003b, 60–68).

Once the scenarios from either method are developed, they should be ranked in order from highest consequence to lowest consequence. The scenarios can be ranked on a simple numerical scale (e.g., 1–5), or a risk matrix can be used to rank each scenario based on likelihood and consequences.

Identifying Countermeasures

The final step in the security-vulnerability analysis is to consider the adequacy of existing countermeasures to manage risk and recommend additional countermeasures when there are shortcomings. Countermeasures can be proposed that deter an attack, detect an attack if it occurs, or delay an attack until an intervention can occur. The team should determine whether there are ways to reduce the profile of the facility or apply the principles of inherently safer design. As with recommendations to prevent accidents, recommendations to prevent terrorist actions should be feasible and written so that individuals who were not part of the analysis team are able to clearly understand the proposed action. Cost-benefit analysis can be conducted on recommendations based on the potential likelihood and consequences of scenarios.

In their paper, "Site Security for Chemical Process Industries," Gupta and Bajpai note that countermeasures can be proposed that address vulnerabilities in a number of areas (Gupta and Bajpai, 2005, 301–309). Some examples are shown in Figure 7.

SPECIAL HAZARDS

Much of this chapter has dealt with addressing the general hazards presented by flammable and toxic materials. There are additional groups of materials that, due to the insidious nature of the hazards they present, require specific approaches to minimize risks. These approaches may include special considerations during hazard assessment and design or additional procedural safeguards. This section addresses three of these classes of materials: reactive materials, asphyxiants, and combustible dusts, and it borrows heavily from work conducted by the United States Chemical Safety and Hazard Investigation Board. While this section is not intended to be a comprehensive list of special hazards, these materials have been responsible for a number of deaths and injuries over the years, and a body of knowledge has been accumulated regarding good practices.

Reactive Chemicals

Reactivity can be defined as the tendency of a material (or combination of materials) to undergo chemical changes under the right conditions (CCPS 2001d, 2). Materials can be reactive by themselves—for example, unstable materials that decompose when exposed to heat. Another example is reactive interactions that occur when stable materials are combined to produce products that react to give off heat, pressure, or a volume of vapor. Reactive chemicals have been responsible for some of the highest-profile accidents in the chemical industry, such as the reaction between methyl isocyanate and water in Bhopal, India, in 1984. The Chemical Safety and Hazard Investigation Board (CSB) conducted a study of reactive chemical incidents and

Vulnerable System	*Potential Countermeasures*
Information and cyber security	• Provide adequate physical security and control access to computer and server rooms • Protect networks with firewalls and password controls
Physical Security	• Improve perimeter fencing and ensure proper lighting • Restrict movement of vehicles within the plant
Policies and Procedures	• Establish strict procedures for visitor and contractor entry into the facility • Create a program to survey surrounding area • Conduct background investigation on all employees • Train employees and contractors on their duties in addressing emergencies, bomb threats, hostage situations, etc. • Encourage employees and contractors to report unknown personnel, unidentified vehicles and packages

FIGURE 7. Vulnerability systems and potential countermeasures (*Source:* Gupta and Bajpai 2005)

found that 165 such incidents between 1980 and 2002 resulted in an average of five deaths each year.

In the safety alert *Reactive Material Hazards: What You Need to Know*, the CCPS notes that the determination of what action needs to be taken to address reactive hazards at either chemical or manufacturing facilities starts with an analysis that answers four questions:

1. How do we handle reactive materials?
2. Can we have reactive interactions?
3. What data do we need to control these hazards?
4. What safeguards do we need to control these hazards? (CCPS 2001, 2)

The first step in this analysis is to determine whether a facility contains any materials that are intrinsically reactive, independent of any interactions with other materials. Material safety data sheets (MSDSs) are a good starting point; however, because the information on them varies, a good practice is to consult multiple MSDSs from a variety of sources. Descriptions such as *unstable, polymerizing, pyrophoric, water-reactive,* and *potential to be an oxidizing agent* should be listed on MSDSs to alert practitioners to such hazards. Other useful references include *Sax's Dangerous Properties of Industrial Materials* (Lewis 2004), NFPA 704 (2007c) and the U.S. Department of Transportation's *Emergency Response Guidebook* (DOT 2008).

The next step is to determine whether there is a potential for dangerous reactions due to the interaction between materials that may come into contact with each other. Consideration must be given to materials that may be present intentionally but in the wrong concentrations (such as charging too much catalyst), as well as those that may be present by accident. Also, varying conditions, such as temperature and pressure, should be considered, since these changes can alter the behavior of materials. This part of the process commences with determining what materials are on site and then determining which ones can react violently when mixed. The likelihood of such mixing can then be determined and necessary safeguards described. Once all the materials on site are inventoried, the consequences of their various interactions can be considered with tools such as compatibility charts. In a simple compatibility chart, a matrix is created in which all the materials on site are listed on the horizontal and vertical axes, and then their interactions are considered and recorded. While creating a compatibility chart in a matrix format is a relatively straightforward method, it does have limitations. The chart is only as valuable as the quality of the sources used to determine reactivity; multiple sources should be considered when possible. Practitioners should be aware that the chart considers only mixtures of two materials, whereas hazardous interactions may not occur until three or more chemicals combine. Air, water, oil, and other materials that may be present inadvertently (such as after maintenance) should be included. Other tools to assist with assessing chemical interactions include the Chemical Reactivity Worksheet, available from the U.S. National Oceanic and Atmospheric Administration (NOAA 2010), and the American Society for Testing and Materials (ASTM) *Standard Guide for Preparation of Binary Chemical Compatibility Chart and Materials* (ASTM 2000).

Once it is determined that there is an intrinsic or interaction-reactive hazard, the next step is to compile the information necessary to determine whether a facility is protected against a reactive incident. Such data includes compatibility with different materials of construction, contaminants to avoid, proper spill and emergency response procedures, and other special considerations. Some of this information may be available from MSDSs, technical bulletins from chemical suppliers, or other data sources. Some information may require chemical testing. Heat-of-mixing information can often be used to determine how much heat or gas will be given off from a chemical interaction.

When appropriate information has been gathered, the final step is to identify and implement safeguards. The principles of inherent safety, which were discussed earlier in this chapter, can decrease the risks associated with reactive materials. Eliminating such materials as feasible and reducing inventories can decrease the chances of a reactive chemical incident. Also, good practices from the material supplier and codes and standards should be referenced and implemented. Multiple safeguards should be in place to prevent catastrophic reactive incidents. Compatible materials of construction and adequate emergency venting must be part of the design strategy. Storage of such materials should be remote from operating areas if possible, and positive separation strategies for incompatible materials must be employed. Dedicated fittings can be used to ensure that incompatible materials are not inadvertently mixed. Reactive materials must be monitored constantly for temperature and pressure excursions. Storage and process areas must have appropriate fire protection, and facilities must consider the possibility of a reactive chemical incident in their emergency response plans.

Practitioners should be aware that handling practices can often play a role in these types of incidents, and that good practices must be followed during all phases of operation, including when a processing unit is shut down. The CSB investigated an incident in Pascagoula, Mississippi, that involved mononitrotoluene (MNT), a material that reacts when heated (CSB 2003a, 11). The material had been left in a distillation column while the unit was shut down, but only a single manual valve was closed to isolate the steam supply from the column. Steam leaked through the valve and the material inside the column reacted energetically, destroying the column and propelling shrapnel off site and onto the property of neighboring facilities. This incident speaks to several issues involved in managing reactive chemical hazards. If the MNT had been evacuated from the column while it was shut down, if the steam supply had been better isolated (perhaps isolated automatically based on the temperature in the column), or if pressure relief had been adequate, the incident could have been prevented.

Asphyxiants

Asphyxiants present the hazard of displacing oxygen in the lungs, thereby essentially smothering victims. Asphyxiants are not poisons in the sense that chemicals like hydrogen sulfide are, but in elevated levels, they can be just as deadly. A variety of materials used in chemical and manufacturing facilities, such as carbon dioxide and steam, can act as asphyxiants. However, one of the most common scenarios involves nitrogen asphyxiation, and it will be discussed in more detail below. The good practices that prevent nitrogen asphyxiation also can be applied to other asphyxiants.

Nitrogen asphyxiation is a particularly insidious hazard because nitrogen is present in the air around us, so its risks are not always fully appreciated. Nitrogen is also used in chemical and manufacturing plants to make the facilities safer. Nitrogen is used to keep equipment free of contaminants through inerting and to purge toxic materials from equipment prior to opening. However, when elevated levels of nitrogen enter the breathing zone, victims can quickly become incapacitated. The CSB conducted a study of the issue and determined that, in the ten-year period between 1992 and 2002, nitrogen-asphyxiation incidents accounted for an average of eight deaths each year. The CSB found that the majority of victims were working in and around confined spaces. Specific causes of nitrogen-asphyxiation incidents included failure to detect an oxygen-deficient atmosphere, mistaking nitrogen for breathing air, and attempted rescue involving entering spaces that contained elevated levels of nitrogen without proper breathing protection (CSB 2003b, 3–5).

Good practices must be employed to prevent incidents of nitrogen asphyxiation. A continuous monitoring system must be used in and around confined spaces that personnel will enter to ensure that the atmosphere is fit for breathing upon entry and that it does not change over time. The entire space should be monitored to the extent practicable, not just the entry portal. Protective systems, such as alarms and auto-locking entryways that prevent access, can be used to warn workers of hazardous atmospheres. Personnel monitors can also measure oxygen concentration and activate audible or vibration alarms. Fresh-air ventilation should be maintained in spaces where personnel will enter, not just at the commencement of jobs, but throughout them as well. Ventilation systems must be properly designed and maintained.

Rescue methods should be planned before personnel enter confined areas. Harnesses and lifelines must be attached to personnel so they can be retrieved quickly from such areas. This approach benefits the potential rescuers as well since they probably will not have to enter the confined area to retrieve personnel inside. Personnel should attempt rescue only if they are trained appropriately, have the correct rescue equipment, and have a dependable source of breathing air. The CSB study showed that approximately 10 percent of the fatalities in such incidents happened to personnel attempting rescue (CSB 2003b, 5).

When workers are using supplied air, the integrity of the air source must be preserved, and the air must be protected from interruption. Air compressors should have alternate sources of power, and the air supply should be continuously monitored. Air hoses must be routinely inspected and replaced, and vehicular traffic should be restricted in the area of supply hoses. Escape packs worn by workers allow them an additional five to ten minutes of breathing air in the event of failure of the primary source. Management systems must be in place to prevent the mix-up of nitrogen and breathing air. Special incompatible fittings must be used for cylinders containing nitrogen and breathing air. Personnel should understand that the fittings are in place for a reason and that adaptors defeating their purpose will not be tolerated. Cylinders should be clearly labeled, and color-coding helps to identify systems. An incident occurred at a nursing home when a nitrogen cylinder was mistakenly delivered with a batch of oxygen cylinders. Even though the nitrogen cylinder had nitrogen-compatible fittings, an employee reportedly removed a fitting from an empty oxygen cylinder and used it as an adaptor to connect the nitrogen cylinder to the oxygen systems. Four deaths occurred as a result of pure nitrogen being delivered to patients (CSB 2003b, 6).

Finally, a comprehensive training program must be implemented (CSB 2003b, 8–9). Good practices are effective only if personnel are adequately trained. Personnel must be trained on appropriate confined-space-entry procedures. They also should be trained on atmospheric monitoring systems—both how to use them and how to tell if they are not working properly. Safe handling of air and nitrogen delivery systems should be stressed, as well as precautions to take when working around equipment that may contain elevated levels of nitrogen. Personnel should also be trained on rescue/retrieval systems and understand the warning not to enter atmospheres that may be hazardous unless they are properly trained and equipped. Finally, training should cover new and revised procedures for entering confined spaces. Contractors and employees should be trained, and personnel should be trained in a language and with a method that they can comprehend.

Combustible Dusts

Dust in high concentrations can be explosive. This hazard is well known in some industries, such as agriculture and coal mining, but has not been widely recognized in many manufacturing sectors. A common scenario with dust explosions is that some initiating event lofts accumulated dust into the air, and it explodes upon contact with an ignition source. Facilities that use powdery raw materials or slurries containing such materials are at risk for dust explosions. Since the lofting of accumulated dust is a common element in dust explosions, the design, operation, and cleaning practices at facilities must act collectively to minimize such accumulations. The principles of inherent safety should be applied, if possible, to select the least-hazardous materials. Less-hazardous materials include those with larger particulate sizes, higher minimum ignition energies, and higher K_{st} values. (***Note:*** K_{st} is the maximum rate of pressure rise normalized to a 1.0 cubic meter volume and is a measure of explosion severity.) If possible, dust should be handled in closed systems that do not allow an accumulation of material. If this is not possible, surfaces where material could accumulate, such as I-beams, should be minimized. Fire walls, blast-resistant construction, and deflagration venting should be installed in production areas.

Production areas where dust can accumulate should be cleaned frequently, including areas above production lines. It is important to note that dust can accumulate in areas not readily visible from floor level. Beams, conduit lines, and false ceilings are all areas that should get frequent attention. Tools that disperse dust, such as compressed air tools, should be avoided. Workers must be trained in the hazards of combustible dusts so that they recognize hazardous situations.

Dust explosions have been the cause of a number of catastrophic incidents in the manufacturing sector. Design, operation, maintenance, and cleaning strategies should be employed to minimize the risks. NFPA 654, *Standard for the Prevention of Fire and Dust Explosions from the Manufacturing, Processing, and Handling of Combustible Particulate Solids*, contains essential guidance on the subject (NPFA 2006).

References

American Petroleum Institute (API). 2002. RP 2009, *Safe Welding, Cutting, and Hot Work Practices in the Petroleum and Petrochemical Industries*. 7th ed. Washington, D.C.: API.

______. 2003. RP 2201, *Procedures for Welding or Hot Tapping on Equipment in Service*. 5th ed. Washington, D.C.: API.

______. 2007. RP 753, *Management of Hazards Associated with Location of Process Plant Portable Buildings*. Washington, D.C.: API.

______. 2008. API 620, *Design and Construction of Large, Welded, Low-Pressure Storage Tanks*. 11th ed. Washington, D.C.: API.

______. 2009a. RP 576, *Inspection of Pressure-Relieving Devices*. 3d ed. Washington, D.C.: API.

______. 2009b. Std 653, *Tank Inspection, Repair, Alteration, and Reconstruction*. 4th ed. Washington, D.C.: API.

______. 2009c. RP 752, *Management of Hazards Associated With Location of Process Plant Buildings*. 3d ed. Washington, D.C.: API.

______. 2009d. API 570, *Piping Inspection Code: Inspection, Repair, Alteration, and Rerating of In-service Piping Systems*. 3d ed. Washington, D.C.: API.

______. 2009e. RP 580, *Risk-Based Inspections*. 2d ed. Washington, D.C.: API.

American Society of Mechanical Engineers (ASME). 2008. ASME B31.3, *Process Piping*. New York: ASME.

American Society for Testing and Materials (ASTM). 2000. E2012-06, *Standard Guide for Preparation of Binary Chemical Compatibility Chart*. West Conshohocken, PA: ASTM.

Center for Chemical Process Safety (CCPS). 1993. *Guidelines for Engineering Design for Process Safety*. New York: American Institute of Chemical Engineers (AIChE).

______. 1994. *Guidelines for Evaluating the Characteristics of Vapor Cloud Explosions, Flash Fires, and BLEVEs*. New York: AIChE.

______. 1995. *Guidelines for Safe Process Operations and Maintenance*. New York: AIChE.

______. 1996. *Guidelines for Evaluating Process Plant Buildings for External Explosions and Fires*. New York: AIChE.

______. 2001. *Reactive Material Hazards: What You Need to Know*. New York: AIChE.

______. 2003a. *Essential Practices for Managing Chemical Reactivity Hazards*. New York: AIChE.

______. 2003b. *Guidelines for Analyzing and Managing the Security Vulnerabilities of Fixed Chemical Sites*. New York: AIChE.

______. 2003c. *Guidelines for Fire Protection in Chemical, Petrochemical, and Hydrocarbon Processing Facilities*. New York: AIChE.

Chemical Safety and Hazard Investigation Board (CSB). 2001 (March). Report No. 99-014-I-CA, *Refinery Fire Incident, Tosco Avon Refinery, Martinez, CA*. Washington, D.C.: CSB.

______. 2002a (October). Report No. 2001-05-I-DE, *Refinery Incident, Motiva Enterprises LLC, Delaware City, DE*. Washington, D.C.: CSB.

______. 2002b (June). Report No. 2001-03-I-GA, *Thermal Decomposition Incident, BP Amoco Polymers, Inc. Augusta, GA*. Washington, D.C.: CSB.

______. 2003a (October). Report No. 2003-01-I-MS, *Explosion and Fire, First Chemical Corporation, Pascagoula, MS*. Washington, D.C.: CSB.

______. 2003b (June). Report No. 2003-10-B, *Hazards of Nitrogen Asphyxiation*. Washington, D.C.: CSB.

______. 2007 (March). Report No. 2005-04-I-TX, *Refinery Explosion and Fire, Texas City, TX*. Washington, D.C.: CSB.

Cote, Arthur E., ed. 2008. *Fire Protection Handbook*. vols I and II. 20th ed. Quincy, MA: NFPA.

Department of Homeland Security (DHS). 2007. *Chemical Facility Anti-Terrorism Standards*. Washington, D.C.: DHS.

Department of Transportation (DOT). 2008. *Emergency Response Guidebook*. Washington, D.C.: DOT.

Environmental Protection Agency (EPA). 1986a. Emergency Planning and Community Right-to-Know Act. 42 USC 116. Washington, D.C.: EPA.

______. 1986b. Superfund Amendment and Reauthorization Act of 1986. 42 USC 103. Washington, D.C.: EPA.

______. 1990. Clean Air Act Amendments of 1990. P.L. 101–549. Washington, D.C.: EPA.

______. 2004. *Chemical Accident Prevention Program; Risk Management Plan*. 40 CFR Part 68, Subpart G. Washington, D.C.: EPA.

Gupta, J. P., and S. Bajpai. 2005. "Site Security for Chemical Process Industries." *Journal for Loss Prevention in the Process Industries*. (Jul–Nov) 18(4–6):301–309.

Industrial Risk Insurers (IRI). 1991. *IR Information Manual. 2.5.2: Plant Layout and Spacing for Oil and Chemical Plants*. Hartford, CT: IRI.

International Society of Automation (ISA). 2004. ANSI/ISA-TR84.00.01-2004. *Standard—Safety Instrumented Systems for the Process Industry Sector Parts 1 and 2*. Research Triangle Park, NC: ISA.

Lewis, R. 2004. *Sax's Dangerous Properties of Industrial Materials*. 11th ed. New York: John Wiley and Sons, Inc.

Lindeburg, Michael R. 1995. *Fire and Explosion Protection Systems: A Design Professional's Introduction*. 2d ed. Belmont, CA: Professional Publications, Inc.

Mannan, Sam. 2005. *Loss Prevention in the Process Industries.* 3d ed. Oxford, UK: Elsevier.

National Fire Protection Association (NFPA). 2006. NFPA 654, *Standard for the Prevention of Fire and Dust Explosions from the Manufacturing, Processing, and Handling of Combustible Particulate Solids.* Quincy, MA: NFPA.

______. 2007a. NFPA 15, *Standard for Water Spray Fixed Systems for Fire Protection.* Quincy, MA: NFPA.

______. 2007b. NFPA 16, *Standard for the Installation of Foam-Water Sprinkler and Foam-Water Spray Systems.* Quincy, MA: NFPA.

______. 2007c. NFPA 704, *Standard System for the Identification of the Hazards of Materials for Emergency Response.* Quincy, MA: NFPA.

______. 2008a. NFPA 12, *Standard on Carbon Dioxide Extinguishing Systems.* Quincy, MA: NFPA.

______. 2008b. NFPA 25, *Standard for the Inspection, Testing, and Maintenance of Water-Based Fire Protection Systems.* Quincy, MA: NFPA.

______. 2008c. NFPA 30, *Flammable and Combustible Liquids Code.* Quincy, MA: NFPA.

______. 2009a. NFPA 1, *Uniform Fire Code.* Quincy, MA: NFPA.

______. 2009b. NFPA 12A, *Standard on Halon 1301 Fire Extinguishing Systems.* Quincy, MA: NFPA.

______. 2009c. NFPA 101, *Life Safety Code.* Quincy, MA: NFPA.

______. 2009d. NFPA 220, *Standard on Types of Building Construction.* Quincy, MA: NFPA.

______. 2010a. NFPA 11, *Standard for Low, Medium, and High-Expansion Foam.* Quincy, MA: NFPA.

______. 2010b. NFPA 13, *Standard for the Installation of Sprinkler Systems.* Quincy, MA: NFPA.

______. 2010c. NFPA 72, *National Fire Alarm Code.* Quincy, MA: NFPA.

National Institute of Standards and Technology (NIST). 2005 (September). *Final Report on the Collapse of the World Trade Center Towers.* Washington, D.C.: NIST.

National Oceanic and Atmospheric Administration (NOAA), Office of Response and Restoration. 2010 (January). *Chemical Reactivity Worksheet (CRW).* Version CRW 2.1. Washington, D.C.: NOAA.

National Safety Council (NSC). 2009. *Accident Prevention Manual: Engineering and Technology.* 13th ed. Itasca, IL: NSC.

Occupational Safety and Health Administration (OSHA). 1992. 29 CFR 1910, *Standards for General Industry.* Washington, D.C.: OSHA.

______. 1996a. 29 CFR 1910.119, *Process Safety Management of Highly Hazardous Chemicals.* Washington, D.C.: OSHA.

______. 1996b. 29 CFR 1910.147, *The Control of Hazardous Energy (Lockout/Tagout).* Washington, D.C.: OSHA.

______. 1998a. 29 CFR 1910.146, *Permit-Required Confined Spaces.* Washington, D.C.: OSHA.

______. 1998b. 29 CFR 1910.252, *Welding, Cutting & Brazing; General Requirements.* Washington, D.C.: OSHA.

Wallace, S. 1994. "Optimize Facility-Siting Evaluations." *Hydrocarbon Processing: A Journal of Gulf Publishing* (May) 73(5):85–96.

______. 1999. "Take Action to Resolve Safety Recommendations." *Chemical Engineering Progress: A Monthly Journal of the American Institute of Chemical Engineers* (March) 99(3):67–71.

______. 2000. "Catching Near Hits." *Professional Safety.* 11:30–34.

______. 2001. "Using Quantitative Methods to Evaluate Process Risks and Verify the Effectiveness of PHA Recommendations." *Process Safety Progress: A Quarterly Journal of the American Institute of Chemical Engineers* (March) 20(1):57–62.

Wallace, S. et. al. 2003. "Know When to Say "When": A Review of Safety Incidents Involving Maintenance Issues." 2003. *Process Safety Progress: A Journal of the American Institute of Chemical Engineers* (December) 22(4):212–219.

Appendix: Best Practice Resources

Following is a list of some sources that may be beneficial to practitioners. This list is not meant to be comprehensive; however, it presents a number of organizations that develop important standards and guidance on a variety of subjects as well as useful books and pamphlets. Some Web-site addresses are provided, although organizational names and contact information are subject to change and it is not possible to guarantee the continuing accuracy of this list. Much of this information is taken from the organization's promotional literature and is not meant to endorse any particular organization but rather to raise awareness of the mission of each one. Practitioners are encouraged to ensure that the reference cited is the appropriate one for their purposes.

American Petroleum Institute (API), www.api.org

The American Petroleum Institute is a trade organization representing the oil and natural gas industry in the United States. It is based in Washington, D.C. It develops a variety of standards for the industry (available for purchase) that can also be used for other industries. It has developed a number of standards regarding safe maintenance and design of equipment.

Center for Chemical Process Safety (CCPS), www.aiche.org/ccps

The Center for Chemical Process Safety has published several books to assist practitioners in the field of process safety, and a number of those publications were referred to throughout this chapter. One of the publications, *Guidelines for Engineering Design for Process Safety* (1993), focuses specifically on design for process safety. Other publications focus on analyzing appropriate layers of protection, building design and location, and maintenance.

American Society of Safety Engineers (ASSE), www.asse.org

The American Society of Safety Engineers is a professional organization dedicated to assisting safety professionals. Its members manage, supervise and consult on safety, health, and environmental issues in industry, insurance, government, and academia. ASSE has specialty divisions and a number of chapters around the country. ASSE is responsible for the creation of this reference handbook and numerous safety publications and is the ANSI Secretariat for many national standards. The society's headquarters are in Des Plaines, Illinois.

American Chemistry Council (ACC), www.americanchemistry.com

The American Chemistry Council, formerly the Chemical Manufacturers Association, is a major trade organization in the chemical industry. Based in Arlington, Virginia, the council is committed to improved environmental, health, and safety performance through Responsible Care, commonsense advocacy designed to address major public policy issues, and health and environmental research and product testing.

American Society for Testing and Materials (ASTM), www.astm.org

ASTM International was originally known as the American Society for Testing and Materials. It is one of the largest voluntary standards-development organizations in the world, and it has developed standards that provide guidance on design and manufacturing. ANSI standards developed at ASTM are the work of ASTM members, including technical experts representing producers, users, consumers, government, and academics from several countries.

National Fire Protection Association (NFPA), www.nfpa.org

The National Fire Protection Association is the premier organization in the United States for publishing standards regarding fire protection and emergency response. The association publishes various standards, including those regarding sprinkler systems, storage tank spacing, and the uniform fire code. The association is also responsible for the *Fire Protection Handbook* (Cote 2008). NFPA holds several seminars throughout the year. Its information can be purchased.

International Society of Automation (ISA), www.isa.org

The International Society of Automation (formerly the Instrumentation, Systems, and Automation Society) is an educational organization that fosters advancement in the theory, design, manufacture, and use of sensors, instruments, computers, and systems for automation. The society hosts conferences to promote the subject of automation and publishes a number of books, magazines, and standards. Of particular interest to safety practitioners is ISA-84 (2004), which can be used to establish safety integrity levels for instruments in hazardous material services.

National Safety Council (NSC), www.nsc.org

The National Safety Council is dedicated to influencing society to adopt safety, health, and environmental policies, practices, and procedures that prevent accidents. The council is located in Itasca, Illinois, and has several chapters throughout the United States. NSC is responsible for several safety publications, including the *Supervisors' Safety Manual* (NSC 2009).

American Welding Society (AWS), www.aws.org

The American Welding Society is a nonprofit organization whose goal is advancing the technology and application of welding and related disciplines. The society produces a number of standards related to welding, cutting, and brazing.

National Association of Corrosion Engineers (NACE) International, www.nace.org

NACE International, originally known as the National Association of Corrosion Engineers, is dedicated to the study of corrosion issues. NACE has developed several corrosion prevention and control standards and conducts several workshops, and classes each year. It also has a number of technical committees.

Occupational Safety and Health Administration (OSHA), www.osha.gov

The Occupational Safety and Health Administration is a regulatory body dedicated to protecting workers in the United States. OSHA produces regulations and technical assistance bulletins. Of particular interest to safety practitioners regarding process safety is OSHA 1910.119, *Process Safety Management of Highly Hazardous Chemicals* (1972).

Chemical Safety and Hazard Investigation Board (CSB), www.csb.gov

The Chemical Safety and Hazard Investigation Board is a nonregulatory federal agency dedicated to preventing accidents in the chemical industry by investigating incidents that occur and making recommendations to prevent recurrence. The board produces public reports of the incidents and studies they conduct that are available free of charge from their Web site.

American Society of Mechanical Engineers (ASME), www.asme.org

The American Society of Mechanical Engineers is a professional society that sets internationally recognized industrial and manufacturing codes and standards that enhance public safety, including the boiler and pressure vessel code and several codes on designing and maintaining piping.

The Chlorine Institute, Inc., www.chlorineinstitute.gov

The Chlorine Institute, Inc., is dedicated to promoting safe practices in industries that produce and handle chlorine and various other chemicals. The institute produces a number of pamphlets recommending good safety practices. The institute is headquartered in Arlington, Virginia.

Insurance Companies

A variety of companies, such as Factory Mutual and Zurich, insure manufacturing and chemical facilities. Many of these companies develop good practices based on their research and observations, which are often available for purchase but are sometimes considered proprietary.

INDEX

D

E

V

W

Z